Self-Constitution of European Society

'This book makes a vital intervention in the debate on European constitutionalism at a time when the foundations seem to be crumbling under the combined pressure of the Eurozone crisis, the refugee crisis and the latest terrorists massacres. It shows a deeper and multi-faceted self-constitutionalization of Europe at work: a self-constitutionalization which is not limited merely to the surface of law and politics. The contributors move far beyond the by-now almost arid ground of constitutional pluralism.'

Kaarlo Tuori, University of Helsinki, Finland

'This fascinating book mirrors the ongoing European crisis, oscillating in its reaction between normalisation and contestation. This creates constructive tensions: normalisation is not simply defensive Union praise but seeks fundamental theoretical renewal; contestation documents suffering, empathy and passion. With such dynamics, there is still hope for a European future.'

Christian Joerges, Hertie School of Governance, Germany

Recent social and political developments in the EU have clearly shown the profound structural changes in European society and its politics. Reflecting on these developments and responding to the existing body of academic literature and scholarship, this book critically discusses the emerging notion of European constitutionalism, its varieties and different contextualization in theories of EU law, general jurisprudence, sociology of law, political theory and sociology.

The contributors address different problems related to the relationship between the constitutional state and non-state constitutionalizations and critically analyze general theories of constitutional monism, dualism and pluralism and their juridical and political uses in the context of EU constitutionalism. Individual chapters emphasize the importance of interdisciplinary and socio-legal methods in the current research of EU constitutionalism and their potential to re-conceptualize and re-think traditional problems of constitutional subjects, limitation and separation of power, political symbolism and identity politics in Europe.

This collection simultaneously describes the EU and its self-constitution as one polity, differentiated society and shared community and its contributors conceptualize the sense of common identity and solidarity in the context of the post-sovereign multitude of European society.

Jiří Přibáň is Professor of Law at the School of Law and Politics at Cardiff University and author of numerous legal philosophical and socio-legal publications, such as *Sovereignty in Post-Sovereign Society* (2015), *Legal Symbolism* (2007) and *Dissidents of Law* (2002). His research interests include social theory and philosophy of law, constitutional theory, philosophy of rights and constitutionalism.

Applied Legal Philosophy Series
General Editor: Tom D.Campbell, Professional Fellow,
Centre for Applied Philosophy and Public Ethics,
Charles Sturt University, Canberra

The principal objective of this series is to encourage the publication of books which adopt a theoretical approach to the study of particular areas or aspects of law, or deal with general theories of law in a way which is directed at issues of practical, moral and political concern in specific legal contexts. The general approach is both analytical and critical and relates to the socio-political background of law reform issues.

The series includes studies of all the main areas of law, presented in a manner which relates to the concerns of specialist legal academics and practitioners. Each book makes an original contribution to an area of legal study while being comprehensible to those engaged in a wide variety of disciplines. Their legal content is principally Anglo-American, but a wide-ranging comparative approach is encouraged and authors are drawn from a variety of jurisdictions.

Legal Evidence and Proof: Statistics, Stories, Logic
Hendrik Kaptein, Henry Prakken and Bart Verheij

Holy Writ: Interpretation in Law and Religion
Arie-Jan Kwak

Cultural Difference on Trial: The Nature and Limits of Judicial Understanding
Anthony J. Connolly

The Concept of Law from a Transnational Perspective
Detlef von Daniels

Ratio and Voluntas: The Tension Between Reason and Will in Law
Kaarlo Tuori

The Right Not to be Criminalized: Demarcating Criminal Law's Authority
Dennis J. Baker

Basic Equality and Discrimination
Nicholas Mark Smith

The Vantage of Law: Its Role in Thinking about Law, Judging and Bills of Rights
James Allan

Constitutional Life and Europe's Area of Freedom, Security and Justice
Alun Howard Gibbs

Legitimizing Human Rights: Secular and Religious Perspectives
Angus J.L. Menuge

Principled Engagement: Negotiating Human Rights in Repressive States
Morten B. Pedersen and David Kinley

Self-Constitution of European Society

Beyond EU politics, law and governance

Edited by Jiří Přibáň

LONDON AND NEW YORK

First published 2016
by Routledge
2 Park Square, Milton Park, Abingdon, Oxon OX14 4RN

and by Routledge
711 Third Avenue, New York, NY 10017

Routledge is an imprint of the Taylor & Francis Group, an informa business

© 2016 selection and editorial matter, Jiří Přibáň; individual chapters, the contributors

The right of Jiří Přibáň to be identified as the author of the editorial material, and of the authors for their individual chapters, has been asserted in accordance with sections 77 and 78 of the Copyright, Designs and Patents Act 1988.

All rights reserved. No part of this book may be reprinted or reproduced or utilised in any form or by any electronic, mechanical, or other means, now known or hereafter invented, including photocopying and recording, or in any information storage or retrieval system, without permission in writing from the publishers.

Trademark notice: Product or corporate names may be trademarks or registered trademarks, and are used only for identification and explanation without intent to infringe.

British Library Cataloguing in Publication Data
A catalogue record for this book is available from the British Library

Library of Congress Cataloging in Publication Data
Names: Jiří Přibáň, 1967- author.
Title: Self-constitution of European society : beyond EU politics, law and governance / By Jiří Přibáň.
Description: Burlington, VT : Routledge, 2016. | Series: Applied legal philosophy | Includes bibliographical references and index.
Identifiers: LCCN 2015042299|
Subjects: LCSH: Constitutional law—European Union countries. | Constitutional law—European Union countries—Interpretation and construction. | European Union.
Classification: LCC KJE5034 .P75 2016 | DDC 342.24—dc23
LC record available at http://lccn.loc.gov/2015042299

ISBN: 978-1-4724-5850-6 (hbk)
ISBN: 978-1-315-60827-3 (ebk)

Typeset in Times New Roman
by Swales & Willis Ltd, Exeter, Devon, UK

Printed in the United Kingdom
by Henry Ling Limited

Contents

Notes on contributors	vii
Acknowledgements	x

Introduction: on Europe's crises and self-constitutions   1
JIŘÍ PŘIBÁŇ

PART I
The European self-constitution: concepts and theories   11

1   **The European Constitution and the *pouvoir constituant*: no longer, or never, *sui generis*?**   13
CHRIS THORNHILL

2   **The concept of self-limiting polity in EU constitutionalism: a systems theoretical outline**   37
JIŘÍ PŘIBÁŇ

3   **A political–sociological analysis of constitutional pluralism in Europe**   66
PAUL BLOKKER

PART II
European constitutional jurisprudence   91

4   **Pluralist constitutional paradoxes and cosmopolitan Europe**   93
JOXERRAMON BENGOETXEA

5   **The pluralist turn and its political discontents**   116
MARCO GOLDONI

vi *Contents*

6 Why supra-national law is not the exception: on the grounds of legal obligations beyond the state 138
GEORGE PAVLAKOS

7 Declaratory rule of law: self-constitution through unenforceable promises 159
DIMITRY KOCHENOV

PART III
EU constitutionalism and governance 181

8 Constitutionalising expertise in the EU: anchoring knowledge in democracy 183
STIJN SMISMANS

9 Bringing politics into European integration: the unvoiced issues of market-making 201
GARETH DAVIES

10 A technocratic tyranny of certainty: a preliminary sketch 218
MICHELLE EVERSON

PART IV
Crises of EU constitutionalism 237

11 The European dual state: the double structural transformation of the public sphere and the need for repoliticization 239
HAUKE BRUNKHORST

12 Societal conditions of self-constitution: the experience of the European periphery 274
PIERRE GUIBENTIF

13 The empire of principle 314
PETR AGHA

Index 332

Contributors

Petr Agha is deputy director of the Centre for Law and Public Affairs (CeLAPA) at the Institute of State and Law, Czech Academy of Sciences and senior lecturer, Faculty of Law, Charles University in Prague. He is interested in the intersections between law and politics, identities and human rights. He has edited a book *Human Rights between Law and Politics: The Margin of Appreciation in Post-National Contexts* (forthcoming in 2016).

Joxerramon Bengoetxea is professor of jurisprudence and sociology of law at the University of the Basque Country. He is the Secretary General of the Basque Council of the European Movement and directs the ehuGune "rethinking together" programme on interaction between academia and civil society. His major research interests are in pluralisms in Europe, the legal reasoning of the Court of Justice of the EU, the theories of European integration and social justice issues within Europe. His major publications are *The Legal Reasoning of the European Court of Justice* (1993), *La Europa Peter Pan* (2005) and *Neil MacCormick y la Razón Práctica Institucional* (2015).

Paul Blokker is associate professor in sociology at the Institute of Sociological Studies, Charles University in Prague. He is co-editor of the journal *Social Imaginaries*. He inter alia published the book *New Democracies in Crisis? A Comparative Constitutional Study of the Czech Republic, Hungary, Poland, Romania and Slovakia* (2013). His research interests are democratization, multiple democracies, critique and dissent, constitutional sociology, constitutional politics and change, pragmatic sociology, political theory and social imaginaries.

Hauke Brunkhorst is professor of sociology at the European-University Flensburg, Germany. His research fields are social evolution, sociology of constitutions, legal and political theory. He is the author of *Solidarity: From Civic Friendship to a Global Legal Community* (2005); *Legitimationskrisen: Verfassungsprobleme der Weltgesellschaft* (2012); *Das doppelte Gesicht Europas. Zwischen Kapitalismus und Demokratie* (2014); and *Critical Theory of Legal Revolutions – Evolutionary Perspectives* (2014).

viii *Contributors*

Gareth Davies is professor of European law at VU University Amsterdam, the Netherlands. His interests are in EU constitutional and free movement law. He is a co-author of Chalmers, Davies and Monti, *EU Law* (2010).

Michelle Everson is professor of law at Birkbeck College, University of London. She has researched and published widely in the sphere of European economic law and European constitutional law. Currently, she is researching the role of financial services regulation in financial crises.

Marco Goldoni is lecturer in legal theory at the University of Glasgow and a research fellow at the Centre for Law and Public Affairs at the Academy of Sciences of the Czech Republic. He researches legal and constitutional theory, EU public law and comparative constitutional law. He is currently writing a monograph on the role of national parliaments in EU law making.

Pierre Guibentif is associate professor at the School for Sociology and Public Policies of ISCTE-IUL and researcher at Dinâmia'CET-IUL. Fields of interest are sociology of law, social policies and theories of society. His latest book is *Foucault, Luhmann, Habermas, Bourdieu. Une génération repense le droit*. Paris: Lextenso-LGDJ, 2010.

Dimitry Kochenov is Martin and Kathleen Crane Fellow in Law and Public Affairs at the Woodrow Wilson School, Princeton University (2015–2016). He holds the Chair in EU Constitutional Law, University of Groningen. He is also visiting professor, College of Europe, Natolin campus. He is mainly engaged with principles of EU law and the role of the individual in the evolution of the EU legal order. He is the editor, most recently, of *EU Citizenship and Federalism: The Role of Rights* (2016); *Reinforcement of the Rule of Law Oversight in the European Union* (with C. Closa, 2016); *The Enforcement of EU Law and Values: Ensuring Compliance* (with A. Jakab, 2016) and *Europe's Justice Deficit?* (with G. de Búrca and A. Williams, 2015).

George Pavlakos is professor of law and philosophy at the School of Law, University of Glasgow. He is the author of *Our Knowledge of the Law* (2007) and has recently edited *Reasons and Intentions in Law and Practical Agency* (2015). George is general editor of the book series *Law and Practical Reason* at Hart Publishing and joint general editor of the journal *Jurisprudence*, published by Routledge.

Jiří Přibáň is professor of law at the School of Law and Politics at Cardiff University and author of numerous legal philosophical and socio-legal publications, such as *Sovereignty in Post-Sovereign Society* (2015), *Legal Symbolism* (2007) and *Dissidents of Law* (2002). His research interests include social theory and philosophy of law, constitutional theory, philosophy of rights and constitutionalism.

Stijn Smismans is professor at the School of Law and Politics and director of the Centre for European Law and Governance at Cardiff University. Publications include *Law, Legitimacy and European Governance* (2004), *Civil Society and*

Legitimate European Governance (editor, 2006) and *The EU and Industrial Relations* (editor, 2012).

Chris Thornhill is professor in law at the University of Manchester, UK. He is the author of a number of publications on the sociological origins of constitutional law and transnational public law, especially *A Sociology of Constitutions* (2011). His works on legal sociology and jurisprudence have been translated into many languages. He is currently researching a book on the sociology of transnational constitutional law.

Acknowledgements

I want to thank Cardiff Law School for its financial, organizational, professional and moral support of this project. The idea of the edited book originated in a research project on self-constitutionalization of European society funded by the school's Research Grant Scheme in June 2013. Furthermore, this project and subsequent book editing was funded by the Cardiff Law School's Centre for European Law and Governance, a Jean Monnet Centre of Excellence. I am particularly grateful to my friend and colleague Stijn Smismans for his help and assistance. Most of all, though, I wish to thank Sian Edwards for her language editing of the whole volume.

Introduction

On Europe's crises and self-constitutions

Jiří Přibáň

The Euro-Greek crisis became an enduring feature of European reality, profoundly challenging the economic and political operations and institutions of the European Union (EU), in the second decade of this century. Every EU summit promises a groundbreaking, definite and decisive solution, which, however, is immediately questioned and overtaken by new economic data and political events. Nobody wants to risk an economic and political collapse caused by Greece's possible exit from the Eurozone. At the same time, everybody expects the Union and Greece to put an end to this extremely high level of economic and political contingency and push for a definite solution, restoring the economic and political stability and credibility of the EU. Nevertheless, the only certainty offered to the EU's citizens is another summit dealing with another critical moment for the Union.

Similarly, the long-standing refugee and migrant crisis, which led to the loss of thousands of lives and the presence of hundreds of thousands of refugees on the EU's territory in the summer of 2015, revealed the shocking incapacity of the Union and member states' institutions to effectively cope with such social development and offer adequate help to the political asylum seekers. Fractures between old and new member states reappeared when the French Foreign Minister, Laurent Fabius, called the reluctance of some East European states, most notably Hungary, to accept more refugees and a compulsory quota system for migrants, as proposed by the EU, scandalous and disrespectful of Europe's common values.

More radical commentators, while challenging hostile responses to the migrant crisis in new member states, added their criticism by asking the inconvenient question as to whether solidarity within the EU should now amount to an obligation on EU states to cope with the consequences of imperialist policies, military interventions, wars and bombings conducted by some of the old European powers. What are these common values in the name of which France, Britain and other members of the EU launched military interventions in recent decades? Are they the same values as those of the Prime Minister of Hungary, Viktor Orbán, who promised to protect against the refugees massing at his country and the EU's borders?

While the levels of hypocrisy among European politicians almost matched the scale of the humanitarian crisis, legal regulations and agreements coordinating

2 *Jiří Přibáň*

and handling the EU's asylum policy, such as the Dublin Regulation[1] determining member states' responsibility for individual asylum claims, were suspended for Syrian refugees by some member states, both old and new, such as Germany and the Czech Republic in the late summer of 2015. Furthermore, the Schengen Treaty guaranteeing the free movement of all persons on the signatory states' territory, and abolishing internal borders while keeping a single external border, became openly questioned vis-à-vis the refugee crisis and the lack of action and coordination of political and administrative agencies within the EU. Border controls subsequently became a reality even within the Schengen zone and armies were mobilized to handle the flow of migrants in Austria, Croatia, the Czech Republic, Germany, Hungary and other EU countries in 2015.

In light of the Eurozone and Schengen zone crises, the risk of the United Kingdom leaving the EU and the growing popularity of secessionist movements in regions such as Catalonia, Flanders and Scotland, appear almost benign and of secondary importance. Nevertheless, they are equally important for the EU's economic, political and administrative constitution. For instance, the political success of secessionist movements in some member states invites a whole set of questions regarding their commitment to democratic coexistence and collaboration at EU level, where these potentially new seceded countries would inevitably have to sit next to the states they separated from in their struggle for independence. In other words, what constitutes member states' loyalty to the supranational EU and how different is it from a country's loyalty to democratically constituted bodies and institutions at nation-state level?

What is today commonly presented as Europe's *crisis* actually should be called its *stasis* – a state of social strife and disturbance in which opposing forces are equal and cancel out each other. While the state of crisis signifies an unstable and dangerous situation and a moment of decision leading to the death or survival of a patient in medical terms, or a radical resolution responding to the highest tensions and conflicts in a drama story, the state of stasis mainly demonstrates a higher level of contingency and irresolution.

Current critical dysfunctions in complex systems of European economy, politics and law should therefore be treated as a specific form of social stasis informed by irresolution and growing social tension. Decisions to deal with these dysfunctions are urgently sought, yet their causes and solutions are unknown, and every decision subsequently involves a high risk of causing more social harm and instability. However, calls on all agents to 'come to their senses' and act 'reasonably' only perpetuate the current European stasis, a kitsch symbol of which has become politicians' futile promises of reforms.

The most important lesson from recent crises in and of the EU, and political responses to them, is the recognition of the complexity of contemporary European society and the operational limitations of its political, administrative, legal,

---

1 The Dublin Regulation (Regulation No. 604/2013; sometimes referred to as the Dublin III Regulation; previously the Dublin II Regulation and the Dublin Convention).

economic, educational and other systems. There is no question as to the existence of a European society of which the EU is the most important organizational subsystem. However, this society does not depend on the EU and its policy making. It is evolving irrespective of the functionality or dysfunctionality of one of its organizational subsystems.

Furthermore, this society does not depend on some foundational and commonly shared values, despite the political declarations and warnings of political leaders and public figures. The very existence of European society is not determined by a specific set of values it chooses to economically promote, politically enforce and legally regulate within and beyond the EU.

Europe as a moral project is just one of many projects in contemporary complex European society. It will select its common values independently of the will of its self-proclaimed guardians and there is no guarantee that these values will always be liberal and democratic. Democratic elections can easily bring anti-democratic and illiberal parties and movements to power at both member state and EU levels, and their leaders may offer unsettling political and social alternatives to our current constitutional democratic and liberal settlement in Europe.

Today, European politicians are only gradually recognizing the disturbing fact that the EU's future may be governed by values completely different from, if not totally opposed to, the original values and ethos of European integration. As discussed in this book, the EU's founding values are politically and socially vulnerable. The concept of liberal democracy is even questioned by senior politicians in some countries of the Union. The rise of populist parties across the continent and their growing willingness to coordinate policies in a paradoxically supranational, yet profoundly anti-EU manner serve as persuasive evidence of this recent development.

Writing and editing a book on Europe's self-constitution at this time of profound tensions and risks of disintegration, and of political and social turmoil, may seem like either a naïvely prescriptive gesture, or evidence of a more profound intellectual ineptitude and ignorance of social realities. Emerging crises reveal the failures as well as the limits of European and member state institutions, and politicians' desperate promises of reform testify strongly to *the powerlessness of the powerful* in Europe's constitution, today.

However, this brief sketch of recent economic, political, legal and even ethical crises and exceptional events both inside and outside the EU also illustrates a more general possibility of rethinking and reconsidering the general function and specific importance of constitutions, constitutionalizations and constitutionalism in Europe. Observing the current state of Europe, one can critically revisit the classical topics of political and legal science and rethink both the methodological and conceptual frameworks of constitutional theory, political and legal philosophy, and sociology.

Recent social and political developments in the EU, especially since the collapse of its official political constitution-making process in 2005, clearly show the profound structural changes in European society and its politics. In its post-Maastricht post-national constellation, the EU has been described as a 'constitution

4   *Jiří Přibáň*

without constitutionalism'[2] by some scholars, yet also as a 'constitutionalism without constitution'[3] by others.

European constitutional pluralism, multi-level legal and political structures, and governance-driven post-constituent constitutionalizations within and beyond the state have been explored and analysed in great detail by many political and legal theorists.[4] Post-Maastricht European integration has been typical of both official constitution making and the unofficial spontaneous constitutionalizations of different systems and regimes in European society. Some scholars have explored profound structural links between the EU's governance and the self-constitutionalizations of these social systems and subsystems. Others have become much more sceptical about the common meaning of constitutionalism and invite their readers to consider contemporary complex society's administration 'beyond constitutionalism'.[5]

The concept and values of modern constitutionalism are challenged by social and political realities to such an extent that scholars even ask whether the system of global economy and politics removing traditional powers and legitimation from the nation-state necessarily lead to 'the twilight of constitutionalism'.[6] In this context, EU constitution-making efforts may resemble a useless act of modern political and legal nostalgia doomed to be rejected by the peoples of Europe. However, the EU's unique constitutional condition also invites a more radical departure from the canon of constitutional theory by reinterpreting the concepts of constitution, constitutionalization and constitutionalism beyond their traditional political and juridical meaning as part of general social theoretical thinking and sociological observations.

This sociological turn in studies of constitutions and constitutionalism is profoundly informed by the difference between political and other societal constitutions and constitutionalizations. EU constitutional politics may be in crisis, yet constitutionalizations of the different subsystems of European society

---

2   J.H.H. Weiler, *The Constitution of Europe* (Cambridge, UK: Cambridge University Press, 1999), p. 298.

3   Antonin Cohen, 'Constitutionalism without constitution: Transnational elites between political mobilization and legal expertise in the making of a constitution for Europe (1940s–1960s)', *Law & Social Inquiry* 32(1) (2007): 109–135.

4   Among many books and articles, see, for instance, Neil MacCormick, 'Beyond the sovereign state', *The Modern Law Review* 56(1) (1993): 1–18; Richard Bellamy and Dario Castiglione (eds) *Constitutionalism in Transformation: European and Theoretical Perspectives* (Oxford, UK: Blackwell Publishers, 1996); Ingolf Pernice, 'Multilevel constitutionalism and the Treaty of Amsterdam: European constitution-making revisited', *Common Market Law Review* 36 (1999): 703–750; Neil Walker, 'The idea of constitutional pluralism', *Modern Law Review* 65(3) (2002): 317–359; Miguel Poiares Maduro, 'Interpreting European law: Judicial adjudication in the context of constitutional pluralism', *European Journal of Legal Studies* 2(1) (2007): 1–21; Matej Avbelj and Jan Komárek (eds) *Constitutional Pluralism in the European Union and Beyond* (Oxford, UK: Hart Publishing, 2012).

5   Nico Krisch, *Beyond Constitutionalism: The Pluralist Structure of Postnational Constitutional Law* (Oxford, UK: Oxford University Press, 2010).

6   Petra Dobner and Martin Loughlin (eds) *The Twilight of Constitutionalism?* (Oxford, UK: Oxford University Press, 2010).

Introduction 5

evolve beyond and independently of EU policy making. Sociological studies of constitutions and constitutionalism in their national, supranational and transnational contexts have flourished in recent years and the EU is used as one of the most persuasive examples of the fact that structural changes in globalized and Europeanized economy, politics and law require new theoretical responses and conceptualizations.

The first aim of this book, then, is to contribute to this reinterpretation of European constitutional processes and constitutionalism as concepts with both legal and social theoretical meaning. The EU's political constitution and both its written and unwritten principles and rules are to be perceived as part of evolving European society and not as its ultimate normative settlement, existential precondition and value legitimation.

Reflecting on recent developments in the EU and responding to the existing body of academic literature and scholarship, this volume of essays by distinguished legal and social theorists, political scientists, sociologists and philosophers of law critically discusses the emerging notion of European constitutionalism, its varieties and different contextualization in theories of EU law, general jurisprudence, sociology of law, political theory and sociology. These scholars are interested in examining the function of constitutions and processes of constitutionalization in contemporary complex European society, instead of intellectually supporting the myth of a society constituted by political will and legal norms, expressing commonly shared ways of life, which still persists among some constitutional theorists and political philosophers.

The second aim of this book is to rethink the concepts of constitution and constitutionalization as metaphors for European unity and integration. The process of Europe's self-constitution can hardly be considered merely a political instrument confronting the growing risk of disintegration and fragmentation in the EU and beyond. Instead, theorists and sociologists of European constitutionalism should analyse even disintegration and fragmentations and various policy opt-outs as specific processes of self-constitutionalization. European constitutionalism thus involves processes of both integration and disintegration and needs to be studied, even in its fragmented forms, beyond the common paradoxes of political constitutionalism and its grand dichotomy between constituent and constituted power.

The fact that societal fragmentations actually contribute to the process of constitutionalization and therefore need to be analysed as part of constitutionalism was highlighted recently by Gunther Teubner in his study of global societal constitutionalism and constitutional fragments.[7] Despite criticisms of the concept of societal constitutions, some of them raised by individual contributors to this book, contemporary theory of global and European constitutionalism is hard to imagine without the radical conceptual and methodological innovations of Teubner's theory of societal constitutionalism.

---

7 Gunther Teubner, *Constitutional Fragments: Societal Constitutionalism and Globalization* (Oxford, UK: Oxford University Press, 2012).

6   *Jiří Přibáň*

The third aim of this volume is to describe the processes of constitutionalization as pluralistic self-constitutionalizations of different systems of European society. These processes often collide and result in systemic asymmetries commonly described as crises, such as the financial and economic crisis which hit European and global society in 2008. The self-constitution of European society thus has to be comprehended as profoundly pluralistic and typical of societal differentiation full of systemic collisions and structural irritations, with no prospect of creating some ultimate societal harmony and normative stability.

The self-constitution of Europe consists of the differentiated and pluralistic constitutionalizations of specific organizations, regimes and operations evolving within European society. The concept of constitutional pluralism, so easily adopted by legal scholars since the mid-1990s, particularly by theorists of European law, therefore needs to be reformulated and reconceptualized vis-à-vis societal pluralism and the impossibility of limiting problems of legal pluralism to the dilemmas of normative validity and political authority. The diversity and pluralism of European constitutionalism stretches far beyond the difference between the transnational self-constitution of the EU and national member state constitutions, because the self-constitution of Europe is profoundly pluralistic in itself and covers European economy, politics, social welfare and security, science and other social systems.[8]

In short, there are many self-constitutions of Europe today.[9] Several chapters in this book therefore address different problems connected with the relationship between the constitutional state and non-state constitutionalizations, and critically analyse general theories of constitutional monism, dualism and pluralism and their juridical and political uses in the context of EU constitutionalism.

Finally, this book aims to emphasize the basic fact that European society is just a segment of global society. Constitutional processes in Europe therefore cannot be separated from the outside world and may be comprehended only within the global context. After all, one can ask the provocative question of whether European integration is just an example of retro-political dreams of a fully integrated society living under one constitution and its normative principles and ethical ideals. Instead, European constitutionalism should be analysed as part of global legal pluralism with a specific constitutional imagination, institutional framework, and economic, political, juridical and other societal operations.

Individual contributors to this book emphasize the importance of interdisciplinary methods in the current research into EU constitutionalism and their ability to reconceptualize and rethink traditional problems of constitutional theory. The opening part of the volume therefore addresses the EU's post-national constellation beyond state sovereignty and its self-proclaimed 'non-state' character and supranational polycentric governance framework. The meaning of European constitutionalism beyond the constitutional state is profoundly questioned, as well as

---

8 Kaarlo Tuori, *European Constitutionalism* (Cambridge, UK: Cambridge University Press, 2015).

9 Kaarlo Tuori and Suvi Sankari (eds) *The Many Constitutions of Europe* (Farnham, UK: Ashgate, 2010).

Introduction   7

the alleged power of EU law to neutralize and depoliticize national constitutional politics. EU constitutionalism is discussed as both a juridical form of the Union's political integration and an example of the plurality of European society and its functional differentiation.

Chris Thornhill's chapter questions the terminology of EU constitutional theory, including the paradox of constituent and constituted power and the magic formula of the *sui generis* character of European constitutionalism. Insisting on the sociological perspective of the EU's legal system, Thornhill states that the judicial institutions of the EU have acquired authority almost matching that of a constituent power determining the EU's distinctive multi-original constitution, shaped by the multiple legislative and interpretive acts of these institutions. However, this sociological analysis of the European constitution is used as just an example of the general social processes of the construction of legal reality.

In the second chapter, Jiří Přibáň analyses the concept of polity in European constitutionalism as another traditional concept of constitutional and political theory, and offers reconceptualization from the social systems theoretical perspective. Přibáň distinguishes between European polity and society and argues that the European constitutional polity, unlike the general concept of society, is just a specific concept constituted by structural coupling between the systems of EU law and politics. Critical of the depoliticizing tendencies of theories of European governance and societal constitutionalism, he concludes that the concept of European polity is profoundly linked to the political notion of constitutionalism, and highlights the function of modern political constitutions as organizations channelling political power through law while limiting exactly the same power by legal rules.

The final chapter of the opening part, focusing on concepts and theories of European constitutionalism, is written by Paul Blokker who pursues a political sociological analysis of constitutional pluralism in Europe. Blokker's contribution to a political sociology of European constitutionalism emphasizes the plurality of interactions between law, politics and society and the importance of transnational civic engagement, movements and mobilization in Europe's constitutional project. Critically discussing the EU's constitutional deficit, Blokker points to the emerging transnational public sphere and its capacity to formulate alternative constitutional claims beyond the formal institutions of the EU.

The second part of the volume focuses on European constitutional jurisprudence, pluralism and legal theoretical reflections on the European constitution's evolution and transformation. Joxerramon Bengoetxea discusses specific paradoxes emerging in European legal and constitutional pluralism and new forms of cultural and political normative pluralism in the EU. A pluralist normative field of different communities living on the EU's territory is contrasted to nationalist populism and Euroscepticism and assessed as potentially contributing to the self-constitution of Europe and its post-national pluralist constellation. Drawing on MacCormick's institutional theory of law, Bengoetxea finally argues that Europe's normative pluralist challenges do not rule out the possibility of a hermeneutic method and legal reasoning legitimately dealing with legal problems and cases in the cosmopolitan European spirit.

8   *Jiří Přibáň*

In the next chapter, Marco Goldoni addresses the political context and consequences of the pluralist turn in European transnational jurisprudence. Where Bengoetxea looks for argumentative and hermeneutical reconciliation between normative pluralism and legal reasoning, Goldoni boldly states that the language of pluralism is a deceptive device leading to more conflicts rather than limiting them in the EU's pluralist legal and political environment. Distinguishing between weak and strong forms of constitutional pluralism, Goldoni sceptically concludes that the normative promise of constitutional pluralism to open up new forums for previously neglected political problems and conflicts cannot materialize within European constitutional politics and contribute to Europe's self-constitution.

Goldoni's critique of pluralist constitutional politics is followed by George Pavlakos's elaborate jurisprudential treatise on the grounds of legal obligation beyond the state, and the extension of Dworkin's 'associative relation' concept from the domestic state to the international and transnational European and global levels. The use of the argumentative scheme of analytical jurisprudence, Pavlakos argues, replaces the factual, sovereignty-based conception of coercion by the normative conception of coercion as a structure of reciprocal and relational action-direction independent of state institutions and norms. Outlining this non-state ground of legal obligation and drawing a distinction between factual enforcement and normative enforceability, Pavlakos shows state enforcement's limited role in grounding and legitimizing obligations in any legal system, including the European constitution.

In the final chapter of the second part of the book, Dimitry Kochenov takes common jurisprudential arguments further into the domain of constitutional politics when he identifies the self-constitution of Europe, rather than the force of law and political authority, with the declaratory rule of law and normative promises which remain politically and legally unenforceable. Kochenov contrasts the EU's official rule of law policies to the structural deficiency of the rule of law as an area of European values, and argues that the difference between the values and the *acquis* (the law) of the EU highlights an excessive preoccupation with the practical enforcement of values. According to him, however, it is the intrinsic tension between the enforceability and ephemerality of values that makes the question of the basis of EU law, integration and self-constitution extremely complicated, yet important and unavoidable.

The third part of the book addresses a number of issues close to European constitutional jurisprudence and politics, but considers them in the context of primarily non-juridical technocratic governance and expert knowledge. The rationality and multi-level operations of EU governance are scrutinized and juxtaposed with the concepts of constitutionalism, democratic legitimacy and legality. This part opens with Stijn Smismans's chapter on the constitutionalization of expertise. According to Smismans, the theory of the EU's multi-level constitutionalism must accommodate the neglected question of the role of expert knowledge in European governance and policy making. European agencies, integrated impact assessments and the open method of coordination are discussed by him to show the different roles of expertise in European governance and the impossibility of

Introduction 9

simply accommodating it within the holistic perspective of traditional constitutionalism and interest-based political theory. The dichotomy of expert knowledge and political interests thus calls for a more complex theory of European constitutionalism and for rethinking the European constitution's meta-function.

In the following chapter, Gareth Davies radicalizes a critique of technocratic governance and its depoliticizing effects on the EU. Davies identifies the constitutionalization of Europe with its politicization and the political contestations reshaping the current constitutional entrenchment. Like Blokker in the opening part of the book, Davies criticizes the reduction of European constitutional politics to Treaty text changes and calls for the voices of the public to be heard during the EU's legislative process, so that its legislation may be considered an outcome of democratic political deliberation. According to Davies, the second politicization of the European constitutional domain needs to evolve in the European Court of Justice's interpretation of the Treaty, by taking into account the public values and political preferences formulated before the Court. For Davies, the separation of politics and expertise, and keeping political emotion and ideology at a national level while preserving the Union's regulatory and technocratic role, is impossible. The EU and its institutions, such as the Court, need to abandon the depoliticized technical space and adopt a political interpretation of their legal and administrative functions.

In the final chapter of this part by Michelle Everson, the gloves are off as she attacks with extraordinary intellectual force what she calls 'a technocratic tyranny of certainty'. Though her chapter is subtitled 'a preliminary sketch', it fundamentally criticizes the most recent developments in European economy and politics triggered by the Eurozone crisis and theorizes them in the context of political economy and critique of ideology. Everson takes the Eurozone crisis as a case study of the general tendencies of global society when she contrasts the technocratic certainty of the globalized market with the moral indeterminacy of globalization and the abdication of the pursuit of universal welfare, and concludes that this is a failure of the symbolically-constrained imagination of European and global politics.

The final part of the book further elaborates on criticisms of recent events and developments in the EU and analyses the impact of crises in Europe's centres and peripheries. Hauke Brunkhorst's chapter is no less passionate and theoretically important than Michelle Everson's previous critique of EU technocracy and market hegemony. Brunkhorst also draws on the same critical concepts as Davies when he calls for the repoliticization of the EU and, in the Habermasian tradition, the double structural transformation of the European public sphere. According to Brunkhorst, this structural transformation and repoliticization of the public sphere needs to happen in both public law and public opinion and, as proved by the Greek–Eurozone crisis, cannot proceed without serious social struggles, contestations, crises and conflicts.

In the next chapter, Pierre Guibentif invites the reader back to the sociological analysis of transnational European constitutionalism, yet keeps his text profoundly informed by both systems-theoretical and critical analysis and offers a disturbing picture of the impact of the financial crisis on 'peripheral' Portuguese

10 *Jiří Přibáň*

society. This most impressive collection of empirical data is subsequently interpreted through the lens of the theory of societal constitutionalism and offers the most innovative sociology of constitutional processes at times of economic and social crisis. According to Guibentif, the strong dynamics and impact of the economic and financial systems on other social systems poses serious questions for the possibility of societal self-constitutionalization, and the forces generated by the operations of the economic and financial systems create serious asymmetries and limit the operations of both national and European politics.

In the final chapter of the volume, Petr Agha returns to the recent economic crisis and examines its impact on the European constitution, including its philosophical, jurisprudential and ideological aspects. The idea of European integration through law combined with cosmopolitan constitutionalism is contested by Agha's critical legal approach and use of, particularly, Žižek and Hardt and Negri's philosophies. Agha points to the similarities between European market arrangements and European constitutionalism beyond the state, informed by the discourse of human rights, the rule of law and democracy, and warns against a 'post-democratic regime of bureaucrats' – a dystopia which several contributors to this book strongly warn their readers against.

Bibliography

Avbelj, Matej and Jan Komárek (eds) *Constitutional Pluralism in the European Union and Beyond.* Oxford, UK: Hart Publishing, 2012.

Bellamy, Richard and Dario Castiglione (eds) *Constitutionalism in Transformation: European and Theoretical Perspectives.* Oxford, UK: Blackwell Publishers, 1996.

Cohen, Antonin. 'Constitutionalism without constitution: Transnational elites between political mobilization and legal expertise in the making of a constitution for Europe (1940s–1960s)'. *Law & Social Inquiry* 32(1) (2007): 109–135.

Dobner, Petra and Martin Loughlin (eds) *The Twilight of Constitutionalism?* Oxford, UK: Oxford University Press, 2010.

Krisch, Nico. *Beyond Constitutionalism: The Pluralist Structure of Postnational Constitutional Law.* Oxford, UK: Oxford University Press, 2010.

MacCormick, Neil. 'Beyond the sovereign state'. *The Modern Law Review* 56(1) (1993): 1–18.

Maduro, Miguel Poiares. 'Interpreting European law: Judicial adjudication in the context of constitutional pluralism', *European Journal of Legal Studies* 2(1) (2007): 1–21.

Pernice, Ingolf. 'Multilevel constitutionalism and the Treaty of Amsterdam: European constitution-making revisited', *Common Market Law Review* 36 (1999): 703–750.

Teubner, Gunther. *Constitutional Fragments: Societal Constitutionalism and Globalization.* Oxford, UK: Oxford University Press, 2012.

Tuori, Kaarlo. *European Constitutionalism.* Cambridge, UK: Cambridge University Press, 2015.

Tuori, Kaarlo and Suvi Sankari (eds) *The Many Constitutions of Europe.* Farnham, UK: Ashgate Publishing, 2010.

Walker, Neil. 'The idea of constitutional pluralism'. *Modern Law Review* 65 (2002): 317–359.

Weiler, J.H.H. *The Constitution of Europe.* Cambridge, UK: Cambridge University Press, 1999.

Part I
The European self-constitution
Concepts and theories

1 The European Constitution and the *pouvoir constituant*

No longer, or never, *sui generis*?[*]

Chris Thornhill

Introduction

Early debate about the rise of European public law was focused on the fact that the European Union (EU) initially evolved as a political order framed by a distinctive, even *sui generis* corpus of legal norms. In the first instance, this debate was mainly centred on the attempt to define the position occupied by European law in relation to the classical distinction between domestic law and international law, and, on this basis, to explain the sources of its authority. Underlying this debate, initially, was an uncertainty about the grounds for the direct effect of European law in member-state societies. Most participants in this debate were concerned with evaluating the legitimacy of interference by the European Court of Justice (ECJ) in areas of jurisprudence traditionally reserved for domestic courts. This part of the debate was settled, at least judicially, by the ruling in *Van Gend en Loos* (1963)[1] stating:

> The Community constitutes a new legal order of international law for the benefit of which the states have limited their sovereign rights, albeit within limited fields, and the subjects of which comprise not only member states but also their nationals.

This construction of European law as a normative order not dependent on constant and express state volition for authority, and able to stabilize itself as a free-standing legal order, penetrating some legal domains within national societies, ultimately gave rise to a large volume of influential literature, which examined the EU as a political order created, distinctively, by judicial bodies and especially by the ECJ.[2] Indeed, the rise of European law as an autonomous legal system, and the salient

---

[*] Research for this Chapter was funded by the European Research Council (Advanced Grant: 323656-STC).

[1] Algemene Transporten Expeditie Onderneming van Gend en Loos v. Nederlandse Administratis der Belastingen [1963] ECR 1.

[2] See, for example, Joseph H.H. Weiler, 'The transformation of Europe', *Yale Law Journal* 100 (1991): 2419, 2430; Eric Stein, 'Lawyers, judges and the making of a transnational constitution', *American Journal of International Law* 75 (1981); Alec Stone Sweet, *The Judicial Construction of Europe* (Oxford, UK: Oxford University Press, 2004).

14   *Chris Thornhill*

position of courts in the emergence of this system, have usually been observed, side by side, as equally distinctive features of the EU qua legal structure.

At the same time, debates about the atypical characteristics of EU public law also focused on the standing of constituent power in the EU, and the lack of a single and distinct constituent power to give authority to European public law became a matter of broad concern in legal analysis. This concern was concentrated in particular around the suspicion that the ECJ itself had arrogated powers usually associated with the constituent people, and that the ECJ, which, as a court, was a classical embodiment of *pouvoir constitué*, had begun to project de facto constitutional norms, both for the EU as polity and for its member states. This early consternation about the EU's absent constituent power might now of itself be seen as rather ironic and historically ill-timed. Notably, in the waves of democratic-constitutional transition in post-war Europe and Asia, few states had paid much attention to the need for a constituent power to give legitimacy to national systems of public law. In fact, the constitutions of most post-1945 post-authoritarian states, up to those of Portugal and Spain in the 1970s, were drafted through processes in which actual constituent acts played only a negligible role and in which inter-elite pacts and, above all, international organizations, international courts and even occupying military forces, established the essential premises for popular will formation. Nonetheless, the rise of the EU as an autonomous legal order forged by the acts of the ECJ seems to have revived long-suppressed memories of the deep hostility to judicial norm setting, which inhered in the origins of modern European constitution making.[3] At an early stage in its formation, accordingly, anxiety about weak constituent power assumed a central role in analyses of the political system that eventually became the EU.[4] Progressively, then, constituent power was slowly institutionalized as a core concept in research on the EU, and much criticism of the EU, both in theory and in practice, has been linked to the fact that it could not refer to a European demos as primary grounds for its jurisdiction.[5]

Over a longer time, reflection on the European constituent power has generated a series of very different, often conflicting, perspectives. For example, Theodor Schilling argued that, owing to the absence of a constituent power, the EU could not lay claim to legitimacy.[6] Dieter Grimm, taking the existence of a constituent power as the basic foundation of legitimate government, also adopted a critical

---

3 In the French Constituent Assembly in 1790, it was observed scathingly that in the *ancien régime* the judiciary had emulated functions proper to 'legislative power' and thus 'disturbed the operations' of the administration: Jacques-Guillaume Thouret, *Discours. En ouvrant la discussion sur la nouvelle organisation du pouvoir judiciaire* (Paris: Imprimerie nationale, 1790), pp. 2–3. Throughout the Revolution, few revolutionary law makers expressed anything but contempt for lawyers and for the judicial system.

4 See for example, Joseph Kaiser, 'Zur gegenwärtigen Differenzierung von Recht und Staat', *Österreichische Zeitschrift für öffentliches Recht* 10 (1960).

5 See the ruling of the German Constitutional Court in *Maastricht-Urteil* (BVerfGE 89, 155,12. 10.1993, Az: 2 BvR 2134, 2159/92).

6 See Theodor Schilling, 'The autonomy of the community legal order: An analysis of possible foundations', *Harvard International Law Journal* 37 (1996): 394.

European Constitution: sui generis? 15

approach to the denationalization of public law in the EU.[7] In parallel to such critical stances, however, some theorists began to argue for a nuanced construction of constituent power in the context of European law, and claimed that the EU might be seen as legitimated by post-traditional expressions of constituent power. Notably, Ingolf Pernice saw the EU as possessing an organic constituent power, based in the devolved powers of all citizens of the member states, resulting in the formation of a distinctively validated European Constitution, formed as an 'association of constitutions'.[8] This approach was extended by Andreas Voßkuhle to include an account of the European Constitution as resulting from an association of Constitutional Courts.[9] Neil Walker contributed to this debate by arguing that in the EU there is 'no scope for creation *ex nihilo* of a distinctive constituent power'. Despite this, however, he argued that the EU should be seen as a pluralistically authorized legal system.[10] Anne Peters echoed this approach. She claimed that in the EU constituent power and constituted power cannot be fully separated. However, she accorded to the ECJ the role of 'permanent *pouvoir constituant*', capable of producing normative authority for European public law.[11] More recently, Fossum and Menéndez developed a theory that observes the constituent power of the EU as residing in the synthesis of all constitutional arrangements in the member states.[12]

Underlying all these perspectives on the European legal system is the claim, albeit variably accentuated, that in the emergence of the EU the judicial branch of government has extended its reach beyond the classical constitutional limits of legitimate judicial authority. As a result, the public-legal order of the EU is partly constructed by judicial institutions, notably the ECJ, sometimes interacting with national courts embedded in national systems of public law, and the legitimacy of the EU cannot easily be traced to an original constituent act, or even to an original *demos*, positioned *outside the law*.[13] Pernice, Voßkuhle,

---

7   Dieter Grimm, 'The constitution in the process of denationalization', *Constellations* 12 (2005).
8   Ingolf Pernice, *Kompetenzabgrenzung im europäischen Verfassungsverbund: Antrittsvorlesung* (Berlin, Germany: Humboldt-Universität zu Berlin, 2000), 11; Ingolf Pernice, *Das Verhältnis europäischer zu nationalen Gerichten im europäischen Verfassungsverbund* (Berlin, Germany: de Gruyter, 2006), p. 18.
9   Andreas Voßkuhle, 'Multilevel cooperation of the European Constitutional Courts: *Der Europäische Verfassungsgerichtsverbund*', *European Constitutional Law Review* 6 (2010).
10 Neil Walker, 'Post-constituent constitutionalism? The case of the European Union', in *The Paradox of Constitutionalism. Constituent Power and Constitutional Form*, eds. Martin Loughlin and Neil Walker (Oxford, UK: Oxford University Press, 2007), p. 259; Neil Walker, 'Reframing EU constitutionalism', in *Ruling the World? Constitutionalism, International Law, and Global Governance*, eds. Jeffrey L. Dunoff and Joel P. Trachtman (Cambridge, UK: Cambridge University Press, 2009), p. 172.
11 Anne Peters, *Elemente einer Theorie der Verfassung Europas* (Berlin, Germany: Dunker und Humblot, 2001), p. 410.
12 John Erik Fossum and Agustín José Menéndez, *The Constitution's Gift. A Constitutional Theory for a Democratic Union* (Lanham, UK: Rowman & Littlefield, 2011), p. 53.
13 Joseph H.H. Weiler, 'In defence of the status quo: Europe''s constitutional *Sonderweg*', in *European Constitutionalism beyond the State*, eds. J.H.H. Weiler and Marlene Wind (Cambridge, UK: Cambridge University Press, 2003), p. 9.

16 *Chris Thornhill*

and Fossum and Menéndez have certainly shown dexterity and imagination in locating a European demos and bringing it conceptually into view. Whether critical or affirmative, however, different analyses ultimately converge around that claim that the European courts establish norms with effective constitutional standing, both for the EU and for individual member states. As a result, the judicial institutions of the EU, condensed around the ECJ, have acquired authority close to that of a constituent power, and the European Constitution is created, not by a single constituent event but by the multiple formative acts, both interpretive and quasi-legislative, of judicial bodies. Accordingly, the system of public law resulting from this constituent power necessarily has a highly distinctive character.

Beyond constituent power

This chapter accepts the diagnosis common to these different lines of literature that in the EU classical patterns of constituent power have been elided into judicial functions: the constitutional order of the EU has indeed been primarily constructed through autonomous judicial acts, acting as separate articulations of a *judicial constituent power*. Constituent power has thus largely become an *inner-juridical function*. However, this chapter proposes three arguments that deviate from more established perspectives on the standing of constituent power in the EU. First, it seeks to disarticulate a number of quite distinct ways in which judicial bodies, especially the ECJ or courts deriving authority from the ECJ, have assumed constitution-making power in the EU. Implied in this reconstruction is the claim that the simple centration of analysis on the absence of a constituent power has obstructed nuanced inquiry into the very varied lines of constitutional legitimation that have characterized the rise of the EU. Second, it argues that it is an error to see the exercise of constituent power by judiciaries as absolutely exclusive to the EU. In fact, the debate about the *sui generis* quality of European public law has tended to obscure the fact that many of the patterns of public law production in the EU have now become quite widespread, and can be identified in many national legal/political systems. On this basis, third, this chapter seeks to show that the EU and its legal system need to be examined in a wide sociological lens. Analysis of the EU and its distinctive multi-original judicial constitution should not be confined to the EU, and it can be productively used to understand much broader, sociologically embedded processes of legal construction.

To approach these questions, first, we can divide the judicial exercise of constituent power in the EU into five separate categories. In each of these categories, albeit distinctly, judicial acts of the ECJ have assumed the authority to set norms, either for the EU as a whole or for one or more member states, which would classically have been reserved for designated holders of constituent power. In each of these categories, thus, constituent agency is translated into a mode of inner-juridical agency. These categories are examined below.

European Constitution: sui generis?   17

Single rights in domestic societies

The first exercise of *inner-juridical constituent power* in the rise of the EU can be seen in the fact that the ECJ obtained power to create constitutional law in the member states because, under the body of European law that it incrementally created, it attributed a series of *single rights* directly to individual persons within their own national societal locations. In so doing, the ECJ stated that national courts were required to protect rights secured under EU law, at the risk of being overruled by European courts, and it enabled single persons to appeal directly from national courts to the European courts if they considered that their rights had been violated. What this meant, initially, was that, in constructing single persons as holders of rights under European law, the European judiciary was able to cut through national legal structures and implant a body of European constitutional law in the middle of national constitutional systems. The European judiciary used rights to extract single persons from their national environments and place them in an immediate relation to the European legal order, thus establishing, through rights, a direct constituent channel in which citizens could activate European laws in domestic litigation, seek redress against national laws in European courts and even individually reshape domestic public laws through invocation of European norms. The direct attribution of rights to single persons elaborated, or, more properly, *constituted*, a hard legal structure, able to penetrate and redefine basic norms of national public law and to revise basic patterns of legal obligation in national jurisdictions: under the European order of rights, citizens in member states entered a multi-tier system of legal inclusion.

Originally, rights offered by European courts were mainly restricted to rights required to secure the four pillars of the European market. In *Salgoil* (1968),[14] for example, the ECJ stated that Articles of EU law regulating movement of goods in national societies created rights in favour of individuals, which national courts were required to protect, regardless of any rule existing in national law. Ultimately, however, as it gradually fleshed out a distinct body of more general human rights law to support its rulings, the ECJ began to distribute rights to single individuals, which were not based solely in market freedoms, and it used more broadly constructed human rights to reach into domestic jurisdictions. By 2011, the ECJ openly applied rights that had little to do with the four basic freedoms. In *Ruiz Zambrano*,[15] it ruled that that 'the genuine enjoyment' of rights obtained by persons 'by virtue of their status as citizens of the Union' should be taken as a normative ideal for legal finding across the EU and its member states as a whole.[16] Through this ruling, implicitly, the ECJ construed itself as a Constitutional Court for the political right holders (citizens) of the EU, and it

---

14 SpA Salgoil v Italian Ministry of Foreign Trade [1968] ECR 453.

15 Case C-34/09 Gerardo Ruiz Zambrano v Office national de l'emploi (ECJ, 8 March 2011).

16 On the implications of this, see Armin von Bogdandy et al., 'Reverse Solange: Protecting the essence of fundamental rights against EU member states', *Common Market Law Review* 49 (2012).

18   *Chris Thornhill*

assumed the capacity to instil a free-standing rights-based constitution in different dimensions of member-state societies.

Autonomous use of international instruments

In the expansion of its authority, both in the EU polity itself and across the jurisdictions of member states, the ECJ repeatedly explained its authority through reference to international conventions, and it began to exercise *inner-juridical constituent power* by constructively appropriating principles from international conventions to secure legitimacy for European law. Manifestly, the ECJ initially had no relation to the Council of Europe; the accession of the EU to the European Convention on Human Rights (ECHR) still remains legally problematic.[17] Nonetheless, the ECJ has increasingly aligned itself to the ECHR, and it has borrowed widely from the case law of the European Court of Human Rights (ECtHR). Generally, use of the ECHR by the ECJ has formed part of a strategy through which the ECJ has endeavoured to justify its encroachment on the domestic law of member states, and it has appealed to international human rights norms as a legitimating basis for its own cross-jurisdictional penetration. In other words, it has utilized international human rights law as a source of inner-juridical constituent power. This process began in the key early case of *Stauder v City of Ulm* (1969),[18] in which the ECJ defined human rights as 'general principles' of European law,[19] implicitly promoting an incorporation of human rights norms in the Union's treaties. Subsequently, in *Internationale Handelsgesellschaft* (1970),[20] the ECJ declared that rights were included in the corpus of 'constitutional principles common to the Member States', and the ECJ was authorized both to interpret these rights and to apply them as common law across the states in the Union.[21] Progressively, the ECJ gradually defined human rights as elements of a wide moral horizon for the EU and its organs, and it freely utilized rights as justification for its rulings. In *Nold* (1974),[22] *Rutili* (1975)[23] and *Hauer* (1979),[24] the ECJ explained its judgments as drawing legitimacy from international treaties, in particular the ECHR, to which member

---

17 See Gráinne de Búrca, 'The road not taken: The European Union as a global human rights actor', *The American Journal of International Law* 105(4) (2011).

18 Stauder v City of Ulm [1969] ECR 419.

19 Andrew Williams, *EU Human Rights Policies: A Study in Irony* (Oxford, UK: Oxford University Press, 2004), p. 145. It is widely agreed that through the cases described above the ECJ 'fleshed out' an effective Bill of Rights to support its rulings: Henri de Waele, 'The role of the European Court of Justice in the integration process: A contemporary and normative assessment', *Hanse Law Review* 3(5) (2010).

20 Internationale Handelsgesellschaft v Einfuhr- und Vorratsstelle Getreide [1970] ECR 1125.

21 See Demetrios G. Metropoulos, 'Human rights, incorporated: The European Community's new line of business', *Stanford Journal of International Law* 29 (1992–1993): 136.

22 Nold v Commission, [1974] ECR 491.

23 Rutili v. Minister for the Interior, [1975] ERC 12.

24 Liselotte Hauer v. Land Rheinland Pfalz, [1979] ECR. 3727.

European Constitution: sui generis? 19

states were signatories.[25] Eventually, the ECJ bolstered its authority by tying its jurisprudence to the case law of the ECtHR.[26] By 1989, in *Hoechst,*[27] the ECJ expressly accorded elevated status to the ECHR as a source of jurisprudence. Through this proximity, the ECJ was able to acquire a number of functions usually allotted to Constitutional Courts, and it progressively conferred *upon itself* the power to review EU legislation for conformity with human rights norms, thus effectively grafting a rights-based judicial constitution onto the legal order of the member states.[28] By the 1980s, the ECJ was often described as having powers of a European Constitutional Court,[29] and it projected its constitutional authority, lacking any evident constitutional foundation, as the result of a mandate to protect human rights.[30]

In this process, the ECJ, in essence, extracted from international human rights norms a distinctive constituent authority *for itself.* It used these norms to build a constitutional basis for its functions, to accompany its rulings and to vindicate and stabilize penetration of its rulings across the societies within the EU. Ultimately, the judicial protection of basic rights in the EU was placed on firmer constitutional footing, and the standing of rights was set out in a series of treaties. From 1992 onwards, the EU witnessed a 'remarkable expansion of fundamental rights protection', reflected in particular in the Treaties of Maastricht and Lisbon.[31] Initially, however, rights were constituted by the ECJ alone. The ECJ in fact *constituted itself* as a court bound by human rights norms and, in so doing, it constituted

---

25 The ECJ declared in the *Nold* decision that 'international treaties for the protection of human rights' (thus including the European Convention) were to be taken as 'guidelines which should be followed within the framework of community law'. See Laurent Scheeck, 'Relationship between the European Courts and integration through human rights', *Zeitschrift für ausländisches öffentliches Recht und Völkerrecht* 65 (2005): 850.

26 Simon Denys, 'Des influences réciproques entre CJCE et CEDH: "Je t'aime, moi non plus"?', *Pouvoirs* 96 (2001): 35–36.

27 Hoechst v Commission [1989] ECR 2859.

28 See classic comment in Joseph H.H. Weiler, 'Eurocracy and distrust: Some questions concerning the role of the European Court of Justice in the protection of fundamental human rights within the legal order of the European Communities', *Washington Law Review* 61 (1986): 1105.

29 Christian Walter, 'Die europäische Menschenrechtskonvention als Konstitutionalisierungsprozeß', *Zeitschrift für ausländisches öffentliches Recht und Völkerrecht* 59 (1999): 962. On the status of the ECJ as a self-appointed Constitutional Court more generally, see Marcus Höreth, 'Stille Revolution im Namen des Rechts? Zur Rolle des Europäischen Gerichtshofes (EuGH) im Prozess der europäischen Integration', Zentrum für Europäische Integrationsforschung, Universität Bonn, Discussion Paper C78 (2000), p. 11; Bo Vesterdorf, 'A Constitutional Court for the EU?', *International Journal of Constitutional Law* 4 (2006): 607. Note the description of the ECJ as a 'comprehensive Constitutional Court' in Lukas Bauer, *Der Europäische Gerichtshof als Verfassungsgericht?* (Baden-Baden, Germany: Nomos, 2008), p. 174.

30 Elenia Simina Tanasenscu, 'Role des droits fondamentaux dans la constitutionnalisation de l'ordre juridique de l'UE', in *The Court of Justice and the Construction of Europe. Analyses and Perspectives on Sixty Years of Case-Law*, eds. Allan Rosas, Egils Levits and Yves Bot (The Hague, The Netherlands: Asser, 2013), p. 217.

31 Sybe A. De Vries, 'Balancing fundamental rights with economic freedoms according to the European Court of Justice', *Utrecht Law Review* 9 (2013): 169.

20   Chris Thornhill

the material constitution, which it construed itself as authorized to interpret and to apply. The early treaties of the EEC, tellingly, gave no particular primacy to human rights, and it was only by extracting authority from international instruments that the ECJ could elevate itself into its broadly constituent role. Having constituted itself, then, the ECJ also constituted other components of the EU as parts of a unitary legal system bound by recognition of human rights. In each respect, the ECJ recursively utilized the constituent power of rights to place itself at the centre of a European constitutional order, and it projected a constitutional system of rights across the entire Union.

Preliminary rulings and legal structure building

The inner-juridical exercise of constituent power in the EU is also evident in the ECJ's practice of handing down preliminary rulings to national courts. These rulings are normally used, pre-emptively, to bring national courts into line with principles developed in the ECJ and to ensure that norms established by the ECJ are constitutively co-implied throughout the domestic legal systems of member states.[32] This practice has acquired manifest constituent impact on national law as it has reduced the basic autonomy of national courts. However, this practice has also played a constituent role in the EU as it has changed the position of the judicial branch within national societies, typically enabling domestic courts to expand their authority against national executives, national policy makers and even national legislatures. The classic example of this can be found in the suite of *Factortame*[33] cases in the UK, in which a single preliminary ruling of the ECJ effectively dislodged the historically immovable commitment to the sovereignty of the Westminster parliament.

Comity and dialogue with national courts: the Solange method

The ability of the ECJ to constitute a system of human rights in European society was largely due, initially, to the paradoxical fact that its penetration into national legal systems was originally resisted by the superior courts of some member states. In particular, by the 1960s, Italian and German Constitutional Courts, motivated by deep ideological commitment to the protection of entrenched rights, had begun to challenge the primacy of EU law on the basis that it was insufficiently compliant with international human rights agreements, notably the ECHR. This controversy was first formally expressed in the Italian Constitution Court, especially in the judgment in *Frontini* (1973).[34] In this judgment, the Italian Court recognized the primacy of European law, but it claimed that it retained authority to review all cases in which there was a conflict between EU law and domestic

---

32 Karen J. Alter, 'Who are the "Masters of the Treaty"? European governments and the European Court of Justice', *International Organization* 52 (1998).

33 Please see especially Factortame Ltd and others v Secretary of State for Transport – [1989] 2 All ER 692.

34 Italian Constitutional Court, Case 183/73 – Frontini.

European Constitution: sui generis? 21

constitutional or human rights law: transfer of sovereign powers did not include transfer of powers to violate human rights and discretionary powers of EU institutions were always, lastly, constrained by rights norms and subject to domestic review. This process of contestation culminated, famously, in the first *Solange* ruling of the West German Constitution Court (1974).[35] Hardening the logic of *Frontini*, the West German Court claimed that it retained the right to review Community laws *as long as* the ECJ did not fully reflect human rights protection thresholds derived from the ECHR. At a manifest level, these rulings distilled a particular conflict between supranational and national courts, and, prima facie, they may have appeared to place a brake on the rising autonomy of the European system of public law. In some respects, however, these jurisdictional frictions ultimately assumed a de facto constituent role, and they also provide evidence of an *inner-juridical constituent power*, shaping the basic laws of the EU in several respects.

First, clearly, the ECJ refracted the challenge to its authority posed by powerful national courts by solidifying the protection that it gave to human rights, and by defining rights more conclusively as inner components of its jurisprudence. Indeed, the ECJ's absorption of human rights from international instruments described above was directly triggered by the *Solange* controversy. Through the course of its long *turn to rights*,[36] the ECJ borrowed a corpus of rights jurisprudence from other courts and generally heightened the standing of human rights across the EU, in order to underscore its own legitimacy and its own constituent influence vis-á-vis judiciaries in member states, which also extracted authority from rights. Rights thus distilled a line of contestation in which the ECJ accepted thresholds of rights' protection defined by national courts and, in so doing, usurped some functions which these courts aimed to reserve to themselves. This was eventually recognized in the second *Solange* ruling (1986),[37] in which the German Constitutional Court agreed to recognize the rulings of the ECJ, because it was content that the ECJ had satisfactorily internalized rights norms.

Second, these contests created a legal system in which different courts, located at different tiers of the EU as supranational polity, were able to mark out spheres of comity and discretion, and different courts, national and supranational, began to accept the rulings of others if these were measurably shaped by recognition of an overarching culture of human rights derived from the ECHR.[38] Notably, this meant

---

35 Solange I – Internationale Handelsgesellschaft von Einfuhr- und Vorratsstelle für . . . Futtermittel, decision of 29 May 1974, BVerfGE 37, 271 [1974] CMLR 540.

36 For this concept see Mikael Rask Madsen, 'The protracted institutionalization of the Strasbourg Court: From legal diplomacy to integrationist jurisprudence', in *The European Court of Human Rights between Law and Politics*, eds. Jonas Christoffersen and Mikael Rask Madsen (Oxford, UK: Oxford University Press, 2011), p. 59.

37 Solange II (BVerfG v. 22.10.1986 – 2 BvR 197/83, BVerfGE 73, 339).

38 See Gráinne de Búrca, 'The European Court of Justice and the International Legal Order after *Kadi*', *Harvard International Law Journal* 51 (2010): 43; Nikolaos Lavranos, 'The *Solange*-Method as a tool for regulating competing jurisdictions among international courts and tribunals', *Loyola Los Angeles International and Comparative Law Review* 30 (2008): 312; Türküler Isiksel, 'Fundamental rights in the EU after *Kadi and Al Barakaat*', *European Law Journal* 16 (2010): 562.

22   *Chris Thornhill*

that each level of jurisdiction was defined internally by rights norms, and different courts assumed responsibilities for the recursive checking of other courts, thus ensuring internal conformity to rights obligations across the entire European legal system. As a result of this, the ECJ spelled out a basic diction of multilaterally recognized rights to create a many-tiered constitution, in which different courts operated within designated, internally legitimated, spheres of competence, ceaselessly reproducing constituent norms to bind the system together. Of course, relations between the supranational and the national courts remained intermittently strained, and there were further turbulent episodes.[39] On the whole, however, different courts acted in consort to form a multi-judicial constitution, in which rights were constantly articulated to check the authority of legislation and judicial verdicts and to form a basic constitutional grammar for the EU as a whole. Ultimately, in *Kadi* (2008),[40] the ECJ turned the *Solange* method outwards, and it argued that other international organizations, in this case the United Nations (UN), could not issue directives in EU member states unless these were consonant with the ECJ's expectations regarding the foundation of legal norms in fundamental rights. The *Solange* method thus became an integral part of both the inner and the outer constitution of the EU.

Proportionality

The exercise of inner-juridical constituent power in the growth of the EU is also manifest in the importance of proportionality in European law, which is applied by European courts in twofold fashion and for a twofold purpose. On the one hand, use of proportionality forms part of the subsidiarity doctrine, and it allows courts to measure the justification of national deviations from EU directives. On the other hand, use of proportionality has been influenced by practices of the ECtHR, and it has been applied by the ECJ to assess cases in national polities in which there occurs a derogation from fundamental rights guaranteed under European law.[41] This is formalized in Art 52 of the Charter of Fundamental Rights. At a most obvious level, use of proportionality in the first category acquired constituent importance for the legal order of the EU, because it formed a matrix in which legal decisions throughout the entire European judicial system were loosely co-ordinated and in which norms of EU law could be interactively transmitted through different courts at different tiers of the EU polity.[42] At the same time, use of proportionality

---

39 See note 6 above.
40 Joined Cases C-402/05 P and C-415/05 *P Kadi and Al Barakaat International Foundation v Council and Commission* [2008] ECR I-6351.
41 See use of rights-based proportionality in *Association Belge des Consommateurs Test-Achats and Others* (Social policy) [2011] EUECJ C-236/09 (1 March 2011). For comment, see Bruno de Witte, 'The past and future role of the European Court of Justice in the protection of human rights', in *The EU and Human Rights*, ed. Philip Alston (Oxford, UK: Oxford University Press, 1999), p. 861.
42 See Karen Alter's claim in a memorandum for the UK parliament that: 'National courts and the ECJ will jointly negotiate the meaning of the terms of "subsidiarity" and "proportionality", as they have negotiated the meaning of EU law supremacy'. http://www.publications.parliament.uk/pa/ld200304/ldselect/ldeucom/47/47we02.htm.

European Constitution: sui generis? 23

in the second category became a constitutional force in a more diffuse, pervasive fashion. The rise of rights-based proportionality has inevitably drawn domestic courts and European courts into a direct, legally constitutive judicial dialogue. However, proportionality relating to fundamental rights also assumed importance, as considered above, because it allowed different national courts to internalize principles, derived from supranational legal norms, which they could invoke as a recursive basic law for their own polities and which even obliged them, in some cases, to act autonomously against their own executives.[43] Increasingly, use of proportionality in the ECJ has replicated some aspects of the proportionality juris-prudence of the ECtHR, and it has defined basic rights as goods requiring even higher judicial protection than basic freedoms. Together with the ECtHR, there-fore, the ECJ has instilled an obligation to basic rights across domestic courts in member states.[44] Overall, owing to their increasing use of proportionality, dif-ferent courts began to enact a *running constitutional code*, which enabled them recursively to evaluate, to criticize, to pre-define and, under some circumstances, to overrule the acts of decision takers in national polities. Through proportional-ity, courts internalized an overarching constituent power, which was endlessly co-implied in judicial acts, and this allowed the entire EU polity, otherwise very diffusely structured, to assume a degree of inner constitutional consistency, often at variance with the constitutional law of member-state polities.

In each of these categories, the rise of the EU can surely be seen as a distinc-tive process of constitutional formation. In particular, the rise of the EU can be seen as a process in which public law was increasingly produced *by and within the legal system itself*. This process was focused around the ECJ, which is widely identified, quite accurately, as a motor of European constitutionalization. More broadly, however, the public-legal form of the EU was abstracted and defined by many different interactions inside the European legal system, and the EU's basic legal structure – that is, its constitution – was cemented, as judicial actors interactively elevated the norms underpinning their own powers to constitutional rank. In each of the above categories of constituent agency, constitutional laws have been produced through an inner-systemic translocation of norms, in which constituted actors have been able to establish and enforce basic constitutional provisions, both for the EU and for its single member states, using powers already stored within the legal system. The rise of the EU's legal system can thus be seen as a process in which an existing legal structure recursively extended and reproduced itself and recursively generated normative constructs to support its self-extension and its self-reproduction. In this process, above all, the construc-tion of singular rights played the most vital role in extending and reconstituting the legal system. The deepening penetration of European constitutional norms

---

43 See Gráinne de Búrca, 'Proportionality and *Wednesbury* unreasonableness: The influence of European Legal Concepts on UK public law', *European Public Law* 3 (1992): 585.
44 See C-112/00 *Schmidberger Internationale Transporte und Planzüge v Austria* [2003] ECR I-5659.

24   *Chris Thornhill*

was induced largely by the fact that the ECJ and other courts *internalized* international human rights norms as sources of constituent power, which these courts then stored and articulated to widen the legal-inclusionary structure of the EU. Rights, in fact, *became the constituent power* for the European legal system, and, through the judicial internalization of rights norms, the European Constitution was able at once to solidify itself and to preserve normative consistency, yet also to dispense with all more classical exercise of constituent agency.

Is this constitution *sui generis*?

As discussed, the reliance of the European legal system on internalized sources of authority is usually taken as a sign of its unique composition, or of its *sui generis* structure, forming a pronounced contrast to conventional national constitutions. It is widely presupposed that the constitution of the EU has been formed through entirely distinctive processes.

In many respects, however, the perception of the EU as a wholly distinctive public-legal order is based on a rather simplified set of premises. On the one hand, first, this conception of the EU can be criticized for historiographical reasons. In fact, the EU was formed before most nation states existed, and even those states that did exist when the EU was founded were, with few exceptions, loosely integrated. It is thus surely inaccurate to imagine that the EU fell short of some commonly established model of national-democratic institution building. Second, from a more conceptual perspective, the sharp counter-position of European public law to more standard patterns of constitution making is only sustainable if we adopt a simplified construction of classical (national) public law: that is, the public-legal order of the EU only appears fundamentally distinctive if classical constitutions are perceived as literally defined normative documents, produced, through identifiable constituent acts, to satisfy reasoned interests of national societies. As I have observed elsewhere, this classical view of constitutions reflects a deeply reductive construction of the social processes that actually impacted on public-legal norm production in most constitution-making situations.[45] Most constitutions in fact developed through a process of deepening social inclusion in which political systems, as they began to penetrate more deeply into society, were required to construct and preserve generalized norms to support their increasingly inclusive transmission of legal decisions and rulings more across complex social environments. To this degree, most classical constitutions developed as inner elements of society's *inclusionary structure*, acting to heighten the integrative reach and capacities of national political systems. In its first formulation in the eighteenth century, the concept of constituent power may have acted to promote this structural widening of society. However, it is illusory to assume that the legal orders of

---

45 Chris Thornhill, 'A sociology of constituent power: The political code of transnational societal constitutions', *Indiana Journal of Global Legal Studies* 20 (2013); Chris Thornhill, 'The dialectic of constituent power in contemporary constitutionalism', *Global Constitutionalism* 1 (2012).

modern societies drew factual legitimacy from constituent actors, or from legal norms resulting from single constituent acts. In consequence, it is perhaps more sociologically realistic if we observe the formation of constitutional laws, not as the deliberate construction of reasonable norms but as a process of *inclusionary structure building*, oriented towards the establishment of a system of legal inclusion for complex societies. From this perspective, the categorical distinction between the public law of the EU and the public law of nation states begins rapidly to dissolve.

Third, however, the suggestion of a strict antinomy between European law and other constitutions is losing validity, because more conventional processes of constitution making are becoming less common, and most public law is now constituted by non-traditional means. In fact, in contemporary societies, a broad range of legal entities has started to emulate the multi-focal, inner-juridical patterns of structural formation, which have played a central role in the EU. This invites a paradigm change in the way in which the public-legal system of the EU is observed: in its internal reconfiguration of constituent power, the EU can now be examined, not as a fully *sui generis* legal order but – instead – as *a precursor* of lines of legal-structural formation that are now becoming more widespread, across very different political systems.

To illustrate this claim, first, the EU has obviously lost some constitutional distinctiveness, because patterns of legal formation pioneered by the EU have migrated into other *supranational legal orders*. For instance, it is well documented that formation of constitutional structures by judicial institutions has been copied in other cross-national legal communities; in other supranational legal systems, rights are widely applied to bring structural cohesion to the legal system as a whole and to link different components of the system to shared founding norms.[46] At a more fundamental level, however, the EU has lost constitutional distinctiveness, because *individual nation states* have begun to deploy modes of constitutional formation devised in the EU. In many cases, in fact, nation states have begun to create their domestic constitutions on multiple, commonly *inner-juridical* foundations, often abandoning all pretence of extracting authority from an external constituent power. In particular, nation states are increasingly confronted with highly complex demands for law making, in which external forms of acclamation or legitimation for law cannot easily be mobilized, and, to address these demands, they are obliged to produce and legitimate their legal structures in recursive, internalistic fashion. In confronting these pressures, many states have assimilated techniques for internalizing constituent agency, which are more typical of cross-national legal entities in general and of the EU in particular.

In recent years, all the distinctive characteristics of public-legal formation in the EU have become, in a number of different settings, quite pronounced aspects of national-democratic polity building and national constitutional formation.

---

46 See Karen J. Alter, Laurence R. Helfer and Osvaldo Saldías, 'Transplanting the European Court of Justice: The experience of the Andean Tribunal of Justice', *American Journal of Comparative Law* 60 (2012).

26   *Chris Thornhill*

Indeed, many national polities now openly extract their constitutional structure through the exercise of an *inner-juridical constituent power*, and many rely on inner-juridical constructions of their authority to compensate for their inability to derive legitimacy for their laws from a clearly manifest demos. The separate categories of inner-juridical constituent power that can be observed in the EU are all replicated in national polities. Some examples of this are outlined below.

Single rights in domestic societies

The extraction of constituent power from the direct judicial application of single rights is now evident in many societies, and it forms an increasingly common pattern of constitutional structure building. Of course, during the first formation of modern national societies, individual rights helped to cement a dense nexus between national political institutions and other parts of society, placing individuals, in different functional domains, in a more immediate relation to centralized organs of the political system.[47] In this context, the ability of state institutions to use rights as instruments to derive legitimacy from, and apply power to, single social agents was a vital precondition for the stabilization of national constitutional order. From this time on, single rights were widely deployed to intensify the constituent link between state and society, and modern political systems have typically relied on singular rights as a foundation for their constitutional structure. In post-1945 history, however, the circulation of individual rights through society has assumed an increasingly important constituent role for national political systems. Most obviously, first, after 1945, the direct allocation of rights to individual persons facilitated the solidification of constitutional order in societies which had traditionally proved resistant to uniform legal inclusion. For example, the post-authoritarian polities created after the Second World War relied on their allocation of singular rights (partly extracted from international law) to cement a constitutional nexus between the state and society and to subordinate disparate, traditionally highly centrifugal, sectors of society to centralized state control and uniform legal inclusion.[48] At the same time, in fact, some relatively established democracies, such as the USA, utilized single rights to harden the structural link between the national state and different sub-national authorities, sectors and regions.[49] Quite generally, singular rights have acted as vital sources of constitutional density across a range of polity types.

In very recent history, however, many states, especially those with a historically diffuse character, and overarching multiple and complexly connected

---

47 See Chris Thornhill, *A Sociology of Constitutions* (Cambridge, UK: Cambridge University Press, 2011), ch. 3.

48 Notably, in both post-1945 Italy and post-1945 Japan the jurisprudence of superior courts was partly focused on restricting the countervailing power of regions and of private actors assuming privileged positions in localities. In Japan, in fact, the growth of rights jurisprudence accompanied policies designed to remove feudal residues from society.

49 See David Sloss, 'How international norms transformed the U.S. Constitution', *Human Rights Quarterly* 37 (2015).

territories have made distinctive use of human rights, often borrowed in part from international law, to strengthen their constitutional basis in society. This can be seen, for example, in contemporary Russia, where rights derived from international law have been strategically applied to bring unity to the national legal system. In Russia, the executive, despite its partial authoritarian position, has specifically encouraged rights-based litigation against public agencies, and it has created procedures to facilitate public law litigation, in particular against local authorities, for violation of rights. In 2002, importantly, Putin introduced the Civil Procedure Code, which established procedures for litigation against administrative decisions, including presidential decrees. This created new opportunities for the mobilization of human rights law in Russian society.[50] A new law to facilitate administrative litigation has recently come into effect, and this law gives extensive powers to courts to simplify access to justice and ensure transparency in administrative functions. One, seemingly intentional, consequence of these processes is that litigation over rights by single individuals has weakened the powers exercised by intermediary actors and local powers (often marked by high levels of corruption), and, in so doing, it has allowed the central state to reach more cohesively into different parts of society.[51] The state has thus consciously promoted single rights in order to generate legal unity across society and to pull different actors in society into a more direct, structured relation to the central authority of the legal-political system. As in the EU, therefore, the fact that individual persons in society are able to claim rights serves, to some degree, to extract these persons from their particular social location and to incorporate them in a widening system of legal inclusion, spanning all parts of society. Even societies at a very early stage of constitutional formation, such as China, have begun to promote singular rights through society, because this integrates different social sectors more fully in the political system and creates an encompassing inclusionary structure through society.[52] Furthermore, in some Latin American societies, nation states have recently utilized international human rights to solidify their hold on society and generally to constitute robust inclusionary structures.[53]

---

50 For information about Russia, I wish to thank my brilliant Research Associate, Dr Maria Smirnova.

51 Notably, Putin's judicial reforms were designed as part of an anti-corruption drive. See Jeffrey Kahn, 'Russia's "Dictatorship of Law" and the European Court of Human Rights', *Review of Central and East European Law* 29 (2004).

52 See the resolutions of the Plenary Committee of the CCP in late 2014. In these resolutions, strengthening the rule of law and protection of human rights were clearly linked to a policy of structural reinforcement.

53 Colombia is the classic example of this. In Colombia, assimilation of rulings from the Inter-American Court of Human Rights (IACtHR) has been promoted, successfully, to raise domestic state capacities. In some cases, the Colombian government has adopted recommendations of the IACtHR in order to intensify its legal control of its own territories, and, despite its initial resistance, it has followed a policy of accepting liability for paramilitary violence in order to assert a domestic monopoly of power. See as illustration observations of the court in *The Case of Afro-Descendant Communities Displaced from the Cacarica River Basin (Operation Genesis) v. Colombia* (Judgment), Inter-Am. Ct. H.R., Ser. C, No. 270, (20 November 2013).

28   *Chris Thornhill*

Overall, therefore, the immediate application of rights (often of international provenance) to single social agents has become a common technique for hardening constitutional structure in society.

Autonomous use of international instruments

The judicial use of international human rights instruments to construct and exercise an inner-juridical constituent power is also an increasingly prominent tendency in national constitution making. For example, in many democratic transitions in recent decades, courts have utilized reference to international human rights instruments to establish basic norms for the political system, to interpret and elaborate national legislation, and even to instruct national legislatures as to their legislative duties. In such cases, courts have proposed themselves as holders of constituent power, they have invoked international human rights norms as a basis for their exercise of this power, and they have often applied human rights norms as internalistic sources of constitutional law. Clear evidence of this can be found in transitional Poland, Hungary and South Africa.[54] Most strikingly, in the longer process of democratic transition in Kenya, the Kenyan High Court invoked international law to *designate itself* as protector of the constituent power for the new constitution, and it defined the procedural conditions under which this power was to be activated.[55] Even in established democracies, however, courts have extracted from international human rights the authority quite fundamentally to reorganize constitutional conditions in their own polities. An important example of this is the UK. In the UK, manifestly, the power of the courts has been greatly expanded by the Human Rights Act (HRA) (1998) in which parliament expressly allows courts to review legislation in light of international rights law and even to declare some acts of primary law making in breach of the ECHR. Long before the HRA, however, courts had begun, in relative autonomy, to alter the classical parliamentary design of the UK constitution. Progressively, and of their own volition, the courts in the UK utilized increasing presumptions in favour of international human rights law to shape a corpus of public law which, although it was underpinned neither by a formal constitution nor by a formal catalogue of rights, acknowledged the existence of *constitutional rights*, which the legislature had only very limited, or *exceptional*, authority to overrule.[56] The courts increasingly promoted the view that, whatever their constitutional position, legislatures are only permitted to act in breach of international rights norms in cases of great emergency and only where they declare this intention in express terms: where this is not the case, statutes must be interpreted as compliant with

---

54   See Mark F. Brzezinski and Lezek Garlicki, 'Judicial review in post-communist Poland: The emergence of a *Rechtsstaat?*', *Stanford Journal of International Law* 31 (1995); András Sajó, 'Reading the invisible constitution: judicial review in Hungary', *Oxford Journal of Legal Studies* 15 (1995).
55   *Njoya and Others* v. *Attorney-General and Others* (2004) AHRLR 157 (KeHC 2004).
56   *R* v. *Lord Chancellor ex p Witham* [1997] EWHC Admin 237 (7 March 1997).

European Constitution: sui generis?   29

human rights norms, and the will of parliament must be seen as a will intrinsically proportioned to rights.[57] The promotion of this doctrine ultimately opened the ground for the courts to declare that the UK polity contains an implicit hierarchy of statutes, in which some laws have constitutional standing and are relatively entrenched against repeal[58] and so quite substantially to restrict time-honoured assumptions regarding the final sovereignty of parliament.[59] In *Simms* (1999), one Justice went as far as to suggest that the courts had acquired powers to assess the constitutionality of statutes not far removed from those exercised in polities with a codified constitution.[60]

Across a range of different political systems, therefore, there is clear evidence that courts are often capable of exercising constituent power. Moreover, courts typically assume the position of constituent power, because they distil authority from international human rights instruments, and they apply rights as the primary source of legitimacy for political structure. In the cases above, as in the EU, courts have repeatedly *constituted themselves* as constituent actors, and, in so doing, they have acquired the ability to create constitutional norms either within the form of an existing constitution or *ex nihilo*.

Preliminary rulings and legal structure building

Analogues to the use of preliminary rulings as an inner-juridical source of constitutional structure can also be identified in a wide range of constitution-making situations. Most clearly, this is now an important part of polity building within supranational legal systems. In many cases, laws of national polities located in a supranational legal system are strictly pre-determined by supranational judicial rulings, and national judiciaries typically form a sluice through which external norms enter and re-configure domestic law. In extreme cases, supranational courts even influence the composition of national courts, and the linkage of national courts to extra-national judicial bodies is established de facto as part of a system of constitutional rights.[61] In addition, however, the promotion of norms by preliminary rulings can also be observed as a source of constitutional structure within nation states, outside supranational jurisdictions. This is especially prominent in states whose penetration across diffuse territories is historically rather strained and whose constitutional foundation in society is precarious. In China, for example, the government has devised a particular strategy for consolidating the inclusionary force of the national political system, which entails the promulgation of sample case rulings by national courts, to be copied and adhered to in

---

57 *R* v. *Secretary of State For The Home Department ex p Daly* [2001] UKHL 26 (23 May 2001).
58 *Thoburn* v. *Sunderland City Council* [2002] EWHC 195 (Admin) (18 February 2002).
59 *Rantzen* v. *Mirror Group Newspapers (1986) Ltd.* [1993] EWCA Civ 16 (31 March 1993).
60 *R* v. *Secretary of State for The Home Department ex p Simms*; H.L. 11 February 1999.
61 See the landmark case in the Inter-American system: *Case of the Dismissed Congressional Employees (Aguado-Alfaro et al.)* v. *Peru*, Inter-American Court of Human Rights (2006).

30   Chris Thornhill

lower-court rulings.[62] These rulings, often partly based on international standards of administrative law, are made public by superior courts, and they are used to provide guidelines for litigation, both to lower courts and to potential litigants, indicating probable outcomes in particular cases of challenge, appeal and litigation. One notable function of this use of sample rulings is that they are intended both to simplify litigation by single social agents against administrative bodies and to bring consistency to the legal system as a whole: to reinforce the basic inclusionary structure of the political system. On the one hand, as in Russia, this publication of sample cases in China is conceived as a means to stimulate litigation by single persons against the state, so that the national government can intensify the immediacy of its relation to particular social agents. On the other hand, however, this promotion of public law litigation is often conceived as a technique by which the central government can augment its supervisory powers over local government: that is, the government publicizes sample case judgments in order to encourage litigation against peripheral public agencies, so that the central state can ensure that these are acting in accordance with formally defined legal codes. In both respects, sample rulings forms a device for hardening the position of the national political system in society and for enabling constitutional norms to penetrate all levels of the political system and all sectors of society. In this example, court rulings are clearly accorded constitutional authority, and litigation through the courts is expressly used as a means of transplanting norms across society as a whole and, in so doing, of elaborating a binding constitutional structure.

Comity and dialogue with national courts: the Solange *method*

Parallels to the *Solange* method as a source of inner-juridical constitutional norm formation can also be found, to an increasing degree, in other legal and political systems. In different ways, some national courts have now begun to use a technique similar to the *Solange* method in order both to mark out spheres of discretion between domestic and supranational courts and to constitutionalize the inner structure of the political system in which they are located.

A significant example of this is the judgment of the UK Supreme Court in *Ahmed* v. *HM Treasury* (2010).[63] In this case, the Supreme Court used norms formalized in the ECHR to strike down domestic orders used to give effect to anti-terrorism directives imposed by the UN. The Court concluded that, although UN directives are traditionally accorded primacy over the ECHR, in this instance these directives were implemented without provision for a judicial remedy for affected parties, and, under the ECHR, the UK courts were obliged to reject these directives as invalid, at least in their application in domestic society.

---

62 Kevin J. O'Brien and Lianjiang Li, 'Suing the local state: Administrative litigation in rural China', *China Journal* 51 (2004): 87.

63 *Ahmed and others v HM Treasury; al-Ghabra v HM Treasury; R (on the application of Youssef) v HM Treasury;* (No 2); Note – [2010] 4 All ER 829.

European Constitution: sui generis? 31

In this instance, notably, the Supreme Court deployed the *Solange* method to borrow rights from international law (the ECHR) and, through these rights, both to harden rights protection in the UK constitution and to project new conditions for comity between the UK and the UN. A reconstructed *Solange* method, strongly influenced by the earlier ruling of the ECJ in *Kadi*, thus became a principle of national constitutional formation. Similar approaches can be discerned in other constitutional systems – notably, in Canada. In *Canada (Justice)* v. *Khadr* (2008), a case regarding disclosure of documents to a Canadian detainee in Guantánamo, it was decided by the Canadian Supreme Court that Canada's human rights obligations must be assigned higher rank than other international obligations and, as a result, that all human rights cases involving Canadians, even if concerned with acts committed extra-territorially, must be judged under domestic law. The Canadian Charter of Rights and Freedoms, thus, was defined by the Court as the constitutional *Grundnorm* for all acts of all Canadians, regardless of their physical location, and in human rights cases conventions of inter-judicial comity were ruled invalid. This was expressed in the following terms:

> The principles of international law and comity of nations, which normally require that Canadian officials operating abroad comply with local law and which might otherwise preclude application of the Charter to Canadian officials acting abroad, do not extend to participation in processes that violate Canada's binding international human rights obligations. . . . The comity concerns that would normally justify deference to foreign law do not apply in this case.[64]

In this context, an approach with similarities to the *Solange* method was used both to define lines and limits of comity between domestic and national courts and to consolidate the strength of national rights jurisprudence. Indeed, in this case, a modified *Solange* method was utilized to project the Canadian Charter as an effective *extraterritorial constitution*, with inclusionary reach beyond the borders of national jurisdiction.

Contest between different judicial systems over lines of discretion is now an increasingly common pattern of constitution making and constitutional reinforcement. Such contest provides a distinct channel through which national courts can cement provisions for constitutional rights in domestic politics and even augment the authority of their own constitutional structure. Hypothetically, in fact, it is imaginable, at least, that judicial insistence on recognition of human rights as the basis of comity could impact transformatively on extra-national constitutional law. As in the EU, it is perfectly conceivable that international bodies, or even other nation states, may be compelled to tighten their constitutional recognition of rights norms in situations in which their directives are rejected by courts in particular nation states on the grounds that they are insufficiently anchored in rights.

---

64 *Canada (Justice)* v. *Khadr* [2008] 2 S.C.R. 125, 2008 SCC 28.

32 *Chris Thornhill*

Proportionality

The inner-juridical constituent force of proportionality is now also a near-universal source of structural and constitutional formation, in a variety of different legal systems. Indeed, almost all national polities, albeit for different reasons, are internally susceptible to the influence of proportionality. Notably, for example, proportionality has assumed a vital structure-building role in societies in which, historically, judiciaries have struggled to preserve and uphold constitutional norms. The fact that proportionality rulings are backed by rulings in international courts has often played a key role in stabilizing historically weak judiciaries, and proportionality is widely used to consolidate judicial authority in new, relatively fragile states, especially in Africa.[65] In addition, proportionality has assumed great significance in societies in which confidence in judiciaries is normally low and where judicial deference to the executive is traditionally high – for example, in Russia. In such cases, proportionality has been used to regularize judicial rulings and to elevate the normative authority of the legal system as a whole. Indeed, even in periods marked by relatively high government repression, the use of proportionality has been increasingly promoted in Russia, partly as a means for eradicating the prevalence of local or private power across society.[66] In societies traditionally defined by weak constitutional structure, therefore, proportionality is an important source of constituent force. It acts as a principle which consolidates basic constitutional norms through acts of judicial evaluation, which symbolically accentuates the legitimacy of governmental acts, and which intensifies the penetration of constitutional norms into domestic society. In addition, however, proportionality has acquired a distinctive constituent role in common-law constitutions traditionally hostile to formal rights-based restrictions on legislation and executive discretion. In the USA, in which proportionality is still at times derided as *foreign law*, analogues to proportionality reasoning have entered even the highest levels of the judiciary.[67] In the UK, although it is still restricted in reach, proportionality has also had a clear constitutional impact, significantly elevating the standing of the judicial branch and establishing human rights norms as co-implied elements of all judicial acts.[68] Indeed, proportionality has fundamentally recast the basic statutory nature of UK constitutional law, elevating the standing of international human rights as binding norms across all areas of statutory law making.

---

65 See, as a key example, the case before the Ugandan Constitutional Court: *Charles Onyango Obbo and Another* v. *Attorney General* (Constitutional Petition No. 15 of 1997).

66 The judicial reforms conducted by Putin have seen a steady rise in the number of cases ruled on proportionality grounds. In 2011, by way of example, circa 80 per cent of decisions on merit in the Russian Constitutional Court involved proportionality reasoning, referring to Art 55.3 of the constitution.

67 See the dissenting opinion in *District of Columbia* v. *Heller*, 554 U.S. 570 (2008). For comment, see Iddo Porat and Moshe Cohen-Eliya, 'The hidden foreign law debate in *Heller*: The proportionality approach in American constitutional law', *San Diego Law Review* 46 (2009).

68 The main trigger for this was of course *Smith and Grady v UK* (1999) 29 EHRR 493, which came close to prescribing a *right to proportionality* in human rights cases.

Generally, in short, proportionality has become a pervasive constituent force both in national and supranational legal and political systems. In flexible fashion, proportionality acts to formalize the constitutional authority of rights, to elevate the norm-setting powers of courts and, in particular, to extend the inclusionary reach and normative penetration of the legal system into different parts of society.

Conclusion

On this basis, it can be concluded, first, that we need to abandon the idea that the system of public law created in the EU is simply a legal order *sui generis*. This presupposition results from a rather simplified analysis of national constitution making. It is doubtful if this characterization was ever accurate. Today, however, what is striking in the public law of the EU is not its *distinction from*, but its paradoxical *similarity to*, national systems of public law. If we observe constitution making not, in classical, literal perspective, as the formalization of objective legal agreements about broad societal ideals and values, but, instead, as a process of *structural formation* on which societies rely to maintain sustainable levels of legal inclusion, then the relation between national constitutions and the constitutional order of the EU is increasingly marked by common adaptive characteristics. Many patterns of constitutional formation in the EU are now quite widespread. In fact, second, it can be concluded that the constitutional mechanism at the core of European public law – the transformation of constituent power into rights and the resultant inner-systemic, *inner-juridical* construction of constitutional legitimacy – has become a prevalent legal phenomenon in global society. The self-authorization and self-reproduction of legal structures can now be observed as defining features of many legal and political systems, whether national or extra-national, even in polities with little resemblance to the EU. Third, it can be concluded that analysis of the legal order of the EU requires a categorical change of paradigm. If we closely observe the growing similarities between the legal order of the EU and the emergent legal/political orders of global society more widely, we need to approach the public law of the EU in more strictly sociological terms, that is, we need to address the sociological questions: *Why* does global society increasingly generate legal structures in internalistic fashion? *Why* does society cover its legislative functions with systemically internalized rights? *Why* has constituent power become a typically inner-juridical agency? and *Why* do courts establish the basic constitutional structure of society? The answer to some of these questions might lie in a fundamental refocusing of constitutional analysis, through which we begin to interpret constitutions as inclusionary structures, insulating society against unmanageable, increasingly contingent demands for legislation and regulation. Through this refocusing of constitutional analysis, the constitutional order of the EU might, in fact, disclose much about the basic sociological functions of public law in contemporary society. The precondition for this analysis, however, is that we stop observing EU law as a priori unique.

34   Chris Thornhill

Bibliography

Alter, Karen J. 'Who are the "Masters of the Treaty"? European Governments and the European Court of Justice'. *International Organization* 52 (1998): 121–147.

Alter, Karen J., Laurence R. Helfer and Osvaldo Saldías. 'Transplanting the European Court of Justice: The experience of the Andean Tribunal of Justice'. *American Journal of Comparative Law* 60 (2012): 629–664.

Bauer, Lukas. *Der Europäische Gerichtshof als Verfassungsgericht?* Baden-Baden, Germany: Nomos, 2008.

Brzezinski, Mark F. and Lezek Garlicki. 'Judicial review in post-communist Poland: The emergence of a *Rechtsstaat*?' *Stanford Journal of International Law* 31 (1995): 13–59.

De Búrca, Gráinne. 'Proportionality and *Wednesbury* unreasonableness: The influence of European legal concepts on UK public law'. *European Public Law* 3 (1992): 561–586.

De Búrca, Gráinne. 'The European Court of Justice and the International Legal Order after *Kadi*'. *Harvard International Law Journal* 51 (2010): 1–49.

De Búrca, Gráinne. 'The road not taken: The European Union as a global human rights actor'. *The American Journal of International Law* 105(4) (2010): 649–693.

De Vries, Sybe A. 'Balancing fundamental rights with economic freedoms according to the European Court of Justice'. *Utrecht Law Review* 9 (2013): 169–192.

De Waele, Henri. 'The role of the European Court of Justice in the integration process: A contemporary and normative assessment'. *Hanse Law Review* 3(5) (2010): 3–26.

De Witte, Bruno. 'The past and future role of the European Court of Justice in the protection of human rights'. In *The EU and Human Rights*, edited by Philip Alston, pp. 859–897. Oxford, UK: Oxford University Press, 1999.

Denys, Simon. 'Des influences réciproques entre CJCE et CEDH: "Je t'aime, moi non plus"?' *Pouvoirs* 96 (2001): 31–49.

Fossum, John Erik and Augustín José Menéndez. *The Constitution's Gift. A Constitutional Theory for a Democratic Union*. Lanham, UK: Rowman & Littlefield, 2011.

Grimm, Dieter. 'The constitution in the process of denationalization'. *Constellations* 12 (2005): 447–463.

Höreth, Marcus. 'Stille Revolution im Namen des Rechts? Zur Rolle des Europäischen Gerichtshofes (EuGH) im Prozess der europäischen Integration'. Zentrum für Europäische Integrationsforschung, Universität Bonn, Discussion Paper, C78 (2000).

Isiksel, Türküler. 'Fundamental rights in the EU after *Kadi* and *Al Barakaat*'. *European Law Journal* 16 (2010): 551–577.

Kahn, Jeffrey. 'Russia's "Dictatorship of Law" and the European Court of Human Rights'. *Review of Central and East European Law* 29 (2004): 1–14.

Kaiser, Joseph. 'Zur gegenwärtigen Differenzierung von Recht und Staat'. *Österreichische Zeitschrift für öffentliches Recht* 10 (1960): 413–423.

Lavranos, Nikolaos. 'The *Solange*-method as a tool for regulating competing jurisdictions among international courts and tribunals'. *Loyola Los Angeles International and Comparative Law Review* 30 (2008): 275–334.

Madsen, Mikael Rask. 'The protracted institutionalization of the Strasbourg Court: From legal diplomacy to integrationist jurisprudence'. In *The European Court of Human Rights between Law and Politics*, edited by Jonas Christoffersen and Mikael Rask Madsen, pp. 42–60. Oxford, UK: Oxford University Press, 2011.

Metropoulos, Demetrios G. 'Human rights, incorporated: The European Community's new line of business'. *Stanford Journal of International Law* 29 (1992–1993): 131–164.

European Constitution: sui generis? 35

O'Brien, Kevin J. and Lianjiang Li. 'Suing the local state: Administrative litigation in rural China'. *China Journal* 51 (2004): 75–96.

Pernice, Ingolf. *Kompetenzabgrenzung im europäischen Verfassungsverbund: Antrittsvorlesung.* Berlin, Germany: Humboldt-Universität zu Berlin, 2000.

Pernice, Ingolf. *Das Verhältnis europäischer zu nationalen Gerichten im europäischen Verfassungsverbund.* Berlin, Germany: de Gruyter, 2006.

Peters, Anne. *Elemente einer Theorie der Verfassung Europas.* Berlin, Germany: Dunker und Humblot, 2001.

Porat, Iddo and Moshe Cohen-Eliya. 'The hidden foreign law debate in *Heller*: The proportionality approach in American constitutional law'. *San Diego Law Review* 46 (2009): 367–415.

Sajó, András. 'Reading the invisible constitution: Judicial review in Hungary'. *Oxford Journal of Legal Studies* 15 (1995): 253–267.

Scheeck, Laurent. 'Relationship between the European Courts and integration through human rights'. *Zeitschrift für ausländisches öffentliches Recht und Völkerrecht* 65 (2005): 837–885.

Schilling, Theodor. 'The autonomy of the community legal order: An analysis of possible foundations'. *Harvard International Law Journal* 37 (1996): 389–409.

Sloss, David. 'How international norms transformed the U.S. constitution'. *Human Rights Quarterly* 37 (2015). Santa Clara Univ. Legal Studies Research Paper No. 4–15. Available at SSRN: http://ssrn.com/abstract=2570566.

Stein, Eric. 'Lawyers, judges and the making of a transnational constitution'. *The American Journal of International Law* 75 (1981): 1–27.

Stone Sweet, Alec *The Judicial Construction of Europe.* Oxford, UK: Oxford University Press, 2004.

Tanasenscu, Elenia Simina. 'Role des droits fondamentaux dans la constitutionnalisation de l'ordre juridique de l'UE'. In *The Court of Justice and the Construction of Europe. Analyses and Perspectives on Sixty Years of Case-Law*, edited by Allan Rosas, Egils Levits and Yves Bot, pp. 207–228. The Hague, The Netherlands: Asser, 2013.

Thornhill, Chris. *A Sociology of Constitutions.* Cambridge, UK: Cambridge University Press, 2011.

Thornhill, Chris. 'The dialectic of constituent power in contemporary constitutionalism. *Global Constitutionalism* 1 (2012): 369–404.

Thornhill, Chris. 'A sociology of constituent power: The political code of transnational societal constitutions'. *Indiana Journal of Global Legal Studies* 20 (2013): 551–603.

Thouret, Jacques-Guillaume. *Discours. En ouvrant la discussion sur la nouvelle organisation du pouvoir judiciaire.* Paris: Imprimerie nationale, 1790.

Vesterdorf, Bo. 'A constitutional court for the EU?' *International Journal of Constitutional Law* 4 (2006): 607–617.

Von Bogdandy, Armin, Matthias Kottmann, Carlino Antpöhler, Johanna Dickschen, Simon Hentrei and Maja Smrkolj. 'Reverse Solange: Protecting the essence of fundamental rights against EU member states'. *Common Market Law Review* 49 (2012): 489–519.

Voßkuhle, Andreas. 'Multilevel cooperation of the European Constitutional Courts: *Der Europäische Verfassungsgerichtsverbund*'. *European Constitutional Law Review* 6 (2010): 175–198.

Walker, Neil. 'Post-constituent constitutionalism? The case of the European Union'. In *The Paradox of Constitutionalism. Constituent Power and Constitutional Form*, edited by Martin Loughlin and Neil Walker, pp. 247–268. Oxford, UK: Oxford University Press, 2007.

36   *Chris Thornhill*

Walker, Neil. 'Reframing EU constitutionalism'. In *Ruling the World? Constitutionalism, International Law, and Global Governance*, edited by Jeffrey L. Dunoff and Joel P. Trachtman, pp. 149–176. Cambridge, UK: Cambridge University Press, 2009.

Walter, Christian. 'Die europäische Menschenrechtskonvention als Konstitutionalisierungsprozeß'. *Zeitschrift für ausländisches öffentliches Recht und Völkerrecht* 59 (1999): 962–983.

Weiler, Joseph H.H. 'Eurocracy and distrust: Some questions concerning the role of the European Court of Justice in the protection of fundamental human rights within the legal order of the European Communities'. *Washington Law Review* 61 (1986): 1103–1142.

Weiler, Joseph H.H. 'The transformation of Europe'. *Yale Law Journal* 100 (1991): 2404–2483.

Weiler, Joseph H.H. 'In defence of the status quo: Europe's constitutional *Sonderweg*'. In *European Constitutionalism beyond the State*, edited by Joseph H.H. Weiler and Marlene Wind, pp. 7–26. Cambridge, UK: Cambridge University Press, 2003.

Williams, Andrew. *EU Human Rights Policies: A Study in Irony*. Oxford, UK: Oxford University Press, 2004.

2 The concept of self-limiting polity in EU constitutionalism

A systems theoretical outline

Jiří Přibáň

Introduction

At the Václav Havel European Dialogues' second annual conference in Prague in May 2015, Elmar Brok, one of the most senior and experienced members of the European Parliament, commented on the current critical state of the EU by stating that it is a fully-fledged democracy and the problem is that people in Europe do not know it. Echoes of political leaders accusing their people of ignorance while exaggerating the legitimacy and extent of their power could hardly be expressed more clearly at these times, when the EU's institutions have accumulated enormous decision-making powers over the Union's citizens and critically determined the quality of their economic and social living conditions.

Detachment between the governed and those who govern the EU these days is just one of the many symptoms of its current economic, political and social crisis. Today, the EU is a post-national organization, the increasing power of which is not matched by a growing sense of responsibility for the lives of the people living in it. Blaming people for insufficient political support, when citizens of the Union actually seek various ways of voicing their protests, amount to yet another blunder by the current EU political élites who have taken the Lisbon Treaty's enhancement of democratic legitimacy as a mere invitation to further their self-empowerment.

Confronting this legitimation crisis and the political deficits of the supranational EU is complicated, because juridical and political concepts of constitution, democracy and polity are being reconfigured and critically examined beyond the typically modern social organization in which law and politics meet, namely, the democratic constitutional state.[1] European politics enhances specific modes of legal legitimacy without typical normative and power hierarchies of state politics. It is commonly described as the self-constitutionalization of European polity beyond the nation state and its constitutional form.

The EU's legal and political framework calls for significant constitutional re-conceptualizations, especially after the failure to ratify what was supposed to

---

1 Jean-Claude Piris, *The Constitution for Europe. A Legal Analysis* (Cambridge, UK: Cambridge University Press, 2006).

38   Jiří Přibáň

become the EU's Constitutional Treaty.[2] Despite occasional claims suggesting that the Lisbon Treaty is similar to the failed Constitutional Treaty in everything but name and format,[3] the constitutional imagination has significantly changed in the EU. The very project of the basic law and normative foundations for a supranational European polity constituting itself into an ever more federal state-like form has turned out to be far too ambitious. Nevertheless, the concepts of constitutionalism,[4] constitution making and constitutionalization have prevailed and the contemporary EU is commonly described as having a judicially constructed supranational constitution[5] or post-constituent constitutionalism[6] normatively binding the EU's post-national constellation.

At the turn of this century, Jürgen Habermas dramatically and unsuccessfully argued that Europe needed a constitution.[7] Today, theorists of European constitutionalism and political integration hardly dispute the fact that Europe has its constitutional settlement even without a written document. However, theoretical contestations and polemics regarding the meaning and structures of European constitutionalism indicate that the very concept of constitutionalism is theoretically challenged. It often has to accommodate non-juridical conceptualizations, processes and forms of decision making, especially governance evolving outside both the EU's legal and political systems, and the paradox of further political constitutionalization evolving through increasing societal differentiation.[8]

While some scholars continue to perceive European constitutionalism as a critical project of cosmopolitan political identity building and moral mobilization of solidarity,[9] other theories of constitutionalism abandon the concept of constitutionalism as a meeting point of legal normativity, political will and moral aspirations and push for alternative sociological explorations of the great variety of self-constitutionalizations within European society. Social theories of constitutionalism[10] draw on the basic distinction of constitutional polity and society

---

2 Gráinne de Búrca, 'The European Constitution project after the referenda', *Constellations* 13 (2006).

3 The statement made by Valéry Giscard d'Estaing, former French President and President of the Constitutional Convention, in several European newspapers, 27 October 2007.

4 Richard Bellamy, 'The European Constitution is dead, long live European constitutionalism', *Constellations* 13 (2006).

5 Alec Stone Sweet, *The Judicial Construction of Europe* (Oxford, UK: Oxford University Press, 2004). See, especially, chapter 2: 'Constructing a supranational constitution'.

6 Neil Walker, 'Post-constituent constitutionalism? The case of the European Union', in *The Paradox of Constitutionalism. Constituent Power and Constitutional Form*, eds Martin Loughlin and Neil Walker (Oxford, UK: Oxford University Press 2007).

7 Jürgen Habermas, 'Why Europe needs a constitution', *New Left Review* 11 (2001).

8 Christine Landfried, 'Difference as a potential of European constitution making', *European Law Journal* 12 (2006).

9 Ulrich Beck and Edgar Grande, 'Cosmopolitanism: Europe's way out of crisis', *European Journal of Social Theory* 10 (2007).

10 David Sciulli, *Theory of Societal Constitutionalism: Foundations of a Non-Marxist Critical Theory* (Cambridge, UK: Cambridge University Press, 1992).

and consider even non-political societal processes in systems of economy, science, education and administration as part of non-state European and global societal constitutionalism.

This chapter, therefore, primarily focuses on transformations of the concept of constitutionalism and constitutional polity vis-à-vis the supranational and transnational organization of the EU and its legal and political systems. The impossibility of identifying the EU and its organizational framework with European society is paradoxically a great conceptual benefit of European societal constitutionalism. European society is not identical to the semantics and structures of the EU. The EU actually forms part of European society as one of its many organizations. Any kind of polity constituted by the Union's structures subsequently must be analysed within the framework of European society and not as its ultimate normative precondition and settlement.

The EU's legal and political systems facilitate the evolution of European society, but do not constitute it. This society is functionally differentiated and, apart from politics and law, constituted by other systems, such as economy, science and education. Critically drawing on the theory of societal constitutionalism, I use the distinction of polity and society to argue that the European constitutional polity is constituted by structural coupling between the systems of EU law and politics. European constitutionalism, therefore, is not a coupling between European law and other social sub-systems as some theorists of societal constitutionalism may suggest. It cannot be exclusively constituted by the sub-system of supranational European governance. However, neither can it be considered a community of foundational values permeating and legitimizing all aspects and levels of European society, as proclaimed, for instance, by those who perceive the EU as an avant-garde organization of cosmopolitan constitutionalism.

European post-constituent constitutionalism is thus self-limiting in terms of both societal expansionism and moral fundamentalism. Its operations are not existentially predetermined and legitimized by constituent polity. Nevertheless, this self-constitution of European polity by self-limitation highlights the general function of modern constitutions, namely, the channelling of political power through law and its limitation by law at local, national or supranational level. European constitutionalism, therefore, is not to be mistaken for the general constitution of functionally differentiated European society and needs to be treated as a specific self-limiting coupling between the systems of European law and politics.

Political or social theory of constitutionalism? On polity, society and governance by reason

In 1960, Sheldon Wolin described the history of Western political thought as a process of shifting the boundaries between politics and other social spheres and the gradual replacement of the concept of *polity* by the more general concept of *society*.

40   *Jiří Přibáň*

According to Wolin, the original definition of the political as a sphere of what is common to the whole community[11] has been fundamentally challenged, especially since the rise of social science and sociology in the nineteenth century.[12] The early modern Hobbesian definition of politics as fictional contractual communication between political sovereignty and civil society, which leads to the constitution of polity, has been criticized by sociologists contrasting the specific realm of politics and its laws to the general concept of society and social needs.

Instead of politically enforced positive laws, sociological theories focus on societal laws operating irrespective of political will and constitution. No wonder some sociologists of law are still profoundly inspired by these close links between the sociological and natural law theories.[13] Nevertheless, the tension between polity and society as part of the sociological tradition has deeper historical and more general theoretical roots. It dates back to the Enlightenment philosophy of Condorcet and others who prioritized mathematical and statistical methods and wanted them applied in the field of social policy and political administration to eliminate cruelty and oppression and establish the reign of scientific truth, political virtues and human happiness.[14]

Condorcet's rational men – 'sophisters', empowered by calculation skills – were to be the true rulers of modern society whose knowledge would entitle them to political leadership, instead of monarchs and priests. Condorcet's disciple, Saint-Simon, summarized the revolutionary force of science, economy and industrial organization in his famous view that the government of persons will be succeeded by the administration of things.[15] At that moment in modern history, legitimation by rational governance fostered by social science became an important force, challenging all other political forces. Saint-Simon's view became a point of reference to both Auguste Comte's ideal of the positivistic religion of sociology replacing liberal and democratic ideals and Karl Marx's revolutionary vision of communist society without the repressive state, politically encompassing the totality of society participating in its self-organization of productive forces and delivering ultimate collective happiness.[16]

Saint-Simon had already contrasted industrialists and scientists – as the productive classes of the new industrial society – to the old groupings of the 'metaphysicians', the lawyers and professional politicians continuing with the politics of power and mere changes of government, from the absolutist monarchy to the Jacobin revolutionary terror and violence. He and many others after him believed

---

11 Sheldon Wolin, *Politics and Vision: Continuity and Innovation in Western Political Thought* (Princeton, NJ: Princeton University Press, 1960), p. 4.
12 See, also, W.G. Runciman, *Social Science and Political Theory* (Cambridge, UK: Cambridge University Press, 1969).
13 Philip Selznick, 'Sociology and natural law', *Natural Law Forum* 6 (1961).
14 Wolin, *Politics and Vision*, p. 281.
15 For further details see, for instance, Eric Voegelin, 'The religion of humanity and the French Revolution', in *From Enlightenment to Revolution*, ed. Eric Voegelin (Durham, NC: Duke University Press, 1975), pp. 192–194.
16 For further details see, for instance, Isaiah Berlin, *The Crooked Timber of Humanity: Chapters in the History of Ideas* (London: Pimlico, 2003), pp. 239–241.

Concept of self-limiting polity 41

that the politics of power was the politics of the old regime which needed to be replaced by a new order governed by the productive industrialists and scientists, drawing exclusively on universal principles of reasoning and impartial calculation.

From ancient times, the government of laws has been contrasted to the government of man. While politics governed by laws is considered to be the first precondition of a just and civil polity, societies governed by personal will and the interests of those in power constitute tyrannical regimes. However, Saint-Simon's modern call for the industrial administration of things radically challenged this ancient wisdom and the normative political difference between the sovereignty of laws and the arbitrary power of men. Modern governments based on the rule of law were to be replaced by social science and engineering. The men of science, because of their knowledge, would rule the modern polity. They would not issue political orders and commands but, rather, merely declare what conformed to the nature of things.[17]

According to this view, government – the rule of people over people – can be replaced by administration, namely, the self-management of society and its scientific guidance provided for by a new science of sociology.[18] Generations of social engineers, utopians and revolutionaries subsequently emphasized the primacy of industrial reason in modern society, and the eventual demise of political reason vis-à-vis the historical progress in social organization and society's ability to respond to social and individual needs. They believed that the universal totality of society preceded all social particularities, including politics, and that the laws of industrial modernity were universally valid, thus constituting a new 'nature' of humankind determining all particular forms of political life.

Instead of the irrational political quarrels dominating the process of democratic deliberation, change and progress were to be achieved by rationalization and the better productivity of society in its totality. As Isaiah Berlin commented:

> Condorcet once observed that all real issues of the future could be decided on the basis of rational calculation of utilitarian consequences. *Calculemus* was to be the new watchword, the key to the solution of both social and personal problems. This method, with its stress on systems analysis, cost-effectiveness, reduction to statistical and quantitative terms, reliance on the authority and power of organization and experts, is today the common property ... The application of technological techniques in organizing the lives and productive activities of human beings is the policy of governments, of industrial enterprises, indeed of all large-scale economic (and cultural) activities ... Scientific knowledge and scientific organization ... can surely be made to rationalize social life and so bring about the maximum satisfaction of discoverable human needs, provided the system is organized by disinterested experts.[19]

---

17 Krishan Kumar, *Prophecy and Progress: The Sociology of Industrial and Post-Industrial Society* (London: Penguin, 1978), p. 42.
18 Ibid. pp. 35–36.
19 Berlin, *Crooked Timber*, pp. 255–256.

42   Jiří Přibáň

The universal legitimacy of scientific and administrative reason prevails over the state's particularity and, while the state is expected to gradually 'wither away', the scientific, instrumental and technological administration of society constitutes its legitimate polity without any hierarchies of authority except the authority of reason, professionalism and impersonal technology.[20]

Theories of transnational governance

The paradigmatic shift from polity to society has been accelerated by globalization and its theoretical reflections, especially in theories of transnational governance.[21] For some theorists, governance is any act of governing, from corporate governance of business organizations and non-profit governance of charities and NGOs to governance conducted by political organizations, including the state and its government.[22] Governance thus stretches from economy and education to science, environmental policies and general politics. It is considered a form of social steering not confined to the political system, yet typical of social expectations, management power and decision making, and various forms of self-regulation and performance assessment.[23]

According to theories of governance, responsive and/or good governance aims at strengthening both the democratic legitimacy of input values and/or processes and the efficiency of outputs. It combines market principles of competition, civic horizontal networks and principles of partnership, negotiation and deliberation or bureaucratic principles of impersonal and politically disinterested administration.[24] Despite the variety of social and political science definitions and contextualizations,[25] the initial disjunction of governance from

---

20 Frank E. Manuel, *The Prophets of Paris* (New York: Harper, 1965), p. 96.
21 Arthur Benz and Ioannis Papadopoulos, eds, *Governance and Democracy: Comparing National, European and International Perspectives* (Oxford, UK: Routledge, 2006).
22 Jan Kooiman, *Governing as Governance* (London: Sage, 2003).
23 Stephen Bell, *Economic Governance and Institutional Dynamics* (Oxford, UK: Oxford University Press, 2002); James Evans, *Environmental Governance* (Oxford, UK: Routledge 2012); Jan Kooiman, ed., *Modern Governance: New Government-Society Interactions* (London: Sage, 1993).
24 See, for instance, Philip Selznick, *A Humanist Science: Values and Ideas in Social Inquiry* (Stanford, CA: Stanford University Press, 2008), pp. 71–82. It is noteworthy that Selznick easily switches from responsive government to responsive governance.
25 Different meanings of the concept of governance are summarized, for instance, by Stoker who turns them into the following five theoretical propositions:

> 1. governance refers to a set of institutions and actors that are drawn from but also beyond government; 2. governance identifies the blurring of boundaries and responsibilities for tackling social and economic issues; 3. governance identifies the power dependence involved in the relationships between institutions involved in collective action; 4. governance is about autonomous self-governing networks of actors; and 5. governance recognizes the capacity to get things done which does not rest on the power of government to command or use its authority. It sees government as able to use new tools and techniques to steer and guide.

> Gerry Stoker, 'Governance as theory: Five propositions', *International Social Science Journal* 50 (1998): 18.

Concept of self-limiting polity 43

government[26] and transfer of governmental authority to non-governmental institutions at national and international level[27] has been constitutive of the meaning of governance, including its different forms evolving at global level. It is considered a process of steering and organization in the absence of political power and enforcement authority.[28]

Furthermore, governance theories often use the government/governance difference to contrast official state institutions and laws with alternative methods of policy making, benchmarking, partnership between public and private actors, and networks coordinating the actions of governmental and non-governmental bodies. This difference contrasts the hierarchical power structures used by governmental institutions with the heterarchical governance networks of coordination and cooperation processes. The political rule of government and its institutions is contrasted with horizontal forms of social interactions stretching beyond politics and engaging in non-political forms of societal constitutionalization and administration.

Associating governance particularly with the processes of Europeanization and globalization of social structures, communication networks and systems, theories of transnational governance question the structural and organizational limitations of national governments in global society and urge us to rethink global politics and law as systems unconstrained by the state's authority,[29] officially declared law and enforcement institutions. The constitutional state operating through formal law making and political representation is allegedly dated, and transnational governance regimes are described as 'spaces' and 'assemblages'[30] that engage in all sorts of hybrid norm making involving public and private actors and creating constitutional regimes beyond national and political constituencies. They operate independently of the territorial boundaries of sovereign states and their internationally negotiated and recognized treaties.[31]

Transnational regimes recombine private coordination and public regulation and dismantle the traditional distinction between private and public law – business and the state, respectively.[32] They are neither purely global nor purely national

---

26 James N. Rosenau, 'Toward an ontology for global governance', in *Approaches to Global Governance Theory*, eds Martin Hewson and Thomas Sinclair (Albany, NY: SUNY Press, 1999), pp. 295–296.

27 James N. Rosenau, 'Governance, order, and change in world politics', in *Governance without Government in World Politics*, eds James N. Rosenau and Ernst-Otto Czempiel (Cambridge, UK: Cambridge University Press, 1992).

28 Roderick A.W. Rhodes, 'The new governance: Governing without government', *Political Studies* 44 (1996).

29 James N. Rosenau, 'The state in an era of cascading politics: Wavering concept, widening competence, withering colossus, or weathering change?' in *The Elusive State: International and Comparative Perspectives*, ed. James A. Caporaso (London: Sage, 1990).

30 Saskia Sassen, *Territory-Authority-Rights. From Medieval to Global Assemblages* (Princeton, NJ: Princeton University Press, 2006).

31 Peer Zumbansen, 'Comparative, global and transnational constitutionalism: The emergence of a transnational legal-pluralist order', *Global Constitutionalism* 1 (2012).

32 Gralf-Peter Callies and Peer Zumbansen, *Rough Consensus and Running Code: A Theory of Transnational Private Law* (Oxford, UK: Hart Publishing, 2010), pp. 112–123.

44   *Jiří Přibáň*

and incorporate diverse and multiple assemblages in which the global is often detectable inside the national.[33] Furthermore, they do not need any political authority at transnational level to guarantee and administer governance goals and coordination networks. They are self-evolving and self-constituting horizontally interconnected forms of social steering and engineering.

Theories of transnational governance commonly think of global society as a heterarchical, post-polemical society engaged in problems of administration and distribution of resources and products, rather than with power conflicts and relations between sovereign states. According to this view, transnational global governance represents the final stage of political disenchantment, replacing the political theology of sovereign power with the technical administration of depoliticized rational decisions. Enchanted nostalgia for the politics of the sovereign state allegedly gives way to rational arbitration of public choices at the transnational level of global society 'operated by a professional personnel which lacks . . . the capacity to bring to prevalence any type of power-mediated politics'.[34]

For these theories of governance, which echo the views of Condorcet, Saint-Simon and others, the differentiation between politicization and depoliticization mirrors the Weberian difference between the enchantment and disenchantment of politics.[35] Power is considered the medium of political enchantment, drawing on premises of grand theoretical designs, identities, struggles and conflicts to be won and will to be imposed on subjects. Unlike power politics, the depoliticized expert knowledge of professionals allegedly liberates politics from the logic of power conflicts and turns the whole political enterprise into problems of European or global calculation, distribution, administration and arbitration.[36]

Europe beyond statehood: the dilemma of technical governance and cosmopolitan ideals in the EU

In his response to Thorstein Veblen's theory of business enterprise,[37] Max Weber warned against 'the new serfdom' and a 'benevolent feudalism'[38] of bureaucracy conducting our modern political life. Weber conceived the process of social modernization as the differentiation of economy and politics and considered

---

33 Saskia Sassen, 'Neither global nor national: Novel assemblages of territory, authority and rights', *Ethics & Global Politics* 1 (2008): 79.

34 Jean Clam, 'What is modern power?', in *Luhmann on Law and Politics: Critical Appraisals and Applications*, eds Michael King and Chris Thornhill (Oxford, UK: Hart Publishing, 2006), p. 152.

35 For a critical account of rationalization as disenchantment, see Ralph Schroeder, 'Disenchantment and its discontents: Weberian perspectives on science and technology', *Sociological Review* 43 (1995).

36 For an original insight into one specific field of EU policy, see Christina Boswell, 'The political functions of expert knowledge: Knowledge and legitimation in European Union immigration policy', *Journal of European Public Policy* 15 (2008).

37 Thorstein Veblen, *The Theory of the Business Enterprise* (New Brunswick, NJ: Transaction Books, 1904).

38 Max Weber, 'On the situation of constitutional democracy in Russia', in *Weber: Political Writings*, eds Peter Lassman and Ronald Speirs (Cambridge, UK: Cambridge University Press, 1994), 68.

Concept of self-limiting polity 45

their mutual structural coupling as complementing and stabilising one another. Nevertheless, he also considered this general process of modern rationalization as a loss of general meaning caused by growing differences between validity claims simultaneously arising in different types of rationality in economy, politics, law and science.

According to Weber, rationalization as social differentiation leads to increasing antagonisms among different value systems, ultimate destruction of reason's universality and the rise of a 'new polytheism'.[39] Increasing specialization and different validity claims cannot be reconciled by some form of universally valid rationality, and Weber concludes, 'For then it might be said of the "last men" of this cultural development: "Specialists without spirit, sensualists without heart"; this nullity imagines that it has attained a level of civilization never before achieved'.[40]

Despite this sociological scepticism,[41] theories of European and global governance often aim at tackling 'the new serfdom' risk of depoliticized expert knowledge by constructing the generally valid normative foundations for European and global society, which have commonly been associated with modern democratic statehood. The emergence of supranational and transnational governance recursively calls for public accountability and representative decision making – overtly political demands, turning allegedly depoliticized governance into political communication and replicating specific operations and institutional settings of the constitutional state at European or global level.

One eventually wonders if this pronounced historical triumph of social steering and governance over politics actually indicates the final victory of administrative politics over constitutional law.[42] For instance, Alexander Somek speaks of the historical victory of the state over both politics and law. According to him, the depoliticized global administration adopts the administrative function formerly performed by the modern state, and the principle of steering and efficiency finally takes over legal normativity.[43]

In this context, theories of cosmopolitan democracy and global human rights represent specific normative responses to the political challenges and depoliticizing effects of supranational and transnational governance beyond statehood in Europe and elsewhere. Responding to the techniques of governance and the *politics of depoliticization*,[44] the ideals of cosmopolitan democracy and human

---

39 Max Weber, 'Science as a vocation', in *The Vocation Lectures*, eds David S. Owen and Tracy B. Strong. (Indianapolis, IN: Hackett Publishing, 2004), p. 23.

40 Max Weber, *The Protestant Ethic and The Spirit of Capitalism* (London: Routledge, 1992), p. 124.

41 For original reflections on Weber's concept of rationalization and contemporary culture, see Nicholas Gane, *Max Weber and Postmodern Theory: Rationalization Versus Re-Enchantment* (Basingstoke, UK and New York: Palgrave, 2002).

42 Nico Krisch, *Beyond Constitutionalism: The Pluralist Structure of Postnational Law* (Oxford, UK: Oxford University Press, 2010).

43 Alexander Somek, 'Administration without sovereignty', in *The Twilight of Constitutionalism?* eds Petra Dobner and Martin Loughlin (Oxford, UK: Oxford University Press, 2010).

44 Jiří Přibáň, *Legal Symbolism: On Law, Time and European Identity* (Aldershot, UK: Ashgate, 2007), pp. 116–119.

46   *Jiří Přibáň*

rights[45] serve the speculative goal of reformulating the concept of polity in a holistic manner as a reservoir of 'good intentions' unified by humanistic principles, unconfined by the territorial boundaries of states or any other political organizations and therefore evolving within contemporary supranational and transnational legal and political structures as their new constitutional regime.[46]

Allegedly, new supranational and transnational polities can retain their democratic legitimacy, and the transnationalization of popular sovereignty is expected to challenge the asymmetry between economic and political globalization. International law and politics theories proclaim the 'demise' of the nation state and the constitutionalization of international law by alternative means of democratizing global governance.[47] The UN Charter is treated as the constitution of the international community and this community relies on ethical normative foundations equally respected by the states as members of the international community.[48] The states have the political and legal responsibility of protecting and enforcing the substantive worldwide interests of the international community, which already needs to be treated as the cosmo-polity – a polity constituted by cosmopolitan values and normative expectations formulated by the body of international law.[49] International law standards and the protection of human rights are expected both to protect individuals against their states and to guarantee the normative standards and justifications of specific policies and global governance.[50]

The re-description of international law in the language of constitutionalism and democracy, actually represents one of the most typical idealizations of law as 'a gentle civilizer of nations',[51] and the juridification of brutish state force in both international and internal relations[52] is treated as the historical victory of global justice over state politics and its international power contestations.[53] According to these views, global society forms its distinct forms of constitutionalism regulating global political and societal issues.[54] The EU and its constitutionalization is then

---

45 Alexander Somek, *The Cosmopolitan Constitution* (Oxford, UK: Oxford University Press, 2014), pp. 9–12.

46 Gerard Delanty, *The Cosmopolitan Imagination: The Renewal of Critical Social Theory* (Cambridge, UK: Cambridge University Press, 2009), p. 51.

47 Jan Klabbers, Anne Peters and Geir Ulfstein, *Constitutionalization of International Law* (Oxford, UK: Oxford University Press, 2009).

48 Bardo Fassbender, 'The United Nations Charter as constitution of the international community', *Columbia Journal of Transnational Law* 36 (1998).

49 Christian Tomuschat, *International Law: Ensuring the Survival of Mankind on the Eve of a New Century* (The Hague, The Netherlands: Martinus Nijhoff, 2001).

50 Errol P. Mendes, *Global Governance, Human Rights and International Law: Combating the Tragic Flaw* (Oxford, UK: Routledge, 2014).

51 Martti Koskenniemi, *The Gentle Civilizer of Nations: The Rise and Fall of International Law 1870–1960* (Cambridge, UK: Cambridge University Press, 2001).

52 Theodor Meron, 'International criminalization of internal atrocities', *American Journal of International Law* 89 (1995).

53 Martti Koskenniemi and Susan Marks, *The Riddle of All Constitutions: International Law, Democracy, and the Critique of Ideology* (Oxford, UK: Oxford University Press, 1999).

54 Ronald St. John Macdonald and Douglas M. Johnston, eds, *Towards World Constitutionalism: Issues in the Legal Ordering of the World Community* (Leiden, The Netherlands: Martinus Nijhoff, 2005).

Concept of self-limiting polity 47

used as a specific example of the possibility of preserving the democratic legitimacy of the transnational polity by constitutionalizing three components of every democratic polity: 'the horizontal association of free and equal legal persons, a bureaucratic organization for collective action, and civic solidarity as a medium of political integration'.[55]

European federalists consider the EU's post-national constellation a normatively-driven and historically optimistic farewell to the nation state, and Europe in general as a 'borderland'.[56] The internal dynamics of the EU's 'polycentric polity'[57] cannot copy legitimation patterns of modern democratic statehood, including its search for the constituent power of the European demos represented through the institutional framework of its political constitution. However, it is equally impossible to continue basing the EU's legitimacy on governance-generated efficiency rather than democratic accountability and civic control of ever more powerful European institutions.[58] The ideals of cosmopolitan democracy and global human rights are then expected to successfully tackle the typically modern formula of 'things administering themselves',[59] which has been an intrinsic part of European governance. If the original function of European governance was to legitimize European integration, with transnational efficiency and common benefits substituting for the absence of the democratically representative framework associated with the modern constitutional democratic state, the European constitution of transnational democratic institutions and human rights is a retrospective attempt to address the EU's notoriously discussed democratic deficit.[60]

Advocates of the EU's democratic ascendency and ever stronger legitimacy do not simply explore the possibility of popular sovereignty and the constitution of European demos as a constituent power of the EU and its post-state constitutionalism. Instead, they construct a new concept of 'originally shared' sovereignty, that is, the sovereignty shared between the European peoples and European citizens.[61] This democratically legitimate transnational polity of European citizens and peoples is to be increasingly detached from their member states and evolve as a genuinely political and constitutionally sovereign polity beyond the organizational limits of modern statehood. Strengthening this civic transnational

---

55 Jürgen Habermas, 'The crisis of the European Union in the light of a constitutionalization of international law', *European Journal of International Law* 23 (2012): 339.
56 Delanty, *The Cosmopolitan Imagination*, p. 225.
57 See, for instance, Marlene Wind, 'The European Union as a polycentric polity', in *European Constitutionalism Beyond the State*, eds Joseph H.H. Weiler and Marlene Wind (Cambridge, UK: Cambridge University Press, 2003).
58 For the view that EU does not need demos but efficiency, see Jens Steffek, 'Sources of legitimacy beyond the state: A view from international relations', in *Transnational Governance and Constitutionalism*, eds Christian Joerges, Inger-Johanne Sand and Gunther Teubner (Oxford, UK: Hart Publishing, 2004).
59 Carl Schmitt, *Legality and Legitimacy* (Durham, NC: Duke University Press, 2004), pp. 5–6.
60 James Bohman, 'Constitution making and democratic innovation: The European Union and transnational governance', *European Journal of Political Theory* 3 (2004).
61 Habermas, 'The crisis of the European Union', p. 342.

48   *Jiří Přibáň*

solidarity apparently has the potential to transform the existing 'executive federalism' of the EU into a transnational constitutional democratic polity.[62]

Constitutions beyond politics: the de-juridification and depoliticization of the EU in societal constitutionalism

Despite these normative theoretical aspirations and recent modest attempts at democratization, such as the Lisbon Treaty's commitment to the principles of democracy as the Union's foundations, administrative governance drawing on expertise and efficiency remains the EU's source of both legitimation and de-legitimation as witnessed, for instance, in the persisting Eurozone crisis and the risks of Grexit, Brexit and any other potential 'exits' from the current EU. These crises persuasively reveal the limits and potentially self-destructive effects of expert knowledge, which, instead of operating as the ultimate source of legitimation, often turns out to be merely ignorant and dangerously de-legitimizing wishful thinking.

Attempts at constituting and legitimizing transnationally governed European polity through shared cosmopolitan values and human rights paradoxically draw on the same holistic notion of a polity of shared foundational values as propounded by some theories of the constitutional democratic state. The originally functionalist concept of transnational law as a concept covering legal frameworks which stretch beyond the relations of one nation to other nations and transcend national frontiers[63] has acquired critical meaning and became associated with normative political and legal expectations and alternatives to state law, national sovereignty, and international law and politics.

Coincidently, the concept of a transnational constitution for a self-integrating Europe was born out of the supranational federalist vision of European statehood and drew on European legal monism and the supremacy of the European basic norm. It would describe the increasing juridification of the EU and its hierarchical 'federal-type' political structure.[64] Since the 1960s, a constitution for Europe was to support the legitimacy of European integration[65] and open further space for this 'ever closer' Union.[66]

However, the current meaning of transnational law and constitutionalism in Europe and elsewhere is mainly associated with the idea of legal and political pluralism and the impossibility of establishing one supreme basic norm to rule the

---

62 Jürgen Habermas, *The Crisis of the European Union: A Response* (Cambridge, UK: Polity, 2012), pp. 12–53.

63 Philip C. Jessup, *Transnational Law: Storrs Lectures on Jurisprudence* (New Haven, CT: Yale University Press, 1956).

64 Eric Stein, 'Lawyers, judges, and the making of a transnational constitution', *American Journal of International Law* 75 (1981).

65 Miguel P. Maduro, 'The importance of being called a constitution: Constitutional authority and the authority of constitutionalism', *International Journal of Constitutional Law* 3 (2005).

66 Federico G. Mancini, 'The making of a constitution for Europe', *Common Market Law Review* 26 (1989).

legal sub-systems of member states. These recent conceptualizations and critical aspirations have serious implications for both political and legal theory, because they consider politics and law not only beyond the nation state organization but also beyond the public/private, procedural/substantive and official/non-official law distinctions. Instead of the jurisprudential view of laws constituting society, recent theories of European and global law and governance thus often adopt the sociological view of constitutionalism as a system of spontaneously evolving social rules and regulations beyond the systems of law and politics.

The theory of societal constitutionalism elaborated by Sciulli and Teubner subsequently reformulates the very notion of polity by stripping it of its original and long-standing political meaning. According to Gunther Teubner, the concept of constitutionalism, 'also refers to non-political institutions of civil society, of the economy, of science, education, health, art, or sports – of all those social sites where constitutionalising takes place'.[67]

According to this view, polity is a by-product of societal self-constitutionalization. Polities are therefore many and unlimited by structural coupling between law and politics typical of the constitutional state. They evolve in any sectors of society in which law provides for the external assistance of primarily non-legal societal self-constitutionalizations. As Teubner comments:

A non-statal, non-political, civil society-led constitutionalization thus occurs to the degree that reflexive social processes, which determine social rationalities through their self-application, are juridified in such a way that they are linked with reflexive legal processes. Understood in this way, it makes sense to speak of the existence of constitutional elements – in the strict sense of the term – within economic regimes, within the academic system, and within digital regimes of the Internet.[68]

According to this description, polity is not a political or legal concept. It is another name for societal processes of systemic, sectorial, regime and organizational self-constitution. Instead of state-centred constitutionalism, societal constitutionalism draws on a fragmented multiplicity of civil constitutions beyond politics.[69]

Another important hallmark of societal constitutionalism is the epistemological shift from state hierarchies and authority-driven vertical forms of communication to horizontal relations between law and society. This shift has been inspired by Georges Gurvitch[70] whose work is interpreted by Teubner as changing the perspective of the sociology of law by studying the horizontal relations of law to other social processes of norm making and a multitude of social normativities

---

67 Gunther Teubner, 'Fragmented foundations: Societal constitutionalism beyond the nation state', in *The Twilight of Constitutionalism?*, eds Dobner and Martin Loughlin, p. 333.

68 Ibid.

69 Gunther Teubner, *Constitutional Fragments: Societal Constitutionalism and Globalization* (Oxford, UK: Oxford University Press, 2012).

70 Georges Gurvitch, *The Sociology of Law* (London: K. Paul, Trench, Trubner & Co., 1947).

50 *Jiří Přibáň*

within the code of law. This horizontalization of law in society replaces the vertical perspective of law and society, focusing on the processes of formalization of informal and diffuse social norms into specific legal norms.[71]

In societal constitutionalism, *calculemus*-based governance is thus considered only one of multiple forms of constitutionalization. Unlike the exclusive Enlightenment philosophy-inspired view of sociology as the science of a rational organization of modern society, the theory of societal constitutionalism is also inspired by the other constitutive part of the sociological imagination, namely, the Romantic idea of the replacement of political society and its state organization by living communities with their traditions, folkways and customary laws.[72]

This sociological turn to ethnological and ethnographic studies is almost completely opposite to the rationalist zeal of social engineering and calculation, yet it shares with it the same criticism of modern politics as a system of conflicts, negotiations and power struggles mainly organized through the state and its official laws. The principal difference is that this Romantic sociology of community, rather than the universal force of reason, considers the particular force of folk histories and collective bonds a real alternative to the modern politics of power contestations.[73]

This supplanting of polity's formal laws by the informal laws of particular communities and groups or social networks and regulatory regimes has always been strong within some streams of the sociology of law and its close relatives, such as theories of legal pluralism or, more recently, transnational law and governance theories.[74] For instance, the recent popularity of Eugen Ehrlich's classic distinction of living law and legislated law among theories of transnational governance and constitutionalism only confirms the sociological and socio-legal shift from formal to informal laws, and from the general polity and its constitutional form to particular communities and their forms of life.[75]

Drawing on these complexities and different sociological traditions, the theory of societal constitutionalism, nevertheless, radicalizes the concept of constitution by removing it from the domain of jurisprudence and legal science and making it part of sociological methodology. It persuasively demonstrates that, for instance, the economy and other social systems of European and global society can claim legal validity without any recourse to the founding values and legitimizing force of polity. Society does not need the semantics of polity as a precondition of its

---

71 Gunther Teubner, 'The two faces of Janus: Rethinking legal pluralism', *Cardozo Law Review* 13 (1992).

72 Philip Allott, *The Health of Nations: Society and Law Beyond the State* (Cambridge, UK: Cambridge University Press, 2002), p. 70.

73 Michael Löwy and Robert Sayre, *Romanticism against the Tide of Modernity* (Durham, NC: Duke University Press, 2001), p. 83.

74 Peer Zumbansen, 'Neither "public" nor "private", "national" nor "international": Transnational corporate governance from a legal pluralist perspective', *Journal of Law and Society* 38 (2011).

75 For further details see, for instance, Emmanuel Melissaris, 'The more, the merrier? A new take on legal pluralism', *Social and Legal Studies* 13 (2004).

Concept of self-limiting polity 51

constitutionalization. Instead of a single constitution of polity, society enhances different processes of self-constitutionalization for fragmented constitutional regimes. It is constitutional evolution without enforcement, best described not just as constitutionalism without polity but, rather, as constitutionalism without politics.

From self-constituted polities of society to the societal constitution of power

This theorization of constitutionalism without politics actually radicalizes governance theories which also treat the concept of governance as different from both the juridification logic of the system of positive law and the power logic of the political system. European and global transnational and supranational forms of governance appear to be just specific forms of multiple societal constitutionalizations.[76]

Reflecting on this peculiar consequence of governance and other non-political societal self-constitutionalizations, Christian Joerges correctly and critically notes that, 'While governance arrangements seek the law's support, they also challenge the law's rule through a de-juridification of the polity'.[77] The level of depoliticization of constitutionalism by governance and other societal constitutions is hard to accept, if only because it neglects theoretical contextualization of the typically modern social process of the evolution of a specific system of organizing political power and the delimited political realm of the secular, self-descriptive and self-regulated modern constitutional state and the supranational or transnational political processes of constitutionalization, such as the process of EU legal integration.

The failure to make theoretical distinctions between legally constituted political society and socially self-constituted, non-political polities of global traders, sportspersons or environmentalists raises a crucial question of what exactly is polity-like in these non-political polities, other than the semantic paradox of non-political politics. The greatest theoretical achievement of societal constitutionalism thus equally turns out to be its greatest weakness.

Teubner successfully criticizes the link between constitutional theory and the politics of identity by showing that juridical processes of constitutionalization actually do not need to be supported by any form of identity politics and political existentialism and/or the essentialist notion of culture and nation. This critical contribution cannot be ignored by any theory of European constitutionalism addressing the profound structural and semantic changes in European society. However, associating the concept of polity with any form of social self-constitution deprives it of conceptual distinction and clarity. Societal constitutions may be defined as opposites of state hierarchy and power politics. Nevertheless,

---

76 For an early view of European governance as constitutionalization, see Alec Stone Sweet and Thomas L. Brunell, 'Constructing a supranational constitution: Dispute resolution and governance in the European Community', *American Political Science Review* 92 (1998).

77 Christian Joerges, 'Constitutionalism and transnational governance: Exploring a magic triangle', in *Transnational Governance*, eds Joerges, Sand and Teubner, p. 341.

52   *Jiří Přibáň*

their heterarchical and/or polyarchical networks of coordination, negotiation, consultation, reasoning and deliberation continue to be confronted by two simple questions: 'How do you enforce decisions made within these networks?' and 'What makes them collectively binding in the absence of power as a political medium?'.

Societal constitutionalism claims of politics without power, and soft law without legal enforcement, avoid an important aspect of the life of any collectivity, namely, the binding character of internal decision making and its general recognition. It thus remains an intriguing question whether the separation of politics and society and the marginalization or even disappearance of concepts such as democratic polity, citizenship, loyalty, representative government and the constitutional state from social and legal theory actually lead to the constitution of polities beyond politics and law. In other words, does the death of *homo politicus* and the fragmentation of political sites and regimes necessarily mean the end of politics, or just its reconfiguration (which has to be carefully studied and analysed, especially against the background of the recent flood of new conceptualizations and theories of law, politics and society)?

Anti-political and anti-formalist perspectives are an intrinsic part of the sociological tradition, and their persistence and recent popularity show the depth of their typically modern roots. The theory of societal constitutionalism avoids the political questions of: 'By whom am I governed?' (the subject of power), 'How much am I governed?' (the extent of power) and 'How well am I governed?' (the efficiency of power), by claiming that it is society and the laws of its evolution that govern and constitute any polity.

Nevertheless, the process of depoliticization through societal constitutionalization means the transformation, but not the end, of politics. Instead of disappearing from modern society, politics can now be traced anywhere in social organizations, families, schools and other social settings. Despite the attempt to eliminate the power problem in societal constitutionalism, the constitution of polity in multi-dimensional and both sectorially and functionally differentiated society of non-political constitutions persists as a political and juridical question impossible to neutralize by sociologically expanding the meaning of constitutionalism.[78]

European constitutional polity: assessment of theoretical responses

From the analysis of European and global governance and constitutionalism and theoretical reflections, it is clear that there are several responses to the challenges regarding the constitution of polity. The first insists on the constitutional semantics of polity traditionally associated with modern statehood and its concepts of sovereign rule, shared political destiny, foundational values and collective solidarity. These cosmopolitan theories mainly adjust major ideas and concepts to

---

78 Neil Walker, 'The idea of constitutional pluralism', *Modern Law Review* 65 (2002): 347.

the transnational political and legal structures and constitute a new cosmo-polity beyond the now insufficient, if not defunct, structures of national or sub-national politics.

Like any other polity, European polity, indeed, can be semantically constructed as an 'imagined community'[79] invoking the sense of collective identity and moral solidarity. As a foundationalist concept, European polity can facilitate the production and circulation of what are considered the constitutive cultural values, moral norms and political principles of society. However, all images of the European polity's unity are confronted by the communal inclusion/exclusion distinctions and boundaries,[80] even if formulated in the prescriptive language of cosmopolitanism and human rights.

The polyarchies of EU governance are not self-justifying and self-enforcing. Rather, they contribute to the organizational complexity of the EU's political system with distinct mechanisms of inclusion/exclusion and decision making. Like state governments, EU governance organizations can determine which subjects and agencies may be involved in its decision making and set up specific conditions for them and their actions. They thus mainly contribute to the political system's elasticity by extending the process of decision making.

Reflecting on this paradox in the concept of European polity as territorially limited, yet founded on unlimited cosmopolitan values, the second response is sociologically informed and abandons the very concept of polity as a political community both constituent of and constituted by a basic legal document. This approach looks more radical, but actually reintroduces a number of normative expectations associated with civil constitutions beyond statehood and politics.[81] One cannot but keep asking what is 'civil' about European or global commerce, science and sport, especially in the wake of crises and scandals, such as the Grexit or FIFA corruption scandals which could not be addressed without state power and jurisdiction.

The structures and operations of these non-political civil constitutions actually constitute their specific 'hidden structures' of politics.[82] They cannot avoid the meta-political question of constitutionalism as commonality. Neil Walker addresses the problem in the following terms:

> At the intersubjective level, too, participants will lack the common 'we' perspective and point of commitment from which to address all questions of the common interest. Instead, we are bound to accept in a post-holistic context that questions of the common interest in collective decision making are simply not questions that, at the deepest level of political self-interrogation, we can

---

79 Benedict Anderson, *Imagined Communities: Reflections on the Origin and Spread of Nationalism* (London: Verso, 1983).

80 Hans Lindahl, 'European integration: Popular sovereignty and a politics of boundaries', *European Law Journal* 6 (2000): 253–256.

81 Gunther Teubner, 'Societal constitutionalism: Alternatives to state-centred constitutional theory?', in *Transnational Governance*, eds Joerges, Sand and Teubner, pp. 27–28.

82 Martin Krygier, 'The rule of law: Legality, teleology, sociology', in *Relocating the Rule of Law*, eds Gianluigi Palombella and Neil Walker (Oxford: Hart, 2009), pp. 51–52.

54   *Jiří Přibáň*

envisage all interested constituencies affected addressing comprehensively *in common* . . . constitutional language retains a crucial longstop function as a kind of 'placeholder' for certain abiding concerns we have. These concerns are, quite simply, that unless we can address the meta-political framing of politics in a manner that remains wedded to ideas of the common interest, however difficult this may be to conceive and however far we have travelled from our most familiar and perhaps most conducive framework for such a task, something of great and irreplaceable value will have been lost from our resources of common living.[83]

No theory of constitutionalism can ignore the political aspects of social steering and governance regimes and obscure them by wide sociological extensions of the constitutional self-reference of rules on rules.[84]

Instead of normatively searching for democratic alternatives to the modern state or fictionalizing new 'constitutional subjects' or 'constitutional actors'[85] beyond politics and law, the concept of polity, like the concept of the state, needs to be studied as a self-referential concept of the emerging systems of transnational law and politics in Europe and elsewhere.[86] It needs to be considered a semantic construct produced by internal operations of the functionally differentiated political and legal systems operating both within and beyond structural limitations of the nation state.

Whether new post-state forms of constitutionalism and the current state of global legal and constitutional pluralism lead to the formation of 'hybrid polities,'[87] or the establishment of 'a jurisprudence of hybridity' as a jurisprudence preferable to both the hierarchies of the hegemonic state and the separatist tendencies of different communities searching for their autonomy,[88] is not too important after all. What is much more important is the fact that the process of constitution making establishes its constituency even without substantive claims of cultural identity or the structures of a nation state.

Multiple normative claims, communal bonds and political recognition are operationalized instead of being either simply subjected to the basic norm or dissolved in the plurality of contested normative preferences. In transnational politics and law, the clearly delineated constitutional form of statehood as the organization legally regulating the process of collective decision making in the common interest, is blurred, and no political substitutes can replicate this specific social organization of political and legal modernity. In practice, any common

---

83 Neil Walker, 'Beyond the holistic constitution?', in *The Twilight of Constitutionalism?*, eds Dobner and Loughlin, p. 307.
84 Teubner, *Constitutional Fragments*, p. 63.
85 Ibid. p. 1.
86 Niklas Luhmann, 'The "state" of the political system', in *Essays on Self-Reference* (New York: Columbia University Press, 1990), p. 166.
87 Walker, 'The idea of constitutional pluralism', p. 304.
88 Paul S. Berman, 'Toward a jurisprudence of hybridity', *Utah Law Review* 1 (2010): 14–15.

Concept of self-limiting polity 55

interest of polity, however, is reformulated as the multiplicity of particular interests presented at different forums and specified by different institutions of European or global society and their supranational and transnational structures and networks.

The third and, in my view, most realistic response, therefore, is to adopt societal constitutionalism's position, which considers polity an outcome of multiple constitutionalizations and not its existential precondition and limitation. However, the processes of constitutionalization do not happen everywhere in society and polities are not emerging beyond the political system of society.

Theories of European constitutionalism and governance cannot eliminate power as an intrinsic part of constitution making and the constitutionalization of different sub-systems of society. Constitutionalizations in society therefore need to be analysed by social science methodologies, yet have to be treated as a distinctly political and juridical process which involves power in its societal productivity and creativity both within the nation state and beyond its structural limitations at supranational and transnational levels. In the next section, I therefore want to show how European legal and political integration, and the polycentric polity constituted by it, demonstrate both the recent transformations and persistence of the constitutional democratic state as a social organization with the capacity to operate constitutionally at supranational and transnational levels.

Europe's self-constitutionalization beyond the imagined polity of values

The historical process of *integration as constitutionalization* shows that the EU has the self-generating power to extend its competence and capacity – the power of self-constitutionalization. The politically and legally integrated EU therefore deserves to be called a polity, even without subscribing to the holistic concept of a European demos as both the missing constituent power in integration and the desired goal of constitutionalization.

The heterarchy of a European polity combines diversity and unity, transcends territorial boundaries and images of collective identity, and projects a polycentric and pluri-dimensional configuration of authority.[89] These characteristics of a European polity beyond statehood and nationhood actually signify the systemic limitation of politics and law in European society and their functional differentiation from other social systems evolving at European level, such as economy, education, science and technology.

As already indicated, the constitution of a European polity is therefore not to be confused with the constitution of a European society, which stretches far beyond structural limitations, political aspirations and legal regulations of the EU.[90] What constitutes a European polity is very different from the constitution

---

89 Neil Walker, 'Sovereignty and differentiated integration in the European Union', *European Law Journal* 4 (1988): 357.

90 Chris Rumford, *The European Union: A Political Sociology* (Oxford, UK: Blackwell, 2002), p. 83.

56 Jiří Přibáň

of societal totality. What keeps its sense of commonality cannot be explained by moral and political philosophy.

There are no identity surrogates for the fiction of the self-governing sovereign people at EU level except the weak ethical language of the common values and shared destiny of European peoples. However, this normative language of political justice and ethics is not enough to take the place of constituent political will and its containment in some form of European statehood. The self-constitution of the EU, therefore, does not and cannot replicate the self-constitution of modern societies in nation states and their conceptualization as national polities.[91]

The concept of a European polity signifies the systemic self-description and self-referential image of society as a unity semantically established by the systems of European positive law and politics. Nevertheless, this image cannot fully grasp the totality of society and therefore needs to be perceived as only recursively describing political and legal operations and semantic constructions at EU level. Political ontology searching for normative societal foundations for a European polity is therefore best abandoned in favour of a social theory of functionally differentiated and heterarchical systems of European law and politics, constituting the polity as their internal construct.

A European polity is to be treated as a construct of structural coupling between the EU's legal and political systems, which, despite the post-national and post-state character of European governance, includes the governing capacities and legal regulations of its member states.[92] Member states continue to exercise significant powers and actively shape the EU's existing political and legal systems despite the radical transformation and limitation of their governing capacities. The failure of the process of EU constitution making and the active popular resistance to attempts to create a written constitution for the Union, clearly signify both the limitations of EU formal institution building and the informal evolutionary processes of the self-constituted legal order benefiting the EU, its member states, individual citizens and different communities.

State-based political constitutionalism has not been replaced by supranational European self-constitutionalization. Constituent popular power and democratic polities formed within the EU's member states persist and even increasingly oppose EU transnational policies and thus recursively turn the EU into a space of serious conflicts and contestations. These tensions between member state and EU institutions are actually an intrinsic part of EU multi-level self-constitutionalization, which leads to the shared governing between EU and member state institutions.

EU governance regimes and different self-constitutionalizations searching for their legitimation still reach out to member state polities, with institutions and

---

91 Erik Oddvar Eriksen, ed., *Making the European Polity: Reflexive Integration in the EU* (Oxford, UK: Routledge, 2005).

92 Beate Kohler-Koch, ed., *Linking EU and National Governance* (Oxford, UK: Oxford University Press, 2003).

Concept of self-limiting polity 57

practices fully conforming to liberal and democratic principles.[93] The European polity thus finds its specific multi-level forms of democratic legitimacy, policy making and justification balancing typically modern dualities traditionally established at state and local levels, such as individual autonomy and collective goals, liberal and republican principles or democratic and administrative policy making.[94]

In this respect, it should be noted how the most recent Lisbon Treaty of the EU recognized the persisting operative capacity of the constitutional state and subsequently enhanced the role of member states and their democratically elected and representative parliaments in EU law making. The current constitutional settlement of the EU, including the Lisbon Treaty, demonstrates that the sovereign state's powers have certainly been weakened in some areas because of Europeanization and globalization processes, most notably in the domain of economy, monetary policies, taxation, health, environment, education, science, technology and the mass media. At the same time, the sovereign state's ability to exercise power has not been diminished in many areas of national security, intelligence and military policies or international relations and law.[95]

Announcements of the end of the nation state are as old as its historical emergence and evolution into the most prevalent political organization. The nation state has always been questioned and its historical limitations and/or eventual disappearance predicted by radical anarchists, syndicalists and communists, but also by sociologists who, like Herbert Spencer, contrasted the person and the state,[96] or Emile Durkheim who believed that repressive state solidarity was giving way to the organic solidarity of social cooperation.[97]

In its legitimate attempts to analyse the state as only one of many social organizations and not the ultimate constitution and representation of social totality, the sociological perspective often falls victim to the opposite extreme, namely, denying the social and political importance of political power and state organization as such. The nation state may be becoming too small for the big problems of life in global society and too big for the small problems of our increasingly complex life in a globalized society.[98] Despite its structural limitations vis-à-vis the processes of political and legal globalization, the modern state's operative capacity of delineating between politicization and depoliticization, nevertheless, remains indispensable even in European and global society.

---

93 Klaus Dieter Wolf, 'Defending state autonomy: Intergovernmental governance in the European Union', in *The Transformation of Governance in the European Union*, eds Beate Kohler-Koch and Rainer Eising (London: Routledge, 1999).

94 Fritz W. Scharpf, *Governing in Europe: Effective and Democratic?* (Oxford, UK: Oxford University Press, 1999).

95 Alexander Wendt, *Social Theory of International Politics* (Cambridge, UK: Cambridge University Press, 1999).

96 Herbert Spencer, *The Man versus the State, with Six Essays on Government, Society and Freedom* [1884]. (Indianapolis, IL: Liberty Fund, 1981).

97 Emile Durkheim, 'The concept of the state' in *Durkheim on Politics and the State*, ed. Anthony Giddens (Cambridge, UK: Polity, 1986).

98 Daniel Bell, 'The world and the United States in 2013', *Daedalus* 116(3) (1987): 14.

58   Jiří Přibáň

Concluding remarks: on the sociological concept of European constitutionalism

The EU context persuasively demonstrates that the concept of polity, rather than some form of societal constitutionalism, continues to be part of political constitutionalism. The process of European self-constitutionalization primarily responds to the need for public accountability and democratization of the EU's supranational and transnational governing bodies.[99] Instead of the erosion and withering powers of the constitutional state, the process of EU integration, rather, promotes various forms of multi-level constitutionalization responding to the polycentric structures of European law and politics and reflecting on both the external limitations and self-limitations of national member state constitutions vis-à-vis the EU's post-national legal and political configurations.

Critically drawing on some ideas of societal constitutionalism, especially its most original and inspiring misreading of autopoietic social systems theory, it is then possible to radically rethink and reconceptualize the EU's self-constitutionalization and polity building. The first lesson of autopoietic social systems theory is the impossibility of pretending that European constitutionalism will eventually lead to the constitution of a European democratic polity replicating structural, semantic and normative patterns of state constitutionalism in the post-national European constellation. The idea of constituting supreme legal and political authority at EU level is present in some theories of European federalism in its executive, legislative or any other form. The idea of the reorganization of nation state structures and transforming the EU's political and legal organization into some form of federal or confederative statehood for Europe disappeared with the rejection of the Constitutional Treaty by the French and Dutch referenda in 2005.

The EU's constitutionalization and polity formation, rather, shows both the practical and theoretical limits of the normative idea of the people constituting its state as a distinct form of socio-cultural existence and identity. This idea of a polity's existence, legitimized by politically enforced moral principles and cultural values, contradicts the process of functional differentiation in modern society.

Modern society is not integrated by the sovereign power of Leviathan and political rationality of its legislative machine – *machina legislatorum*. It is functionally differentiated by the systemic rationality of different social sub-systems. Politics and law therefore have specific social functions and cannot guarantee the general normative integration of modern society. The concept of polity is not a prescriptive precondition of politics in the sense of common identity establishing a political system, its hierarchies and legally defined constitutional limitations. It can scarcely be treated in the essentialist sense as the social or moral foundation of politics and its cultural legitimation. Unlike persons, societies do not have their categorical imperatives and cannot be integrated through moral principles and

---

99 Stijn Smismans, ed., *Civil Society and Legitimate European Governance* (Cheltenham, UK: Edward Elgar, 2006).

Concept of self-limiting polity 59

norms into one political body which could be considered analogous to the human body and soul, and its existence and commitment to the ethical life.

The second lesson is no less important, though it contradicts societal constitutionalism's non-political conceptualization of constitutionalization and constitution making. The history of European integration shows that there are profound differences between political constitutions, whether formal or informal, of the state or any supranational or transnational political organization, such as the EU, and the societal non-political constitutions of a golf club, the Scouts, business associations or global traders and consumer groups. The concept of societal constitutionalism obscures the fact that political and legal operations and communication are part of society and its functional differentiation and therefore need to carefully analysed and not ignored by any social theory of constitutionalism.

One of the first paradigmatic rules of autopoietic systems theory states that, 'Everything that happens belongs to a *system* (or many systems) and *always at the same time* to the *environment of other systems*'.[100] The system's relationship to the environment is constitutive for systemic operation and system formation. The internal operations of the EU systems of law and politics constantly differentiate between the system and its environment. The autonomy and constitutional self-reference of EU law and politics can only be described as the system/environment differentiation and structural irritation between law and politics; it cannot be reformulated by the theory of societal constitutionalism as merely the external assistance of law to the internal constitutionalization of other social systems.

The final and most important lesson of autopoietic social systems theory is its sociological reformulation of the typically modern problem of constitutionally limited government. According to this theory, the modern political problem of limitation of power becomes a social problem of the self-limitation of politics in democratic society. The political system needs to protect itself from the totalizing tendencies of society. Modern society, therefore, increasingly uses its internal operations to differentiate between the systems of positive law and politics and their social environment, and to escape both the totalizing utopia of popular self-government and the risk of the technology of power legitimized by the equally totalizing canon of depoliticized rationality present in legal validity or administrative governance.

While profoundly inspired by Luhmann's theory of autopoietic social systems, Teubner's theory of societal constitutionalism downplays the persisting role of the state, this 'device for holding together what has emerged as the self-reinforcing dynamics in the political system and the legal system',[101] and political constitutionalism in European and global society. Teubner's identification of constitutionalism with general social processes of self-reference and self-production

---

100 Niklas Luhmann, *Social Systems* (Stanford, CA: Stanford University Press, 1995), p. 177.
101 Niklas Luhmann, *Law as a Social System* (Oxford, UK: Oxford University Press, 2004), p. 365.

60   Jiří Přibáň

eliminates the problem of political power as a specific code of social communication and its legal validation through constitutional procedures.

However, the political system cannot operate without power as its medium. The state's operative capacity to respond to all three questions of politics – subject, extent and efficiency of power – has made it the most prominent political organization of modernity.[102] Nevertheless, while the democratic subject's legitimacy question, despite globalization, continues to be persistently rooted in nation state semantics and decision-making procedures, the question of the extent and efficiency of state power is radically reformulated by the operations of functional systems and the structural limitations of EU politics and law, and their further coupling with the systems of global politics and law.

European post-constituent constitutionalism is self-limiting in terms of both societal expansionism and moral fundamentalism. Its operations are not existentially predetermined and legitimized by constituent polity. This self-constitution of European polity by its self-limitation actually highlights the general function of modern constitutions, communicating political power through law and limiting it by law. Within the EU context, it is communicated at the same time at local, national or supranational levels. However, rather than marginalizing the state, the structures and organizations of transnational, supranational and international law and politics, such as the EU, recognize the persistence of modern nation states and use their operative capacity adjusted to 'new modes of global governance'.[103]

In this new political and legal condition, however, the biggest challenge to the constitutional state, its ruling authority and people, is the constant deterritorialization of European and global law and politics and the emergence of new political spaces and legal regimes irrespective of nation state borders.[104] When focusing on this particular problem of law and politics beyond statehood, it appears that the project of European integration as constitutionalization and multi-level polity making is actually less avant-garde and more anachronistic than many of its advocates would want to admit.

The global drive towards the deterritorialization of law and politics shows that European society is just one of many segments of functionally differentiated global society. Its polity, therefore, is just a systemic construct of political constitutionalization limited by the territorially segmented differentiation of Europe, yet channelled through the general constitutional processes of evolving global society.

---

102 For general views, see, for instance, Gregor McLennan, David Held and Stuart Hall, eds, *The Idea of the Modern State* (Milton Keynes, UK: Open University Press, 1984).

103 Abram Chayes and Antonia Chayes, *The New Sovereignty: Compliance with International Regulatory Agreements* (Cambridge, MA: Harvard University Press, 1995).

104 James Anderson, ed., *Transnational Democracy: Political Spaces and Border Crossings* (London: Routledge 2002).

Concept of self-limiting polity 61

Bibliography

Allott, Philip. *The Health of Nations: Society and Law Beyond the State*. Cambridge, UK: Cambridge University Press, 2002.

Anderson, Benedict. *Imagined Communities: Reflections on the Origin and Spread of Nationalism*. London: Verso, 1983.

Anderson, James, ed. *Transnational Democracy: Political Spaces and Border Crossings*. London: Routledge, 2002.

Beck, Ulrich and Edgar Grande. 'Cosmopolitanism: Europe's way out of crisis'. *European Journal of Social Theory* 10 (2007): 67–85.

Bell, Daniel. 'The world and the United States in 2013'. *Daedalus* 116(3) (1987): 1–31.

Bell, Stephen. *Economic Governance and Institutional Dynamics*. Oxford, UK: Oxford University Press, 2002.

Bellamy, Richard. 'The European constitution is dead, long live European constitutionalism'. *Constellations* 13 (2006): 181–189.

Benz, Arthur and Ioannis Papadopoulos, eds. *Governance and Democracy: Comparing National, European and International Perspectives*. Oxford, UK: Routledge, 2006.

Berlin, Isaiah. *The Crooked Timber of Humanity: Chapters in the History of Ideas*. London: Pimlico, 2003.

Berman, Paul S. 'Toward a jurisprudence of hybridity'. *Utah Law Review* 1 (2010): 11–29.

Bohman, James. 'Constitution making and democratic innovation: The European Union and transnational governance'. *European Journal of Political Theory* 3 (2004): 315–337.

Boswell, Christina. 'The political functions of expert knowledge: Knowledge and legitimation in European Union immigration policy'. *Journal of European Public Policy* 15 (2008): 471–488.

Callies, Gralf P. and Peer Zumbansen. *Rough Consensus and Running Code: A Theory of Transnational Private Law*. Oxford, UK: Hart Publishing, 2010.

Chayes, Abram and Antonia Chayes. *The New Sovereignty: Compliance with International Regulatory Agreements*. Cambridge, MA: Harvard University Press, 1995.

Clam, Jean. 'What is modern power?' In *Luhmann on Law and Politics: Critical Appraisals and Applications*, edited by Michael King and Chris Thornhill. Oxford, UK: Hart Publishing, 2006, pp. 145–162.

De Búrca, Gráinne. 'The European Constitution project after the referenda'. *Constellations* 13 (2006): 205–217.

Delanty, Gerard. *The Cosmopolitan Imagination: The Renewal of Critical Social Theory*. Cambridge, UK: Cambridge University Press, 2009.

Durkheim, Emile. 'The concept of the state'. In *Durkheim on Politics and the State*, edited by Anthony Giddens. Cambridge: Polity, 1986, pp. 32–72.

Eriksen, Erik Oddvar, ed. *Making the European Polity: Reflexive Integration in the EU*. Oxford, UK: Routledge, 2005.

Evans, James. *Environmental Governance*. Oxford, UK: Routledge, 2012.

Fassbender, Bardo. 'The United Nations Charter as constitution of the international community'. *Columbia Journal of Transnational Law* 36 (1998): 529–619.

Gane, Nicholas. *Max Weber and Postmodern Theory: Rationalization Versus Re-Enchantment*. Basingstoke, UK and New York: Palgrave, 2002.

Gurvitch, Georges. *The Sociology of Law*. London: K. Paul, Trench, Trubner & Co., 1947.

Habermas, Jürgen. 'Why Europe needs a constitution'. *New Left Review* 11 (2001): 5–26.

Habermas, Jürgen. *The Crisis of the European Union: A Response*. Cambridge, UK: Polity, 2012.

62   Jiří Přibáň

Habermas, Jürgen. 'The crisis of the European Union in the light of a constitutionalization of international law'. *European Journal of International Law* 23 (2012): 335–348.

Jessup, Philip C. *Transnational Law: Storrs Lectures on Jurisprudence*. New Haven, CT: Yale University Press, 1956.

Joerges, Christian. 'Constitutionalism and transnational governance: Exploring a magic triangle'. In *Transnational Governance and Constitutionalism*, edited by Christian Joerges, Inger-Johanne Sand and Gunther Teubner. Oxford: Hart Publishing, 2004, pp. 343–375.

Klabbers, Jan, Anne Peters and Geir Ulfstein. *Constitutionalization of International Law*. Oxford, UK: Oxford University Press, 2009.

Kohler-Koch, Beate, ed. *Linking EU and National Governance*. Oxford, UK: Oxford University Press, 2003.

Kooiman, Jan, ed. *Modern Governance: New Government-Society Interactions*. London: Sage, 1993.

Kooiman, Jan. *Governing as Governance*. London: Sage, 2003.

Koskenniemi, Martti. *The Gentle Civilizer of Nations: The Rise and Fall of International Law 1870–1960*. Cambridge, UK: Cambridge University Press, 2004.

Koskenniemi, Martti and Susan Marks. *The Riddle of All Constitutions: International Law, Democracy, and the Critique of Ideology*. Oxford, UK: Oxford University Press, 1999.

Krisch, Nico. *Beyond Constitutionalism: The Pluralist Structure of Postnational Law*. Oxford, UK: Oxford University Press, 2010.

Krygier, Martin. 'The rule of law: Legality, teleology, sociology.' In *Relocating the Rule of Law*, edited by Gianluigi Palombella and Neil Walker. Oxford, UK: Hart, 2009, pp. 45–69.

Kumar, Krishan. *Prophecy and Progress: The Sociology of Industrial and Post-Industrial Society*. London: Penguin, 1978.

Landfried, Christine. 'Difference as a potential of European Constitution making'. *European Law Journal* 12 (2006): 764–787.

Lindahl, Hans. 'European integration: Popular sovereignty and a politics of boundaries'. *European Law Journal* 6 (2000): 239–256.

Löwy, Michael and Robert Sayre. *Romanticism Against the Tide of Modernity*. Durham, NC: Duke University Press, 2001.

Luhmann, Niklas. 'The 'state' of the political system'. In *Essays on Self-Reference*, by Niklas Luhmann. New York: Columbia University Press, 1990.

Luhmann, Niklas. *Social Systems*. Stanford, CA: Stanford University Press, 1995.

Luhmann, Niklas. *Law as a Social System*. Oxford, UK: Oxford University Press, 2004.

MacDonald, Ronald St. John and Douglas M. Johnston, eds. *Towards World Constitutionalism: Issues in the Legal Ordering of the World Community*. Leiden, The Netherlands: Martinus Nijhoff, 2005.

Maduro, Miguel P. 'The importance of being called a constitution: Constitutional authority and the authority of constitutionalism'. *International Journal of Constitutional Law* 3 (2005): 332–356.

Mancini, Federico G. 'The making of a constitution for Europe'. *Common Market Law Review* 26 (1989): 595–614.

Manuel, Frank E. *The Prophets of Paris*. New York: Harper, 1965.

McLennan, Gregor, David Held and Stuart Hall, eds. *The Idea of the Modern State*. Milton Keynes, UK: Open University Press, 1984.

Melissaris, Emmanuel. 'The more, the merrier? A new take on legal pluralism'. *Social and Legal Studies* 13 (2004): 57–79.

Concept of self-limiting polity 63

Mendes, Errol P. *Global Governance, Human Rights and International Law: Combating the Tragic Flaw*. Oxford, UK: Routledge, 2014.

Meron, Theodor. 'International criminalization of internal atrocities'. *American Journal of International Law* 89 (1995): 554–577.

Piris, Jean-Claude. *The Constitution for Europe. A Legal Analysis*. Cambridge, UK: Cambridge University Press, 2006.

Přibáň, Jiří. *Legal Symbolism: On Law, Time and European Identity*. Aldershot, UK: Ashgate, 2007.

Rhodes, Roderick A.W. 'The new governance: Governing without government'. *Political Studies* 44 (1996): 652–667.

Rosenau, James N. 'The state in an era of cascading politics: Wavering concept, widening competence, withering colossus, or weathering change?' In *The Elusive State: International and Comparative Perspectives*, edited by James A. Caporaso. London: Sage, 1990, pp. 17–48.

Rosenau, James N. 'Governance, order, and change in world politics'. In *Governance Without Government in World Politics*, edited by James N. Rosenau and Ernst-Otto Czempiel. Cambridge, UK: Cambridge University Press, 1992, pp. 1–29.

Rosenau, James N. 'Toward an ontology for global governance'. In *Approaches to Global Governance Theory*, edited by Martin Hewson and Thomas Sinclair. Albany, NY: SUNY Press, 1999, pp. 287–296.

Rumford, Chris. *The European Union: A Political Sociology*. Oxford, UK: Blackwell, 2002.

Runciman, W.G. *Social Science and Political Theory*. Cambridge, UK: Cambridge University Press, 1969.

Sassen, Saskia. *Territory-Authority-Rights. From Medieval to Global Assemblages*. Princeton, NJ: Princeton University Press, 2006.

Sassen, Saskia. 'Neither global nor national: Novel assemblages of territory, authority and rights'. *Ethics & Global Politics* 1 (2008): 61–79.

Scharpf, Fritz W. *Governing in Europe: Effective and Democratic?* Oxford, UK: Oxford University Press, 1999.

Schmitt, Carl. *Legality and Legitimacy*. Durham, NC: Duke University Press, 2004.

Schroeder, Ralph. 'Disenchantment and its discontents: Weberian perspectives on science and technology'. *Sociological Review* 43 (1995): 227–250.

Sciulli, David. *Theory of Societal Constitutionalism: Foundations of a Non-Marxist Critical Theory*. Cambridge, UK: Cambridge University Press, 1992.

Selznick, Philip. 'Sociology and Natural Law'. *Natural Law Forum* 6 (1961): 84–108.

Selznick, Philip. *A Humanist Science: Values and Ideas in Social Inquiry*. Stanford, CA: Stanford University Press, 2008.

Smismans, Stijn, ed. *Civil Society and Legitimate European Governance*. Cheltenham, UK: Edward Elgar, 2006.

Somek, Alexander. 'Administration without sovereignty'. In *The Twilight of Constitutionalism?* edited by Petra Dobner and Martin Loughlin. Oxford: Oxford University Press, 2010, pp. 267–278.

Somek, Alexander. *The Cosmopolitan Constitution*. Oxford, UK: Oxford University Press, 2014.

Spencer, Herbert. *The Man Versus the State, with Six Essays on Government, Society and Freedom* [1884]. Indianapolis, IL: Liberty Fund, 1981.

Steffek, Jens. 'Sources of legitimacy beyond the state: A view from international relations'. In *Transnational Governance and Constitutionalism*, edited by Christian Joerges, Inger-Johanne Sand and Gunther Teubner. Oxford, UK: Hart Publishing, 2004, pp. 81–101.

64   *Jiří Přibáň*

Stein, Eric. 'Lawyers, judges, and the making of a transnational constitution'. *American Journal of International Law* 75 (1981): 1–27.

Stoker, Gerry. 'Governance as theory: Five propositions'. *International Social Science Journal* 50 (1998): 17–28.

Stone Sweet, Alec. *The Judicial Construction of Europe*. Oxford, UK: Oxford University Press, 2004.

Stone Sweet, Alec and Thomas L. Brunell. 'Constructing a supranational constitution: Dispute resolution and governance in the European Community'. *American Political Science Review* 92 (1998): 63–81.

Teubner, Gunther. 'The two faces of Janus: Rethinking legal pluralism'. *Cardozo Law Review* 13 (1992): 1443–1462.

Teubner, Gunther. 'Societal constitutionalism: Alternatives to state-centred constitutional theory?' In *Transnational Governance and Constitutionalism*, edited by Christian Joerges, Inger-Johanne Sand and Gunther Teubner. Oxford, UK: Hart Publishing, 2004, pp. 3–28.

Teubner, Gunther. 'Fragmented foundations: Societal constitutionalism beyond the nation state'. In *The Twilight of Constitutionalism?*, edited by Petra Dobner and Martin Loughlin. Oxford, UK: Oxford University Press, 2010, pp. 327–341.

Teubner, Gunther. *Constitutional Fragments: Societal Constitutionalism and Globalization*. Oxford, UK: Oxford University Press, 2012.

Tomuschat, Christian. *International Law: Ensuring the Survival of Mankind on the Eve of a New Century*. The Hague, The Netherlands: Martinus Nijhoff, 2001.

Veblen, Thorstein. *The Theory of the Business Enterprise*. New Brunswick NJ: Transaction Books, 1904.

Voegelin, Eric. 'The religion of humanity and the French Revolution'. In *From Enlightenment to Revolution*, by Eric Voegelin. Durham, NC: Duke University Press, 1975, pp. 160–194.

Walker, Neil. 'Sovereignty and differentiated integration in the European Union'. *European Law Journal* 4 (1998): 355–388.

Walker, Neil. 'The idea of constitutional pluralism'. *Modern Law Review* 65 (2002): 317–359.

Walker, Neil. 'Post-constituent constitutionalism? The case of the European Union'. In *The Paradox of Constitutionalism: Constituent Power and Constitutional Form*, edited by Martin Loughlin and Neil Walker. Oxford, UK: Oxford University Press, 2007, pp. 247–267.

Walker, Neil. 'Beyond the holistic constitution?' In *The Twilight of Constitutionalism?*, edited by Petra Dobner and Martin Loughlin. Oxford, UK: Oxford University Press, 2010, pp. 291–308.

Weber, Max. *The Protestant Ethic and The Spirit of Capitalism*. London: Routledge, 1992.

Weber, Max. 'On the situation of constitutional democracy in Russia'. In *Weber: Political Writings*, edited by Peter Lassman and Ronald Speirs. Cambridge, UK: Cambridge University Press, 1994, pp. 29–74.

Weber, Max. 'Science as a vocation'. In *The Vocation Lectures*, edited by David S. Owen and Tracy B. Strong. Indianapolis, IN: Hackett Publishing, 2004.

Wendt, Alexander. *Social Theory of International Politics*. Cambridge, UK: Cambridge University Press, 1999.

Wind, Marlene. 'The European Union as a polycentric polity'. In *European Constitutionalism Beyond the State*, edited by Joseph H.H. Weiler and Marlene Wind. Cambridge, UK: Cambridge University Press, 2003, pp. 103–131.

Wolf, Klaus Dieter. 'Defending state autonomy: Intergovernmental governance in the European Union'. In *The Transformation of Governance in the European Union*, edited by Beate Kohler-Koch and Rainer Eising. London: Routledge, 1999, pp. 231–248.

Wolin, Sheldon. *Politics and Vision: Continuity and Innovation in Western Political Thought*. Princeton, NJ: Princeton University Press, 1960.

Zumbansen, Peer. 'Neither "Public" nor "Private", "National" nor "International": Transnational corporate governance from a legal pluralist perspective'. *Journal of Law and Society* 38 (2011): 50–75.

Zumbansen, Peer. 'Comparative, global and transnational constitutionalism: The emergence of a transnational legal-pluralist order'. *Global Constitutionalism* 1 (2012): 16–52.

3 A political–sociological analysis of constitutional pluralism in Europe[*]

Paul Blokker

Introduction

The original constitutional moment of the early 2000s has faltered, not least due to a popular rejection of the European Draft Constitution in the referenda held in France and the Netherlands in 2005. In terms of constitutional and political theory, the rejection has spawned a discussion on the status and form of EU constitutionalism, the complexities involved with post-national constitutionalism, as well as normative views on its future. In empirical-sociological terms, much investigation has gone into reasons behind rejection and popular support for the EU project. The rejection has thus been widely discussed in terms of the process (the Convention, referenda), the constitutional product (the Draft Constitution) and the status of the EU in public opinion. In all this, however, there has been relatively little political–sociologically informed analysis linking constitutional politics with political activities and positive constitutional claims beyond formal institutions.

This chapter contributes to a political sociology of European constitutional politics, which takes into account a plurality of constitutional subjects, emphasizes the interaction between law, politics and society, and underlines the importance of civic constitutional engagement. The claim is that a political–sociological approach develops a more comprehensive perspective on constitutional politics in Europe, bringing to the fore a 'constitutional deficit' in the EU that is not always appreciated in theoretical debate, relating to the sociological – and not merely the normative – legitimacy of the EU. It further helps to bring into the picture alternative constitutional subjects, next to the 'usual suspects' (political and legal actors), including (transnational) pro-democracy movements. And perhaps most importantly, it sheds light on the emergence of a transnational public sphere, which includes civic projects that put existing institutions 'to the test', not least by means of the articulation of positive, alternative constitutional claims. Such claims might be particularly relevant in times of multi-faceted

---

[*] The author recognizes a Unità di Ricerca grant from the *Provincia Autonoma di Trento* for the 'Constitutional Politics in Post-Westphalian Europe' (CoPolis) project at the Department of Sociology, University of Trento.

Constitutional pluralism in Europe 67

crisis in which the instituted constitutional language has grown tiresome, and an instituting[1] language is more likely to be drawn upon.

The chapter starts with a discussion of a few theories of European constitution making, contrasting different understandings of constitutionalism with regard to relations between law and politics, the role of self-government and the constitutional subjects involved (discussing statist, freestanding or universalist, and democratic constitutionalism). Second, the chapter will outline a political sociology of constitutional politics, emphasizing the relevance of a 'constitutional deficit' on the EU level and the importance of scrutinizing foundational claims also beyond formal institutions. Third, I will draw attention to and concisely analyse a number of constitutional claims that have emerged in the transnational public arena, endorsed by transnational pro-democracy movements. These movements indicate both an emerging transnational, constitutional public debate and provide substantive examples of different understandings of constitutionalism on the European level.

Theories of EU constitutionalism

The literature on the European Constitution has exploded,[2] particularly since the formal constitution-making experience. Below, I will discuss a few relevant theories of constitutionalism that address the supranational context, with no attempt to be exhaustive. The point is, rather, to explore three very different takes on (supranational) constitutionalism, in particular with regard to dimensions of the relations between law and politics, the role of self-government and identified constitution-interpreting subjects. I discuss these theories with a view to taking seriously Brunkhorst's statement that:

> While Europe is constitutionally organized, it is not particularly democratic. The already quite advanced status of European constitution making is simultaneously increasing both the chance for a transition from a weak to a very strong European public sphere, and the danger of constitutionally solidifying the de-democratization of Europe and its nations.[3]

I thus attempt to tease out how three different interpretations of (European) constitutionalism – statist, universal and democratic constitutionalism – relate to the dual potentiality of constitutionalism, that is, as both a source of order and legality and as a source of democratic participation.

---

1 In the terms of Cornelius Castoriadis. Instituting society refers to the creative dimension of society, which is expressed in the ceaseless creation of new institutions as well as in the constitution of society as such, while instituted society refers to the creation or final product in terms of an instituted world. See Cornelius Castoriadis, *The Imaginary Institution of Society* (London: Polity Press, 1987).

2 One recent addition to the debate is Gráinne de Búrca and Joseph H.H. Weiler, eds., *The Worlds of European Constitutionalism* (Cambridge: Cambridge University Press, 2012).

3 Hauke Brunkhorst, *Solidarity. From Civic Friendship to a Global Legal Community* (Cambridge, MA: MIT Press, 2005), 163–164.

68   *Paul Blokker*

Statist or foundationalist constitutionalism

A well-known, but contested and largely negative, take on the possibilities for a European Constitution is the 'statist paradigm'[4] or foundational constitutionalism.[5] According to Mattias Kumm, the statist paradigm of understanding constitutions, or the 'way national constitutional lawyers imagine constitutional law',[6] consists of the following set of ideas:

> [t]he constitution establishes the supreme legal norms of the national legal system. It constitutes the legal system of the sovereign nation-state. That rank is justified with reference to 'We The People', the demos as the *pouvoir constituant*, and the foundation of constitutional authority. The statist paradigm establishes an analytical link among the constitution as a legal document, democracy as a foundational value, and the sovereign state as an institution.

Relation law and politics

In important ways, the statist view is intertwined with, or actually consists of, the idea of modern, Westphalian constitutionalism.[7] The idea is that modern constitutionalism is strictly related to the Westphalian triptych of territory, people and jurisdiction. Constitutionalism on this view is only meaningful when understood as involving the 'capacity to legitimise and regulate comprehensively the public power that takes effect within the territory of the state'.[8] In this, the statist view emphasizes the higher law status and the 'submission of politics to law',[9] and, one could add, the submission of society to law. In this, 'constitutionalism neither recognise[s] any extra-constitutional bearer of public power, nor any extra-constitutional ways and means to exercise power vis-à-vis citizens'.[10] As argued by James Tully, one key feature of modern constitutionalism is that a modern constitution is regarded as a 'structure of law' that is in important ways *separate from its subjects*. Whereas the modern constitution is ultimately dependent on the people for its legitimation, once constituted, it becomes a

---

4   Mattias Kumm, 'The cosmopolitan turn in constitutionalism: On the relationship between constitutionalism in and beyond the state', in *Ruling the World? Constitutionalism, International Law, and Global Governance*, eds. Jeffrey L. Dunoff and Joel P. Trachtman (Cambridge, UK: Cambridge University Press, 2009).

5   Michael A. Wilkinson, 'Political constitutionalism and the European Union', *Modern Law Review* 76 (2013); compare Neil Walker, 'Beyond the holistic constitution', in *The Twilight of Constitutionalism*, eds. Petra Dobner and Martin Loughlin (Oxford, UK: Oxford University Press, 2010).

6   Kumm, 'The cosmopolitan turn', p. 261.

7   Compare Walker, 'Beyond the holistic constitution'.

8   Dieter Grimm, 'The achievement of constitutionalism and its prospects in a changed world', in *The Twilight of Constitutionalism*, eds. Petra Dobner and Martin Loughlin (Oxford, UK: Oxford University Press, 2010), p. 21.

9   Ibid. p. 5.

10   Ibid. p. 7.

relatively autonomous set of meta-norms and rules that constitutes social and political interaction. James Tully calls this relative autonomy or externality the 'formality' of modern constitutions.[11]

Autonomy or self-rule

A further and related essential idea behind the constitution is to channel and express popular sovereignty. In this, popular sovereignty in statist constitutionalism is widely understood in a monist way, that is, as the expression of a singular people or demos.[12] In addition, a singular understanding of the people presupposes a shared civic or ethno-cultural identity, which is symbolically reflected in the constitution, either implicitly or explicitly so.[13] At any rate, the act of the constitution transfers this popular sovereignty from the *pouvoir constituant* to the *pouvoir constitué*. As Grimm argues, 'Popular sovereignty was the legitimating principle of the new order. But unlike the sovereign monarch, *the people were incapable of ruling themselves*. They needed representatives who governed in their name. *Democratic government is government by mandate*'.[14]

Furthermore, while constitutions also provide for a positive, democratic dimension, including civil and political rights which politically enable citizens and political actors, this positive dimension is confined within the limits set by the very same constitution. Thus, as Tully remarks, 'if people wish to change the laws, they must go to a separate institutionalized procedure such as a court, a legislature, and formal amending procedure or judicial review'.[15]

Constitution-interpreting subjects

What emerges from the statist view on constitutionalism is that – beyond the revolutionaries in, for instance, the American and French Revolutions – the range of constitution-interpreting subjects is a limited one. As argued by Grimm, once established, 'no extra-constitutional bearers of public power and no extra-constitutional ways and means to exercise this power are recognised'.[16] The relevant constitutional subjects become formal political actors and legal institutions, not least national Constitutional Courts. In the European context, this means that constitutionalism is related to member states as the 'Masters of the Treaty' and constitutional democracy is defended by states and national courts.[17]

---

11 James Tully, *Public Philosophy in a New Key, Vols. 1 and 2* (Cambridge, UK: Cambridge University Press, 2008).
12 Compare Walker, 'Beyond the holistic constitution'.
13 Compare Joseph H.H. Weiler, *Un'Europa cristiana. Un saggio esplorativo* (Milan, Italy: BUR Saggi, 2003).
14 Grimm, 'The achievement of constitutionalism', p. 8; emphasis added.
15 Tully, *Public Philosophy*, p. 199.
16 Grimm 'The achievement of constitutionalism', p. 9.
17 Compare Wilkinson, 'Political constitutionalism', pp. 197–200.

70 *Paul Blokker*

A constitution beyond the state becomes, according to a statist view, grounded in modern constitutionalism, a contradiction in terms as the transnational sphere cannot refer back to the constituent power of the people (not even in the European context, as held by the 'no-demos' thesis), does not relate to a closed cultural background, does not contain an ultimate legal authority (in the case of the European Court of Justice (ECJ), its status is evidently contested) and does not relate to principles of self-government and democratic participation. Indeed, the 'most straightforward application of the foundationalist mindset to the European constitution consists in the blunt denial of its plausibility in the absence of an accompanying "demos" or political unity'.[18] Foundational constitutionalism needs a 'relatively stable and coherent political community, or at least a community that is capable of exercising collective self-rule'.[19] In addition, the community is itself embedded in a deeper lying unity, a 'symbolic unity'.[20]

Universal constitutionalism

A strong contrast to a statist view of constitutionalism is provided by what Wilkinson calls 'free-standing constitutionalism' or Avbelj's 'best fit universal constitutionalism'.[21] This form of constitutionalism entails a form that 'rejects the premise that constitutional authority is based on the will of the constituent power, or "the people" as a collective entity, however this might be construed'.[22] The most pronounced exponent of this view – which I will simply label universal constitutionalism here – is found in the work of Mattias Kumm. A universal-constitutionalist understanding of the European integration project sees constitutionalism as based on a set of 'universal moral-legal values or basic principles that are essential to human flourishing' or 'constitutional essentials', which are, however, part of an 'autonomous legal order'.[23] On the universalist view, the EU as a legal-constitutional order consists of: (i) a set of essential constitutional – republican – principles that enshrine human rights, democracy and the rule of law;[24] (ii) a pluralistic juridical system that is responsible for the interpretation and application of these principles (the European Court of Justice (ECJ) as well as national courts); and (iii) the idea of a pluralistic European constitutional order, comprising EU and national levels, which contains various constitutions that express universal principles or constitutional essentials.

---

18 Ibid. p. 194.
19 Ibid.
20 Ibid.
21 Matej Avbelj, 'Questioning EU constitutionalisms', *German Law Journal* 9(19) (2008): 15.
22 Wilkinson, 'Political constitutionalism', p. 200.
23 Kumm, 'The cosmopolitan turn'.
24 Compare Mattias Kumm, 'Beyond golf clubs and the judicialization of politics: Why Europe has a constitution properly so called', *American Journal of Comparative Law* 54 (2006).

Constitutional pluralism in Europe 71

Relation law and politics

Part of the view of freestanding constitutionalism as the basis of European constitutionalism seems to overlap with a Dworkinian view of constitutionalism, in which legal norms are prioritized over a democratic-participatory dimension of constitutionalism, as the deeper (supposedly uncontestable) principles that the constitutional order is based on provide the preconditions of functioning democracy. Political democracy appears then reduced to a knowable end form, of which no extensive discussion is necessary, and which merely needs to be guaranteed by a constitutional meta-frame. Indeed, Kumm argues that it is the:

> [i]dea that legally constraining the relationship between Member States is an effective remedy against the great evils that have haunted the continent throughout much of the 19th and first half of the 20th century . . . [and that] . . . legal integration can be seen as a mechanism which tends to immunize nationally organized peoples from the kind of passionate political eruptions that have led to totalitarian or authoritarian governments and/or discrimination of minorities that have characterized European history in the 19th and 20th century.[25]

What 'freestanding constitutionalism' offers is a commitment to both legality and democracy on the basis of an institutionalization of republican principles, such as human rights, democracy and the rule of law, without recourse to any form of direct democratic identification of such principles. Rather, the principles are indirectly derived from a democratic genealogical basis, as they are supposedly based on a 'common heritage of the European constitutional tradition as it has emerged in the second half of the 20th century'.[26] Kumm invokes article 6 TEU as evidence of such a freestanding dimension to the European constitutional order.

Autonomy or self-rule

In Kumm's opinion, a democratically informed constitutionalism, which he calls 'emphatic republicanism', 'connects the idea of an ultimate legal authority with a strong conception of democratic self-government, [and] is mistaken and needs to be modified'.[27] In the context of what Kumm labels 'cosmopolitan constitutionalism', he has argued:

> What might domestic constitutionalism be, if it was imagined not within the conventional statist paradigm, but within a cosmopolitan paradigm? What if the idea of sovereignty as ultimate authority, a conception of constitutional law tied to the coercive institutions of the state and a conception of legitimacy

---

25 Ibid. pp. 514–515.
26 Ibid. p. 517.
27 Ibid. p. 515.

72 Paul Blokker

and democracy reductively tied to the self-governing practices of 'We the People', is *deeply flawed and implausible?*[28]

Kumm argues that the 'emphatic republican conception of constitutional self-government' (one that places a strong emphasis on constituent power, or what Kumm refers to as 'genealogy') encounters three problems. The first problem is that of an inability to overcome a statist conception. It apparently suffers from a 'statist fallacy'.[29] According to Kumm, the insistence on a demos and democratic self-government make this conception unfit for the imagining a post-national form of constitutional order.[30] Second, he argues that the republican conception is 'unhelpfully focused on genealogy', that is, the original founding of a constitutional order. According to Kumm, this leads to a 'genealogical fallacy'. Third, democracy is prioritized 'over all other concern, in particular the value of legality'.[31] Kumm argues that the 'absolutist fallacy' entails an 'exclusive focus on democratic self-government as the alpha and omega of constitutionalism'.[32] Instead, universal constitutionalism 'treats [no concern] as absolute: human rights, democracy and the rule of law are conceived as complementary principles'.[33] The democratic dimension of constitutionalism does then come to the fore not in decisions 'by directly electorally accountable national actors',[34] but on occasions in which 'concerns relating to democracy and human rights may provide countervailing reasons for limiting the authority of EU Law in certain circumstances'.[35]

Constitution-interpreting subjects

In universal constitutionalism, it is particular legal actors – predominantly national Constitutional Courts, the ECJ and the ECHR – who are responsible for the interpretation of 'constitutional essentials' or principles.[36] Universal or 'cosmopolitan constitutionalism' (Kumm's own term) seems 'to put a lot of faith in the powers of the judiciary'.[37] More generally, the constitutional subjects engage in a 'rights practice [which] is a highly cooperative endeavor in which courts and other politically accountable institutions are partners in joint enterprise and different institutions assume different roles'. Indeed, 'courts, legislators, and administrative agencies are conceived of as partners in a joint enterprise to give meaning to the abstract

---

28 Kumm, 'The cosmopolitan turn', p. 261; emphasis added.
29 Kumm, 'Beyond golf clubs', p. 518.
30 It does not seem to occur to Kumm that it might be his own inability to imagine a meaningful democratically or self-governing order of this kind beyond the statist order that makes him project a statist fallacy on the 'emphatic republican tradition'.
31 Kumm, 'Beyond golf clubs', p. 518.
32 Ibid. p. 522.
33 Ibid.
34 Ibid. p. 526.
35 Ibid. p. 527.
36 Ibid. p. 507.
37 Kumm, 'The cosmopolitan turn', p. 305.

Constitutional pluralism in Europe 73

rights guarantees in concrete contexts'.[38] But the relationship is not balanced, in that, 'national-level courts generally *accord* the democratic legislator or administrative agencies *some degree of discretion*, particularly when it comes to assessing competing policy considerations within the proportionality framework'.[39]

What a freestanding view of European constitutionalism ignores, sees as outdated or conceptualized away is, first of all, a normative commitment to 'autonomy', which understands democracy as a system in which the ruled can in some way understand themselves as co-authors of the law (including foundational norms). In such a perspective, the emphasis is on how political communities determine their own constitutions contextually, following their own needs, traditions and political aspirations.[40] The universal-constitutional view, 'takes as basic a commitment to rights-based public reason and interprets acts by the democratic legislator as an attempt to spell out what that abstract commitment to rights amounts to under the circumstances addressed by the legislative act'.[41]

Legislation is thus evaluated from the point of view of a universally oriented public reason and not from 'within the framework of an authoritative will'.[42] Second, universal constitutionalism lacks a sociological account of democratic society which relates a politico-legal community to wider society through different forms of legitimacy. Legitimacy takes both an empirical and a normative form.[43] It is then not sufficient to argue that a particular constitutional arrangement enjoys normative legitimacy as it reflects universal principles and is grounded in public reason. The normative legitimacy dimension needs to be linked to the empirical dimension, meaning that actors 'on the ground' actually adhere to the normative principles and base their evaluations and justifications on them.

Democratic constitutionalism

In contrast to both statist constitutionalism and universal constitutionalism, democratic constitutionalism puts the democratic-participatory dimension of constitutions upfront. That is, not least in the face of tendencies of juridification and neo-liberal economic colonization, it endorses constitutional engagement and control by civic actors.

Relation law and politics

Democratic constitutionalism emphasizes the open-endedness of the democratic process and the difference in public points of view that 'goes all the way down'. In this, it includes an ultimately open-ended view of rights. For democratic

---

38 Ibid.
39 Ibid. pp. 305–306; emphasis added.
40 Andrew Arato, 'Multi-track constitutionalism beyond Carl Schmitt', *Constellations*, 18 (2011): 324.
41 Kumm, 'The cosmopolitan turn', pp. 304–305.
42 Ibid. p. 305.
43 Andrew Arato, 'Redeeming the still redeemable: Post sovereign constitution making', *International Journal of Politics, Culture and Society*, 22 (2009).

74   *Paul Blokker*

constitutionalism, this means that the nature of the constitution itself is understood in a radically different way from modern constitutionalism's foundationalism. That is, whereas modern constitutionalism understands 'constitution making as an "act of completion", the constitution as a final settlement or social contract in which basic political definitions, principles, and processes are agreed, as is a commitment to abide by them' and democratic constitutionalism entails a 'conversation, conducted by all concerned, open to new entrants and new issues, seeking a workable formula that will be sustainable rather than assuredly stable'.[44] While the foundational nature of modern constitutionalism is not dissolved completely, the idea of a 'final act of closure' is replaced by one of flexibility and a 'permanently open process'.[45] This derives from an unwillingness to tie down democracy to choices made by previous generations, the recognition of the continuously changing nature of society and identity, as well as the realization of the ultimate impossibility of grounding foundational principles once and for all.

Reflecting on a democratic-constitutional approach to European constitution making, Jo Shaw suggests that, 'we could adopt the mathematical perspective of seeing the European constitution as a vector rather than as a point, and supplement that with the challenge posed by the seafaring metaphor of "building the ship at sea"'.[46] In this, post-national constitutionalism could be based on the 'reinforcement of a constitutional politics which is specifically non-teleological and accepts contestation and non-fixity as a way of life, not a deviant practice'.[47]

Autonomy or self-rule

Democratic constitutionalism departs significantly from statist constitutionalism in that it judges representative constitutional politics as insufficient. Instead, democratic constitutionalism endorses a more open democratic settlement, which aims at the 'extension of democratic process to include, free, open, and responsive discussion of the constitutional settlement'. The latter provides the framework under which 'diverse and disagreeing groups can live, while continuing to engage in a freely accessible debate about that settlement itself'.[48] If, then, both political and democratic constitutionalism understand the constitution not as fully entrenched and pre-political, but as an outcome of the continuous political process itself, it is only in the latter that democratic politics is understood in its radical sense as the 'rule of people extended to all matters . . . including the

---

44 Vivian Hart, 'Democratic constitution making' (Washington, DC: United States Institute for Peace, 2003), pp. 2–3. Available at http:// www.usip.org.

45 Ibid. p. 3.

46 Jo Shaw, 'Process, responsibility and inclusion in EU constitutionalism', *European Law Journal*, 9 (2003): 47.

47 Ibid. p. 48.

48 Hart, 'Democratic constitution making', pp. 5, 3.

Constitutional pluralism in Europe   75

creation and re-creation of the fundamental laws'.[49] In democratic constitutionalism, the democratic dimension of constitutional democratic legitimation clearly has the upper hand, even if the constitutional ordering type of legitimacy is not abandoned.

Constitution-interpreting subjects

A democratic-constitutional approach points to practices beyond existing institutions and sees as relevant a 'multiplicity of sites' where citizens can engage in democratic practice.[50] In this, democratic constitutionalism understands as relevant constitutional subjects a range of subjects, including non-formal and/or marginalized ones.[51] Democratic constitutionalism puts forward a critical, normative suggestion of how radically to rebalance the legal and democratic dimensions in the contemporary situation in favour of the democratic-participatory dimension. In this, the approach builds in part on a rehabilitation of non-modern, alternative experiences of 'customary constitutionalism' and grassroots struggles 'in the most effective forums' against inequalities and heteronomy that are continued through informal imperialism.[52]

In its emphasis on a multiplicity of relevant sites of democratic practice, democratic constitutionalism has a combative ring and goes beyond the emphasis on judicial supremacy in freestanding constitutionalism, or the restricted popular sovereignty of statist constitutionalism.[53] A radical democratic view of constitutional democracy claims that democracy would need to entail a more direct and substantive participation of citizens in the democratic process, including a constitutional or meta-politics that aims at transforming existing institutions.[54] Specifically geared to the European project, Shaw argues that EU citizenship might form a basis on which a democratic-constitutionalist dimension might be enhanced:

> [t]he constructive potential of Union citizenship posits the possibility of processes and practices of citizenisation operating within a virtuous circle enhanced by the synergies between the formal legal figure of Union citizenship under the Treaties and the wider legal and political rights of citizenship established under the Treaties and secondary legislation.[55]

---

49 Joel Colon-Rios, 'The three waves of the constitutionalism-democracy debate in The United States (and an invitation to return to the first)', *Willamette Journal of International Law and Dispute Resolution* 18 (2011).

50 Tully, *Public Philosophy*, p. 98.

51 James Tully, 'A new kind of Europe?: Democratic integration in the European Union', *Critical Review of International Social and Political Philosophy* 10 (2007).

52 Tully, *Public Philosophy*, p. 103.

53 For the latter, see Jan-Werner Mueller, 'Beyond militant democracy?', *New Left Review* 73 (2012).

54 Compare Joel Colon-Rios, 'The second dimension of democracy: The people and their constitution', *Baltic Journal of Law & Politics* 2(2) (2009).

55 Shaw, 'Process, responsibility and inclusion', p. 50.

76   *Paul Blokker*

To sum up, the three theoretical understandings of (European) constitutionalism all combine a normative thrust with a set of empirical observations that support the normative argument. Thus, statist constitutionalism puts emphasis on popular sovereignty and the national cultural and linguistic community; universal constitutionalism emphasizes constitutional principles and court dialogue; and democratic constitutionalism prioritizes self-government and bottom-up struggles for rights (compare Table 3.1 below). But in this they all tend to favour a specific dimension of constitutional reality and ignore other dimensions. Thus, the statist view hardly engages with how actors actually engage with constitutional practices beyond the state. The universal-constitutionalist view is strongly biased towards the interaction between courts on different levels and courts (and legislatures), but ignores extra-institutional democratic claims (also regarding national democratic systems under strain), while democratic constitutionalism prioritizes bottom-up, civic engagement, but engages much less with legal dialogue or formal constitutional change.

The political–sociological approach to constitutional politics that I outline below starts from a more comprehensive focus, even if it does not pretend to cover the whole panorama.[56] Normatively, the political–sociological approach presented here shares many of the democratic-constitutionalist concerns regarding the importance of self-government, civic engagement in constitutional politics, the processual nature of constitutions and, particularly important, the salience of the idea of a 'constitutional deficit' on the European level. Empirically, the political–sociological approach attempts to contribute to a broader, pluralistic picture of various constitutional subjects and their constitutional interpretations, ongoing constitutional interaction and conflict on the European, as well as on national, levels.

A political sociology of European constitutional politics

A constitutional sociology endorses the study of constitutions beyond a predominantly legalistic analysis, as can be found in constitutional law (in which there is a largely internalistic perspective on constitutions) as well as beyond the political-scientific approach (which largely understands constitutions as frameworks for the rule of law), and emphasizes the functional correspondence of constitutions to a variety of societal needs as well as studying the contextual and historical differences in the emergence of constitutions and constitutionalism. A political sociology of constitutions can help to conceptualize changing relations between constitutions and wider society and new constitutional forms by: (i) exploring

---

56 In this chapter, I focus mostly on non-institutionalized transnational movements. A comprehensive political sociology of constitutions would need to analyse such movements in their relations with other actors and institutions. In a research project 'Constitutional Politics in Post-Westphalian Europe' (CoPolis) at the University of Trento, we do look at both pro-democracy movements' constitutional claims and the constitutional discourses of political elites and juridical actors. See http://www.paulblokker.eu/CoPolis.html.

Constitutional pluralism in Europe   77

a range of socio-functional dimensions of constitutions with regard to political order, participation, rights, social cohesion, values and identity (also beyond the national level); (ii) studying various constitutionally relevant actors and their interrelations; and (iii) analysing a related plurality of understandings of constitutionalism.

The political–sociological approach outlined here emphasizes ongoing interpretational differences and conflict over constitutions and constitutional reform pathways, in particular on the post-national level. The idea of the constitution is relevant on the transnational level in that a variety of social actors actively uses constitutional concepts, conceptions and language to describe and act in a transnational reality of constitutional 'law-in-the-making'.[57] The extensive debate on constitutional pluralism attests to the increased importance of post-national constitutionalism, but also makes clear that there is no consensus on what guise post-national constitutionalism takes. In this debate, however, there is ample attention for the formal legal dimension in the formation of post-national constitutional regimes (that is, the role of courts such as the ECJ and the European Court of Human Rights), while the transnational social-civic dimension of post-national constitutionalism is hardly analysed and remains relatively unexamined to date. Therefore, in the rest of the chapter, I propose to focus on non-institutional actors and their engagement with European constitutionalism. Important dimensions are an increased usage of constitutionalist language by social movements as well as increasing calls for civic participation in constitutional change in a number of contexts, including the European one. What becomes important is to understand the different viewpoints, narratives and understandings of constitutionalism held and expressed by significant actors, which inform their actions. These actors include constitutionalists as well as politicians and technocrats but also, importantly, social movements and wider civil society.

What I attempt to develop here builds on, inter alia, Jo Shaw's idea of a 'responsible and inclusive constitutionalism' for the EU context,[58] Ulrike Liebert and Hans-Joerg Trenz's work on a 'logics of contentious transnational constitution-making',[59] Hauke Brunkhorst's work on 'democratic solidarity'[60] and Michael Wilkinson's 'political constitutionalism'.[61] The normative thrust is towards a constitutionalism that is inclusive, bottom-up and of a processual nature. The assumptions are – contrary to the statist and universal views – that law and politics interact, that wider public engagement with constitutional politics is mandatory for a viable constitutional order and that an understanding of what constitutionalism is and what it is supposed to achieve differs between groups of actors. A key

---

57 Compare Kaarlo Tuori, 'The European financial crisis: Constitutional aspects and implications', EUI Working Papers, LAW 2012/28 (2012).
58 Shaw, 'Process, responsibility and inclusion', p. 45.
59 Ulrike Liebert and Hans-Joerg Trenz, 'Mass media and contested meanings: EU constitutional politics after popular rejection', EUI Working Paper, RSCAS 2008/28 (2008), p. 1.
60 Brunkhorst, *Solidarity*.
61 Wilkinson, 'Political constitutionalism'.

78   *Paul Blokker*

notion is that of sociological legitimacy.[62] Sociological legitimacy is understood here as a 'matter of justifications of rule empirically available, one that the citizens, groups, and administrative staffs are likely to find valid, under the given historical circumstances'.[63] Attention needs to be paid to the prevailing norms in society and views of legitimacy as held by relevant actors.

The empirical-sociological thrust in this chapter is towards the identification of societal constitution-making subjects that operate in an interlocking set of European public spheres in which constitutional claims towards an emerging transnational polity are made. More generally, however, a political–sociological approach is equally concerned with the interaction of societal claims, formal institutions and processes of constitutionalization.

The political–sociological approach towards constitutional politics taken here further builds on pragmatic sociology,[64] in particular Luc Boltanski's work on critique.[65] As mentioned, the focus in this chapter is particularly on bottom-up constitutional claims. One of the assumptions is that, in particular in the current times of EU crisis (a foundational crisis?), non-institutional forms of critique could become salient contributions to a debate on the future of Europe. As I have argued elsewhere,[66] a focus on grassroots, non-institutional claims and narratives can be particularly useful in a number of ways. First, the significance of more radical, non-institutionalized forms of 'anti-politics', including civil disobedience, lies not least in its bringing into clear relief the *increasing gap* between European citizens and European elites[67] but also in terms of understanding the foundations of the European project. This also points to the (problematic) lack of 'civic voice' in the European political system. Second, some of the articulated critique can provide a valuable resource for the elaboration of critical ideas on existing or instituted reality in that it 'tests' democracy, points to structural imperfections and helps to reimagine European democracy.[68] Third, grassroots constitutional claims might provide a not insignificant and promising counter-trend in times of general 'depoliticization' and a turning away from politics. In a more general sense, I suggest that it is particularly in times of crisis, when existing, instituted

---

62 Andrew Arato, *Civil Society, Constitution, and Legitimacy* (Lanham, MD: Rowman & Littlefield Publishers, 2000); Andrew Arato, 'Regime change, revolution and legitimacy in Hungary', in *Constitution for a Disunited Nation: On Hungary's 2011 Fundamental Law*, ed. Gábor A. Toth (New York and Budapest, Hungary: Central European University Press, 2012).

63 Arato, 'Regime change', p. 40.

64 Luc Boltanski and Laurent Thévenot, *On Justification: Economies of Worth* (Princeton, NJ: Princeton University Press, 2006).

65 Luc Boltanski, *De La Critique. Précis de sociologie de l'émancipation* (Paris: Gallimard, 2009).

66 Paul Blokker, 'A political sociology of European "anti-politics" and dissent', *Cambio. Rivista sulla Trasformazioni Sociali*, II/4 (2013).

67 Compare Tamsin Murray-Leach, 'Reimagining Europe: Reimagining democracy', *Open Democracy* (2012). Available at http://www.opendemocracy.net/tamsin-murray-leach/re-imagining-europe-re-imagining-democracy.

68 Compare Mary Kaldor et al., 'The "bubbling up" of subterranean politics in Europe' (London: LSE, 2012). Available at http://eprints.lse.ac.uk/44873/1/The%20%E2%80%98bubbling%20up%E2%80%99%20of%20subterranean%20politics%20in%20Europe%28lsero%29.pdf.

Constitutional pluralism in Europe 79

imaginaries tend to lose their grip on reality, that critical perspectives can provide fruitful hints as to alternative trajectories.

A related normative claim is that if we want to imagine a democratic European order, it needs to involve what Rainer Forst has called a 'basic structure of justification' in which everyone has the right to be part of justificatory practices.[69] What makes foundational politics and non-institutionalized claims in the European order of constitutional and legal norms so salient, is that – as Forst puts it:

> [t]he basic question of justice is about how these norms came about and who is being ruled by them – and thus the question is about the power of setting up these norms in the first place and of changing them, not primarily the power of using and interpreting them (important as it is). Justice is a constructive and creative human force, not just an interpretive one. And where there are norms that bind all citizens equally, justificatory procedures have to be in place in which these citizens can be authors of these norms.[70]

A political sociology of constitutions and constitutional politics moves beyond the theoretical and normative debate by putting emphasis on the dynamic nature of European constitutional politics and the interrelatedness of law and politics. The constitutionalization of Europe is neither reducible to a creeping juridification of the European polity (integration through law) nor to a political mandate for formal political actors (European constitution making). The picture is more complex in that constituent politics and judicialization interact and react to each other (as with the drafting process and the subsequent Lisbon Treaty, but also the existing EU order and grassroots constitutional claims). What is more, it is impossible to conceive of European constitution making as based on the expression of the will of a monolithic European 'people', in that there is no such thing as a 'people', neither on the national nor on the supranational level.[71] Constituent power needs to be related not to the modern constitutional idea of the sovereign people but to a fragmented and variegated set of relevant actors and interests engaging in a continuous struggle over the European polity.[72]

What is important in European constitution making is not the identification of and convergence towards a set of universal principles, nor the attempt to recreate the conditions for a European demos to emerge, but, rather, the exploration of possibly emerging contributions to an emerging transnational public sphere in which constitutional claims are made and justifications for different constitutional scenarios expressed. As Wilkinson puts it, the:

---

69 Rainer Forst, 'Justice and democracy. Comment on Juergen Neyer', in *Political Legitimacy and Democracy in Transnational Perspective*, eds. Rainer Schmalz-Bruns and Rainer Forst (Oslo, Norway: ARENA, 2012), p. 39.

70 Ibid. p. 40.

71 Compare Pierre Rosanvallon, *Democracy Past and Future* (New York: Columbia University Press, 2006).

72 Compare Wilkinson, 'Political constitutionalism', pp. 207–208.

80   *Paul Blokker*

[p]ublic sphere is not framed by any culturally unified demos or elite accord of moral principle; it is constituted by the practice and discourse of political right, which, put simply, consists in competing claims, more or less plausible, of collective self-government.[73]

As Hauke Brunkhorst has pointed out, the communicative power that emerges from a public sphere, which is not related to formal political or administrative power nor to economic power, is crucial for a 'strong public in the making'.[74] Such a strong public is important for those who endorse a democratic understanding of European constitutionalism, but more importantly allows a *reconnection* between formal European institutions and the wider European public or multitude. What is equally crucial to a functioning public sphere is the potential to generate communicative power that speaks to and criticizes existing arrangements, without ultimately being reducible to political or economic interests. It does relate to public creativity as well as enabling a reflexive and critical view on the status quo, a view that, from the inside of institutions, is very hard to produce.[75] As Wilkinson states, the:

[m]ore apposite and amorphous concept of 'public sphere' [is] to function as a political form for the modern secularised and disenchanted constitutional order [and] provides a context for this reflexivity [that is the 'iteration and interplay between the constitutional surface and structure, or between constitutional text and context'].[76]

A public sphere beyond the state points to the importance of sociological legitimacy for the European polity. Statist constitutionalism equates such a legitimacy with a thick, culturally levelled community and therefore denies its potential beyond the nation-state. Universal constitutionalism ignores sociological legitimacy altogether, as it sustains the unlikely idea that normative legitimacy can do all the work. Sociological legitimacy, however, conceptualizes the idea that if a constitutional framework is to integrate a larger polity and is to make such a polity meaningful to its participants, important linkages between formal institutions and wider society need to exist. The public sphere is then an intermediary that facilitates sociological legitimacy. As Fossum and Trenz have stated (they refer to 'political legitimacy' rather than 'sociological legitimacy'):

Legitimacy is a core component in the linking of the polity and social constituency. Political legitimacy refers to popular approval and to the way in which public authority is *justified.* Such justifications open a basic communicative relationship between political authorities and their constituent publics. This replicates a basic sociological insight that the exercise of political power in

---

73 Ibid. pp. 208–209.
74 Brunkhorst, *Solidarity*, p. 151.
75 Ibid.
76 Wilkinson, 'Political constitutionalism', p. 208.

Constitutional pluralism in Europe   81

modern societies can no longer be derived from a given and stable ('divine') order. Political legitimacy stems instead from a *contingent* societal order that places substantial constraints on the exercise of political power.[77]

Transnational civil society

Constitutional claims by transnational civic actors involve a dialogue between institutions and wider European society and potentially point to important deficits in the current status quo, thereby 'testing' existing arrangements. Returning to Boltanski's *On Critique*, he distinguishes between three types of tests of the existing institutional order, that is, a 'test of truth', a 'test of reality' and a 'test of existentiality'.[78] The first two tests tend to either confirm the 'rituality' and imaginary of the existing order or point to ways of reforming institutions to reconfirm reality. It is only in the last type of test – the test of existentiality – that innovative, novel ways of seeing the world are appearing. Radical forms of critique are related to such a 'test of existentiality' – in the dual sense of a test (*épreuve*) as a form of testing and as a challenge[79] – which is situated on the 'margins of reality', and in this way offers a means to open up a 'pathway to the world', that is, to a non-institutionalized social reality.[80] In this, radical critique 'endangers the comprehensiveness of established definitions and puts into doubt the universal character of confirmed relations'.[81]

An example of a 'test of truth' of the European project is a statement by the outgoing president of the European Commission, José Manuel Barroso, in October 2014:

> Over the past ten years, the European Union has endured a series of unprecedented crises, the likes of which we are unlikely to see again. But other, no less daunting challenges lie ahead, and we would do well to remember the lessons learned along the way. One lesson is that unity is not an option; it is a *condition sine qua non* of the EU's economic prosperity and political relevance . . . While integration must deepen further, especially in the eurozone, this can and should be done in a way that preserves the integrity of Europe's single market.[82]

The response to the financial, economic and constitutional crisis is to intensify the existing project, rather than significant change. A similar view emerges in

77 John-Erik Fossum and Hans-Joerg Trenz, 'The EU's fledging society: From deafening silence to critical voice in European constitution-making', *Journal of Civil Society* 2 (2006): 59.

78 Boltanski, *De La Critique*.

79 Luc Boltanski and Axel Honneth, 'Soziologie der Kritik oder Kritische Theorie? Ein Gespraech mit Robin Celikates', in *Was ist Kritik?* eds. Rahel Jaeggi and Tilo Wesche (Frankfurt am Main, Germany: Suhrkamp, 2009), p. 103.

80 Boltanski, *De La Critique*, p. 163.

81 Ibid. p. 164.

82 Available at http://www.euractiv.com/sections/eu-priorities-2020/europes-essential-unity-309305.

82   *Paul Blokker*

Barroso's discussion of the Constitutional Treaty in his speech at the European parliament on 21 October 2014:

> I think you can agree with me that these have been exceptional and challenging times. Ten years of crisis, and response of the European Union to this crisis. Not only the financial and sovereignty debt crisis – let's not forget at the beginning of my first mandate we had a constitutional crisis, when two founding members of the European Union rejected, in referenda, the Constitutional Treaty. So we had a constitutional crisis, we had a sovereign debt and financial crisis, and in the most acute terms we now have a geopolitical crisis, as a result of the conflict between Russia and Ukraine. The constitutional crisis that we had was in fact solved through the Lisbon Constitutional Treaty. The reality is that at that time, many people were saying that it would be impossible for the European Union to find a new institutional setting. And in fact there were moments of ambiguity and doubt. But basically, we could keep most of the acquis of the European Union, including most of the new elements of the Lisbon Constitutional Treaty, which was ratified by all Member States including those that today seem to have forgotten that they have ratified the Lisbon Treaty.[83]

An example of a 'test of reality' is a statement by Bruce Ackerman and Miguel Maduro[84] in *The Guardian* newspaper in October 2012 in which they propose a new attempt at European constitution making. They argue that 'longer-term solutions demand democratic legitimation' and that in the past, 'nothing was done to encourage citizens to deliberate seriously on the fateful choice before them [the Draft Constitution]'. Ackerman and Maduro suggest that a new constitutional moment might build on the South African 'three-stage experiment in constitutional creation'. In the European context, this would mean 'organising a convention – representing national and European parliaments, heads of state and governments, and the European commission' to formulate general principles; a 'second-stage convention that hammers out the final text' (the national representatives of which will be voted for by the citizenry); while a 'final judicial check is provided by a special court, headed by the president of the ECJ'.[85] Ackerman and Maduro clearly indicate the need for doing things differently, but their approach is not to suggest a wholesale alternative, but, rather, a 'calibration' of the earlier European constitution-making attempt by making principles clear and offering (somewhat) more opportunities for civic engagement. The prior attempt at constitution making is questioned, but not the European edifice.

Below I will engage with what I see as a number of societal claims and initiatives that engage in a 'test of existentiality'. The first example is the European

---

83 Available at http://europa.eu/rapid/press-release_SPEECH-14-707_en.htm.
84 *The Guardian*. 'How to make a European constitution for the 21st century'. *The Guardian*, 3 October 2012.
85 See http://www.guardian.co.uk/commentisfree/2012/oct/03/european-constitution-21st-century.

Commons Movement. The movement can be included in a more general critical attempt to contrast European institutions and the European austerity policy by means of a mobilization from below, claiming that the 'European dream' has been abandoned by the institutions and is now to be reclaimed by 'movements, by activists, by collective experiences of action and thought', who are the promoters of 'a new radical and democratic constituent process of European integration, within and against, or better beyond the institutions of the EU'.[86] In 2011, the European project Commons Sense, of Italian origin, launched a 'European Charter of the Commons', with the (so far non-materialized) intention of starting a European Citizens' Initiative for the Commons. The Charter criticizes the fact that 'Liberal constitutionalism fails to provide a shield against private interests [and that citizens remain unprotected], without the active constituent role of the people to enforce public purpose guarantees'.[87] It follows the insight that, particularly on the European level, citizens have fewer means of influencing the law with regard to forms of (economic, political) domination, as the European constitutional order is largely a legalistic one in which democratic channels and the possibilities of forming a European political will are reduced.[88] This seems a particularly valid argument in the context of the current multiple crises, in which the EU intervenes in national economies on the basis of a largely neo-liberally inspired view of economic adjustment. This is, as Jan-Werner Mueller argues, a both quantitatively and qualitatively novel fact. Such interference is not backed by 'any overarching supranational architecture to generate legitimacy'.[89]

The aim of the Commons Sense movement is to provide a 'strategy for reclaiming fundamental common goods (like water, culture, and education) and the democratic processes and spaces, which govern their access and distribution'.[90] Commons Sense argues that a true commonwealth of Europe is possible only by means of constitutional safeguards for the Commons through a direct participatory process (see Table 3.1). The existential dimension of the critique of the Commons consists of a call for a redefinition of the public and the private by reference to the idea of 'common goods', which can be understood as 'more similar to a change of paradigm rather than a rediscovery of something that has never ceased to be present in juridical systems'.[91] The Charter states:

---

86 Federico Tomasello, 'Una Carta per l'Europa: note sull'incontro di Madrid e sulla rottura possibile di un'evidenza' (2014). Available at http://www.euronomade.info/?p=1930.
87 Ugo Mattei, 'Protecting the commons: Water, culture, and nature: The Commons Movement in the Italian struggle against neoliberal governance', *South Atlantic Quarterly* 112 (2013): 375.
88 Compare Brunkhorst, *Solidarity*, ch. 7.
89 Mueller, 'Beyond militant democracy?', p. 44.
90 Saki Bailey and Ugo Mattei, 'Social movements as constituent power: The Italian struggle for the commons', *Indiana Journal of Global Legal Studies* 20 (2013).
91 Stefano Rodotà, *Il diritto di avere diritti* (Bari, Italy: Laterza, 2012), p. 120.

84   *Paul Blokker*

9. It is necessary that the commons are understood not only as living resources, such as forests, biodiversity, water, glaciers, seabeds, shores, energy, knowledge and cultural goods, but also as organized public services, such as schools, healthcare facilities, and transportation.

. . .

13. Such catalogue must be an integral part of a *Constitutional process*, based on the irreversibility of ecological legal protection, eventually to be granted *constitutional status* as heritage of Europe in trust for future generations.

. . .

20. We hereby require the Commission to *transform* this popular citizen's initiative *into a new form of legitimate and democratic European Constitutional Law*. The Commission must take all the necessary steps in order for the European Parliament, to be elected in 2014, to be granted *Constitutional Assembly Status* in order to adopt a *Constitution of the Commons.*[92]

A related initiative is that of the first successful European Citizens' Initiative for the Right to Water, which managed to collect almost 2 million votes by September 2013. The initiative called for a legal redefinition of water as a public rather than a private good, which is 'not [to] be subject to "internal market rules" [while] water services are [to be] excluded from liberalisation':

> Water is a *public good*, not a commodity. We invite the European Commission to propose legislation implementing the *human right to water and sanitation* as recognised by the United Nations, and promoting the provision of water and sanitation as essential public services for all. The EU legislation should require governments to ensure and to provide all citizens with sufficient and clean drinking water and sanitation.[93]

In the same vein, the European Water Movement argues in its Manifesto for the Commons in the European Union:

> Common goods are universal: they belong to everyone and they must not be monopolised by private interests. European Institutions, as *guarantors of fundamental civil liberties*, peace, cultural diversity and *the rule of law*, must ensure respect for, and the preservation of, these common goods . . . In a context of crisis and austerity, where privatisation is often encouraged, a political approach based on respect for common goods represents an opportunity to establish a *new democratic project for European society*, one based on citizen

92 European Charter of the Commons. Available at http://www.commonssense.it/emend/european-charter-of-the-commons-eng/; emphasis added.
93 Available at http://www.right2water.eu/; emphasis added.

Constitutional pluralism in Europe 85

participation, *respect for fundamental rights* and cultural, moral and intellectual development. This is why we propose the recognition of common goods by the European Parliament and its integration into *European judicial texts*.[94]

A related set of initiatives, with a more comprehensive and general political outlook, is promoted by the European network, European Alternatives. This initiative includes a strong bottom-up, extra-institutional thrust in its call for a Democratic Assembly and the creation of a grassroots, citizen-driven constitution for Europe. Here, a foundationalist/constitutionalist language appears in a reaction to what is understood as an ongoing 'quasi constitutional process happening on the European level in which the citizens are barely having any say'. It is interesting to see that the top-down, elite-driven initiative of constituent politics, as also attempted in the European Convention on the Future of Europe, is explicitly criticized: 'We need to move beyond the unsatisfactory experience of the European Convention'.[95] The promoters of the initiative:

> [b]elieve there is an alternative – the demand for a Europe where *citizens, social forces, movements and associations have a say over their collective future*. The construction of a Europe based on real democratic and political processes, able to interrupt the hegemony of austerity and reformulate a response to the crisis and open another road to Europe. We don't need a Fiscal Pact, *we need a Citizen Pact*. A real pact of European citizens and residents leading to substantial reforms of the decision-making processes and institutions of the European Union.[96]

There is a clear allusion here to a *bottom-up constitutional order* (see Table 3.1) with an emphasis on self-government as the higher common principle. The promoters go on to state:

> Such a Pact can only be drafted by the *activation of a real participatory and democratic process*. We need to imagine – and begin constructing – the tools of transnational democracy in Europe. That is why we imagine a process that builds a real public debate, that engages citizens in local assemblies and that mobilises local authorities and institutions of proximity. There is no Citizen Pact without European Citizens.[97]

Finally, a recent initiative, promoted by L'Internationale (a collaboration of a number of European museums) and the Fundación de los Comunes, envisages a

---

94 Available at http://europeanwater.org/it/home/91-english/news/news-from-the-ground/395-manifesto-for-the-commons-in-the-european-union; emphasis added.
95 European Alternatives, 'Refounding Europe: A democratic assembly towards a citizen pact', statement distributed at European Social Forum, 10+10, November 2012, Florence; on file with the author.
96 Ibid., emphasis added.
97 European Alternatives, 'Refounding Europe'; emphasis added.

86   *Paul Blokker*

charter for Europe, which consists of the 'networked writing of a charter and its attempt at collectively elaborating on the central problems for political organization and agency outside the representational sphere'. The organizers:

> [g]athered to rethink practices of the political imagination within the European situation, starting from the territory of making (making society, making the common of human beings) rather than from ideological organization or the diffuse elaboration of slogans. For this [they] used a series of tools that allow for the construction of a transeuropean political techné, common to many, different and a priori discordant subjects.[98]

The drawing up of the Charter is understood as a bottom-up and open process:

> 21. We want to initiate a different kind of constituent process on the basis of social and political struggles across the European space, a process towards a radical political and economic change for Europe focusing on the safeguarding of life, dignity and democracy. It is a contribution to the production and creation of the commons, a *process of democratic regeneration in which people are protagonists of their own lives*. In the squares and the networks we have learnt something simple that has changed our way of inhabiting the world forever. We have learnt what 'we' can achieve together. We invite people across and beyond Europe to join us, to contribute to this charter, to make it live in struggles, imagination, and *constituent practices* (emphasis added).[99]

To sum up, this cursory exploration of distinctive legal and constitutional claims by transnational movements suggests the potential richness of some of the forms of radical critique of the European project. While most are not amenable to being directly translated into institutional forms, they indicate some significant dimensions of the imperfections of the current order, putting the current order to the 'test', not least with regard to the incapacity of existing political institutions and actors for action, the problematic and shifting distinctions between the public and the private, and the deeply problematic nature of the relations between formal political society and wider civil society. In this, they point to a 'constitutional deficit' that seems largely off the radar of both statist and universal constitutionalism. In Table 3.1, I have summed up and counterposed these various views of a European constitutional order, highlighting the different principles of legitimation, democratic rationale, institutional imagination and understandings of the scope of politics.

Concluding remarks

In this chapter, I have suggested that a political sociology of European constitutional politics can help us develop a more comprehensive grasp on constitution

---

98 Available at http://www.internationaleonline.org/research/real_democracy/charter_for_europe_1_2.
99 Ibid. clause 21.

Table 3.1 European constitutional orders

EU as a:	Statist constitutional order	Free-standing constitutional order	Commons constitutional order	Grassroots constitutional order
Principles of legitimation	Stability, rule of law	Public reason	Commonality, community	Self-government
Main democratic rationales	Individual liberty, popular sovereignty	Essential, universal principles of equality, individual liberty	Access to fundamental common goods	Public autonomy
Institutional imagination	European constitutional order grounded in state constitutions	Key charters, conventions, national constitutions	Charter of the Commons, European Constitution, social rights	Plurality of channels of civic input; various forms of basic guarantees
Scope of politics	Political participation based on rights	Formal politics within scope allowed by juridical frame	Bottom-up, extra-constitutional, dispersed participation	Politics beyond formal institutions

making, constitutional conflict and constitutional deficits in Europe. My review of three legal theories of European constitutionalism shows the diversity of interpretations of (and consequent lack of consensus on) how European constitutionalism is to relate to (European) politics, collective autonomy, and a variety of political and social actors. It is perhaps unsurprising that the relation between constitutionalism and democracy cannot be seen as clear cut. Statist foundationalism sees a robust relation between democracy and constitutionalism as only possible in the context of the nation-state, while universal constitutionalism does away with the idea of collective self-government by democratic means altogether. Only democratic constitutionalism understands comprehensive collective self-government as a possibility and necessity, which is also beyond the nation-state. It is often overlooked, however, that (normative) approaches tend to provide only partial pictures of the European constitutional landscape.

In the political–sociological approach to European constitutionalism developed in the chapter, I attempt to offer a more comprehensive approach, which analyses constitutional politics in practice; acknowledges legal, political and societal actors as relevant constitutional subjects; explores diverse justifications for a constitutionalized Europe; and understands constitutionalism as a field of tensions. In other words, the political–sociological approach recognizes various constitution-interpreting subjects, in both institutionalized and non-institutionalized domains, who make a variety of claims (some critical) with regard to an emergent European constitutional order. A focus on the interaction

88   *Paul Blokker*

and conflict between constitutional subjects becomes particularly relevant in current times of multiple crises, in which the instituted language of the European project is increasingly growing thin and contested, and therefore a multiplicity of alternative, instituting languages are a crucial source for a reflective, reinvigorating and inclusive exercise in constitution making.

What becomes clear from the concluding, brief, empirical analysis of transnational constitutional critique and resistance is that the constitutional status quo, increasingly related to, but also in tension with, what Habermas calls 'post-democratic executive federalism', is contested from more reformist points of view (calling for a political constitutionalization of the EU) and also by radical narratives of an alternative Europe (as articulated by, among others, the Commons movement). While these radical views are mostly linked to non-institutionalized civil society, the relation between the formal, political world of the European institutions and member states on the one hand, and the informal world of social movements and associations on the other, is evidently changing as a result of the crisis and its consequences. This has become particularly clear with the electoral victory of Syriza in Greece in January 2015.

In sum, a political sociology of constitutional politics intends to explore the changing relations and conflicts between political and civil society, as well as legal institutions, regarding the constitutionalization of Europe. The European constitutional adventure is clearly far from over, and sociological reflections on ongoing struggles can help to discern the contours of possible trajectories.

Bibliography

Arato, Andrew. *Civil Society, Constitution, and Legitimacy.* Lanham, MD: Rowman & Littlefield Publishers, 2000.

Arato, Andrew. 'Redeeming the still redeemable: Post sovereign constitution making'. *International Journal of Politics, Culture and Society* 22 (2009): 427–443.

Arato, Andrew. 'Multi-track Constitutionalism beyond Carl Schmitt'. *Constellations* 18 (2011): 324–351.

Arato, Andrew. 'Regime change, revolution and legitimacy in Hungary'. In *Constitution for a Disunited Nation: On Hungary's 2011 Fundamental Law*, edited by Gábor A. Toth. New York and Budapest, Hungary: Central European University Press, 2012, pp. 35–58.

Avbelj, Matej. 'Questioning EU constitutionalisms'. *German Law Journal* 9(19) (2008): 1–26.

Bailey, Saki and Ugo Mattei. 'Social movements as constituent power: The Italian struggle for the commons'. *Indiana Journal of Global Legal Studies* 20 (2013): 965–1013.

Blokker, Paul. 'A political sociology of European "anti-politics" and dissent'. *Cambio. Rivista sulla Trasformazioni Sociali* II/4 (2013): 17–32.

Boltanski, Luc. *De La Critique. Précis de sociologie de l'émancipation.* Paris: Gallimard, 2009.

Boltanski, Luc and Laurent Thévenot. *On Justification: Economies of Worth.* Princeton, NJ: Princeton University Press, 2006.

Boltanski, Luc and Axel Honneth. 'Soziologie der Kritik oder Kritische Theorie? Ein Gespraech mit Robin Celikates'. In *Was ist Kritik?*, edited by Rahel Jaeggi and Tilo Wesche. Frankfurt am Main, Germany: Suhrkamp, 2009, pp. 81–116.

Constitutional pluralism in Europe   89

Brunkhorst, Hauke. *Solidarity. From Civic Friendship to a Global Legal Community.* Cambridge, MA: MIT Press, 2005.

Colon-Rios, Joel. 'The second dimension of democracy: The people and their constitution'. *Baltic Journal of Law & Politics* 2(2) (2009): 1–30.

Colon-Rios, Joel. 'The three waves of the constitutionalism-democracy debate in the United States (and an invitation to return to the first)'. *Willamette Journal of International Law and Dispute Resolution* 18 (2011): 1–37.

De Búrca, Gráinne and Joseph H.H. Weiler, eds. *The Worlds of European Constitutionalism.* Cambridge, UK: Cambridge University Press, 2012.

European Alternatives 2012. 'Refounding Europe: A democratic assembly towards a citizen pact'. European Social Forum, Florence 10+10, November 2012.

Forst, Rainer. 'Justice and democracy. Comment on Juergen Neyer'. In *Political Legitimacy and Democracy in Transnational Perspective*, edited by Rainer Schmalz-Bruns and Rainer Forst. Oslo, Norway: ARENA (2012), pp. 37–42.

Fossum, John-Erik and Hans-Joerg Trenz. 'The EU's fledging society: From deafening silence to critical voice in European constitution-making'. *Journal of Civil Society* 2 (2006): 57–77.

Grimm, Dieter. 'The achievement of constitutionalism and its prospects in a changed world'. In *The Twilight of Constitutionalism*, edited by Petra Dobner and Martin Loughlin. Oxford, UK: Oxford University Press, 2010, pp. 1–27.

Hart, Vivian. 'Democratic constitution making'. Washington, DC: United States Institute for Peace, 2003. Available at http://www.usip.org.

Kaldor, Mary, Sabine Selchow, Sean Deel and Tamsin Murray-Leach. 'The "bubbling up" of subterranean politics in Europe'. London: LSE, 2012. Available at http://eprints. lse.ac.uk/44873/1/The%20%E2%80%98bubbling%20up%E2%80%99%20of%20 subterranean%20politics%20in%20Europe%28lsero%29.pdf.

Kumm, Mattias. 'Beyond golf clubs and the judicialization of politics: Why Europe has a constitution properly so called'. *American Journal of Comparative Law* 54 (2006): 505–530.

Kumm, Mattias. 'The cosmopolitan turn in constitutionalism: On the relationship between constitutionalism in and beyond the state'. In *Ruling the World? Constitutionalism, International Law, and Global Governance*, edited by Jeffrey L. Dunoff and Joel P. Trachtman. Cambridge, UK: Cambridge University Press, 2009, pp. 258–325.

Liebert, Ulrike and Hans-Joerg Trenz. 'Mass media and contested meanings: EU constitutional politics after popular rejection'. EUI Working Paper, RSCAS 2008/28, 2008.

Mattei, Ugo. 'Protecting the commons: Water, culture, and nature: The Commons Movement in the Italian struggle against neoliberal governance'. *South Atlantic Quarterly* 112 (2013): 366–376.

Mueller, Jan-Werner. 'Beyond militant democracy?' *New Left Review* 73 (2012): 39–47.

Murray-Leach, Tamsin. 'Reimagining Europe: Reimagining democracy'. *Open Democracy* (2012). Available at http://www.opendemocracy.net/tamsin-murray-leach/re-imagining-europe-re-imagining-democracy.

Rodotà, Stefano. *Il diritto di avere diritti.* Bari, Italy: Laterza, 2012.

Rosanvallon, Pierre. *Democracy Past and Future.* Manhattan, NY: Columbia University Press, 2006.

Shaw, Jo. 'Process, responsibility and inclusion in EU constitutionalism'. *European Law Journal* 9 (2003): 45–68.

The Guardian. 'How to make a European constitution for the 21st century'. *The Guardian*, 3 October 2012.

90 Paul Blokker

Tomasello, Federico. 'Una Carta per l'Europa: Note sull'incontro di Madrid e sulla rottura possibile di un'evidenza', (2014). Available at http://www.euronomade.info/?p=1930.

Tully, James. 'A new kind of Europe?: Democratic integration in the European Union'. *Critical Review of International Social and Political Philosophy* 10 (2007): 71–86.

Tully, James. *Public Philosophy in a New Key, Vols. 1 and 2.* Cambridge, UK: Cambridge University Press, 2008.

Tuori, Kaarlo. 'The European financial crisis: Constitutional aspects and implications'. EUI Working Papers, LAW 2012/28, 2012.

Walker, Neil. 'Beyond the holistic constitution'. In *The Twilight of Constitutionalism*, edited by Petra Dobner and Martin Loughlin. Oxford University Press, 2010, pp. 1–24.

Weiler, Joseph H.H. *Un'Europa cristiana. Un saggio esplorativo.* Milan, Italy: BUR Saggi, 2003.

Wilkinson, Michael A. 'Political constitutionalism and the European Union'. *Modern Law Review* 76 (2013): 191–222.

Part II

European constitutional jurisprudence

4 Pluralist constitutional paradoxes and cosmopolitan Europe

Joxerramon Bengoetxea

This contribution[1] analyses the impact on EU constitutionalism of different forms of normative and legal pluralism. The first section deals with the classical accounts of legal pluralism, closely linked to the centrality of the state. It then moves on to analyse new forms of pluralism at all levels of governance, from the local to the transnational and European. These new forms are of two types: constitutional pluralism and new forms of normative pluralism. As regards the constitutional dimension, there are two major challenges to the current division of the EU into member states. One relates to territorial autonomy and to regional or national claims for internal enlargement of the EU through secession from multinational member states. The other comes from nationalist populism and claims for withdrawal from the EU, from the eurozone, or from the project of an 'ever closer union amongst the peoples of Europe'. I argue that the way the EU is dealing with these types of challenges is paradoxical, if not incoherent. The normative pluralist or multicultural challenge comes from the existence of different communities or groups of people who wish to regulate aspects of their everyday life according to normative standards that can clash with official law. The resulting complex picture is analysed as a pluralist field. If adequately addressed, it could reinforce the self-constitution of Europe. Having analysed the challenges and the pluralist field, I will suggest an analytical framework for the study of the resulting pluralist constellation, based on Neil MacCormick's theory of law as an institutional normative order, and will suggest a normative method to deal with pluralist challenges highlighting the human rights dimension as a hermeneutic standard that could work as a meeting point or forum where concrete cases can be debated on the basis of legal reasoning.

---

1 This contribution is dedicated to Volkmar Gessner, who passed away in November 2014. Volkmar, whom I had the honour of succeeding as director, was a driving force for the Oñati International Institute for the Sociology of Law. He co-edited (with David Nelken) *European Ways of Law. Towards a European Sociology of Law* (Oxford, UK: Hart, 2007), where some of the ideas discussed in this chapter are discussed in different ways by authors like Jiří Přibáň, Mikael Madsen, the editors and Roger Cotterrell, among others. This contribution was written in Kansai University on a visiting scholar scheme in the autumn of 2014. I am grateful to Kansai University and to Professor Tsunoda Takeshi for their generous hospitality.

94   *Joxerramon Bengoetxea*

Introduction: pluralist paradoxes

Traditional legal pluralism in Europe studied forms of living law that co-existed with official state law. Ehrlich[2] was the first to point out and attempt to systematize the fact that the sources of the law's authority are plural, some are political or institutional and encompass norms of decision like statutes or judgments while others are cultural, arising from popular consciousness and generating customary and social norms of conduct. Norms of decision, or positive rules, and social legal norms, or legal postulates, can enter into conflict or avoid each other, depending on the facts of the law. The realm of officialdom in Europe was clearly dominated by the centrality of the state.[3] Yet, to be fair, Ehrlich was considering a very special type of state and of official law, living in Bukovina at the time of the Austro-Hungarian Empire, a truly multinational complex system, arguably closer to the EU than to the classical nation-state.

The evolution of Europe in the EU has witnessed a transformation of state centrality. Europe can now be seen as a complex network of constitutional systems and official forms of governance comprising the member states at a national level, regions and cities at the sub-state level,[4] and international, intergovernmental and supranational organizations at the suprastate level. All these levels, whether hierarchically structured or not, would make up the official legal orders or forms of law, ultimately created by, or emanating from, the states or composing them. Alongside these official laws, however, we can still detect other forms of law or institutional normative orders operating in state or national societies, but we can also detect forms of law that transcend state boundaries, so-called transnational, informal orders that are not necessarily circumscribed by the states, *lex mercatoria* being the most cited example.[5] The resulting unstructured network of legalities is diverse, plural and complex, perhaps better represented as a constitutional constellation. The issue of hierarchical relationships between all these constitutional orders is not solved, not even in the EU, which is often referred to as a multi-level governance system, or a composite constitution.[6] How other

---

2   Eugen Ehrlich, *Fundamental Principles of the Sociology of Law* (Cambridge, MA: Harvard University Press, 1936); see Marc Hertogh, ed., *Living Law: Reconsidering Eugen Ehrlich* (Oxford, UK: Hart, 2009).

3   For non-Western approaches, see Masaji Chiba, 'Legal pluralism in Sri Lankan society. Toward a general theory of non-Western law', *Journal of Legal Pluralism* 33 (1993). Chiba explains how Western law and jurisprudence have been believed to be the authoritative type of law and of justification of the law, the standard. Whereas Chiba seems to downplay the relevance of pluralism too within Western law, his classification of official law in non-Western contexts into state law, religious law and tribal or indigenous law, and his awareness of unofficial law in various forms, like local law, family law and minority law, are really advanced.

4   See Stephen Weatherill and Ulf Bernitz, eds., *The Role of Regions and Sub-national Actors in Europe* (Oxford, UK: Hart, 2005).

5   See A. Fischer-Lescano and G. Teubner, 'Regime collisions: The vain search for legal unity in the fragmentation of global law', *Michigan Journal of International Law* 25 (2004): 999.

6   See Leonard Besselink, *A Composite European Constitution* (Groningen, The Netherlands: Europa Law Publishing, 2007). Besselink discards the term 'multilevel' constitutional order since

sources of authority are treated in Europe will depend on how each system reacts to international, supranational or national laws, adopting monist positions (automatic deference) or dualist positions (deferred deference), or even pluralist ones where the issue of ultimate authority is left unsolved or diluted into other issues, as in constitutional pluralism.[7]

At any rate, the very complexity of the legal and constitutional situation makes it difficult for the European constellation to be constituted from a single external source. The EU was set up by the member states attributing it important powers, which they formally retain, but are no longer entitled to act upon on their own. The Union is thus the creation of its members. Moreover, this vesting of power has the aim of creating an *ever closer union* amongst the peoples, not the states, of Europe; this indicates that the Union becomes an entity with a legal personality of its own, independently but not regardless of its founders. Citizenship of the Union adds a new legitimation dimension by making the Union dependent on member state nationality laws, but adding a new identity and an incipient constitutional sphere of rights that is solely supranational. The EU is soon to be structurally linked with the Council of Europe through its membership of the European Convention of Human Rights, and it also relates structurally with EFTA through the creation of the EEA.[8]

In an important sense, therefore, Europe, and not just the EU, is constituting itself. Not only by means of symbols, politics and law but by the networks of

it implies separate, autonomous constitutional orders and thinking in 'levels' as a symptom of hierarchical relations, and this does not properly account for the current constitutional European make-up. See, also, Giuseppe Martinico, *The Tangled Complexity of the EU Constitutional Process: The Frustrating Knot of Europe* (Oxford, UK: Routledge, 2013). The term composite has its own difficulty; it is seldom used in jurisprudence and the multi-level vision is itself still composite in some way. Similar difficulties can be predicated of terms like the contrapunctual law that Maduro has proposed for EU law.

7 Neil MacCormick coined the term 'constitutional pluralism' in *Questioning Sovereignty* (Oxford, UK: Oxford University Press, 1999) to indicate this view of shared and permanently negotiated, as opposed to ultimate or hierarchically superior, that is sovereign, authority. See Joachim Nergelius, *The Constitutional Dilemma of the European Union* (Groningen, The Netherlands: Europa Law Publishing, 2009), p. 36, identifying MacCormick's article, 'Beyond the sovereign state', *Modern Law Review* 56 (1993) and his book, *Questioning Sovereignty*, as the first to suggest a version of legal pluralism or genuine co-existence of institutional normative orders. This idea of constitutional pluralism has been developed by many authors: to mention only two, MacCormick's successor in the Edinburgh Regius Chair, Neil Walker, 'The idea of constitutional pluralism', *Modern Law Review* 65 (2002), and the former Advocate General, Miguel Poiares Maduro, *A Constituição Plural. Constitucionalismo e União Europeia* (Cascais, Portugal: Principia, 2006).

8 See, for example, the two EEA opinions (Opinion 1/91 and Opinion 1/92), and, more recently, Opinion 1/09 on the creation of a unified patent litigation system (2011). As regards the accession of the EU to the ECHR, the ECJ has been occupied with the question of whether the Draft Accession Agreement negotiated by the CoE and the EU Commission, mandated by the Council, encroaches upon its own position and prerogatives under the Treaties, especially its monopoly on the interpretation of Union law or upon the autonomy of the Union's legal order. The hearing took place in May 2014 and the Opinion of the Court was delivered at the end of 2014.

96   Joxerramon Bengoetxea

relationships that are being forged in the internal market,[9] in the areas of freedom, security and justice, and in the area without frontiers where citizens can, in principle, move freely and reside. The elimination of discrimination on the basis of nationality, the progressive dismantling of barriers and obstacles to free movement, the possibility of testing the human rights standards of one's state against mutually accepted European standards all contribute to an image of an autonomous legal space in Europe. The formal absence of a European demos as the mythical political subject does not deprive this new space of its political relevance and its dynamic projection of a pluralist constellation of demoi.

Democratic power is being transformed, because a civil democratic culture has emerged in Europe and is informing the EU as a hybrid mixture of political identification with a culture of civil liberties and democratic values and the persistence of national and regional communal identities. Issues like the independence referendum in Scotland, the Catalan citizen consultation process, the proposed referendum on UK membership of the EU, the prohibition of the full veil in French public spaces, the electoral success of UKIP and the Front National, the issue of quotas on immigrants, the same-sex marriage legislations, the legislative bill to control the internet in Hungary, the demonstrations against the war in Iraq in 2003, the Occupy movement, to name but a few examples, are now being discussed with interest not only locally and not only at the European Parliament, but throughout the European arena.

Of these, two contrasting movements are paradoxically contributing to this discursive process of the self-constitution of Europe. Some European regions like Scotland, Catalonia and the Basque Country are undergoing 'constitutional' processes led by sovereignty movements of citizens and political parties where claims are being made to secede from the member states of which they are a part, the UK or Spain in this case, but to remain in the EU as new member states. The 'unofficial' reply often given to these processes from EU and national circles is that secession from an existing member state implies automatic withdrawal from the EU. For instance, Spanish Premier, M. Rajoy, said that these processes are torpedoes aimed at the waterline of the EU. They are seen as a threat to the member states, thus sounding the alarm that member states are falling apart. Not quite so. Interestingly enough, these secessionist movements are in fact reaffirming the EU; they want to (continue to) be part of it as equal members and thus they tend to reinforce the EU and highlight its relevance. By threatening these region-nations with the penalty of withdrawal from the EU if freely voted secession prevails, some EU officials and national politicians are undermining the democratic value of the EU and the very project of an ever closer union between the peoples of Europe, which is at the heart of European integration and incorporated into the preamble and Article 1 of the Treaty establishing the EU.

---

9 The internal market can be seen as a public good with beneficial consequences for not only private autonomy, extending commercial opportunity and allowing for contractual freedom but also for social goods, such as consumer choices, lower prices, wider availability of employment, wider opportunities for residence, access to welfare services.

Pluralist constitutional paradoxes 97

At the opposite end, political movements have developed in many member states of the EU that are actually seeking withdrawal from the EU, because they are profoundly against the project of European integration and they reject most, if not all, of the 'liberal' and 'centralizing' policies developed at EU level. In the European Parliamentary elections in May 2014, these political parties obtained the largest number of votes in two member states, UKIP in the United Kingdom and Front National in France. There are other similar parties in most member states, and some with similar views on the EU are in power in some of them. These movements pose a real threat to the whole project of European integration, and they should cause the EU and all the forces sustaining it to react and reaffirm the European democratic project and distinguish it from nationalist europhobia. It is paradoxical that EU institutions and officials do not build decisively on the claims of regions like Scotland, Catalonia or the Basque Country who reaffirm their EU vocation, and remain passive and content at the fierce criticism to which they are subjected from the right-wing nationalism and populism.

The pluralistic constitutional scene that obtains from these processes is not the subject of most works on constitutional pluralism in the EU. They tend to focus instead on the relationships between member states' constitutional elites (constitutional courts and constitutional jurists), which normally claim ultimate authority to decide on issues like nationally understood fundamental rights considered essential to national constitutional identity, and the EU judicial and political elite, which claim authority resulting from the attribution of powers, given the need for the uniform application of EU law throughout the member states and the primacy and effectiveness of the rights recognized under EU law (including pan-European fundamental rights). Behind the clashes of political authority, there are also cultural differences, highlighted when some of the new phenomena of pluralism like multiculturalism are analysed, as we see in the next section.

Cultural, legal and constitutional pluralism in Europe

European legal culture is individualistic in a normative sense, where individuals are autonomous 'legislators' of their morality. But fundamental rights and obligations in Europe are assigned to individuals by social or institutional normative systems, independent of individual will or choice. In a very important sense not only European legal culture but, as Lawrence Friedman argues, *human rights culture* itself is individualistic.[10] Still, individuals are not *noumenal* or atomistic self-standing cultural or social units, independent of their participation in collective

---

10 Lawrence Friedman, *The Human Rights Culture* (New Orleans, LA: Quid pro Quo, 2012). Along with individualism, Friedman considers we are living in 'the age of plural equality' and free choice (p. 123). I am not taking issue with Friedman's liberal optimism but, rather, with the troubling fact that this optimism falls short of a convincing strategy to tackle the anti-minority feelings and attitudes that are taking root almost everywhere in Europe.

98   *Joxerramon Bengoetxea*

entities.[11] Many, if not all, of their rights and obligations become meaningless without the social, community or group dimension.[12] Still, the normative mix of value preferences each individual constructs from these group influences is often very diverse in modern societies. Some individuals conceive of freedom and personal autonomy as precisely ridding themselves of the bonds, normative expectations and pressures they feel that the cultural groups into which they are assigned as members by language, ethnicity, religion or origin, exert upon them. In that sense, they might relate to the broader, more impersonal modern liberal 'society' as their normative framework for expressing a free lifestyle. They will become normatively individualistic even though they remain cognitively social or communitarian. Their assigned identity and their identity of choice tend to diverge.

Even if rights are normative individual imputations, they still have a social source and a collective dimension. Some, if not most, individuals still conceive of, and lead, more valuable lives and build their normative understandings through their membership of groups and communities, including language communities and nations. In other words, they acquire 'rights through a group' rather than being left on their own to devise their own vision of the good life from a blank or a void.

Europe is characterized by diversity, plurality and complexity in this cultural and social normative sense. There are over 30 widely used languages in the EU, not all of them official; a handful of major world religions together with a plethora of non-religious, neutral, secular, anti-clerical and anti-religious beliefs; and a rich collection of traditions, histories of communities and groups of ethnic and national minorities, new and old, alongside other liberal, urban, global and cosmopolitan forms of life. Some of these territorial national minorities often, but not always, happen to be majorities in their territories;[13] others are territorially separated from the state of their national identity.[14] Some of the ethnic and religious majorities tend to concentrate geographically into urban spaces, as we can see in many European cities. Others are non-territorial minorities like the Roma and, scattered mostly in the major metropolitan areas, there are communities of immigrants and urban subcultures.

All these cultural groups or 'peoples' co-existing in the same modern societies make important normative claims from the law and from the normative responses of majority cultures. Those responses take an official or unofficial institutional form, often depending on the availability of normative standards at more local or more global levels, as the case may be. These claims, responses and standards come from individuals organized in institutions or in informal associations.

---

11 The point is not, therefore, that rights are vested in groups, but neither can it be that groups cannot possibly be holders of rights. 'Group rights' is a hotly debated issue and is not the subject of this work.

12 As Habermas puts it (in *Between Facts and Norms*, (Cambridge, MA: MIT Press, 1996), p. 88): '*At a conceptual level*, rights do not immediately refer to atomistic and estranged individuals who are possessively set against one another'.

13 For example, Catalonia, Scotland, the Basque Country.

14 This is the case, for instance, of Hungary and the Magyar in Romania, or of Serbian Kosovars and Muslim Serbians in Kosovo and Serbia, a thorny reminder of the complex linguistic, ethnic, national and religious mosaic in the Balkans.

Pluralist constitutional paradoxes   99

The study of all these processes and actors can be seen as a field, the pluralist field, which one could analyse by looking at the history of the discipline, at the internal structure shaped by power relations of actors, like political activists, legal scholars, judges, and movements and different schools of thought.[15]

The pluralist field

Cultural diversity in Europe springs from a diversity of sources like: (i) national, cultural or linguistic minorities; (ii) immigrant groups with organized religious claims; (iii) non-territorial ethnic minorities with a special way of life; (iv) other heterogeneous groups: sub-urban minority groups and subcultures, rights groups claiming accommodation and recognition of their difference based on gender, sexual orientation, disabilities, lifestyles, ideologies, age; (v) other cases that are hard to classify, for example, Gibraltarians in the UK resisting Spanish sovereignty claims and maintaining privileges under the Commonwealth and the Crown, or Russians in Latvia; and, obviously (vi) social class.

This is a pan-European classification. The classification may differ if we zoom into each of the European member states. It will be different, for example, in Portugal, Finland, Slovakia, Latvia, Austria or Greece; and in the UK and within the UK it will be different in Scotland, Wales or Northern Ireland. In other parts of the world, multicultural studies focus on other major sources of diversity, and indigenous peoples and migrant groups are often in focus. In the USA's melting pot, indigenous peoples, migrant communities and racial groups, or LGBTs, get more attention than national 'minorities' other than First Nations; but in Canada, national minorities are brought to the fore, because of the strong link between national community based on language and territory. In India, religious, cultural and national minorities, along with the class stratification, are highlighted.[16] Multiculturalism calls for political accommodation by the state and/or a dominant group of all minority cultures and co-existence between groups, by reference to race, ethnicity, religion, language, nationality or aboriginality.

Studies of cultural diversity or plurality and normative proposals of multiculturalism draw from each of these different groups. There are methodological

---

15 The concept of a legal field was developed by Pierre Bourdieu, 'The force of law: Toward a sociology of the juridical field', *Hastings Law Journal* 38 (1987): 805.

16 Werner Menski, in his Osaka lecture ('Immigration and multiculturalism in Britain: New issues in research and policy'. Lecture delivered at Osaka University of Foreign Studies, 25 July 1992), makes an interesting comparison of the multicultural models:

> In the USA, the image of the 'melting-pot' is still relevant, but has quietly been replaced by the 'salad bowl' model, in which cultural and ethnic identities do not just disappear through a process of blending the elements of the multicultural salad. The cucumber is still a cucumber, and the tomato still a tomato, but they have taken on a different flavour, too. In Canada, the 'mosaic' model has been applied to create an image of Canadian society as composed of all kinds of immigrants and their descendants. Australia has begun to recognize this pluralizing fact, too, and various European countries are experimenting with different models of respect for ethnic minority groups and their socio-cultural needs.

100 *Joxerramon Bengoetxea*

risks when analysing the social space of confusing descriptive and normative discourses of pluralism or of prioritising one type of minority over the others,[17] or even ignoring the presence of 'other' minority groups when advancing claims of one particular group.

On a practical normative dimension, these groups all make social, political and legal claims on rights and policies in various ways. They all claim (official) recognition of their difference, non-discrimination and resistance to assimilation or forced equality patterned by the majority culture; they all aim at participation in the social and political life of the wider organized society and call for a nuanced understanding of the principle of equality as non-discrimination and awareness to difference – treating like cases alike and not treating unlike cases alike.[18]

Depending on their identities and their perceived needs and interests, each of the identified categories of groups make specific claims.

i   National minorities make territorial, cultural and linguistic claims, demands for devolution and self-government, and for official recognition and constitutional accommodation.

ii Religious groups claim respect, tolerance and the freedom to pursue and practise in their daily lives and social patterns their own, distinct view of the good.

iii Ethnic minorities claim non-discrimination and equality and special measures of inclusion or positive discrimination, and indigenous people have special claims related to their territories and local knowledge and way of life, whereas non-territorial ethnic minorities have cultural and recognition claims.

iv Other groups claim non-discrimination, respect and support for their special social and cultural needs.

v   Underprivileged social classes claim a substantial reduction of inequality and increased life chances, which is not only an economic claim but a much broader claim about how resources, symbolic capital and power relations are distributed and stratified in society.

These claims to access, power, empowerment, recognition, tolerance, respect and equality are made before different institutions: legislatures, policy-makers, jurisdictions and administrations, and also before non-public organizations, for instance, the mass media and telecommunications, the cultural industry, the

---

17 Nasar Meer and Tariq Modood, two sophisticated and methodologically aware scholars, seem to prioritize immigration (and thus religion) over substate nations in the West: 'Despite Kymlicka's attempt to conceptualize multiculturalism as multinationalism, the dominant meaning of multiculturalism in politics relates to the claims of post-immigration groups'. Nasar Meer and Tariq Modood, 'The multicultural states we're in: Muslims, "multiculture" and the "civic re-balancing" of British multiculturalism', in *European Multiculturalisms. Cultural, Religious and Ethnic Challenges*, eds. Anna Triandafyllidou, Tariq Modood and Nasar Meer (Edinburgh, UK: Edinburgh University Press, 2011), p. 181.

18 See Sandra Fredman, 'Substantive equality revisited', Oxford Legal Studies Research Paper no. 70/2014 (2014).

Pluralist constitutional paradoxes 101

educational sector, the labour environment, political parties, trades unions and NGOs. Public institutions, organizations, agencies and bodies with authority to make general norms and determine public policies or to apply those general rules and generate individual norms, respond to these claims in different ways:[19]

i containing demands for difference, by supporting the majority facing minority claims;
ii reinforcing equality as 'uniformity' or assimilation, denying the relevance of difference and making everyone 'the same';
iii reconstructing equality as non-discrimination, recognizing a claimed difference;
iv granting special rights of representation for collectives, seeing these as special privileges;
v recognizing and accommodating differences, from reasonable accommodation to full-blown pluralism and programmes for inclusion;
vi mainstreaming the differences and encouraging a normative and communicative situation between the majority and minority positions, through legislative measures or judicial recourse to equity and exceptions.

These responses take place at different levels, before different institutions and involve different legal strategies, like the adoption of general, universal norms or dispute resolution through litigation or alternative methods. They also vary according to territorial-institutional perspectives. They have a lot to do with access to power and power sharing. Academic disciplines like constitutional theory, administrative law and sociologically informed legal theory, amongst others, ought to analyse such responses and do so in an inter-disciplinary and comparative way.

Depending on the powers or competences assumed by each institutional arrangement, the types of demand and the types of norms and decisions adopted, reactions vary greatly according to the institutional levels:

i at the local level, for example, permits for the building or opening of a new mosque, family counselling services, school boards, in which case accommodation or rejection of the claim will take the form of an administrative decision, but other forms like mediation can also solve individual conflicts;
ii at the regional level, for example, housing and social benefits, provision of health care, taxes, education policy, infrastructures, cultural promotion,

---

19 The *Stanford Encyclopedia of Philosophy* entry on 'Multiculturalism' mentions the following supply-side examples of cultural accommodations or 'group-differentiated rights': exemptions from generally applicable law (for example, religious exemptions); assistance to do things that the majority can do unassisted (for example, multilingual ballots, funding for minority language schools and ethnic associations, affirmative action); representation of minorities in government bodies (for example, ethnic quotas for party lists or legislative seats, minority-majority Congressional districts); recognition of traditional legal codes by the dominant legal system (for example, granting jurisdiction over family law to religious courts); or limited self-government rights (for example, qualified recognition of tribal sovereignty and federal arrangements recognizing the political autonomy of Quebec).

102   *Joxerramon Bengoetxea*

social inclusion policy, where accommodation or containment can take the form of legally recognized and enforceable rights, or promotion policies, but also administrative decisions and judicial individual norms;

iii at the member state or national level, for example, immigration control, labour laws, justice and, of course, human rights constitutional control, where legislative accommodation is achieved through universal norms, social and cultural policies, and individual judicial decisions at highest courts;

iv at the European level with the EU and Council of Europe and other organizations, a very complex system of governance or composite constitution: for example, the harmonization of laws, free movement (especially of workers and their dependents), internal market, non-discrimination directives,[20] but also judicial decisions from Luxembourg and Strasbourg;

v at the international level by means of Human Rights Treaties and International Organizations;

vi at the transnational level, in norms that are being developed in formal or non-formal ways, depending on the issues, but by other bodies, and which in practice determine the conditions for exercising many rights: for example, *lex mercatoria*, forms of arbitration dealing with copyright or investment, or access to public lands and contracts that affect indigenous people's ability to safeguard their traditional forms of life.

Evaluative approaches within the pluralist field

'Pluralist' studies aim at understanding and analysing the types of claims and the responses – legal and political strategies, reasons and techniques – to those claims and deferring the evaluation of these debates to a latter, normative, stage of the analysis. Multiculturalism can be seen as a comprehensive *normative* theory guiding public policy and decision making in many different domains.[21] These different responses are then also controlled, overseen or supervised by European

---

20 The EU Antidiscrimination directives do not provide an equal level of protection: (Race) Directive 2000/43/EC prohibits discrimination on the grounds of race in the areas of employment, education, social protection, social advantages and access to goods and services, but (Framework Employment) Directive 2000/78/EC forbids discrimination on the grounds of religion only in the area of employment. The European Commission put forward a proposal for a new general anti-discrimination Directive on 2 July 2008, covering sexual orientation, age, disability and religion or belief in the areas of access to goods and services, education, social protection and social advantages.

21 Julie Ringelheim has carried out one of the most impressive research projects in Europe trying to see how this theory informs all areas of Belgian law; see her excellent introduction: 'Droit et la diversité culturelle: Cartographie d'un champ en construction' in *Le droit et la diversité culturelle*, ed. Julie Ringelheim (Brussels, Belgium: Bruylant 2011), p. 6, where she explains how:

> *le multiculturalisme est conceptualisé comme une politique publique particulière qui peut se traduire par différentes mesures, comme le financement d'associations socio-culturelles regroupant des personnes d'une même origine ethnique, l'aménagement de certaines règles générales pour éviter d'entraver la pratique de religions minoritaires ou la modification des programmes scolaires pour mieux tenir compte de la pluralité de la population.*

Pluralist constitutional paradoxes   103

supranational institutions by reference to commonly shared European values and standards, as recognized by and interpreted from important human rights instruments. The most important standard setters in this context are the European Court of Human Rights (ECtHR) and the European Court of Justice (ECJ). Within the Council of Europe, there are a number of institutions that elaborate a discourse on issues related to pluralist situations: the Human Rights Convention, the ECtHR and the Venice Commission on democracy through law are the most significant. Depending on the existence or the absence of a European consensus, there will be a greater or smaller margin of appreciation left to the states, for example, special constitutional traditions like Turkish or French *laïcité*, or radical secularism or special Catholic culture in Italy.

Within the EU we see a number of institutions pursuing the values of integration, that is, the ever closer union of peoples; the subsidiarity principle; the margin of appreciation or institutional autonomy of the member states or justifications explicitly allowed on the basis of public morality; the technique of harmonization through directives that leave the choice of form and methods to the member states; the solidarity, loyalty and cooperation clauses; the principle of mutual recognition; prohibition of discrimination on grounds of nationality or other grounds; the principle of equal treatment; and the rights and liberties contained in the Charter of Fundamental Rights of the EU and in the Social Charter, the HR Agency.

But there are other standard setters like the (Peace and) Security and Cooperation at the European level (OSCE), based on the rationale of the democratization of Central and Eastern Europe and, at the global level, many UN legal instruments, Conventions on Human Rights, individual and collectively understood, and UN soft law on human rights.

Interesting tensions and dynamics obtain as to the descriptive-interpretative question of who is actually setting the standards and highlighting the values and as to the normative question of who should be setting those standards: local versus European or global actors. As mentioned above, to the extent that a 'European' consensus may have emerged, the local – meaning national – margin of appreciation will decrease, and to the extent that the challenges need to be, and actually are, tackled effectively on a wider regional European scale, the scope for subsidiarity and proximity of decision making to the citizens will diminish.

As regards standard setting by the ECtHR, we can look at some of the many interesting cases like the headscarf prohibition in French (*Dogru*) and Swiss (*Dahlab*) schools or in Turkish universities (*Sahin*), the issue of the crucifix in Italian public schools (*Lautsi*), or the question of gypsies in the United Kingdom (*Connors*), or in Spain (*Muñoz Diaz*).[22] There are other cases including

> (Multiculturalism is conceptualized as a particular public policy that can mean different measures, such as the financing of socio-cultural associations of persons of the same ethnicity, the development of some general rules to avoid interference with the practice of minority religions or modification of curricula to better reflect the plurality of the population.)

22 *Dogru* v. *France, ECtHR* (2008) and *Dahlab* v. *Switzerland*, 2001-V *ECtHR* 447; *Sahin* v. *Turkey*, 2005-XI *EctHR* 173; *Lautsi and Others* v. *Italy*, ECHR judgment of 18 March 2011; (Application

104 Joxerramon Bengoetxea

the treatment of national minorities as in Silesia (*Gorzelik*), the way the Court has dealt with languages, or with the thorny issue of banned political parties, and even the human rights review of UN Security Council resolutions reinforced by the Contracting States (*Al-Jedda*).[23]

In the ECJ as well we find interesting 'pluralist' cases, such as the language cases,[24] same-sex marriage cases,[25] fundamental rights in the single market[26] and citizenship[27] cases that raise the issue of tension between regional social welfare and the internal market.[28] There are cases that raise regional constitutional issues, such as the tension between regional taxation and state-aid controls and anti-trust[29] and even the human rights review of the UN Security Council reinforced at EU and member state level (*Kadi*).[30]

We engage in the evaluation of these normative questions from the standpoint of critical discourse theory and from a new understanding of law and its legitimacy. The result of this complex situation of multiple forums, arenas or public spaces of debate where multiple sovereign authorities are trying to find their way in this complex institutional patchwork, is a diversity of normative claims. It is not only a question of who gets to interpret and decide on the extent of the competences (or powers): the difficult question is where sovereignty itself lies and whose normative standards are going to be followed. Is it, as the state-nationalists claim, on the side of the member states or, as the European federalists claim, on the side of the EU? Looking at the cases where European supranational courts have reviewed UN Security Council resolutions on the basis of human rights, or at the cases where the ECtHR has controlled an EU member state's normative standards and practices or their wrongful implementation of EU policies,[31] one might conclude that the question is, rather, who is to be the legitimate interpreter?

---

no. 66746/01), judgment of 27 May 2004; (Application no. 66746/01), judgment of 27 May 2004; (Application no. 66746/01), judgment of 27 May 2004; (Application no. 49151/07), judgment of 8 Dec 2009.

23 *Gorzelik and Others* v. *Poland*, (Application no. 44158/98) judgment of the ECHR 17 Feb 2004; *Belgian linguistic case* (A/6), (1979–1980) 1 EHRR. 252; *Refah Partisi and Others* v. *Turkey* (Applications nos. 41340/98, 41342/98, 41343/98 and 41344/98), judgment of 13 Feb 2003, and *EAE-ANV* c. *ESPAGNE* (Requêtes nos 51762/07 et 51882/07), arrêt du 7 décembre 2010; *Al-Jedda* v. *United Kingdom*, Application no. 27021/08, ECHR judgment of 7 July 2011.

24 Criminal proceedings against Horst Otto Bickel and Ulrich Franz C-274/96 [1998] ECR I-07637.

25 T-58/08P *Commission* v. *AP Roodhuijzen*, judgment of 5 Oct 2009 and W v. Commission F-86/09 judgment of 14 Oct 2010.

26 *Omega Spielhallen* C-36/02, [2004] ECR I-09609.

27 Ruiz Zambrano, C-34/09 judgment of 8 March 2011.

28 Viking case *International Transport Workers' Federation and Finnish Seamen's Union* v. *Viking Line ABP and OÜ Viking Line Eesti* C-438/05 [2007] ECR I-10779 and *Laval* C-341/05 [2007] ECR I-11767.

29 Basque Historic Territories Taxation, joined cases C-428/06 to C-434/06, judgment of 11 Sep 2008.

30 C-402/05 P *Kadi and Al Barakaat International Foundation* v *Council and Commission* [2008] ECR I-06351.

31 *Hirsi Jamaa* v. *Italy* (Application no. 27765/09) ECHR judgment of 23 Feb 2012.

Thus, according to Alec Stone Sweet, *Al-Jeddah* extends the reach of cosmopolitan pluralist constitutionalism into a realm beyond the ECHR.[32]

Take issues like the banning of political parties, or the treatment of detainees and the recognition of certain fundamental rights to prisoners, or the imposition of certain penalties and the definition of certain crimes. These issues might be less controversial within a homogeneous society or a seemingly consensual society where divergent voices do not get much media attention – according to the principle that national authorities know better and thus need a margin of appreciation. They might be much more controversial and closely examined from a wider European perspective where such consensus is regarded with more scepticism – according to the need for European-wide standards on the core of the rights recognized. In addition, sometimes at the local level in even well-established democracies, this European control might be seen as offensive, as when important parts of British public opinion push for a revision of the terms of accession to the European Convention of Human Rights on the basis of their different local appreciation of the standards (UK Commission on a Bill of Rights).[33]

Who is to be master? Challenges to supremacy and constitutional pluralism

As we saw in the introduction, there are interesting challenges to the legitimate authority of the EU, such as setting the fundamental values of a liberal democratic society – individual freedom, non-discrimination, equality and solidarity. These values are not always interpreted in the same way by different normative systems; clashes occur between the moralities and ways of life of minority groups and the norms of the official majority. There are also the territorial autonomy challenges from stateless European nations making claims for the internal enlargement of the EU, and there are claims from nationalist populist movements to withdraw from and break down the Union. Internal enlargement claims do not question the current constitutional make-up, or the project of integration or the ever closer union, whereas nationalist populism is a challenge to the very project of sharing sovereignty in the EU, since it involves a return to classical state sovereignty.

Plural demos

The main idea of the 'constitutional pluralists' is that there is no, nor should there be any, final authority or sovereignty; there is no clear European demos that could self-proclaim its identity or constitute itself by an illocutionary act. On the other hand, there are no longer sovereign nation-states on the old one-dimensional Westphalian model of Europe but, rather, European *member states*. Statehood in

---

32 Alec Stone Sweet, 'A cosmopolitan legal order: Constitutional pluralism and rights adjudication in Europe', *Global Constitutionalism* 1 (2012). See also, Sabino Cassese, *When Legal Orders Collide: The Role of Courts* (Seville, Spain: Global Law Press, 2010).
33 Ministry of Justice, *Commission on a Bill of Rights Final Report* (2012). Available at http://www.justice.gov.uk/about/cbr.

106 *Joxerramon Bengoetxea*

Europe has simply become member statehood, and the different demoi of those member states are at the same time the citizenry of the Union: pluralism and *heterarchy* prevail. Yet, as Avbelj and Komarek concede:

> [t]he world pervaded by plurality also requires a minimum degree of coherence and, more importantly, it calls for a meta-language through which the actors situated at different (epistemic) sites could reflexively engage with each other by recognising their differences with a simultaneous commitment to a certain shared framework of co-existence.[34]

In other words, although descriptively they are pluralists, many of these positions become normatively more nuanced.

In my view, there are good cognitive and normative reasons for giving up the nation-state claim to sovereignty. It is true that we find in the EU at least 28 ultimate authorities, each claiming legitimacy and supremacy. It is nevertheless the case that each of them is part of a wider union where they share their sovereignty and their constitutional values, and are also part of the European Convention of Human Rights to whom they are jointly and severally accountable. Each of them abides by the supranational decisions of its Court, based in Strasbourg. Soon, following the Treaty of Lisbon (Article 6), the EU will formally and legally abide by these decisions, as it does now as a matter of general principle.[35] Perhaps then, where the highest domestic jurisdictions see heterarchical relations, and our non-conflictual, meta-constitutionalist scholars see bridled pluralism (and dead metaphors), the European courts, especially the ECJ,[36] see an understandable national reluctance to digest the 'systemic necessity' of supranational primacy, a foot-dragging to be cured with time, patience, modesty and well-grounded pedagogic judgments. In my opinion, this constitutional pluralism devised by public lawyers can also be seen as a new 'ideology' in the sense of the term used by Clifford Geertz, provoked by the difficulty of providing an adequate image of the political process according to traditional models, like that of the sovereign nation-state.[37]

---

34 See Matej Avbelj and Jan Komarek, 'Introduction', in *Constitutional Pluralism in the European Union and Beyond*, eds. Matej Avbelj and Jan Komarek (Oxford, UK: Hart, 2012).

35 See note 8, above.

36 Cormac MacAmhlaigh, 'Questioning constitutional pluralism', University of Edinburgh School of Law Working Paper Series no. 2011/17 (2011), p. 30, points out that with regard to the ECHR, domestic courts can claim that they are upholding the values of the Convention while disagreeing with the Strasbourg Court's interpretation thereof, but with regard to EU normative conflicts, domestic courts must uphold the rule of EU law, which will not always be easy and may lead to occasional institutional disobedience. But this can be viewed as the normal development and evolution of any (hierarchical) constitutional system.

37 Clifford Geertz considers ideology as a response to the cultural, social and psychological strain provoked by a loss of orientation derived from an inability to comprehend – for lack of models – the universe of civic rights and responsibilities in which one finds oneself, and says (in *The Interpretation of Cultures* (New York: Basic Books, 1973), p. 219): 'The development of a differentiated polity may and commonly does bring with it severe social dislocation and psychological

Pluralist constitutional paradoxes 107

If we add to this picture the gradual development of a forum or agora, which becomes the instance where the decisions required to face the economic and financial crisis can become effective, and where the social solidarity necessary for inclusive strategies to manage cultural diversity inspires harmonizing measures, then gradually we will see the waning of the nation-state as the only, perhaps even the main, forum of sovereignty, deliberation and decision making on these issues of practical reason.

We the People

The US standard, 'We the People',[38] has two relevant facets related to our pluralist discussion: its monism and its inclusiveness. As to monism, 'the people' becomes *one* by virtue of its own illocutionary force; it conceives of itself as One, *unified*, as a single entity, not as a plural ontology. Perhaps in its origins it was plural, there were several peoples and perhaps they were together, united in diversity, like Europe would like to think it is right now, but that was before it was merged or unified, before the demos (con)formed. It is not really the Constitution that united and *unified* the people; it is its very reflexivity and self-description as a People; for, without this People, the Constitution would not have been possible. The people continued to be a melting pot,[39] culturally plural but constitutionally one. What is crucial is that there was a political aspiration to be seen as one nation, and this will was not eternally valid, as the Civil War made clear.

The US Constitution confirmed the constituency that proclaimed the Constitution. Pluralism of legitimacies or of constitutional authorities was out of the question, because there is one demos and *it* is sovereign. There is no question of constitutional pluralism under 'We the People'; at most you can have a discussion

---

tension. But it also brings with it conceptual confusion, as the established images of political order fade into irrelevance'. I believe this is what has happened to nation-state constitutionalists vis-à-vis European constitutionalism: constitutional pluralism and meta-constitutionalism are ideological adaptations in order to avoid the traditional and dated position of state nationalism or the promised supranationalism and cosmopolitanism to come.

38 Two fabulous studies of this symbolic reflexivity are James Tully, *Strange Multiplicity. Constitutionalism in an Age of Diversity* (Cambridge, UK: Cambridge University Press, 1995) and Hans Lindhal, 'Democracy and the symbolic constitution of society', *Ratio Juris* 11 (1998). 'We the people' is the self-proclaimed source of validity of constitutionalism. One does not question it because, once assumed as valid, the whole constituted order appears to work. If one rejects the autonomous validity of the constitutional system, then validity can be derived from a larger and higher system of which it is a part or a deeper norm, like Natural Law or a Hegelian sense of History, or Kelsen's monism of international law: the source of validity of state constitutions and the ultimate *Grundnorm* of international law could be the norm *pacta sunt servanda*. Under international law, the systemic pluralism of constitutional sovereignties (Krisch) seems thus reconciled, at least in the 'Pure Theory of Law'. The Kantian inspiration is here expressed in the transcendental category of the *Grundnorm* and in the ideal of a cosmopolitan order, an ideal attempt to dissolve pluralism.

39 On cultural pluralism in the USA, critically responding to assimilationist or separatist calls, see Bill Ong Hing, 'Beyond the rhetoric of assimilation and cultural pluralism: Addressing the tension of separatism and conflict in an immigration-driven multiracial society', *California Law Review* 81 (1993), largely anticipating his book *To Be an American* (New York: NYU Press, 1997).

108 *Joxerramon Bengoetxea*

as to the extent of the conferred and the retained powers, or a discussion as to how pluralistic the Constitution itself is; in other words, to what extent does it pretend to safeguard political, religious and cultural pluralism? But although the people are now 'one', everyone can be part of the people: no one is excluded.[40] This second feature is perhaps related to the first, and this is the inclusive potential of the illocution. Perhaps when it was first expressed, it encompassed a certain category of white men, who saw themselves as embodying sovereignty. But the trend has been to favour inclusion of more and more 'people' into the We. Not only that: more crucially, the ideal has been resorted to by those excluded to demand inclusion. All groups identify with a *We the People* standard to claim being part of the (civic) demos.

Perhaps this is what we miss and lack in Europe. Our national and constitutional identities are not always and not necessarily the result of a rational illocutionary will but, rather, of the power games of historically conditioned national majorities. Furthermore, we face the challenge of inclusion where all individuals and groups share a liberal citizenship ethos. Pluralism there might well be, but there is nothing constitutional about it. The EU Treaty is the product of the Heads of European member states (many of them 'majesties'). A constitutionally pluralist preamble would read something like 'We the nations' or better 'We the peoples of Europe'. But we are not there yet. But is this what pluralism is about? How to bring in all the underlying diversity, in other words: We the territorial national minorities, We the immigrants, We the non-territorial minorities, We the indigenous peoples, We the ethnic groups, We the religious groups, We the alternative subcultures, We the sexual minorities, above all, We the citizens? We all are part of the European demos under construction, and we do not relinquish our particular demoi.

If pluralism were limited to the constitutional *topos* – the nations or peoples constituted through the member states versus the Union – it would still be normatively and institutionally relevant under the subsidiarity principle and the federal, globalising dynamics, but it would fail to capture the cultural and legal diversity and plurality that characterizes Europe. In order to capture those pluralisms we need a perspectival and aspectival (kaleidoscopic) approach. We know that the most important aspect of pluralism is not this constitutional 'exceptionalism' of contested, but coordinated, supremacies. Rather, it is the diversity of institutional normative orders that may obtain in any given social field at multiple levels involving multiple regulators and which can be analysed following the methods developed by cultural anthropology, even if, as legal theorists or philosophers, we might consider it desirable to strive for some form of 'coherence' and meta-systematicity. The external and internal (cognitive and volitional) points of view need to be combined.[41]

---

40 We know that historically this is not so, that in fact many classes of people lacked the status of citizenship. But what is interesting is that the tendency has been to formally include more and more categories into citizenship, up until a certain point in (recent) time when the non-citizen becomes 'illegal'. This trend of expulsions is, sadly, common to the USA and the EU. The term 'expulsions' is inspired by a lecture given by Saskia Sassen at Stanford on 2 May 2012, presenting her new line of research.

41 Habermas, *Between Facts and Norms.*

MacCormick's theoretical framework for pluralism

Part of Neil MacCormick's legacy,[42] for the purposes of our discussion, is a concept of law as 'institutional normative order', a theory that is very well suited to all forms of pluralism and to this diversity and this sociologically inspired practical reason, in a domain where different norms interact discursively, directing socially meaningful action. This approach allows us to address under a single theory the two dimensions of pluralism: plurality of normative orders and legal orders, and a principled strategy for integrating such plurality. We will address both perspectives.

The diversity of institutional normative orders in Europe

As we saw in the introduction, by bringing in ideas from Ehrlich, people guide their social behaviour by relation to norms and, to that extent, order and *normal*ity result. When conflict arises, norms develop to deal with it, and sometimes the norms according to which people guide their behaviour are modified as a result. Norms are at the same time action-guiding and action-justifying reasons. The domain of the normative ranges from the moral norms, *mores*, to the highly institutionalized legal norms of modern state administrations and supranational organizations, and from the relatively few precepts following from a given religious domain of social life to the comprehensive and extensive domain of contemporary state legal orders covering practically all areas of social life. Where we fix the line between social, moral, aesthetic, ethical, economic, political, religious and legal norms is not always pellucid; it can be a matter of degree rather than category. All of these norms have social sources, action-guiding, justificatory and critical dimensions, and at given times all of these can clash in any given social space and in any given situation involving social actors. To the extent that those norms become institutionalized and involve institutions for their recognition, change and application, they tend to *juridify*. Rather than legal pluralism, such situations are better described or captured under the concept of *normative pluralism*, but the practical issues raised are much the same.

State (official) positive law appears historically as the most complex and highly institutionalized of all normative orders. State law has very refined, all-encompassing (comprehensive) and commonly shared rules of recognition; a system of legislatures and of distribution of legislative powers to adapt and adjust the normative order to changing environmental and institutional circumstances; a network of administrative authorities to implement such general and universal norms as more concrete policies and individual acts; and a system of courts to adjudicate authoritatively upon possible disputes between citizens and/or administrations and a monopoly on the (authorized) use of power to enforce such decisions.

---

42 Neil MacCormick, *Rhetoric and the Rule of Law* (Oxford, UK: Oxford University Press, 2005); Neil MacCormick, *Institutions of Law: An Essay in Legal Theory* (Oxford, UK: Oxford University Press, 2007).

110 *Joxerramon Bengoetxea*

But this is a gradual scale rather than an absolute category of state law. It might be the case that a less complex normative order manages to regulate certain spheres of social life and operates within the confines of the state with its latent consent or even without the state officials acknowledging its existence. If actors guide their action and solve their disputes according to those orders, they can be considered forms of law. On top of these 'normative orders'[43] we observe that there are other regulators or standard setters alongside state administrations and legislatures. We also observe that there are other forums or instances of dispute resolution besides state courts. These regulators and dispute resolvers operate within and outwith the state, from the local level to the transnational one, and they are the subject of new legal pluralism studies and new governance.[44]

It might also be the case that above the legal order of the state we witness the development of an even more sophisticated, multi-level and multi-actor system of governance and network of regulators. State law purports to be the centralized regulator, the 'chief enabler',[45] the hub of all forms of legal recognition. For the moment, it seems that this is (still) a plausible claim; however, the types of regulatory challenges we have seen regarding cultural and legal pluralism and the authority challenges posed by constitutional pluralism could lead us to nuance this statement, especially in the EU context.

Pluralist claims to validity and the search for cosmopolitan frameworks

The description of the diversity of normative orders captures an important aspect of law as an institutional action-guiding and action-justifying order, but the law adds an important dimension: the claim to legitimacy or validity. Normative orders make a claim to their correctness, legitimacy or validity, and it would be pragmatically self-contradictory and self-defeating for a normative order not to make such a claim, or to claim otherwise. A normative order that makes no claim to legitimacy would be considered incomplete, lacking, self-defeating or merely technical, like traffic regulations: the only reason to follow it would be utilitarian and prudential, but it could be forborne whenever it failed to accomplish its given utility functions, because it withdraws the claim to legitimacy.[46] In contrast, the internally binding character of the law is based on its claim to acceptability and to relative validity within a given community. In making such claim, the law enters the broader and deeper domain of practical reason, where, in ideal discourse conditions, it can be contrasted with other co-existing normative orders

---

43 See Maleiha Malik's report, *Minority Legal Orders in the UK. Minorities, Pluralism and the Law* (London: British Academy, 2012).

44 See Paul Schiff Berman, 'The new legal pluralism', *Annual Review of Law and Social Sciences* 5 (2009) and the classic by Sally Engle Merry, 'Legal pluralism', *Law & Society Review* 22 (1988).

45 This is the term used by Dani Rodrik, 'Who needs the nation-state?', Arrow Lecture on Ethics and Leadership, Stanford, 24 May 2012. Questioning hyper-globalization, Rodrik insists on the nation-state's resilience as the principal locus of governance.

46 This point is convincingly made by Habermas, *Between Facts and Norms*, pp. 121, 130.

Pluralist constitutional paradoxes 111

making equally forceful claims to validity. We now face a new dimension of the issue of plurality of validity claims, not only of constitutional systems but also of all normative domains of practical reason – ethical theories, moral systems, religious codes, political moralities and ideologies, different law-like orders within the same social space, or also transnationally.

Again, if each makes a claim to validity and legitimacy, and some of the normative systems – for instance, major world religions – make an additional claim to *universal* validity, we might be interested in asking whether there might indeed be meta-normative or transcendental practical criteria to deal with such contrasting legitimacy claims and, if we conclude affirmatively, in setting out to look for them. Are there – and can we find any – common, shared criteria independent of the normative claims and premises of each order, according to which we may critically evaluate such claims and premises?

If we answer in the negative, then we probably cling to incommensurability and ethical relativism, a position some have wrongly identified with multi-culturalism. If we answer affirmatively, we need to substantiate our position with credible candidate criteria and theories for a cross-system evaluation.[47] These could be found in theories and normative proposals like Rawlsian liberalism or versions of it; MacIntyre communitarianism or versions of it; Hayekian libertarianism or versions of it; social welfarism; different conceptions of the common good; and Aristotelian communal or general justice as opposed to particular justice.[48]

Alternatively we could envisage procedural criteria that focus on the discursive conditions for making and testing validity claims, like Rawls's veil of ignorance and reflective equilibrium, Kant's golden mean and categorical imperative, Habermas's ideal discourse and MacCormick's Smithian Categorical Imperative,[49] or we could even envisage substantive criteria like Dworkin's and Alexy's rights thesis. Perhaps the human rights culture is the hermeneutical synthesis, culminating in a celebration of cosmopolitanism and individual autonomy. Similarly, Tuori considers that ethical fragmentation, the differentiation of conceptions of the good life, is not in conflict with the possibility of a wide-reaching consensus on fundamental moral principles, and that it is on the very basis of such a possibility that human rights principles are able to exercise their harmonizing effects in diverse legal contexts.[50] Yet this wide-reaching consensus on human rights, interpreted from different genealogies, philosophical schools or religious and cultural traditions, will crumble and fade away the moment we start discussing actual cases. Settling for less-than-optimal solutions may be the price we have

---

47 See Paul van Seters, 'Introduction', in *Communitarianism in Law and Society*, ed. Paul van Seters (Lanham, MD: Rowman & Littlefield, 2006).

48 Claudio Michelon, 'The virtuous circularity between positive law and particular justice', Edinburgh University School of Law Working Paper Series, no. 2011/11 (2011).

49 Neil MacCormick, *Practical Reason in Law and Morality* (Oxford, UK: Oxford University Press, 2008).

50 See Kaarlo Tuori, 'Legal culture and the general societal culture', in *Private Law and the Many Cultures of Europe*, eds. Thomas Wilhelmsson, Elina Paunio and Annika Pohjolainen (Utrecht, The Netherlands: Kluwer, 2007), p. 35.

112   *Joxerramon Bengoetxea*

to pay. Could we at least work out the steps necessary to identify the key actors and issues in our pluralist and hopefully not incommensurable debates?

Hermeneutic pluralism and cosmopolitan Europe

After these explorations of diversity and the search for normative coherence and legitimacy in Europe, we might conclude that normative and constitutional pluralism – heterogeneity and diversity[51] – are structural features of the EU. To capture the full 'diversity of pluralism' in Europe, five steps could be adopted, hermeneutically combining both the descriptive and the normative approaches.

i   To begin with, and remaining in the institutional level, we need to bring in the wealth of pluralities at a *vertical* territorial and governance axis, from the local to the global.

ii   Next, we need to examine the inclusiveness claims at each of these levels – from the local to the European – and ask ourselves whether important communities or groups might be excluded from each of the pluralistic mosaics of 'we the peoples'; for instance, is this EU only a club of nation-states? Are nation-regions or national minorities forced into the straitjackets of their member states like, for example, Quebec in Canada, Scotland in the UK or the Basque Country in Spain and in France? Are towns and cities encouraging the participation of all their individuals and communities in, say, town planning, financing cultural events or environmental issues?

iii We would need to be aware of the fact that these territorial jurisdictions, at each level, are implicitly contested or challenged by legal pluralism at the level of norms or even normative orders that are competing if not as global regulators, at least in specific areas of social regulation (typically, family law, but also commercial law) and at local, regional, national, state, transnational, supranational and international levels. This raises, again, the classical issue of legal pluralism, or the co-existence of normative orders that could be called minority legal orders.[52] There is not only a plurality of norms but also alternative *forums* and methods of dispute resolution at each of these levels.

---

51 Ulrich Beck and Edgar de Grande, *Cosmopolitan Europe* (Cambridge, UK: Polity Press, 2007).

52 In the UK context, see the thorough report by Maleiha Malik (Malik, *Minority Legal Orders*), where minority legal order is a non-state normative field of social action that may refer to cultures or religious groups that regulate their social life by reference to norms that are coherent and consistent, rather than random or arbitrary. In some situations, the state legal system may recognize or incorporate the minority legal order's norms, with the consequence that these 'norms' become 'law' in the official and ordinary sense, although many of these cultural or religious groups do not seek to compete with the state. If there is some mechanism, albeit informal, for resolving disputes about validity, interpretation and enforcement, then this institutional aspect will make it more likely that there is a minority legal order. Despite the public anxiety that minorities are following their own 'parallel' laws that could be a threat to the unity of the state, there is no necessary tension or conflict between a minority community's understanding of itself as having 'law' and the state's claim that the national legal system is 'sovereign'.

Pluralist constitutional paradoxes 113

'Where the practices of communities or individuals do not conform to state law requirements, or where communities turn to their own legal regimes or tribunals, the reasons behind these developments need to be understood'.[53]

iv Then, we could continue on a *horizontal* axis of inclusiveness to study if there might be groups or collectives that are not territorially based, but are neglected or ignored since they are unnoticed by the institutional bodies that do get formal representation in the commonwealth. It might be that in new forms of governance the same type of stake-holding elite regulators (repeat players) get to set the standards, because they are more visible, better mobilized or consulted more regularly – or more powerful. We would be inspired by theories of multiculturalism or inter-culturalism, even by more group-oriented communitarian theories to push towards inclusiveness and participation.

v Finally, the wind of freedom blows within minorities as well; this inclusiveness has to be carried deeper, as an ideal normative framework, to each of the communities claiming recognition of difference, and enquire how each of these groups is itself handling internal endogenous claims of difference and of participation and exercises of individual autonomy or personal self-determination (internal minorities[54]). This is where we reintroduce important values of liberalism and individualism as enshrined in most of our human rights instruments. Here, obviously, we are ideologically loaded by the value of autonomy.

In doing so, we also reintroduce popular mobilizations and claims for human rights, for participation and deliberative democracy, but also the supervision and control by the key European supranational institutions, the ECJ and the ECtHR; and these are important aspects of the cosmopolitan vision of Europe as opposed to fundamentalism and nationalist, europhobic and xenophobic populism. As Beck and Grande argue in *Cosmopolitan Europe*:

> [e]verything that the fundamentalists hate is to be celebrated and cherished as what is authentically European: the much lamented 'vacuum of meaning', the 'decadence', the 'loss of the middle', the rejection of the metaphysical image of 'the' human being and 'the' European West. Why? Because the cosmopolitan-European character of a society consists in the fact that nobody lays down what is right and good and how people should live their lives as long as they do not harm others.[55]

As Alec Stone Sweet aptly observes,[56] in a cosmopolitan legal order every public authority, including the UN, bears a duty to justify acts that would have the effect

---

53 Religare Project. On religious plurality, see, generally, the works of Prakash Shah and of the RELIGARE project and network. Available at www.religareproject.eu.
54 See Sarah Song, *Justice, Gender, and the Politics of Multiculturalism* (Cambridge, UK: Cambridge University Press, 2007).
55 Beck and Grande, *Cosmopolitan Europe*, p. 105.
56 Stone Sweet, 'A cosmopolitan legal order'.

114   *Joxerramon Bengoetxea*

of violating the fundamental rights of individuals. This brings us back to the need for the justification of normative claims to validity, made by all normative orders in the pluralist constellation, on the basis of practical and legal reasoning.

Bibliography

Avbelj, Matej and Jan Komárek, eds. *Constitutional Pluralism in the European Union and Beyond*. Oxford, UK: Hart, 2012.

Beck, Ulrich and Edgar de Grande. *Cosmopolitan Europe*. Cambridge, UK: Polity Press, 2007.

Berman, Paul Schiff. 'The new legal pluralism'. *Annual Review of Law and Social Sciences* (2009): 225–242.

Besselink, Leonard. *A Composite European Constitution*. Groningen, The Netherlands: Europa Law Publishing, 2007.

Bourdieu, Pierre. 'The force of law: Toward a sociology of the juridical field'. *Hastings Law Journal* 38 (1987): 805–853.

Cassese, Sabino. *When Legal Orders Collide: the Role of Courts*. Seville, Spain: Global Law Press, 2010.

Chiba, Masaji. 'Legal pluralism in Sri Lankan society. Toward a general theory of non-Western law'. *Journal of Legal Pluralism* 33 (1993): 197–212.

Ehrlich, Eugen. *Fundamental Principles of the Sociology of Law*. Cambridge, MA: Harvard University Press, 1936.

Engle Merry, Sally. 'Legal pluralism'. *Law and Society Review* 22 (1988): 869–896.

Fischer-Lescano, Andreas and Gunther Teubner. 'Regime collisions: The vain search for legal unity in the fragmentation of global law'. *Michigan Journal of International Law* 25 (2004): 999–1046.

Fredman, Sandra. 'Substantive equality revisited'. Oxford Legal Studies Research Paper No. 70/2014.

Friedman, Lawrence. *The Human Rights Culture*. New Orleans, LA: Quid pro Quo, 2012.

Geertz, Clifford. *The Interpretation of Cultures*. New York: Basic Books, 1973.

Gessner, Volkmar and David Nelken, eds. *European Ways of Law. Towards a European Sociology of Law*. Oxford, UK: Hart Publishing, 2007.

Habermas, Jürgen. *Between Facts and Norms*. Cambridge, MA: MIT Press, 1996.

Hertogh, Marc, ed. *Living Law: Reconsidering Eugen Ehrlich*. Oxford, UK: Hart, 2009.

Lindhal, Hans. 'Democracy and the symbolic constitution of society'. *Ratio Juris* 11 (1998): 12–37.

MacAmhlaigh, Cormac. 'Questioning constitutional pluralism'. University of Edinburgh School of Law Working Paper Series no. 2011/17, 2011.

MacCormick, Neil. 'Beyond the sovereign state'. *Modern Law Review* 56 (1993): 1–18.

MacCormick, Neil. *Questioning Sovereignty*. Oxford, UK: Oxford University Press, 1999.

MacCormick, Neil. *Rhetoric and the Rule of Law*. Oxford, UK: Oxford University Press, 2005.

MacCormick, Neil. *Institutions of Law: An Essay in Legal Theory*. Oxford, UK: Oxford University Press, 2007.

MacCormick, Neil. *Practical Reason in Law and Morality*. Oxford, UK: Oxford University Press, 2008.

Malik, Maleiha. *Minority Legal Orders in the UK. Minorities, Pluralism and the Law*. London: British Academy, 2012.

Pluralist constitutional paradoxes 115

Martinico, Giuseppe. *The Tangled Complexity of the EU Constitutional Process: The Frustrating Knot of Europe*. Oxford, UK: Routledge, 2013.

Meer, Nasar and Tariq Modood. 'The multicultural states we're in: Muslims, "multiculture" and the "civic re-balancing" of British multiculturalism'. In *European Multiculturalisms. Cultural, Religious and Ethnic Challenges*, edited by Anna Triandafyllidou, Tariq Modood and Nasar Meer. Edinburgh, UK: Edinburgh University Press, 2011, pp. 61–87.

Menski, Werner. 'Immigration and multiculturalism in Britain: New issues in research and policy'. Lecture delivered at Osaka University of Foreign Studies, 25 July 1992.

Michelon, Claudio. 'The virtuous circularity between positive law and particular justice'. Edinburgh University School of Law Working Paper Series, no. 2011/11, 2011.

Nergelius, Joachim. *The Constitutional Dilemma of the European Union*. Groningen, The Netherlands: Europa Law Publishing, 2009.

Ong Hing, Bill. 'Beyond the rhetoric of assimilation and cultural pluralism: Addressing the tension of separatism and conflict in an immigration-driven multiracial society'. *California Law Review* 81 (1993): 863–925.

Ong Hing, Bill. *To Be An American*. New York: New York University Press, 1997.

Poiares Maduro, Miguel. *A Constitução Plural, Constitucionalismo e União Europeia*. Cascais, Portugal: Principia, 2006.

Ringelheim, Julie, ed. *Le Droit et la Diversité Culturelle*. Brussels, Belgium: Bruylant, 2011.

Rodrik, Dani. 'Who needs the nation-state?' Arrow Lecture on Ethics and Leadership, Stanford, 24 May 2012.

Seters, Paul van, ed. *Communitarianism in Law and Society*. Lanham, MD: Rowman & Littlefield, 2006.

Song, Sarah. *Justice, Gender, and the Politics of Multiculturalism*. Cambridge, UK: Cambridge University Press, 2007.

Song, Sarah. 'Multiculturalism'. In *The Stanford Encyclopedia of Philosophy*, edited by Edward N. Zalta. Stanford, CA: CSLI, Stanford University, 2014 edition. Available at http://plato.stanford.edu/archives/spr2014/entries/multiculturalism/.

Stone Sweet, Alec. 'A cosmopolitan legal order: Constitutional pluralism and rights adjudication in Europe'. *Global Constitutionalism* 1 (2012): 53–90.

Tully, James. *Strange Multiplicity. Constitutionalism in an Age of Diversity*. Cambridge, UK: Cambridge University Press, 1995.

Tuori, Kaarlo. 'Legal culture and the general societal culture'. In *Private Law and the Many Cultures of Europe*, edited by Thomas Wilhelmsson, Elina Paunio and Annika Pohjolainen. Utrecht, The Netherlands: Kluwer, 2007, pp. 23–36.

Walker, Neil. 'The idea of constitutional pluralism.' *Modern Law Review* 65 (2002): 317–359.

Weatherill, Stephen and Ulf Bernitz, eds. *The Role of Regions and Sub-national Actors in Europe. Essays in European Law*. Oxford, UK and Portland, OR: Hart Publishing, 2005.

5 The pluralist turn and its political discontents

Marco Goldoni

The pluralist turn in European Union (EU) and supranational studies

This chapter does not intend to criticize legal pluralism as a general theory of law but, rather, to focus on the discourse of pluralism at the supranational level and its impact on political action as conceived by a recent wave of key publications on this topic. The purpose is to test the strength of theories linked to legal or constitutional pluralism when applied to the European scenario and, more specifically, to the EU. The main point put forward is that the language of pluralism is a deceptive heuristic device.

Legal pluralism has been revitalized in different forms by current versions of constitutional or legal pluralism. It has become one of the main theoretical frameworks available to international and constitutional lawyers to grapple with the realities of transnational legal orders.[1] It is, however, essential to note that in the pluralist realm there are important differences between those whose starting point is the recognition of the 'fact' of legal pluralism (*qua* descriptive statement) and those who actually celebrate and embrace some form of legal or constitutional pluralism (normative stance). This chapter tackles only the latter cohort of pluralists, for two reasons. First, among these authors, there are outspoken supporters of highly original and distinctive forms of contemporary pluralism; second, in these works, and despite their pretensions, the suppression of the political tenet of constitutionalism is at its peak. The core argument put forward in this chapter is an invitation to resist the celebration of legal and constitutional pluralism as an emancipatory move, but, rather, to see it as a direct attempt at depleting the resources of meaningful political action. This is the case despite the fact that in constitutional pluralism a lot of emphasis is put on the role of contestation among different sites, all claiming authority over the same conduct. Dialogic exchanges among different layers of governance on the one hand, and interactions between institutional and non-institutional subjects on the other, make supranational law increasingly more tolerant and rich. Even

---

1 For an overview, see Ralf Michaels, 'Global legal pluralism', *Annual Review of Law and Social Science* 5 (2009).

Pluralist turn and political discontents   117

more, it is often advocated within this discourse that legal interactions in a pluralist environment are open to severe contestation by a multiplicity of subjects. As such, this kind of legal pluralism would open new avenues for conflicts rather than limiting them.

However, as we shall see in the following paragraphs, these versions of legal and constitutional pluralism cannot deliver what they promise. In particular, the framework adopted by legal pluralists cannot accommodate (it actually undercuts) the two main features of a political kind of constitutionalism, that is, the possibility of constituent power[2] and the staging of ordinary political conflict.[3] The writings of legal pluralists of the constitutional or global kinds extol the virtues of social groups and agents and plead for the opening up of that space to such forces. The logic of the argument is simple: releasing previously constrained social forces produces beneficial effects to the legitimacy of transnational law. In this respect, globalization has offered a new opportunity to make visible claims previously not recognized or left unregistered at the political level. However, strong forms of pluralism postulate that this promise can be redeemed only if politics is not allowed to impact on other systems or if it is displaced by new forums which are supposed to illuminate aspects of social reality previously neglected. In a nutshell, constitutional and legal pluralism challenge directly the capacity of the political constitution to recognize, shape and address political conflict. In the next sections, I will broach the main proposals concerning first constitutional and then global legal pluralism; I will then try to show why they cannot open up politics at the European level.

The constitutional version of pluralism

A first wave of thinkers who intended to give a pluralist twist to traditional legal theory emerged out of the need to cope with the porousness of state borders vis-à-vis supranational law and, in particular, in the case of European integration. The multiplication of sites of authority within the European legal space was perceived as a controversial legal construction. The constitutional question after the Maastricht Treaty came into force, along with the challenges from rising public and private actors, took the form of a conflict among different levels of authorities.[4] It was therefore the reaction of the German Constitutional Court to the claims contained in that Treaty that actually triggered the debate on this form of pluralism through a seminal article by Neil MacCormick.[5] MacCormick resorted to an

---

2 Constituent power expresses the idea that politics should be reflexive. See Jacques Rancière, *Disagreement* (London: Verso, 2006); Emilios Christodoulidis, 'Against substitution: The constitutional thinking of dissensus', in *The Paradox of Constitutionalism*, eds. Martin Loughlin and Neil Walker (Oxford, UK: Oxford University Press, 2007).

3 For the importance of a space of appearance for political action, see Hannah Arendt, *The Human Condition* (Chicago, IL: Chicago University Press, 1958), ch. V.

4 For an accurate overview of the debate, see Jan Komárek and Matej Abelj, eds. *Constitutional Pluralism in the European Union and Beyond* (Oxford, UK: Hart, 2012).

5 Neil MacCormick, 'Beyond the sovereign state', *Modern Law Review* 56 (1993).

118   *Marco Goldoni*

institutionalist theory of law in order to account for these ambiguous conflicts.[6] What was deemed to be pluralistic about European integration was that the EU legal order (taken as an autonomous one) claimed supremacy over national constitutions against the opinions of other national constitutional courts. Most of these claims were made by the European Court of Justice and other national constitutional courts in the course of adjudicating on particular cases.[7]

Constitutional and legal theorists have taken these conflicts very seriously.[8] Over 20 years, the reflections initially advanced by MacCormick have been developed and unpacked by many other scholars and commentators in what has become an autonomous stream of contemporary legal theory. Neil Walker, the torchbearer of this tradition, has offered an epistemic version of constitutional pluralism,[9] which claims to be valid beyond the realm of EU constitutionalism.[10] It should be noted that Walker does not rule out either the explanatory or the normative dimension of constitutional pluralism, for both flow from epistemic pluralism.[11] Pluralism is first and foremost *epistemic*, because it is a discourse shaped by and through the development of constitutionalism. Its main virtue lies in its being the least imposing perspective on other first-order points of view. The accent is on the *how* of the constitutional discourse rather than on the *what* and the *who*. This is because, as a form of pluralist thinking, the constitutional pluralist discourse cannot impose substantial principles. It limits itself to providing a thin meta-discourse as a shared discursive platform for all legal entities to interact meaningfully. Yet, the deep grammar of Walker's constitutional pluralism is based on the recognition of a set of seven standards that betray a specific and circumstantial genealogy. In fact, despite any allegiance to formal proceduralism, some of these standards do refer to substantive contents, whereas others stem from the resolution of actual conflicts among existing legal orders.[12] Finally, the other necessary requirement for this version of constitutional pluralism establishes that every constitutional

---

6 For the last statement on his own institutional theory of law, see Neil MacCormick, *Institutions of Law* (Oxford, UK: Oxford University Press, 2007).

7 To sum up, the ECJ has made three claims to supremacy: first, that within its area of competence, European law enjoys supremacy over all conflicting rules of national law, including the constitution; second, the ECJ has exclusive competence to decide what counts as a matter of European law, that is, what falls within its competence (*kompetenz-kompetenz*); third, that it has ultimate authority to decide all matters on European law. On the national side of the judicial divide, both the first and second of these claims have been challenged.

8 Mattias Kumm, 'Who is the arbiter of constitutionality in Europe?', *Common Market Law Review* 36 (1999).

9 Neil Walker, 'The idea of constitutional pluralism', *Modern Law Review* 65 (2002): 339.

10 Ibid.

11 On this point, see the reconstruction offered by Jaklic Klemen, *Constitutional Pluralism in the EU* (Oxford, UK: Oxford University Press, 2014), 58–59.

12 For example, the fourth standard tenet establishes the requirement of interpretive autonomy, a claim 'to the entitlement of an organ internal to the polity or political process to construe the meaning and extent of these competences' and the fifth requires that 'there is the constitution and regulation of an institutional structure to govern the polity'. See Walker, 'The idea of constitutional pluralism', p. 342.

Pluralist turn and political discontents   119

site can claim 'internal sovereignty', but cannot claim any superiority vis-à-vis other constitutional sites. This means that the novelty of constitutional pluralism has to be seen in *the absence of any claim of absolute or supreme authority* among interacting orders. As a way of facing the uncertainties generated by the lack of a supreme institution, Walker's project is to adapt the language and mindset of constitutionalism to the pluralist imperatives. One might wonder why this discourse should successfully vindicate pluralism when none of the pluralist tenets can really ensure that new voices or new subjectivities can actually have access to the second-order discourse to which Walker makes reference. It is revealing that, in the end, this thin meta-discourse is compatible with standard forms of governance as those embodied, for example, by comitology.[13] While the interactions among different legal regimes can actually produce valuable outcomes in terms of the quality of legal reasoning and interpretation, nothing really ensures that a dialogue or any other form of interaction among these established institutions will be able to register voices and subjectivities that are not expressions of already constituted legal rationalities.

A different version of constitutional pluralism, whose starting point and problems are basically the same as Walker's, but explicitly rests on substantive normative principles, is Mattias Kumm's. His argument is clearly underpinned by universalist tones, as it is based on the following assumption: the philosophical underpinnings of modern constitutionalism are always the same, despite the changes of institutional design, because of the validity of certain principles that can be deduced with reference to the normative status of free and equal individuals. Against this larger background, traditional state-centred constitutional systems assume a more modest significance. Constitutionalism is decoupled from its state template, and the state itself remains just one of the players in a wider stage.[14] Based on this account, Kumm derives a set of universal constitutional commitments to the principles of legality, subsidiarity, democracy and rights protection. In this reading, collisions among different normative claims are unavoidable, because pluralists 'insist that the different legal orders making up the world of public law are not hierarchically integrated'.[15] The absence of hierarchy and the recognition of principles of autonomy and democratic self-government bring about constitutional collisions and these make up the horizon of substantive constitutional pluralism. The answer to these potential conflicts is inspired by the following approach:

---

13 'The Comitology system creates inclusive decision-making contexts which allow for mutual accommodation and mutual learning between different types of supranational and non-aligned actors': Neil Walker, 'Late sovereignty in the European Union', in *Sovereignty in Transition*, ed. Neil Walker (Oxford, UK: Hart, 2003), p. 30.

14 Mattias Kumm, 'The best of times and the worst of times: Between constitutional triumphalism and nostalgia', in *The Twilight of Constitutionalism?*, eds. Petra Dobner and Martin Loughlin (Oxford, UK: Oxford University Press, 2009).

15 Mattias Kumm, 'The moral point of constitutional pluralism', in *Philosophical Foundations of European Union Law*, eds. Julie Dickson and Pavlos Eleftheriadis (Oxford, UK: Oxford University Press, 2012), p. 216.

120 *Marco Goldoni*

Constitutional pluralists insist that different legal orders don't simply coexist beside one another, as self-enclosed Leibnizian monads with at best contingent relationships between them. Notwithstanding the pluralist nature of legal practice, the relevant actors – and courts in particular – have established mechanisms and designed doctrines that allow for constructive mutual engagement between different legal orders. Legal pluralism . . . is guided, constrained, and structured in a way that justifies describing that practice in constitutional terms, even in the absence of hierarchical ordering.[16]

Kumm suggests dealing with those constitutional orders by resorting to a rationality which is *immanent* to the practice of modern constitutionalism. In particular, one can find an instantiation of this rationality in the interplay among courts, understood as a communicative and principled practice. At the same time, the reference to a common template imposes a limit on pluralism's antinomian tendencies. Moreover, in terms of adjudicative practices, pluralism can be managed through the application of the principle of proportionality.[17] The latter is understood as the third stage of the balancing process, where competing rights or principles are compared and assessed on the basis of a common scale. These two elements seem to indicate that pluralists defend an institutional conception of law (meaning, one based on legal institutions) which shares some important features with a certain strand of legal positivism. More specifically, Kumm rejects any hierarchy and therefore jettisons both legal positivism and legal monism if these are understood (as in Hans Kelsen's pure theory) as conditions for the intelligibility of law. However, the identification of a common juridical space created by communication among courts and the emphasis on norm-applying institutions, betray strong affinities with H.L.A. Hart's and Joseph Raz's conceptions of the legal system.[18] From this perspective, one might reasonably question the pluralist nature of a type of constitutionalism which is so redolent with the grand theories of legal monism. Contrary to Walker's project, in this substantive type of constitutional pluralism the pluralist element emerges out of constitutional rationality and is therefore already contained and predetermined by the principles and rules inherited from modern constitutionalism. MacCormick corrected his original institutional pluralism by placing it under the banner of a higher law, that is, international law.[19] On the same wavelength, Kumm subsumes pluralism under the higher norm of modern constitutionalism.

In this respect, both versions of constitutional pluralism aim to keep the tension between constitutionalism and pluralism alive and productive. Yet, given this

---

16 Ibid. p. 217.

17 Mattias Kumm, 'Institutionalising Socratic contestation: The rationalist human rights paradigm, legitimate authority and the point of judicial review', *European Journal of Legal Studies* 1 (2007).

18 H.L.A. Hart, *The Concept of Law* (Oxford, UK: Clarendon Press, 1961); see also Raz's definition of a legal system as requiring at least one necessary kind of institution, to wit, norm-applying institutions: Joseph Raz, *Practical Reason and Norms* (Oxford, UK: Oxford University Press, 1975), pp. 122–125.

19 Neil MacCormick, 'Risking constitutional collision', *Oxford Journal of Legal Studies* 18 (1998).

Pluralist turn and political discontents   121

aim, the normative promises of this strand of legal thought can be delivered only as long as neither of the two elements prevails. Therefore, the risk involved in constitutional pluralism is that it will either be colonized by its constitutional tendencies or will simply be reduced to a form of constitutional plurality. As will be shown again below, at the European level constitutional pluralism does not open up new channels of political action. Rather, its descriptive virtues are severely undermined by the starting premises of this strand of pluralism. As it is the case for the following pluralist theories, constitutional pluralism does not provide an account of the relevant plurality of constitutions.

Towards radical pluralism

An alternative to the constitutional version of pluralism is provided by a radical form of legal pluralism, sometimes dubbed 'global legal pluralism'. This theory of pluralism applies to the EU, but it is more ambitious in its scope. A standard account of global legal pluralism has recently been proposed by Paul Schiff Berman.[20] It presents some of the classic tenets of legal pluralism and applies them to supranational law. Berman's methodology is rooted in the tradition of socio-legal studies and adopts a cultural analysis of law.[21] Within this framework, law is part and parcel of the construction of social reality, and its analysis cannot be detached from this aspect. The aim of this kind of enterprise is to recap how legal meaning is produced (and the condition of legal intelligibility) rather than test legal validity. The second tenet is a direct consequence of the former: legal pluralism is neither state-centred nor fully cosmopolitan (at least not in the universalist version of cosmopolitanism). The idea of an ultimate legal authority and of state sovereignty (at every level, national or international) has to be abandoned precisely because it can be supported neither by legal fictions nor by factual monopoly of power.[22]

Berman's starting point is the recognition that legal orders in a globalized age cannot exhaust the phenomenology of legal activities taking place across and beyond jurisdictions. At the beginning of his recent monograph, it is indeed stated that 'we live in a world of multiple overlapping normative communities'.[23] This entails that different legal orders might claim the right to regulate the same social field or the same activity. He defines this condition as 'normative hybridity'. No definition is provided for that idea, but it can be loosely reconstructed as the

---

20 See Paul Schiff Berman, *Global Legal Pluralism. A Jurisprudence of Law Beyond Borders* (Cambridge, UK: Cambridge University Press, 2012); see, also, Paul Schiff Berman, 'The globalization of jurisdiction', *University of Pennsylvania Law Review* 151 (2002); Paul Schiff Berman, 'A pluralist approach to international law', *Yale Journal of International Law* 32 (2007).

21 See Paul Kahn, *The Cultural Study of Law* (Chicago, IL: Chicago University Press, 1999); Robert Cover, 'Nomos and narrative', *Harvard Law Review* 94 (1983).

22 For a recent take on this issue and the development of the idea of relative authority, see Nicole Roughan, *Authorities* (Oxford, UK: Oxford University Press, 2013).

23 Berman, *Global Legal Pluralism*, p. 3.

122 *Marco Goldoni*

phenomenon of 'the relationship among multiple communities and their decision makers'.[24] The examples offered by Berman are conspicuous: from state versus state conflict to state versus international norms and state versus non-state law. It remains an open question whether normative hybridity is a peculiar phenomenon of the age of globalization which requires a new approach to law. Nonetheless, for the sake of the argument, we can even concede to Berman that this is the case. Legal hybridity is first a de facto reality with which it is necessary to become familiar. The point is that global legal pluralism is a more ambitious theory and it advances stronger claims than just descriptive ones. It is indeed a normative theory, because it praises the virtues of a pluralist understanding of legal interactions.

What are the virtues of this form of global legal pluralism? The first one is indeed epistemic: recognizing the multiplicity of sources of law beyond the states means respecting social groups as autonomous creators of law and recognizing their legal impact. The second main virtue is that, according to Berman, this form of pluralism is empowering, because it creates new opportunities for contestation and creative adaptation.[25] Berman believes that pluralism should cope with the phenomenon of hybridity with procedural and not substantive means. Because normativity is pervasive, and the production of legal meanings relentless, substantive principles have to yield to normative proceduralism.[26] No agreement on the content of substantive principles is indeed possible. The recognition of this state of affairs is part and parcel of how the response to legal hybridity takes shape, 'to create or preserve spaces for productive interaction among multiple, overlapping legal systems by developing procedural mechanisms, institutions, and practices that aim to manage, without eliminating, the legal pluralism we see around us'.[27]

The purpose of global legal pluralism is to manage legal hybridity by devising procedures in which the voices of different communities can be heard. Berman believes that this approach can tame conflict between staunchly different and contrasting views of the law and also reply to the democratic objection to the legitimacy of such a pluralist framework. The first point concerns the capacity of procedural forms to channel and eventually tame conflict between opposing normative commitments by building a common social space through the expansion of the range of voices heard or considered.[28] In this way, relations of enmity would be turned into adversarial relationships.[29] As for the second point, the democratic objection, Berman replies by adopting an array of tools for coping with pluralism without suppressing it and at the same time giving voice

---

24 Ibid. p. 117.
25 Ibid. p. 118.
26 Alexis Galán and Dennis Patterson, 'The limits of normative legal pluralism', *International Journal of Constitutional Law* 11 (2013): 786.
27 Berman, *Global Legal Pluralism*, p. 10.
28 Ibid. p. 18.
29 Berman here adapts to his theory an argument formerly put forward by Chantal Mouffe, *On the Political* (London: Verso, 2005).

Pluralist turn and political discontents 123

to all those affected by decisions: procedural mechanism, institutional designs and discursive practices. These mechanisms provide the framework for enabling and at the same time constraining legal pluralism at the global level. Berman concedes also that these procedures are not completely formal, but they cannot decide any issue by introducing substantive reasons. As rightly noted by Galán and Patterson, this requirement makes Berman's pluralism mild and basically grounded in a liberal political philosophy.[30] Not every new voice is legitimate, just those who put forward reasonable arguments. In the end, the purpose of these mechanisms lies in being 'sites for continuing debates about pluralism, legal conflicts, and mutual accommodation'.[31] The examples of instantiations of continuing debates put forward by Berman are quite telling. They all point to interactions between different sites of authority or institutional power and rarely discuss informal (meaning social but not institutional) movements. The use of the margin of appreciation is understood as a form of communication between the Strasbourg Court and the constitutional courts of member states. It can be used as a way to signal dissatisfaction with current decisions, but it is also a way to calibrate the protection of fundamental rights among different layers. Another example concerns the relationship between North American Free Trade Agreement panels and US state courts in cases,[32] which generated new trilateral relations between them and federal institutions. What is valuable in these cases, according to Berman, is the reciprocal influence among different bodies based not on coercion or the threat of sanctions but on dialogue and criticism among these institutions. Of course, interactions are not limited to institutions but can also occur between informal agents and formal bodies. We are even informed by Berman that this informality can be stretched as far as to the point where 'the decisions of arbitral panels may, over time, exert influence on the decisions of more formal state or international bodies, and vice versa'.[33] Given the problematic status of arbitral panels, in particular in the case of investment treaty law (which is certainly affecting the supranational level), one wonders how these 'dialectical interactions' can instantiate any form of political conflict or even contestation at the supranational level.[34] In fact, most of the examples provided by Berman do not actually make visible any form of political conflict. On the contrary, they are usually ways of coping with potential conflict 'by stealth', that is, by avoiding the staging of disagreement.

In light of these remarks, the overall upbeat tone deployed by Berman is unwarranted. The containment of pluralism by a series of liberal constraints is not given

---

30 Galán and Patterson, 'Limits of normative legal pluralism', p. 787.
31 Berman, *Global Legal Pluralism*, p. 153.
32 *Loewen Group* v. *United States*, ICSID case No. Arb(Af), 98/3, 42 ILM 811 (2003).
33 Berman, *Global Legal Pluralism*, p. 160.
34 As known, in certain cases there is no duty to make the motivations of panels' decisions public, a feature which makes treaty investment law apolitical. For a strong criticism of investment treaty law along these lines, see David Schneiderman, *Constitutionalizing Economic Globalization* (Cambridge, UK: Cambridge University Press, 2008).

124   *Marco Goldoni*

proper consideration despite the fact that this framework is essential for making global legal pluralism operative.[35] Berman seems to postulate a form of public reason as a framework for the development of global legal pluralism. Yet, even if one were to consider appropriate the thin requirements for the validity of reasons exchanged in public reasoning, it would still be difficult to understand how these reasons came into being in the first place. In other words, Berman takes these requirements of public reasoning as a given, a structural feature of certain practices which, in the end, turn out to be already inscribed within a liberal horizon. It is not possible to put into question this framework, and therefore the kind of politics envisaged by global legal pluralism is not fully reflexive. In the end, the political added value of this version of global legal pluralism can be summed up as 'the more, the merrier'.[36] A proliferation of viewpoints, once channelled through certain devices, will improve the representation and quality (in terms of its contents) of law. Yet, this claim just replicates the logic of competition as a system for enhancing knowledge which is usually embedded into the rationality of system markets.

While Berman's proposal is still attached to some form of liberal constitutionalism, the case of Nico Krisch's[37] work on pluralism appears as partially different. At a certain level, Krisch's understanding of pluralism is definitely more radical than Berman's. He embraces and supports a normative perspective on systemic pluralism. Institutional pluralism is a form of plurality of institutions: different parts of one order operate on a basis of coordination, in the framework of common rules, but without a clearly defined hierarchy.[38] Berman's pluralism, in the end, would be just another version of institutional pluralism, because it recognizes a common framework. Systemic pluralism eschews a common framework in favour of a decentred management of diversity. In this kind of pluralism, there are no common rules of recognition,[39] but only competing rules coming from a number of different layers. Krisch's starting point is the new regulatory reality of transnational law. Regulations have become the main legal source for governing supranational or transnational phenomena. One aspect of this landscape is that the state has become much less important as the main site of both legal and

---

35 See Berman's reply to Galán and Patterson, 'How legal pluralism is and is not different from liberalism: A response to Alexis Galán and Dennis Patterson', *International Journal of Constitutional Law* 11 (2013).

36 Emmanuel Melissaris, 'The more the merrier? A new take on legal pluralism', *Social & Legal Studies* 13 (2004).

37 Nico Krisch, *Beyond Constitutionalism: The Pluralist Structure of Postnational Law* (Oxford, UK: Oxford University Press, 2010).

38 According to Krisch, this is another version of the weak kind of legal pluralism identified in John Griffiths, 'What is legal pluralism?', *Journal of Legal Pluralism*, 1 (1986): 4–5. In the debate on supranational law, this position is powerfully represented by Mattias Kumm, 'The cosmopolitan turn in constitutionalism: In the relationship between constitutionalism in and beyond the state', in *Ruling the World*, eds. Jeffrey Dunoff and Joel Trachtman (Cambridge, UK: Cambridge University Press, 2009).

39 According to Krisch, this version of pluralism is closer to the one proposed by Boaventura de Sousa Santos, *Toward a New Legal Common Sense* (London: Butterworths, 2002).

Pluralist turn and political discontents 125

political authority.[40] Another essential feature (at least, for the solidity of Krisch's argument) is the proliferation of global regulatory bodies, such as international courts, international organizations and supranational regulatory agencies. This point seems to be rather uncontroversial: just to mention one example, according to Karen Alter, 85 per cent of the total number of international decisions, opinions and rulings have been issued in the last two decades.[41] At the descriptive level, Krisch is basically starting from the thesis of the fragmentation of international law. At the normative level, he is fundamentally advocating the superiority of systemic pluralism to hierarchical and foundational constitutional systems, inter-state systems and forms of institutional pluralist law which rest upon general legal rules and/or principles. Once he has abandoned any reference to a common language or framework, it becomes necessary to provide an alternative explanation for enlightening the interactions among different legal claims.

Two normative principles are conjured up by Krisch in order to support his global legal pluralism. The first one is *toleration* and it is directly linked to the epistemic status of systemic pluralism. According to this principle, 'regulatory bodies should tolerate, and respect, the standards and decisions of other bodies'.[42] This is a standard prescription for many versions of legal pluralism. In order to operate (and, as we shall see later, to flourish), pluralism needs reciprocal and conditional recognition of at least the prima facie value of the legal orders and institutions involved in a transnational legal conflict.

The second principle pertains to the normative justification of systemic pluralism. Here, what is most relevant for the economy of this chapter is that this justification comes wrapped in a political language. Pluralism, in contrast to constitutionalism, is related to 'political deliberation', because it is supposed to augment the openness to and hence the inclusiveness of many voices. This is how Krisch sums up his position in contrast with the constitutional approach:

> [c]onstitutionalism and pluralism are distinguished . . . by the different extent to which [each] formally link[s] the various spheres of law and politics. While pluralism regards them as separate in their foundations, global constitutionalism, properly understood, is a monist conception that integrates those spheres into one. As a result, rules about the relationship of national, regional, and global norms are immediately applicable in all spheres, and neither political nor judicial actors can justify non-compliance on legal grounds.[43]

---

40 It has to be noted that Krisch's treatment of the role of the state is very superficial and inaccurate. He basically accepts the common but shallow interpretation of the decline of the state without really engaging with the topic of the restructuring of the state. For an insightful and still relevant analysis of the state within supranational orders, see Nicos Poulantzas, 'Internationalization of capitalist relations and the nation-state', *Economy and Society* 3 (1974).

41 Karen Alter, 'The multiple roles of international courts and tribunals', in *International Law and International Relations*, eds. Jeffrey Dunoff and Mark Pollack (Cambridge, UK: Cambridge University Press, 2013).

42 Patrick Capps, 'The problem of global law', *Modern Law Review* 74 (2011): 798.

43 Nico Krisch, *Beyond Constitutionalism*, p. 242.

126   *Marco Goldoni*

Global legal pluralism, by respecting the separation between different domains, is allegedly political, because it promotes the value of *public autonomy*. Much of the argument in support of systemic pluralism revolves around this ideal. Yet, it is striking how poorly this ideal is developed. The argument follows this line of reasoning: social practices alone are not a sufficient ground for the legitimacy of a post-national order. It is necessary to introduce an added value, which is provided, in this case, by the ideal of public autonomy, which among other things has to be compatible with the principle of toleration. But at this stage, Krisch's argument becomes vague and too thin to meet the expectations that radical pluralism has generated in the first place. Social practices are instantiations of public autonomy when 'they concretize the discursive requirements that allow all to be the authors of the rules to which they are subject'.[44] Therefore, social practices realize public autonomy when they are substantiated by a particular kind of political deliberation. In other terms, social practices instantiate public autonomy when they are the specification of the idea of self-legislation.[45] This is a demanding claim, but it should be recognized that Krisch confronts directly the objection of democratic accountability, which is immediately raised when a heavy normative principle like public autonomy is conjured up. Global legal pluralism is supposed not to translate standard conceptions of democracy (that is, representative democracy within the framework of the nation-state) to the transnational sphere, but to adapt democratic politics to a new context. In response to the difficulties of post-national democracy, Krisch advocates the virtues of systemic pluralism: openness to revision, contestation, and checks and balances. Openness to revision is ensured by the lack of ultimate authority, while checks and balances are operational through the proliferation of sites of authority. However, for the argument put forward in this article, contestation is the most interesting of the three.

Contestation is supposed to be the main political component of global legal pluralism and ensures that accountability is properly in place in the interaction between different legal orders and institutions. Only through contestation is it possible to counter the lack of trust that is created by the absence of a direct representative link between agents and supranational institutions, that is, by the distance between the governing supranational institutions and those governed. To be fair, Krisch does not advocate pluralism's virtues as valid in an absolute sense, but only as comparatively stronger when compared to the constitutionalist approach: 'thus a pluralist structure does not, in and of itself, allow for more effective contestation than a constitutionalist one'.[46] Note that it is accepted that most global regulation and standard setting in areas such as manufacturing, banking, taxation, bankruptcy, money laundering or air transport is today generated through processes that connect the decision making of transnational actors,

---

44 Ibid. p. 99.
45 Ibid. Krisch follows and quotes Habermas on this point, but adding that 'there is no need to limit this approach to the discourse within a pre-established association'.
46 Ibid. p. 85.

Pluralist turn and political discontents 127

organizations and state actors, configuring a process which may be pluralist, but is certainly not properly political. There is no public forum where positions are articulated, or disagreements become visible, but the effects of global legal pluralism are produced just through interactions between different actors and institutions.

Bearing in mind this background picture, one might conclude that Krisch adopts a conflict-of-laws perspective.[47] However, his allegiance to global legal pluralism commits him to an admittedly stronger stance. The conflict-of-laws approach understands the relation between different legal claims as a conflict between autonomous orders, with a neat distinction between inside and outside.[48] Global legal pluralism's starting point is categorically different, because it is concerned with orders that are intermeshed and interconnected and which accept forms of common decision making. This is reflected in the terminology chosen by Krisch: interactions at the supranational level are not regulated by collision between norms, but by 'interface norms' which signal enmeshment and joint engagement in a common space. For courts, for example, this means a move from a perception of themselves as the guardians of their legal orders, to the role of mediators or arbiters between orders as they start seeing themselves as increasingly belonging to many legal identities at the same time.

As such, the structure of a post-national order is likely to be complex and fluid, but it also lacks any constitutional mechanism to cope with and recognize the contestation which is supposed to be pervasive throughout the regulatory landscape. In fact, Krisch's main point is that regulatory bodies disagree, compete or contest with each other within global legal pluralism. But what is the object of contestation? This is not immediately clear, but as noted by Patrick Capps, it seems that regulatory bodies, at the transnational level, do actually regulate types of activity rather than legal subjects.[49] Competition and contestation arise in a multiplicity of activities. This proliferation secures global legal pluralism's efficacy. Regulatory bodies compete around what a particular legal subject should do, or they conflict in an attempt to impose standards on each other. But Krisch believes that this is a great advantage for pluralism as it allows for greater flexibility and an improved capacity for adaptation.

In order to assess the virtues of this kind of legal pluralism, two factors need to be taken into account. First, it is necessary to describe accurately the nature and content of those interface norms, which are supposed to regulate the conflicts ensuing from different legal standpoints. Krisch recognizes that interface norms are based on the principle of public autonomy. They:

---

47 The standard version of this approach is Christian Joerges, '*Sozialstaatlichkeit* in Europe: A conflict-of-laws approach to the law of the EU and the proceduralisation of constitutionalisation', *German Law Journal* 10 (2009).

48 For an analysis of the EU as comprised of many autonomous legal systems, see Julie Dickson, 'Toward a theory of European Union legal systems', in *Philosophical Foundations of EU Law*, eds. Julie Dickson and Pavlos Eleftheriadis (Oxford, UK: Oxford University Press, 2012).

49 Capps, 'Problem of global law', p. 801.

128 *Marco Goldoni*

[w]ill also reflect other factors, such as the degree of prior formal acceptance of other norms (for example, through ratification), the proximity of
values (for example, equivalence or identity in the interpretation of rights),
or functional considerations, such as the utility of cooperation in a regime.
Yet, these should be secondary factors, operating within the autonomy-based
framework I have just outlined. If a polity has a strong autonomy pedigree, its
norms are due respect even if they are based on distinct values or compliance
with them does not have immediate benefits.[50]

How are different claims from various legal standpoints going to be adjudicated?
Krisch's reliance on the principle of public autonomy reveals itself to be again a
liberal answer to the question of pluralism. Conflict rules do not have an overarching legal character, but they are 'normative, moral demands that find (potentially
diverging) legal expressions only within the various sub-orders'. How these
demands are put forward and then channelled is a question which is left completely unexplored.

Here the second issue kicks in: who is going to adjudicate these difficult cases
and how? The answer is rather predictable and it gets Krisch's solution very close
to the one proposed by global administrative law. Courts and regulatory bodies
are the best-suited agents for dealing with these conflicts, for two reasons. The
first is a matter of institutional design: in the process of interpreting the law,
courts often collect claims from different legal orders, something that usually
does not happen to other kinds of more overtly political institutions. The idea is
that courts thus provide a common space where parties may speak. Through this,
contestation can take place and be articulated according to a common grammar.
The second point is that legal reasoning provides a common language very well
suited to deal with contestation. Revealingly, Krisch admits that judicial minimalism is often the right attitude for dealing with issues of social and political
conflict. Against a teleological interpretation of the law, he suggests a case-by-
case evolutionary, but minimalist, approach to legal interpretation. Given that it is
not always possible to easily reconcile conflicting claims, decisions should refrain
from addressing principles and be restricted to the circumstances of the particular
case without developing any wider theory of law. This is very similar to Cass
Sunstein's judicial minimalism, based on the so-called 'incompletely theorised
agreements', which may help shape a common solution even if disagreement
over fundamental issues remains.[51] This approach is instantiated by the European
human rights regime and, in particular, by the use of the margin of appreciation
by the European Court of Human Rights. No grand theory of interpretation is
employed by the Court, but constant adjustment sensitive to the context involved

---

50 Krisch, *Beyond Constitutionalism*, p. 296.
51 Cass Sunstein, *Legal Theory and Political Conflict* (Oxford, UK: Oxford University Press, 1996);
Cass Sunstein, *One Case at a Time: Judicial Minimalism on the Supreme Court* (Cambridge, MA:
Harvard University Press, 2001).

Pluralist turn and political discontents 129

in a dispute. The dialogue between the Court and the member states is based on interface norms, but these do not function as rules. In fact:

> [l]egally, the relationship between the parts of the overall order in pluralism remains open – governed by the potentially competing rules of the various sub-orders, each with its own ultimate point of reference and supremacy claim, the relationships between them are left to be determined ultimately through political, not rule-based processes.[52]

This is a form of balancing case by case which takes place in a judicial setting.[53] In the end, the political test for public autonomy is left to a kind of judicial and administrative politics, which is performed on a case-by-case basis.[54] The idea is that in supranational and global law, the judicial channel opens up spaces for political action. The innovative aspect of this approach is that it creates new possibilities for actors in spheres from which they were previously excluded. However, nothing is said by Krisch on whether and how the judicial language colonizes political action either in terms of offering a platform for disagreement[55] or in allowing any room for the reflexivity of politics, to the possibility of discussing the terms of the framework within which contestation takes place.[56] A minimalist understanding of the judicial management of interface norms, even if coupled with rules which make sure that interactions are open to negotiation, seems hardly an effective way to politicize global legal pluralism. It might create a multiplicity of channels open to strategic actions from various actors, but this dispersion does not enhance the visibility of political conflict.

Pluralism as fragmented constitutions

The last kind of pluralist discourse to be taken into account is the one celebrated by Gunther Teubner, in particular in his recent *Constitutional Fragments*.[57] Teubner's work is extremely ambitious (and certainly not limited to the European space), because it merges legal pluralism and the sociology of constitutions in a highly innovative approach to law and globalization.[58] His starting point is rather different from the previous two theories. He adopts (but modifies) Luhmann's theory of systems, which puts an emphasis on the autopoiesis or self-generation of every functional system and on the importance of communication for their stability.[59]

---

52 Krisch, *Beyond Constitutionalism*, p. 23.
53 For the idea of 'balancing *ad hoc*', see Alexander Aleinikoff, 'Constitutional law in the age of balancing', *Yale Law Journal* 96 (1984): 979–980.
54 Alec Stone Sweet, *Governing with Judges* (Oxford, UK: Oxford University Press, 2000), p. 78.
55 This point has been raised, among many others, by Rancière, *Disagreement*, p. 77.
56 It is probably unfair to demand something of legal pluralism that it does not promise. But one of the main tenets of Krisch's argument is the claim to a political quality of pluralism.
57 Gunther Teubner, *Constitutional Fragments* (Oxford, UK: Oxford University Press, 2012).
58 Compare Marcelo Neves, *Transconstitutionalism* (Oxford, UK: Hart, 2013).
59 Niklas Luhmann, *Law as a Social System* (Oxford, UK: Oxford University Press, 2002).

130   *Marco Goldoni*

Consequently, law plays an essential role since, once coupled with other systems, it provides the stabilization of normative and communicative expectations and it also protects the autonomy of each system. Teubner links societal constitutions to the problem of double reflexivity. Societal constitutions are defined as 'structural coupling between the reflexive mechanisms of the law (that is, secondary legal norm creation in which norms are applied to norms) and the reflexive mechanisms of the social sector concerned'.[60] In practice, societal constitutions emerge when their reflexivity is supported by legal norms. Globalization has shown how productive the coupling of law and other systems can be beyond the horizon of the nation-state. In this way, it has changed the experiences of the nation-state itself. State-based constitutionalism is now threatened by a centrifugal force defined as the double fragmentation of world society. The first fragmentation coincides with the autonomy of global social sectors; the second fragmentation concerns the consolidation of regional cultures and it pre-empts any possibility of a unitary global constitution. Moreover, the development of global social sub-systems has not been realized at the same pace. Social systems still tied to nation-state level have not been globalized, creating an asymmetry between different media. However, according to Teubner, this gap is not negative in itself as it can actually enrich contemporary constitutionalism by containing the ambition of the nation-state.

As is evident, the main target of Teubner's work is the political version of constitutionalism, and more specifically, the political constitution of the nation-state. His main concern is to liberate the idea of the constitution from the grip of the state, because only in this way will it be possible to redeem the promises of constitutionalism.[61] According to him, the drawbacks of political constitutionalism are many: at the epistemic level, political constitutions obscure the role of other societal formations, distorting our knowledge of society; at the normative level, they empower only individuals through public law and, in the best case scenario, social groups through norms of private law; theoretically, they are understood in a strictly formalist way to the detriment of the undergirding material constitution. Finally, political constitutionalism is always verging on the brink of a totalitarian turn, that is, a reshaping of the constitution from a liberal one, where society is just left to the regulation of private law, to one where society is completely controlled by the state constitution.

The conceptual underpinning of this position is that, as Teubner recognizes, political constitutions do claim a double function: to constitute power and to limit it. But the methodology of constitutional sociology suggests that this double function cannot be limited to the constitution of the nation-state. The main insight provided by a sociological study of constitutions is that societies are much more complex than can be captured by formal constitutions, and they contain multiple non-state social orders. The foundation of an autonomous order and its self-limitation are required for vast numbers of institutions. Note that, according

---

60 Teubner, *Constitutional Fragments*, p. 105.

61 Therefore, it is clear that the EU, together with other supranational institutions, offers the opportunity of disentangling constitutionalism from its state-based origins.

Pluralist turn and political discontents 131

to Teubner, this is actually the main difference between juridification and constitutionalization. Juridification requires only first-order rules, that is, rules that regulate the behaviour of subjects. Constitutionalization requires the creation of second-order rules (in H.L.A. Hart's sense), which serve as a containment of the power engendered by the first-order rule. Therefore, constitutionalization brings about the full autonomy of the system. Teubner's fear is that the political constitutionalization of social systems may engender new forms of totalitarianism, because these claims of social autonomy would not be recognized. State-based constitutionalism is the only form of constitutional law which claims to be able to regulate, at least in principle, all aspects of life. This is what Teubner fears and why he extols the virtue of global legal pluralism.

Despite its various merits, Teubner's proposal is quite troubling when it comes to his assessment of the role of politics as a limit to the expansionist tendencies of social sub-systems.[62] If the logic of functional differentiation is considered as absolute – something that cannot be excluded, given that it represents the logic undergirding each societal constitution – then what is left of politics? Teubner draws a distinction between external and internal politicization of systems, clearly lending his support to the latter. On top of that, Teubner disaggregates constitutions and political power at the supranational level, in the sense that the former does not generate the latter. No space is left for external re-politicization. It is clear that the separation among different functional systems is an essential and sufficient condition for the effectiveness of the same systems. This is why the kind of global legal pluralism advocated by Teubner remains in deep tension with political constitutions.

It is striking to see how Teubner underestimates the effects of this separation when it comes to assessing the functioning of politics within market systems. We are even told that:

> [a] strengthened politics of reflection is required within the economy, and this has to be supported by constitutional norms. Historically it was collective bargaining, co-determination and the right to strike which enabled new forms of societal dissensus. In today's transnational organisations, ethical committees fulfil a similar role. Societal constitutionalism sees its point of application wherever it turns the existence of a variety of 'reflections centres' within society, and in particular within economic institutions, into the criterion of a democratic society.[63]

---

62 This criticism of societal constitutionalism has already been put forward by Jiří Přibáň, 'Constitutionalism as fear of the political?', *Journal of Law and Society* 39 (2012): 457:

> Societal constitutionalism thus involves a paradox of criticizing the political and legal form while using its concepts to describe non-political processes of self-limitation and self-constitution of different sub-systems and sectors of global society . . . it is important to ask if Teubner's most fascinating and original concept of constitutional fragments expresses either an alternative concept of the politics of societal constitutionalism, or fear of the political.

63 Teubner, *Constitutional Fragments*, p. 17.

132 *Marco Goldoni*

We are therefore reminded that politicization can take place internally, that is, within social sub-systems, through politicizing consumer preferences, ecologizing corporations and placing monetary policy in the public domain. It is apparent that internal politicization cannot account for political reflexivity, because it folds seamlessly back into the logic of the reproduction of the system.[64]

Teubner argues that institutionalized politics has an innate tendency to suppress opportunities and impulses coming from within the social sub-systems. In other terms, the political system receives and translates the external impulses into its own code, weakening, in this way, the transformative potential (of the impulses). While Teubner is right in stressing the reductionist (and exclusionary) potential of constituted powers, he does not recognize the fact that by pleading for the proliferation and decentralization of politics he is actually proposing to leave many areas outside the possibility of becoming politicized. His indictment of the political constitution does not leave any space for politics beyond the national state on the basis of sociological and normative arguments. It is better to leave it to the social sub-system itself to signal the moment of introducing limitations (usually in the forms of rights) through internal processes. The moment when this happens is described as the moment where the system 'hits the bottom'. However, the idea of having hit the bottom is rather insidious. How is it possible to know ex ante what the bottom is? Is there anything in social systems that functions as a warning mechanism for signalling when the bottom is being reached? Here, a certain unjustified optimism is at work when Teubner assures that:

> [i]n the long run ... the one-sided 'neo-liberal' reduction of global constitutionalism to its constitutive function cannot be sustained. It is only a matter of time before the systemic energies released trigger disastrous consequences ... a fundamental readjustment of constitutional politics will be required to deal with the outburst of social conflicts.[65]

It is sufficient to think of the new European Economic Governance to see how optimistic Teubner's prescription is. It is extremely hard to define the measures adopted by the EU and its member states to cope with the economic and financial crisis as a counter-movement.[66] Even if one postulated that the system had hit the bottom, the question of whether there would be a basis left upon which to build the counter-movement of limitation would remain open.[67]

---

64 Emilios Christodoulidis, 'The politics of societal constitutionalism', *Indiana Journal of Global Legal Studies* 20 (2013): 659.

65 Teubner, *Constitutional Fragments*, p. 78.

66 See, for penetrating analyses, Kaarlo Tuori and Klaus Tuori, *The Eurozone Crisis: A Constitutional Analysis* (Cambridge, UK: Cambridge University Press, 2012); Massimo Fichera, Sakari Hänninen and Kaarlo Tuori, eds. *Polity and Crisis: Reflections on the European Odyssey* (Farnham, UK: Ashgate, 2014).

67 In another essay, Teubner remarks that a concern for catastrophe is part and parcel of societal constitutionalism: 'Constitutionalizing polycontexturality', *Social & Legal Studies* 19 (2011).

What constitutional and legal pluralism do not register and why

It is time to take stock of the remarks made in the previous three sections. As already noted, the strategy adopted by constitutional and global legal pluralists is two-fold. But both the invitation to look at the interaction among different institutional layers or to keep functionally differentiated systems separated, favour the destitution of traditional constitutionalism and the main characters of modern political law. Both options also undercut the possibility of any meaningful and effective political constitutionalism. The kind of constitutionalism advocated by pluralists is either politically very thin or even paralysing for future innovative political action. First, the possibility of staging political disagreement is severely constrained, when not completely impeded. The circumstances of politics are either ignored or masked under the fact of pluralism. There is, in other words, a severe misunderstanding of the 'perspective' character of political action. Global legal pluralists believe that opening up to pluralism is by itself a sufficient enabling device for politicization, either because of the opening up of channels for voices previously unheard or because the competition between different perspectives will generate the right kind of political conflict.

As a consequence of these remarks, a second important criticism emerges. Pluralists do not take into account the possibility of any kind of meaningful constituent power.[68] Within a pluralist understanding of constitutional law, there is no traction for constituent power, but only the possibility of taking advantage of the normative interstices left open in the interactions between different sites of authority. It is no surprise, for example, that none of these theorists takes into account the role played by the rationality of economic actors. In the end, the politics of pluralism is in danger of being shaped by the principles of competition and proliferation or, in the case of Teubner, by the politicization of consumers' behaviours and the creation of ethical committees. From these perspectives, the rationality of markets cannot be questioned as an appropriate register for dealing with many contemporary issues. In such a context, it is predictable that social conflicts are not thematized or consistently tempered.[69]

One of the reasons behind this blindness towards political and social conflicts is the conception of the constitution taken up by pluralists, based on the common assumptions of liberal constitutionalism. An alternative approach might be employed to understand European constitutionalism and its dynamics. The EU can also be described as a polity. Indeed, even its constant transformation is part of the construction of its constitutional order as a polity. Here, a socio-political

---

One is left wondering how social systems would register the signals of an imminent catastrophe when strict functional differentiation is still in place.

68 Teubner, for example, is explicit when he advocates the overcoming of the dichotomy between constituent power and constituted powers.

69 Marco Dani, 'Rehabilitating social conflicts in European public law', *European Law Journal* 18 (2012).

134　*Marco Goldoni*

understanding of the constitution[70] is extremely helpful for deciphering the nature of the European polity and represents the best possible reading of pluralism in the EU. A political sociology of the constitution indicates that the creation of political power is part and parcel of the process of polity building. This process usually enables the structuring of conflicts along certain axes and creates the condition for the visibility of these conflicts.

A more accurate instrument to map the constitutional space of the EU is provided by the concept of the material constitution. This is a non-formal understanding of the constitution which points at the arrangement among social and political forces with a clear sense of political trajectory.[71] In this respect, the material constitution is the outcome of a compromise between political and social forces, which structures the space of political action around certain conflictual axes. In this respect, the EU already has a material constitution (as opposed to a formal constitution). Mike Wilkinson, for example, has noted that this constitution is already well established and functioning: 'Whatever constitutional order is adopted or emerges in this new domain has an expressive and polity-building dimension. Politics is not abolished, only transformed, or concealed'.[72] European constitutionalism operates according to a particular political rationality dictated by certain imperatives. The problem is that constitutional or global legal pluralism does not capture the relevant plurality of constitutions, which is the equivalent of saying that the framing of the European constitutional question in terms of compatibility among different seats of authority is misleading or, at best, reductive. What is defining the material constitution of the EU is, on the one side, the detachment of the economic constitution from the political constitution (which is still mostly left at national level) and, on the other, the empowerment of national executives as the leading actors in Eurozone economic governance.[73] Such a material constitution enables the internal market, competition law and the governance of the common currency to heavily restructure member states and their societies.[74] Of the conflicts generated by these transformative processes, pluralists do not have much to say at the descriptive and normative levels. This is probably due to the given underlying formalist and often liberal assumptions guiding their approach to constitutional studies.[75]

---

70 Two books, while adopting different perspectives, have recently revived the interest in the socio-political approach to constitutions: Chris Thornhill, *A Sociology of Constitutions* (Cambridge, UK: Cambridge University Press, 2011); Martin Loughlin, *Foundations of Public Law* (Oxford, UK: Oxford University Press, 2010).

71 Costantino Mortati, *La costituzione in senso material*e (Milan, Italy: Giuffré, 1998): p. 5. Negri and Hardt note that the term material constitution refers to 'the continuous formation and re-formation of the composition of social forces' in the state: Antonio Negri and Michael Hardt, *Empire* (Cambridge, MA: Harvard University Press, 2000), p. xiv.

72 Michael Wilkinson, 'Political constitutionalism and the European Union', *Modern Law Review* 76 (2013).

73 Uwe Puetter, *The New Intergovernmentalism* (Oxford, UK: Oxford University Press, 2014).

74 This is the main point made by Chris Bickerton, *European Integration* (Oxford, UK: Oxford University Press, 2012).

75 Martin Loughlin, 'Constitutional pluralism: An oxymoron', *Global Constitutionalism* 3 (2014): 30.

Pluralist turn and political discontents 135

All of this entails that constitutional and legal pluralism does not provide a solid perspective to describe the 'self-constitution' of Europe.

Bibliography

Abelj, Matej and Jan Komárek, eds. *Constitutional Pluralism in the European Union and Beyond*. Oxford, UK: Hart, 2012.

Aleinikoff, Alexander. 'Constitutional law in the age of balancing'. *Yale Law Journal* 96 (1984): 943–1005.

Alter, Karen. 'The multiple roles of international courts and tribunals'. In *International Law and International Relations*, edited by Jeffrey Dunoff and Mark Pollack. Cambridge, UK: Cambridge University Press, 2013, pp. 345–370.

Arendt, Hannah. *The Human Condition*. Chicago, IL: Chicago University Press, 1998.

Berman, Paul Schiff. 'The globalization of jurisdiction'. *University of Pennsylvania Law Review* 151 (2002): 311–529.

Berman, Paul Schiff. 'A pluralist approach to international law'. *Yale Journal of International Law* 32 (2007): 301–322.

Berman, Paul Schiff. *Global Legal Pluralism. A Jurisprudence of Law beyond Borders*. Cambridge, UK: Cambridge University Press, 2012.

Berman, Paul Schiff. 'How legal pluralism is and is not different from liberalism: A response to Alexis Galán and Dennis Patterson'. *International Journal of Constitutional Law* 11 (2013): 801–808.

Bickerton, Chris. *European Integration*. Oxford, UK: Oxford University Press, 2012.

Capps, Patrick. 'The problem of global law'. *Modern Law Review* 74 (2011): 794–810.

Christodoulidis, Emilios. 'Against substitution: The constitutional thinking of dissensus'. In *The Paradox of Constitutionalism*, edited by Martin Loughlin and Neil Walker. Oxford, UK: Oxford University Press, 2007, pp. 189–208.

Christodoulidis, Emilios. 'The politics of societal constitutionalism'. *Indiana Journal of Global Legal Studies* 20 (2013): 629–663.

Cover, Robert. 'Nomos and narrative'. *Harvard Law Review* 94 (1983): 4–68.

Dani, Marco. 'Rehabilitating social conflicts in European public law'. *European Law Journal* 18 (2012): 621–643.

Dickson, Julie. 'Toward a theory of European Union legal systems'. In *Philosophical Foundations of EU Law*, edited by Julie Dickson and Pavlos Eleftheriadis. Oxford, UK: Oxford University Press, 2012, pp. 25–53.

Fichera, Massimo, Sakari Hänninen and Kaarlo Tuori, eds. *Polity and Crisis: Reflections on the European Odyssey*. Farnham, UK: Ashgate, 2014.

Galán, Alexis, and Dennis Patterson. 'The limits of normative legal pluralism'. *International Journal of Constitutional Law* 11 (2013): 783–800.

Griffiths, John. 'What is legal pluralism?' *Journal of Legal Pluralism* 1 (1986): 1–16.

Hart, H.L.A. *The Concept of Law*. Oxford, UK: Clarendon Press, 1961.

Joerges, Christian. '*Sozialstaatlichkeit* in Europe: A conflict-of-laws approach to law of the EU and the proceduralisation of constitutionalisation'. *German Law Journal* 10 (2009): 335–360.

Kahn, Paul. *The Cultural Study of Law*. Chicago, IL: Chicago University Press, 1999.

Klemen, Jaklic. *Constitutional Pluralism in the EU*. Oxford, UK: Oxford University Press, 2014.

Krisch, Nico. *Beyond Constitutionalism: The Pluralist Structure of Postnational Law*. Oxford, UK: Oxford University Press, 2010.

136 *Marco Goldoni*

Kumm, Mattias. 'Who is the arbiter of constitutionality in Europe?' *Common Market Law Review* 36 (1999): 351–386.

Kumm, Mattias. 'Institutionalising Socratic contestation: The rationalist human rights paradigm, legitimate authority and the point of judicial review'. *European Journal of Legal Studies* 1 (2007): 1–24.

Kumm, Mattias. 'The best of times and the worst of times: Between constitutional triumphalism and nostalgia'. In *The Twilight of Constitutionalism?*, edited by Petra Dobner and Martin Loughlin. Oxford, UK: Oxford University Press, 2009, pp. 201–220.

Kumm, Mattias. 'The cosmopolitan turn in constitutionalism: In the relationship between constitutionalism in and beyond the state'. In *Ruling the World*, edited by Jeffrey Dunoff and Joel Trachtman. Cambridge, UK: Cambridge University Press, 2009, pp. 258–324.

Kumm, Mattias. 'The moral point of constitutional pluralism'. In *Philosophical Foundations of European Union Law*, edited by Julie Dickson and Pavlos Eleftheriadis. Oxford, UK: Oxford University Press, 2012, pp. 216–246.

Loughlin, Martin. *Foundations of Public Law*. Oxford, UK: Oxford University Press, 2010.

Loughlin, Martin. 'Constitutional pluralism: An oxymoron'. *Global Constitutionalism* 3 (2014): 9–30.

Luhmann, Niklas. *Law as a Social System*. Oxford, UK: Oxford University Press, 2002.

MacCormick, Neil. 'Beyond the sovereign state'. *Modern Law Review* 56 (1993): 1–18.

MacCormick, Neil. 'Risking constitutional collision'. *Oxford Journal of Legal Studies* 18 (1998): 517–532.

MacCormick, Neil. *Institutions of Law*. Oxford, UK: Oxford University Press, 2007.

Melissaris, Emmanuel. 'The more the merrier? A new take on legal pluralism'. *Social & Legal Studies* 13 (2004): 57–79.

Michaels, Ralf. 'Global legal pluralism'. *Annual Review of Law and Social Science* 5 (2009): 243–262.

Mortati, Costantino. *La costituzione in senso materiale*. Milan, Italy: Giuffré, 1998.

Mouffe, Chantal. *On the Political*. London: Verso, 2005.

Negri, Antonio and Michael Hardt. *Empire*. Cambridge, MA: Harvard University Press, 2000.

Neves, Marcelo. *Transconstitutionalism*. Oxford, UK: Hart, 2014.

Poulantzas, Nicos. 'Internationalization of capitalist relations and the nation-state'. *Economy and Society* 3 (1974): 145–179.

Přibáň, Jiří. 'Constitutionalism as fear of the political?' *Journal of Law and Society* 39 (2012): 441–471.

Puetter, Uwe. *The New Intergovernmentalism*. Oxford, UK: Oxford University Press, 2014.

Rancière, Jacques. *Disagreement*. London: Verso, 2006.

Raz, Joseph. *Practical Reason and Norms*. Oxford, UK: Oxford University Press, 1975.

Rougane, Nicole. *Authorities*. Oxford, UK: Oxford University Press, 2013.

Santos, Boaventura de Sousa. *Toward a New Legal Common Sense*. London: Butterworths, 2002.

Schneiderman, David. *Constitutionalizing Economic Globalization*. Cambridge, UK: Cambridge University Press, 2008.

Stone Sweet, Alec. *Governing with Judges*. Oxford, UK: Oxford University Press, 2000.

Sunstein, Cass. *Legal Theory and Political Conflict*. Oxford, UK: Oxford University Press, 1996.

Sunstein, Cass. *One Case at a Time: Judicial Minimalism on the Supreme Court*. Cambridge, MA: Harvard University Press, 2001.

Teubner, Gunther. 'Constitutionalizing polycontexturality'. *Social & Legal Studies* 19 (2011): 210–219.

Teubner, Gunther. *Constitutional Fragments*. Oxford, UK: Oxford University Press, 2012.

Thornhill, Chris. *A Sociology of Constitutions*. Cambridge, UK: Cambridge University Press, 2011.

Tuori, Kaarlo and Klaus Tuori. *The Eurozone Crisis: A Constitutional Analysis*. Cambridge, UK: Cambridge University Press, 2012.

Walker, Neil. 'The idea of constitutional pluralism'. *Modern Law Review* 65 (2002): 317–359.

Walker, Neil, ed. *Sovereignty in Transition*. Oxford, UK: Hart, 2003.

Wilkinson, Michael. 'Political constitutionalism and the European Union'. *Modern Law Review* 76 (2013): 191–222.

6 Why supra-national law is not the exception

On the grounds of legal obligations beyond the state

George Pavlakos[*]

Vademecum

Whether we should best make sense of the global legal order as a unitary whole or as a plurality of independent (possibly interconnected) legal orders, is a highly contested issue. However, a lot is at stake: a monist understanding of the global legal order would entail that what binds us, as individual persons or in our associations, are obligations that may have been generated independently of our own domestic legal practices. To that extent, the normative authority of the EU or the UN may not be left up to an act of acceptance or consent on behalf of sovereign states. In contrast, a dualist or *a fortiori* pluralist understanding would entail that states are only bound by *perspectival* obligations or obligations that are generated from within the domestic legal order. For any other practice to produce binding obligations, it would be required to be recognized or adopted from some domestic point of view. In other words, the dualist/pluralist approach submits that the EU, the UN and so on, bind states only to the extent that these have agreed to them.

In a recent, posthumously published paper[1] Ronald Dworkin sought to challenge the latter mode of presentation. He argued against consent as the ground of international legal obligations. Instead, he suggested that those obligations be understood as an instance of associative obligation. These are obligations pertaining to agents who form a political association.[2] While associative relations mainly

---

[*] An earlier draft was presented in June 2013 at the Cardiff one-day conference on 'Self-constitution of Europe: Symbols, politics and law'. I am indebted to Jiří Přibáň and the other participants for valuable comments which have led to considerable improvement in the final version of the argument. Research was supported by the long-term strategic development financing of the Institute of State and Law of the Academy of Sciences of the Czech Republic (RVO: 68378122). Finally, I would like to acknowledge permission to reprint portions of: George Pavlakos, 'Transnational legal responsibility: Some preliminaries', in *Challenging Territoriality in Human Rights Law. Foundational Principles for a Multi Duty-Bearer Human Rights Regime*, ed. Wouter Vandenhole (Abingdon, UK and New York: Routledge, 2015), p. 136.

[1] Ronald Dworkin, 'A new philosophy for international law', *Philosophy and Public Affairs* 41 (2013).

[2] Associative relations pertain not only to political associations but also to other associations, such as the family, friendship and so on; see Ronald Dworkin, *Law's Empire* (London: Fontana Press, 1986); also Ronald Dworkin, *Justice for Hedgehogs* (Cambridge, MA: Harvard University Press,

Supra-national law is not the exception   139

pertain to those living within the state, they can reach out beyond the state to include any kind of obligation that would enhance the legitimacy of the relevant domestic associative bond. To that extent, Dworkin subscribes to the following exceptionalist claim: namely, that there is something special about the role of the state to the grounding of legal obligation,[3] which renders domestic law the standard site of legal obligation with supra- or international law being the exception.

In this chapter, I want to defend a version of non-exceptionalism with respect to the grounds of legal obligation. While Dworkin – despite departing from the idea of state consent – still takes the domestic level as the main site of legal obligation, I shall claim that there exists nothing special about the domestic level when it comes to determining the grounds of legal obligation: those may be located at any level of governance (domestic, regional or international) and amongst different kinds of actors (state, individuals or corporations). To reach that conclusion, I shall argue that the kind of relation or bond, which Dworkin deems appropriate for legal obligation ('the associative relation'[4]), is not exclusively confined to the domestic level. To the extent to which my argument succeeds, legal obligations can also arise independently of domestic state practices.[5]

Here is how the argument will proceed: in the first instance, I shall draw a contrast between the site and the scope of legal obligations. While considerations of site generate what I shall label a 'pedigree test for grounds', considerations of scope set out to detect salient normative relations amongst agents, which ground reciprocal claims and responsibility between them.

Next, I will argue that such normative relations pertain to any context of action, in which agents can direct one another's actions. I will coin the term 'normative conception of coercion (NCC)' for this structure of reciprocal action-direction and will contrast it to another, more standard conception of coercion which tracks mere facts of (state) enforcement (which I will label 'facts of sovereignty').[6] This will give me the opportunity to dispel the view that the salient associative bond requires facts of sovereignty, which seems to be a common ground of those accounts that attribute special role to state practices.[7]

Finally, I will propose a fresh way of reconceiving the salient associative relation that grounds legal obligations. I will suggest that the associative relation that

---

2011), ch. 14. For present purposes, I am only interested in political associations, so when I employ 'association', it is political association I have in mind.

3 Arguably, the exceptionalist claim is shared by the theories he targets: consent theorists, in deeming consent a key ground of legal obligation, also highlight the special role of the domestic level (the state).

4 While I accede to Dworkin's terminology of associative obligation, I am not committed to the term: my project aims precisely at unpacking the content of the concept, which Dworkin has left rather opaque. Later in the chapter, I shall employ the concept of *proto-legal relation* to give more flesh to the type of association that gives rise to legal obligations.

5 The claim here is not that state practices are not instances of the associative bond, but only that they are just one amongst many possible instances of associative bond.

6 Henceforth, I shall use force and enforcement as synonymous terms.

7 Including Dworkin's own account, as I will try to demonstrate.

140   *George Pavlakos*

gives rise to legal obligations be better redescribed as a *proto-legal* relation,[8] which does not necessarily involve the state. Proto-legal relations involve interactions between individuals such as those that generate *enforceable* claims amongst the participants, along the lines of the claims we usually attach to ordinary legal obligations. I will spend some time clarifying the conditions under which a class of interactions between persons may produce that effect. Interestingly, it will turn out that while state-based norms are sufficient for enforceability, they are not necessary for it; many other instances of interaction between agents are capable of producing that effect. The chapter will conclude by drawing a distinction between enforcement and enforceability and offering an account of the limited role that enforcement plays in the grounding of legal obligations.

Associative obligations: site and scope

In his 'A new philosophy for international law', Ronald Dworkin writes:

> I draw this conclusion: we cannot take the self-limiting consent of sovereign nations to be the basic ground of international law . . . That conception of legitimacy generated the social contract tradition in political philosophy and the artificial conceptions of consent that were necessary to sustain that tradition. I have argued elsewhere that these accounts all fail and are anyway unnecessary because consent is neither a necessary nor a sufficient ground of legitimacy. We must locate the source of political obligation elsewhere: in my view, we must locate it in the more general phenomenon of *associative obligation* (emphasis added).[9]

The phenomenon of associative obligation is called upon to answer the question about the grounds of legal obligation by moving beyond the standard statist view, which designates the self-limitation of the sovereign state as the key determinant of the grounds of legal obligation. Instead of looking into the facts of state practice and grouping them into a formula or litmus test for the existence of obligations, Dworkin suggests taking on board a more substantive criterion, that is, the associative bond that pertains between citizens living under a sovereign entity. This bond will then point the way to those principles of public morality which can legitimize the associative relationship in the eyes of those living under the state. It is those principles that, together with the facts of the practice of the community, will ground the legal obligations we have.[10]

In opting for this solution, Dworkin arguably was exploiting the findings of his long-standing criticisms against a positivist understanding of law: the standard

---

8 The proto-legal relation is ultimately a political relation, but the term proto-legal is more illuminating in the present context. By adopting that terminology, I also wish to suggest that the scope of legal relations is wider than the boundaries of state sovereignty.

9 Dworkin, 'A new philosophy', pp. 10–11.

10 Dworkin's view has been developed in a long line of works, starting with *Taking Rights Seriously* (1978) and culminating with *Justice for Hedgehogs* (2011).

Supra-national law is not the exception   141

positivist view argues that providing an answer to the question, 'what counts as law?' requires one to arrive at a salient description of the law-giving practice of a community which would then function as a pedigree test for picking out legal rules that, in turn, ground legal obligations. Very early on in his intellectual career, Dworkin launched a wholesale attack on that model and argued instead that legal obligations are grounded not on pedigree tests but on the substantive moral reasons (principles of political morality) we have for living together in a community. Thus, what better captures the relevance of our social living together to the explanation of legal obligation is not its formal aspect qua social fact but its more substantive significance qua associative bond: that is, a relation between agents which can only be sustained if it delivers legitimacy to the parties involved. Further, the requisite amount of legitimacy derives from the appropriate principles of political morality, which justify the association. In this light, what grounds obligations in law are not the facts of a practice but the principles that justify it qua associative practice.[11]

Two methods of inquiry

Drawing on broadly Dworkinian ideas for the explanation of legal obligations, we can distinguish between two lines of inquiry into the grounds of legal obligation. In doing so, I shall aim to illustrate that one of them is more apposite for capturing the associative dimension which Dworkin deems crucial for the explanation of obligations we incur under the law. However, I will also use my analysis to suggest that, when moving on to discuss the global/international level, Dworkin switched to the least fruitful line of inquiry, which led him to conclude that domestic law is the primary site of legal obligation with international law being the exception.[12] I will conclude the section by questioning the coherence of his exceptionalism.

Instructively, inquiry on the grounds of legal obligations can be conducted in one of two ways: it can start as a question about the *site* or as one about the *scope* of obligations.[13] Considerations of site relate to those social facts which obtain when legal obligations are already at work (call these *facts of sovereignty*). In contrast, scope depicts the range of persons that are reciprocally connected (be it

---

11 Famously, the facts of the practice are relevant too, but only in the manner in which they are 'lit' by the relevant principles. To that extent it is accurate to say that social practice does not *ground* legal obligation, but rather only becomes *salient* to the grounding thereof.

12 More precisely: Dworkin's discussion of international law reveals a deep-rooted belief in the special role of the state, which is also at work, even though less visibly so, in his analysis of the domestic level. As I argue below, the origins of that belief may lie in the role he accrues to state coercion as being uniquely relevant to the grounding of legal obligations.

13 Compare with the analysis of Arash Abizadeh in his 'Cooperation, pervasive impact, and coercion: On the scope (not site) of distributive justice', *Philosophy & Public Affairs* 35 (2007). Although Abizadeh discusses the obligations of justice, this should not raise major concerns as, in following the Dworkinian line of reasoning, we have already accepted the premise that the obligatory force of the law rests with principles of political morality.

142   *George Pavlakos*

as addressees or issuers) through legal obligations. Unsurprisingly, the question about the grounds of the law involves considerations of both site and scope. Yet, the picture we get with respect to the grounds of legal obligation depends crucially on the emphasis one places on either site or scope.

Accordingly, someone who takes considerations of site to determine the grounds of the law focuses on social facts (facts of sovereignty), which obtain when legal obligations are at work, and counts them as *existence conditions* for legal obligations. Those existence conditions are further grouped together to form a pedigree test which is used to assess the existence of legal obligations for an unlimited range of cases.[14] Thus, if a social arrangement does not instantiate the conditions enumerated in the test, then it falls outwith the purview of legal obligation. Hence, the question of site – as one asking about the existence of conditions of legal obligation – becomes, on this conception, antecedent to the question of scope, that is, the question about the range of persons who have claims on and responsibilities to each other arising from legal obligations.[15] To judge whether an agent has standing in law, we must ascertain whether the existence conditions of legal obligation have been fulfilled in the particular situation, antecedent to what agents owe one another. Positivist lawyers tend to abide by such pedigree tests when they wish to capture the site of legal obligations. Famously, H.L.A. Hart[16] identified a social rule of recognition, which depicts a set of facts about the practice of legal officials that in turn function as existence conditions (or criteria) for the obtaining of obligation-imposing rules. Such positivist views bear the mark of exceptionalism, in that they deem domestic law to form the standard site of legal obligation, wedded to facts of sovereignty, with supra-national law remaining an odd exception in need of explanation.[17]

But why should the direction of fit between site and scope be that one? To begin with, should it be true that site determines scope, something like the site/scope thesis would obtain, that is, the thesis that the scope of legal obligations coincides with their site. However, as Abizadeh observes in the context of obligations of global justice, this substantive claim is far from being a conceptual truth; thus, it needs to be specifically argued for in order to ground its truth.[18]

Contrariwise, as I take a broadly Dworkinian line to suggest this, one may have good reasons to start the inquiry on the side of 'scope'. It is actually a substantive question whether two agents stand in a relation of obligation, which is

---

14 Think here of rules of recognition or other formal positivist criteria. Notably, such tests may support a formal monism in law, whereby all law flows out of the same category of properties or facts, which count as the uniquely identified set of existence conditions for 'law'.

15 Compare Abizadeh, 'Cooperation, pervasive impact', p. 323.

16 H.L.A. Hart, *The Concept of Law* (Oxford, UK: Clarendon Press, 1961).

17 See Richard Collins, 'No longer at the vanishing point? International law and the analytical tradition in jurisprudence', *Jurisprudence* 5 (2014).

18 Further, it would seem that drawing inferences from the actual sites to the potential scope of legal obligations of justice might open one to the charge of a naturalistic fallacy (in case S1: conditions XYZ exist when obligation O obtains → lack of XYZ in S2 → no obligation O).

Supra-national law is not the exception   143

not exhausted by the obtaining of any set of facts of sovereignty as we encountered earlier. Along these lines, site does not list existence conditions but merely enabling or instrumental conditions: it points at those facts which in a particular context instantiate the salient normative bond between the agents. Furthermore, this account tallies better with our intuition that questions of obligation are 'practical', hence must be determined not by some agent-independent properties, but by agent-relevant considerations about what should be done with respect to the effects of our actions on others.

There is a further reason to question the primacy of site over scope. Recent phenomena, which we categorize under the heading of globalization, strengthen the intuition that it becomes increasingly difficult to formalize the grounds of legal obligation into sets of criteria, which can generate some invariable formula that determines what counts as the site of legal obligation. This is quite revealing in respect of views that render the state the primary site of legal obligation. Such views, usually originating in the positivist tradition, as we saw, take the facts of sovereignty to belong to the set of existence conditions that fix a pedigree test for legal obligation. Yet, as Mattias Risse submits when discussing obligations of justice:

> At a time when states share the world stage with a network of treaties and global institutions, philosophers have had to consider not only whether the state can be justified to those living under it but whether the whole global political and economic order consisting of multiple states and global institutions can be justified to those living under it. And in a world in which the most salient inequalities are not within states but among them, philosophers have had to broaden their focus for justice, too, asking not only what counts as a just distribution within the state but also what counts as a just distribution *globally*.[19]

Replace 'justice' with 'legal obligation' and the salient point turns out to be common to obligations of law and justice, namely, that any focus on state practices will not explain obligations at the international level.

It comes as a surprise then when Dworkin, in his discussion of international law, treats associative relations as limited to the site of the sovereign nation state. In the same paper mentioned earlier, he openly argues that in order to identify the scope of obligations in international law, we must ask the question from within the site of the nation state: 'what could justify the exercise of coercion by the state to its citizens?'[20] It would seem then that the scope of the associative relation, that is, the relation capable of grounding legal obligations, must remain confined to the site of the nation state which mainly includes facts about state practice. This is wanting, however, pending a more satisfactory explanation as to why associative relations ought to be identified with the state bond.

---

19 Mathias Risse, 'Introducing pluralist internationalism: An alternative approach to questions of global justice' (2013), p. 3. Available at http://www.hks.harvard.edu/fs/mrisse/Papers/Current%20 Research/IntroducingPluralistInternationalismWZBJuly2013.pdf.
20 Dworkin, 'A new philosophy'.

144 *George Pavlakos*

One plausible reason might be that Dworkin takes the existence of an associative bond to require coercive imposition by the state, initially at the domestic and derivatively at the international level.[21] This allows two interpretations. The first submits that coercion is relevant only in its instantiation as a fact of state enforcement. Or it can mean that coercion has special normative significance that makes it relevant to the grounding of legal obligations. But if the latter is the case, the normative significance of coercion should be intelligible over and above any particular instantiations thereof. Besides, taking the former route would be suspicious according to Dworkin's own lights: we know that he rejects the claim that facts about state consent can ground legal obligation. But if facts about state consent are insufficient for grounding legal obligation, why should facts about state coercion be deemed to be sufficient? Alternatively, if coercion allows some intrinsic normative significance, then *that* should be attributed to the deeper structure it has; but if so, then that structure should be capable of plural instantiations, not merely through facts about state coercion.

The second interpretation sits far better with the scope-directed inquiry into the grounds of legal obligation, one that focuses on the claims and responsibilities of agents, and was shown to be consistent with a broadly Dworkinian understanding of law. Further, it entails an explanation of legal obligation that is non-exceptionalist in rejecting the primacy of domestic state practices to the grounding of legal obligations. In what follows, I shall explore the latter line of argument, with an eye to illustrating that coercion, if at all relevant to the explanation of the associative relation and the grounding of legal obligation, is so because of the deeper normative structure it possesses.

Associative obligations: the NCC

When does the associative bond obtain? I will assume, along broadly Dworkinian lines, that political associations are coercive in a very special sense: in their interactions over time, the members of such associations are involved in mutually coercive action, as a result of which they incur a special duty of explanation or justification which they reciprocally owe to one another. That is to say, the relations between each and every member of a political association are marked by the possibility of coercion, which is arguably linked to a claim to and corresponding duty of justification. I shall discuss two candidate conceptions of coercion and ask which of the two succeeds in better explaining this relation.

The first conception takes coercion to track facts of sovereignty. This conception is at the core of a venerable tradition in legal and political philosophy, which argues that state institutions generate genuine obligations only to the extent to which they coerce citizens legitimately. Dworkin himself falls squarely in this tradition when he maintains time and again that law is about the legitimate exercise of institutional coercion. Call this *the standard account of coercion*. The standard

---

21 See Ibid. and Dworkin, *Law's Empire*, pp. 195–218.

Supra-national law is not the exception 145

account assumes that facts of enforcement trigger off principles of political morality by virtue of their purporting to direct the action of autonomous agents: those can be properly directed if, and only if, the coercive direction 'relies' on sound moral principles which govern independently the relation between the agents. Thus, the obtaining of legal obligation requires justification in the light of the appropriate principles of political morality. Along these lines, for a legal obligation to obtain, it takes the facts of enforcement to 'activate' appropriate principles of political morality.

Now a surprising conclusion of this line of thought is that, absent any fact of state enforcement, somehow the principles that govern the relations between agents remain inapplicable or, to use a figurative expression, 'silent'. This generates a paradox: all along under the standard account, coercive imposition by the state was not grounding the relevant principles. It was merely 'triggering off' or 'activating' them. Accordingly, one could plausibly assume that the relevant principles were grounded elsewhere, or in different ways.

But the assumption, if true, generates a fresh worry: by virtue of what are these principles supposed to enter the lives of the relevant agents? How are they supposed to become salient in their relations in the absence of state enforcement? In other words, even if state coercion is not necessary for grounding the said principles, it might still remain necessary for making them salient. Were that true, the absence of the state would be crucial for the existence of those principles in our lives, even though not necessary for their existence *simpliciter* (that is, in determining existence conditions for those principles). What is more, absent any fact of enforcement, no associative bond would be substantiated between interacting agents, for no justification could be demanded.[22]

Reference to facts of state enforcement gets the relation between coercion and the associative bond the wrong way round. This account starts from a pedigree test (composed by reference to some facts of sovereignty) and concludes that when those facts exist, then a normative associative relation obtains between agents. And yet, it is the normative relation we need to grasp first in order to be able to conclude which particular facts instantiate it and hence which contexts count as coercive. In other words, we are interested in the normative structure of coercion antecedent to its empirical instantiations.[23]

There is a further reason to find the standard account of coercion unsatisfactory. Recall that pedigree tests bear the mark of inquiries which focus on the site of obligations. Such accounts conclude from some pedigree test, composed of the facts of a social practice, the scope of obligations, that is, the range of

---

22 One could reconstruct one of the aspects of the recent *Kadi* case (Case T-315/01 *Kadi* v. *Council and Commission* [2005] ECR II-3649), to reflect this problem: international law in holding traditionally that only states are its subjects, cannot explain why Mr. Kadi ought to have standing before the UN. The structure of the problem generalizes to all types of non-state actors.

23 I suggest, but cannot develop further here, that the relation between the normative structure of coercion and the associative relation is constitutive: that is, a relation between agents will count as associative if it displays the normative structure of coercion.

146   *George Pavlakos*

persons who are connected by reciprocal normative claims and duties. Yet the thesis that the scope coincides with the site of an obligation is not a conceptual truth, but a substantive thesis which needs to be specifically argued for. To my knowledge, there is no such argument to be found within the standard account of coercion.

Given the shortcomings of the standard account of coercion, we may turn to another conception of coercion, which focuses on the dimension of the scope of obligations. Recall that a scope-directed inquiry is interested in such grounds of legal obligations as are capable of explaining reciprocal normative demands amongst agents. It is a kind of practical shift of focus, which moves one away from lists of existence conditions towards substantive, agency-oriented considerations that identify reasons for the evaluation of actions in the relevant contexts of appraisal.

Navigating towards substantive reasons as grounds of obligations requires that we occupy a standpoint from which substantive reasons make sense as the appropriate kind of ground. A plausible candidate is the standpoint of justification: in other words, substantive reasons make sense as the right kind of ground if they respond to demands for justification that originate in anyone whose agency is affected by the range of actions which are the subject matter of appraisal in the relevant contexts. These justificatory claims form part of a deeper normative structure of justification which links any agents who can reciprocally direct one another's actions. This, as it were, second-person[24] structure of justification plays a crucial role in determining grounds for obligations and explaining the reciprocal normative demands amongst agents. Further, it constitutes the normative standpoint through which states of affairs in the world become salient *and* serve as guides for identifying relevant grounds of legal obligation.

The conception of coercion that tracks the second-person structure of justification is a Normative Conception of Coercion (or NCC).[25] More specifically, the structure of justification which NCC tracks can be illustrated through principle 'C':[26]

> C: I should not (do y, intend by y'ing to bring it about that you do x, and fail to believe with warrant that, for some reasons R independent of me, my y'ing facilitates your [doing x because you take R as giving you sufficient reason to x]).[27]

---

24 For lending the term its philosophical significance, see Stephen Darwall, *The Second Person Standpoint: Morality, Respect, and Accountability* (Cambridge, MA: Harvard University Press, 2006).

25 See George Pavlakos and Joost Pauwelyn, 'Principled monism and the normative conception of coercion under international law', in *Beyond the Established Legal Orders: Policy Interconnections Between the EU and the Rest of the World*, eds. Malcolm Evans and Panos Koutrakos (Oxford, UK and Portland, OR: Hart Publishing, 2011); George Pavlakos, 'Legal obligation in a global context', EUI Working Papers: RSCAS 2012/16 (2012). Available at http://hdl.handle.net/1814/21758.

26 Alexander J. Julius, 'Nagel's atlas', *Philosophy & Public Affairs* 34 (2006); for discussion in the legal context, see Pavlakos, 'Legal obligation in a global context'.

27 Alexander J. Julius, 'The possibility of exchange', *Politics, Philosophy & Economics* 12 (2013): 363.

'C' is a structural principle which places agents in a reciprocal normative relation that determines, in turn, the grounds of the relevant, domain-specific legal obligations.[28] Such relations between agents, mediated by principle 'C', capture the deep structure of justification that lies in the core of political associations.

Let me take stock of the argument in the last few paragraphs: I argued earlier that political associations are coercive in the sense that their members owe special justification to one another. Having exposed the limitations of a conception of coercion that tracks facts of enforcement, I introduced the NCC as one that better captures the justificatory structure of the associative bond. No sooner, however, have we taken on board NCC than we realize that the associative relation cannot be confined to domestic law. Associative relations can materialize in any context in which NCC is at work through principle 'C', be it domestic, regional or international. Further, they may vary in density and content, depending on the domain of interaction. Accordingly, we may experience variations in the subjects and the site of obligations: whether it is the individual, a company, the state or finally the global community that bears responsibility is a matter left to substantive judgement; however, such judgement is not unrestricted but bounded by the structure of the NCC, which is given through principle 'C'.

The NCC points the way towards identifying associative relations which may obtain independently of facts of sovereignty. In the section that follows, I will proceed to adumbrate a fresh way for conceptualizing such relations and reaping their explanatory significance. I will explore in some more detail the type of relation that can generate instances of coercion in the normative sense proposed earlier, while suggesting that the constraint of justification generated by principle 'C' ultimately signifies a constraint from permissibility. Using a slightly different vocabulary, I coin the term *proto-legal relation* to characterize any instance of joint activity between agents which is subject to a constraint of permissibility. My claim will be that proto-legal relations are capable of instantiating the properties of Dworkin's associative relations and generating enforceable (legal) obligations in a manner that is independent of facts of sovereignty.

The proto-legal relation

I shall refer to a relation as *proto-legal* when it obtains between agents independently of facts of sovereignty.[29] Importantly, the proto-legal relation is capable of grounding obligations which share a core feature with standard legal obligations,[30]

---

28 Principle 'C' operates in a similar manner to a definite description. To demonstrate this point consider the case of water. A definite description of the concept 'water' would be: 'water is the odourless stuff that surrounds us'. That description helps us pick out the right property in the relevant domain (H_2O on earth; or XYZ on twin-earth and so on).

29 To put it more sharply: facts of sovereignty are not *necessary* for the proto-legal relation to obtain even though their obtaining can also ground the proto-legal relation (in other words they are *sufficient* for proto-legality).

30 'Standard legal obligation' is intended here as a useful shortcut for depicting obligations which are grounded on facts of sovereignty, along the lines of the site-oriented model of explanation.

148   *George Pavlakos*

that is, the property of *enforceability*. I will first discuss what renders a relation proto-legal and subsequently propose a way for understanding the property of enforceability.

First, proto-legal relations obtain through patterns of action which engage two or more individuals (*joint patterns of action*). Such patterns are ubiquitous in our lives: from cooking or moving a heavy table together to constructing a levee that contains the flood or planning the economy of our community, we all become subjects of such patterns. Significantly, the set of processes which are usefully captured under the label of globalization, has *created* many new instances of joint patterns of action while typically expanding the circle of actors involved in them: parent companies set up subsidiary companies in distant locations, which in turn engage with the local people through plural and complex patterns of action; immigration policies establish new patterns of action that direct the choices of foreign populations and so on. Crucially, in compressing the space between agents, globalization has significantly contributed to transforming many otherwise 'unilateral' choices and actions to instances of joint patterns of action. That is to say, globalization has intensified joint patterns of action, not just those that are grounded in some shared intention of the parties involved to participate in them (as in the cooking example) but, in addition, those that join together the actions of agents who do not partake in the same intention, by virtue of the impact their actions have on one another.[31]

What is the salient normative effect of those occurrences? Joint patterns of action impose normative constraints on the agency of the parties involved, along the lines that were suggested by principle 'C' earlier. Usefully these constraints can be understood as constraints of permissibility: that is to say, they constrain both parties to perform only actions that are permissible within the joint pattern. This applies to both types of joint pattern of action – those covered by shared intention but also, and more interestingly so, those that join the action of different agents independently of their sharing a common intention. To that extent, the constraint of permissibility becomes part of, or even constitutes, the *normative structure* of joint patterns of action.[32] Before I attempt a more detailed formulation

---

31 For the standard account of joint action, as based on shared intentions, see the work of Michael Bratman: Michael Bratman, *Intention, Plans, and Practical Reason* (Cambridge, MA: Harvard University Press, 1987); Michael Bratman, 'Intention, practical rationality, and self-governance', *Ethics* 119 (2009). For a prominent re-statement of Bratman's theory in the realm of law, see Scott Shapiro, *Legality* (Cambridge, MA: Harvard University Press, 2011). The account of joint action that forms the background of this chapter renders the idea of shared intention insufficient for capturing joint action.

32 Although I cannot discuss this further, it should be noted in passing that the normative structure is itself grounded on the autonomy of the agents engaged in the joint pattern. The capacity of joint undertakings for mutual impact on the agency of the parties involved renders them answerable to reasons, thus subjecting them to justification. To that extent, joint endeavours have a second-person structure in the sense that the parties who engage in them should look to take on board, or respect, the reasons of one another, ultimately aiming to help one another to realize the reasons each independently has. In other words, exchange, not coercion, should be the outcome of the

Supra-national law is not the exception   149

of the constraint of permissibility, let me first cast a closer look at the success and pathology of the joint patterns of action.[33]

On a good day, joint patterns turn out to be *exchanges* between the parties. This roughly means that each party engages in the pattern for reasons they have independently of the doings and sayings or the motives of the other parties.[34] During an exchange, the parties, in engaging in the joint pattern, help realize the reasons each of them independently has. Take for instance the joint action, 'You drive me to the station, I pay the fare', in which we often engage when hiring a taxi. Here the passenger and the driver partake in the joint action, 'You drive . . . I pay the fare', for reasons each has independently of the sayings and doings of the other.[35] Alas, good days are often few and far between.

On a bad day, the joint pattern fails to amount to an exchange and deteriorates into some kind of *exploitative* or *coercive* scenario: a clear instance would be something like, 'You drive . . . I refrain from shooting you'. But other, subtler instances of deterioration come to mind when, for instance, the driver is driving the taxi for an exploitative taxi owner; here the joint activity between taxi owner and taxi driver might take the form, 'You drive the taxi 15 hours a day and give the earnings to me; I let you drive it for 3 more hours in order to make a living'. What makes this activity exploitative is the fact that the driver does not have any independent reason to perform their part of the joint pattern (that is, to drive the taxi 15 hours for another person), other than the fact that the taxi owner has rendered that a condition for the driver to earn a living. A more blunt case of exploitation is blackmail: when the boss says to the employee 'You sleep with me, I promote you', the pattern proposed thereby lacks independent justification vis-à-vis the employee who is *coerced* to perform their part as a result of the employer's making it a condition for performing their part.[36]

The pathology of coercion/exploitation contributes to an understanding of the salience of the *constraint of permissibility* in the context of joint patterns of action. Let me explain how: joint patterns of action succeed (qua exchanges) if, and only if, they do not contribute to the exploitation/coercion of any of the

---

joint endeavour. For accounts that make autonomy the basis of joint action in law and politics, see Rainer Forst, 'The justification of human rights and the basic right to justification: A reflexive approach', *Ethics* 120 (2010); Kai Möller, *The Global Model of Constitutional Rights* (Oxford, UK: Oxford University Press, 2012).

33 I would not have arrived at this account had it not been for the seminal work of A. J. Julius; see: Julius, 'The possibility of exchange'; Alexander J. Julius, *Reconstruction* (book draft, 12 July 2013), p. 145. Available at http://www.ajjulius.net/reconstruction.pdf.

34 Julius, 'The possibility of exchange'.

35 Such reasons may be explained either by reference to the reciprocal promises actors make (contract) or – on a deeper explanation – the reasons that predate the promissory act (my reason to go to place X; the driver's reason to make a good living and so on).

36 These pathologies are cases in which principle 'C' is violated. It is precisely in this manner that one or some of the parties are 'coerced' in the normative sense, by being directed to act in violation of the reasons they have independently of the pattern of action at hand.

150   *George Pavlakos*

parties involved.[37] Otherwise, cases of coercion/exploitation count as instances of wrongdoing.[38] For the purposes of the present discussion, a plausible way of understanding wrongdoing is through the idea of hindrance of freedom.[39] Under this explication, exploitative or coercive patterns hinder the freedom of the coercee in disregarding the coercee's independent reasons for participating in the pattern.

What may count as a hindrance of freedom, on this understanding, is determined by the impact it has on the capacity of the coercee to determine their participation in the joint pattern according to the reasons they have. Thus, any manipulation of the environment by the coercer, or any other intervention that modifies the reasons of the coercee in a manner that prevents the latter from acting on the reasons she actually has, would count as hindrance of freedom.[40] If a corporation imposes exploitative terms on its employees or otherwise coerces those who live in the environment in which it is active, these actions would constitute hindrances of freedom, violating the constraint of permissibility of the relevant joint pattern of action.[41]

The most important normative consequence of the constraint of permissibility is that it requires joint patterns of action to contribute to each person's acting consistently with the actions of others.[42] Contribution of the required kind takes place when patterns of action facilitate exchange and, conversely, hinder coercion/exploitation. Patterns that facilitate exchange do so by virtue of certain features they possess (facilitating features), which are shared by each of them. These facilitating features can be formulated through general principles that generate obligations akin to those we encounter in human rights and other precepts of justice. Importantly, those obligations are jointly shared by everyone who partakes in the relevant patterns.

---

37 Julius further requires that these patterns help realize the reasons of those involved; see Julius, *Reconstruction*. We may remain agnostic about this stronger condition for present purposes.

38 Recall that the account was deemed wrongdoing-sensitive precisely for that reason. See earlier in the chapter.

39 Wrongdoing is often defined through harm (see, for instance, the so-called 'Maastricht principles on extraterritorial obligations of states in the area of economic, social and cultural rights'). To the extent that the definition relies on a standard understanding of harm as reduction of welfare, one should caution against it. Wrongdoing does not overlap with reduction of harm so conceived, for wrongdoing aims to cover instances of interference with freedom/autonomy which do not amount to any loss of welfare (so-called instances of harmless wrongdoing: say, if I avail myself of your car without your permission, damage it, and subsequently replace it with a better one, I will still count as having wronged you). See, for an excellent discussion of the relevant conceptual distinction, Arthur Ripstein, *Force and Freedom* (Cambridge, MA: Harvard University Press, 2009), pp. 42–50.

40 Julius, *Reconstruction*.

41 A more specific aspect of wrongdoing relates to the various kinds of means we each use to achieve our ends. The use of any material resources must comply with such conditions, which ensure that the use of, say, chattels and land does not hinder the freedom of others. Notably, Kant believes that any unilateral use of property that is not based on publicly promulgated rules would count as wrongful. See for extensive discussion, Ripstein, *Force and Freedom*.

42 There exists, of course, a class of joint patterns of action in which permissibility does not feature prominently or at all. Such cases include *de minimis* infringements or special relations within which the hindrance of freedom is justified through some thick moral reasons (special relations, such as family or club membership).

Supra-national law is not the exception   151

Let me take stock and gesture at an interim conclusion. I argued that the proto-legal relation pertains to joint patterns of action such as those that trigger off a constraint of permissibility.[43] The normative environment of the proto-legal relation grounds general principles that impose obligations which are jointly shared by every actor that partakes of joint patterns of action of the kind described. If my account were sound, then it would seem that something like the proto-legal relation meets all the requirements of what I earlier labeled 'legal relation' without requiring any dedication to institutional facts of a certain kind. Focusing on the proto-legal relation would also take us beyond a site-oriented inquiry that is wedded to facts of sovereignty. What, instead, would become salient is the normative relation between agents in itself, not the social facts that determine one version of that relation (that is, within the domestic state). Finally, the account would be able to draw the conclusion that joint patterns of action *plus* the condition of permissibility (the two key ingredients of 'proto-legality') are capable of grounding obligations whose content and normative force is not dissimilar to the kind of obligation we usually call legal. Accordingly, it would open our eyes to all those other instances of interaction which can generate legal obligations, a fact that had been obfuscated by the dedication of the standard picture to one specific site for legal obligation. For, in disentangling the content of the salient normative relation from a preconceived test of site, proto-legality helps us recover the normative space, which is prominent in and largely constituted by transnational contexts.

Let me linger on the structural similarities between the proto-legal and legal relation before I turn to the property of enforceability, which I believe is a core feature shared by the obligations that are grounded in the legal and proto-legal relation alike. Famously, Kant took instances of wrongdoing in the interaction between actors to constitute the opposite of the *rightful condition* as the condition that enables each actor to act consistently with the actions of everyone else. [44] Leaving out a lot of detail, Kant considered the rightful condition to be possible only within a system of publicly authorized norms which can exist only within the confines of a positive legal order. Legal norms, in being equipped with sanctions, have the capacity to 'hinder the hindrance of freedom' and thus restore instances of wrongdoing to the rightful condition. The details of the Kantian account aside, it turns out that what I have called a proto-legal relation aims precisely at the whereabouts of the rightful condition, in Kant's terms. The proto-legal relation displays a normative structure that is identical to that of the rightful condition, that of enabling each actor to act consistently with the actions of everyone else. Does this entail that the obligations grounded by the proto-legal relation be legal in the full sense, that is, share the features of the obligations we have in the rightful condition?

---

43 Such constraints of responsibility include human rights obligations and obligations from distributive justice alike. The formulation needs to remain general in order to capture any obligation-imposing principle which aims to enable exchange and/or disable exploitation.

44 See Immanuel Kant, '"The Doctrine of Right", Part I of the metaphysics of morals', in *Practical Philosophy*, trans. and ed. Mary Gregor (Cambridge, UK: Cambridge University Press 1996); also the very instructive overview in the first chapter of Ripstein, *Force and Freedom*, pp. 1–29.

152   *George Pavlakos*

A careful Kantian might caution against such an equation on two grounds: first, she would argue, obligations in the rightful condition take off the ground only as *publicly (omnilaterally) authorized* norms which are enshrined in positive rules of law.[45] If that objection were sound it would be damaging for the present account, as it would make state-related institutions a fresh part of the condition for the obtaining of the kind of obligations I am interested in. The second objection is somewhat different, albeit related: nothing can be called a legal obligation unless it is equipped with enforcement. Thus, even if one could conceive something like the proto-legal relation as a source of public or omnilateral obligations, these would not be the obligations of the rightful condition. Ultimately, a crude version of the objection would run: legal obligations require states and their institutions.

The objection from public authorization is challenging. To begin with, Kant does not give any democratic gloss to public or omnilateral authorization. Rather, his concern is that the norms introducing obligations should not originate unilaterally from any individual actor, or else they would impose, in their unilateral character, an impermissible constraint on others. Whether the property of publicity requires a particular kind of institution (a state) is a further issue that cannot be resolved solely by reference to publicity itself, not at least to the extent to which publicity does not require democratic authorization. The structure of the proto-legal relation, as outlined earlier, can deal with the challenge of omnilateral authorization without requiring reference to the state: we saw there that *that* relation grounds general principles which outline the general features of joint patterns of action that facilitate mutual consistent action. Such principles make it the case that, when acting within the joint pattern of action, agents are acting out of reasons they themselves share, thereby rendering their joint endeavour an exchange rather than exploitation/ coercion. To that extent, the obligations entailed by the principles that facilitate exchange purport to be omnilaterally authorized, for they purport to prevent wrongdoing. While the precise nature of omnilateral authorization will need to be elaborated further, it suffices for now to point out that it does not stand in opposition to the normative structure of the proto-legal relation.

The second objection is stronger, but for that reason perhaps easier to rebut: it says, in a nutshell, that no obligation can be rendered legal unless it is coupled with enforcement. I believe that this view rests on a misunderstanding which I will seek to dispel in the subsection that follows. Very briefly, the point will be that proto-legal obligations share with law a property with a much deeper significance than enforcement: that is, the property of enforceability. I will argue that enforceability is distinct from enforcement and also a more fundamental feature of legal obligation than the latter. It is more fundamental to the extent to which it meets the conditions set by the rightful condition when it comes to the grounding of legal obligations. Conversely, enforcement plays no role in the grounding of legal obligations and only refers to the various factual possibilities for the realization of enforceable obligations. That said, enforcement still retains a normative

---

45 For the idea of omnilateral authorization, see Ripstein, *Force and Freedom*, pp. 148–159.

Supra-national law is not the exception   153

significance, however it is one that can be appreciated only in the light of the normative significance of enforceability.

Enforceability and enforcement

I shall now turn to argue that a key feature of the obligations grounded by proto-legal relations is enforceability. Earlier I argued that the proto-legal relation grounds principles that account for the general features of joint patterns of action which help persons to act consistently with the actions of others. Further, I submitted that those principles entail obligations which are jointly shared by everyone within the overall scheme of joint patterns of action. I will now seek to explain a further claim about such obligations, that is, the claim that they are enforceable. Subsequently, I shall suggest that the same property of enforceability is shared by the obligations of the rightful condition, which are the standard instances of legal obligation. This will help me to corroborate the conclusion that proto-legal obligations are much like the obligations of the rightful condition. I will conclude with some remarks on the significance of enforcement.

Proto-legal obligations are *enforceable* in the sense that the coercee has a claim vis-à-vis the coercer that she abide by the relevant course of action or that she be made to perform some other action/omission for failing to do so. The claim/right of the coercee is part of the content/meaning of the obligation, which makes it the case that there arises an authorization or 'standing' over the coercer's agency that she be made to do as the obligation says. That is to say, the precise content of any such obligation to Φ is 'you ought to Φ and *can be made* to Φ'. Suppose, for the sake of demonstration, that I pass on to someone false information in the context of a promise or, more broadly, some other assurance-evoking exchange: for example, I indicate to Mary that she can have my car tomorrow in order to pick up her friend from the airport, but proceed to give my car to John instead. My obligation to Mary is enforceable, for part of its content is that I be made to comply with it, irrespective of whether I am motivated (intend, etc.) to do so or not.[46] While the objection of the standard picture theorist is that lack of any mechanism of enforcement would deprive those obligations of enforceability, there is an emerging consensus amongst scholars that this is not so.[47]

---

46 This case can be helpfully contrasted with one of a purely moral, non-enforceable obligation. Take a general obligation not to lie: suppose I am boasting to someone about being very prominent in some way (say, in being on first-name terms with President Obama). Should it turn out that I am lying, the other person may think ill of me or pass negative judgement about my character. However, there is no ground to suggest that they have a claim that I retract my lie or that I otherwise compensate them for having lied to them. As a result, enforceability sets apart the relevant joint obligations from other moral obligations which are owed in a first instance merely unilaterally.

47 The argument has been developed with regard to the binding force of *jus cogens* and its impact on determining the scope of obligations under international law. In summary, it is argued that *jus cogens* determines the content and scope of international law obligations irrespective of the consent of actors, or the undertaking of any institutional acts relating to its validation or enforcement. Compare with Dworkin, 'A new philosophy'.

154   *George Pavlakos*

Arguably, this is what obligations are like in the rightful condition. The rightful condition, much as the proto-legal relation, aims to facilitate persons' acting in a way that is consistent with the actions of others. In it, legal norms formulate patterns of action which regulate the action of everyone in a manner that is consistent with the action of every other person, much as the patterns established by the proto-legal relation do. Crucially, what generates enforceability in the strictly legal case (that is, the rightful condition) is not the possibility of enforcement, which is attached to institutional norms, but the normative structure of the relation that pertains amongst agents: enforceability is part and parcel of any joint pattern that aims to help agents to engage in a consistent scheme of coinciding actions. For, in any such scheme, the reasons for acting are removed from the disposal of each agent individually and become subject to a normative constraint about what counts as an action that is consistent with the action of every other.

Notice what may, at first glance, strike us as paradoxical: what would count, within a joint scheme/pattern, as acting for the reasons I have (and not as a 'reaction' to others' coercive moves) would after all be determined not by me but by the pattern in which I partake. There is no paradox here, however, because acting (as part of a joint pattern) for the reasons 'I have' does not mean that the reasons I choose to act on are 'up to me'. The reasons I have are the reasons I *may* (as in: may permissibly) have; and I may have only those reasons that make my action compossible with the actions of others, or else permissible. Such reasons turn out to be determined by the principles that outline the general features of the joint scheme of compossible action.

Helpfully, this way of understanding enforceable obligations sheds a lot of light on a feature of law, which often is expressed by saying that the law aims to regulate *external conduct* leaving outwith its purview the internal conviction of agents. Now, if regulating 'external conduct' just meant that the law imposes on people obligations irrespective of the reasons they have, the law would be achieving consistency of action without aiming at exchange. Such an interpretation – consistent as it may be with the standard picture of legal obligation – falls massively short of the standard set by the *rightful condition*. Rather, to grasp the point about law's focus on 'external conduct', in a manner consistent with the rightful condition, we need to interpret legal obligations as proto-legal, that is, enforceable obligations that aim to safeguard joint patterns of action through which consistency of action is achieved. Now, at last, the point about confining legal regulation to external conduct becomes clear: in the proto-legal relation, the reasons of the agents and the obligations imposed by the joint pattern do not come apart. The agents are jointly obligated to act on patterns of external conduct which secure consistency of action. These are their reasons and, at that, they are external reasons.[48]

---

48 See, for an attempt to spell out this argument in the context of Kant's legal philosophy, George Pavlakos, 'Coercion and the grounds of legal obligation: Arthur Ripstein's *Force and Freedom*', *Jurisprudence* 1 (2010); George Pavlakos, 'Why is willing irrelevant to the grounding of (any) obligation? Remarks on Arthur Ripstein's conception of omnilateral willing', in *Freedom and Force: Essays on Kant's Legal Philosophy*, eds. Sari Kisilevsky and M.J. Stone (Oxford, UK and Portland, OR: Hart Publishing, 2016).

Supra-national law is not the exception 155

Accordingly, any obligations that arise from proto-legal relations already 'have one foot' in the legal realm, because they possess the same property of enforceability as do legal obligations. A key feature of this property, you will recall, is that the content of the obligation contains an authorization over the conduct of the agent who is subject to it. If the earlier analysis is correct, then there is no independent account of the legal relation or 'legality' upon which a distinction between some special legal and other enforceable obligations can rest. Any account of the legality of an obligation will first have to demonstrate its enforceability before it can lay claim to its legality. But if that is the right order of explanation, then 'legality' is on course to a slippery slope which makes it very difficult to recover its autonomy through reference to more facts (including facts of enforcement) about the state and its institutions.

The role of enforcement

It turns out that the proto-legal relation can ground by itself the property of enforceability, which arguably counts as the key feature of legal obligations. I argued that in two steps, first by suggesting that the legal relation, qua relation that grounds legal obligations, aims to secure a rightful condition. In a further step, I suggested that the rightful condition is simply a proto-legal relation. To the extent to which the conclusion stands, it supplies a strong indication against any views that wish to distinguish legal obligation as a special kind of enforceable obligation. Typically, such views focus on enforcement (or sanctions) in order to support that distinction.

For the moment, I will rely on the strong indication that my account offers against such views and, instead of putting forward a more detailed argument, shall seek to explore the function and role of enforcement with respect to enforceable obligations. For, even though my account suggests that enforcement does not play any special role in the grounding of (any) enforceable obligation, it still considers enforcement to have normative significance in respect of enforceable obligations, which otherwise are grounded independently of it. What is interesting is that the role of enforcement I am about to adumbrate is not confined to only some enforceable obligations. Having argued against any fundamental distinction between legal and any other enforceable obligation, I will suggest that the normative significance of enforcement, whatever that turns out to be, will attach, in principle, to all enforceable obligations.[49]

The relation that accounts for the property of the enforceability of obligations needs to be strictly divorced from enforcement (actual or possible, within

---

49 I need to draw a caveat here: for some enforceable obligations, it might even be inappropriate actually to introduce enforcement. Take, for instance, a joint pattern of action aimed at moving a heavy object (for example, a large table). In this case, and despite the fact that an enforceable obligation is in place, it would be otiose to argue that some enforcement mechanism ought to be in place – at least for as long as the stakes remain low.

156   *George Pavlakos*

some available institutional context). Facts of enforcement are not constitutive to the proto-legal relation, hence, to the obligations pertaining to it. However, enforcement remains normatively relevant in the following sense: the proto-legal relation, in realizing the rightful condition, cannot afford a unilateral imposition of enforceable obligations; in other words, it frowns upon any of the actors involved who take upon themselves the task of enforcing the obligation. For any such unilateral enforcement would make it impossible for a scheme to act consistently with the action of everyone else which, after all, is part of what the rightful condition requires. Instead, enforcement should be entrusted to institutional arrangements which form a public or omnilateral scheme for realizing the relevant enforceable obligations. Accordingly, the requirement for the publicity of enforcement in fact becomes part of the content of the principles that formulate the general features of the joint scheme which aims at consistency of action.

While the requirement of publicity confers a prima facie presumption in favour of state-based enforcement, nothing precludes other institutional arrangements from taking up that role. To that extent, a certain amount of *pluralism* is in order: it is conceivable that public/omnilateral institutions of a non-state (that is, sub-state or supra-state) nature can meet the task of enforcement. As a result, different parts of the existing international legal order can be combined with a view to addressing instances of wrongdoing which cut across the established domestic legal orders.[50]

Finally, one other aspect of the normative significance of enforcement comes into play: because public or omnilateral enforcement is a requirement grounded in the principles that determine the scheme for the consistency of action, it can be plausibly argued that the actors involved incur secondary obligations to set up institutions which can appropriately enforce the obligations that arise from those principles.[51] Notice, however, that here again it is the force of the enforceable

---

50 A prominent example of combining the enforcement mechanisms of different institutional orders is displayed by the reasoning strategy of the ECJ in Case T-315/01 *Kadi* v. *Council and Commission* [2005] ECR II-3649. For additional examples and some useful comparisons, see the discussion in Pavlakos and Pauwelyn, 'Principled monism'.

51 A comparison with Kant's obligation to enter the rightful condition might be instructive at this juncture. Kant famously argued that everyone in the state of nature has an obligation, and, at that, one that is enforceable, to enter the rightful condition. This formulation might give rise to a misunderstanding that Kant's obligation merely focuses on setting up institutional mechanisms of enforcement. The account of the chapter helpfully dispels the misunderstanding: Kant's obligation to enter the rightful condition is explained as the sum of all those obligations which are generated by the principles that formulate the general features of the rightful condition (that is, a joint scheme of action that aims to generate consistency). For, on the present account, we become subject to those principles each time we engage in joint patterns of action by virtue of the constraint of permissibility that such patterns trigger. Accordingly, enforcement makes no distinct contribution to the existence conditions of the rightful condition. The obligation to set up appropriate mechanisms of enforcement is just one amongst the obligations of the rightful condition and, at that, one that serves an instrumental goal.

Supra-national law is not the exception 157

obligations of the proto-legal relation that explain the secondary obligation to set up institutions of enforcement, rather than the other way round.

Bibliography

Abizadeh, Arash. 'Cooperation, pervasive impact, and coercion: On the scope (not site) of distributive justice'. *Philosophy and Public Affairs* 35 (2007): 318–358.

Bratman, Michael. *Intention, Plans, and Practical Reason.* Cambridge, MA: Harvard University Press, 1987.

Bratman, Michael. 'Intention, practical rationality, and self-governance'. *Ethics* 119 (2009): 411–443.

Collins, Richard. 'No longer at the vanishing point? International law and the analytical tradition in jurisprudence'. *Jurisprudence* 5 (2014): 265–298.

Darwall, Stephen. *The Second Person Standpoint: Morality, Respect, and Accountability.* Cambridge, MA: Harvard University Press, 2006.

Dworkin, Ronald. *Law's Empire.* London: Fontana Press, 1986.

Dworkin, Ronald. *Justice for Hedgehogs.* Cambridge, MA: Harvard University Press, 2011.

Dworkin, Ronald. 'A new philosophy for international law'. *Philosophy and Public Affairs* 41 (2013): 2–30.

Forst, Rainer. 'The justification of human rights and the basic right to justification: A reflexive approach.' *Ethics* 120 (2010): 711–740.

Hart, H.L.A. *The Concept of Law.* Oxford, UK: Clarendon Press, 1961.

Julius, Alexander J. 'Nagel's atlas'. *Philosophy & Public Affairs* 34 (2006): 176–192.

Julius Alexander J. *Reconstruction.* Book draft, 12 July 2013. Available at http://www.ajjulius.net/reconstruction.pdf.

Julius, Alexander J. 'The possibility of exchange'. *Politics, Philosophy & Economics* 12 (2013): 361–374.

Kant, Immanuel. '"The Doctrine of Right", Part I of the metaphysics of morals'. In *Practical Philosophy*, translated and edited by Mary Gregor. Cambridge, UK: Cambridge University Press, 1996.

Kumm, Mattias. 'The moral point of constitutional pluralism'. In *Philosophical Foundations of EU Law*, edited by Julie Dickson and Pavlos Eleftheriadis. Oxford, UK: Oxford University Press, 2012, pp. 216–246.

Möller, Kai. *The Global Model of Constitutional Rights.* Oxford, UK: Oxford University Press, 2012.

Pavlakos, George. 'Coercion and the grounds of legal obligation: Arthur Ripstein's *Force and Freedom*'. *Jurisprudence* 1 (2010): 305–316.

Pavlakos, George. 'Legal obligation in a global context'. EUI Working Papers, RSCAS 2012/16, 2012. Available at http://hdl.handle.net/1814/21758.

Pavlakos, George. 'Transnational legal responsibility: Some preliminaries'. In *Challenging Territoriality in Human Rights Law. Foundational Principles for a Multi Duty-Bearer Human Rights Regime*, edited by Wouter Vandenhole. Abingdon, UK and New York: Routledge, 2015, pp. 136–157.

Pavlakos, George. 'Why is willing irrelevant to the grounding of (any) obligation? Remarks on Arthur Ripstein's conception of omnilateral willing'. In *Freedom and Force: Essays on Kant's Legal Philosophy*, edited by Sari Kisilevsky and M.J. Stone. Oxford, UK and Portland, OR: Hart Publishing, 2016.

Pavlakos, George and Joost Pauwelyn. 'Principled monism and the normative conception of coercion under international law'. In *Beyond the Established Legal Orders: Policy Interconnections between the EU and the Rest of the World*, edited by Malcolm Evans and Panos Koutrakos. Oxford, UK and Portland, OR: Hart Publishing, 2011, pp. 317–341.

Ripstein, Arthur. *Force and Freedom*. Cambridge, MA: Harvard University Press, 2009.

Risse, Mathias. 'Introducing pluralist internationalism: An alternative approach to questions of global justice' (2013). Available at http://www.hks.harvard.edu/fs/mrisse/Papers/Current%20Research/IntroducingPluralistInternationalismWZBJuly2013.pdf.

Shapiro, Scott. *Legality*. Cambridge, MA: Harvard University Press, 2011.

7 Declaratory rule of law
Self-constitution through unenforceable promises[*]

Dimitry Kochenov

Introduction

The EU is presumed to be a rule of law[1] Union. This is the traditional vision[2] pre-dating the first references to the rule of law in the Treaties and also the *Les Verts* judgment of the Court of Justice (ECJ).[3] The self-vision of the Union in this regard is absolutely solid. While the very assumption, which is seemingly built into this solidity, that the rule of law in the EU should amount to mere legality – internal rule-making coherence in a largely autopoietic system of rules[4] – can

---

[*] I would like to thank all the colleagues who engaged with my thoughts, presented, inter alia in Amsterdam, Berlin, Cardiff, Florence, New York, Princeton and Tilburg, especially Professors Carlos Closa, Jan-Werner Müller, Gianluigi Palombella, Laurent Pech, Wojciech Sadurski and Kim Lane Scheppele. Special thanks to Jiří Přibáň for patience and kind support. An extended version of the same argument will appear at the beginning of 2016 in a collection edited by Maurice Adams *et al.*, entitled 'Constitutionalism and the rule of law, bridging idealism and realism'.

[1] For a most comprehensive treatment of EU Rule of Law, see Laurent Pech, 'The rule of law as a constitutional principle of the European Union', Jean Monnet Working Paper no. 04/09 (2009). For a special 'Eastern-European' perspective, which is particularly important in the context of the on-going developments in the EU, see Jiří Přibáň, 'From 'which rule of law?' to 'the rule of which law?': Post-communist experiences of European legal integration', *Hague Journal on the Rule of Law* 1 (2009).

[2] Lord Mackenzie Stuart, *The European Communities and the Rule of Law* (London: Stevens and Sons, 1977). See also, Gerhard Bebr, *Rule of Law within the European Communities* (Brussels, Belgium: Institut d'Etudes Européennes de l'Université Libre de Bruxelles, 1965). For more classical accounts, see Maria Luisa Fernandez Esteban, *The Rule of Law in the European Constitution* (The Hague, The Netherlands: Kluwer Law International, 1999); also, Ulrich Everling, 'The European Union as a federal association of states and citizens', in *Principles of European Constitutional Law*, eds. Armin von Bogdandy and Jürgen Bast (second edition, Oxford, UK and Munich, Germany: Hart Publishing/CH Beck, 2010); Manfred Zuleeg, 'The advantages of the European constitution', in Von Bogdandy and Bast, eds., ibid., pp. 772–779.

[3] Case 294/83 *Partie Ecologiste 'Les Verts'* v. *Parliament* [1986] ECR 1339, 23. See, also, Opinion 1/91 *EEA Agreement* [1991] ECR I-6079.

[4] See, for the most recent proof, Opinion 2/13 (*ECHR Accession II*) [2014] ECLI:EU:C:2014:2454. See also, Marco Goldoni, 'The pluralist turn and its political discontents', in this volume; G. Letsas, 'Harmonic law: The case against pluralism', in *Philosophical Foundations of European Union Law*, eds. Julie Dickson and Pavlos Eleftheriadis (Oxford, UK: Oxford University Press, 2012).

160 *Dimitry Kochenov*

certainly be questioned, as has been done, for instance, in the scholarship of Gianluigi Palombella on the rule of law as an 'institutional ideal',[5] this chapter will not venture into the terrain of attacking the starting premise, something the author has done elsewhere.[6] What it aims at, instead, is mapping a somewhat more complex picture of the practical operation of the rule of law in the context of EU constitutionalism and of the promises it entails, which, it is submitted, is closer to the reality on the ground than the official eurospeak of the 'EU has rule of law because it is bound by law' – which would be a rough summary of most of the literature on the subject. Indeed, the picture is bound to be (much) more complex than that as 'the rule of law cannot mean just the self-referentiality of a legal order',[7] as Palombella rightly pointed out. In this context, once one admits that simple tautologies do not always work, a stricter scrutiny of the whole operation of the principle is necessary – the necessity, which this chapter aims to clarify and bring to light. It is thus crucial to move beyond the focus on enforcement,[8] which seems to be holding the rule of law literature hostage at the moment.

The argument of this chapter is that Europe's structural constitutional vulnerability stretches far beyond rule of law enforcement issues per se.[9] The EU is thus facing, it is argued, a structural deficiency in the rule of law field,

---

5 Gianluigi Palombella, *È possibile la legalità globale?* (Bologna, Italy: Il Mulino, 2012); Gianluigi Palombella, 'The rule of law and its core', in *Relocating the Rule of Law*, eds. Gianluigi Palombella and Neil Walker (Oxford, UK: Hart Publishing, 2009). See, also, Gianluigi Palombella, 'Beyond legality – before democracy: Rule of law caveats in the EU two-level system', in *Reinforcing Rule of Law Oversight in the European Union*, eds. Carlos Closa and Dimitry Kochenov (Cambridge, UK: Cambridge University Press, 2016).

6 Dimitry Kochenov, 'EU law without the rule of law: Is the veneration of autonomy worth it?', *Yearbook of European Law* 34 (2015).

7 Gianluigi Palombella, 'Beyond legality – before democracy: Rule of law caveats in the EU two-level system', in Closa and Kochenov, eds., ibid. Compare with Krygier: 'To try to capture this elusive phenomenon by focusing on characteristics of laws and legal institutions is, I believe, to start in the wrong place and move in the wrong direction': M. Krygier, 'The rule of law. An abuser's guide', in *Abuse: The Dark Side of Fundamental Rights*, ed. András Sajó (Utrecht, The Netherlands: Eleven International Publishing, 2006), p. 131.

8 For a detailed analysis of all the key proposals related to the improvement of the enforcement of the rule of law in the EU, see, C. Closa, D. Kochenov and J.H.H. Weiler, 'Reinforcing rule of law oversight in the European Union', EUI Florence: RSCAS Paper No. 2014/25 (2014); Editorial comments, 'Safeguarding EU values in the member states – is something finally happening?', *Common Market Law Review* 52 (2015): 619. See, also, Closa and Kochenov, eds., *Reinforcing Rule of Law*; Jan-Werner Müller, 'The EU as a militant democracy, or: Are there limits to constitutional mutations within the member states?', *Revista de Estudios Políticos* 164 (2014). Kim Lane Scheppele, 'Enforcing the basic principles of EU law through systemic infringement actions', in Closa and Kochenov, eds., ibid. See, also, Armin von Bogdandy and Pál Sonnevend, eds., *Constitutional Crisis in the European Constitutional Area: Theory, Law and Politics in Hungary and Romania* (Oxford, UK: Hart Publishing, 2015).

9 On the latter, see, for example, the contributions in András Jakab and Dimitry Kochenov, eds., *The Enforcement of EU Law and Values: Methods against Defiance* (Oxford, UK: Oxford University Press, forthcoming).

Self-constitution: unenforceable promises   161

which concerns both the supranational and the national legal orders to an equal degree. In the light of this structural deficiency, one can argue that the much analysed 'systemic deficiency'[10] in the area of values and, especially, the rule of law, was bound to emerge sooner or later, whether in Hungary or elsewhere,[11] as the Union matured.[12] Dealing with it will necessarily require the reinvention of the place that values actually occupy in the edifice of EU integration, thus reforming the integration project as such,[13] moving beyond the enforcement of particular rules and re-constitutionalizing the substance of the Union in Europe.

Several starting points need to be clarified right away, to make it absolutely clear where this contribution is going. It presumes (rightly, it argues) that the *acquis* on *values* is not quite the same as 'ordinary' *acquis*. This presumption is reached by observing the process of the distillation of the substance of the two, as well as the obvious *ratione materiae* limitations, which arise in the context of reading Article 2 of the Treaty of European Union (TEU) with a practice-oriented eye.[14] This chapter states that the difference between the two – that is, the values and the *acquis* ('the law') – is not confined to that of the scope of the EU's possible intervention, but obviously covers the *substance* of the rules in question: the latter is infinitely clearer, once the letter and the spirit of the *acquis* is at stake, as opposed to the 'values'. This holds true even for the pre-accession context, where the institutions, most notably the Commission, made an important (and markedly unsuccessful) attempt to bridge this divide.[15] There is a third difference between the two: values are infinitely more difficult to enforce (as well as to breach, one would presume) than the 'law'. What is relatively easy and straightforward with the latter is – still – an unchartered terrain with the former, which explains the excessive focus on the enforcement aspects of the practical operation of values in the literature today. The starting point of this contribution is thus the triple difference

---

10 Armin von Bogdandy and Michael Ioannidis, 'Systemic deficiency in the rule of law: What it is, what has been done, what can be done', *Common Market Law Review* 51 (2014).

11 On the Hungarian developments, in particular, see, László Sólyom, 'The rise and decline of constitutional culture in Hungary', in von Bogdandy and Sonnevend, eds., *Constitutional Crisis in the European Constitutional Area: Theory, Law and Politics in Hungary and Romania*; Miklós Bánkuti, Gábor Halmai and Kim Lane Scheppele, 'Hungary's illiberal turn: Disabling the constitution', *Journal of Democracy* 23 (2012): 138. See also, Renata Uitz, 'Can you tell when an illiberal democracy is in the making? An appeal to comparative constitutional scholarship from Hungary', *I-CON* 13 (2015): 279.

12 For a broad discussion, see Dimitry Kochenov, Gráinne de Búrca and Andrew Williams, eds., *Europe's Justice Deficit?* (Oxford, UK: Hart Publishing, 2015).

13 For a much more critical restatement of this particular argument, see Dimitry Kochenov, 'EU law without the rule of law' and Joseph H.H. Weiler, 'Epilogue: Living in a glass house: Europe, democracy and the rule of law', both in Closa and Kochenov, eds., *Reinforcing Rule of Law*.

14 See also Christophe Hillion, 'Overseeing the rule of law in the EU: Legal mandate and means', in Closa and Kochenov (eds.), *Reinforcing Rule of Law*.

15 Dimitry Kochenov, *EU Enlargement and the Failure of Conditionality: Pre-Accession Conditionality in the Field of Democracy and the Rule of Law* (The Hague, The Netherlands: Kluwer Law International, 2008).

162 *Dimitry Kochenov*

between the law and values of European integration: scope, substance and enforceability. The key point the contribution is making is, then, overwhelmingly simple: looking at one of the three in isolation from the other two will most likely be meaningless, which adds complexity to the standard picture of the EU as a rule of law Union.

A much more fundamental problem plaguing the EU, whether we notice it or not, is the elephant in the room: once the 'values' emerge as ephemeral – and thus even possibly inoperable – at the three levels mentioned above, what is then the basis of the 'law'? This question, which is very far from rhetorical, is worthy of serious consideration, but will not be the central feature of this chapter.[16] It should necessarily be kept in mind at all times, when any issues of values are brought up in the context of European integration.

Founding ideas and contemporary presumptions

It is not for nothing that, thinking about the EU, democracy or human rights protection is the last thing that comes to mind, lagging far behind bananas, motorcycle trailers or the prohibition on deporting foreign prostitutes (as long as they are not a burden on a social security system). This is because democracy and the rule of law are *not* the EU's founding ideas or, paraphrasing Joseph Weiler, are not in the EU's DNA,[17] notwithstanding constant rhetorical adherence to both. They are thus seemingly left entirely as the concern of the member states.[18] This is a serious design flaw, which was probably difficult to anticipate from the very beginning. The issue only became problematic as a result of a certain path that the Union has followed throughout its history, emerging as a dynamic federal constitutional system and digesting more and more competences, turning into an indispensable element of the legal-political climate in Europe.[19]

The EU's gradual rise to its current constitutional prominence is connected to a most fundamental deficiency of the Union related to its professed values. By and large, they do not inform the day-to-day functioning of EU law, either

---

16 For more on this and related questions, see Andrew Williams, *The Ethos of Europe* (Cambridge, UK: Cambridge University Press, 2009) and Kochenov, de Búrca and Williams, eds., *Europe's Justice Deficit?*

17 Joseph H.H. Weiler, 'The Schuman declaration as a manifesto of political messianism', in *Philosophical Foundations of European Union Law*, eds. Julie Dickson and Pavlos Eleftheriadis (Oxford, UK: Oxford University Press, 2012).

18 The issue underlined by the Council Legal Service in its Opinion on the Commission's pre-Article 7 procedure.

19 Robert Schütze, *From Dual to Cooperative Federalism: The Changing Structure of European Law* (Oxford, UK: Oxford University Press, 2009). See, also, Koen Lenaerts and Kathleen Gutman, '"Federal common law" in the European Union: A comparative perspective from the United States', *American Journal of Comparative Law* 54 (2006); Jean-Claude Piris, 'L'Union européenne: Vers une nouvelle forme de fédéralisme?', *Revue trimestrielle de droit européenne* 41 (2004).

internally[20] or externally.[21] Indeed, unless we take the Commission's propaganda for granted, the EU's steering of countless issues directly related to the values at hand is more problematic than not: the EU itself is obviously not about the values Article 2 TEU preaches, which any student of EU law and politics will readily confirm.[22] The EU's very self-definition is not about human rights, the rule of law or democracy. EU law functions differently; there is a whole other set of principles which actually matter and are held dear: supremacy, direct effect and autonomy is the key trio that comes to mind. Operating together, they can set aside both national constitutional[23] – and international human rights[24] and UN law constraints.[25] In the current crisis-rich environment[26] it seems almost self-evident that, for the Union to survive, this will most likely have to change.

Assuming a particular type of constitutionalism

Such a change will mean, at least partially, a return to the promise of EU integration made in the days of the Union's inception.[27] A *fédération européenne* (the one mentioned in the Schuman Declaration) to be brought about via the creation of the internal market, stood for something significantly more far reaching than the idea of economic integration as such. The former is value based, while the latter

---

20 Joseph H.H. Weiler, 'Europa: "Nous coalisons des Etats, nous n'unissons pas des hommes"', in *La sostenibilità della democrazia nel XXI secolo*, eds. Marta Cartabia and Andrea Simoncini (Bologna, Italy: Il Mulino, 2009); Williams, *The Ethos of Europe*.

21 For critical engagements, see Ester Herlin-Karnell, 'EU values and the shaping of the international legal context', in *The European Union's Shaping of the International Legal Order*, eds. Dimitry Kochenov and Fabian Amtenbrink (Cambridge, UK: Cambridge University Press, 2013); Marise Cremona, 'Values in EU foreign policy', in *Beyond the Established Legal Orders: Policy Interconnections between the EU and the Rest of the World*, eds. Malcolm Evans and Panos Koutrakos (Oxford, UK: Hart Publishing, 2011); Päivi Leino and Roman Petrov, 'Between "common values" and competing universals', *European Law Journal* 15 (2009).

22 The crucial argument in this vein has been made, most powerfully, by Andrew Williams, 'Taking values seriously: Towards a philosophy of EU law', *Oxford Journal of Legal Studies* 29 (2009). See, also, Joseph H.H Weiler's unpublished paper 'On the distinction between values and virtues in the process of European integration' (2010), available at www.iilj.org/courses/documents/2010Colloquium.Weiler.pdf

23 *Pace Bundesverfassungsgericht.*

24 Opinion 2/13 (m) [2014] ECLI: EU:C:2014:2454; Kochenov, 'Is there EU rule of law?'.

25 On the *Kadi* saga, see Gráinne de Búrca, 'The European Court of Justice and the International Legal Order after *Kadi*', *Harvard International Law Journal* 51 (2010). See, also, C-584/10 *Kadi II* [2013] ECLI:EU:C:2013:518.

26 Three equally important facets of the current crisis can be outlined: values, justice, and economic and monetary. On the crisis of values, see, for example, Williams, 'Taking values seriously' and Weiler, 'On the distinction'. On the crisis of justice: Kochenov, de Búrca, and Williams, eds., *Europe's Justice Deficit*. On the economic side of the crisis, Agustín Menéndez, 'The existential crisis of the European Union', *German Law Journal* 14 (2013); Maurice Adams, Federico Fabbrini and Pierre Larouche, eds., *The Constitutionalisation of European Budgetary Constraints* (Oxford, UK: Hart Publishing, 2014).

27 On the key aspects of the dynamics of the EU's legal history, see Bill Davies and Morten Rasmussen, 'Towards a new history of European law', *Contemporary European History* 21 (2012).

164 Dimitry Kochenov

is probably not (at least not based on the values of Article 2), as Andrew Williams explained in his seminal work.[28]

Although, the Union's ambition has gradually been scaled down to the market – call it a hijacking of the ends by the means[29] – de facto the Union started playing, mostly through negative integration, the role of the promoter of liberal and tolerant nationhood, as rightly characterized by Will Kymlicka, assuming (if not indirectly promoting) a very clear idea of constitutionalism based on proportionality, tolerance and the glorification of reason, the idea that the law should make sense.[30] Besides, at the core of the Union there lay basic mutual respect among the member states: the Union would be impossible, should they obstruct the principle of mutual recognition.[31] This came down to frowning upon the ideology of 'thick' national identities, however glorified in some schoolbooks. The ultimate result is that the EU, sub-consciously as it were, emerged as a promoter of *one* particular type of constitutionalism,[32] which is based on the rule of law understood through national democracy and the culture of justification, implying human rights protection and strong judicial review. To be a member state of the EU in the context of these developments came to signify one thing, at least, when approached from a systemic point of state-organization: namely, to stick to this particular type of constitutionalism, which is now reflected in Article 2 TEU and which also represents the most important condition to be fulfilled before joining the EU, as hinted at in Article 49 TEU.[33]

The EU thus emerged as a vehicle of a negative market-based approach to the 'values' question, for which it is rightly criticized by, for example, Alexander Somek and Andrew Williams, among numerous others.[34] Clearly, creating a market and questioning the state is not sufficient as a basis for a mature constitutional system. Characteristically, among many other drawbacks, it potentially creates a justice void at the supranational level,[35] also perpetuating the Union's inability

---

28 Williams, *The Ethos of Europe*.

29 Dimitry Kochenov, 'The citizenship paradigm', *Cambridge Yearbook of European Legal Studies* 15 (2012–13).

30 Will Kymlicka, 'Liberal nationalism and cosmopolitan justice', in Seyla Benhabib, *Another Cosmopolitanism*, ed. Robert Post (Oxford, UK: Oxford University Press, 2006), p. 134. See also, Gareth Davies, 'Humiliation of the state as a constitutional tactic', in *The Constitutional Integrity of the European Union*, eds. Fabian Amtenbrink and Peter van den Bergh (The Hague, The Netherlands: T.M.C. Asser Press, 2010).

31 Miguel Poiares Maduro, 'So close yet so far: The paradoxes of mutual recognition', *Journal of European Public Policy* 14 (2007). For a very sophisticated analysis of the Union's effects on the member states, see Alexander Somek, 'The argument from transnational effects I', *European Law Journal* 16 (2010); Alexander Somek, 'The argument from transnational effects II', *European Law Journal* 16 (2010).

32 Vlad Perju, 'Proportionality and freedom: An essay on method in constitutional law', *Global Constitutionalism* 1 (2012).

33 See, for example, Kochenov, *EU Enlargement*, ch. 2.

34 For example, Alexander Somek, 'The preoccupation with rights and the embrace of inclusion: A critique', in Kochenov, de Búrca and Williams, eds., *Europe's Justice Deficit?*

35 Dimitry Kochenov and Andrew Williams, 'Europe's justice deficit introduced' and Sionaidh Douglas-Scott, 'Justice, injustice and the rule of law in the EU', both in Kochenov, de Búrca, and Williams, eds., ibid.

Self-constitution: unenforceable promises 165

to help the member states labouring hard to inflict a justice void on themselves, either through an outright embrace of Putin-style 'illiberal democracy', or through failing to build a well-ordered and functioning modern state. Outright defiance is thus not required to fall out of adherence to Article 2 TEU aspirations.

Enforcing the values in the face of an ideological choice not to comply

Moving beyond Article 7 TEU, which has been analysed in the literature in overwhelming detail (with much of this analysis convincingly questioning the provision's effectiveness),[36] ordinary enforcement mechanisms designed to ensure that EU law works well in the member states – most notably, Articles 258, 259 and 260 of the Treaty on the Functioning of the European Union (TFEU) – are always at our disposal. There is a very important problem here, however; it is too easy to expect more from these provisions than they can deliver.

Even if it is presumed that violations of Article 2 TEU can be subject to the aforementioned procedures along with Article 7 TEU[37] – indeed, the very existence of Article 7 TEU clearly testifies to the intention of the drafters of the Treaty to ensure that Article 2 TEU is an enforceable legal provision, not merely a declaration[38] – the fact that Article 2 law is somewhat different from the rest of the *acquis* is impossible to hide. The same applies to the violations: Article 2 TEU violations are not the same as ordinary *acquis* violations. Such differences are particularly acute in the context of one specific type of chronically non-compliant states where, as in Hungary, non-compliance is *ideological* and cannot be explained with reference to lack of capacity, 'simple' corruption and outright sloppiness, as in the context of some south-east European countries. Where chronic non-compliance is ideological, Article 260 TFEU becomes the *crux* of the whole story, as simple restatements of the breach under Article 258 TFEU (or Article 259 TFEU, for that matter) will presumably not be enough.[39] The question of how effective fining member states that have made an ideological choice favouring non-compliance has been, is likely to remain open.[40]

---

36 Bojan Bugarič, 'Protecting democracy inside the EU: On Article 7 TEU and the Hungarian turn to authoritarianism', in Closa and Kochenov, eds., *Reinforcing Rule of Law*; Leonard F.M. Besselink, 'The Bite, the bark and the howl: Article 7 and the rule of law initiatives', in Jakab and Kochenov, eds., *Enforcement of EU Law*. See also, most importantly, Wojciech Sadurski, 'Adding bite to a bark: The story of Article 7, EU enlargement, and Jörg Haider', *Columbia Journal of European Law* 16 (2010).
37 Christophe Hillion, 'Overseeing the rule of law in the EU: Legal mandate and means', in Closa and Kochenov, eds., *Reinforcing Rule of Law*.
38 Ibid.; Jean-Claude Piris, *The Lisbon Treaty* (Cambridge, UK: Cambridge University Press, 2010), p. 71.
39 On the main deficiencies of the system, see, most importantly, Brian Jack, 'Article 260(2) TFEU: An effective judicial procedure for the enforcement of judgments?', *European Law Journal* 19 (2013); Pål Wennerås, 'Sanctions against member states under Article 260 TFEU: Alive, but not kicking?', *Common Market Law Review*, 49 (2012).
40 See Kim Lane Scheppele, 'Enforcing the basic principles of EU law through systemic infringement actions', in Closa and Kochenov, eds., *Reinforcing Rule of Law* (defending the potential effectiveness of fines, if wisely applied).

166   *Dimitry Kochenov*

The fact thus seems to be that the EU suffers from an inability to approach the values question, thereby supplying a legitimate answer concerning what it stands for beyond the market – or a procedure to come up with such an answer by itself. It also lacks any ability to enforce the values as mentioned in Article 2 TEU in legal terms: the particular type of constitutionalism the member states seemingly embrace with the Union's blessing is thus not guaranteed at all. Indeed, in some cases it amounts to a mere proclamation. The limitations of both Article 7 TEU and of the standard enforcement procedures in this context are clear as day.[41] For many decades, the Union has been consistently denying the very possibility that any Article 2 TEU problems could ever arise, presenting itself as solely working within the paradigm of the internal market, which denies serious treatment of the majority of the values and principles listed in Article 2 TEU. Only in the context of the preparation of the Eastern enlargement did a fascinating situation arise, when the EU de facto ended up seemingly enforcing its foundational values through the pre-accession conditionality policy – to highly questionable effect. The failure of conditionality in the fields of democracy and the rule of law, analysed elsewhere,[42] now stands overwhelmingly proven by the Hungarian developments.[43]

The broader danger of ideologically informed non-compliance

The Union is thus generally powerless concerning the *enforcement* of values and, more importantly, also their *content*. The very fact that we are now concerned with enforcing them seriously amounts to nothing more than conceding that the presumption that all member states form a level playing field in terms of rule of law, etc. – that is, the fact that all of them actually adhere to the specific type of constitutionalism the EU set out to promote – does not always hold. This is something the European Court of Human Rights (ECtHR) has already clearly hinted at in *M.S.S.* v. *Belgium and Greece*.[44] Acknowledging this, alongside the EU's obvious powerlessness as far as values are concerned, is a potentially explosive combination in a Union built on member-state equality and the principle of

---

41 For a restatement, see, for example, Dimitry Kochenov, 'On policing Article 2 TEU compliance – Reverse *Solange* and systemic infringements analyzed', *Polish Yearbook of International Law* 33 (2013).

42 Kochenov, *EU Enlargement.*

43 While scholars tend to disagree with this point, I submit that it is precisely the *lasting* nature of transformation that the Union's involvement had to guarantee, not mere window-dressing, which it provided in abundance. See e.g. Eline De Ridder and Dimitry Kochenov, 'Democratic conditionality in Eastern enlargement: Ambitious window dressing', *European Foreign Affairs Review* 16 (2011).

44 *MSS v. Belgium and Greece* [2011] Application No. 30696/09. ECtHR confirmed its position in *Tarakhel v. Switzerland* [2014] Application No. 29217/12, dealing with the same issue and restating that the ECJ's 'systemic' standard articulated in *N.S. and others* (C-411/11 ECLI:EU:C:2011:865) and restated in *Abdullahi v. Bundesasylamt* (C-294/12 ECLI:EU:C:2013:813) is unacceptable under the ECHR.

mutual recognition.[45] In a situation when the core values are not respected by Hungary, for instance, we are not dealing with a member state revolting, for one reason or another, against a binding norm of European law. At the level of values, we are dealing with a *member state which is different in principle*; with the Belarusization of the EU from the inside.[46] Once the principles of Article 2 TEU are not observed, the essential presumptions behind the core of the Union do not hold any more, undermining the very essence of the integration exercise.[47] Mutual recognition becomes an untenable fiction, which the member states, nevertheless, are bound by EU law to adhere to. This is an important element of the core of what the autonomy of EU law stands for, as confirmed by the Court in the infamous Opinion 2/13.[48] As we know from every textbook, autonomy considerations in the context of EU law are usually likely to prevail over human rights and other values – including the rule of law – cherished in the national constitutional systems of the member states. Indeed, it would probably not be incorrect to argue that this would be the shortest possible summary of Opinion 2/13, which, in turn, summarized a crucially important aspect of EU law as it stands.[49] As Eleanor Sharpston and Daniel Sarmiento say:

> [i]n the balance between individual rights and primacy, the Court in Opinion 2/13 has fairly clearly sided with the latter. The losers under Opinion 2/13 are not the Member States of the signatory States of the Council of Europe, but the individual citizens of the European Union.[50]

This is so, one must add, not only because of the potential reduction of the level of human rights protection. Rather, it is because the EU, as Opinion 2/13 made crystal clear, boasts an overwhelming potential to undermine the rule of law at national level, and this potential impact is not an empty threat.[51]

---

45 For a most insightful analysis, see Valsamis Mitsilegas, 'The symbolic relationship between mutual trust and fundamental rights in Europe's area of criminal justice', *New Journal of European Criminal Law*, forthcoming.

46 Jan-Werner Müller, 'Safeguarding democracy inside the EU: Brussels and the future of liberal order', *Working Paper* No. 3 (Washington, DC: Transatlantic Academy, 2013); Uladzislau Belavusau, 'On age discrimination and beating dead dogs: *Commission v. Hungary*', *Common Market Law Review* 50 (2013).

47 This is where the enforcement talk enters the picture. See, most importantly, Müller, 'The EU as a militant democracy'.

48 This point has been forcefully restated in the ECJ's Opinion 2/13 (ECHR Accession II) [2014] ECLI:EU:C:2014:2454. See, for example, para. 192.

49 This is strikingly similar to the key ideas behind the Judgment of the Constitutional Court of the Russian Federation of 14 July 2015, which allowed Russia not to comply with ECtHR judgments if the Constitutional Court finds that such judgments are in contradiction with the Constitution of the Federation: the autonomy of the Russian Federal legal order has to be respected.

50 Eleanor Sharpston and Daniel Sarmiento, 'European citizenship and its new union: Time to move on?', in *EU Citizenship and Federalism: The Role of Rights*, in Dimitry Kochenov, ed., (Cambridge, UK: Cambridge University Press, forthcoming).

51 See, further, Kochenov, 'EU law without the rule of law'.

168 *Dimitry Kochenov*

The question, then, is how to ensure that the EU's own rule of law does not undermine, if not destroy, the adherence to the principle of the rule of law in the member states, which are, in fact, compliant with the values listed in Article 2 TEU.[52] Mutual trust without too much checking and the principle of the autonomy of a legal order based on presumptions, but offering no enforcement of the bases of such presumptions, is an inalienable part of the EU's own rule of law.

Clearly, horizontal *Solange*, if ever implemented – that is, allowing the member states to check each other's adherence to the values of Article 2 TEU and the *acquis* with the use of their own national system of courts and other institutions – means nothing else but the end of all that we cherish in the Union, all its imperfections notwithstanding.[53] The legal fiction of 'all the member states are good enough' is absolutely worth fighting for. But the only way to do it, it seems, is to incorporate the values of Article 2 TEU in full into the realm of the EU's *acquis*, thus rethinking our understanding of the scope of EU law and also approaching the difficult questions of the substance of values and of their effective enforcement.[54] Dealing with the values emergency should become the most important and immediate task of the Union and the member states combined, should the core idea of the Union withstand the test of rule of law non-compliance, which, in turn, could result in undermining the rule of law in perfectly compliant states.

On defining the scope: an argument for acknowledging EU law's plasticity

All normative grounds for Union intervention to uphold values notwithstanding,[55] the issues of the substance and scope of the law will have to be resolved first, before any serious talk about enforcement. Adopting an approach which is too inflexible in restating this, however, hardly helps anyone in an atmosphere where changing the Treaties to bring about a different legal reality is no doubt impossible: unanimity is of course required and potentially problematic states cannot be expected, rationally speaking, to throw their weight behind a meaningful values-enforcement reform.

Having said this, numerous examples of sound logical constructions come to mind, which could clearly be deployed to back much wider inclusion of the values of Article 2 TEU within the scope of the *acquis* compared with what has been seen so far. The most important example from the history of EU law which could inform our thinking is the embrace of human rights by the supranational legal system in Europe. Something that had not been within the realm of EU law – remember

---

52 For a detailed discussion of this dilemma, see ibid.
53 But, see Iris Canor, 'My brother's keeper? Horizontal *Solange*: "An ever close distrust among the peoples of Europe"', *Common Market Law Review* 50 (2013).
54 See, in the same vein, the contributions in Von Bogdandy and Sonnevend, eds., *Constitutional Crisis*.
55 Carlos Closa, 'Reinforcing the rule of law: Normative arguments, institutional proposals and procedural limitations', in Closa and Kochenov, eds., *Reinforcing Rule of Law*.

Stork[56] – entered this realm and stayed.[57] It is easy to answer why: EU law would not be operational without human rights. This is not simply to exaggerate the importance of *Solange* threats from the *Bundesverfassungsgericht* and *Corte Costituzionale*:[58] any *effet utile* hopes could be laid to rest without it, just as in the crucial transformation that turned the EU from an atypical international organization into a constitutional system.[59]

Approached in this sense, the rule of law (including at member-state level) does not seem in any way different: can the EU exist without the rule of law? As long as it cannot, the power to police the rule of law in the member states is to be assumed as well – exactly what happened with the human rights story. This is not about reinventing the wheel, just a repetition of a necessary step, well tested in the past. The crucial difference is that the first step was taken under pressure from national courts, ready for *ideological* non-compliance for reasons concerned with respecting the law and the values of the legal systems entrusted to their care, which are now reflected in Article 2 TEU; step number two is to be taken under pressure from equally ideological non-compliance, but rooted, as opposed to the first step, in failure to respect the law and values on which the Union and all its member states are built. The fact that one context of non-compliance was 'positive', while the second is undoubtedly 'negative', cannot possibly change the nature of non-compliance with the values (and the law, for that matter), or diminish the EU's eagerness and desire to solve the resulting problems.

Plentiful sources could be outlined for turning values into a somewhat more binding part of the law of the Union. It would be absolutely wrong to approach the rule of law – which is the air any legal system breathes – as a luxury, which its *own law* seemingly prevents the EU from acquiring. Such an approach should be dismissed outright as lacking in coherence and potentially dangerous for both levels of law in the EU, the supranational and the national, given the EU's essential conditioning – in all that it does – which makes it entertain and foster the presumption that there is something akin to an equal level of compliance with the values throughout the Union. In the atmosphere where *the presumption – not the compliance* is policed by the use of EU law under the banner of EU rule of law, the fundamental stance on this issue taken by the majority of institutions and commentators today will have to change.[60]

---

56 Case 1/58, *Stork* v. *High Authority* [1959] ECR 17.

57 For details, see P. Alston, ed., *EU Law and Human Rights* (Oxford, UK: Oxford University Press, 1999).

58 See Bill Davies, *Resisting the European Court of Justice* (Cambridge, UK: Cambridge University Press, 2012).

59 Joseph H.H. Weiler, 'The transformation of Europe', *Yale Law Journal* 100 (1991). See, also, Joseph H.H. Weiler, *The Constitution for Europe* (Cambridge, UK: Cambridge University Press, 1998) and Joseph H.H. Weiler and Gráinne de Búrca, eds., *The Worlds of European Constitutionalism* (Cambridge, UK: Cambridge University Press, 2011).

60 For a number of crucial exceptions, see, for example, the contributions in Von Bogdandy and Sonnevend, eds., *Constitutional Crisis*, as well as the contributions in Closa and Kochenov. eds., *Reinforcing Rule of Law*.

170 *Dimitry Kochenov*

Turning to other analogies from which the EU can rightly draw inspiration in these difficult times, the pre-accession context should also be named. The story of the pre-accession monitoring of democracy, the rule of law and other values is overwhelmingly telling, not just because of how dysfunctional the monitoring was. Indeed, it landed us with all the countries we now criticize as non-compliant with Article 2 TEU in the Union in the first place. While the Commission's regular reports were applauding compliance with what was then Article 6(1) TEU among all the member states-to-be, there was a failure to ensure maturation of the institutions and lasting continuity of the change achieved. The Commission unquestionably enjoyed the competence to police Article 2 TEU matters, since Article 49 TEU then (and also now) requires it to ensure that new member states are fully compliant with the EU's values, not merely those elements thereof which happen to fall within the scope of the *acquis*. Otherwise – remember Weiler's DNA argument – we would not have had *any* checks at all on compliance with democracy or the rule of law in the context of pre-accession.

What is of crucial importance is that such a competence was then enjoyed by the Union institutions, for the first time in the EU's history. The use of the competence thus acquired led to the gradual forming of a quasi-*acquis* on values, which can be vaguely distilled from the pre-accession monitoring documents.[61] While critics would no doubt point to the important differences which exist between the 'internal' and the 'external' realms of the *acquis* in the competences field, what empowered the Commission to act in the realm of what is now Article 2 TEU, treating this provision as directly enforceable law, was a request from the European Council at Copenhagen in 1993 and the pre-accession reorientation of the Europe agreements,[62] that is, a strong political decision and the rethinking of the law in force. No change was deemed necessary in primary law. Even now, Article 49 TEU still does not expressly mention either the principle of conditionality or the fact that the classical standard limitations of the scope of EU law do not apply to the pre-accession context, which this provision (very) vaguely regulates.

Both the example of the introduction of human rights protection into the edifice of EU law by the ECJ and the attempt to endow the values of what is now Article 2 TEU with substance by the Commission clearly testify to the plasticity of EU law, when the very *effet utile*, if not the survival of this legal system is at stake. More examples could be given to support this point:[63] like the human

---

61 For an attempt, see, for example, Dimitry Kochenov, 'Behind the Copenhagen façade: The meaning and structure of the Copenhagen political criterion of democracy and the rule of law', *European Integration Online Papers* 8 (2004). Available at http://eiop.or.at/eiop/texte/2004-010a.htm.

62 Kirstyn Inglis, 'The Europe agreements compared in the light of their pre-accession reorientation', *Common Market Law Review* 37 (2000).

63 Especially the concept of the 'essence of rights' comes to mind, emerging from EU citizenship law and other fields: Martijn van den Brink, 'The origins and the potential effects of the substance of rights test', in Kochenov, ed., *EU Citizenship and Federalism*; Dimitry Kochenov,

brain, the EU legal system is flexible enough to multiply its chances of effective functioning. When push comes to shove and the legal system experiences a series of important shocks at its very base, there is no room for excluding systemic legal arguments based on the considerations of the functionality of the law, and the scope of the *ratione materiae* of EU rule of law should be reassessed in this vein.

On reconsidering the values' substance and enforcement effectiveness

Should we view the scope of the supranational law more flexibly, the change brought about as a result of such reinterpretation will most likely be incapable of reversing the politics of consistent rule of law non-compliance in 'ideologically different' member states undergoing Belarusization. An emphasis on at least four aspects of why this is most likely to be the case can be made. As has been demonstrated, the EU does not actually have any *acquis* on values (outside of the pre-accession framework, which failed to produce sound results precisely in the field of values); the EU does not have tools to formulate such *acquis*; the enforcement of values is lacking; and the effectiveness of the current enforcement mechanisms – in particular the fines and lump sums deployed against ideologically non-compliant member states – is inadequate in the values-enforcement field. Consequently, should the EU be serious about solving the rule of law crisis, the key elements to consider should reach beyond mere enforcement, to include the following aspects:

a   the substance of values;
b   the procedure to alter the *acquis* on values and unquestionably extend the scope of EU law to cover the systemic departures from what Article 2 TEU presupposes;
c   the elaboration of sound enforcement procedures in the sphere of Article 2 TEU *distinct* from those which Articles 258 and 260 TFEU offer.

In light of the above, several observations are in order once the work aimed at designing a new mechanism commences to enforce the *values*, rather than the *presumption*, of compliance, as is the case today.

'A real European citizenship; A new jurisdiction test; A novel chapter in the development of the Union in Europe', *Columbia Journal of European Law* 18 (2011). For a clear proposal to apply this particular aspect of EU law's plasticity to the solution of Article 2 TEU enforcement problems, see, most importantly, Armin von Bogdandy, Carlino Antpöller and Michael Ioannidis, 'Enforcing European values', in Jakab and Kochenov, eds., *Enforcement of EU Law* (as well as the earlier emanations of Professor von Bogdandy's proposal in the references). See, also, Johanna Croon-Gestefeld, 'Reverse *Solange* – Union citizenship as a detour on the route to European rights protection against national infringements', in Kochenov, ed., *EU Citizenship and Federalism*.

172 *Dimitry Kochenov*

A glance into the future

EU values, objectively speaking, are not (and never have been) part of the *acquis*. This is precisely why the Copenhagen political criteria on democracy, the rule of law and human rights protection were formulated roughly 20 years ago in the first place. The ECJ's attempts to deal inter alia with human rights and the rule of law as if these were part of the ordinary *acquis* are far from sufficient; the rule of law is turning into a purely procedural consideration of basic legality. In one example, paying compensation to the judges replaces the need not to destroy the independence of the courts.[64] Worse still, nods in the direction of the ECtHR even in the most outrageous cases (like *McCarthy*, for instance[65]) are frequent and usually unhelpful, allowing citizens to question the very foundations of what EU law stands for. Where to find justice in the maze of a purely legalistic engagement with crucially important problems, usually reformulated as internal market governance issues, is thus the burning question.[66] In this context, when the *acquis* is not about the values,[67] the EU at times emerges as a potent cause of injustice: the evil power. Consequently, the pre-accession attempts at flirting with values notwithstanding, it would be premature to make any claims with regard to the EU's experience in the values field. We pretty much need to start at square one (and a half).

In this general context, when the *acquis* and values are not synonymous, the application of the Copenhagen criteria in particular in the context of the recent enlargement rounds teaches a lesson of caution. The Commission has emerged as an institution, which, when given all the responsibility for the preparedness of the new member states for accession, failed in the exercise.[68] Here, to the void of substance, was added the lack of any capability to generate such a substance, notwithstanding the lack of virtually any scope of law limitations, as discussed above. Anything could have been done; it has not. Besides illustrating the EU's inbuilt limitations with regard to the ability to generate the substance of Article 2 TEU rules, the pre-accession context thus also raises the alarm regarding institutional capacity: the Commission is probably not the best actor to entrust with the

---

64 Kim Lane Scheppele, 'Enforcing the basic principles of EU law through systemic infringement actions', in Closa and Kochenov, eds., *Reinforcing Rule of Law*.

65 Niamh *Nic Shuibhne*, '(Some of) *the kids are all right*: Comment on *McCarthy* and *Dereci*', *Common Market Law Review* 49 (2012). For a broader presentation of this problem, see Dimitry Kochenov, 'Citizenship without respect', Jean Monnet Working Paper no. 08/10 (2010).

66 For further analysis, see the contributions in Kochenov, Búrca and Williams, eds., *Europe's Justice Deficit?*; as well as, crucially, Gustav Peebles, 'A very Eden of the innate rights of man? A Marxist look at the European Union treaties and case law', *Law and Social Inquiry* 22 (1997).

67 Williams, *The Ethos of Europe*. For a general assessment of the *acquis* to uncover the ideology it reproduces and the biases in the knowledge it favours and blesses, see Marija Bartl, 'Internal market rationality, private law and the direction of the Union: Resuscitating the market as the object of the political', *European Law Journal* 21(5) (2015): 572–598. See, also, for a broader account, Petr Agha, 'The empire of principle', in this volume.

68 Kochenov, *EU Enlargement*.

Self-constitution: unenforceable promises 173

internal monitoring of member states' compliance with Article 2 TEU. It is highly unlikely that the Commission's approach will change radically – so who should be doing this job?

This is a fascinating question. The Copenhagen Commission proposed by Jan-Werner Müller is definitely a workable idea,[69] even given the failure of the Copenhagen criteria, as enforced by the Commission (and made obvious by the very fact that other states were fully subjected to the Copenhagen scrutiny during the accession process). Acting on the assumption that the very ethos of the Copenhagen Commission will be radically different from that of the Commission, Müller's proposal is worthy of the most serious consideration. Of crucial importance here is the understanding that the formulation of the substance of values should not be outsourced, which would be the case if the Venice Commission, for instance,[70] were to be asked to do the job. The drawback of asking the Council of Europe to do something for the EU is obvious: it amounts to *outsourcing key constitutional issues*. Having said that, it is also necessary to keep in mind that given the overarching character of the values and principles established by Article 2 TEU, it is highly unlikely that the provision can be read as a sign of EU specificity, let alone uniqueness. The crucial symbolic value of being in charge of the proclaimed core of the EU's constitutional system is worth defying outsourcing calls, however.

Solving the outstanding value problems should be done with care, gently. However imperfectly, the EU is functioning well, boasting an obvious added value. Any new tools aimed at the enforcement of Article 2 TEU compliance should thus unquestionably respect the key premise of European integration: EU federalism. Federalism's importance is two-fold: it is a guarantee of the preservation of diversity and of the preservation of liberty. Article 2 TEU should not be used as a pretext for a power grab – even if this happens unintentionally. The risks are clear: the EU, with all its deficiencies, is not really very dangerous at the moment from the point of view of liberty and freedom (whatever one's opinion on the Greek bailouts), but only because it is constantly kept in check, whether we like it or not. In this context, putting an emphasis on the Charter of Fundamental Rights, for instance, is highly problematic. The general applicability of the Charter – something Vice-President Reding (as she then was) used to argue for – is likely to create more problems than it would solve; decentralized judicial review is not a panacea, when the value core of the system is flimsy and often irrelevant at a time when key decisions are taken.

Whichever mechanism is put in place to remedy the current problems, it is necessary to look at the likelihood of such mechanism's effectiveness, keeping

---

69 Jan-Werner Müller, 'For a Copenhagen Commission: The case restated', in Closa and Kochenov, eds., *Reinforcing Rule of Law*.

70 Kaarlo Tuori, 'Mutual trust: The virtue of reciprocity. Strengthening the acceptance of the rule of law through peer review', in Closa and Kochenov, eds., ibid.

174   *Dimitry Kochenov*

both member states and EU citizens in mind. Accordingly, it is absolutely clear that copying the Council of Europe's (CoE's) expulsion procedure is not an option; rather than improving the situation, it will amount to little more than making clear that the EU is powerless. Moreover, it will ignore the interests of the EU citizens with the nationality of the expelled state. It is thus wonderful that Article 7 TEU is milder than its CoE Statute counterpart.[71] One should be equally realistic about the effectiveness of financial sanctions. Clearly, when nothing less than a regime change is required in order to comply, a member state will be happy to pay.[72] Moreover, shaming will not work either. The amounts of fines are never unbearable (especially for a captured state). Besides, the 'ability to pay' is one of the criteria used by the ECJ in its case law on determining the amounts of fines and lump sums that defiant member states should pay. The implications of this are far reaching. It does not matter how the substance of Article 2 TEU values is established (by courts, the Commission, the Copenhagen Commission, the Venice Commission, etc.) – enforcement is still a problem in the end if fines are not effective and ejecting a member state (thus seemingly eliminating the problem) is not an option. A better solution is needed.

The most mature answer to these outstanding problems must involve not only reform of the enforcement mechanisms but *reform of the Union as such*, as the supranational law should be made more aware of the values it is obliged by the Treaties to respect and also, crucially, to aspire to protect at national, and also supranational, level. This particularly concerns the basic principles behind drawing the vertical competence boundaries. For the Union to adhere to Article 2, the narrow-minded market-based vision will have to be replaced with some alternative. EU citizenship provides an option to consider.[73]

Ultimately, the very fact that we are facing the problems with values is an extremely good sign: the Union is finally mature enough to take up the issues, the essential importance of which goes far beyond the EU's self-defined sectoral (economic) interests. This is what Joris Larik has insightfully characterized as a 'constitutional sense of purpose'.[74] Solemn proclamations suddenly take on a lot of meaning, including hope for the future.

---

71 Art. 8 of the Statute of the Council of Europe.
72 See, for the analysis of similar issues in the context of EU external relations law, Nathalie Tocci, 'Can the EU promote democracy and human rights through the ENP? The case for refocusing on the rule of law', in *The European Neighbourhood Policy: A Framework for Modernisation?*, eds. M. Cremona and G. Meloni, EUI Working Paper Law 2007/21 (2007), p. 29.
73 Kochenov, 'The citizenship paradigm'.
74 Joris Larik, 'From speciality to a constitutional sense of purpose: On the changing role of the objectives of the European Union', *International & Comparative Law Quarterly* 63 (2014).

Bibliography

Adams, Maurice, Federico Fabbrini and Pierre Larouche, eds. *The Constitutionalisation of European Budgetary Constraints*. Oxford, UK: Hart Publishing, 2014.

Alston, Philip, ed. *EU Law and Human Rights*. Oxford, UK: Oxford University Press, 1999.

Bánkuti, Miklós, Gábor Halmai, and Kim Lane Scheppele. 'Hungary's illiberal turn: Disabling the constitution', *Journal of Democracy* 23(3) (2012): 138–146.

Bartl, Marija. 'Internal market rationality, private law and the direction of the Union: Resuscitating the market as the object of the political', *European Law Journal* 21(5) (2015): 572–598.

Bebr, Gerhard. *Rule of Law within the European Communities*. Brussels, Belgium: Institut d'Etudes Européennes de l'Université Libre de Bruxelles, 1965.

Belavusau, Uladzislau. 'On age discrimination and beating dead dogs: *Commission v. Hungary*', *Common Market Law Review* 50 (2013): 1145–1160.

Besselink, Leonard F.M. 'The bite, the bark and the howl: Article 7 and the Rule of Law Initiatives'. In *The Enforcement of EU Law and Values: Methods against Defiance*, edited by András Jakab and Dimitry Kochenov. Oxford University Press (forthcoming).

von Bogdandy, Armin and Michael Ioannidis. 'Systemic deficiency in the rule of law: What it is, what has been done, what can be done'. *Common Market Law Review* 51 (2014): 59–96.

von Bogdandy, Armin and Pál Sonnevend, eds. *Constitutional Crisis in the European Constitutional Area: Theory, Law and Politics in Hungary and Romania*. Oxford, UK: Hart Publishing, 2015.

von Bogdandy, Armin, Carlino Antpöller and Michael Ioannidis. 'Enforcing European values'. In *The Enforcement of EU Law and Values: Methods against Defiance*, edited by András Jakab and Dimitry Kochenov. Oxford University Press, (forthcoming).

van den Brink, Martijn. 'The origins and the potential effects of the substance of rights test'. In *EU Citizenship and Federalism: The Role of Rights*, edited by Dimitry Kochenov. Cambridge, UK: Cambridge University Press, (forthcoming).

Bugarič, Bojan. 'Protecting democracy inside the EU: On Article 7 TEU and the Hungarian turn to authoritarianism'. In *Reinforcing Rule of Law Oversight in the European Union*, edited by Carlos Closa and Dimitry Kochenov. Cambridge, UK: Cambridge University Press (2016).

de Búrca, Gráinne. 'The European Court of Justice and the International Legal Order after *Kadi*'. *Harvard International Law Journal* 51 (2010): 1–49.

Canor, Iris. 'My brother's keeper? Horizontal *Solange*: "An ever closer *distrust* among the peoples of Europe"'. *Common Market Law Review* 50 (2013): 383–442.

Closa, Carlos and Dimitry Kochenov, eds. *Reinforcing Rule of Law Oversight in the European Union*. Cambridge, UK: Cambridge University Press (2016).

Closa, Carlos, Dimitry Kochenov and Joseph H.H. Weiler. 'Reinforcing rule of law oversight in the European Union'. RSCAS Paper (EUI Florence) No. 2014/25 (2014).

Cremona, Marise. 'Values in EU foreign policy'. In *Beyond the Established Legal Orders: Policy Interconnections between the EU and the Rest of the World*, edited by Malcolm Evans and Panos Koutrakos. Oxford, UK: Hart Publishing, 2011, pp. 275–315.

Croon-Gestefeld, Johanna. 'Reverse *Solange* – Union citizenship as a detour on the route to European rights protection against national infringements'. In *EU Citizenship and Federalism: The Role of Rights*, edited by Dimitry Kochenov. Cambridge, UK: Cambridge University Press (forthcoming).

176   Dimitry Kochenov

Davies, Bill. *Resisting the European Court of Justice*. Cambridge, UK: Cambridge University Press, 2012.

Davies, Bill and Morten Rasmussen. 'Towards a new history of European law'. *Contemporary European History* 21 (2012): 305–318.

Davies, Gareth. 'Humiliation of the state as a constitutional tactic'. In *The Constitutional Integrity of the European Union*, edited by Fabian Amtenbrink and Peter van den Bergh. The Hague, The Netherlands: T.M.C. Asser Press, 2010, pp. 147–174.

De Ridder, Eline and Dimitry Kochenov, 'Democratic conditionality in Eastern enlargement: Ambitious window dressing', *European Foreign Affairs Review* 16 (2011).

Douglas-Scott, Sionaidh. 'Justice, injustice and the rule of law in the EU'. In *Europe's Justice Deficit?*, edited by Dimitry Kochenov, Gráinne de Búrca and Andrew Williams. Oxford, UK: Hart Publishing, 2015, pp. 51–66.

Everling, Ulrich. 'The European Union as a federal association of states and citizens'. In *Principles of European Constitutional Law*, edited by Armin von Bogdandy and Jürgen Bast. Oxford, UK and Munich, Germany: Hart Publishing/CH Beck, 2010, pp. 701–734.

Fernandez Esteban, Maria Luisa. *The Rule of Law in the European Constitution*. The Hague, The Netherlands: Kluwer Law International, 1999.

Herlin-Karnell, Ester. 'EU values and the shaping of the international legal context'. In *The European Union's Shaping of the International Legal Order*, edited by Dimitry Kochenov and Fabian Amtenbrink. Cambridge, UK: Cambridge University Press, 2013, pp. 89–107.

Hillion, Christophe. 'Overseeing the rule of law in the EU: Legal mandate and means'. In *Reinforcing Rule of Law Oversight in the European Union*, edited by Carlos Closa and Dimitry Kochenov. Cambridge, UK: Cambridge University Press (2016).

Inglis, Kirstyn. 'The *Europe agreements* compared in the light of their pre-accession reorientation'. *Common Market Law Review* 37 (2000): 1173–1200.

Jack, Brian. 'Article 260(2) TFEU: An effective judicial procedure for the enforcement of judgments?' *European Law Journal* 19 (2012): 404–421.

Jakab, András and Dimitry Kochenov, eds. *The Enforcement of EU Law and Values*. Oxford, UK: Oxford University Press (forthcoming).

Kochenov, Dimitry. 'Behind the Copenhagen Façade: The meaning and structure of the Copenhagen political criterion of democracy and the rule of law'. *European Integration Online Papers* 8 (2004). Available at http://eiop.or.at/eiop/texte/2004–010a.htm.

Kochenov, Dimitry. *EU Enlargement and the Failure of Conditionality*. The Hague, The Netherlands: Kluwer Law International, 2008.

Kochenov, Dimitry. 'Citizenship without respect'. Jean Monnet Working Paper no. 08/10, 2010.

Kochenov, Dimitry. 'A real European citizenship; A new jurisdiction test; A novel chapter in the development of the Union in Europe'. *Columbia Journal of European Law* 18 (2011) 56–109.

Kochenov, Dimitry. 'The citizenship paradigm'. *Cambridge Yearbook of European Law and Policy* 15 (2012–2013): 197–226

Kochenov, Dimitry. 'On policing Article 2 TEU compliance – Reverse Solange and systemic infringements analyzed'. *Polish Yearbook of International Law* 33 (2013):145–170.

Kochenov, Dimitry. 'EU Law without the rule of law: Is the veneration of autonomy worth it?', *Yearbook of European Law* 34 (2015).

Kochenov, Dimitry and Andrew Williams. 'Europe's justice deficit introduced'. In *Europe's Justice Deficit?*, edited by Dimitry Kochenov, Gráinne de Búrca and Andrew Williams. Oxford, UK: Hart Publishing, 2015, pp. 1–20.

Self-constitution: unenforceable promises 177

Kochenov, Dimitry, Gráinne de Búrca and Andrew Williams, eds. *Europe's Justice Deficit?* Oxford, UK: Hart Publishing, 2015.

Krygier, Martin. 'The rule of law. An abuser's guide'. In *Abuse: The Dark Side of Fundamental Rights*, edited by András Sajó. Utrecht, The Netherlands: Eleven International Publishing, 2006, pp. 129–161.

Kymlicka, Will. 'Liberal nationalism and cosmopolitan justice'. In *Another Cosmopolitanism*, by Seyla Benhabib, edited by Robert Post. Oxford, UK: Oxford University Press, 2006, pp. 128–146.

Larik, Joris. 'From speciality to a constitutional sense of purpose: On the changing role of the objectives of the European Union'. *International & Comparative Law Quarterly* 63 (2014): 1–28.

Leino, Päivi and Roman Petrov. 'Between "common values" and competing universals'. *European Law Journal* 15 (2009): 654–671.

Lenaerts, Koen and Kathleen Gutman. '"Federal common law" in the European Union: A comparative perspective from the United States'. *American Journal of Comparative Law* 54 (2006): 1–121.

Letsas, George. 'Harmonic law: The case against pluralism'. In *Philosophical Foundations of European Union Law*, edited by Julie Dickson and Pavlos Eleftheriadis. Oxford, UK: Oxford University Press, 2012, pp. 77–108.

Mackenzie Stuart, Lord. *The European Communities and the Rule of Law*. London: Stevens and Sons, 1977.

Menéndez, Agustín. 'The existential crisis of the European Union'. *German Law Journal* 14 (2013): 453–526.

Mitsilegas, Valsamis. 'The symbolic relationship between mutual trust and fundamental rights in Europe's area of criminal justice', *New Journal of European Criminal Law* (forthcoming).

Müller, Jan-Werner. 'Safeguarding democracy inside the EU: Brussels and the future of liberal order', *Working Paper* No. 3. Washington, DC: Transatlantic Academy, 2013.

Müller, Jan-Werner. 'The EU as a militant democracy, or: are there limits to constitutional mutations within the member states?' *Revista de Estudios Políticos* (2014): 141–162.

Müller, Jan-Werner. 'For a Copenhagen Commission: The case restated'. In *Reinforcing Rule of Law Oversight in the European Union*, edited by Carlos Closa and Dimitry Kochenov. Cambridge, UK: Cambridge University Press (2016).

Nic Shuibhne, Niamh. '(Some of) the kids are all right: Comment on *McCarthy* and *Dereci*'. *Common Market Law Review* 49 (2012): 349–379.

Palombella, Gianluigi. 'The rule of law and its core'. In *Relocating the Rule of Law*, edited by Gianluigi Palombella and Neil Walker. Oxford, UK: Hart Publishing, 2009, pp. 17–42.

Palombella, Gianluigi. *È possibile la legalità globale?* Bologna, Italy: Il Mulino, 2012.

Palombella, Gianluigi. 'Beyond legality – before democracy: Rule of law caveats in the EU two-level system'. In *Reinforcing Rule of Law Oversight in the European Union*, edited by Carlos Closa and Dimitry Kochenov. Cambridge, UK: Cambridge University Press, 2016.

Pech, Laurent. 'The rule of law as a constitutional principle of the European Union'. Jean Monnet Working Paper no. 04/09 (NYU Law School), 2009.

Peebles, Gustav. 'A very Eden of the innate rights of man? A Marxist look at the European Union treaties and case law', *Law and Social Inquiry* 22 (1997).

Perju, Vlad. 'Proportionality and freedom: An essay on method in constitutional law'. *Global Constitutionalism* 1 (2012): 334–367.

178 Dimitry Kochenov

Piris, Jean-Claude. 'L'Union européenne: Vers une nouvelle forme de fédéralisme?' *Revue trimestrielle de droit européenne* 41 (2004): 243–260.

Poiares Maduro, Miguel. 'So close yet so far: The paradoxes of mutual recognition'. *Journal of European Public Policy* 14 (2007): 814–825.

Přibáň, Jiří. 'From "Which Rule of Law?" to "The Rule of Which Law?": Post-communist experiences of European legal integration'. *Hague Journal on the Rule of Law* 1 (2009): 337–358.

Sadurski, Wojciech. 'Adding bite to a bark: The story of Article 7, EU enlargement, and Jörg Haider'. *Columbia Journal of European Law* 16 (2010): 385–426.

Scheppele, Kim Lane. 'Enforcing the basic principles of EU law through systemic infringement actions'. In *Reinforcing Rule of Law Oversight in the European Union*, edited by Carlos Closa and Dimitry Kochenov. Cambridge, UK: Cambridge University Press (2016).

Schütze, Robert. *From Dual to Cooperative Federalism: The Changing Structure of European Law*. Oxford, UK: Oxford University Press, 2009.

Sharpston, Eleanor and Daniel Sarmiento. 'European citizenship and its new union: Time to move on?'. In *EU Citizenship and Federalism: The Role of Rights*, edited by Dimitry Kochenov. Cambridge University Press (forthcoming).

Sólyom, Lászlo. 'The rise and decline of constitutional culture in Hungary'. In *Constitutional Crisis in the European Constitutional Area: Theory, Law and Politics in Hungary and Romania*, edited by Armin von Bogdandy and Pál Sonnevend.

Somek, Alexander. 'The argument from transnational effects I'. *European Law Journal* 16 (2010): 315–344.

Somek, Alexander. 'The argument from transnational effects II'. *European Law Journal* 16 (2010): 375–394.

Somek, Alexander. 'The preoccupation with rights and the embrace of inclusion: A critique'. In *Europe's Justice Deficit?*, edited by Dimitry Kochenov, Gráinne de Búrca and Andrew Williams. Oxford, UK: Hart Publishing, 2015, pp. 295–310.

Tocci, Nathalie. 'Can the EU promote democracy and human rights through the ENP? The case for refocusing on the rule of law'. In *The European Neighbourhood Policy: A Framework for Modernisation?*, edited by Marise Cremona and Gabriella Meloni. EUI Working Paper Law 2007/21, 2007, pp. 23–35.

Tuori, Kaarlo. 'Mutual trust: The virtue of reciprocity. Strengthening the acceptance of the rule of law through peer review'. In *Reinforcing Rule of Law Oversight in the European Union*, edited by Carlos Closa and Dimitry Kochenov. Cambridge, UK: Cambridge University Press (2016).

Uitz, Renata. 'Can you tell when an illiberal democracy is in the making? An appeal to comparative constitutional scholarship from Hungary', *I-CON* 13 (1) (2015): 279–300.

Weiler, Joseph H.H. 'The transformation of Europe'. *Yale Law Journal* 100 (1991): 2403–2483.

Weiler, Joseph H.H. *The Constitution for Europe*. Cambridge, UK: Cambridge University Press, 1998.

Weiler, Joseph H.H. 'Europa: "Nous coalisons des Etats, nous n'unissons pas des hommes"'. In *La sostenibilità della democrazia nel XXI secolo*, edited by Marta Cartabia and Andrea Simoncini. Bologna, Italy: Il Mulino, 2009.

Weiler, Joseph H.H. 'On the distinction between values and virtues in the process of European integration', 2010. Available at www.iilj.org/courses/documents/2010Colloquium. Weiler.pdf.

Weiler, Joseph H.H. and Gráinne de Búrca, eds. *The Worlds of European Constitutionalism*. Cambridge, UK: Cambridge University Press, 2011.

Weiler, Joseph H.H. 'The Schuman declaration as a manifesto of political messianism'. In *Philosophical Foundations of European Union Law*, edited by Julie Dickson and Pavlos Eleftheriadis. Oxford, UK: Oxford University Press, 2012, pp. 146–149.

Weiler, Joseph H.H. 'Epilogue: Living in a glass house: Europe, democracy and the rule of law'. In *Reinforcing Rule of Law Oversight in the European Union*, edited by Carlos Closa and Dimitry Kochenov. Cambridge, UK: Cambridge University Press (2016).

Wennerås, Pål. 'Sanctions against member states under Article 260 TFEU: Alive, but not kicking?'. *Common Market Law Review* 49 (2012): 145–175.

Williams, Andrew. 'Taking values seriously: Towards a philosophy of EU law'. *Oxford Journal of Legal Studies* 29 (2009): 549–577.

Williams, Andrew. *The Ethos of Europe*. Cambridge, UK: Cambridge University Press, 2009.

Zuleeg, Manfred. 'The advantages of the European constitution'. In *Principles of European Constitutional Law*, edited by Armin von Bogdandy and Jürgen Bast. Oxford and Munich: Hart Publishing/CH Beck, 2010, pp. 763–786.

Part III
EU constitutionalism and governance

8 Constitutionalising expertise in the EU

Anchoring knowledge in democracy

Stijn Smismans

Introduction

Constitutional theory builds bridges to democratic theory and to sociological concepts, such as identity and citizenship. However, as far as it is concerned with democratic procedure, it has mainly focused on democratic electoral representation and aggregating interests. At the same time, it has neglected the question of the role of expertise and knowledge in policy making. Political science and regulatory literature, as well as science and technology (STS) literature, have increasingly paid attention to expertise in policy making while policy makers themselves have developed discourses and procedures aiming at 'sound evidence' and 'scientific expertise'. However, the exact relation between knowledge and democracy, and between the aggregation of evidence and the aggregation of interests, requires still further normative investigation.

In relation to the EU, the multi-level constitutionalism debate has reflected on sovereignty, democratic design, identity and citizenship beyond the nation state, but again paid little attention to the role of expertise and knowledge in European governance. Yet, debates about the place of (scientific) expertise and sound evidence have emerged in other parts of the literature and among policy makers, in particular from the mid-1990s onwards, and have intensified since the 2000s. However, arguments about expertise have been patchy and made in relation to particular institutional settings. More holistic arguments about the place of expertise in democratic governance, in a way one would ideally expect from a constitutionalism perspective, have been rarely made. Moreover, different strands of the literature have focused on different institutional settings of European governance. Hence, arguments about expertise are rarely 'cross-referenced'.

In this chapter, I will first place the debate on multi-level constitutionalism within the context of a wider tendency in EU studies to focus on the aggregation of interests and the way the EU's institutional set-up accommodates national diversity, rather than on how expertise is channelled and functional diversity accommodated. I will then investigate further those parts of the literature, beyond constitutionalism, which have dealt with the role of expertise and knowledge in European governance, and set out three dimensions along which these parts of the literature differ from each other.

184 *Stijn Smismans*

The following two sections analyse how arguments about expertise and knowledge have been framed specifically in relation to different European governance mechanisms. Debates on expertise have developed in relation to three institutional settings in particular, namely, European agencies, integrated impact assessments and the open method of coordination (OMC). The following section deals with the debates on both agencies and impact assessments (IAs). These debates emerged at different moments in time, and the debate on IAs picked up where the one on agencies had left off and, more particularly, extended the discussion on expertise from the implementation stage to the legislative stage. Despite their differences, these two debates have much in common, both in relation to their inspirational origin and the 'rational technical' approach to conceiving the place of expertise in governance, relying mainly on a traditional understanding of democracy focused on aggregating interests via parliament. The debate on the OMC instead is very different in nature. I then analyse how arguments on expertise and democratic accountability have been made in relation to the OMC, both in the (normative) literature and in institutional discourse. In the concluding section, I reflect on whether a more holistic argumentation on expertise in European governance can be made, beyond the specific settings of agencies, IAs and OMC, and whether the language of constitutionalism is the appropriate solution for that.

Expertise and (European) constitutionalism

The debate on constitutionalism in the EU has long been framed in terms of 'multi-level constitutionalism' and 'constitutional pluralism', which mainly focused on the relationship between the legal orders of the EU and its member states, and the resulting constitutional dialogue between the European Court of Justice (ECJ) and national constitutional courts.[1] The 'multi-level' or 'pluralist' adjective mainly refers then to the way in which the EU's institutional design accommodates national diversity. The constitutionalism debate thus reflects a broader trend in EU studies, which is characterised by two elements.

First, the predominant focus of EU studies on studying the way the EU has tried to accommodate *national* diversity has overshadowed questions about how European governance deals with functional differentiation. That modern society is increasingly characterised by functional differentiation is a well-established insight of social theory, going back to Weber, and particularly Talcott Parsons'[2] and Niklas

---

1 Ingolf Pernice, 'Multilevel constitutionalism in the European Union', *European Law Review* 27 (2002); Ingolf Pernice, 'The Treaty of Lisbon: Multilevel constitutionalism in action', *Columbia Journal of European Law* 15 (2009); Neil Walker, 'The idea of constitutional pluralism', *Modern Law Review* 65 (2002); and Neil Walker, 'Multilevel constitutionalism: Looking beyond the German debate', in *The Many Constitutions of Europe*, eds. Kaarlo Tuori and Suvi Sankari, (Farnham, UK: Ashgate, 2010).

2 Talcott Parsons, *The Social System* (Abingdon, UK: Routledge, first published 1951; new edition 2005).

Constitutionalising expertise in the EU 185

Luhmann's[3] systems theory. However, the consequences of such functional differentiation for governance in the EU remain strongly understudied and this despite the functionalist and 'sector-by-sector' origin of the European integration project. Certainly, neo-functionalism featured as the front runner of European integration theory,[4] but its institutional and democratic consequences have not been thought through, while normative debates on the EU were increasingly framed in terms of accommodating national differences, through the focus on intergovernmentalism versus supranationalism and the democratic deficit debate, which evolved from 'no demos' argumentation[5] to conceptualising the European polity in terms of demoi-cracy.[6] The limited attention to questions of functional differentiation within EU studies may be understood by the fact that sociology and social theory, in which theories of functional differentiation are routed, have played a less prominent role in EU studies than political science or law. It must be said, though, that even the (limited) sociological studies of the EU have tended to focus on the 'vertical' multi-level challenges of the European polity, dealing with topics as European citizenship or the European public sphere,[7] although sociological approaches to European studies are now on the rise[8] and sociology of knowledge[9] as well as attention to functional differentiation is slowly trickling into the debate.[10]

Second, the EU institutional debate's focus on the way national diversity is accommodated is related to a focus on conceiving politics and reflections on its democratic nature in terms of aggregating interests, whether territorially or functionally defined. The debate has focused on aggregating national or other territorially defined levels of interests, via electoral representation and expressed

3 Niklas Luhmann (translated by Peter Gilgen), *Introduction to Systems Theory* (Cambridge, UK: Polity Press, 2012); Michael King and Chris Thornhill, *Niklas Luhmann's Theory of Politics and Law* (Basingstoke, UK: Palgrave, 2003); Niklas Luhmann *Social Systems* (translated by J. Bednarz Jr. and D. Baecker). (Stanford, CA: Stanford University Press, 1995).

4 Ben Rosamond, 'Performing theory/theorizing performance in emergent supranational governance: The "live" knowledge archive of European integration and the early European Commission', *Journal of European Integration* 32 (2015).

5 Joseph H.H. Weiler, 'Legitimacy and democracy of Union governance', in *The Politics of European Treaty Reform*, eds. Geoffrey Edwards and Alfred Pijpers (London: Pinter, 1997).

6 James Bohman, 'From demos to demoi: Democracy across borders', *Ratio Juris*, 18(3) (2005); Kalypso Nicolaïdis, 'The new constitution as European "demoi-cracy"?', *Critical Review of International Social and Political Philosophy*, 7 (2004); Francis Cheneval, Sandra Lavenex and Frank Schimmelfennieg, 'Demoi-cracy in the European Union: Principles, institutions and policies', *Journal of European Public Policy* 22 (2015).

7 Maurice Roche, *Exploring the Sociology of Europe* (London: Sage, 2010); Klaus Eder and Berhard Giesen, eds., *National Legacies and Transnational Projects* (Oxford, UK: Oxford University Press, 2001).

8 Sabine Saurugger and Frédéric Mérad, 'Does European integration theory need sociology?', *Comparative European Politics* 8 (2010).

9 Rebecca Adles-Nissen and Kristoffer Kropp, eds., *Making Europe: The Sociology of Knowledge Meets European Integration*, Special issue, *Journal of European Integration* 37(2) (2015).

10 Stijn Smismans, 'European constitutionalism and the democratic design of European governance: Rethinking directly deliberative polyarchy and reflexive constitutionalism', in *The Many Constitutions of Europe*, eds. Kaarlo Tuori and Suvi Sankari (Farnham, UK: Ashgate, 2010).

186   *Stijn Smismans*

through parliament at European, national or regional level. In addition, the political science literature has paid extensive attention to functional interest aggregation via lobbying or civil society activity.[11] However, modern governance is as much about knowledge-based claim making as about interest-based claim making.

The role of 'knowledge' or 'expertise' is discussed in several strands of the literature dealing with European policy making. However, it is not dealt with in a normative and holistic fashion in a way a constitutionalism perspective would provide. More particularly, the democratic challenges related to expertise and knowledge are only dealt with in the literature in a patchy way, rather than by addressing the issue more systemically at the level of the polity as a whole. In the following sections, I will analyse how arguments about expertise and knowledge have been made in relation to specific European governance institutions. As will be illustrated in that institutional analysis, the different strands of literature can be distinguished by three different key dimensions of addressing the question of expertise and knowledge in European governance.

First, the focus can be either on expertise or on knowledge. Expertise assumes a level of authority, the possession of knowledge others do not have, giving the privileged position to speak as an expert. Literature on expertise may focus on how experts are appointed and on the institutional settings authorising some actors to speak as experts, as well as on the relation between different types of experts and expertise. The literature on knowledge in policy making instead is most often framed in terms of learning; knowledge is not the privilege of a particular group of experts, and the debate is particularly focused on the conditions under which learning occurs among the diversity of actors involved in policy making.

Second, studies of the role of expertise and knowledge in governance may be either analytical or normative. Hence, literature may deal with whether the inclusion of experts or the institutional setting for knowledge gathering ensures more efficient governance. At the same time, normative models have been proposed which place knowledge at the centre of democratic design.

Third, and partially related to the two previous points, part of the literature fits with a societal understanding close to systems theory; while another part of the literature does not, or even explicitly distances itself from it. Indeed, a systems-theory perspective naturally raises questions in terms of expertise. The difficulties of communication between different sub-systems imply that expertise is located within each sub-system and rules of authorisation and recognition of expertise abide by the norms of each sub-system. Contrary to that, pragmatic approaches to reflexive governance ignore or deny the systemic nature of society and are based on the belief that learning can emerge among all policy actors; knowledge rather than expertise is the key word in this literature.

---

11 For a literature review on the topic, see Rainer Eising, 'Interest groups in EU policy-making', *Living Review in European Governance* 3(4) (2008), doi: 10.12942/lreg-2008-4; Eva G. Heidbreder, 'Civil society participation in EU governance', *Living Review in European Governance* 7(2) (2012), doi: 10.12942/lreg-2012-2.

Constitutionalising expertise in the EU   187

In the following section, I will analyse how arguments regarding expertise and knowledge have been made in relation to different European governance mechanisms, exemplifying how different strands of the literature have remained rather separate.

The debates on European agencies and IAs

From agencies to IAs

Expertise has always been central to the European integration process. The functional approach to European integration considered the participation of actors with particular expertise in the areas of sectoral integration more important than wider public participation, with the initial parliamentary assembly not being directly elected and only having advisory power. However, as a topic of both institutional and academic debate, expertise only really emerged during the 1990s. Particularly following the bovine spongiform encephalopathy (BSE) crisis, the EU's regulatory framework was strongly contested for not respecting scientific standards and being biased by the interests of member states. In fact, the comitology system is based on a collaboration between the Commission and comitology committees, which are composed of representatives from the national administrations. In the case of the 'mad cow crisis', the UK had managed through comitology to keep the European market open to its beef, which would not have been the case if decision-making had relied more heavily on the available scientific evidence.

Both the institutional and the academic debates that followed have focused on the importance of 'independent expertise', which was assumed to be found in the creation of independent agencies. However, the European agencies, which multiplied from the 1990s onwards, have not taken the form of independent regulatory agencies. They have no regulatory powers, but act as executive or information agencies, either giving advice to the European Commission and comitology, or as a network of exchange of information aimed at improving implementation at a national level. Nevertheless, insofar as European agencies have a role in European regulation, their creation is based on a distinction between risk assessment and risk management. Agencies are supposed to provide 'neutral', 'independent' risk assessment, while it is up to the political decision makers to ensure risk management by taking into account a broader variety of factors, which includes both the independent risk assessment and consideration of other (national, functional) interests. Risk management is thus to be ensured by the European legislator (Commission, European Parliament (EP) and Council), or (much more regularly) by the Commission in interaction with comitology procedures. The relation between expertise and democracy in this case is based on the idea that information can be gathered neutrally and is then made available to politically accountable decision makers. The democratic process is ensured through the aggregation of interests via direct electoral representation (EP), or indirect electoral representation (Council) or by the mandate given by the legislator to the Commission. While most of the democratic accountability argument has focused on such

188 *Stijn Smismans*

territorial representation, it has also been recognised that aggregation of interests can be organised in a functional way, by way of consultation with stakeholders. However, from the 'risk assessment/risk management' perspective, such participation should not be institutionalised via the agencies, which are supposed to gather 'neutral' scientific advice (although some agencies have some stakeholders on their board). It is up to the European Commission to organise wider stakeholder participation; and it is up to the discretion of the Commission, and subsequently the EP and the Council (for legislation), or comitology committees (for comitology), to decide to what extent 'neutral' information gathered through agencies and interest-based arguments gathered through Commission consultation procedures are taken into account in the final political decision.

During the 2000s, the debate on expertise in EU policy has shifted from the focus on agencies during the 1990s to a debate on sound evidence in the context of the 'better regulation' agenda and, more particularly, the use of IAs. The debate on the European agencies, which function mainly as networks of national administrations rather than independent regulatory agencies, has more recently been framed in terms of the development of an 'EU executive order', 'European administrative space' or 'European regulatory space',[12] rather than in terms of their centrality in providing independent expertise for European regulatory action. At the same time, with the better regulation debate, the attention for expertise has turned to EU legislative action, whereas it was previously focused on delegated legislation, with the critique on comitology and then on the implementation stage as it became centred on the role of the European agencies. The better regulation debate emerged gradually during the 1990s as a concern about the regulatory burden of EU intervention, but was placed higher on the political agenda in the context of the 2000 Lisbon Strategy, merging different concerns, namely, regulatory burden, sound evidence for policy making and more participatory procedures (the latter particularly also influenced by the parallel debate on the White Paper on European Governance).[13] The most important instrument of the better regulation agenda has been the system of integrated IAs, which the Commission has systematically applied since 2003. Integrated IAs, considering the economic, social and environmental impacts of new proposals, are required for all main policy initiatives and legislative action in particular.

As in the agencies debate, the IA debate also (and particularly the official discourse about IAs) has to a great extent been framed in terms of a dichotomy between ensuring expertise on the one hand, and democratic participation and the aggregation of interests on the other. According to the 2015 Commission Guidelines on Better Regulation:

---

12 Mark Thatcher and David Coen, 'Reshaping European regulatory space: An evolutionary analysis', in *Towards a New Executive Order in Europe?*, eds. Deirdre Curtin and Morten Egeberg (London: Routledge, 2009).

13 Claudio Radaelli, 'Whither better regulation for the Lisbon agenda?', *Journal of European Public Policy* 14 (2007): 194.

Impact assessment is about gathering and analysing evidence to support policy making. In this process, it verifies the existence of a problem, identifies its underlying causes, assesses whether EU action is needed, and analyses the advantages and disadvantages of available solutions. IA promotes more informed decision-making and contributes to Better Regulation which delivers the full benefits of policies at minimum cost while respecting the principles of subsidiarity and proportionality. However, IA is only an aid to policy-making/decision-making and not a substitute for it.[14]

Similar statements were found in the previous iterations of the IA guidelines, indicating that IAs provide 'neutral' information which is then passed on to the political decision-making level.

Expertise for IAs is gathered in different ways: with 'internal expertise' the Commission refers to knowledge available within the Commission itself, which can be gathered by the creation of an IA Steering Group, bringing together officials from Directorates General (DGs) relevant to the issue.[15] 'External expertise' is instead expected to come from expert groups and, in particular, scientific committees set up by the Commission and EU Agencies, while experts on the Commission expert website SINAPSE can also be used.[16] At the same time, the EU's system of IAs does recognise a role for interested parties within the IA process. In fact, compared to other countries and international organisations, the EU's system of IAs pays more attention to ensuring the participation of stakeholders during the drafting of IAs.[17] 'Consultation with interested parties' is said to be, 'an essential tool for producing high quality and credible policy proposals. Consultation helps to ensure that policies are effective and efficient, and it increases the legitimacy of EU action from the point of view of stakeholders and citizens'.[18]

However, while it is acknowledged that stakeholders or 'interested parties' can provide evidence and can contribute to, for instance, 'finding new ideas (brainstorming), collecting factual data, and validating a hypothesis', their involvement also comes with the warning that 'it is important to distinguish evidence from opinions'.[19] Information provided by stakeholders is considered partisan and not objective, and it is therefore said that DGs should ensure 'peer-reviewing, benchmarking with other studies and sensitivity analysis' in order to 'significantly enhance the quality of data' and ensure 'the robustness of the results'.[20] At the

---

14 European Commission, Commission Staff Working Document, *Better Regulation Guidelines*, COM (2015) 215 final, p. 16. Similar statements were found in previous versions of the Impact Assessment Guidelines.
15 2009 Commission Guidelines on IAs, p. 18.
16 Ibid. p. 19.
17 Radaelli, 'Whither better regulation', p. 194.
18 2009 Commission Guidelines on IAs, p. 19.
19 Ibid. p. 20.
20 Ibid.

190   *Stijn Smismans*

same time, DGs should be sure to 'engage all affected stakeholders' and 'consult all relevant target groups'. Such wide involvement seems to have a representative dimension: it is only through wide participation of all stakeholders that the feasibility and legitimacy of policy proposals are ensured. The EU's system of IAs thus does not entirely rely on 'independent expertise', but also on expertise provided by interested parties. At the same time, it is assumed that some actors, such as scientific committees and agencies, do provide such independent expertise (not requiring a similar check of 'robustness' as in relation to information from stakeholders) and that the DG drafting the IA can provide a neutral overview of stakeholders' positions which can then be forwarded to the political decision-making level, which can use this information at its discretion.

Common features and differences of the agencies and IA debates

Despite the time lapse between the start of the European agencies and the IA debates, they have many common features. More precisely, both debates struggle with two 'pitfalls' that have structured the argumentation in a particular way, namely, a strong inspiration in the US experience with these governance tools and a solid belief in the rational technical model of policy making.

Both the debates on agencies and IAs at EU level have been strongly influenced by arguments concerning these governance tools in the US, where they have been used for a longer time. The debate on European agencies was strongly influenced by arguments about the assumed advantages of using independent regulatory agencies as a governance technique, particularly through the work of Giandomenico Majone.[21] However, as the European agencies did not develop into real independent regulatory agencies, the American-inspired debate on the independence of expertise often sounds out of context. Many European agencies function as networks of national administrative authorities. The latter might also be institutionalised outside the main administration of ministries, on the basis of arguments of independence and expertise. However, such networks do not provide the EU agencies with regulatory decision-making power. Although some agencies have executive decision-making power, and some agencies may de facto weigh heavily on regulatory decisions due to their expert advice, the (final and formal) regulatory decision-making power remains in the hands of the political decision-making bodies, most often the Commission in interaction with comitology committees representing the member states' interests.

In a similar way, the experience with IAs in the US has been regularly referred to as a reference point in the European debate,[22] but IAs in the EU turned out to

---

21 Giandomenico Majone, *Regulating Europe* (London: Routledge, 1996); Giandomenico Majone and Michelle Everson, 'Independent agencies, oversight, coordination and procedural control', in O. De Schutte, N. Lebessis and J. Paterson eds. *Governance in the European Union* (Brussels, Belgium: European Commission, 2001).

22 While the EU's broader Better Regulation debate has also been inspired by national experiences (particularly from the UK and the Netherlands), the debate on IA was particularly coloured by

Constitutionalising expertise in the EU   191

play a very different role than what they have traditionally been used for in the US. In the US, IAs are particularly used as a way to curb the enthusiasm and initiative of the regulatory agencies. It is a way for the President, accountable to the legislature, to control delegated regulation by independent agencies, a control mechanism that is particularly inspired by a deregulatory philosophy. In the EU, by contrast, IAs are not to be drafted by the agencies (which do not have the regulatory power) but by the European Commission. However, this applies in particular when the Commission takes legislative initiatives, unlike in the US where the legislator does not have to draft IAs. This raises very different constitutional questions than in the American case, as IAs in the EU are not simply a way in which the executive (regulatory independent agency) has to justify itself, but is a way of framing the legislative debate itself. It can be argued that IAs oblige the Commission to justify its initiatives in front of the co-legislators, which are the EP and the Council. At the same time, the Commission (protected by its near exclusive right of legislative initiative) thus sets out the cognitive framework within which legislative proposals will be debated. Of course, the EP and Council can bring in totally different arguments. However, in the battle over 'sound evidence' and 'appropriate knowledge', the EP and Council are modestly resourced in counter-arguing the expertise set out in IAs by the Commission. In an effort to counterbalance the Commission's expertise, the EP created a Directorate for Impact Assessment and European Added Value in January 2012, which became in 2014 part of a new European Parliamentary Research Service with 200 staff to support members of parliament with more evidence. While this may improve the EP's ability to engage in the legislative debate on the basis of 'sound evidence', the better regulation agenda of the new Juncker Commission, presented in early 2015, may lead to the EP not even being able to put forward its 'sound' arguments. The new Commission is strongly committed to a thinner regulatory agenda. Armed with IA and evaluation reports, the Commission's first Vice-President, with the responsibility for better regulation, will proactively block initiatives from Commission DGs if considered not fitting the thin regulatory agenda. Hence, 'sound evidence' provided in IA and evaluation reports, particularly in terms of cost-benefit analysis,[23] may be used against EU intervention without the EP even having a say over it.

The second common pitfall in the debates on agencies and IAs is the belief in a rational technical model of policy making, in which a clear line can be drawn between the gathering of neutral expertise and the subsequent political decision-making stage. Such a dichotomy between expertise and aggregating interests fails to acknowledge the many insights from STS studies, sociology of science and

---

its American references. See Jonathan B. Wiener, 'Better regulation in Europe', *Current Legal Problems* 59 (2006): 453.

23 On the deregulatory risks of the Commission's recent commitment to an 'evaluation culture', see Stijn Smismans, 'Policy evaluation in the EU: The challenges of linking ex ante and ex post appraisal', *European Journal of Risk Regulation* 6 (2015).

192   *Stijn Smismans*

policy analysis, so that such a strict distinction does not stand the test of reality.[24] Interest-based participants also possess knowledge and evidence and definitely make knowledge-based claims. There has also been an increased 'politicisation of science' as opposed interest groups make claims on the basis of contradictory scientific arguments using only those supporting their position.[25] In turn, this development makes public that science does not provide the single truth. As a consequence, the neutrality of science and expertise cannot be assumed, and there is plenty of evidence that science can be bent by special interests.[26]

The IA debate has acknowledged that interest groups also provide information, but while it is cautious about the bias of such information, it is less critical of the politics of the gathering of assumed neutral and scientific expertise and interests at play therein. In the agency debate, the belief in the separation of knowledge gathering and interest politics is even more clear-cut. Yet, over the last years, criticism from civil society organisation and from the Court of Auditors and the European Ombudsman on issues of conflict of interest in the functioning of the European agencies has undermined the normative underpinnings of the agencies' institutional set-up.

The debate on the OMC

While the debates on agencies and IAs show many similarities in their arguments on expertise, a very different approach to expertise in European governance emerged in the debate on the OMC. The core of this debate developed in the first half of the 2000s,[27] and thus somewhat in between the key moments of attention of the agency and IA debates. In 2000, the Lisbon Summit had put the OMC centrally on the agenda as a new governance tool. Instead of relying on binding EU intervention, the OMC is based on the definition of European guidelines, for which the member states then have to set out national action plans explaining how they intend to implement or have implemented these guidelines. These action plans are subsequently assessed at the European level (which may lead to a revision of the guidelines) and may be combined with a process of specific recommendations addressed to the member states. This cyclical process is combined with the definition of benchmarks and measurable indicators allowing comparison

---

24 Sabine Maasen and Peter Weingart, eds., *Democratization of Expertise? Exploring Novel Forms of Scientific Advice in Political Decision-making* (Dordrecht, The Netherlands: Springer, 2009); Sheila Jasanoff, *Designs on Nature. Science and Democracy in Europe and the United States* (Princeton, NJ: Princeton University Press, 2005).

25 Maasen and Weingart, ibid. p. 4; Michelle Everson and Ellen Vos, 'The scientification of politics and the politicisation of science', in *Uncertain Risks Regulated*, eds. Michelle Everson and Ellen Vos (Abingdon, UK: Routledge, 2009), p. 8.

26 Thomas McGarity and Wendy Wagner, *Bending Science. How Special Interests Corrupt Public Health Research* (Cambridge, MA: Harvard University Press, 2010).

27 For an overview of the main topics in the numerous pages written on the OMC in that period, see Sandra Kröger, ed., *What We Have Learnt: Advances, Pitfalls and Remaining Questions in OMC Research*, Special Issue 1, *European Integration Online Papers* 13 (2009), doi: 10.1695/2009005.

Constitutionalising expertise in the EU 193

of best practice. Moreover, the OMC is said to be based on a 'fully decentralised approach', in line with the principle of subsidiarity in which the Union, the member states, the regional and local levels, as well as the social partners and civil society, are actively involved, using variable forms of partnership.

In both the institutional and academic debates on the OMC, the question of 'expertise' is rather framed in terms of knowledge and exchange of information. The OMC is conceptualised as a process of learning. From this perspective, all actors in the process are assumed to learn and be capable of providing knowledgeable input. Unlike in the agency and IA debates, there is no strong normative argumentation on the assumed benefit of separating the 'neutral gathering of expertise' from the political decision-making. Both are assumed to emerge through the same bottom-up process. In fact, within the OMC, it is difficult to oppose the traditional democratic aggregation of interests based on an electoral mandate to the neutral gathering of expertise, since parliamentary involvement in the OMC is weak. At EU level, the OMC is driven by the Commission and the (European) Council, with the EP almost entirely absent. One has therefore argued in favour of strengthening the role of national parliaments in the OMC.[28] However, while they can be involved in the implementation of the OMC at the national level, ensuring involvement in the drafting of the EU level guidelines is much more difficult. Hence the OMC's discourse on the importance of bottom-up participation and stakeholder involvement. Whether the OMC's decentralised setting really ensures at the same time the gathering of knowledge and the representative involvement of all stakeholders, has been an issue of academic inquiry, with some evidence of increased stakeholder participation, but leading to an overall picture of an OMC that is mainly technocratically driven by administrators at national and EU level.[29]

At the same time, a more theoretical academic debate on the OMC developed around ideas of reflexive governance and the model of directly-deliberative polyarchy (DDP). Reflexive governance has been discussed in both policy analysis, particularly in environmental policy, and legal theory, particularly based on Gunther Teubner's autopoietic theory of reflexive law.[30] The common ground is the focus on policy and law making as a cyclical and permanent learning process in which experience with the policy or law in practice leads to amendment of that policy or norm (first-order learning) and in which the process of policy and law

---

28 Francesco Duina and Tapio Raunio, 'The open method of coordination and national parliaments: Further marginalization or new opportunities?', *Journal of European Public Policy* 14 (2007).

29 Kerstin Jacobsson and Åsa Vifell, 'Soft governance, employment policy and committee deliberation', in *Making the European Polity. Reflexive Integration in the EU*, ed. Erik Oddvar Eriksen (London: Routledge, 2005); Evelyne Léonard *et al. New Structures, Forms and Processes of Governance in European Industrial Relations* (Luxembourg: European Foundation for Living and Working Conditions, 2007), p. 70.

30 Erik Oddvar Eriksen, ed., *Making the European Polity. Reflexive Integration in the EU* (London: Routledge, 2005); Jan-Peter Voss, Dierk Bauknecht and René Kemp, eds., *Reflexive Governance for Sustainable Development* (Cheltenham, UK: Edward Elgar, 2006); Olivier De Schutter and Jacques Lenoble, eds., *Reflexive Governance. Redefining the Public Interest in a Pluralistic World* (Oxford, UK: Hart, 2010).

194 *Stijn Smismans*

making itself can be revised (second-order learning).[31] Most authors on reflexive law and governance stress the importance of a wide decentralised participation in these learning processes. At the same time, theories on reflexive governance or law are often proposed as analytical, describing the changing nature of modern policy and law making. When they are more normative, it is mainly in proposing the conditions under which learning would best occur. Arguments about the democratic nature of reflexive governance are often made implicitly rather than explicitly. Decentralised and participatory processes ensure the required knowledge and expertise for learning. That they ensure at the same time democratic involvement is often assumed, but not strongly argued.

However, the OMC has also been said to be an example of DDP. The model of DDP is explicitly proposed as a design for modern democratic governance. DDP is a democratic ideal that is based on the idea that:

> [l]ocal-, or more exactly, lower-level actors (nation state or national peak organizations of various kinds; regions, provinces or sub-national associations within these, and so on down to the level of whatever kind of neighbourhood the problem in question makes relevant) are granted autonomy to experiment with solutions of their own devising within broadly defined areas of public policy. In return they furnish central or higher-level units with rich information regarding their goals as well as the progress they are making towards achieving them, and agree to respect in their actions framework rights of democratic procedure.[32]

The system is 'directly-deliberative' since 'citizens must examine their own choices in the light of the relevant deliberations and experiences of others',[33] in contrast to other discursive ideas of democracy of deliberation by an administrative or political elite. The system is 'polyarchic' due to the permanent disequilibrium created by the grant of substantial powers of initiative to lower-level units.[34] The democratic claims of DDP are akin to ideas of participatory democracy[35] and deliberative democracy in that it focuses on direct participation and deliberation in terms of rational argument. DDP aims at decentralisation 'down to the level of whatever kind of neighbourhood the problem in question makes relevant',[36] and postulates 'direct participation by and reason-giving between and among free and

---

31 Voss, Bauknecht, and Kemp, ibid.
32 Oliver Gerstenberg and Charles Sabel, 'Directly-deliberative polyarchy: An institutional ideal for Europe?', in *Good Governance in Europe's Integrated Market*, eds. Christian Joerges and Renaud Dehousse (Oxford, UK: Oxford University Press, 2002), p. 291.
33 Joshua Cohen and Charles Sabel, 'Directly-deliberative polyarchy', *European Law Journal*, 3 (1997): 314.
34 Gerstenberg and Sabel, 'Directly-deliberative polyarchy', p. 292.
35 Carole Pateman, *Participation and Democratic Theory* (Cambridge, UK: Cambridge University Press, 1970).
36 Gerstenberg and Sabel, 'Directly-deliberative polyarchy', p. 291.

Constitutionalising expertise in the EU 195

equal citizens'[37] as a normative ideal. 'There is a presumption in favour of equal membership for affected parties – open meetings, with equal rights to participate in discussion and decision-making for all affected parties'.[38]

DDP does not fit well with the concept of expertise. Instead, knowledge is to emerge through a bottom-up process in which all actors can learn. However, DDP underestimates the systemic nature of knowledge and society. As argued in systems theory, society is constituted by sub-systems with their own language, making interaction between these sub-systems not entirely impossible, but very difficult. Gerstenberg and Sabel argue instead that:

> [l]ocal knowledge is neither tacit nor fully and self-referentially systematic. Co-ordination among local collaborators is necessary because of the diversity of their views and possible because . . . the exploration of the ambiguities internal to each shades into exchange with the others. But as local co-ordination yields new ambiguities of its own, there is both need and possibility for inter-local exchange through a new centre that frames discussion and re-frames it as results permit.[39]

However, the evidence of governance practices, in particular in the context of the EU, shows that the heterogeneity of participants[40] within local units emerges far less spontaneously than DDP seems to suggest, given the systemic expertise that is required. Moreover, a new centre at a higher level that allows inter-local exchange may indeed provide opportunity to reframe discussion, but the (partial) self-referentiality of sub-systems implies that, if not consciously institutionalised, there will be a tendency for such a higher-level centre to be created within the sub-system rather than creating deliberation across sub-systems. As the OMC illustrates, European governance tends to occur through auto-referential deliberation between functional actors structured by the language of each sub-system, rather than as a bottom-up process based on citizen participation and a rather spontaneous process of cross-system interaction.

Conclusion: back to constitutionalism for a holistic approach to expertise?

The analysis above shows how arguments about the role of expertise and knowledge in European governance have been made in relation to specific institutional settings and by different parts of the literature which have not interacted much. Set on track with the debate on European agencies, which was focused on the (regulatory) implementation stage, the debate on expertise was

---

37 Cohen and Sabel, 'Directly-deliberative polyarchy', p. 314.
38 Ibid. p. 333.
39 Gerstenberg and Sabel, 'Directly-deliberative polyarchy', p. 340.
40 Cohen and Sabel, 'Directly-deliberative polyarchy', p. 333.

196   *Stijn Smismans*

extended to the legislative stage by the topic of IAs. In both cases, normative discourse has been based on the idea of a separation between the democratic aggregation of interests on the one hand, and ensuring the input of independent expertise in policy making on the other. A different approach predominated in relation to the third European governance structure that engendered arguments about expertise and democracy, namely, the OMC. In this context, both expertise and interest representation are assumed to emerge bottom-up through the same process.

None of the three governance mechanisms around which arguments of expertise have developed received much attention in the debate on constitutionalism. This raises the question of whether constitutionalism can provide a more holistic approach to the patchy arguments about expertise and democracy which have been framed in function of specific institutional settings and by separate literatures.

Neil Walker describes the essence of constitutionalism by its 'meta-political function of shaping the domain of politics broadly conceived – of literally constituting the body politic'.[41] It is:

> [t]hat species of practical reasoning which, in the name of some defensible locus of common interest, concerns itself with the organization and regulation of those spheres of collective decision-making deemed relevant to the common interest in a manner that is adequately informed by the common interest.[42]

Within the context of the nation state, constitutionalism functioned as a cluster concept, accumulating various distinct layers of situated constitutional practice, namely, juridical (self-constituted legal order), politico-institutional (idea of a secular delimited political realm, free from deference to particular interests), popular (democratic self-constitution) and societal (idea of an integrated society, whether 'thin' political society or 'thicker' cultural society).[43] However, much of contemporary governance does not correspond to the expectation of such holistic constitutionalism.

The debate on multi-level constitutionalism has indeed more recently evolved from multi-level constitutionalism *senso stricto* (focused on the EU and with the option to anchor the multi-levels within democratic processes of the nation state) to multi-level constitutionalism *senso lato*, paying attention to the complexity of modern governance which is often global, transnational, partially based on private regulation and characterised by heterarchical networks (often difficult to anchor within the hierarchical nation state democratic process). The debate on such multi-actor (rather than multi-level) constitutionalism has so far mainly been

---

41 Neil Walker, 'Multilevel constitutionalism: Looking beyond the German debate', in *The Many Constitutions of Europe*, eds. Kaarlo Tuori and Suvi Sankari (Farnham, UK: Ashgate, 2010), p. 152.
42 Ibid.
43 Ibid, pp. 154–155.

initiated in relation to transnational private regulation.[44] However, multi-actor governance plays at all levels, including within the nation state and where public and private sectors interact. In fact, the key challenge of modern governance may well be how knowledge, expertise and cognitive frameworks, which are often functionally defined and increasingly transnational, influence policy making. Put differently, the challenge of multi-actor constitutionalism is how to regulate the interaction between the provision of knowledge and expertise on the one hand, and interest-based politics which answers to the meta-constitutional principle of self-governance, on the other. So far, the literature on multi-level constitutionalism *senso lato* has not been framed in these terms.

At the same time, the literature on transnational private regulation also raises the question of how far the language and meta-political function of constitutionalism can reach. In a special issue on transnational private regulation of the *Journal of Law and Society*, the guest editors, Colin Scott, Fabrizio Cafaggi and Linda Senden investigate the constitutional challenge of such private governance.[45] They argue that private-regulatory power can significantly enhance capacity for developing and implementing public-regarding norms. The legitimacy of such private governance may often not be found in public law forms that traditionally justify regulatory intervention (above all linkage to electoral politics, but also proceduralisation and judicial accountability), but in private law forms and competitive structures. However, while these might provide legitimating discourses, they do so in a much more sectoral way, and one wonders whether it can really live up to the constitutional meta-political function of providing a framework ensuring the common interest. Although the authors refer briefly to the meta-principle of the right to self-governance,[46] which they argue might also be organised in ways other than electoral politics, most of the proposed legitimating discourses stand far from traditional constitutional guarantees.

The analysis by Bomhoff and Meuwese in the same special issue may therefore appear more honestly modest, but is at the same time even more disappointing from a constitutionalist perspective.[47] Here the constitutionalist language is entirely absent. They analyse the meta-norms that develop through different disciplinary and professional lenses, looking in particular at private international law and better regulation. However, in the absence of a constitutionalist discourse as benchmark, it may be too easily taken for granted that such meta-norms (for instance, on consultation requirements on better regulation) live up to democratic benchmarks.

Bringing this back to the analysis above, the debates on agencies, IAs and OMC have all engendered legitimating discourses and, in the language of Bomhoff and

---

44 For example, the special issue of the *Journal of Law and Society* 38(1) 2011.

45 Colin Scott, Fabrizio Cafaggi and Linda Senden, 'The conceptual and constitutional challenge of transnational private regulation', *Journal of Law and Society* 38 (2011).

46 Ibid. p. 14.

47 Jacco Bomhoff and Anne Meuwese, 'The meta-regulation of transnational private regulation', *Journal of Law and Society* 38 (2011).

198 Stijn Smismans

Meuwese, meta-norms among the policy makers involved. None of them, though, has provided a broader normative framework in a way holistic constitutionalism would have done. Not only are these legitimating discourses limited to a narrow range of actors but neither do they reach as far as a narrative 'constituting the body politic'. In the agency debate at least, the broader constitutional challenge has partially been raised with reference to principles of (global) administrative law (which finally links into electoral politics), while the democratic concern in the context of the OMC has been raised via reflexive governance and deliberative democracy. The better regulation debate, instead, has largely developed its own meta-norms, largely independent from constitutionalist language and concerns. In the absence of the constitutionalist language, such narratives risk providing simply a legitimating discourse for functional governance captured by particular interests.

At the same time, given the complexity of modern governance (heterarchical and often transnational), 'traditional' holistic constitutionalism is clearly a framework from the past. The challenge is to rethink constitutionalism in such a way that its core meta-function of shaping the domain of politics in the common interest can be ensured, based on the acknowledgment that policy making is as much about knowledge-based as about interest-based claim making.

Bibliography

Adles-Nissen, Rebecca and Kristoffer Kropp, eds. *Making Europe: The Sociology of Knowledge Meets European Integration*. Special issue of the *Journal of European Integration* 37 (2015).

Bohman, James. 'From demos to demoi: Democracy across borders'. *Ratio Juris*, 18 (2005): 293–314.

Bomhoff, Jacco and Anne Meuwese. 'The meta-regulation of transnational private regulation'. *Journal of Law and Society* 38 (2011): 138–162.

Cheneval, Francis, Sandra Lavenex and Frank Schimmelfennieg. 'Demoi-cracy in the European Union: Principles, institutions and policies'. *Journal of European Public Policy* 22 (2015): 1–18.

Cohen, Joshua and Charles Sabel. 'Directly-deliberative polyarchy'. *European Law Journal* 3(4) (1997): 313–342.

De Schutter, Olivier and Jacques Lenoble, eds. *Reflexive Governance. Redefining the Public Interest in a Pluralistic World*. Oxford, UK: Hart, 2010.

Duina, Francesco and Tapio Raunio. 'The open method of coordination and national parliaments: Further marginalization or new opportunities?'. *Journal of European Public Policy* 14 (2007): 489–506.

Eder, Klaus and Berhard Giesen, eds. *National Legacies and Transnational Projects*. Oxford, UK: Oxford University Press, 2001.

Eising, Rainer. 'Interest groups in EU policy-making'. *Living Review in European Governance* 3(4) (2008). doi: 10.12942/lreg-2008-4.

Eriksen, Erik Oddvar, ed. *Making the European Polity. Reflexive integration in the EU*. London: Routledge, 2005.

Everson, Michelle and Ellen Vos, 'The scientification of politics and the politicisation of science'. In *Uncertain Risks Regulated*, edited by Michelle Everson and Ellen Vos. Abingdon, UK: Routledge, 2009, pp. 1–18.

Constitutionalising expertise in the EU 199

Gerstenberg, Oliver and Charles F. Sabel. 'Directly-deliberative polyarchy: An institutional ideal for Europe?'. In *Good Governance in Europe's Integrated Market*, edited by Christian Joerges and Renaud Dehousse. Oxford, UK: Oxford University Press, 2002, pp. 289–341.

Heidbreder, Eva G. 'Civil society participation in EU governance'. *Living Review in European Governance* 7(2) (2012). doi: 10.12942/lreg-2012-2.

Jacobsson, Kerstin and Åsa Vifell. 'Soft governance, employment policy and committee deliberation'. In *Making the European Polity. Reflexive integration in the EU*, edited by Erik Oddvar Eriksen. London: Routledge, 2005, pp. 214–236.

Jasanoff, Sheila. *Designs on Nature. Science and Democracy in Europe and the United States*. Princeton, NJ: Princeton University Press, 2005.

King, Michael and Chris Thornhill. *Niklas Luhmann's Theory of Politics and Law*. Basingstoke, UK: Palgrave, 2003.

Kröger, Sandra, ed. *What We Have Learnt: Advances, Pitfalls and Remaining Questions in OMC Research*. Special Issue 1, *European Integration Online Papers* 13 (2009). doi: 10.1695/2009005.

Léonard, Evelyne, Ronald Erne, Paul Marginson and Stijn Smismans. *New Structures, Forms and Processes of Governance in European Industrial Relations*. Luxembourg: European Foundation for Living and Working Conditions, 2007.

Luhmann, Niklas. *Social Systems* (translated by J. Bednarz Jr. and D. Baecker). Stanford, CA: Stanford University Press, 1995.

Luhmann, Niklas. *Introduction to Systems Theory* (translated by Peter Gilgen). Cambridge, UK: Polity Press, 2012.

Maasen, Sabine and Peter Weingart, eds. *Democratization of Expertise? Exploring Novel Forms of Scientific Advice in Political Decision-making*. Dordrecht, The Netherlands: Springer, 2009.

Majone, Giandomenico. *Regulating Europe*. London: Routledge, 1996.

Majone, Giandomenico and Michelle Everson. 'Independent agencies, oversight, coordination and procedural control', in *Governance in the European Union*, edited by O. De Schutte, N. Lebessis and J. Paterson. Brussels, Belgium: European Commission, 2001.

McGarity, Thomas O. and Wendy E. Wagner. *Bending Science. How Special Interests Corrupt Public Health Research*. Cambridge, MA: Harvard University Press, 2010.

Nicolaïdis, Kalypso. 'The new constitution as European "demoi-cracy"?'. *Critical Review of International Social and Political Philosophy* 7 (2004): 76–93.

Parsons, Talcott. *The Social System*. Abingdon, UK: Routledge, first published 1951, new edition 2005.

Pateman, Carole. *Participation and Democratic Theory*. Cambridge, UK: Cambridge University Press, 1970.

Pernice, Ingolf. 'Multilevel constitutionalism in the European Union'. *European Law Review* 27 (2002): 511–529.

Pernice, Ingolf. 'The Treaty of Lisbon: Multilevel constitutionalism in action'. *Columbia Journal of European Law* 15 (2009): 349–407.

Radaelli, Claudio. 'Whither better regulation for the Lisbon agenda?' *Journal of European Public Policy* 14 (2007): 190–207.

Roche, Maurice. *Exploring the Sociology of Europe*. London: Sage, 2010.

Rosamond, Ben. 'Performing theory/theorizing performance in emergent supranational governance: The "live" knowledge archive of European integration and the early European Commission'. *Journal of European Integration* 32 (2015): 175–191.

200   *Stijn Smismans*

Saurugger, Sabine and Frédéric Mérad. 'Does European integration theory need sociology?' *Comparative European Politics* 8 (2010): 1–18.

Scott, Colin, Fabrizio Cafaggi and Linda Senden. 'The conceptual and constitutional challenge of transnational private regulation'. *Journal of Law and Society* 38 (2011): 1–19.

Smismans, Stijn. 'European constitutionalism and the democratic design of European Governance: Rethinking directly deliberative polyarchy and reflexive constitutionalism'. In *The Many Constitutions of Europe*, edited by Kaarlo Tuori and Suvi Sankari. Farnham, UK: Ashgate, 2010, pp. 169–193.

Smismans, Stijn. 'Policy evaluation in the EU: The challenges of linking ex ante and ex post appraisal'. *European Journal of Risk Regulation* 6 (2015): 6–26.

Thatcher, Mark and David Coen. 'Reshaping European regulatory space: An evolutionary analysis'. In *Towards a New Executive Order in Europe?*, edited by Deirdre Curtin and Morten Egeberg. London: Routledge, 2009, pp. 168–198.

Voss, Jan-Peter, Dierk Bauknecht and René Kemp, eds. *Reflexive Governance for Sustainable Development*. Cheltenham, UK: Edward Elgar, 2006.

Walker, Neil. 'The idea of constitutional pluralism'. *Modern Law Review* (65) (2002): 317–359.

Walker, Neil. 'Multilevel constitutionalism: Looking beyond the German debate'. In *The Many Constitutions of Europe*, edited by Kaarlo Tuori and Suvi Sankari. Farnham, UK: Ashgate, 2010, pp. 143–168.

Weiler, Joseph H.H. 'Legitimacy and democracy of Union governance'. In *The Politics of European Treaty Reform*, edited by Geoffrey Edwards and Alfred Pijpers. London: Pinter, 1997, pp. 249–287.

Wiener, Jonathan B. 'Better regulation in Europe'. *Current Legal Problems* 59 (2006): 447–518.

9 Bringing politics into European integration

The unvoiced issues of market-making

Gareth Davies

1.

What the European Union should be and do are political questions. The relationship between a group of neighbouring states on a peninsula does not have such a self-evident institutional or legal form that there is nothing to contest, not even given a complex history that brings great normative weight to the question. Neither can agreements made 50 or 60 or even 20 years ago by Treaty be seen as the definitive answer to the big questions of that relationship. Even if – which seems unlikely – there was at some point in the history of European integration a clear and consensual vision of its proper form, and even if – which is certainly not the case – that vision was given clear and legitimated form in Treaty texts, nothing in such a constitutional moment should, or can, prevent all those visions and agreements from being revisited.

Should not, because constitutional entrenchment – the rule of the dead – is only suited to norms so sacred that we would be prepared to sacrifice democracy for them. That claim can perhaps be made about the mission to prevent war in Europe, the driving force behind integration, but it cannot plausibly be made about the how and what of that integration, and the manner in which it is given organizational and legal shape. Even if peace is a goal beyond legitimate challenge, the rules which take us there are inevitably to be arrived at by negotiation and experiment. Whether war comes from emotion or merely interests, to lead a continent to peace without asking its people what they feel and which interests they hold dear, is absurd, almost oxymoronic.

Cannot, because the European Union has never achieved such an entrenched power that its will becomes reality, despite what states may think. Taking effect through national institutions, laws and indeed markets, it depends for its effectiveness upon a certain acceptance and internalization of its dogmas. If these become too rigidly opposed to the normative consensus in the states then it is not the states who will be reshaped so much as the European Union which will be quietly sidelined. At most, both states and Union may deform each other. However, there is nothing in those few institutions in Brussels and Luxembourg which contain the capacity to enforce a fundamentally unwelcome dogma for an unlimited period of time.

202 *Gareth Davies*

Where should this contestation take place? It is not enough to debate the Treaties. They are too vague, necessarily so. With such a diversity of states, opinions and interests, it is hard to imagine how a European Union Treaty could be anything other than an incomplete bargain. This means that debate about the Treaties can certainly take place, but the resulting text is incapable of capturing the outcome of that debate to a sufficiently reliable degree.[1] Treaty texts do not determine predictably what the Union legislature may or should do, nor how the Court will decide Treaty-based litigation. Changes to the Treaties may certainly influence these processes, but only in a broad and general sense. After a Treaty change, it remains uncertain what the outcome of that change will be. The history of European law, as indeed of the constitutional law of any state, is full of instances of exposed indeterminacy, unexpected results and texts used in ways that were not anticipated by their authors.[2]

Politics as an expression of popular will requires more robustly concrete mechanisms. Even if the debating and determining of abstract Treaty principles has some purpose, these are not precise enough to capture and give expression to the real differences about what Europe should be or do. That requires politics to also, in fact primarily, exist within the sphere of the Treaty, in the decisions about how it is to be used, interpreted and implemented.[3]

This entails, above all, two things. First, that the voices of the public should be heard in the process of adopting EU legislation, so that this legislation is genuinely the product of a political process. Second, that when the Court of Justice interprets the Treaty it should have before it arguments which express or contain the views of the public on the values and political preferences at stake, and it should take these into account.[4] Fixing the meaning of such an open text is a matter of choosing between these values and preferences just as much as it is a matter of applying legal technical skills to written rules. Arguments that are essentially, overtly, policy-based or otherwise normative are as relevant and necessary a contribution to the interpretative process as are more traditional legal arguments about the inter-relationship of the words and sentences of the written law. Indeed, in many Treaty contexts, it is the latter form of argument which seems artificial, irrelevant and a dishonest means of justifying a conclusion. The Court may be right to search for coherence between the rules, phrases and constraints which are in play, but often that search will not be enough to determine a decision: only a political choice can explain the final adjudicatory leap.

---

1 Gareth Davies, 'Subsidiarity: The wrong idea in the wrong place at the wrong time', *Common Market Law Review* 43 (2006).

2 See, also, Thomas Wilhelmsson, 'Private law in the EU: Harmonised or fragmented Europeanisation', *European Review of Private Law* 1 (2002).

3 Damian Chalmers, 'The European redistributive state and a European law of struggle', *European Law Journal* 18 (2012).

4 Marco Dani, 'Rehabilitating social conflicts in European public law', *European Law Journal* 18 (2012); Christian Joerges, 'Unity in diversity as Europe's vocation and conflicts law as Europe's constitutional form', LEQS Paper no. 28 (2010). doi: 10.2139/ssrn.1723249.

2.

For most of its history, the most important and politically salient, if not politicized, policy of the European Union has been the creation of an internal market. The decision to remove barriers to the movement of goods, persons, services and capital between the member states has had an enormous impact on the economies of those states and the lives of those living in them, as well as on many public institutions and on the capacities of state governments.[5]

Union activities developed more recently, such as the government of the euro and the policing of national budgets, threaten to have an equally powerful impact, albeit on a more macro scale and with less direct interference in the details of national laws and practices. Yet these activities still take place within a sort of oligarchic field, in which key national and Union actors negotiate and agree largely outside the reach of either representative politics or law.[6] There can be public protest, but with only a marginal role for either the Parliament or Court in the making of policy, there is little role for the formal representation of interests. There is plenty of criticism to be made of this, but it is a different criticism from the one in this chapter, which concerns the inadequacy of representation even when these institutions are involved.

Nevertheless, it is likely that in the years to come both monetary and budgetary governance will normalize; they will become the subject of law to an increasing extent, expressed in directives and judgments and look ever more like normal policy fields.[7] Part of the rhetoric of that process will no doubt be the need for accountability and for political representation in such important policy areas. Yet, unless lessons are learned from the political inadequacies of market regulation, the European history of excluding meaningful contestation will merely repeat itself in another, equally contestable, field.

3.

What would contesting the internal market entail? The thrust of the law has not been essentially deregulatory so much as essentially pro-competition, with the primary effects of legislation and case law being to expose producers, traders and service providers to a wider and fiercer range of competitors – not just from abroad, but also from within their state as changing regulatory frameworks have increased economic diversity.

With competition is believed to have come increased economic dynamism, reduced prices and increased welfare, of a certain kind, but alongside that there has also been arguably increased economic uncertainty and a change in the styles of public economic space as the small, traditional and expensive local firm finds

---

5 Gareth Davies, 'Internal market adjudication and the quality of life in Europe', *Columbia Journal of European Law* 21 (2015).
6 Chalmers, 'The European redistributive state'.
7 Ibid.

204 *Gareth Davies*

itself challenged by the mass-producing, economically efficient, transnational business.[8] There have been, at least relatively, winners and losers among the geographical areas of the EU and among the individuals and social groups. Some experience economic Europeanization and its consequences as life enhancing, and others as harmful to their quality of life. What determines this is not just what happens to those people but also how they value different aspects of life: there is no objectively better or worse market. Contrary to the occasional simplistic economic claim, we do not all just want more for less.

The core political question about the internal market is thus what it should be. That is not to try to undo the Treaty or challenge its fundament. Such challenges would be legitimate, but they belong to the politics of the making of the Treaty, not the politics within it. However, even accepting that there shall be an internal market, and accepting all the Treaty provisions concerning it, leaves an enormous space for discussion about how it should be understood.

These provisions are so brief, and so deceptively simple, that this is easy to show. They fall into three types. First, there is Article 26(2) of the Treaty on the Functioning of the European Union (TFEU), which gives the closest to a definition of the market, but not a very detailed one. It merely tells us that the internal market 'shall comprise an area without internal frontiers in which the free movement of goods, persons, services and capital is ensured'.

What is an internal frontier? Does this refer to physical fences and checks, or is it more metaphorical? What is free movement, that is to say, when is the movement of these factors of production properly described as 'free'? It is hard to think of any context in which freedom has a clear and uncontestable meaning, and this is no different. It cannot have some absolute meaning, for no movement of any kind is ever absolutely free: there are always practical issues, costs, upsides and downsides. Could it be a relative meaning, compared with movement within a member state? But then there is the problem of apples and pears and of comparing different situations. As with any kind of equality assessment, an adjudicator or interpreter must decide which factors to take into account and which to ignore, and these choices embed values which determine what the law really is. There is no 'neutral' equality.[9] In an economic context, to decide what the costs of movement are we must decide which prior advantages and disadvantages to recognize – the extent to which the foreign is to be seen as the same or different from the domestic. This is not a legal decision; it is pure policy.

The second kind of internal market provision may perhaps help. These are the prohibitions of restrictions on movement.[10] Addressed primarily to the member states, although increasingly to private actors too,[11] they disallow measures which restrict the inter-state movement of the internal market factors listed in Article 26.

---

8 Davies, 'Internal market adjudication'.
9 Peter Westen, 'The empty idea of equality', *Harvard Law Review* 95 (1982).
10 Primarily Articles 34, 35, 45, 49, 56, 63 TFEU.
11 Case C-438/05 *Viking Line*, ECLI:EU:C:2007:772.

The wording varies a little from goods to persons to services to capital, but the concepts are clearly similar.

It is thus 'restrictions' on movement which are to be concretely disallowed. Yet almost all regulation of economic activity, and much regulation of other areas of life, restricts economic actors in some sense, imposing costs or limitations.[12] It may decrease or increase economic activity to some extent, in some way, and so may have some consequences for at least some cross-border movement. Is a requirement to have a driving licence before driving a car on the highway a restriction on the movement of persons? An attempt to give 'restrictions' an uncomplicated meaning, to finesse fancy legal arguments by an appeal to a sort of 'plain language' approach leads us into difficult waters.

Alternatively, there can be a focus on some kind of intention. The mere fact that a measure has consequences for trade should not make it a restriction. There should be some evidence that it aims to restrict trade. An interpretation of this kind has a strong normative appeal and reduces the number of measures prohibited to a plausible number, but runs into evidential, and ultimately coherence, difficulties. What does it mean to speak of the intention of a legislature, which is a multi-headed body, a conglomerate of compromising intentions?[13] The situation is made worse when the laws are old, pre-dating the current trade framework.

A third approach is to try and characterize measures as 'essentially' about trade or essentially about something else, to find some kind of policy centre of gravity.[14] This is similar in some ways to what the Court does.[15] Thus, the fact that a measure impacts on movement will not necessarily make it a restriction if it also has some other purpose, for example, protecting safety, the environment or the consumer. Then the movement effects can be seen as incidental. A measure on this logic has one label, determined by its most important effect, so only restrictive measures which do not have some higher consequences too will be prohibited.

None of these readings has any claim to a monopoly of linguistic logic or sense. The prohibitions give us too little to go on: they are vessels waiting to be filled. Even putting them in their wider legal context, from the rest of the Treaty to the structure of global trade law, does not lead to a reading which persuasively excludes the others. There are choices to be made, which take place on the basis of factors outside the Treaty, choices between interpretations such as those above, and perhaps many others.

These choices have consequences for the Union's legislative power. The third kind of internal market provision is the legislative competence, the legal base. These authorize the Council, Commission and Parliament to adopt secondary

---

12 Gareth Davies, 'Understanding market access: Exploring the economic rationality of different conceptions of free movement law', *German Law Journal* 11 (2010).

13 Davies, 'Internal market adjudication', p. 225.

14 See Don Regan 'An outsider's view of "Dassonville" and "Cassis de Dijon": On interpretation and policy', in *The Past and Future of EU Law*, eds. Miguel Poiares Maduro and Loic Azoulai (Oxford, UK: Hart, 2010).

15 Case 120/78 *Cassis de Dijon*, ECLI:EU:C:1979:42.

206 *Gareth Davies*

legislation. There are a range of legal bases relevant to the internal market, allowing legislation specifically to do with, for example, the liberalization of services or the movement of workers.[16] However, a constraining factor in all of them is that legislation must in fact contribute to the internal market. What this may mean was famously discussed by the Court in its *Tobacco Advertising* judgment, interpreting Article 114 TFEU, the most general and most important internal market legal base.[17] It allows legislation which has as its goal the establishment and functioning of the internal market. Interpreting this demands that one consider what kinds of laws are required for a market to exist. What kinds of laws could be said to aim at a Europe without internal frontiers? Those laws are the ones that the Union is entitled to adopt under Article 114.

4.

A minimalist conception of a market is that it requires no more than the possibility of trade, which entails no more than the elimination of protectionism.[18] An essentially economic legal framework, which prohibits all the usual market-closing measures – duties, quotas, discrimination – suffices. A market in this sense is a space where buyers and sellers find each other.[19] A transnational market is a space where they can do so even across borders. The role for the lawmaker is just to ensure that public authorities do not come between those buyers and sellers. This is a laissez-faire conception in which the market is essentially private. It takes place outside the institutions of the state and its creation entails policing that state to ensure that it does not extend its domain into what is properly private.

Such a conception is often appealed to on an ad hoc basis when particular parties object to public measures, but in reality few people in Europe think of markets as self-constituting entities autonomous of public power. Current thinking, even on the economic right, sees a distinct role for the state in regulating market actors, the idea being that private exchange will be hindered by all kinds of factors unless the state actively addresses them. A pure and hardcore theorist might take the approach that the market itself will create the circumstances for its own success if only the state will stay away, but this is a rare view in politics. Rather, there is a consensus that if the state provides a degree of infrastructure – whether physical, intellectual or social – and polices the behaviour of private parties to each other – competition law – then this will optimize the possibilities for private exchange and is hence part of ensuring the 'establishment and functioning' of the market.

The density of the public law framework considered necessary for a market to exist is contested along what may be imagined as a continuum, even though this

---

16 For example, Articles 46, 48, 50, 53, 59, 64, 113, 114, 115, 118 TFEU.
17 Case C-376/98 *Tobacco Advertising*, ECLI:EU:C:2000:544.
18 Regan, 'An outsider's view'.
19 Gareth Davies, 'Freedom of movement, horizontal effect, and freedom of contract', *European Review of Private Law* 20 (2012).

Bringing politics into European integration 207

linear metaphor obscures the variety of different laws which may, it is argued, be needed. On one view, it is essentially economic space which must be regulated so that the measures which Article 114 should allow are those directly related to the acts of exchange. It might be self-evident for such a thinker that matters to do with, for example, culture, language, security or the welfare state would have nothing to do with establishing or creating the internal market.

Yet further along the continuum it may be argued that the market is a socially embedded construct and that creating it entails creating a space within society where it may take place.[20] This may mean thinking about who suffers from competition, and who is made vulnerable, and taking measures to protect them – that could include stricter, or more flexible, labour laws or production standards to prevent a globalization-led race to the bottom, or indeed to allow domestic actors to compete more effectively. It may also mean harmonizing across states to create common standards in all kinds of fields, from labour law to environmental measures to product standards to qualifications. These prevent economic advantage accruing to those in states with low (cheap) standards at the expense of others.

Measures of this kind can be defended on justice or efficiency grounds and are analytically comparable with the competition law that is more conventionally associated with market building.[21] Competition law, as with the more socially oriented measures below, is sometimes defended in justice terms, aiming to prevent the abuse of power and the tyranny of concentrations of economic power. It protects a certain structure which in the longer term is more advantageous for economy and society.

These days it is more fashionable to understand competition law in different terms, as promoting 'welfare' by addressing market imperfections, so that the market can be as close as possible to perfectly efficient.[22] That same argument can be made about the more social measures: the harm to the weak, the environment or quality of life are externalities resulting from free exchange, made possible by market imperfections which prevent proper internalization of the costs of that exchange. Harmonizing maternity leave or the kinds of ladders that a window cleaner can use is part of the same programme of market-perfecting to which anti-cartel law and monopoly-bashing belong.

It is possible to go even further. The market is populated by human beings, and these may be inhibited from moving or trading across borders by factors more subtle and incidental than the socio-economic issues above.[23] Compared with the rather

---

20 Stefano Giubboni, *Social Rights and Market Freedom in the European Constitution* (Cambridge, UK: Cambridge University Press, 2009). See, also, Ioannis Lianos, 'Shifting narratives in the European internal market: Efficient restrictions of trade and the nature of "economic" integration', *European Business Law Review* 21 (2010).

21 Rob van der Laan and Andries Nentjes, 'Competitive distortions in EU environmental legislation: Inefficiency versus inequity', *European Journal of Law and Economics* 11 (2001).

22 See Damian Chalmers, Gareth Davies and Giorgio Monti, *EU Law* (Cambridge, UK: Cambridge University Press, 2014), pp. 944–955.

23 Davies, 'Subsidiarity'.

208   *Gareth Davies*

abstract and speculative theories which often justify much harmonization, there is something very hard-nosed and realistic about looking at people as they actually are and considering what may make it possible or attractive for them to move and trade, rather than building a market on the basis of the newest economic model, no doubt shortly to be changed or replaced by another. The dramatic rise of psychology as one of the primary sciences of markets – albeit under the misleading name of behavioural economics – is part of a turn away from mathematical theory towards a more empirically robust understanding of how markets work.[24] Yet empiricism – realism – is a slippery slope, which can take market making into many surprising areas.

For workers often do not move because of language. If there was one measure that would genuinely contribute to establishing a single European market, to an extent dwarfing most of the legislative programmes pursued in that name, it would be a measure creating a common language. Less apocalyptically, it has long been accepted that workers will not move if they cannot take their families, so that creating rights for partners, children and even parents is part of creating free movement of persons. Yet rights may not be enough: many people are inhibited by educational and welfare differences, the difficulties of transplanting their children from one system to another, or the weaker pension system in one state, or a reluctance to give up their affiliation with a certain healthcare system and be subjected to a new one that they trust less. Hard-nosed market making can easily be understood to require a common welfare framework, a common approach to education and so on.[25]

One of the underlying issues here is of trust.[26] People perhaps cannot be expected to go into business with each other if they do not trust each other – at least that is probably a proposition that could claim much support, perhaps more in some lands than others. The primary measures which contribute to establishing an internal market are then those which make trust across borders possible, by increasing understanding of difference and also reducing that difference: from school exchanges to language classes to common codes of contract, this is, perhaps, real market building. The regulation of competition is skating on the surface compared with these attempts to get at what really divides Europe's economic actors from each other.

One does not even need to argue that without such measures trade will not happen. They can be justified on the basis that without such measures trade *should* not happen: people may be driven to exchange by self-interest, but if that exchange takes place without a framework of trust, fairness and understanding – of community – then it becomes harmful to all, not just creating externalities but forcing the market actor to become two people, a money maker on the one hand and, alienated from this half, hostile to it even, a human being with social and personal values on the other. Creating a market, on this view, is creating a framework

---

24 For example, Ester-Mirjam Sent, 'Behavioral economics: How psychology made its (limited) way back into economics', *History of Political Economy* 36 (2004).

25 Davies, 'Subsidiarity'.

26 See Ioannis Lianos and Okeoghene Odudu, eds., *Regulation of Services in the EU and WTO: Trust, Distrust and Economic Integration* (Cambridge, UK: Cambridge University Press, 2012).

Bringing politics into European integration 209

of rules in which the economic, social and human can be reconciled in the lives of individuals – in which we can have a good life.[27]

The project of making economic activity non-alienating and non-harmful is an ambitious one, and many might think it hopeless. It has, however, a long European history and is still within the mainstream of politics in the form of the ideals of the social-market economy.[28] At its most ambitious, it can lead one to the conclusion that a market needs a state – for what is a state but a structure to police the relationships between private individuals, to minimize the harm of their exchanges and interactions, to allow the different aspects of their lives to be reconciled? A reading of Article 114 which allows the Union legislature to regulate almost all the things that a state does, is just one of the readings of its open and ambiguous words, based, as are they all, on a particular set of values, preferences and political choices.

Measures which could be said to contribute to the establishment and functioning of an internal European market, might therefore vary from those which take down immediate trade barriers, to those which create a sense of community, trust, fairness and solidarity and so address the more social, political and human obstacles to movement.[29]

5.

There are three deep normative issues which underlie the choices above, questions which are the stuff of politics almost everywhere, not confined to Europe or markets.

One is the relationship between the individual and the community. To what extent do we owe obligations of solidarity to each other? When is the majority justified in limiting the activities of the minority? Should those who wish to trade be left alone, or should they be restrained if their activities harm others, in a concrete sense but even in a more emotional one if they create inequality and alienation in society? Do we have the right to pursue our own interests and ignore those of others, or is a right to chase our own goals derived only from the contribution that these make to the welfare of society as a whole? These questions arise everywhere, and many nuanced positions are possible between the extremes. A framework that makes a market possible must be one that makes it acceptable and so must take account of positions on this issue, for so much of market building and its critique is about the management of externalities and the inequalities that arise wherever new opportunities come into being.[30]

---

27 See Floris De Witte, *Justice in the EU: The Emergence of Transnational Solidarity* (Oxford, UK: Oxford University Press, 2015).

28 Wofgang Streeck, 'Beneficial constraints: On the economic limits of rational voluntarism', in *Contemporary Capitalism: The Embeddedness of Institutions*, eds. J. Rogers Hollingsworth and Robert Boyer (Cambridge, UK: Cambridge University Press, 1997).

29 Ioannis Lianos, 'Shifting narratives'.

30 Gareth Davies, 'The process and side-effects of the harmonisation of European welfare states', Jean Monnet Working Paper 02/06 (2006). doi: 10.2139/ssrn.900934.

210   *Gareth Davies*

Another issue is that between the rule of the people and the rule of experts. Perhaps more (post-)modern, less traditional than the issue above, this is nevertheless an emerging classic of politics.[31] When should decisions be in the hands of the public and when in those with expertise? Should we elect judges, vote for mayors or police chiefs, have the possibility to overrule the decisions of scientific experts, remove economic and monetary decisions from the reach of parliaments? Almost everyone agrees that important policy should ultimately be under democratic control, but the people may choose in their own interests to set certain issues outside of their reach. If there is something alarming in the people acknowledging its own infantilism, its decisional incontinence, in this way, it is also reflective of what may be a particularly contemporary democratic narcissism: like spoilt children, we want laws to be vehicles of expression for our values and allegiances, loci for political debate between our representatives, but we also want the hard practical results which come when laws are in more technocratic hands. We want to send messages that crime does not pay, to increase punishments and make jail harsher, but we also want a safer society with less crime, and the fact that the two may not go together is something that we would rather not think about. Yet, in a society with endless data and endless expertise, the conflict between our instincts and our goals is sometimes hard not to see. Anger may be one result. Another may be protected expert governance, which allows the public to let off steam safely and indulge its passions and critique in rhetoric, safe in the knowledge that the results will be limited. We can all rail against globalization, as long as this does not lead to us losing the benefits it brings.[32]

This is particularly pertinent in the context of European integration, which is largely regarded as an interest-promoting project rather than a natural democratic community. States and their populations want the largely economic benefits which may arise from a shared market, but are also still committed to the idea of a national democratic community and national sovereignty over things that matter, and certainly over things that may have cultural or social importance. When it comes to matters such as foodstuffs, the welfare state, cross-border crime, harmonization of social law or GMOs, there is then no good answer. Business and the working of the market would be improved greatly by common European rules, and given that we want Europe primarily to deliver results, rather than deliver symbolic community, it makes sense that these European rules should be as technocratic as possible: EU regulation is not there to send messages, but to make things work.

However, there is still a strong attachment to the idea that these politically salient matters should belong to politics, particularly national politics. There is understandable resistance to local value and culture choices being subordinated to European expert rules, and this is easily framed in democratic terms. Yet if

---

31 See, for example, William Wallace and Julie Smith, 'Democracy or technocracy? European integration and the problem of popular consent', *West European Politics* 18 (1995).

32 Gareth Davies, 'Democracy and legitimacy in the shadow of purposive competence', *European Law Journal* 21 (2015): 21–22.

Bringing politics into European integration   211

Europe cannot deliver an efficient economic framework, then it is no use to us: that is all that we want from it. We want to have our national political cake and eat it.

The third issue at the heart of market making is the most fundamental and the one that resonates most with recent European history and the very purposes of the EU. It is the question of how much difference we can tolerate. To what extent do states or individuals have to agree on values or behaviour in order to be able to be open together? Is it, as one might expect, a sliding scale in which the more open the borders the greater the degree of similarity required, the more common laws and institutions? Or is the degree of difference that a population can accept less a factor of the degree of contact and more dependent on either cultural or temporal factors? On some political visions, a market entails a state, and a state entails common rules and shared values. On others, the essence of exchange is that it takes place between those who dwell in different contexts and want different things – that is what makes it advantageous. Trade is more a way of overcoming difference than something premised on its absence. Finally, perhaps it is just a question of time, although whether we expect that time will make us more inclined to accept shared laws and norms, or more inclined to accept the different laws and norms of our neighbours is, again, contestable.

The difficulty at the heart of this issue is that the difference is not so much between the extreme positions as between the middle and the edges. To insist that removing borders demands an almost complete social or legal commonality is intolerance, the very reason that the EU (ironically a mechanism for delivering social and legal commonality) was created. A perfect market, in this sense, is something that nobody wants. Yet to open borders without caring about what the circumstances in other states may be is a form of indifference to justice and consequences, ultimately indifference to human beings, which is hardly less acceptable and in fact rather similar. If we are to care about our neighbours, then market integration will necessarily be a process of muddling along, negotiating in the shadow of consequences, fairness and respect for difference.

6.

The tragedy in this story is that the Court of Justice has spoken. It has answered all the big questions of market integration in a way that takes them out of the political arena.[33]

For example, it has defined what free movement is and what a restriction on free movement is, and so it has determined the extent to which the Treaty constrains national policies and laws.[34] Its definitions are certainly imprecise in many ways, but they contain a certain hard core of principle. What is striking is that it has made the prohibitions broad, and they apply to measures whose 'centre of

33 Ibid.
34 Ibid.

212   Gareth Davies

gravity' is clearly not economic, and it has established strong presumptions which make it quite hard for a state to resist a Treaty prohibition on grounds that might politically seem quite sensible, such as budgetary or institutional concerns. The definitions are certainly defensible – within the mainstream of possible interpretative choices – but they of course entail contestable political choices.

Similar remarks can be made about the Union's competence to harmonize using Article 114 and other internal market bases. The Court has again taken a strong and principled stand on how far this should go – on what establishing an internal market entails.[35] Its view is again not an extreme or ridiculous one, but it is contestable. It understands these articles in particularly practical, functional terms: they may only be used to eliminate obstacles to trade, or remove distortions of competition, but not for broader contextual purposes. The market, in the Treaty, is not understood as entailing any of the wider considerations or requirements discussed above.

It is tempting to see these as legal technical judgments of limited political significance. Some may think that whatever the result in a particular dispute, politics goes on within the EU. Yet three factors show how 'politics-denying' the Court's interpretation has been.

First, its interpretations are largely fixed. With the notable exception of its judgment in *Keck*, it has shown no desire to revisit any of them, and its caselaw typically takes the form of the repetition of dogmas which have emerged at some point in the past from a particular judgment.[36] This is good for consistency, but not for debate. This catechismic quality of EU jurisprudence has much to do with the nature of the Court, its collective decision making and the problems of language and of widely different legal traditions represented within it.[37] Yet a contrast can be made with the supreme courts of states such as the United States or Germany, where questions of high constitutional principle do not die after a judgment. Each generation debates them anew, and that debate is meaningful, because it is possible to bring them back before the highest courts. Abortion, gun control or states' rights are not rigid dogmas in the way that free movement is, but issues on which a court has taken a stance, but on which all parties know that a subsequent court may take a new one. The law lives. Even if there is a powerful voice in American legal scholarship which argues that constitutional law should always stay the same – to paraphrase the originalists – that voice is strident and important precisely because it is not inevitable that it will. Everything in the system makes it possible for it to change.

Much of this is to do with reasoning. The Court of Justice could also change, of course, but change happens more easily, coherently and plausibly when decisions are based on thorough, discursive and contextual reasoning. That allows

---

35 Ibid.
36 Cases C-267 and C-268/91, *Keck and Mithouard*, ECLI:EU:C:1993:905.
37 Mitchel Lasser, *Judicial Deliberations. A Comparative Analysis of Transparency and Legitimacy* (Oxford, UK: Oxford University Press, 2009).

Bringing politics into European integration 213

changing circumstances to be used to argue which part of the reasoning no longer applies. Attacking an assertion – which is more or less what most EU law consists of – is harder.

This assertive character of Court judgments is the second reason that they are politics-denying. Even courts can be fora for the voicing of interests and arguments, if the courts allow that. The US and German supreme courts are examples of bodies which, in deciding salient constitutional cases, pay great attention to essentially political considerations – arguments about values, public preferences, consequences and history.[38] These are weighed and discussed in the judgments. This may lead to the critique, beloved of some lawyers, that the judgments become political, but when the law requires political choices then unpacking these openly is a more publicly liberating choice than deciding them in silence.

The doctrines of the Court of Justice have never been built on an assessment of such arguments. Only a narrow selection of the issues relevant to interpreting the Treaty articles on the internal market have ever been mentioned by the Court in establishing those doctrines or in cases where they were revisited.[39] Functional considerations and the encompassing goal of integration have always been named, if not discussed in depth. However, the many other aspects of sensibly deciding what achieving free movement and building a market should mean have been consistently ignored.[40]

The third, and perhaps most important, aspect of the Court's impact on political debate is that it constrains the Union legislature.[41] They are unable to take decisions outside of the framework of principle that it creates. If they try, their actions are annulled, and this has happened.[42] The Court is a strict guardian of the law. As a result, the legislature is in fact remarkably obedient to the Court. Perhaps because the Commission still has the monopoly of initiative, proposals for legislation are always carefully crafted to respect everything the Court has said and very often do little more than codify it.[43] There is, it is striking to note, not a single case of legislative override: despite the many ways of reading the Treaty, the legislature has never imposed a view that in any way challenges or contradicts that of the Court.[44]

As a result, there is no space for a debate within the Union's political organs on what the internal market should be, or what kinds of measures it needs to

---

38 See, for example, the German Constitutional Court's discursive and analytic judgment on the Lisbon Treaty in: Treaty of Lisbon, 2 BvE 2/08, Bundesverfassungsgericht, 30 June 2009.
39 Davies, 'Internal market adjudication'.
40 Ibid.
41 Gareth Davies, 'Legislative control of the European Court of Justice', *Common Market Law Review* 51 (2014).
42 Case C-376/98 *Tobacco Advertising*, ECLI:EU:C:2000:544; Case C-236/09 *Test-Achats*, ECLI:EU:C:2011:100.
43 Davies, 'Legislative control'.
44 Ibid.; but see Clifford Carruba, Matthew Gabel and Charles Hankla, 'Understanding the role of the European Court of Justice in European integration', *American Political Science Review* 106 (2012).

214   *Gareth Davies*

take to make trade possible, or what kinds of common laws economic integration entails. These issues are settled. The only question remaining for the legislature is whether or not a given obstacle to movement or distortion of competition (as defined by the Court) should be removed and the technical details of how and the procedural and institutional niceties of this.[45] These details are not always without their importance and may be fiercely debated, but they are something other than the fundamental questions of what a market means. On those, in Europe, there is a judicial monopoly.

7.

The Court's coup d'état does not fit a democratic logic. However, it does fit a certain constitutional logic. Perhaps the most fundamental principle of the European Union is that it is, unlike a state, a creature of conferred powers.[46] It has only the competences that are attributed to it by Treaty. This is more than a technical question – an undefined and open-ended transfer of powers to the EU would allow residual member state sovereignty to be squeezed ever more and would violate constitutional democracy guarantees in at least one member state.[47] Giving the EU the breadth of powers that it has is controversial and challenging enough, but the conventional perspective is that they must be defined in a way that bounds them meaningfully and prevents uncontrolled expansion if membership is to be politically or constitutionally acceptable in the member states. No member state when signing the Treaty wished or intended to grant an open-ended competence to constrain national policy or to legislate.

Hence, it is unsurprising that the Court understands one of its core functions as policing conferral. Determining what the Union can do, and the limits of this, is central to its existence. One may contrast the position with a national supreme court, which will typically prevent policies from infringing higher norms, but will rarely see its function as determining what those policies should be or mean. The difference is that in states policies are rarely constitutionalized; their meaning is not a constitutional issue. [48] The constitutionalization of policy in the European Union is both a logical corollary of conferred powers and the very reason why that policy is removed from meaningful politics.

8.

There is a deal implicit in the way the member states have created the EU. It may be described as 'save us from ourselves'.[49] The EU is not equipped to be a body of political or democratic depth, but rather a regulator that can deliver the policy

---

45 Davies, 'Democracy and legitimacy'.
46 Article 5 TEU.
47 Treaty of Lisbon, 2 BvE 2/08, Bundesverfassungsgericht, 30 June 2009.
48 Davies, 'Legislative control'.
49 Davies, 'Democracy and legitimacy', pp. 20–21.

Bringing politics into European integration 215

rationality which member states often find hard to extract from entrenched domestic political structures. There is a division of labour in which member states do the politics and the Union does the policy: the emotion and ideology is at national level, but the Union ensures that material results are achieved. The cake, again, is to be had and eaten. The point of harmonization is not so much the constraints it imposes on other member states – the competitive or functional significance of such harmonization is usually vastly overstated – but the constraints it imposes on one's own: the externality of the Union allows it to impose policies which cannot be achieved domestically, and the fact that other member states are similarly constrained is what makes this acceptable and gives it political justification. It is not that state X accepts constraints so that Y and Z will: rather, it is that state X needs Y and Z to be constrained, so that it can be too.

This deal is ultimately rotten. It relies on a separation of politics and policy – meaning technocratic policy – that is only coherent if that policy is confined to narrow and politically relatively unimportant fields.[50] Perhaps it was once believed that trade regulation and the creation of a single market fell into this category. Given the way the Court has interpreted it and given the way its breadth and impact have grown, no one could believe that this is the case anymore. On the contrary, the objects of expertise and the objects of politics are intertwined, even co-extensive, and to try to separate them is always to do violence to either democracy or expertise and the output legitimacy that it brings.

The idea of separating politics and expertise offers a vision of the European Union and member states as complementary regulators, giving their citizens a world both expressive and rich. Yet, if the distinction fails, then they become what they currently are: competing regulators, the one using its legal tools of supremacy and direct effect, and the other using institutional inertia and the loyalty of national institutions, to try to exert their will on the societies and institutions of the member states.[51]

Competition can of course be healthy, under the right circumstances. It might lead experts towards humility and member states towards rationality. Creating conflicting levels could be a way of confronting populations with their own conflicting desires and helping them reach an internal compromise.

However, such an ideal relies on the possibility for change. There must be room for movement at both national and Union level. For this, the Court must be prepared to bend, to defer to interpretations of the Treaty coming from the legislature. It must invite and accept the idea that the Parliament, or even on a good day the Council, might have ideas about what a Treaty prohibition or a legal base really means, and that such a political interpretation of such a political Treaty article should be prima facie accepted by courts.[52] Conferral still counts and so

50 Giandomenico Majone, *Rethinking the Union of Europe Post-Crisis. Has Integration Gone Too Far?* (Cambridge, UK: Cambridge University Press, 2014).
51 Davies, 'Internal market adjudication', pp. 232–233.
52 Davies, 'Legislative control'.

216 *Gareth Davies*

does the policing function of the Court, but there could and should be a process of negotiation between conferral and legitimate interpretation; between the need for limits and the need for political organs to make political choices. The Court should not try to interpret the Treaty on its own.

No rule or dogma stops this – it is merely judicial pride and habit. However, it would be hard for the Court to change. When it created its doctrines, they were controversial, but to open them up now to challenge on the overt grounds that they are political and that they require political input, would probably be even more contested. The Court has been given an impossible task in which the sort of neutral, technical space that European courts typically like to occupy is simply not there.

The legislature should help it. What is needed most of all is a legislature that actually proposes its own interpretation of the Treaty, that has the intellectual capacity and commitment to adopt autonomous and reasoned positions on what a market is and should be, and dares to put these forward whether or not they are cut-and-pasted from the Court.[53] It would be easier for the Court to defer if it had a serious authority to defer to. The greatest political failure of the European Union is that its political organs refuse to see their task as political.

Bibliography

Carruba, Clifford, Matthew Gabel and Charles Hankla. 'Understanding the role of the European Court of Justice in European integration'. *American Political Science Review* 106 (2012): 214–223.

Chalmers, Damian. 'The European redistributive state and a European law of struggle'. *European Law Journal* 18 (2012): 667–693.

Chalmers, Damian, Gareth Davies and Giorgio Monti. *EU Law*. Cambridge, UK: Cambridge University Press, 2014.

Dani, Marco. 'Rehabilitating social conflicts in European public law'. *European Law Journal* 18 (2012): 621–643.

Davies, Gareth. 'Subsidiarity: The wrong idea in the wrong place at the wrong time'. *Common Market Law Review* 43 (2006): 63–84.

Davies, Gareth. 'The process and side-effects of the harmonisation of European welfare states'. Jean Monnet Working Paper 02/06, 2006. doi: 10.2139/ssrn.900934.

Davies, Gareth. 'Understanding market access: Exploring the economic rationality of different conceptions of free movement law'. *German Law Journal* 11 (2010): 671–704.

Davies, Gareth 'Freedom of movement, horizontal effect, and freedom of contract'. *European Review of Private Law* 20 (2012): 805–827.

Davies, Gareth. 'Legislative control of the European Court of Justice'. *Common Market Law Review* 51 (2014): 1579–1608.

Davies, Gareth. 'Internal market adjudication and the quality of life in Europe'. *Columbia Journal of European Law* 21(2) (2015): 207.

Davies, Gareth. 'Democracy and legitimacy in the shadow of purposive competence'. *European Law Journal* 21 (2015): 2–22.

---

53 Ibid.

De Witte, Floris. *Justice in the EU: The Emergence of Transnational Solidarity*. Oxford, UK: Oxford University Press, 2015.

Giubboni, Stefano. *Social Rights and Market Freedom in the European Constitution*. Cambridge, UK: Cambridge University Press, 2009.

Joerges, Christian. 'Unity in diversity as Europe's vocation and conflicts law as Europe's constitutional form'. LEQS Paper no. 28/2010 (revised version April 2013).

Lasser, Mitchel. *Judicial Deliberations. A Comparative Analysis of Transparency and Legitimacy*. Oxford, UK: Oxford University Press, 2009.

Lianos, Ioannis. 'Shifting narratives in the European internal market: Efficient restrictions of trade and the nature of "economic" integration'. *European Business Law Review* 21 (2010): 705–760.

Lianos, Ioannis and Okeoghene Odudu, eds. *Regulation of Services in the EU and WTO: Trust, Distrust and Economic Integration*. Cambridge, UK Cambridge University Press, 2012.

Majone, Giandomenico. *Rethinking the Union of Europe Post-Crisis. Has Integration Gone Too Far?* Cambridge, UK: Cambridge University Press, 2014.

Regan, Don. 'An outsider's view of "Dassonville" and "Cassis de Dijon": On interpretation and policy'. In *The Past and Future of EU Law*, edited by Miguel Poiares Maduro and Loic Azoulai. Oxford, UK: Hart, 2010, pp. 465–473.

Sent, Ester-Mirjam. 'Behavioral economics: How psychology made its (limited) way back into economics'. *History of Political Economy* 36 (2004) 735–760.

Streeck, Wolfgang. 'Beneficial constraints: On the economic limits of rational voluntarism'. In *Contemporary Capitalism: The Embeddedness of Institutions*, edited by J. Rogers Hollingsworth and Robert Boyer. Cambridge, UK: Cambridge University Press, 1997, pp. 197–219.

Van der Laan, Rob and Andries Nentjes. 'Competitive distortions in EU environmental legislation: Inefficiency versus inequity'. *European Journal of Law and Economics* 11 (2001): 131–152.

Wallace, William and Julie Smith. 'Democracy or technocracy? European integration and the problem of popular consent'. *West European Politics* 18 (1995): 137–157.

Westen, Peter. 'The empty idea of equality'. *Harvard Law Review* 95 (1982): 537–596.

Wilhelmsson, Thomas. 'Private law in the EU: Harmonised or fragmented Europeanisation?'. *European Review of Private Law* 1 (2002): 77–94.

10 A technocratic tyranny of certainty

A preliminary sketch

Michelle Everson

Shotgun politics

There is no alternative: the brutal imposition upon Greece of a socially unsustainable regime of economic conditionality in July 2015 has been presented as an economic imperative by the governments and technocrats of the Eurozone. The effort made by the Syriza-led Greek government to win for itself a space for a politics of choices, or for the pursuit of solvency through state-stimulated growth has been decisively foreclosed. Economic conditionality and the dissolution of state-funded welfare is an immutable and unforgiving feature of the modern world. Significantly, economic conditionality has also been given added *constitutional* force by courts, such as the European Court of Justice:

> When granting assistance, the ESM 'Board of Governors shall entrust the European Commission – in liaison with the ECB and, wherever possible, together with the IMF – with the task of negotiating, with the ESM Member concerned, a memorandum of understanding ('MoU') detailing the conditionality attached to the financial assistance facility. The content of the MoU shall reflect the severity of the weaknesses to be addressed and the financial assistance instrument chosen. In parallel, the Managing Director of the ESM shall prepare a proposal for a financial assistance facility agreement, including the financial terms and conditions and the choice of instruments, to be adopted by the Board of Governors.[1]

Dependent upon the European Stability Mechanism (ESM) for day-to-day financing, the Greek government has lost its own political functionality, now being subordinate, both in law and in fact, to a governance of technocracy, comprising experts from the European Commission, European Central Bank (ECB) and the International Monetary Fund (IMF).

The brutality of the European Union's post-economic crisis commitment to a shotgun politics whose exact contours are dictated by the unholy technocratic

---

1 Case C-370/12 *Pringle* v. *Government of Ireland, Ireland and the Attorney General*, judgment of 27 November 2012, para.18, not yet reported.

A technocratic tyranny of certainty   219

alliance of Commission, ECB and IMF within the 'Troika', cannot be denied: millions of often poorer European citizens are now subject to an austerity regime of slashed pensions, privatization and unemployment, as well as greatly diminished health care. Yet, brutality cannot be opposed through democratic process or through constitutional complaint: it must be accepted in its entirety. This leaves us with one vital question: what has happened to the European project, one originally founded in peaceful union between the democratic states of the western European continent, and one which was built up on socializing post-war traditions?

> [International] managerialism turns into absolutism: the absolutism of this or that regime, this or that system of preferences. The lawyer becomes a counsel for the functional power-holder speaking the new natural law: from formal institutions to regimes, learning the idiolect of 'regulation', talking of 'governance' instead of 'government' and 'compliance' instead of 'responsibility'. The normative optic is received from a 'legitimacy', measured by international relations – the Supreme Tribunal of a managerial world.[2]

For Martti Koskenniemi, writing more generally about the managerialist quality of international regimes, an end to politics, as well as to democratic process within post-national forms of organization, has its roots in the power of administrative science. Drawing explicitly upon Foucauldian first principles, Koskenniemi attributes the normatively void discourse and fact of internationalist managerialism to the cumulative transfer of administrative capacity from national governments to post-national governance regimes and to the concomitant establishment of the post-national powers of expansive technocratic calculation: 'If 'government' connotes administration and division of powers, with the presumption of formal accountability, 'governance' refers to *de facto* practices and is – like those corporate enterprises in which the term originates – geared to the production of maximal value'.[3] Our modern internationalism has no normative content, is blind to social and democratic value and is concerned simply to expand its powers.

Has the EU also become an instrument of managerial science, a mask for normatively voided managerialism? For all that the Troika may appear to be a purely functionalist body, the immediate answer to this must be no: the Greek sovereign debt crisis has far more complex roots and consequences, above all, with regard to the demands for and limits to the assumption of a joint European liability for Greek debt. In particular, the imposition of economic conditionality upon new debt financing for Greece may also be attributed to political and constitutional demands within the Federal Republic of Germany that any German debt relief to

---

2 Martti Koskenniemi, 'Miserable comforters: International relations as new natural law', *European Journal of International Relations* 15 (2009): 412.
3 Ibid. p. 409.

220   *Michelle Everson*

Greece must be given in accordance with the Republic's historical and continuing dedication to price stability and anti-inflationary monetary and economic policy.[4] The cultural and political constellation of the crisis is infinitely complex and multi-faceted. Yet, and beyond this particular complexity of member state inter-relations, the shotgun politics of the Eurozone and, above all, the dominant *belief* that there is no *economic* alternative to the imposition of austerity, may and will be argued, in the following, to be a feature of a new administrative science; one which masks its own peculiar normative void in technocratic pursuit of newly-postulated economic certainty.

In certain belief . . .

There is no alternative: a striking feature of current crisis is not that it is devoid of politics, but rather that foreclosure of a political space for the establishment of democratically legitimated alternatives (in Greece) has been accompanied by its own aggressively political commitment to pursuit of a market-driven exit from crisis (in creditor nations). The rejection of Keynesian approaches to the overcoming of crisis is as pervasive within the Eurozone as it is politically dominant: the left-leaning Greek government has few if any allies and, more significantly, has been denied any space in which it might pursue its own anti-austerity position. Instead, a political programme of private wealth creation as the solution to Greek malaise is imposed as *credo*; as a faith that cannot fail.

Economic conditionality, or the slashing of state budgets and the privatization of state function, is designed to stimulate private wealth creation and has its own appearance of holiness, or its own apparent normativity: we are imposing pain now so that the working man and woman will enjoy benefit in the future. At the same time, the discourse of austerity projects its own inevitability: we have no choice, this is the way the world is, and this is the only way forward. The economics of the private market have become an objective reality, a space which we cannot contest. Equally, however, the market has also morphed into a machine which, it is asserted, will provide us with a *certainty* of growth and wealth. The duality of the discourse of economic conditionality is immediately striking: the *is* of the market is made inseparable from the *ought* of pursuit of wealth through austerity. This is not, however, a new duality, in particular as regards long-standing efforts to identify a fact of economic certainty.

Risk, uncertainty and profit

The birth of a modern discipline of economics may be argued to date from 1921 and the publication by Frank Knight of his thesis that certain profit might be secured where the uncertainties of market operation can be translated into risks,

---

4 Christian Joerges, 'The European economic constitution and its transformation through the financial crisis', ZenTra Working Paper in Transnational Studies no. 47/2015 (2015).

A technocratic tyranny of certainty 221

such that they can be managed.[5] From the hidden hand to observable and manageable phenomena: the emergence of modern economics as a discipline of objective observation also found its counterpart in the academic endeavour both to project and to control the machine of the market. For Knight himself, this effort was, in his final analysis, utterly illusory. Combining philosophy with his economic observations, Knight characterized the entrepreneurial spirit not as one of pedestrian risk management but, rather, as one of the embracing of the non-quantifiable uncertainties of market operation. Supply and demand remained adjuncts to human interaction and, for that reason, would always be subject to stochastic variation: only the brave would hazard their all in market exposure, because true profit is born of uncertainty. However, for others within the discipline, scientification became an ambitious end in itself, such that economic observation sought its own realities within market operation, more particularly seeking to master the market by identifying and combatting the 'disutility' of market uncertainty.[6]

Ideas, interests, symbolism and science

An interesting counterpart to the scientific tendency within a modern discipline of economics may be found in the writings of one atypical economist of the post-war period, Walter A. Weisskopf. As mainstream economic study increasingly subsumed itself within the effort to master a posited objective reality of markets, Weisskopf turned instead to the business of observing economists. Taking a psychoanalytical approach, Weisskopf identified the existence of uncertainty as a 'psychological malaise'. Uncertainty is unbearable to human nature and this is equally true in the sphere of economics. Asking himself whether ideas or interests led the discipline, Weisskopf concluded that there was no difference between the two and that, in the shadow of uncertainty, symbolism becomes the only and primary tool with which to overcome uncertainty: only in creating symbols can we hope to make any sense of a wholly incomprehensible world. In turn, our symbolism is subsequently legitimated, or systematized with the aid of scientific discourse and method.[7]

The challenge made by Weisskopf to the development of modern economics as a scientific discipline is a deep one: where this analysis is taken to its conclusion, the science of economic method is revealed as a chimera, no more than a mask for a symbolic effort to understand the impossible, to conquer an uncertainty which cannot be mastered. At the same time, symbolism is the product both of ideas and of interests, such that the impartiality of economic method is always in doubt.

---

5 Frank H. Knight, *Risk, Uncertainty, and Profit* (Boston, MA: Houghton Mifflin Co., 1921).
6 Jean-François Outreville, 'We have learned much since Willett and Knight', *Geneva Papers on Risk and Insurance* 36 (2011): 476.
7 Walter A. Weisskopf, 'Normative and ideological elements in social and economic thought', *Journal of Economic Issues* II (1977); Walter A. Weisskopf, 'The method is ideology: From a Newtonian to a Heisenbergian paradigm in economics', *Methodology in Economics* 13 (1979); Walter A. Weisskopf, 'Reflections on uncertainty in economics', *Geneva Papers on Risk and Insurance* 33 (1984).

222 *Michelle Everson*

A new scientific objectivity?

Weisskopf provided two examples of scientifically systematized economic method in post-war thinking. The first was neo-classical economics, which had adopted the certainties of Newtonian physics in support for its assertion that the market would, as a matter of deterministic course, provide general utility; the second, Keynesian variant, was far more subtle, reacting to a Heisenbergian paradigm of complexity within markets, with its notion of steering levers for control of macro-economic directions within the economy.[8] Given these examples, and with the distance of three decades, the assertion that the economic method of the post-war period was not scientific, but was symbolic in its origins, may appear convincing. But what of modern markets and more particularly the modern economic response to them?

From uncertainty to risk in markets

The movement, management and pricing of risk have moved from the periphery to the core of financial activity.[9]

Sovereign debt crisis must be seen in the far broader context of financial crisis: the pressure upon state budgets followed directly on from the general loss of liquidity in banking markets. Financial crisis, in its turn, however, may also be directly linked to modern economic advances and, more particularly, with efforts to combat the disutility of economic uncertainty through the increasingly scientific process of risk management.

Financial crisis was preceded by a comprehensive change in the nature and role of money within the broader economy. Changes in the uses of money are not new, occurring periodically throughout history. Yet, 'Big Bang', or the 1980s' deregulation of the financial services market entailed one of the greatest ever challenges made to our understanding of money, especially with regard to the multiplication of the present and future uses of money and the implication of a traditionally pedestrian banking industry within the technicalities of volatile global capital markets.

Money has always existed twice: traditionally, banks paddled quietly in the backwaters of intra-institutional and inter-institutional lending, wherein the multiple risks associated with the dual disposition of money – its simultaneous existence as debt and credit – were the object of subjectively flavoured in-house management. The various risks associated with the two primary challenges faced by banks – default between creditors and debtors, and maturation mismatch between monies lent and monies earned – were tackled on the basis of the bank's superior information about the moral hazard posed by customers, as well as relative expertise with regard to the prediction of interest rates and pricing movements.

---

8 Weisskopf, 'Reflections on uncertainty',
9 Claudio Borio and Haibin Zhu, 'Capital regulation, risk taking and monetary policy', *Journal of Financial Stability* 8 (2012): 251.

A technocratic tyranny of certainty   223

Upon Big Bang, the sector faced an existential challenge to its competitive dominance, first, in the mastery of informational asymmetries between creditors and debtors, and thereafter in the maximization of capital value for the general economy. Where regulatory liberalization, rapid technological advances, globalization and the increasing refinement of financial products facilitated heightened differentiation of the exogenous and endogenous risks posed to lending operations, it created its own distinct risk pools, thus increasingly substituting the quantitative risk modelling of global capital markets for the subjective risk assessments undertaken within banking firms. Global hazards of interest rate risk, exchange rate risk and sovereign default risk were separated out from the bank internal lending dangers of settlement and payment risk, operational risk, and market and price risk, to be sold within myriad financial instruments. As a result, the exponential multiplication of the dual disposition of money, founded in the creation of a new contractual market for the management of individuated risks, became its own reality. Innovative financial instruments such as over-the-counter derivatives, credit default swaps and securities, and legion futures provided a simultaneous means of packaging out and managing the leveraging risks associated with lending while also multiplying the availability of present and future monies within capital markets.

The certainty of 'futurization'

The common observation that revolutionary change in the global economy was precipitated by the deregulation of financial services markets must be immediately qualified. In the case of banks, 'deregulation' is a misnomer, as the worldwide release of banking from the straitjackets of strict investment controls (prudential supervision) and innovation-restraining material supervision (product approval) was based not upon a rejection of regulation but, rather, upon its technical perfection. Where financial markets had shown the way, recreating the industry with the aid of advanced risk management processes, banking regulation too was reborn within new forms of risk-based supervision of capital adequacy and the governance of banks as well as, to a lesser degree, in new regulatory frameworks built upon the quality of advice given by financial intermediaries and designed to transform once paternalistic conceptions of consumer protection into competitive models of consumer choice. In the case of financial services, less has paradoxically meant more within a technical regime of permissive interventionism wherein regulation and, far more importantly, enhanced supervisory capacity are dedicated to the pursuit of market utility.

New technologies of micro-prudential banking regulation are accordingly founded within the core conviction that the ever-present leverage risks posed by banks can be managed in a market-friendly manner that eschews pre-emptive imposition of regulatory solvency margins for capital adequacy beyond that which is necessary to establish basic confidence. Instead, in addition to a minimum capital requirement, regulators and the regulated work in tandem to establish capital adequacy margins that reflect the true market position of each organization, or

224   *Michelle Everson*

the risks posed by its liabilities relative to its assets. In turn, the technique of market-conform valuation, or economic solvency is not simply concerned with ensuring that banks are safe.[10] Rather, where the assessment of a firm's soundness is measured with reference to its real rather than postulated market exposure, personalized capital adequacy tailored to commercial strategy has a second function of promoting a competitive market discipline within which the strong may be distinguished from the weak and competitive choice is the norm.

Regulatory governance of the banking market is now globalized with the Basel group of banking regulators, together with central bankers, setting the tone for banking regulation worldwide.[11] The choice made by banking regulators to join with the market in a risk-based paradigm of market operation and oversight has had two major consequences. On the one hand, where Big Bang had called into question the profitability of traditional banking models – characterized by the strict regulatory divisions made between retail and investment banking – the new regulatory paradigm for banks similarly allowed them to play their own part in new contractual markets for risk management within their own lending operations. On the other hand, however, where regulation brought an end to the distinction between a public interest in day-to-day financial settlements and more speculative investment activities, it also allowed banks to play their part in the multiplication of monies within the global economy.

This latter fact may similarly be argued to have had its own decisive impact upon the politics of modern economies. Colin Crouch has written convincingly of a process of 'privatized Keynesianism', wherein the ready availability of private credit within the increased liquidity of international capital markets has facilitated state retreat from its welfare function.[12] Where banks are also able to offer ready credit to mass markets, reduced state function can be compensated for through private credit, a process that might also be represented as an act of private economic empowerment.[13] At the same time, the acclaimed end of economic uncertainty within the refinement of regulatory risk management has heightened an on-going process of 'futurization', wherein capital is provided in the here and now, in the certain belief that it will be created in the future:[14] a zero sum game where debt no longer exists, having been replaced instead by a risk which can be managed.

---

10 Shelagh Heffernan, *Modern Banking in Theory and Practice* (Chichester, UK: Wiley, 1996), pp. 217–266.
11 See, for details: www.bis.org/bcbs/about.htm.
12 Colin Crouch, *The Strange Non-Death of Neo-Liberalism* (Cambridge, UK: Polity Press, 2011).
13 This may be a positive development, but must similarly be balanced against the process of provision of mortgages to the indigent in the US, which both precipitated financial crisis and comprehensively dispossessed this grouping of the few resources over which it disposed. See Fred Block, 'Relational work and the law: Recapturing the legal realist critique of market fundamentalism', *Journal of Law and Society* 40 (2013).
14 Elena Esposito, *The Future of Futures: The Time of Money in Financing and Society* (Cheltenham, UK: Edward Elgar, 2013); Elena Esposito, 'The present use of the future: Management and production of risk on financial markets', in *Business Ethics and Risk Management*, eds. Christoph Luetge and Johanna *Jauernig* (Dordrecht, The Netherlands: Springer, 2014).

A technocratic tyranny of certainty 225

Allowing economies and lives to be managed in an expectation of constant capital gain state, the multiplication of money usage and futurization have perhaps become the drugs that the global economy cannot do without, implicating all citizens in immediate gratification as well as the expectation of financed future opportunity. At the same time, however, modern micro-prudential regulation, as well as a still powerful post-crisis interest in combined retail and investment banking, incentivizes and enables the banking sector to play its own important role within capital maximization. The parallel to the waning profitability of traditional banking models is the equal participation of banks within the futurization paradigm, or within the solvency-conform spread of banking sector risks across global financial services markets. Where banks are also free to innovate and move beyond internal risk management in order to securitize and offset lending risks within the highly differentiated products of financial innovation, they may now pose and be exposed to systemically relevant risks of counter-party default, whereby, for example, securitized assets have been revealed as worthless vessels of bad debt. At the same time, the sale of individuated risks on global markets offers up a shareholder value-securing promise of increased competitive efficiency, as banking liabilities, transferred from balance to trading accounts, become assets to be managed in contractual operations by individual counterparties with the greatest proven degree of success in individuated risk management.[15]

A technocratic certainty

A central bank is not an appropriate institution for macro-prudential supervision because central bankers are not legitimate politically to make decisions that involve important trade-offs between political and economic objectives ... Such decisions should be left with finance ministries and other elected officials.[16]

Indispensable futurization

The depth of our reliance upon futurization is perhaps best assessed following a financial crisis. In the view of some, the financial crisis demonstrates 'that financial innovation is of limited value relative to the risks engendered'.[17] This observation captures the painful irony of the financial crisis. The financial instruments within which bad debt had been dissipated – only to re-emerge with

---

15 Heffernan, *Modern Banking*.
16 Eilis Ferran and Kern K. Alexander, 'Can soft law bodies be effective? Soft systemic risk oversight bodies and the special case of the European systemic risk board', *European Law Review* 35 (2010): 771.
17 Luis Garicano and Rosa M. Lastra, 'Towards a new architecture for financial stability: Seven principles', *Journal of International Economic Law* 13 (2010): 603.

226 *Michelle Everson*

disastrous consequences as faith in US mortgage securities collapsed – may not simply be dismissed as the unconscionable creations of commission-obsessed bank employees. Instead, just as such products came into being as advanced risk management tools within financial markets, they were also congruent with the regulatory philosophy developed by a global executive dedicated to the perfection of innovative competition. One commentator unwittingly captured the fundamental paradox associated with contemporary banking regulation shortly before the crisis. Under the impetus of futurization, the 'regulating of risk within the banking sector' could not and should not interfere with the competitive paradigm. Instead, recognition 'of the vibrancy and necessity of financial innovation' remained uppermost, with the consequence that the success of a primary micro-prudential goal to 'limit, if not prevent, the downside of bank failure'[18] resided in the adoption by bankers and regulators of a responsively interactive supervisory paradigm in which the mutual refinement of risk management took central stage.

It is beyond doubt that banking regulation played its own part in precipitating the crisis. Most strikingly, a much celebrated value-at-risk methodology (VaR), designed to ensure the security of market investments by requiring banks to continuously calculate their real-time market exposure, has been identified as encouraging the pro-cyclical behaviour of the sector, or its over-leveraging on the back of rising markets within which securitized assets were subject to overvaluation, such that capital adequacy proved illusionary.[19] At a deeper level, however, the sector was also supported in its overdue reliance on market-based securitization by its particularly close relationship with supervisors, which fostered the catastrophic joint 'cognition failure' that failed to appreciate that individual risk management strategies created systemically relevant risks.[20] Given all this, it highly surprising that 'the essential' – in the crisis, fatal – 'linkage between banks and their supervisory authorities',[21] or their jointly calibrated response to leveraging risks, remains at the core of the supervisory structure introduced by the Basel group following crisis. The much celebrated Basel III Accords significantly increase capital adequacy requirements for bank, but equally continue to place a jointly calibrated process of risk management at the heart of competition-orientated market-supervisor relations.[22]

---

18 Razeen Sappideen, 'The regulation of credit, market and operational risk management under the Basel Accords', *Journal of Business Law* No. 1 [2004]: 61.

19 Julia Black, 'Restructuring Global and EU financial regulation: Capacities, coordination and learning' LSE Legal Studies Working Paper no. 18/2010 (2010).

20 Ibid.

21 Sappideen, 'The regulation of credit', p. 61.

22 Michelle Everson, 'Banking on union: EU governance between risk and uncertainty', in *Beyond the Crisis: The Governance of Europe's Economic, Political and Legal Transformation*, eds. Mark Dawson, Henrik Enderlein and Christian Joerges (Oxford, UK: Oxford University Press, forthcoming).

A certainty of systemic risk?

Futurization is the paradigm that refuses to die, at least to the degree that risk-based supervision remains the preferred means to oversee as well as sustain innovation: Basel III is dedicated to correcting the volatility inducing failings within earlier regulation, in order to ensure that banks are 'shock absorbers rather than risk transmitters' in the face of 'volatile market conditions, or worse still in the time of financial crisis'.[23]

At the same time, however, steps have been taken to address the problem of systemic risk within financial markets. Systemic risk within financial markets – or the rapid transfer of bad debts throughout the financial system – is a new phenomenon for which 'there is [as yet] no universally accepted definition, let alone an accepted measure of quantification'.[24] Although the exact causes and ramifications of systemic risk are to date only dimly perceived within economic literature,[25] policy-makers consider it to equate to financial instability 'so wide-spread that it impairs the functioning of a financial system to the point where economic growth and welfare suffer materially'.[26] As a result, 'waiting was not an option,' and 'policies have moved ahead of academic research',[27] with central banks throughout the world now being given macro-prudential functions and oversight powers within capital markets.

The new supervisory fulcrum of macro-supervision remains as ill-defined as the systemic risk it is designed to combat, but commonly comprises technocratic oversight of rating agencies, the application of stress tests and the setting of additional countercyclical capital buffers and leverage ratios in times of unusual credit growth.[28] The discretionary rather than prescriptive character of macro-prudential supervision is argued to allow for continual corrective adjustment in the oversight function during a period of necessary experimentation.[29] However, where 'the ultimate goals of the policy are still the usual macro-economic ones of output and welfare',[30] post-crisis oversight schemes remain wholly in obeisance to futurization processes; central bankers, including the ECB, have become vital decision makers within the global economy, determining just how much risk the system can or cannot bear.

---

23 Emily Lee, 'Basel III: Post-financial crisis international financial regulatory reform', *Journal of International Banking Law and Regulation* 28 (2013): 434.
24 Bruce Arnold *et al.*, 'Systemic risk: Macroprudential policy frameworks, monitoring financial systems and the evolution of capital adequacy', *Journal of Banking & Finance* 36(12) (2012): 127.
25 Pierre L. Siklos, 'Emerging market yield spreads: Domestic, external determinants, and volatility spillovers', *Global Finance Journal* 22 (2011) 83–100; Benjamin Born, Michael Ehrmann and Marcel Fratzscher, 'Communicating about macro-prudential supervision: A new challenge for central banks', *International Finance* 15 (2012).
26 Jean-Claude Trichet, then ECB Chair, 13th Conference of the ECB-CFC Research network, 2010; cited by Arnold *et al.* 'Systemic risk', p. 127.
27 Ibid.
28 Lee, 'Basel III', pp. 440–442.
29 Siklos, 'Emerging market yield'.
30 Arnold *et al.* 'Systemic risk', p. 132.

228 *Michelle Everson*

The deliberative adjunct?

> Behind the façade of parliamentary democracy, both political conflict and the resolution of policy issues increasingly takes place within organisations which are unknown to democratic theory.[31]

In some highly optimistic analyses, macro-prudential supervision remains a wholly technocratic exercise: 'macro-prudential regulation' concerned with 'interactions between financial institutions, markets, infrastructure and the wider economy . . . complements the micro-prudential focus on the risk position of individual institutions, which largely takes the rest of the financial system as a given.[32]

Technocratic optimism extends even to a highly troublesome problem of the balancing of potentially conflicting monetary and prudential supervisory functions by central banks: according to no less a body than the Bank of International Settlement, the lynchpin role that is now to be played by central banks in addressing 'the close two-way relationship between . . . procyclicality and conducting monetary policy' is legitimated by the banks' technical expertise, or their 'deep experience in system-wide analysis and intervention'.[33]

Others are far less sanguine. Critics of the notion of macro-supervision highlight the inevitable conflict between monetary and macro-prudential economic policy and the alienation of democratic oversight over the balance between innovation and competition. At their most optimistic, many studies accordingly highlight the 'reputational risks'[34] posed to central banks by assumption of macro-prudential functions. At their pessimistic worst, some studies even argue that politicization of the central bank function may eventually wholly overwhelm technocratic independence: 'one can reasonably ask whether, having won the battle to maintain central bank independence, some central banks may in the future lose the war, if and when the next crisis emerges'.[35]

From the Foucauldian perspective, the final colonization of the political sphere by a technology of authorless power, or a rationality of governing which, by the same universal token, posits its own inevitability, is simply a culmination of the alienation of human (political) subjectivity which began with the modern postulation of the sovereignty of the Prince, and was slowly consolidated in the adoption of pastoral functions by the state.[36] Others disagree: although

---

31 Claus Offe, 'The separation of form and content in liberal democratic politics', *Studies in Political Economy* 3 (1980): 8.
32 Bart P.M. Joosen, 'The limitations of regulating macro-prudential supervision in Europe', *Journal of International Law and Banking Regulation* 25 (2010): 498.
33 Bank for International Settlements (BIS), *80th BIS Annual Report 2009/10* (Basel: BIS, 2010), p. 90. www.bis.org/publ/arpdf/ar2010e7.pdf.
34 Born *et al.*, 'Macro-prudential supervision', p. 180.
35 Pierre L. Siklos, 'Communication for multi-taskers: Perspectives on dealing with both monetary policy and financial stability'. Rimini, Italy: Rimini Centre for Economic Analysis, WP 11-04, 2010), p. 7.
36 Michelle Everson, 'The fault of (European) law in economic crisis', *Law and Critique* 24 (2013).

A technocratic tyranny of certainty 229

conceding the loss of ideological battles between command interventionism and market-conform supervision, some authors maintain that typological distinctions made between 'autonomous' regulatory models do matter, to the exact degree they reflect continuing dispute about the end to which steering capacities are to be exercised within the modern economy and to what end.[37] In this view, technocratic governance is not synonymous with depoliticized scientification but, rather, represents the establishment of a 'regulatory enterprise'[38] within which sharp divides between efficiency-led regulation and continuing pursuit of public goods, between public and private spheres have dissolved within a praxis of discretionary supervision in which all competing rationales are still fought out.[39] Politics still finds its place within executive governance. More fundamentally, however – and infamously so in the standoff between the views of Jasanoff and Sunstein[40] – the scientification of modern governance is also represented, not as an alienation of democracy and political self-determination but, rather, as a necessary corrective to public irrationality, as deliberative choices are constrained within a rationalizing decisional framework, which eschews blind pursuit of particularist interest in preferred pursuit of an informed and, thus, universal public good.

Technocratic governance clearly remains suspended within political cultures, such that its discretion will and must be exercised with at least a degree of influence from political bodies. A newly established European Banking Union, whereby the ECB takes enhanced responsibility for macro-prudential supervision within the Eurozone, is now subject to enhanced reporting requirements, not only to the European Parliament but also to its national counterparts: 'This role for national parliaments is appropriate given the potential impact that supervisory measures may have on public finances, credit institutions, their customers and employees, and the markets in the participating Member States'.[41]

However, the deliberative adjunct to technocratic governance must surely be questioned in this context. Above all, history teaches us that confusion about the aims of (European) parliamentary oversight over ECB monetary policy can result in weaker rather than enhanced supervision of discretionary executive powers. Urging caution about the results of their quantitative study of Bank–Parliament dialogue, Amtenbrink and Van Duin are nonetheless sufficiently

---

37 Frank Vibert, 'Regulation in an age of austerity: Reframing international regulatory policies', LSE Global Governance Working Papers 3/2011 (2011).

38 Tony Prosser, *The Regulatory Enterprise: Government, Regulation, and Legitimacy* (Oxford, UK: Oxford University Press, 2010.

39 Ibid.

40 For further details see, for instance, Martin Kusch, 'Towards a political philosophy of risk: Experts and publics in deliberative democracy,' in *Risk: Philosophical Perspectives*, ed. Tim Lewens (Abingdon, UK: Routledge, 2007).

41 Council Regulation (EU) No 1024/2013 of 15 October 2013 conferring specific tasks on the European Central Bank concerning policies relating to the prudential supervision of credit institutions.

230   *Michelle Everson*

confident to highlight the problems arising when parliamentary scrutiny of ECB operation is muddled: in this case, by the question of whether review seeks to assess the quality of ECB monetary performance or, by contrast, is more concerned with the Bank's role in the formulation of EU economic policy.[42] Historically, and despite close cooperation, parliamentary preoccupation with a 'secondary' ECB task to support EU economic policy (Article 127(1) TFEU) has distracted it from review of the technical quality of ECB monetary policy, a trend which does not 'necessarily point towards an effective scrutiny by the EP of the ECB'.[43]

Symbolic ideologies?

Universalism and the democratization of capital

Writing with much hindsight, left-leaning critique of the economic revolution dating from the Thatcherism and Reaganomics of the 1980s was notably myopic, not only to the degree that it failed adequately to weight the democratizing attractions of capital liberalization but also since it was founded on a core misconception, which equated liberalization with deregulation. The UK Gower Report of 1983, presaging the 1986 Financial Services Act and, above all, its author's curt assertion that he was not 'in the business of protecting fools from themselves',[44] may now be viewed as paradigmatic, not simply of the Big Bang unfettering of private capital markets but also of a long-term and globalized trend that has opened up the vital benefits of futurization for a mass population more commonly used to the deprivations of opportunity rationing. The understandable preoccupation with the programme to end nationalized ownership within the establishment of the shareholder society, has thus perhaps found its most unfortunate counterpart in an under-theorizing of the consequences of capital market reform and the revolution in the provision of financial services.

Above all, universalist impulses – or a globalization-driven quest for an objectively universal measure of welfare – together with the increasing dominance of scientific claims to management-mastery of social process, have also played their own important part in inducing the left to implicate itself within, rather than to resist, capitalist hegemony, through its pursuit of a programme of privatized Keynesianism. At the same time, the redefinition of private capital creation (debt) as leverage, or as an objectively definable risk that can be simultaneously fostered and controlled, has allowed governments of the left and the right to abdicate their political responsibility for the pursuit of public

---

42   Fabian Amtenbrink and Kees P.S. Van Duin, 'The European Central Bank before the European Parliament: Theory and practice after ten years of monetary dialogue', *European Law Review* 4 (2009).

43   Ibid, p. 568.

44   Jim Gower, *Review of Investor Protection* (The Gower report) (London: Stationery Office, 1984).

A technocratic tyranny of certainty 231

welfare. This has been achieved within a very modern materialism, or a scientific outlook that posits a reality, or inevitability of social organization that, just like the physical universe, is extraordinarily complex in its composition, but which can likewise be made predictable within ordered method. However, as political ideology has ceded to scientific materialism within the transfer of risk management processes from the physical to the social realm, modern markets have themselves also become increasingly alienated from their inspirational roots in spontaneous social interactions; they have been fatally distanced from a Hayekian normativity of liberating unmanageability, to be constrained and contained, instead, within an increasingly dominant paradigm of technocratic certainty.

Hayek disregarded

A national example proves instructive:

> That firms should be allowed to fail so long as failure is orderly . . . reflects the view that firms should be allowed to fail, and thereby subject to the disciplines of the market. It is important for firms to be able to fail in an orderly way without public funds being put at risk since, apart from being an unwarranted subsidy, the public provision of solvency support to a firm . . . can create an expectation of future assistance. This 'moral hazard' in turn increases the risk of future financial instability, as it provides incentives for excessive risk-taking and reduces market discipline.[45]

Explaining its approach to bank failure, the Prudential Regulatory Authority (PRA), the division of the Bank of England responsible for UK oversight within the European System for Financial Supervision (ESFS), simultaneously enunciates the dominant philosophy of contemporary banking supervision. The PRA demands that banks have a profit-driven risk appetite and expose themselves to failure within a market discipline that simultaneously secures the futurization paradigm. However, 'this risk appetite should similarly be consistent with PRA's objectives' of 'safety and soundness' and the 'continued stability of the financial system'.[46] Any other form of risk appetite – profit motive – is a sinful excess, preferably to be exorcised within the creed of supervisory oversight of bank internal risk management, at worst, to be atoned for within a supervised market exit.

We live in a technical age which has made an orchestrated *homo economicus* of the banking sector: the quantitative modelling of markets for differentiated objects of risk management has largely superseded human judgements made

---

45 The Prudential Regulation Authority's approach to Banking Supervision (Bank of England, June 2014). Available at www.bankofengland.co.uk/publications/Pages/other/pra/supervisoryapproach.aspx.
46 Ibid.

232   *Michelle Everson*

within the firm. Subject also to the desire that they should internalize the risk of potential losses, banks are only further denatured by permissive interventionism, as their risk appetites are simultaneously crafted to the prerogatives of financial stability within economic growth. That security in growth is an illusion and matters not a jot. The UK example is again revealing: 'while quantitative models can play an important role in supporting firms' risk management, the PRA expects firms to be prudent in their use of such models given the inherent difficulties with risk measurement'.[47]

The post-crisis recognition that risk analysis is not always an objectively quantitative exercise, but may be skewed at the outset by subjective assumptions – a pertinent example being that a rising market will continue to rise – and, above all, the amplified awareness that some dangers cannot be foreseen, are perhaps only restatements of the seminal distinction made long ago by Frank Knight between risks and uncertainty. That is, between dangers which can be calculated in probabilistic paradigms (risks), and hazards which defy all statistical accounting (uncertainty). Yet, within the modern paradigm of objective governance, the radical nature of this statement is obscured, subsumed within a science of manageable risk, wherein the full extent of Knight's careful revelation of the profit motive as an unknowable creature of uncertainty, is discounted, reduced to a systemic distortion in the perception of risk. By the same token, the post-crisis reiteration of the dominant futurization paradigm, reacts, first, with enhancement of the supervisory function, which reaches its zenith in the elevation of central bankers to a messianic station; and, second, through its experimental politicization of the regulatory governance complex for money, thus offering up what is still only a fig leaf of democratic legitimation for the welfare losses that necessarily accompany any trade-off between competitive innovation and financial stability.

Render unto the globalized market . . .

The European Union is not alone in the extent of its denial of a Hayekian truth of a market of spontaneously unmanageable human exchange relations. Instead, mainstream political debate in the age of futurization has been remarkable only for its silence about the consequences of the amplified socio-economic expectations that have been levelled at private financial markets following state welfare withdrawal: above all, the inevitability of individual loss due to market failure, but also the difficulties facing the denuded state in the matter of the co-ordination of competing welfare claims. To render unto markets the truth of the uncertainty that is theirs, would appear to be too unpalatable a political utterance. However, both within Europe and far beyond, the attractions of political abdication are only magnified by the material allure of the science of new economic liberalisms,

47 Ibid.

A technocratic tyranny of certainty   233

or their promise of value-neutrality in the positing of universal welfare gain within market disciplines, which are deemed – counterfactually – to be a given force of nature.

As Weisskopf has taught us, the allure of a certainty of welfare maximization within scientific economic process is not new. Whether founded in a Newtonian mechanical determinism, congruent with the invisible hand of universal welfare maximization of neo-classical economics, or more subtly reliant upon the Keynesian levers of direction over a 'Heisenbergian' paradigm of complex organization, the modern system of economics was necessarily blinded from the very outset to indeterminate phenomena which were not and could not be systematized within its own symbolism. Similarly, the chimera of scientific economic modelling often masks a procrustean marriage between interests and ideas, between constructed knowledge and desires, and can only be combatted through development of an 'economic morality':

> Most disputes in economics are about ends. How should resources be allocated? What should be produced and who should get what? There are those who see in these normative questions mere conflicts of interest; they will see economics as the discipline of political economy. Those who believe that such questions are questions of ultimate goals and ends of human life will see economics as a moral science.[48]

Thirty years later, the contemporary marriage between economics and scientific method, in all of its reification of technocratic method and blindness to Hayekian uncertainties, would also seem only to deny the political and the moral dimensions of resource allocation. Weissenberg notably placed much of his own moral faith in the transferral of Habermasian efforts to bridge facts and norms from the philosophical to the economic discipline;[49] yet, just as Habermasian visions of constitutional patriotism can now appear exhausted in their paradoxical closure to the moral indeterminacy of globalization, our contemporary, political and moral abdication for public welfare is perhaps a similar reflection of heightened psychological malaise in the face of the myriad uncertainties of economic globalization. The tyranny of technocratic certainty, its all-too-ready preparedness to abdicate an inspirational pursuit of universal welfare to new processes of capital formation, as well as its chimeric belief in its own powers to oversee and manage debt as risk, is also a failure of symbolically constrained imagination.

---

48 Weisskopf, 'Reflections on uncertainty', p. 360.
49 Weisskopf, 'The method is ideology', pp. 882–883.

234   *Michelle Everson*

Bibliography

Amtenbrink, Fabian and Kees P.S. Van Duin. 'The European Central Bank before the European Parliament: Theory and practice after ten years of monetary dialogue'. *European Law Review* 4 (2009): 561–583.

Arnold, Bruce, Claudio Borio, Luci Ellis and Fariborz Moshirian. 'Systemic risk: Macroprudential policy frameworks, monitoring financial systems and the evolution of capital adequacy'. *Journal of Banking & Finance* 36(12) (2012): 125–139.

Black, Julia. 'Restructuring global and EU financial regulation: Capacities, coordination and learning'. LSE Law, Society and Economy Working Papers 18/2010.

Black, Julia and Robert Baldwin. 'Really responsive risk-based regulation'. *Law & Policy* 32 (2010): 181–213.

Block, Fred. 'Relational work and the law: Recapturing the legal realist critique of market fundamentalism'. *Journal of Law and Society* 40 (2013): 27–48.

Borio, Claudio and Haibin Zhu. 'Capital regulation, risk taking and monetary policy'. *Journal of Financial Stability* 8 (2012): 236–251.

Born, Benjamin, Michael Ehrmann and Marcel Fratzscher. 'Communicating about macro-prudential supervision: A new challenge for central banks'. *International Finance* 15 (2012): 179–203.

Crouch, Colin. *The Strange Non-Death of Neo-Liberalism*. Cambridge, UK: Polity Press, 2011.

Esposito, Elena. *The Future of Futures: The Time of Money in Financing and Society*. Cheltenham, UK: Edward Elgar, 2013.

Esposito, Elena. 'The present use of the future: Management and production of risk on financial markets'. In *Business Ethics and Risk Management*, edited by Christoph Luetge and Johanna Jauernig. Dordrecht, The Netherlands: Springer, 2014, pp. 17–24.

Everson, Michelle. 'The fault of (European) law in economic crisis'. *Law & Critique* 24 (2013): 107–129.

Everson, Michelle. 'Banking on union: EU governance between risk and uncertainty'. In *Beyond the Crisis: The Governance of Europe's Economic, Political and Legal Transformation*, edited by Mark Dawson, Henrik Enderlein and Christian Joerges. Oxford, UK: Oxford University Press, forthcoming.

Ferran, Eilis and Kern K. Alexander. 'Can soft law bodies be effective? Soft systemic risk oversight bodies and the special case of the European systemic risk board'. *European Law Review* 35 (2010): 751–776.

Garicano, Luis and Rosa M. Lastra. 'Towards a new architecture for financial stability: Seven principles'. *Journal of International Economic Law* 13 (2010): 597–621.

Geva, Benjamin. 'Systemic risk and financial stability: The evolving role of the central bank'. *Journal of International Law and Banking Regulation* 28 (2013): 403–417.

Gower, Jim. *Review of Investor Protection* (The Gower report). London: Stationery Office, 1984.

Heffernan, Shelagh. *Modern Banking in Theory and Practice*. Chichester, UK: Wiley, 1996.

Joerges, Christian. 'The European economic constitution and its transformation through the financial crisis'. ZenTra Working Paper in Transnational Studies no. 47/2015, 2015.

Joosen, Bart P.M. 'The limitations of regulating macro-prudential supervision in Europe'. *Journal of International Law and Banking Regulation* 25 (2010): 493–501.

Knight, Frank H. *Risk, Uncertainty, and Profit*. Boston, MA: Houghton Mifflin Co., 1921.

Koskenniemi, Martti 'Miserable comforters: International relations as new natural law'. *European Journal of International Relations* 15 (2009): 395–422.

Kusch, Martin. 'Towards a political philosophy of risk: Experts and publics in deliberative democracy'. In *Risk: Philosophical Perspectives*, edited by Tim Lewens. Abingdon, UK: Routledge, 2007, pp. 131–155.

Lee, Emily. 'Basel III: Post-financial crisis international financial regulatory reform'. *Journal of International Banking Law and Regulation* 28 (2013): 433–447.

Offe, Claus. 'The separation of form and content in liberal democratic politics'. *Studies in Political Economy* 3 (1980): 5–16.

Outreville, Jean-François. 'We have learned much since Willett and Knight'. *Geneva Papers on Risk and Insurance* 36 (2011): 476–487.

Prosser, Tony. *The Regulatory Enterprise: Government, Regulation, and Legitimacy.* Oxford, UK: Oxford University Press, 2010.

Sappideen, Razeen. 'The regulation of credit, market and operational risk management under the Basel Accords'. *Journal of Business Law* No. 1 [2004]: 59–93.

Siklos, Pierre L. 'Communication for multi-taskers: Perspectives on dealing with both monetary policy and financial stability'. Rimini, Italy: Rimini Centre for Economic Analysis, WP 11–04, 2010.

Siklos, Pierre L. 'Emerging market yield spreads: Domestic, external determinants, and volatility spillovers'. *Global Finance Journal* 22 (2011) 83–100.

Vibert, Frank. 'Regulation in an age of austerity: Reframing international regulatory policies'. LSE Global Governance Working Papers 3/2011, 2011.

Weisskopf, W.A. 'Normative and ideological elements in social and economic thought'. *Journal of Economic Issues* II (1977): 103–117.

Weisskopf, W.A. 'The method is ideology: From a Newtonian to a Heisenbergian paradigm in economics'. *Methodology in Economics* 13 (1979): 869–884.

Weisskopf, W.A. 'Reflections on uncertainty in economics'. *Geneva Papers on Risk and Insurance* 33 (1984): 335–360.

Part IV
Crises of EU constitutionalism

11 The European dual state

The double structural transformation of the public sphere and the need for repoliticization

Hauke Brunkhorst

The democratic circle

By the 'public sphere' I mean both the sphere of *public law* (state, constitution) and the sphere of *public opinion* (civil society). In a working democratic regime, political will is formed in a circular manner: bottom-up, from the formation of public opinion – 'the struggle of the orators on the platform . . . evokes the struggle of the scribblers of the press; the debating club in parliament is necessarily supplemented by debating clubs in the salons and the bistros', the 'dance' of 'those down below'[1] – to electoral campaigns and public legislation; back top-down, through the 'concretization'[2] of legal norms (legislation, jurisdiction, administration, government, investment, police and other operations) and then back up again from the bottom. I call this the circle of democratic 'legitimization through legality',[3] or the *democratic circle*. The process must be open to public deliberation and public intervention at *all* levels, bottom-up as well as top-down – in the 'struggle of the orators' on the streets and in the meeting rooms, in the 'debating clubs in the salons and the bistros', in the 'struggle of the scribblers', in the 'debating club in parliament', in court, in confrontation with public authority and the functioning of the police.

The bottom-up process of public opinion formation is *inclusive*. It must include equally, *all voices available*, those of all kinds of citizens and non-citizens (foreigners, inmates, etc.), as well as all kinds of voices and other symbolic forms, the so-called political as well as the so-called non-political, and it must include sensitivity to the signs of silenced voices (present and past).[4]

---

1 Karl Marx, 'The eighteenth Brumaire of Louis Bonaparte'. *Die Revolution* 1 (1852): ch. IV. Available at https://www.marxists.org/archive/marx/works/1852/18th-brumaire/ch04.htm.

2 Hans Kelsen, *Allgemeine Staatslehre*. (Berlin: Springer, 1925), p. 234; see Jochen von Bernstorff, 'Kelsen und das Völkerrecht', in *Rechts-Staat. Staat, internationale Gemeinschaft und Völkerrecht bei Hans Kelsen*, eds Hauke Brunkhorst and Rüdiger Voigt (Baden-Baden, Germany: Nomos, 2008), p. 181.

3 Jürgen Habermas, *Between Facts and Norms: Contributions to a Discourse Theory of Law and Democracy* (Cambridge, MA: The MIT Press, 1996).

4 On the inclusion of the latter with respect to the Love- and Fuck-Parade judgments of the German Supreme Court see: Christoph Möllers, 'Wandel der Grundrechtsjudikatur. Eine Analyse der

240   *Hauke Brunkhorst*

In contrast, the top-down process of legislation and concretization is *exclusive* and delimited by access rules: citizenship, voting-rights (which can include non-citizens, but only under certain conditions), delegation (representative government) and professionalization (lawyers, officials, etc.).[5]

The inclusive as well as the exclusive discourses and decisions are *public, contested and deliberative*. As public processes (normatively speaking), they penetrate (and conflict) with one other within the same circle of democratic legitimization.

The public sphere is at the same time not only normativity but also facticity. It is a sphere of 'discursive power'.[6] However, the democratic power discourse has an *epistemic dimension* that is constitutive for any public dispute, because it is implicit in the public use of language that is always bound by normative commitments to consistent inferences, truth claims, moral principles, explanations and sincerity.[7] Normativity is not the opposite of facticity (or something transcendental), but part of it. All arguments are arguments in a social context of political contestation, class conflict and cultural divides. All arguments are always mixed with strategic and technical power, propaganda, rhetoric and structural violence. 'Telling the truth' or 'speaking truth' is a speech act that may be true or false, but always has some (intended or unintended) perlocutionary, technical and strategic effects.[8] Every real discourse represents at the same time truths and insights as well as 'historically discrete structures of power', and there are only real discourses to check the truth or justification of something.[9] Everyone who ever participated in a scientific discourse (and who is not completely naïve) knows that merely drawing a distinction between true and false has exclusive power effects and is henceforth always contaminated with power and violence (authority, reputation, exclusion of non-normal science, revolutionary strategies and so on).[10] This is so, just because there is no truth, no

---

Rechtsprechung des Ersten Senats des BverfG', in *Neue Juristische Wochenschrift* Issue 28 (2005). On the republican idea of public sphere (or civil society) in general see: Jürgen Habermas, *The Structural Transformation of the Public Sphere*, trans. Thomas Burger (Cambridge, MA: MIT Press, 1989); Jean Cohen and Andrew Arato, *Civil Society and Political Theory* (Cambridge, MA: MIT Press, 1994). Recently Kant's theory of judgment and Machiavelli's political theory have been used for re-reading the theory of bottom-up egalitarian will formation, see Banu Bargu, 'The problem of the republic in Marx and Machiavelli' (lecture given at the Historical Materialism Conference, New York, January 2010). For a similar argument with strong reference to Kant, see Miguel Vatter, 'The people shall be judge: Reflective judgment and constituent power in Kant's philosophy of law', in *Political Theory* 6 (2011).

5 See, recently, Christoph Möllers, *The Three Branches. A Comparative Model of Separation of Powers* (Oxford, UK: Oxford University Press, 2013).

6 See Michel Foucault, *Discipline and Punish. The Birth of the Prison.* (New York: Vintage, 1995).

7 See, recently, Oliver Flügel-Martinsen *et al.*, *Deliberative Kritik – Kritik Der Deliberation: Festschrift für Rainer Schmalz-Bruns* (Wiesbaden, Germany: Springer, 2014).

8 Paul Allen Miller, 'Truth-telling in Foucault's "Le gouvernement de soi et des autres" and Persius 1: The subject, rhetoric, and power', *Parrhesia* 1 (2006): 27.

9 Miller, Truth-telling: pp. 27–28.

10 See Thomas S. Kuhn, *The Structure of Scientific Revolutions* (Chicago, IL: Chicago University Press, 1970); Michel Foucault, *Die Ordnung des Diskurses* (Berlin: Ullstein, 1977).

The European dual state 241

argument and no idea beyond its performance at a specific place and a specific time, performed by living organisms with tongues and teeth.[11]

However, everybody performing a speech act, *also knows* that *everybody* can distinguish between the forceless force of the better argument, the overwhelming forces of linguistic manipulation, the strategic forces of power games and the compelling force of hegemonic pressure. Even if the respective concrete distinction is arguable in many (if not most) cases, there are enough clear cases to draw a distinction between good and bad reasons, true and false statements, legal (and also moral) right and wrong which is *as stable as the language game based on the distinction between yellow, red and green lights.* Moreover, in a similar (not the same) way, contact and contamination with power techniques is factually unavoidable once we give and take reasons – normative commitments, inferential consequences (you are at a ball, you must dance), consistency and universal truth claims are as unavoidable as perlocutionary effects and contamination with power techniques.[12] Therefore, all who participate seriously (and not jokingly) in a dispute over contentious questions counterfactually assumes that their endeavour is a rational discourse which can lead to a solution of an open problem (contest, conflict) – even if they know that they (and others) might have some strategic interests, are sometimes joking, are always a bit ironic, rhetorical or looking for aesthetic brilliance and applause.[13] Again, there is nobody who can not distinguish between serious, ironic and suchlike expressions.

This short reflection on power and discourse is important for the justification of my basic thesis, namely, the argument that Rousseau implicitly made when he distinguished the *general will* from the *will of the majority.* Any *democratic circle of legitimization gains its legitimizing power only from the empirical effects of the forceless force of the better argument*, because it is only the better argument (good reasoning) that provides us with sufficient means to draw a distinction between true and false, right and wrong, legitimated and non-legitimated government.[14] This is no longer Plato's question: who has the *better life*, the tyrant who triumphs

---

11 Jürgen Habermas, 'Das Sprachspiel verantwortlicher Urheberschaft und das Problem der Willensfreiheit', in *Philosophische Texte Bd. 5* (Berlin: Suhrkamp, 2009), p. 333; Jürgen Habermas, *Wahrheit und Rechtfertigung. Philosophische Aufsätze* (Frankfurt, Germany: Suhrkamp, 1999), p. 59; see, also, Ernst Cassirer, *Philosophie der symbolischen Formen* (Darmstadt, Germany: Wissenschaftliche Buchgesellschaft, 1987/1925), Bd. 1, pp. 102, 124ff, 148; Bd. 2, pp. 14ff, 46f; Ernst Cassirer, *Versuch über den Menschen* (Hamburg, Germany: Meiner, 1996/1944), p. 93.

12 Kant already knew when he made his famous statement in *Groundwork* that the *one and only* (or purely) good thing that exists in human life is good will; everything else, any good deed, is always already contaminated or impure (because of its unintended side-effects). His 'mistake' was to decouple the pure will from the impure deed and situate it in a transcendental realm of freedom.

13 See Daniel Gaus, 'Critical theory and reconstruction', *Philosophy and Social Criticism*, Online first, June 2015 (forthcoming).

14 Again, if someone is forced by power to say that '2 + 2 = 4', nobody accepts it as a true statement, even if it is true.

242 *Hauke Brunkhorst*

but does wrong, or his victim who suffers but does right? This is still the difference between right and wrong, true and false that matters, but now it distinguishes democratic from despotic regimes and no longer the totalities of a good or bad life.

The forceless force of the better argument is usually only one (and not the most effective) aspect of the political process of public contestation, struggle, campaigning, debate, decision making and concretization of binding decisions (that is, the democratic circle). However, all power of legitimization stems from the consistency, truth, rightness and convincing justification (explanation) of arguments (deliberations) which can be abstracted from the power discourse that constitutes its performance. To avoid any misunderstandings, I repeat that these abstractions can only be performed by (worldly) speech acts and not by (otherworldly) pure reason, and they can be performed by everybody who can understand (is able to learn) that 'bicycle' and '*Fahrrad*' (or the Morning Star and the Evening Star) are referring to the same thing.

Recognizing the legitimizing power of the democratic circle requires only some robust criteria, available to everybody, and which are deeply entrenched in the democratic language game. A good indication of the dramatic loss of democratic legitimization is the fact that some 50 years ago, between 30 and 40 per cent and more of the electorate participated in public meetings during electoral campaigns, and every candidate had to face serious opposition in open-air marketplaces (living deliberative democracy). Nowadays only some 1 per cent of the electorate participates in public meetings – where party leaders usually give strategically carefully prepared talks in small halls and before a selected audience of supporters (dead deliberative democracy).[15]

Another robust criterion is an observation everybody can make. If leaders argue that decisions concerning money politics (typically made by central banks) must not be settled by democratic majorities, because they are technical questions, the province of experts alone (and members of the political class say the same now about macroeconomic decisions), I bet hardly anybody in any audience of average citizens will accept that argument, because the republican common sense of ordinary citizens is still alive and tells them that these are not *technical* but *political* questions.[16] For the very reason that the people are right with their republican distinction between political and technical questions, their silenced voices have a high (but latent) democratic legitimacy, whereas the democratic legitimacy of their technocratic leaders at the top of the central banks is zero (but manifest). To be sure, social sciences can invent (and have invented) much more complicated and valid measures, but would still come regularly to

---

15 Schröder's last electoral campaign against Merkel was one of the rare counter-examples, when he nearly overturned the predicted result in the marketplace. This gave the whole election a stronger democratic legitimization than any other election in Germany during the early twenty-first century.

16 In the same way, for example, the US Congress thinks that questions of money politics are not technical, but political – but as far as I can see, most of the members of the German Bundestag and the European Parliament see it the other way round.

The European dual state 243

the same result and have done already with very robust measures and extremely high correlations.[17]

Serious *public contestation* is an important, perhaps the *most* important indicator for sufficient democratic legitimization. A second and necessary one is a *low level of direct pressure* by big money and big power, and a third, the degree of *equal access for every voice* (or fair representation) in public debate. Further indicators are the *number of participants* (30 per cent versus 1 per cent), the *turnout*, the opportunities for *deliberative change of opinions* and so on.[18]

Here we have to distinguish again between fact and norm. *Normatively*, nearly all member states of the United Nations have constitutions which prescribe deliberative democracy performed through the democratic cycle. *Factually*, the respective democratic constitutions of these nations are more or less *normative*, often only *nominal* and sometimes even merely *symbolic*.[19] They constitute living, dead, undead, moribund, chronically ill, handicapped, convalescing and other states of deliberative democracy. Theories of deliberative democracy, such as Habermas's, are rational reconstructions of the normative content of these constitutional textbooks (and its factual effects) which transcend the present constitutional reality (and much of the written constitutional law) by far, but from within.[20]

Constitutional facticity: the decoupling of the Eurozone from democratic legislation

The same distinction between fact and norm fits transnational political organizations such as the European Union (EU). *Normatively*, the EU is a democratic federation, and the 'ever closer' united 'peoples of Europe' (Art. 2 Treaty of Rome) now constitute a European citizenry, which as a (differentiated) whole is the Union's subject of legitimization.[21] The democratic circle of the EU entails a 'mixed constituent power' of EU citizens and national peoples in 'personal union', with double representation, general elections, the ordinary (parliamentary) legislative procedure, national and European basic rights.[22]

---

17 See Armin Schäfer, *Der Verlust politischer Gleichheit. Warum sinkende Wahlbeteiligung der Demokratie schadet* (Frankfurt, Germany: Campus, 2015); see also, Armin Schäfer, 'Liberalization, inequality and democracy's discontent', in *Politics in the Age of Austerity*, eds. Wolfgang Streeck and Armin Schäfer (Cambridge, UK: Polity Press, 2013). I will return to this point.

18 For a model, see Bernhard Peters, *Der Sinn von Öffentlichkeit* (Frankfurt, Germany: Suhrkamp Verlag, 2007).

19 On the distinction between normative, nominal and symbolic constitutions, see Karl Löwenstein, *Verfassungslehre* (Tübingen, Germany: Mohr, 1997), pp. 148 ff.

20 See Daniel Gaus, 'Discourse theory's sociological claim: Reconstructing the epistemic meaning of democracy as a deliberative system', *Philosophy and Social Criticism*, Online first, January 2015. Available at http://psc.sagepub.com/content/early/recent.

21 See Christoph Schönberger, *Unionsbürger* (Tübingen, Germany: Moor, 2005).

22 See Jürgen Habermas, *The Crisis of the European Union: A Response* (Oxford, UK: Polity, 2012); Claudio Franzius, *Recht und Politik in der Transnationalen Konstellation* (Frankfurt, Germany: Campus, 2014).

244   Hauke Brunkhorst

Factually, in the present system of the EU, the democratic circle has been transformed one-sidedly into a top-down technocratic regime of 'executive federalism'.[23] It results in a (at least partial) *usurpation of the constituent power of the people by the economic system.*

This has been the case since the invention of the euro, and it became manifest during the present world economic crisis that broke in 2008. But it has a long prehistory (see the next section). With the euro, a dream came true, that is, the dream of ordo- and neo-liberal economists of an economy without government and legislator.[24] It was the accidental result of contradicting political interests. In 1988 France wanted a euro with a fully fledged economic and financial government; Germany wanted a euro only after the development of equal living conditions all over Europe. What they got was the worst possible compromise, a euro without equal living conditions and without an economic government.[25] Since that time, nothing has changed. Living conditions have not converged – to the contrary, social, economic and political inequality between North and South, centre and periphery, has increased dramatically, in particular as a result of the global economic crisis of 2008 and its ordo-liberal therapy – neither has economic government been established. Instead, the intergovernmental power of the ever closer United Executive Bodies of Europe (UEB), especially those of the Eurozone, has increased.

Even if the decisive turning point of 1988 was not due to the plan of the major political actors, it was just what ordo- and neo-liberals and the transnational class of investors had never dared to dream about: an economy checked only by judges.[26] Therefore, the euro was the last cornerstone completing the hegemony of the economic constitution of Europe over the legal, political and social welfare constitution. I will now give a brief overview of the long developmental history of economic hegemony in Europe.[27]

Constitutional evolution under economic hegemony

The EU was founded on the battlefields of the Second World War.[28] It was founded by the *Kantian constitutional mindset* of peoples and social classes who

---

23 On the concept see, further, Habermas, *Crisis of the European Union.*

24 Wolfgang Streeck, 'Zum Verhältnis von sozialer Gerechtigkeit und Marktgerechtigkeit', lecture given in Verona, 20 September 2012.

25 Henrik Enderlein, 'Grenzen der europäischen Integration? Herausforderungen an Recht und Politik', paper presented at Friedrich-Ebert-Stiftung Berlin, 25–26 November 2011.

26 Ernst-Joachim Mestmäcker, 'Einführung', in *Wettbewerb und Monopolkampf. Eine Untersuchung zur Frage des wirtschaftlichen Kampfrechts und zur Frage der rechtlichen Struktur der geltenden Wirtschaftsordnung*, ed. Franz Böhm (Baden-Baden, Germany: Nomos, 2010), 9.

27 For more, see Hauke Brunkhorst, *Das doppelte Gesicht Europas* (Berlin: Suhrkamp, 2014); for the basic idea of constitutional evolution, see Kaarlo Tuori, 'The many constitutions of Europe', in *The Many Constitutions of Europe* eds. Kaarlo Tuori and Suvi Sankari (Farnham, UK: Ashgate, 2010).

28 I use European Union as a notion that covers both the former European Communities and the present European Union.

The European dual state 245

emancipated themselves from fascist rule all over Europe.[29] Their battles and struggles were fought in the name of comprehensive democratic and social self-determination. Liberating violence was transformed into the constituent power of a *new foundation* and the unification of Europe.[30] It was the *new foundation* that replaced the classical peace treaty (which was no longer possible after the European and Asian atrocities of the former Axis Powers).

European unification did not begin with the Treaties of Paris and Rome in 1951 and 1957, nor with the *Method Monet*, but with the *new* national constitutions that all the founding members (France, Belgium, Italy, Luxemburg, the Netherlands and West Germany) had given themselves between 1944 and 1948.[31] All the founding members had changed their political leaders and had replaced great parts of their former ruling classes with former resistance fighters or emigrants who had defected.[32] All the constitutions of the founding members were new or, in important aspects, revised and more democratic than ever before, and all had eliminated the remains (or post-1918 newly invented structures) of a corporatist political representation of society.[33] The German *Grundgesetz* even constituted a completely new state.[34] All the constitutions of the founding members expressed a strong emphasis on human rights and had

29 On the distinction between the Kantian and the managerial mindset, see Martti Koskenniemi, 'Constitutionalism as mindset: Reflections on Kantian themes about international law and globalization', *Theoretical Inquiries in Law* 8(9) (2006).

30 See Alexander Somek, 'Europe: From emancipation to empowerment', LSE, LEQS Paper no. 60/2013. Even the former president of the European Commission, the Portuguese, Barroso, owed his job to a late effect of the emancipation of Europe from fascism in Portugal.

31 Chris Thornhill, *A Sociology of Constitutions. Constitutions and State Legitimacy in Historical-Sociological Perspective* (Cambridge, UK: Cambridge University Press, 2011), pp. 327–371; John Erik Fossum and Augustín José Menéndez, *The Constitution's Gift. A Constitutional Theory for a Democratic European Union* (Plymouth, UK: Rowman, 2011). On the two basic ideas of a constitution (power-founding versus power-limiting), see Hauke Brunkhorst, *Solidarity. From Civic Friendship to the Global Legal Community* (Cambridge, MA: MIT Press, 2005), pp. 67 ff.; Christoph Möllers, 'Pouvoir constituant – constitution – constitutionalization', in *Principles of European Constitutional Law*, edited by Armin von Bogdandy and Jürgen Bast (Oxford, UK: Hart, 2009).

32 Jürgen Osterhammel and Niels P. Petersson, *Geschichte der Globalisierung* (Munich, Germany: Beck, 2007), p. 85; Eric Hobsbawm, *Das Zeitalter der Extreme. Weltgeschichte des 20. Jahrhunderts* (Munich, Germany: Hanser, 1994), pp. 185–187. This does not mean that strong continuities did not remain in all countries; in Germany, in particular, the Nazi continuities of the élites were still strong but were silenced and displaced, strikingly described by Hermann Lübbe as 'kommunikatives Beschweigen brauner Biographieanteile': see Hermann Lübbe, 'Der Nationalsozialismus im politischen Bewußtsein der Gegenwart', in *Deutschlands Weg in die Diktatur*, eds. Martin Broszat *et al.* (Berlin, Germany: Siedler Verlag, 1985).

33 See Dietrich Jesch, *Gesetz und Verwaltung. Eine Problemstudie zum Wandel des Gesetzmäßigkeitsprinzips* (Tübingen, Germany: Mohr, 1961); Thornhill, *A Sociology of Constitutions*, pp. 327–371.

34 See Hans Kelsen, 'The legal status of Germany according to the Declaration of Berlin', *American Journal of International Law* 39 (1945).

246　*Hauke Brunkhorst*

opened themselves (explicitly or implicitly) to international law.[35] They were committed to the egalitarian project of mass democracy and social welfare. Even the programmes of conservative parties advocated ideas of democratic socialism. Already in 1941, Spinelli, Rossi and Colorn, all three communist and socialist resistance fighters, had outlined – in the Manifesto of Ventone[36] – the project of a European federal social welfare state that preceded the later foundation of the national welfare states.[37] Finally, and most crucially for the foundation of the EU, all the founding members of the European Communities bound themselves by the constituent powers of their peoples to the project of European unification.[38]

In consequence, it can be concluded that, from the very outset, the EU was *not* founded as an international association of states. On the contrary, it was founded as a community of peoples who legitimated the project of European unification directly and democratically through their combined, but still national, constitutional powers. At the same time and with the same founding act, these peoples, acting plurally, constituted a single *European citizenry*. Therefore, from the very beginning, the Treaties were not just intergovernmental, but legal documents with a constitutional quality, committed to the democratic circle of legitimization through legality.

However, what followed was the long *Katzenjammer* of gradual incrementalism and the Method Monet. The Kantian mindset of emancipation from fascism was repressed by the rhetoric of peace, reconciliation and anti-communism.

35 See, on the German case, which was not exceptional: Rainer Wahl, *Verfassungsstaat, Europäisierung, Internationalisierung* (Frankfurt, Germany: Suhrkamp Verlag, 2003); Udo Di Fabio, *Das Recht offener Staaten. Grundlinien einer Staats- und Rechtstheorie* (Tübingen, Germany: Mohr, 1998).

36 Ernesto Rossi and Altieri Spinelli, 'Manifest von Ventotene' (August 1941). Available at http://www.europarl.europa.eu/brussels/website/media/Basis/Geschichte/bis1950/Pdf/ Manifest_Ventotene.pdf; see Kolja Möller, 'Die Europäische Sozialunion', in *Interdisziplinäre Europastudien: Eine Einführung*, eds. Ulrike Liebert and Janna Wolff (Wiesbaden, Germany: Springer Fachmedien, 2015), p. 291; see, also,
Agustín José Menéndez, ed., *Altiero Spinelli – From Ventotene to the European Constitution* (Oslo, Norway: RECON Report No 1, 2007).

37 See Möller, 'Die Europäische Sozialunion'; see Lutz Leisering, 'Gibt es einen Weltwohlfahrtsstaat?', in *Weltstaat und Weltstaatlichkeit*, eds. Mathias Albert and Rudolf Stichweh (Wiesbaden, Germany: VS, 2007); see, also, Ulrike Davy, 'The rise of the "global social": Origins and transformations of social rights under UN human rights law', *International Journal of Social Quality* 3(2) (2013). Available at www.journals.berghahnbooks.com/ijsq.

38 Fossum and Menendez appropriately are speaking of a synthetic constitutional moment in Europe, see Fossum and Menéndez, *Constitution's Gift*, pp. 80 ff., 175. The only instance of a founder-member constitution that made no declaration about Europe, that of Luxemburg, is revealing. The Luxemburg *Conseil d'Etat* decided in 1952 that the Constitution implicitly committed the representatives of the people to join the European Coal and Steel Community and to strive for further European unification. It is argued that, even if the constitution of Luxemburg did not contain anything vaguely resembling a proto-European clause, the *Conseil d'Etat* constructed its fundamental law along very similar lines. When reviewing the constitutionality of the Treaty establishing the Coal and Steel Community, the *Conseil* affirmed that Luxembourg not only could, but also should, renounce certain sovereign powers if the public good so required.

The first stage of the constitutional evolution was triggered by the invention of the economic constitution of Europe that consisted in the structural coupling of law and economics.[39] German ordo-liberals in the early 1930s had already 'hijacked' the idea of an economic constitution from the political left, from Hugo Sinzheimer and Franz Neumann.[40] German ordo-liberals – then strongly backed by the conservative American government – took advantage of the 1957 Treaty negotiations to realize their old dream of a mere technical constitution without government and legislator.[41] The economic constitution was centred in competition law and overseen by the Court. There is not a big difference between ordo- and neo-liberalism, except that ordo-liberal rhetoric pays lip-service to a social market economy. However, what ordo- and neo-liberals share is the basic idea of changing law from functioning as the immune system of society into functioning as the immune system of free markets, triggering an auto-immune disease by stigmatizing the rest of the societal body, especially its legislative organs, as a public enemy. Paradigmatic here is the legal theory of Friedrich Hayek and the political praxis of his master student, Margaret Thatcher.

The second stage was the establishment of the rule-of-law constitution (and a rights constitution) for Europe.[42] In systems-theoretical terms, the rule-of-law constitution is based on the (reflexive) structural coupling of law and law, or, more precisely, the structural coupling of law and rights.[43] The growth of European norms and corresponding legal conflicts urged European *and* national courts to construct, apply and implement European rights and the direct effect of European law, together with the corresponding European citizenship. Therefore, the European Court, in *van Gent en Loos*, rightly interpreted the Treaties as an 'agreement between the peoples of Europe that binds their governments and not simply an agreement between the governments that binds the peoples'.[44] Finally, the European rule-of-law constitutionalization resulted in a deeply interpenetration national and European law, now constituting a single legal order.[45] The two decisions of the Court from 1963

---

39 The following reconstruction of stages of the constitutional evolution of Europe was originally introduced by Kaarlo Tuori in 'Multi-dimensionality of European constitutionalism', in *The Many Constitutions of Europe*, eds. Tuori and Sankari; see Brunkhorst, *Das doppelte Gesicht Europas*.

40 Tuori, ibid. p. 16. The hijacking was organized by Franz Böhm, *Wettbewerb und Monopolrecht* (Baden-Baden, Germany: Nomos, 2010/1933).

41 See Streeck, 'Zum Verhältnis', p. 8.

42 Tuori speaks of a juridical constitution: Tuori, 'Multi-dimensionality', pp. 3, 18.

43 Ibid. p. 18.

44 Damian Chalmers, Gareth Davies and Giorgio Monti, *European Union Law* (Cambridge, UK: Cambridge University Press, 2010); see Franzius, *Recht und Politik*, pp. 87 ff.; Claudio Franzius, 'Besprechung von "Habermas, Die Verfassung Europas"', *Der Staat* 2 (2013): 318; Claudio Franzius and Ulrich K. Preuß, *Europäische Demokratie*, (Baden-Baden, Germany: Nomos, 2012), pp. 16 ff.

45 Tanja Hitzel-Cassagnes, *Entgrenzung des Verfassungsbegriffs. Eine institutionentheoretische Rekonstruktion* (Baden-Baden, Germany: Nomos, 2012); see Karen J. Alter, 'The European Court's political power', *West European Politics* 19 (1996); Karen J. Alter, 'Who are the "Masters of the Treaty"'? *International Organization* 52 (1998).

248   *Hauke Brunkhorst*

(*van Gent en Loos*) and 1964 (*Costa*) were emphatically described by the jurists as 'the declaration of independence of Community law',[46] maybe a little prematurely, because as long as there was no fully fledged political European constitution, active citizenship remained virtual and arbitrary. Individual or, more precisely, private legitimization without public legitimization, remains structurally incomplete on the level of the rule-of-law constitution. Normatively, governments were bound by the agreement between the peoples of Europe. Factually, the peoples were bound by the agreement of governments.

However, at the third stage of constitutionalization, a European political constitution was implemented that couples law and politics structurally; even the beginnings of a European social welfare and security constitution – the fourth and fifth stages – are now observable.[47] The Czech Constitutional Court in its judgment on the Lisbon Treaty states that the EU today forms a complete and unbroken system of democratic legitimization and rightly so, at least from the normative (legal) point of view.[48] Normatively, the EU no longer has a common economy without government and legislator, but has become a democratic political community. Unfortunately, just at the moment the hard issues of unequal distribution of wealth, unequal life conditions and unequal life chances came to the fore, the European Council, the German hegemon and the hastily established Troika reached for their guns. An economic state of siege was declared, and factually nothing changed with the hegemony of the economic constitution, the prevailing system of executive federalism and the differences in life chances between centre and periphery. European parliamentarism became façade democracy and constitutional kitsch.[49]

Contradicting systems of power

In particular, the currency without a legislator reinforced the technocratic politics through the establishment of two parallel systems of political power. They are not compatible normatively, and they represent the existing (but still latent)

---

46 Tuori, 'Multi-dimensionality', pp. 3, 17.

47 Ibid.; Sonja Buckel, *'Welcome to Europe' – Juridische Auseinandersetzungen um das Staatsprojekt Europa* (Frankfurt, Germany: Habilitation, 2013); see Phillip Dann, 'Looking through the federal lens: The semi-parliamentary democracy of the EU', Jean Monnet Working Paper no. 5/02 (2002); Jürgen Bast, 'Europäische Gesetzgebung – Fünf Stationen in der Verfassungsentwicklung der EU', in *Strukturfragen der Europäischen Union*, eds. Claudio Franzius, Franz C. Meyer and Jürgen Neyer (Baden-Baden, Germany: Nomos, 2011), p. 173.

48 Isabelle Ley, 'Brünn betreibt die Parlamentarisierung des Primärrechts. Anmerkungen zum zweiten Urteil des tschechischen Verfassungsgerichtshofs zum Vertrag von Lissabon vom 3.11.2009', *Juristen-Zeitung* 65(4) (2010): 170. For a case study that backs the judgment, see Anna Katharina Mangold, *Gemeinschaftsrecht und deutsches Recht. Die Europäisierung der deutschen Rechtsordnung in historisch-empirischer Sicht.* (Tübingen, Germany: Mohr, 2011).

49 Jürgen Habermas, *Zur Verfassung Europas.* (Berlin: Suhrkamp 2011); Martti Koskenniemi, 'International law in Europe: Between tradition and renewal', *European Journal of International Law* 16(1) (2005): 122.

The European dual state 249

contradiction of the EU.[50] They emerged through the spin-off and systemic closure of the top-down process of norm-generation from the democratic circle.

The first system is the democratic circle, centred in the normative bottom-up procedure of democratic self-legislation (input legitimization) that was completed (even if not perfectly) in the Lisbon Treaty with the ordinary and parliamentary legislative procedure.[51] The normative structure of legitimization consists of a system of checks and balances between the European Parliament, the Commission, the Council of Ministers (which all are integrated within the ordinary legislative procedure) and the European Court of Justice (ECJ) that (like every court) is activated only by individual complaints (and is, in this way, part of the legislative procedure). The normative centre of the democratic system is the parliament, particularly because it represents the cultural, political and social plurality of European citizens adequately (and not despite, but because of its not being a one-person-one-vote electoral system, the normative ideal of the German Constitutional Court).[52] Normatively, the EU is a regime of (Rousseauian/ Kantian) popular sovereignty, reconstructed by Inge Maus and Jürgen Habermas as the completely decentred procedural sovereignty of all addressees of legal norms (that is, people).[53] In the EU, procedural sovereignty has the specific form of a mixed constituent power (*pouvoir constituant mixte*) of European citizens and national peoples (that is, two political roles for each political subject).[54]

However, in political terms of facticity, the democratic system of power today is at best counter-hegemonic, and as far as it is counter-hegemonic, it is not only kitsch and façade. However, it is also the kitsch façade of a second system of institutions, mechanisms and organizations which are largely decoupled from the ordinary legislative procedure.

The second system of power influences European legislation deeply. It is to a considerable extent a soft-law regime with hard-law effects.[55] The second system of power is the informal legislator of the EU, and especially the Eurozone, the system of technocratic top-down government of the executive federalism that

---

50 'Existing contradiction' is the explication of Hegel's (more esoteric) *Science of Logic* for the 'existing concept' of law that Hegel defines in his (more exoteric) *Philosophy of Law* as 'existence of free will' (*Dasein des freien Willens*).

51 Bast, 'Europäische Gesetzgebung'; for the distinction between (democratic) input legitimization and (technocratic) output legitimization, see Fritz Scharpf, *Regieren in Europa – Effektiv und demokratisch?* (Frankfurt, Germany: Campus, 1999), pp. 18 ff., 33 f., 111, 167 f.

52 Jelena von Achenbach, 'Vorschläge zu einer Demokratietheorie der dualen demokratischen Legitimation europäischer Hoheitsgewalt', in *Interdisciplinary Research in Jurisprudence and Constitutionalism. Archiv für Rechts und Sozialphilosophie*, eds. Stephan Kirste *et al.* (Baden-Baden, Germany: Nomos, 2012), p. 205.

53 Ingeborg Maus, *Zur Aufklärung der Demokratietheorie. Rechts- und demokratietheoretische Überlegungen im Anschluß an Kant* (Frankfurt, Germany: Suhrkamp, 1992); Habermas, *Between Facts and Norms*.

54 Habermas, *Crisis of the European Union*.

55 See Christoph Möllers, 'European governance: Meaning and value of a concept', *Common Market Law Review* 43 (2006).

250   *Hauke Brunkhorst*

has its centre in the European Budgetary Regime (EBR).[56] It has released itself from (or never really connected with) the democratic circle of legitimization. It consists of the closely cooperating institutions of the European Central Bank (ECB), the Eurogroup of Eurozone finance ministers (that has become more and more important since the 2000s) and the European Council, all connected closely, but largely informally, with the European Commission. With the exception of the Commission and the ECB, these institutions are only partly and indirectly connected with the ECJ. The ECB (as well as the Commission) is under ECJ jurisdiction, whereas the Eurogroup and the European Council are barely touched by ECJ jurisdiction.

The legal basis of the system of technocratic top-down government is the Stability Growth Pact of the Lisbon Treaty (Arts. 121 and 126) and the 2012 Treaty on Stability, Coordination and Governance in the EMU (EMU = European Monetary Union = Eurozone), that is, the so-called Fiscal Compact. The Fiscal Compact enables a special regime of emergency measures separate from the constitutional law of the Lisbon Treaty without derogating from or amending a word of that Treaty.[57]

There is no question that the technocratic system of executive federalism is the hegemonic one. Up to now, it has had the final say in every important matter. It has the formal and (even more) informal power to shape European as well as national parliamentary legislation and governance. It bypasses national and transnational elections and electoral campaigns.[58] It is a regime that frequently uses exceptional measures (prerogative state/*Maßnahmestaat*), even if all its actions are regularly backed by the normative state (*Normstaat*). Fraenkel's old distinction, originally developed in his theory of the dual state in an analysis of pre-war fascism in Germany, fits (far too) nicely with the technocratic regime of European (and not only the European) political system today.[59] The EBR acts as a self-referentially closed social system. In particular, the EBR is closed against

---

56 See Jonathan White, 'Emergency Europe', *Political Studies* 63 (2015): pp. 304–305.

57 Ibid. p. 308.

58 See Brunkhorst, *Das doppelte Gesicht Europas*.

59 Ernst Fraenkel, *The Dual State. A Contribution to the Theory of Dictatorship* (Oxford, UK: Oxford University Press, 1941). Dual state theory applies not only in the extreme case of the first five years of German fascism and other twentieth-century terrorist regimes but on broad continuum of cases such as the German (or English) constitutional monarchy of the nineteenth century, all of which have reserved certain prerogative powers to the state or the monarch, described by statuary positivists, such as Paul Laband or Georg Jellineck, as a sphere of 'non-law' (Paul Laband, *Das Staatsrecht des deutschen Reiches, Bd. II* (Tübingen, Germany: Laupp, 1877), p. 200). For a critical account, see Dietrich Jesch, *Gesetz und Verwaltung* (Tübingen, Germany: Mohr, 1961), p. 90; Christoph Gusy, 'Der Vorrang des Gesetzes', *Juristische Schulung* 23 (1983): 189 ff; Christoph Schönberger, *Das Parlament im Anstaltsstaat* (Frankfurt, Germany: Klostermann, 1997), pp. 234 ff.; see, also, Christoph Schönberger, 'Ein Liberaler zwischen Staatswille und Volkswille. Georg Jellinek und die Krise des staatsrechtlichen Positivismus um die Jahrhundertwende' in *Georg Jellinek – Beiträge zu Leben und Werk*, eds. Stanley L. Paulsen and Martin Schulte (Tübingen, Germany: Mohr, 2000).

The European dual state   251

the disturbing white noise that is produced by the circle of democratic legitimization: the 'struggle of the orators, the struggle of the scribblers, the debating club in parliament', the 'debating clubs in the salons and the bistros', the 'dance' of 'those down below'.

The Commission and the ECJ are operating in both systems, and therefore they fulfil the important function of mediating and stabilizing the contradicting systems of technocratic and democratic rule. However, they cannot change the hegemonic structure and, therefore, must stabilize it, whether they want to or not. In Habermasian terms, one could describe the system of democratic legitimization as the political lifeworld of the Union, and the system of technocratic governance as the colonial power that colonized the lifeworld, thereby transforming the democratic circle into its kitsch façade.

Who is the sovereign of the EU and its member states? The masters of the Treaty (as in the opinion of the German Constitutional Court) are not the sovereign, neither normatively nor factually. The factual sovereign and constituent power of the EU does not reside in one, or a distinct number of subjects. Jonathan White's reconstruction of the European legal facticity as an emergency regime without a sovereign comes closer to the truth than the traditional theory of the German Constitutional Court.[60] However, there exists a constituent power that is sovereign, but that power resides in the interactive, communicative, decentred and procedural performance of power that has no specific subject any longer. The sovereign is the system of formal-informal interaction of European actors, organizations, institutions and legal mechanisms. Reconstructed from the normative perspective of existing constitutional law, the second system of top-down technocratic power is a perversion of the procedural sovereignty of the European citizens and peoples that is internal to their political lifeworld.

Since 1957, a gradually growing amount of national state-power ('sovereignty') has been transferred formally to the Union. Sovereign states (under the legal 'principle of sovereign equality', Art. 2, Para. 1 UN) finally became member states (under EU law) and the citizens of the EU as a whole the subject that gave it legitimization (that is, not a substantial 'subject', but a performative procedure/ process including all EU citizens and all voices, publicly articulated in the European discourse).

However, as we have seen, the lion's share of power went to the institutions of the technocratic circle, in particular to its centre, namely, the EBR. The UEB and the EBR now control the EU bottom-up process of democratic will-formation; at the same time they have also gained even more control over its national parliaments, which have increasingly found themselves in the classical blackmailing position of 'take it or leave it'.[61] This happens every day, but there have been some paradigmatic hypes in recent time:

---

60 White, 'Emergency Europe', p. 311.
61 Klaus Dieter Wolf, *Die neue Staatsräson – Zwischenstaatliche Kooperation als Demokratieproblem der Weltgesellschaft* (Baden-Baden, Germany: Nomos, 2000).

252   Hauke Brunkhorst

- Merkel calls, Monti comes (2011);
- Papandreou announces a referendum in the name of parliament, European institutions say No with a German accent and 'in the name of the gravity of the stakes' (2012);[62]
- The Greek Parliament plans elections, the informal leader of the Eurozone (again with a German accent) postpones Greek elections (2012);
- In the same year, on 17 May, former ECB President, Jean-Claude Trichet, in the Eleventh Annual Niarchos Lecture (Peterson Institute of International Economy, Washington DC), affirmatively celebrates the European 'quantum leap of governance' that re-founds the EU as a 'federation of exception'.[63]

Thus, the main effect of the European dual state is that for 'a crucial and potentially open-ended length of time, the normal rules of government and opposition are effectively suspended'.[64]

With the growth of the power of the UEB, the EBR has become indistinguishable from economic power (that is, the power of the economic system and its main actors). On the European level, economic, especially financial, power is vested in the normatively and factually independent ECB that operates in close cooperation with the Eurogroup and the heads of government of the Eurozone (the latter two acting under the informal leadership of Germany with its overly powerful economy). In Europe, only the ECB is government, and not governance. Through these (highly flexible) institutions, including the much weaker Commission, and supplemented occasionally by global institutions such as the International Monetary Fund (IMF), the ever closer UEB of Europe has replaced the ever closer union of the peoples and citizens of Europe that still is Europe's normative constitution. UEB exercises direct legislative and executive power in particular through:

- intergovernmental treaties and mechanisms, which are ad hoc contracted and effective as European law, such as the European Stability Mechanism (ESM), rightly called a 'firewall' in a Brussels language game which combines nicely the language of emergency with that of personal computers;
- ad hoc established transnational special regimes, such as the Troika (now 'Brussel Group', 'institutions'), the Schengen regime of border control and many others (with a long-standing agenda).[65] They are implemented by ad hoc

---

62 White, 'Emergency Europe', p. 305.
63 Quoted in White, 'Emergency Europe', p. 305.
64 Ibid.
65 On the special regimes: Jürgen Bast, 'Einheit und Differenzierung der europäischen Verfassung – Der Verfassungsvertrag als reflexive Verfassung', in *Die Europäische Verfassung – Verfassungen in Europa*, eds. Jürgen Bast and Yvonne Becker (Baden-Baden, Germany: Nomos, 2005), pp. 43 ff., 46 ff.; with the example of the ECB as an 'Institution sui generis'; Charlotte Gaitanides, 'Die Verfassung für Europa und das Europäische System der Zentralbanken', in *Europa und seine Verfassung*, eds. Charlotte Gaitanides, Stefan Kadelbach and Gil Carlos Rodriguez Iglesias (Baden-Baden, Germany: Nomos, 2007).

emergency meetings of the heads of the UEB (such as the emergency meeting of the German Chancellor, the French President, the President of the ECB, the President of the European Commission and the President of the IMF on 2 June 2015 in Berlin, making a final offer to Greece);

- the binding decisions of the ECB, which presides over the whole range of European legislative measures (Art. 110 EGV), depending only on a simple majority of Eurozone members. The ECB can implement its legislative decisions immediately. Therefore, the ECB decision-making process is a perfect union of legislative and executive powers. The ECB was legally established through the Treaty of Amsterdam as an executive body, endowed with exactly the same legislative competencies as the institutions which participate in the ordinary legislative procedure of democratic self-legislation. The decisions of the ECB are only subject to judicial review and very soft and indirect parliamentary control that (up to now) has not mattered much. This situation is completely different from that which national parliaments face vis-à-vis their (now disempowered) national central banks. National parliaments can regulate them, amend them and even abolish them with a simple majority. In contrast, to regulate, amend or abolish the ECB politically requires a *unanimous* decision of all European member states, including a couple of referenda[66];
- the specific combination of international and constitutional law that is characteristic of the European Treaties since Paris and Rome. The constitutional basic decision of European law is *competition law first*. This brings me to the next section.

Constitutional technocracy

The European dual state constitutes a new (and so far culturally more or less progressive) regime of authoritarian liberalism.[67] The more Europe grew together as a single legal order of deeply interpenetrating subnational, national, inter-, trans- and supranational law, the less democratic it became as a whole. Constitutionalization regressed from democratic constitutionalism into constitutional technocracy. As we have seen, constitutional technocracy (a constitutional formation strongly favoured by German ordo-liberalism) has its unique legal basis in the constitutional law of the Treaties, in particular because the Treaties since Rome (1957) constitutionalize a huge amount of economic and social law that in a working parliamentary system should be at the disposition of parliamentary legislation, campaigns and referenda. That is why the Treaties are so long. Technically, they combine the legal form of international law with the legal form of constitutional

---

66 See Fritz Scharpf, 'Regieren im europäischen Mehrebenensystem – Ansätze zu einer Theorie', *Leviathan* 30 (2002): 74.
67 Michael A. Wilkinson, 'Authoritarian liberalism in the European constitutional imagination: Second time as farce?' *European Law Journal* 21 (2015). ('Extremely liberal' in historical comparison.)

254   *Hauke Brunkhorst*

law, resulting in a (further) marginalization of parliamentary power.[68] In recent decades, parliamentarianism in Europe has faded away silently and without changing or abolishing its constitution.

There are historical paradigms of the specific combination of international treaties and law, which today constitutes the political community of European peoples.[69] However, the number of *democratic* constitutions based on international treaties is small. From a democratic point of view, most of them are authoritarian federations of authoritarian regimes, such as the British Union of 1707, the German Bund of 1815, the Deutsche Zollverein of 1833 and the German Reich of 1871. One (at the beginning, at least) of the two (half)-democratic exceptions is the United States Constitution, which, unlike the European Treaties, does not constitutionalize ordinary law and does not concretize the enlisted reserved powers of the member states. The same is true of the other (half)-democratic exception, namely, the Swiss Confederation from 1848. This is fundamentally important for democracy, because the legislative concretization and implementation of the (more or less nationwide) meaning of 'reserved powers', of the US commercial clause and due-process clause, must be to the result of permanent contestation and legislative change, that is, change through the 'struggle of the orators, the struggle of the scribblers, the debating club in parliament', the 'debating clubs in the salons and the bistros', the 'dance' of 'those down below'.

Like the United States Constitution, the Treaty of Lisbon constitutes a transnational democratic community. However, what lies at the centre of European constitutional law is not the system of democratic legitimization, rights, and check and balances, but, as we have seen, the system of competition law.[70] Claus Offe has rightly called it the 'hidden curriculum' of Europe.[71] Due to the constitutional priority of competition law, and reinforced by the dramatically growing blackmailing power of the globalized economy, state-embedded democratic class struggle has been replaced by the disembedded competition of national member states over locational advantages, such as low taxes, flexible employment, cheap

---

68 See Dieter Grimm, 'Die Stärke der EU liegt in einer klugen Begrenzung', *Frankfurter Allgemeine Zeitung*, 11 August 2014.

69 See Schönberger, *Unionsbürger*; on the specific form of constitutional treaties, see Günther Frankenberg, 'Die Rückkehr des Vertrages. Überlegungen zur Verfassung der Europäischen Union', in *Die Öffentlichkeit der Vernunft und die Vernunft der Öffentlichkeit*, eds. Lutz Wingert and Klaus Günther (Frankfurt, Germany: Suhrkamp, 2001), pp. 507–508.

70 Nevertheless, we must be aware that, in historical comparison, the situation of early transnational constitutionalism in Europe is not so different from early republican (and reluctantly democratic) state formation in the United States or France. The Marshall Court (in accordance with most federal and state legislative agencies) has established over a long period (150 years) an unchangeable interpretation of the Constitution in accordance with the class interests of big money and private property, and the Code Civil established the same constitutional facticity in France, lasting until 1944 (for a brief account, see Hauke Brunkhorst, *Critical Theory of Legal Revolutions – Evolutionary Perspectives* (London: Bloomsbury, 2014), pp. 294–316.

71 Claus Offe, 'The European model of "social" capitalism: Can it survive European integration?', *Journal of Political Philosophy* 11 (2003): 463.

The European dual state 255

manpower, constitutional debt breaks, etc. Of most importance since the introduction of the euro is national competition regarding labour costs.[72] As a result, member states are dispossessed of all their means of macroeconomic steering. They are no longer able to decide democratically on, for example, neo-classical or neo-Keynesian macroeconomic policies.[73] Neo-classical/ordo-liberal economic theory has become an unchangeable eternal clause of European (and not only European) constitutional law (which is harder to change than that of Art. 79, Para 3, German Basic Law). The last Greek elections were paradigmatic. These days, the German Minister of Finance, Wolfgang Schäuble, uses the word 'democracy' only to refer to an obstacle, with a grimace.

European member states now rely on microeconomic politics alone, and that allows them only a choice of alternatives *within* the neo-classical paradigm of political economy. 'Great choice', as they congratulate you in the shopping malls once you have decided to buy the same schlock you get everywhere for more or less the same price, a price that is far too high anyway.

> The policy preferences of the Union are constitutionally entrenched. Examples abound: monetary policy is geared towards 'prize stability' instead of 'full employment', energy policy focuses on competitiveness and energy security instead of democratic access, non-discrimination policy fosters labour market access over dignity in the workplace, the Court's interpretation of Article 125 TFEU entails that financial assistance must be based on conditionality instead of solidarity, the excessive deficit procedure prefers austerity over Keynesian solutions, and the free movement provisions themselves already express a very particular understanding of the interaction between state and market.[74]

Whatever it takes

Since the 2000s, ever more constituent power has been transferred from the European citizens and peoples of Europe to the UEBs of the Eurozone. A spectacular case marked the shift of political and constituent power from the public sphere of the people to the economic system. It consists of three words: 'whatever it takes', spoken by Mario Draghi into the microphones of an investor's meeting in the City of London at the height of the euro-crisis on 26 July 2012. Minutes later, he added: 'and believe me, it will be enough'.[75] The three words changed

---

72 It seems that the ironic deconstructionists who gave the Nobel Peace Prize to the EU had just this in mind.
73 Fritz Scharpf, 'Rettet Europa vor dem Euro', *Berliner Republik* 2 (2012). Available at http://www.b-republik.de/aktuelle-ausgabe/rettet-europa-vor-dem-euro.
74 Mark Dawson and Floris de Witte, 'From balance to conflict: A new constitution for the EU', *European Law Journal* 21 (forthcoming).
75 Mario Draghi, President of the European Central Bank, speaking at the Global Investment Conference at the British Business Embassy on 26 July 2012. Available at https://www.youtube.com/watch?v=hMBI50FXDps.

256   *Hauke Brunkhorst*

the constituted power of the ECB into constituent power, exactly 223 years, 1 month and 10 days after Emmanuel Joseph Sieyès in the Assembly of Estates had declared that the Third Estate is the Nation, and the Assembly of States the National Assembly. The implementation of what Draghi's three words meant (macroeconomic monetary policies on the European level), was a clear breach of the treaty constitution (as those few words of Sieyès in June 1789 were a clear breach of the statutes of the Assembly of Estates). However, *post festum*, Draghi's breach of the constitution was healed legally by the ECJ on 6 June 2015. Here too, the parallel with 1789 is stunning, because the King healed the breach of the constitution two months after the revolutionary act of the Third Estate.[76] This did not help monarchy then, as it will not help democracy now. In the case of Sieyès, monarchy was replaced by parliamentary democracy; in the case of Draghi, parliamentary democracy will be replaced by economic technocracy. On this day, European citizens became clients and its nations firms.[77]

However, Sieyès misunderstood popular sovereignty as the sovereignty of a substantial subject. The same is true in the case of Draghi. He or his organization cannot perform sovereign constituent acts as a subject (that is a misconception). They can only perform sovereignty as legal or illegal acts *within* an existing legal code (and by finally changing the constitutional code), but they can never become the sovereign. Sieyès could not, and neither can Draghi, avoid procedural sovereignty that has always been decentred; they can only pervert and distort it, and that is, as we will see in the final two sections, the only good news in this big, bad game. Today, political sovereignty tends to be transformed into a decentred procedure of political and economic actors, agencies and networks, which form regionally closed systems within a global network of politico-economic institutions based on a new mix of public international and transnational civil law.[78] Whereas in the EU, public law is still the basis of transnational combines, in the global order, transnational civil law tends to trump international public law.

In the worst case, this could lead to the end of the (no longer – if ever) only Western legal tradition that once combined the religious law of universal and egalitarian salvation with the civil law of the Roman Empire. This was (as is any civil law) a law of coordination of the ruling classes, which later (in its secularized version) was defined by Rousseau and Sieyès, Kant and Hegel, paradoxically, as a law that is the realization of egalitarian freedom (*Dasein des freien Willens*).[79]

---

76 See Horst Dreyer, 'Revolution und Recht', *Zeitschrift für öffentliches Recht* 69 (2014): 805.

77 This was anticipated already with Merkel's infamous play with words: 'If the euro fails, Europe fails'.

78 In *this* respect the time diagnosis of Hardt and Negri's *Empire* is appropriate.

79 See Harold Berman, *Law and Revolution. The Formation of the Western Legal Tradition* (Cambridge, MA: Harvard University Press, 1983); Harold Berman, *Law and Revolution II: The Impact of the Protestant Reformation on the Western Legal Tradition* (Cambridge, MA: Harvard University Press, 2006); Hauke Brunkhorst, *Critical Theory*. For *Dasein des freien Willens*, see n. 50, above.

With the (counter)-revolutionary turn of world law from public to private law, this tradition could come to an end at the price of its emancipatory dimension.[80]

'Go Right!' Social inequality causes political inequality

The great global transformation from state-embedded markets to market-embedded states has strongly reinforced the turn from social mass democracy to a constitutional technocracy.[81] The global disembedding of markets (an important exception is China and South-East Asia in general) has led to a dramatic increase in social inequality worldwide, together with a much less impressive decrease in absolute poverty.[82] However, the absolute decrease of poverty does not matter when it comes to the disastrous political effects of social inequality. Social inequality causes political inequality.[83]

Nearly everywhere in the world of (relatively) free and equal democratic elections, and not only in Europe, turnout is decreasing from election to election – and there are no significant differences between European transnational and national parliaments. However, the effect of shrinking turnout is very different at the top in comparison with 'those down below' at the bottom of the social-class pyramid.

Class matters again, and more than ever before in the second half of the twentieth and early twenty-first centuries. Whereas the least populous upper-class district (the rich quarter of the four quarters of a city, for example) has a turnout of often more than 90 per cent, sometimes close to 100 per cent – all (as in the former GDR) voting for the same unity party of neo-liberal austerity politics – the turnout of the most populous lower classes (the least advantaged quarter of a city) shrinks towards 30 per cent, sometimes even 20 per cent.

The effect on political parties and electoral campaigns is a 'timidity trap'.[84] This means that the major parties of the political left lose most of their core voters, whereas the major parties of the political right retain most of theirs. Therefore, for the right-wing parties (like the German CDU and FDP, the

---

80 This diagnosis is the truth and the strong point of Gunther Teubner, *Constitutional Fragments. Societal Constitutionalism and Globalization* (Oxford, UK: Oxford University Press, 2012). However, instead of appraising civil law constitutionalism as democratic progress, one should assess it as a regression to the old Roman stage of legal evolution (see Michael Geyer, '"Creative destruction"': Some thoughts on Hauke Brunkhorst's legal revolutions', talk at a workshop on 'Critical Theory in Critical Times', Evaston, Northwestern University, 27 February 2015, forthcoming in *Ethics & Global Politics*).

81 Wolfgang Streeck, 'Sectoral specialization: Politics and the nation state in a global economy' (2005), paper presented at the 37th World Congress of the International Institute of Sociology, Stockholm, Sweden.

82 Richard Wilkinson and Kate Pickett, *The Spirit Level. Why Greater Equality Makes Societies Stronger* (New York: Bloomsbury, 2010); Tony Judt, *Ill Fares the Land* (New York: Penguin, 2010); Thomas Piketty, *Capital in the Twenty-First Century* (Cambridge, MA: Harvard University Press, 2014), pp. 23–26, 195 f., 402 f.

83 Schäfer, *Der Verlust politischer Gleichheit*; Schäfer, 'Liberalization, inequality', strongly backed by historical political economy; Piketty, ibid.

84 Paul Krugman, 'The timidity trap', *New York Times*, 21 March 2014, A29.

258   Hauke Brunkhorst

American Republicans and British Conservatives) there is no need for change, but the parties on the left (SPD, Greens, Socialists, Labour, Democrats) are forced to change themselves faster than ever before. Their final goal becomes to go *as far right as the parties on the right.*

This destination was reached in Germany with the Great Coalition of the constitutional debt break from November 2005, energetically pushed by Social Democrats. 'Go Right!' became the hidden theme of campaigns driven by political inequality. In the language of political propaganda, Schröder, Blair and Clinton called it euphemistically a move to the centre ground, and their definition of progress became structural reform, hijacked from their own former leftist party programmes of the 1950s and 1960s. Finally, Blair, Clinton and Schröder became the most radical neo-liberal reformers ever, half-forced, half-fascinated by the blackmailing power of global economy.

The reforms, by the way, not only increased national inequalities but also the inter- and transnational North-South divide, impacting dramatically on the global (boat people) as well as on the European level (PIGS). Wages in southern member states of the EU increased too quickly. Northern – in particular, German – wages decreased too far. Germany and the North (due to export competition between European nations in Europe and beyond) were the winners, the South the losers. Austerity politics (wage-dumping) in the South led to structural deflation and proved the wrong cure, whereas wage growth in Germany would (most probably) be the right cure to end the euro-crisis, but is blocked constitutionally by European and (reformed) national constitutional law, ideological prejudices (ordo-/neoliberal doctrines) and the unique order of constitutional technocracy in Europe.[85]

The effect was that the growth of social inequality could not be stopped: the formerly left-wing parties lost even more voters, moving further right from election to election, and the political system ran out of alternatives. So far, the timidity trap is still stabilizing the first transformation of the public sphere of public law (political institutions). Where does the leader of the German Social Democratic Party in 2015 go, to get voters back to the ballot boxes? He goes far right, to the fascist movement of Pegida. This was, in a way, consistent with his and his party's attempts to stay in power, especially as the party's programme had tacitly replaced socialism, the socialization of the means of production, and social equality with empty formulas of political justice, basic rights with basic values, democratic legitimization with personal respect and the Sunday sermons of recognition.[86] People do not fight for values; they fight for their rights.

The general result of political inequality is that parliaments, citizens and trade unions lose power, whereas executive bodies and political and economic elites

---

85   Briefly and concisely: interview with Martin Höpner, 'Der Euro überfordert die Lohnpolitik systematisch', *MPIfG – Aus der Forschung – Standpunkte* (2015). Available at http://www.mpifg.de/aktuelles/forschung/standpunkt/hoepner_interview.asp.

86   *Hamburger Programm der SPD 2007.* Available at https://www.spd.de/linkableblob/1778/data/hamburger_programm.pdf. Wolfgang Thierse, 'Kultur der Anerkennung' *SPD News*, 31 August 2010.

The European dual state   259

gain power. The more dramatic the changes, the faster *all* (the big as well as the small powers) run out of political alternatives. The scope of alternatives shrinks to the margin, and the one in absolute charge who has no alternatives, finally loses all their power, just when they reach the peak of their power – the final destination of Angela Merkel.

The structural transformation of the public sphere I: public law

Despite the growing (for the first time) public relevance and visibility of the EU Parliament (and other EU institutions), the public face of Europe is still the face of its UEBs, especially its leading national presidents and prime ministers (those of Germany and France), and now, more than ever, the face of the President of the ECB. The moment Draghi became the face of Europe, and the six million jobless young in the EU (nearly four million in the Eurozone) its moving body (having the right to move!), the decline of a transnational European public sphere became irreversible (or at least as irreversible as the regime of the ECB).[87]

The intuition of protesting groups often reveals secret truths about the system of power. For the first time, protesters no longer addressed governments but banks and financial centres, as in the 'Occupy Wall Street' movement. In more than one way, they rightly believe that it is the big banks who are now really in charge of the political system.

However, those who are in charge do not engage in discussion. The public medium of the UEB is not debate, contestation, struggle, polemic and campaigning for political alternatives. Once the European Parliament in a vivid and heated debate comes close to a publicly controversial decision that could lead to deep conflict, divide and finally a strong change of politics (as in the debate on the Transatlantic Trade and Investment Partnership (TTIP) on 10 June 2015), the President of the Parliament stops the debate and postpones it forever.

The public medium of the UEB is advertisement, representative statements without opposition, declarations of consent and announcements of indisputable and immutable decisions. The entire institutional design of the EU is programmed for avoiding any public conflict, for bypassing public opinion and public law, and for making contested decisions exclusively in the arcane sphere of diplomatic negotiations, fireside chats and the shadow world of hundreds and thousands of commissions.[88] These commissions, in particular those of the EU Parliament, are

---

87 There are 12 per cent unemployed in the EU, 23 per cent of these are young people (youth unemployment is about 50 per cent in Greece, Spain, Croatia and Italy); the total for the EU is 21 per cent among the young in total and 24 per cent in the Eurozone. Available at http://de.statista.com/statistik/suche/?q=Jugendarbeitslosigkeit.

88 Dawson and de Witte, 'From balance to conflict'; White, 'Emergency Europe'. See, also, Fritz Scharpf: 'The [macro-economic] choices are taken in an institutional setting that provides near-perfect protection against the interference of input-oriented political processes and of democratic accountability in the constituencies affected': 'Political legitimacy in a non-optimal currency area' (Cologne, Germany: MPIfG, 2013), p. 23. Available at http://www.mpifg.de/pu/mpifg_dp/dp13-15.pdf.

260 *Hauke Brunkhorst*

more often legally *accessible* to the public than national parliamentary commissions, but are never ever really reached by the public. People know nothing of their existence. The same has become true of national parliamentary commissions (at least in Germany), but this was not so in former times. Unknown rights are dead rights.

Avoiding public conflict and contestation through transnationalization, structural reforms and emergency regimes, which allow the UEB and its Budgetary Regime to bypass public law, is the main feature of the first structural transformation of the public sphere of public law and institutionalized political discourse.

The structural transformation of the public sphere II: public opinion

At the same time and for the same reasons (namely, the transformation of state-embedded markets into market-embedded states, European executive federalism and the constituent power of the economy), the public sphere of public opinion is structurally transformed, reinforced by huge programmes of privatization, the new system of private-public partnerships that now deeply interpenetrate the whole sphere of public law and, last but not least, the electronic media revolution and other technical innovations.

Here, again, private law trumps public law. High-grade journalism is completely marginalized. Under the exponentially growing pressure of electronic media, global media markets and media groups, it came close to extinction everywhere. High-grade journalism did came back innovatively, intellectually strengthened and interactive on the internet, together with a critical public and vivid opposition, but the internet is still highly fragmented, and its contributions to political will-formation remain incalculable, more or less accidental, and increasingly colonized by capital and secret services. China is only the tip of the iceberg. However, the internet is still a source of new democratic hope, and rightly so, in particular because it dissolves national identities and functions as a means to extend solidarity beyond national borders in various formations. The suddenness and speed of the Arab Rebellion, and its completely spontaneous transnational coordination must (at least partly) be explained as a result of advanced electronic communication. As usual, the first waves of insurgencies were quickly put down, but more (in Arab countries and elsewhere) will follow. One of the effects of the internet seems to be that nationalism becomes a peripheral (and therefore an even more regressive and terrorist) phenomenon of (transnationally networked) fundamentalist sects.

Nevertheless, the global political, economic, financial, media and celebrity classes still form a dense network of communication and shape public opinion nationally and transnationally. The (privatized) media system operates in the same way, as the system of top-down technocratic and politico-economic power is closed against all bottom-up voices from its public environment.

The (Western) media are far from being *gleichgeschaltet* (compliant). They act autonomously (even in China, thanks to the internet). However, they stabilize their systemic autonomy through different mechanisms of reducing complexity.

The European dual state 261

My rough thesis is: whereas the mass media are structurally coupled with the politico-economic system, guaranteeing close exchange and cooperation on an equal footing with the politico-economic ruling classes, they are closed against the bottom-up system of democratic legitimization, excluding bottom-up voices as arguments, including them only as technically manipulable white noise.

The political, economic and media elites have studied Luhmann. They now know that they are not living in a state, but in a society (just compare the use of the two words 'state' and 'society' in 1960 and 2000 in the German Bundestag), and they draw a sharp distinction between their own communicative *system* of political deliberation and the *environment* of the human beings out there. They refer to themselves using the system/environment difference. They no longer talk *with* the people but only *about* them, even if they are present in their campaigns and talk shows, such as Charcot's hysterics in his famous *Leçons du mardi* in Paris in the late 1880s. Everything can be said, but nothing has any effect on the deliberations of the politico-economic-media class. A new stage of Herbert Marcuse's 'repressive tolerance' has been reached.

For example, hundreds and thousands of articles were written, critical of the Bologna reforms of the European university education system, a lot of them in the ever smaller preserves of high-grade newspapers. These newspapers sometimes attacked governments sharply, because of the planned reforms. However, unlike the nationwide and population-wide debates on university reforms in the 1960s (including under-classes and their unions), little or nothing of the academic debate reached the sounding board of the political elites and their voters, and the structurally coupled TV media forums in the 1990s and early twenty-first century. Yet, (in Germany) one could make the interesting observation that the structural transformation of the public sphere of public law had already reached the managerial structure of the universities and reprogrammed the university management's mindset from a Kantian to a managerial one. Who then wonders, if the sovereign parliament of the German State of Schleswig-Holstein writes in the draft for a new university law that the 'Bologna Process' (what is the legal status of a process?) 'has to be implemented' by the legislator – even if it is neither a European regulation nor a European directive (hence higher European law)?[89]

Whereas freelance journalists can no longer make a living from writing, leading journalists make more money than ever before in history and move up to the class of global political and economic players. Journalism today mirrors exactly the new social differentiation of world society, but no longer exposes it. The same is true about universities. For example, the managerial staff of science-politics departments know from their own research fellows how bad their social situation has become, and that this is a direct effect on the structural (microeconomic) reforms of the universities. However, nine of ten say that what is needed is not

---

89 Hauke Brunkhorst, *Legitimationskrisen. Verfassungsprobleme der Weltgesellschaft* (Baden-Baden, Germany: Nomos, 2012), pp. 369–372.

262   *Hauke Brunkhorst*

an end to the reforms that have produced the disaster – but more of the same.[90] Public opinion has been shaped by the same logic during the present Greek crisis of 2015: the reforms failed, the prognoses were falsified, the austerity measures proved to be counter-productive and the conclusion is – we need more of them.

The effect of social differentiation in the sphere of public opinion is the same as in the sphere of public institutions and public law. As regards journalistic output, audience ratings shrink from talk show to talk show, from news programme to news programme, from newspaper edition to newspaper edition (like the industrial growth rate). To increase the ratings of the diminishing number of high-quality publications, the secret slogan becomes ever louder: 'Go Right!' Moreover, instead of protesting, organizing, striking, fighting, journalists copy the strategies of global capitalism to advance growth in times of structurally shrinking growth, by internalizing economic pressure and letting it take over their entire life, including intimate relations, family life and leisure time, increasing working hours by individual self-exploitation, dedicating their whole (increasingly drug-enhanced) life to competing ever better.[91] The message of bio-politics is: the cure for the ailments of capitalism is more capitalism.

Journalism that is structurally coupled with the politico-economic class, but closed against the 'debating clubs in the salons and the bistros' and the 'dance' of 'those down below' is the feature of the second structural transformation of the public sphere of public opinion.

The contradictions of the public sphere

Given the two transformations of the public sphere, some stunning public effects, based on empirical research and summarized here, are easy to explain.

On the one hand, it is not only the Euro-barometers that show trust in European and national political institutions has been shrinking continuously over the last 30 years, the decades of neo-liberal reforms, accompanied by worldwide mob-inciting campaigns against the state, state representatives and officials. The media coverage of this topic is extensive and leads to – mostly helpless and self-pitying – critical debates, which are regularly reported by television, newspapers and other mass media.[92] The favoured cure, reported by the hegemonic media, is

---

90 See Michael Hartmann, 'Elitenreproduktion in der Postdemokratie', workshop lecture (TU-Darmstadt, Germany, 5 July 2013).

91 See Wolfgang Streeck, 'Coping, doping, hoping, shopping: Prolegomena to a theory of capitalist legitimacy in the face of system disintegration', talk at a conference on 'The legitimation crisis of capitalism', Bergische University, Wuppertal, 31 May 2015.

92 Gary S. Schaal, 'Vom Vertrauensverlust in die Vertrauenskrise', *Berliner Republik*, April 2008. Available at http://www.b-republik.de/archiv/vom-vertrauensverlust-in-die-vertrauenskrise. See also, Serge Embacher 'Einstellungen zur Demokratie' in *Demokratie in Deutschland 2011 – Ein Report der Friedrich-Ebert-Stiftung*. Available at http://www.demokratie-deutschland-2011. de/common/pdf/Einstellungen_zur_Demokratie.pdf; European Commission, *Standard-Eurobarometer 80 – Autumn 2013: Public Opinion in the European Union*. Available at http://ec.europa.eu/public_opinion/archives/eb/eb80/eb80_first_en.pdf.

The European dual state   263

always the same: a smaller state (as if increasing bureaucracy is only a problem in public organizations), more markets, lower taxes for profits and assets, and lower wages, especially in the remaining public sectors (railway workers, teachers, social services).

On the other, in a transnational comparative study, Gerhards and Lengfeld have found that, after the outbreak of the economic crisis, and parallel to the decrease of trust in political institutions, feelings of shared commitment, political and social solidarity and a transnational cultural sense of belonging among Europeans has increased to an astonishing degree. To mention only one significant result: the citizens of the European hegemonic state of Germany support in general (and in accordance with a high majority of other Europeans) European-wide reciprocal help, support, equality of life chances and a European welfare state. Moreover, more than 58 per cent of the German population are in favour of the idea of Europe-wide minimum wages, even if they themselves were to lose income.[93]

Why? This is an open question, but at least one reason seems more or less evident and worthy of further research. The global economic crisis, reinforced by the Euro-Greek crisis, caused a heated, conflicting Europe-wide debate: the 'struggle of the orators, the struggle of the scribblers', even 'the debates in parliament', much more 'the debates in the salons and the bistros', and last but not least, the 'dance' of 'those down below'. The latent contradiction between the democratic circle of legitimization and the technocratic system of the dual state became manifest. Suddenly, horizons opened up for public struggle, dispute and deliberation over political alternatives, macroeconomics and the future of Europe. As its by-product, the legend of European identity (that is, an identity of non-identity and conflict) became fact, the legal form of European citizenship gained political meaning, European solidarity, having had cheap lip-service paid to it again and again in the treaties, struck back on the streets and in the marketplaces of Madrid, Lisbon and Athens.

However, the double transformation of the public sphere is challenged, but still functioning, as a strong means of repressing public debate and silencing the 'struggle of the orators', 'the scribblers' and the 'debating clubs' everywhere. Unlike the findings showing shrinking trust in institutions, the findings of Gerhards and Lengfeld (and other similar observations) have been completely silenced – and not only by the mass media. Even within the small social sciences community (and despite the high reputation of the researchers), their findings are practically unknown.

Why is the decrease in trust so widely reported, particularly by the mass media, whereas the increasing civic solidarity is not only not reported, but even silenced? As we have seen, the public sphere of political institutions and public law is open only for manageable problems, which seem to be resolvable by experts and

---

93 Jürgen Gerhards and Holger Lengfeld, 'European integration, equality rights and people's beliefs: Evidence from Germany', *European Sociological Review* 29 (2013); Jürgen Gerhards and Holger Lengfeld, *Wir, ein europäisches Volk? Sozialintegration Europas und die Idee der Gleichheit aller europäischen Bürger* (Wiesbaden, Germany: Springer VS, 2013).

264   *Hauke Brunkhorst*

top-down technocratic improvements of efficiency and the usual means of output legitimization. This is the tacitly accepted common perspective of the UEBs of Europe and the greater part of its mass media. However, at the same time, the public sphere (of the institutions and the media) is almost totally closed to any political (and macroeconomic) alternative. Moreover, it is even closed against any lasting, serious, ferocious and passionate debate about alternatives that could contest and endanger the hegemonic politics of structural reform, austerity measures and the 'peaceful improvement' of national competitiveness.[94] This explains the mass media's blind spot (without any reference to conspiracy and class-interest, even if the latter enhances the effect): if there is no normatively effective bottom-up input legitimization, that is, legitimization through campaigns for real and, in particular, macroeconomic alternatives, and if the whole political system is designed to avoid public conflict, then there is no longer any reason for the mass media to pay attention to the dissenting opinions of the majority, for the very reason that they are not represented but, rather, excluded from public observation. The double structure of structural coupling and exclusion re-stabilizes itself. The system simply cannot observe opinions excluded from systemic communication.

Even the strongest feelings of civic solidarity can become public and political only in a bottom-up process of (in this case) transnational deliberative will-formation and (finally) parliamentary legislation. To understand that, we must distinguish the individualizing (atomizing) *observer's* perspective from the intersubjective perspective of the political *participant*. As long as the bottom-up process within the democratic circle of legitimization is smothered, the silencing will be successful, because the spiral of silence cannot be broken, with the paradoxical effect that I know that I think European solidarity is a great thing – but at the same time, I believe that my neighbour does not think so. To become fact, the legend of European identity must be printed.[95] Otherwise, it remains an observation that is beyond the perspective (lifeworld horizon) of the participant, and it is this perspective that matters for politics (vis-à-vis policies).

The problem of the spiral of silence was already being discussed in 1970s' survey research and has impacted on international follow-up research. A simple, but convincing, model of this pathology of communication can be found in Ronald D. Laing's studies on the reciprocal ascription of opinions/expectations.[96] The one-sided public reception of the different studies (Eurobarometer versus Gerhards and Lengfeld) fits exactly the distinction between the private expression of public opinion in individualized surveys (observers' perspective), and its

---

94 On the 'peaceful improvement of competition' see Marx, 18th Brumaire, ch. I

95 'If legend becomes fact, print the legend', is the famous statement of the editor of the *Shinbone Star* at the end of John Ford's masterpiece, *The Man who shot Liberty Valence*.

96 See Kurt Neuwith, Edward Frederick and Charles Mayo, 'The spiral of silence and fear of isolation', *Journal of Communication* 57 (2007); Dietram A. Schäufele, James Shanahan and Eujung Lee, 'Real talk: Manipulating the dependent variable in spiral of silence research', *Communication Research* 28 (2001). For a more sophisticated theoretical layout, see Ronald D. Laing, H. Phillipson and A.R. Lee, *Interpersonal Perception* (London: Tavistock, 1966).

The European dual state 265

public expression around the water cooler, on the street and in the mass media (participants' perspective). If people start public debate and 'those down below' begin to 'dance', everything can change. However, to start dancing, they must think that public debate makes sense. They must hear the 'play [of] the fiddle'.[97]

The repoliticization of the public sphere?

However, who will be able to make the still latent and individualized contradictions of the European public sphere manifest? Who will make public the secret that conceals their expectations of European transnational solidarity? 'Who will activate this conflict zone' and 'make it tend towards the repoliticization of the desiccated public sphere'? as Habermas asked himself, facing a similar kind of conflict between a silencing administrative technocracy and the repressed political discourse of the democratic people of Western late capitalist democracies in the late 1960s.[98]

In the course of the 1960s, it quickly became evident that technocratic policies (instead of democratic politics) is limited, and its limit is reached once a desiccated public sphere is flooded with political (and anti-political) speech acts. With the Euro-Greek crisis, this limit seems to have been reached in the EU. Therefore, and despite all its executive concentration of power and the sophisticated filter of the double transformation of the public sphere, the weakness of the European system of intergovernmental technocratic governance now becomes obvious.[99]

To state the basic assumption of this chapter: a crisis occurs in the top-down system of manipulated will-formation once a serious debate is provoked that cannot be silenced by the combination of technocratic policies and the media. If such a debate is caused by an economic crisis that hits a structurally coupled complex of legal, political and economic systems (a high level of functional systems' integration), which are, however weakly integrated socially through procedures of democratic legitimization (the democratic circle), the existing but colonized and perverted structure of the democratic circle can be reactivated and used for sound and effective criticism and democratic (class)-struggle against the existing politico-economic regime.[100] Foucaultian 'speak truth' as a direct expression of power can then be disconnected from its specific power structure, generalized and turned against the wielders of political, economic and media power. Distorted and perverted procedures of democratic legitimization can be reactivated in many ways:

---

97 Marx, 18th Brumaire, ch. IV.
98 Habermas, 'Technology and science', p. 263.
99 See Hauke Brunkhorst, 'Collective Bonapartism: Democracy in the European crisis', *Reset Doc – The Web Magazine For All Tribes of the World*. Available at www.resetdoc.org/story/00000022418; Hauke Brunkhorst, 'Unbezähmbare Öffentlichkeit. Europa zwischen transnationaler Klassenherrschaft und egalitärer Konstitutionalisierung', *Leviathan*, January 2007.
100 On the distinction between social and system integration, see Habermas, *Theory of Communicative Action, Vol. II* (Cambridge, UK: Polity Press, 1984).

266 *Hauke Brunkhorst*

- They can 'strike back', for example, just by 'strengthening the rule of law'.[101] Court decisions, such as those in a series of cases before the ECJ on the rights of movement of European citizens, are as good an example for a step-by-step process of democratic inclusion of (in this case) workers, students, prostitutes and homeless people, as the *Hirsi* case of the European Court of Human Rights, in respect of the democratic inclusion of asylum-seeking people from the other side of the Mediterranean, Derrida's 'other heading'.[102]
- The early 2000s' effort to create an EU constitution was in the beginning kept totally under the control of the technocratic system, but during the French campaign in 2005, it suddenly ran out of control and became a matter of democratic, bottom-up deliberation and decision making.[103] However, immediately after the (negative) election results were published on the front pages of all European newspapers, public debate was silenced successfully by an explicit and publicly announced agreement of the UEBs not to talk publicly any longer with their kids, the citizens of Europe, and to wait a couple of years before signing the same Treaty in Lisbon, without the C-word and without a French referendum.
- Silencing public debate was challenged for a second time after the last European elections in May 2014, when Angela Merkel stepped into the press conference and said that she had never heard from a man called Jean-Claude Juncker, but only knew that *pacta sunt servanda*. Nevertheless, this time silencing did not work; the journalists present became angry, and Juncker was elected by Parliament. This made it harder to keep Parliament under technocratic control.
- Parliament failed the defining moment of becoming a widely perceived opposition against the prevailing technocratic system on 9 June 2015 (TTIP vote) by only two votes. A time can now be foreseen when technocratic postponing by presidential prerogative will no longer work.
- The next cases followed immediately, and probably more will follow in an even shorter period of time. The Greek elections of January 2015 brought a leftist government to power, who (as the European executive and media combined immediately alleged) had no professional and economic competencies – except talking publicly at the wrong places about the wrong things. And that was too much.

The Greeks just took the chance to pose publicly, and in the middle of the structurally coupled systems of politics, economy and media, the question of democratic alternatives. They talked before the doors were closed about austerity measures and deflationary dangers. They expressed that there are alternatives just by breaching the official diplomatic dressing code. Overnight, deliberative democracy was back

---

101 Friedrich Müller *Wer ist das Volk?: Die Grundfrage der Demokratie – Elemente einer Verfassungstheorie VI* (Berlin: Duncker & Humblot, 1997); White, 'Emergency Europe', p. 313.
102 Jacques Derrida, *L'autre cap* (Paris: Les Éditions de Minuit, 1991). Brief account in Brunkhorst, *Critical Theory*, pp. 454–457 (with further literature).
103 See Brunkhorst, 'Unbezähmbare Öffentlichkeit'; White, 'Emergency Europe', p. 313.

The European dual state 267

within the distorted structure of procedural sovereignty, once the Greek Prime Minister and his Secretary of Finance and other representatives appeared at the European public forums, repeating again and again that the cure was wrong; that there are macroeconomic alternatives; that they should be discussed; that economic questions are not technical, but political questions; hence, they have to be decided democratically. Democracy matters on all (transnational, international, national and subnational) levels, if we want to solve the tremendous problems of Europe within an overly complex world society.[104] There is no technocratic alternative, in particular, not when it comes to questions of money, private property, the distribution of wealth and (the participatory structures of) its production. These are questions of politics and truth.

The Greeks brought considerable turbulence into the technocratic system just by insisting, like a stubborn kid, that electoral outcomes are the expression of the will of the people and therefore should be taken seriously everywhere in a democratic union of states and peoples. That was new in Brussels and Berlin. Brussels and Berlin gave the formally correct answer that there are more democratic opinions in Europe than just those of the Greek people. However, the answer was expressed so sheepishly that it immediately became obvious that the speakers in Berlin and Brussels did not even believe their own assertion that the united executive bodies of the Eurozone represent the democratic will of the ever closer united peoples of Europe. Just by saying 'No', the Greeks tore up the existing European constitution that leaves everything to the UEBs and prohibits any contested and deliberative will-formation that transcends the eternal clause of national competitiveness. Schäuble declared that it was the 'end of the debate', administratively. As in 2005, the political class agreed, but this time the agreement lasted only a couple of hours. The heads of the hegemon powers of Germany, the ECB, the IMF, France and the Commission later met in Berlin, making a final offer at night, and the next morning, newspapers reported the next offer. The debate goes on, for the good of democracy, and is the first step in solving Europe's currency problems, financial problems, economic problems and social problems. This first step is the insight that these problems are not technical, but political.

The Greeks, even it they did everything else wrong, reminded Europe that there is no social integration of modern societies without (class) struggle, serious contestation, crisis and conflict. The conflict over Greece, that could destroy Europe, showed the limits of intergovernmental technocracy. Therefore, this is the beginning of European democracy.

Ironically, during the Euro-Greek crisis, it was only Mario Draghi, the man who came from Goldman Sachs, who argued that we are in need of real European government, and – as he added, paying (important) lip-service – it must be democratically legitimated, directly and on the European level.[105] Right. Whatever it takes.

---

104 On the internal relation of problem-solving (questions of truth) and democracy, see Flügel-Martinsen *et al.*, *Deliberative Kritik.*
105 See Markus Zydra, 'Draghi's mission – Notenbanker sollen sich eigentlich aus der Politik raushalten. Doch der EZB-Präsident fordert: Die Mitgliedstaaten der EU müssen Souveränität aufgeben – sonst zerbricht der Euro', *FAZ-Wirtschaft*, 17 April 2015, p. 15.

268   *Hauke Brunkhorst*

Bibliography

Alter, Karen J. 'The European Court's political power'. *West European Politics* 19 (1996): 458–487.

Alter, Karen J. 'Who are the "Masters of the Treaty"?'. *International Organization* 52 (1998): 121–147.

Bargu, Banu. 'The problem of the republic in Marx and Machiavelli'. Lecture given at the Historical Materialism Conference, New York, January 2010.

Bast, Jürgen. 'Einheit und Differenzierung der europäischen Verfassung – Der Verfassungsvertrag als reflexive Verfassung'. In *Die Europäische Verfassung – Verfassungen in Europa*, edited by Jürgen Bast and Yvonne Becker. Baden-Baden, Germany: Nomos, 2005, pp. 34–60.

Bast, Jürgen. 'Europäische Gesetzgebung – Fünf Stationen in der Verfassungsentwicklung der EU'. In *Strukturfragen der Europäischen Union*, edited by Claudio Franzius, Franz C. Meyer and Jürgen Neyer. Baden-Baden, Germany: Nomos, 2011, pp. 173–180.

Berman, Harold. *Law and Revolution. The Formation of the Western Legal Tradition.* Cambridge, MA: Harvard University Press, 1983.

Berman, Harold. *Law and Revolution II: The Impact of the Protestant Reformation on the Western Legal Tradition.* Cambridge, MA: Harvard University Press, 2006.

Bernstorff, von Jochen. 'Kelsen und das Völkerrecht', in *Rechts-Staat. Staat, internationale Gemeinschaft und Völkerrecht bei Hans Kelsen*, edited by Hauke Brunkhorst and Rüdiger Voigt. Baden-Baden, Germany: Nomos, 2008, pp. 167–190.

Böhm, Franz. *Wettbewerb und Monopolrecht.* Baden-Baden, Germany: Nomos, 2010.

Brunkhorst, Hauke. *Solidarity. From Civic Friendship to the Global Legal Community.* Cambridge, MA: MIT Press, 2005.

Brunkhorst, Hauke. 'Unbezähmbare Öffentlichkeit. Europa zwischen transnationaler Klassenherrschaft und egalitärer Konstitutionalisierung'. *Leviathan*, January 2007, pp. 12–29.

Brunkhorst, Hauke. *Legitimationskrisen. Verfassungsprobleme der Weltgesellschaft.* Baden- Baden, Germany: Nomos, 2012.

Brunkhorst, Hauke. *Critical Theory of Legal Revolutions – Evolutionary Perspectives.* London: Bloomsbury, 2014.

Brunkhorst, Hauke. *Das doppelte Gesicht Europas.* Berlin: Suhrkamp, 2014.

Brunkhorst, Hauke. 'Collective Bonapartism: Democracy in the European crisis'. *Reset Doc – The web magazine for all tribes of the world*, 24 June 2014. Available at www.resetdoc.org/story/00000022418.

Buckel, Sonja. *'Welcome to Europe' – Juridische Auseinandersetzungen um das Staatsprojekt Europa.* Frankfurt, Germany: Habilitation, 2013.

Cassirer, Ernst. *Philosophie der symbolischen Formen.* Darmstadt, Germany: Wissenschaftliche Buchgesellschaft, 1987/1925.

Cassirer, Ernst. *Versuch über den Menschen.* Hamburg, Germany: Meiner, 1996/1944.

Chalmers, Damian, Gareth Davies and Giorgio Monti. *European Union Law.* Cambridge, UK: Cambridge University Press, 2010.

Cohen, Jean and Andrew Arato. *Civil Society and Political Theory.* Cambridge, MA: MIT Press, 1994.

Dann, Phillip. 'Looking through the federal lens: The semi-parliamentary democracy of the EU'. Jean Monnet Working Paper no. 5/02 (2002).

Davy, Ulrike. 'The rise of the "global social": Origins and transformations of social rights under UN human rights law'. *International Journal of Social Quality* 3(2) (2013): 41.

The European dual state   269

Dawson, Mark and Floris de Witte. 'From balance to conflict: A new constitution for the EU'. *European Law Journal* 21, forthcoming.

Derrida, Jacques. *L'autre cap*. Paris: Les Éditions de Minuit, 1991.

Di Fabio, Udo. *Das Recht offener Staaten. Grundlinien einer Staats- und Rechtstheorie.* Tübingen, Germany: Mohr, 1998.

Dreyer, Horst. 'Revolution und Recht'. *Zeitschrift für öffentliches Recht* 69 (2014): 805–831.

Embacher, Serge. 'Einstellungen zur Demokratie'. In *Demokratie in Deutschland 2011 – Ein Report der Friedrich-Ebert-Stiftung.* Available at http://www.demokratie-deutschland-2011.de/common/pdf/Einstellungen_zur_Demokratie.pdf.

Enderlein, Henrik. 'Grenzen der europäischen Integration? Herausforderungen an Recht und Politik'. Paper presented at Friedrich-Ebert-Stiftung Berlin, 25–26 November 2011.

Flügel-Martinsen, Oliver, Daniel Gaus, Tanja Hitzel-Cassagnes and Franziska Martinsen, eds. *Deliberative Kritik – Kritik Der Deliberation: Festschrift für Rainer Schmalz-Bruns.* Wiesbaden, Germany: Springer, 2014.

Fossum, John Erik and Augustín José Menéndez. *The Constitution's Gift. A Constitutional Theory for a Democratic European Union.* Plymouth, UK: Rowman, 2011.

Foucault, Michel. *Die Ordnung des Diskurses.* Berlin: Ullstein, 1977.

Foucault, Michel. *Discipline and Punish. The Birth of the Prison.* New York: Vintage, 1995.

Fraenkel, Ernst. *The Dual State. A Contribution to the Theory of Dictatorship.* Oxford, UK: Oxford University Press, 1941.

Frankenberg, Günther. 'Die Rückkehr des Vertrages. Überlegungen zur Verfassung der Europäischen Union'. In *Die Öffentlichkeit der Vernunft und die Vernunft der Öffentlichkeit*, edited by Klaus Günther and Lutz Wingert. Frankfurt, Germany: Suhrkamp, 2001, pp. 507–538.

Franzius, Claudio. 'Besprechung von "Habermas, Die Verfassung Europas"'. *Der Staat* 2 (2013): 317–321.

Franzius, Claudio. *Recht und Politik in der Transnationalen Konstellation.* Frankfurt, Germany: Campus, 2014.

Franzius, Claudio and Ulrich K. Preuß. *Europäische Demokratie.* Baden-Baden, Germany: Nomos, 2012.

Gaitanides, Charlotte. 'Die Verfassung für Europa und das europäische System der Zentralbanken'. In *Europa und seine Verfassung*, edited by Charlotte Gaitanides, Stefan Kadelbach and Gil Carlos Rodriguez Iglesias. Baden-Baden, Germany: Nomos, 2007, pp. 550–558.

Gaus, Daniel. 'Discourse theory's sociological claim: Reconstructing the epistemic meaning of democracy as a deliberative system'. *Philosophy and Social Criticism*, Online first, 20 January 2015. doi:10.1177/0191453714567733.

Gerhards, Jürgen and Holger Lengfeld. 'European integration, equality rights and people's beliefs: Evidence from Germany'. *European Sociological Review* 29 (2013): 19–31.

Gerhards, Jürgen and Holger Lengfeld. *Wir, ein europäisches Volk? Sozialintegration Europas und die Idee der Gleichheit aller europäischen Bürger.* Wiesbaden, Germany: Springer VS, 2013.

Geyer, Michael. '"Creative Destruction": Some thoughts on Hauke Brunkhorst's legal revolutions'. Talk at a workshop on 'Critical Theory in Critical Times', Evaston, Northwestern University, 27 February 2015 (forthcoming in *Ethics & Global Politics*).

Grimm, Dieter. 'Die Stärke der EU liegt in einer klugen Begrenzung', *Frankfurter Allgemeine Zeitung*, 11 August 2014.

270   *Hauke Brunkhorst*

Gusy, Christoph. 'Der Vorrang des Gesetzes'. *Juristische Schulung* 23 (1983): 189–194.
Habermas, Jürgen. *Theory of Communicative Action, Vol. II*. Cambridge, UK: Polity Press, 1984.
Habermas, Jürgen. *The Structural Transformation of the Public Sphere*, translated by Thomas Burger. Cambridge, MA: MIT Press, 1989.
Habermas, Jürgen. 'Technology and Science as "Ideology"'. In *Jürgen Habermas: On Society and Politics*, edited by Steven Seidman. Boston, MA: Beacon, 1989, pp. 237–265.
Habermas, Jürgen. *Between Facts and Norms: Contributions to a Discourse Theory of Law and Democracy*. Cambridge, MA: The MIT Press, 1996.
Habermas, Jürgen. *Wahrheit und Rechtfertigung. Philosophische Aufsätze*. Frankfurt, Germany: Suhrkamp, 1999.
Habermas, Jürgen. 'Das Sprachspiel verantwortlicher Urheberschaft und das Problem der Willensfreiheit'. In *Philosophische Texte Bd. 5*. Berlin: Suhrkamp, 2009.
Habermas, Jürgen. *Zur Verfassung Europas*. Berlin: Suhrkamp. 2011.
Habermas, Jürgen. *The Crisis of the European Union: A Response*. Oxford, UK: Polity, 2012.
Hartmann, Michael. 'Elitenreproduktion in der Postdemokratie'. Workshop lecture, TU-Darmstadt, 5 July 2013.
Hitzel-Cassagnes, Tanja. *Entgrenzung des Verfassungsbegriffs. Eine institutionentheoretische Rekonstruktion*. Baden-Baden, Germany: Nomos, 2012.
Hobsbawm, Eric. *Das Zeitalter der Extreme. Weltgeschichte des 20. Jahrhunderts*. Munich, Germany: Hanser, 1994.
Jesch, Dietrich. *Gesetz und Verwaltung. Eine Problemstudie zum Wandel des Gesetzmäßigkeitsprinzips*. Tübingen, Germany: Mohr, 1961.
Judt, Tony. *Ill Fares the Land*. New York: Penguin, 2010.
Kelsen, Hans. *Allgemeine Staatslehre*. Berlin: Springer, 1925.
Kelsen, Hans. 'The legal status of Germany according to the Declaration of Berlin'. *American Journal of International Law* 39 (1945): 518–526.
Koskenniemi, Martti. 'International law in Europe: Between tradition and renewal'. *European Journal of International Law* 16(1) (2005): 113–124.
Koskenniemi, Martti. 'Constitutionalism as mindset: Reflections on Kantian themes about international law and globalization'. *Theoretical Inquiries in Law* 8(9) (2006): 9–36.
Krugman, Paul. 'The timidity trap'. *New York Times*, 21 March 2014, A29.
Kuhn, Thomas S. *The Structure of Scientific Revolutions*. Chicago, IL: Chicago University Press, 1970.
Laband, Paul. *Das Staatsrecht des deutschen Reiches, Bd. II*. Tübingen, Germany: Laupp, 1877.
Laing, Ronald D., Herbert Phillipson and Russell Lee, *Interpersonal Perception*. London: Tavistock, 1966.
Leisering, Lutz. 'Gibt es einen Weltwohlfahrtsstaat?' In *Weltstaat und Weltstaatlichkeit*, edited by Mathias Albert and Rudolf Stichweh. Wiesbaden, Germany: VS, 2007, pp. 185–205.
Ley, Isabelle. 'Brünn betreibt die Parlamentarisierung des Primärrechts. Anmerkungen zum zweiten Urteil des tschechischen Verfassungsgerichtshofs zum Vertrag von Lissabon vom 3.11.2009'. *Juristen-Zeitung* 65(4) (2010): 165–173.
Löwenstein, Karl. *Verfassungslehre*. Tübingen, Germany: Mohr, 1997.
Lübbe, Hermann. 'Der Nationalsozialismus im politischen Bewußtsein der Gegenwart'. In *Deutschlands Weg in die Diktatur*, edited by Martin Broszat, Ulrich Dübber and Walther Hofer. Berlin: Siedler Verlag, 1985, pp. 329–349.

The European dual state 271

Mangold, Anna Katharina. *Gemeinschaftsrecht und deutsches Recht. Die Europäisierung der deutschen Rechtsordnung in historisch-empirischer Sicht.* Tübingen, Germany: Mohr, 2011.

Marx, Karl. 'The eighteenth Brumaire of Louis Bonaparte'. *Die Revolution* 1 (1852): ch. IV. Available at https://www.marxists.org/archive/marx/works/1852/18th-brumaire/ch04.htm.

Maus, Ingeborg. *Zur Aufklärung der Demokratietheorie. Rechts- und demokratietheoretische Überlegungen im Anschluß an Kant.* Frankfurt, Germany: Suhrkamp, 1992.

Menéndez, Agustín José, ed. *Altiero Spinelli – From Ventotene to the European Constitution.* Oslo, Norway: RECON Report No 1, 2007.

Mestmäcker, Ernst-Joachim. 'Einführung'. In *Wettbewerb und Monopolkampf. Eine Untersuchung zur Frage des wirtschaftlichen Kampfrechts und zur Frage der rechtlichen Struktur der geltenden Wirtschaftsordnung*, edited by Franz Böhm. Baden-Baden, Germany: Nomos, 2010, pp. 5–14.

Miller, Paul Allen. 'Truth-telling in Foucault's "Le gouvernement de soi et des autres" and Persius 1: The subject, rhetoric, and power'. *Parrhesia* 1 (2006): 27–61.

Möller, Kolja. 'Die Europäische Sozialunion'. In *Interdisziplinäre Europastudien: Eine Einführung*, edited by Ulrike Liebert and Janna Wolff. Wiesbaden, Germany: Springer, 2015.

Möllers, Christoph. 'Wandel der Grundrechtsjudikatur. Eine Analyse der Rechtsprechung des Ersten Senats des BverfG'. In *Neue Juristische Wochenschrift* Issue 28 (2005): 1973–9.

Möllers, Christoph. 'European governance: Meaning and value of a concept'. *Common Market Law Review* 43 (2006): 313–336.

Möllers, Christoph. 'Pouvoir constituant – constitution – constitutionalization'. In *Principles of European Constitutional Law*, edited by Armin von Bogdandy and Jurgen Bast. Oxford, UK: Hart Publishing, 2009, pp. 169–204.

Möllers, Christoph. *The Three Branches. A Comparative Model of Separation of Powers.* Oxford, UK: Oxford University Press, 2013.

Müller, Friedrich. *Wer ist das Volk?: Die Grundfrage der Demokratie – Elemente einer Verfassungstheorie VI.* Berlin: Duncker & Humblot, 1997.

Neuwith, Kurt, Edward Frederick and Charles Mayo. 'The spiral of silence and fear of isolation'. *Journal of Communication* 57 (2007) 450–468.

Offe, Claus. 'The European model of "social" capitalism: Can it survive European integration?'. *Journal of Political Philosophy* 11 (2003): 437–469.

Osterhammel, Jürgen and Niels P. Petersson. *Geschichte der Globalisierung.* Munich, Germany: Beck, 2007.

Peters, Bernhard. *Der Sinn von Öffentlichkeit.* Frankfurt, Germany: Suhrkamp Verlag, 2007.

Piketty, Thomas. *Capital in the Twenty-First Century.* Cambridge, MA: Harvard University Press, 2014.

Rossi, Ernesto and Altieri Spinelli. 'Manifest von Ventotene'. August 1941. Available at http://www.europarl.europa.eu/brussels/website/media/Basis/Geschichte/bis1950/Pdf/Manifest_Ventotene.pdf.

Schaal, Gary S. 'Vom Vertrauensverlust in die Vertrauenskrise'. *Berliner Republik*, April 2008. Available at http://www.b-republik.de/archiv/vom-vertrauensverlust-in-die-vertrauenskrise.

Schäfer, Armin. 'Liberalization, inequality and democracy's discontent'. In *Politics in the Age of Austerity*, edited by Wolfgang Streeck and Armin Schäfer. Cambridge, UK: Polity Press, 2013, pp. 169–195.

272 Hauke Brunkhorst

Schäfer, Armin. *Der Verlust politischer Gleichheit. Warum sinkende Wahlbeteiligung der Demokratie schadet.* Frankfurt, Germany: Campus, 2015.

Scharpf, Fritz. *Regieren in Europa – Effektiv und demokratisch?* Frankfurt, Germany: Campus, 1999.

Scharpf, Fritz. 'Regieren im europäischen Mehrebenensystem – Ansätze zu einer Theorie'. *Leviathan* 30 (2002): 65–92.

Scharpf, Fritz. 'Rettet Europa vor dem Euro'. *Berliner Republik* 2 (2012). Available at http://www.b-republik.de/aktuelle-ausgabe/rettet-europa-vor-dem-euro.

Scharpf, Fritz. 'Political legitimacy in a non-optimal currency area'. Cologne, Germany: MPlfG, 2013. Available at http://www.mpifg.de/pu/mpifg_dp/dp13-15.pdf.

Schäufele, Dietram A., James Shanahan and Eujung Lee. 'Real talk: Manipulating the dependent variable in spiral of silence research'. *Communication Research* 28 (2001): 304–324.

Schönberger, Christoph. *Das Parlament im Anstaltsstaat.* Frankfurt, Germany: Klostermann, 1997.

Schönberger, Christoph. 'Ein Liberaler zwischen Staatswille und Volkswille. Georg Jellinek und die Krise des staatsrechtlichen Positivismus um die Jahrhundertwende'. In *Georg Jellinek – Beiträge zu Leben und Werk*, edited by Stanley L. Paulsen and Martin Schulte. Tübingen, Germany: Mohr, 2000, pp. 3–32.

Schönberger, Christoph. *Unionsbürger.* Tübingen, Germany: Moor, 2005.

Somek, Alexander. 'Europe: From emancipation to empowerment'. LSE, LEQS Paper no. 60/2013.

Streeck, Wolfgang. 'Sectoral specialization: Politics and the nation state in a global economy'. Paper presented at the 37th World Congress of the International Institute of Sociology, Stockholm, Sweden, 2005.

Streeck, Wolfgang. 'Zum Verhältnis von sozialer Gerechtigkeit und Marktgerechtigkeit'. Lecture given in Verona, 20 September 2012.

Streeck, Wolfgang. 'Coping, doping, hoping, shopping: Prolegomena to a theory of capitalist legitimacy in the face of system disintegration'. Talk at The Legitimation Crisis of Capitalism conference, Bergische University, Wuppertal, Germany, 31 May 2015.

Teubner, Gunther. *Constitutional Fragments. Societal Constitutionalism and Globalization.* Oxford, UK: Oxford University Press, 2012.

Thierse, Wolfgang. 'Kultur der Anerkennung'. *SPD News*, 31 August 2010.

Thornhill, Chris. *A Sociology of Constitutions. Constitutions and State Legitimacy in Historical-Sociological Perspective.* Cambridge, UK: Cambridge University Press, 2011.

Tuori, Kaarlo. 'The many constitutions of Europe'. In *The Many Constitutions of Europe*, edited by Kaarlo Tuori and Suvi Sankari. Farnham, UK: Ashgate, 2010, pp. 3–30.

Vatter, Miguel. 'The people shall be judge: Reflective judgment and constituent power in Kant's philosophy of law'. *Political Theory* 6 (2011): 749–776.

Von Achenbach, Jelena. 'Vorschläge zu einer Demokratietheorie der dualen demokratischen Legitimation europäischer Hoheitsgewalt'. In *Interdisciplinary Research in Jurisprudence and Constitutionalism. Archiv für Rechts und Sozialphilosophie*, edited by Stephan Kirste, Anne van Aaken, Michael Anderheiden and Pasquale Policastro. Baden-Baden, Germany: Nomos, 2012, pp. 205–218.

Wahl, Rainer. *Verfassungsstaat, Europäisierung, Internationalisierung.* Frankfurt, Germany: Suhrkamp Verlag, 2003.

White, Jonathan. 'Emergency Europe'. *Political Studies* 63 (2015): 300–318.

Wilkinson, Michael A. 'Authoritarian liberalism in the European constitutional imagination: Second time as farce?'. *European Law Journal.* 21 (2015): 313–339.

Wilkinson, Richard and Kate Pickett. *The Spirit Level. Why Greater Equality Makes Societies Stronger.* New York: Bloomsbury, 2010.

Wolf, Klaus Dieter. *Die neue Staatsräson – Zwischenstaatliche Kooperation als Demokratieproblem der Weltgesellschaft.* Baden-Baden, Germany: Nomos, 2000.

Zydra, Markus. 'Draghi's mission – Notenbanker sollen sich eigentlich aus der Politik raushalten. Doch der EZB-Präsident fordert: Die Mitgliedstaaten der EU müssen Souveränität aufgeben – sonst zerbricht der Euro'. *FAZ-Wirtschaft,* 17 April 2015, p. 15.

12 Societal conditions of self-constitution
The experience of the European periphery

Pierre Guibentif

Introduction

Recent political trends in Europe's periphery raise questions about the scope and effectiveness of political rights in Europe; or, in other words, about the current state of Europe's constitutionalization. This chapter aims at contributing to the analysis of this political experience at the European periphery, trying to relate this analysis to current debates about the constitutionalization of international and European law and politics.

The argument is that the experience of the European periphery calls for several developments of the conceptual framework underlying some of the main approaches defended in these debates, approaches briefly introduced in the next section. The following sections unfold this argument.

First, the Portuguese experience offers an illustration of a phenomenon already abundantly discussed: the force of transnational economic dynamics, which generate factual and normative constraints on the national constitutional orders. The measures taken in reaction towards the sovereign debt crisis offer impressive illustrations of this force. Second, the analysis of the measures at stake leads to the hypothesis that they might be linked, not only to economic and financial dynamics but also to trends within a social domain which crosses the economic system, as well as other functionally differentiated social systems: the universe of formalized organizations. Third, the discussion of these organizational dynamics requires us to revisit Gunther Teubner's theory of the separation of organized and spontaneous components of functionally differentiated social systems. The analysis of the Portuguese case emphasizes the relevance, within the spontaneous component – which, in this period, has been severely challenged by the organized one – of the experiences and practices of individuals.

Fourth, such an analysis, apart from possible political implications, has implications for the development of sociology. More density should be given to the conceptual tools addressing the human individual, and models of societal processes should be improved in order to better articulate them with the conceptualization of individual experience. In this exercise, sociology should take advantage, in particular, of the theory of the relationship between individual perception and societal communication supplied by Niklas Luhmann's systems theory.

The experience of the European periphery   275

Research carried out on the basis of such a psycho-sensitive sociological conceptual framework could be in a condition to appreciate the current European social situation from the point of view of the following question: what mechanisms and factors could favour, within the relevant social systems, processes likely to re-equilibrate their spontaneous and organized components? Or, in other words, more directly linked to the formulation of the main topic of the present volume: what are the societal conditions for self-constitutionalization processes and what could favour or hamper such processes?

Three approaches to transnational constitutionalism

The perception of an accelerated process of globalization has sharpened the traditional opposition between two views of constitutional issues: on the one hand, the defence of the states and their national constitutions as main pillars of the world order; on the other, the defence of the possibility of an overarching world constitutional order. This opposition has strongly stimulated theoretical debates since the 2000s. Three different intermediate approaches, in particular, have deserved particularly careful and extensive formulation. I shall call them here the *systemist*, the *law and politics centred*, and the *critical* approach. All three are discussed at length in other contributions to the present volume. A short summary of each of them will serve here as a starting point.

The systemist approach

National constitutions, since they exist, only constitute national states and political systems. Other social systems have developed beside the political systems and, in increasing measure over the last two centuries, beyond the borders of national states. If there is such a thing as constitutionalism, it lies in the potential of these systems, as well as of the political systems, to define and to limit themselves by their own means; to 'self-constitute'. In the best possible case, each system would bring about one single 'fragment' in a wider world constitutionalization process: its own constitution. The world constitutionalization process, as such, could by no means be subjected to a general integrating design. This approach has been mainly developed by Gunther Teubner.[1] Other authors work on the basis of this

---

1 Constitutions became a central topic in Teubner's work at around 2000. See, in particular, Gunther Teubner, 'Global private regimes: Neo-spontaneous law and dual constitution of autonomous sectors?', in *Public Governance in the Age of Globalization*, ed. Karl-Heinz Ladeur (Ashgate, UK: Aldershot, 2004). For a comprehensive discussion, see Gunther Teubner, *Constitutional Fragments: Societal Constitutionalism and Globalization* (Oxford, UK: Oxford University Press, 2012). For more recent developments, see Gunther Teubner and Anna Beckers, 'Expanding constitutionalism', *Indiana Journal of Global Legal Studies* 20 (2013) and Gunther Teubner, 'Exogene Selbstbindung: Die Konstitutionalisierung von Gründungsparadoxien gesellschaftlicher Teilsysteme', *Zeitschrift für Rechtssoziologie* 35 (2015).

276   *Pierre Guibentif*

model, combining it with their own research agenda, notably Poul F. Kjaer[2] and Jiří Přibáň.[3]

The law and politics centred approach

National constitutions, whatever their relevance for the shaping of national states since the early modernity, can no longer be approached as self-standing institutions. Nowadays, they are part of a larger normative fabric – 'transconstitutionalism', as Marcelo Neves would call it.[4] The development of this normative fabric, however, is beyond the reach of any single collective or individual actor; it is the ever moving result of the establishment and management of the relations between states, as well as between states and other relevant players in our globalized world. Its legitimacy derives from the fact that the impulsions to its development are acts of the defence of human rights: 'Rights thus act, *ex nihilo*, as the founding principle for the politicality of today's deeply acentric society'.[5] This approach is defended, in particular, by Chris Thornhill.[6] Mattias Kumm, within a different conceptual framework, defends similar conclusions, giving a prominent position to notions such as 'human dignity and autonomy' or 'just relations between free and equal persons'.[7]

---

2 Poul F. Kjaer, 'The structural transformation of embeddedness', in *Karl Polanyi. Globalization and the Potential of Law in Transnational Markets*, eds. Christian Joerges and Josef Falke (Oxford, UK: Hart Publishing, 2011); Poul F. Kjaer, 'Law and order within and beyond national configurations', in *The Financial Crisis in Constitutional Perspective: The Dark Side of Functional Differentiation*, eds. Poul F. Kjaer, Gunther Teubner and Alberto Febbrajo (Oxford, UK: Hart Publishing, 2011).

3 Jiří Přibáň, *Legal Symbolism. On Law, Time and European Identity* (Aldershot, UK: Ashgate, 2007); Jiří Přibáň, 'The juridification of European identity, its limitations and the search of EU democratic politics', *Constellation* 16 (2009); Jiří Přibáň, 'The self-referential European polity, its legal context and systemic differentiation: Theoretical reflections on the emergence of the EU's political and legal autopoiesis', *European Law Journal* 15 (2009).

4 Marcelo Neves, *Tranconstitucionalismo* (São Paulo, Brazil: Martins Fontes, 2009).

5 Chris Thornhill, 'A sociology of constituent power: The political code of transnational societal constitutions', *Indiana Journal of Global Legal Studies* 20 (2013): 585; on the relevance of rights in the global constitutional discourse, see also, Neves, ibid. p. 249 f.

6 See the different papers, which give substance to the second part of the ambitious socio-legal work of Thornhill on constitutions, starting with *Sociology of Constitutions. Constitutions and State Legitimacy in Historical-Sociological Perspective* (Cambridge, UK: Cambridge University Press, 2011), p. 19: the part focusing on 'the constitutional order of increasingly internationalized societies': Chris Thornhill, 'The future of the state', in Kjaer, Teubner and Febbrajo, eds. *The Financial Crisis*; Chris Thornhill, 'Politische Macht und Verfassung jenseits des Nationalstaats', *Zeitschrift für Rechtssoziologie* 32 (2011); Chris Thornhill, 'National sovereignty and the constitution of transnational law: A sociological approach to a classical antinomy', *Transnational Legal Theory* 3 (2012); Chris Thornhill, 'A sociology of constituent power'. For a comparison of Thornhill and Teubner, see Jiří Přibáň, 'Constitutionalism as fear of the political? A comparative analysis of Teubner's *Constitutional Fragments* and Thornhill's *A Sociology of Constitutions*', *Journal of Law and Society* 39 (2012).

7 Mattias Kumm, 'The legitimacy of international law: A constitutionalist framework of analysis', *European Journal of International Law* 15 (2004): 931. Mattias Kumm, 'The cosmopolitan turn in constitutionalism: An integrated conception of public law', *Indiana Journal of Global Legal Studies* 20 (2013): 614.

The critical approach

Globalization consists of transnational processes, in particular, economic and financial dynamics, which threaten humanity and its natural environment. They call for urgent answers that cannot be given by single states, but require coordinated action involving multiple players in the global arena. Current societal and institutional trends suggest that such coordinated action is possible, could be strengthened and made more rational, that is, submitted to designs consciously formulated by the players involved. In other words, it is necessary and admittedly possible to constitutionalize this coordinated action. However, the design of the institutional settings to be developed with that aim has to be based on our most recent experience of transnational politics and cannot be the result of a mere transposition on a supranational level of the institutional arrangement characterizing modern nation-states, including national constitutions. This approach has been defended notably by Jürgen Habermas[8] and Hauke Brunkhorst.[9] It is possible to relate it to the approach developed by Michelle Everson: transnational jurisprudence could contribute to the formation of transnational politics by institutionalizing transnational conflicts, thus giving expression to the 'competing rationalities of political agonism'.[10] The common trait between these two critical

---

8 The two main papers on this topic are Jürgen Habermas, 'Hat die Konstitutionalisierung des Völkerrechts noch eine Chance?', in *Idem, Der gespaltene Westen* (Berlin: Suhrkamp, 2004) and Jürgen Habermas, 'Eine politische Verfassung für die pluralistische Weltgesellschaft?', in *Idem, Zwischen Naturalismus und Religion* (Frankfurt, Germany: Suhrkamp, 2005). For a more recent formulation, see Jürgen Habermas, 'Demokratie oder Kapitalismus?', in *Idem, Im Sog der Technokratie* (Berlin: Suhrkamp, 2013). In Habermas's conceptual scheme, regional organizations, formed by groups of states, could play a crucial role. He is particularly concerned with the role of the European Union, the recent evolution of which he criticizes against the background of his broader concepts of world citizenship and constitutionalization of international law: see, in particular, Jürgen Habermas, *The Crisis of the European Union* (Cambridge, UK: Polity Press, 2012) and Jürgen Habermas, 'Democracy in Europe Today', (speech delivered in Lisbon, Portugal, Fundação Calouste Gulbenkian, 29 October 2013). For a discussion of Habermas, 'Konstitutionalisierung', see James Bohman, 'Volkerrechtsverfassung und Politik', in *Habermas-Handbuch*, eds. Hauke Brunkhorst, Regina Kreide and Cristina Lafont (Stuttgart, Germany: J.B. Metzler, 2009). On the constitutionalization of international law in the work of Habermas, see Jean L. Cohen, 'Völkerrechtsverfassung'; on Habermas's concept of European citizenship, see Christian Joerges, 'Europäische Staatsbürgerschaft', both articles published in *Habermas-Handbuch*, ibid.

9 Hauke Brunkhorst, 'Zwischen transnationaler Klassenherrschaft und egalitärer Konstitutionalisierung. Europas zweite Chance', in *Anarchie der kommunikativen Freiheit. Jürgen Habermas und die Theorie der internationalen Politik*, eds. Peter Niesen and Benjamin Herborth (Frankfurt, Germany: Suhrkamp, 2007); Hauke Brunkhorst, 'Cosmopolitanism and democratic freedom', in *Legality and Legitimacy: Normative and Sociological Approaches*, eds. Chris Thornhill and Samantha Ashenden (Baden-Baden, Germany: Nomos, 2010); Hauke Brunkhorst, 'The European dual state: The double structural transformation of the public sphere and the need for repoliticization', in this volume.

10 Michelle Everson, 'The fault of (European) law in (political and social) economic crisis', *Law and Critique* 24 (2013): 126; see also, Michelle Everson and Christian Joerges, 'Reconfiguring the politics-law relationship in the integration project through conflicts-law constitutionalism', *European Law Journal* 18 (2012).

278 *Pierre Guibentif*

approaches is the identification of transnational political dynamics, which need to be institutionalized in order to counterbalance transnational economic dynamics. One version emphasizes the integrative trends in these dynamics, the other the conflictual trends.

Evaluation of the three approaches

This set of three approaches does not pretend to offer a complete picture of the ongoing debates. What justifies this selection is that, apart from the coherence of each of them, the three approaches form a meaningful starting point. The order chosen aims at highlighting two dimensions, according to which they may be characterized, and which discussion of could help the formulation of the approach defended here.

On the one hand, the three approaches differ according to the place attributed to law and politics, and to the relationship established between these two domains. In the first approach, law and politics are two among many other social systems, all equally important for the composition of the social reality. In the second approach too, modern societies are viewed as the result of the functioning of many differentiated systems; however, among them, law and politics play a somehow coordinating role. In the third approach, the role of law and politics is given even more prominence. This relates to the two following assumptions: first, a close link is established between law and politics – politics here in the narrow sense, that is, the functioning of organs of sovereignty and political parties according to a distinction between government and opposition – with both spheres being central parts of a broader political sphere; second, this broader political sphere is supposed to institutionalize social forces, generated, at least to a significant extent, outside of it, which are able to condition, thanks to this institutionalization, other components of the social reality.

In the face of these differences, the present approach aims at combining the three models. It recognizes the reality of a broad scope of differentiated social systems, and all of them should be, as far as possible, included in the analysis. It also admits, however, that law and politics both play a special role, and that it is important to understand this specificity. In addition, it assumes that the dynamics of social reality cannot be accurately grasped taking only into account the functioning of social systems.

On the other hand, the three approaches differ in their normative content. The first develops a sophisticated version of systems theory, aiming at giving a cognitive account of the social reality. This cognitive interpretation of the reality, however, can easily be used for the justification of normative statements, such as: 'Let each system function in its differentiated ways'. The second approach accepts as a starting point the modern norm, which requires societies to be 'constituted', and puts forward new proposals for the foundation of that norm: 'Societies ought to have constitutions, because constitutions make the production of political power possible, which is necessary for most of their operations'. It also extends the scope of that norm: 'Societies ought to have constitutions, because the practice of constitutional provisions contributes, in the long run, to the formation a global order'. The third approach makes the strongest normative statement, in the sense

The experience of the European periphery 279

that this statement is maintained against a significant part of the facts discussed in its cognitive account of current social reality. Despite the poor results of international cooperation between national political systems and the weakness of transnational political movement, 'something similar to national constitutions has to be created at a global level, because this is the only way to warrant people's self-government in a globalized world'.

At this normative level, this chapter would like to follow the example of systems theory: to develop a picture of reality which could possibly suggest normative implications. It should be, as a sociological contribution to current debates, sufficiently precise to inspire practical initiatives, which means having normative implications.[11] But such implications should be worked out in other debates, linked to, but differentiated from, scientific discussion. Differently from Luhmann's disenchanted and ironic approach, it borrows from the third approach the notion of the need for normative discussion, inside and outside the academy, as an indispensable environment for sociological theory.

The force of the financial system and the experience of the loss of sovereignty

Recent European history has provided us with striking examples of the interplay between social systems, notably between economic and political systems, allowing us to appreciate the accuracy of the approaches introduced above. I shall focus here on the Portuguese case, where the crisis had severe social consequences and where, therefore, the debate on the causes and nature of the crisis is particularly intense.

One crucial moment is the signing, on 17 May 2011, of the Memorandum of Understanding between the Portuguese government and the European Commission, the European Central Bank and the International Monetary Fund (IMF) – the so-called Troika – by which Portugal, in exchange for financial assistance, committed itself to reduce its public deficit and to undertake a broad scope of structural reforms.[12]

---

11 If the cognitive conclusions likely to be derived from systems theory have this normative and practical potential, it is because systems theory, arguably, is originally motivated by a normative and practical concern: to contribute to the establishment of the social conditions of thought. Thought requires differentiation of consciousness and communication, and for the construction of meaning at these two levels, differentiation of signs. Therefore, thought requires a theory of differentiation, which is what systems theory aims at offering: differences are generated by operating systems. Luhmann did not explicitly develop such an argument. The work where ideas close to this reasoning are defended is Niklas Luhmann, *Grundrechte als Institution. Ein Beitrag zur politischen Soziologie* (Berlin: Duncker & Humblot, 1965), which can be interpreted as a defence of functional differentiation as a condition for open societies.

12 For a discussion of the set of official documents which form what is usually called the Memorandum of Understanding, as well as of the subsequent revisions of these documents, see Alexandre Abreu *et al., A Crise, A Troika e as Alternativas Urgentes* (Lisbon, Portugal: Tinta-da-China, 2013), p. 63 f. Available at http://ec.europa.eu/economy_finance/assistance_eu_ms/portugal/index_en.htm and http://www.portugal.gov.pt/pt/os-temas/memorandos/memorandos.aspx.

280 Pierre Guibentif

The last steps of the economic process that led to this exceptional measure may be summarized in the following terms. After the subprime crisis (summer 2007) and the bankruptcy of Lehman Brothers (September 2008), governments around the world took measures to restore the stability of the banking system and to stimulate economic activity in order to avoid a recession comparable to that of 1929–1932.[13] The expenses required for the implementation of these measures, however, increased the public debt of the countries concerned, in particular the European countries, which led to the sovereign debt crisis. The reactions of investors to this crisis affected, in the first place, countries with a particularly high public deficit and debt, Greece being the most acute case. In the aftermath of the bail-out undertaken to respond to this first case, in April/May 2010, the government bond yields of several highly indebted countries, among them Portugal, reached levels compromising their access to the financial markets and obliging them to request international financial assistance.[14]

Let us now briefly recall the political process which took place at European level and in Portugal during the same period. After the subprime crisis and the Lehman Brothers bankruptcy, a European Council in December 2008 decided on a set of measures aimed at restoring confidence in the banking system and stimulating economic growth. According to these European guidelines, the Portuguese government, at that time formed by the Socialist Party, issued in January 2009 an 'Initiative of investment and employment'. This countercyclical policy option was legitimated in October 2009, when the Socialist Party won the general election (see Table 12.1). In the election campaign, the Socialist Party defended that option against the criticisms of the right-wing Social Democrat Party.[15] In the course of the Greek crisis, however, the European strategy changed radically,[16] requiring member states, from February 2010 onwards, to give top priority to the consolidation of their budgets.[17] From that moment on, the new Socialist

---

13 Robert Boyer, 'The unsustainable divergence of national productive systems', in *Structural Change, Competitiveness and Industrial Policy. Painful Lessons from the European Periphery*, eds. Ricardo Paes Mamede, Ester G. Silva and Aurora A.C. Teixeira (London and New York: Routledge, 2014), p. 36.

14 Abreu *et al.*, *A Crise*, p. 45 f.; Fernando Teixeira dos Santos, 'Convergence and imbalances in the EMU: The case of Portugal,' in Mamede, Silva and Teixeira, ibid. pp. 49 ff.; Ana Costa and José Castro Caldas, 'A União Europeia e Portugal entre os resgates bancários e a austeridade: Um mapa das políticas e das medidas', in *A Economia Política do Retrocesso. Crise, Causas e objectivos*, ed. José Reis (Coimbra, Portugal: Almedina/Centro de Estudos Sociais, 2014), p. 87 f.

15 Paulo Pedroso, *Portugal and the Global Crisis. The Impact of Austerity on the Economy, the Social Model and the Performance of the State* (Lisbon: Fundação Friedrich Ebert, 2014), p. 3.

16 Even if the relevance of this fact should not be overestimated, it is worth remembering the following sequence here. Elections for the European Parliament were scheduled for June 2009; decisions on a European strategy aiming at stimulating the economy were taken a few months before these elections, in December 2008; the European turn to budgetary consolidation policy took place a few months after them, in early 2010.

17 Abreu *et al.*, *A Crise*, p. 55; Costa and Caldas, 'A União Europeia e Portugal', p. 124; Pedro Hespanha, Sílvia Ferreira and Vanda Pacheco, 'O Estado Social, crise e reformas', in Reis, *A Economia Política*, p. 199 f.; Pedroso, *Portugal and the Global Crisis*, p. 2 f.; Alain Supiot,

Portuguese government, this time a minority administration, had to interrupt the 'Initiative of investment and employment' and launch successive, and increasingly restrictive, 'Programmes for stability and growth', aiming at reducing the public debt.[18] The project for a fourth programme was presented in March 2011 to the Parliament and was rejected. As a consequence of this rejection, the Prime Minister resigned, and snap elections were scheduled for June 2011. The markets reacted negatively to that political crisis: 'government bond yields skyrocketed to an unsustainable level, (and) rating agencies downgraded the country's sovereign debt'.[19] This forced the caretaker government to open negotiations with the Troika, even before the election, which was announced on 6 April 2011. The negotiations took place with the participation of the leading opposition party at that time, the Social Democrat Party.[20] The Memorandum, signed on 17 May 2011, is said to be strongly inspired by the 'Fourth Programme for Stability and Growth',[21] rejected a few weeks earlier by Parliament, with the votes of the Social Democrat Party. After the elections of 5 June 2011 (see Table 12.1), the Social Democrat Party was able to form a coalition with the other major right-wing party, the Centre Democratic Social Party. This coalition government has been in office ever since (state of affairs on September 2015) and had to implement the Memorandum under the control of the Troika.[22]

The measures taken in accordance with the Memorandum were manifold. State agencies were partly suppressed – notably at local government level – and partly re-engineered, particularly in the domains of education, health and social security.[23] The territorial organization of the justice system was redesigned.[24] Labour law was thoroughly reformed: the dismissal of employees was made easier and less costly; working hours were made more flexible; and collective agreements lost their significance.[25] In the domain of social security, unemployment and social assistance benefits were reduced and conditions of eligibility tightened. Pensions and earnings of civil servants were reduced.[26] Taxes on individuals (VAT as well as income taxes) were increased, and taxes on firms lowered.[27] Public sector

---

'Towards a European policy on work', in *Resocializing Europe in a Time of Crisis*, eds. Nicola Countouris and Mark Freedland (Cambridge, UK: Cambridge University Press, 2013).

18 For a compared analysis of the four 'Programmes of Stability and Growth', see Costa and Caldas, 'A União Europeia e Portugal'.

19 Pedroso, *Portugal and the Global Crisis*, p. 3.

20 Costa and Caldas, 'A União Europeia e Portugal', p. 101; Pedroso, ibid.

21 Abreu *et al.*, *A Crise*, p. 82, Costa and Caldas, ibid. p. 88.

22 On the implementation of the *Memorandum*, as well as on changes negotiated during its period of validity, see Abreu *et al.*, ibid. p. 77 f.

23 Hespanha, Ferreira and Pacheco, 'O Estado Social', p. 210 f.

24 Susana Santos, 'Novas reformas, velhos debates. Análise das políticas de justiça e dos seus impactos no sistema judicial', *Configurações* 13 (2014).

25 Pedroso, *Portugal and the Global Crisis*, p. 13 f., p. 18; Jorge Leite *et al.*, 'Austeridade, reformas laborais e desvalorização do trabalho', in Reis, *A Economia Política*.

26 Hespanha, Ferreira and Pacheco, 'O Estado Social'; Pedroso, ibid. p. 23.

27 Costa and Caldas, 'A União Europeia e Portugal', p. 116.

282   *Pierre Guibentif*

Table 12.1 Results of recent parliamentary elections in Portugal (%)

	European Parliament June 2009	Portuguese Parliament October 2009	Portuguese Parliament June 2011	European Parliament May 2014
Participation	36.77	59.68	58.03	33.67
PSD-CDS – Social Democratic Party and Centre Democratic Social Party (centre-right)*	40.07	39.54	50.37	29.95
PS – Socialist Party	26.53	36.56	28.05	34.01
CDU-PEV – Communist Party and Ecologists	10.64	10.43	11.71	13.71
BE – *Bloco de Esquerda* (radical left)	10.72	9.81	5.17	4.93
Others	5.43	0.67	0.62	9.98
Blank	4.65	1.74	2.66	4.38
Void	1.96	1.25	1.42	3.04
Total	100.00	100.00	100.00	100.00

* Separate lists apart from the May 2014 elections

	June 2009	Oct. 2009	June 2011
PSD	31.71	29.11	38.66
CDS	8.36	10.43	11.71

Sources: Portugal. Comissão Nacional de Eleições.
Resultados Eleitorais. Assembleia da República. Acto realizado em: 27/09/2009. Resultados Nacionais Oficiais. http://eleicoes.cne.pt/raster/index.cfm?dia=27&mes=09&ano=2009&eleicao=ar
Resultados Eleitorais. Assembleia da República. Acto realizado em: 05/06/2011. Resultados Nacionais Oficiais. http://eleicoes.cne.pt/raster/index.cfm?dia=05&mes=06&ano=2011&eleicao=ar
Eleições para o Parlamento Europeu 2009. http://www.cne.pt/content/eleicoes-para-o-parlamento-europeu-2009
Eleições para o Parlamento Europeu 2014. http://www.cne.pt/content/eleicoes-para-o-parlamento-europeu-2014

companies were privatized.[28] The implementation of these measures was effectively monitored by representatives of the Troika, thus giving permanent visibility to the power of these external entities.[29]

---

28 Pedroso, *Portugal and the Global Crisis*, p. 33.
29 The economic and social impact of the austerity imposed by the Memorandum will not be discussed in this chapter. On this issue, see the report prepared under the auspices of the Directorate-General for Economic and Financial Affairs: John Berrigan, Stefan Kuhnert and Peter Weiss, dirs, *The Economic Adjustment Programme for Portugal 2011-2014. European Economy – Occasional Papers 202* (Brussels, Belgium: European Commission – Directorate-General for Economic and Financial Affairs, 2014), as well as the other official reports published during

The experience of the European periphery 283

All these measures, which hit the population of Portugal directly and painfully, were the result of decisions taken outside democratic will-formation procedures and even jeopardizing them. As can be seen, the procyclical programmes for stability and growth were designed, under European requirement, by a government originally elected on the basis of a countercyclical economic programme. The elections of June 2011 took place when the complete action programme of the government to be elected had already been decided – by the Memorandum, which had been published for the first time on 3 May 2011,[30] two weeks before its signature. During the first period of implementation, the only version of the document made available to the public by the Portuguese government was in English, which meant that the text was accessible only to a minority of the citizens. Its content could not be – and was not supposed to be – discussed by the citizenry.[31]

During this period, several massive demonstrations took place, some of them linked to general strikes: on 24 November 2010, 12 March 2011, 15 October 2011, 24 November 2011, 22 March 2012, 15 September 2012, 14 November 2012 and 2 March 2013.[32] These demonstrations, against the measures taken by the government and against the Troika, attracted many hundreds of thousands in Lisbon and in Portugal generally.[33] A remarkable feature of the demonstrations of March 2011, October 2011, September 2012 and March 2013 is that they were the result of the initiatives of small groups with no recognized position in the institutional political landscape of Portugal. Trades unions and political parties played a

---

the implementation of the programme (available on 'Post-programme surveillance of Portugal'). Available at http://ec.europa.eu/economy_finance/assistance_eu_ms/portugal/index_en.htm. For a – very critical – global assessment, see, among others, Abreu *et al.*, *A Crise*, p. 95 f.; Costa and Caldas, 'A União Europeia e Portugal', p. 113 f.; José Reis *et al.*, 'Compreender a crise: a economia portuguesa num quadro europeu desfavorável', in Reis, *A Economia Política*. See also, the materials issued by the *Observatório sobre Crises e Alternativas*. Available at http://www.ces.uc.pt/observatorios/crisalt/.

30 Costa and Caldas, ibid. p. 101.

31 On the translation problems in Portugal, see 'Desconhecimento de segundo texto do acordo da troika é "inacreditável", diz Ribeiro e Castro'. *Público*, 27 May 2011. Available at http://www.publico.pt/economia/noticia/desconhecimento-de-segundo-texto-do-acordo-da-troika-e-inacreditavel-diz-ribeiro-e-castro_1496335. It is worth noting here that the whole documentation on the EU financial assistance programmes on the official website of the EU is available only in English (for Portugal, see http://ec.europa.eu/economy_finance/assistance_eu_ms/portugal/index_en.htm). It would be a measure of sound governance to produce at least a translation in the official language of the country whose population is affected.

32 Mentions of these demonstrations in Leite *et al.*, 'Austeridade, reformas laborais'; more details on the chronology of the crisis on the website of the Observatory of the Crises and of the Alternatives: 'Cronologia das crises'. Available at http://www.ces.uc.pt/observatorios/crisalt/index.php?id=6522&id_lingua=1&pag=6555.

33 Two examples: 15 September 2012, between 300,000 and 500,000 people in Lisbon ('Os muitos números da manifestação de 15 de Setembro em Lisboa', *Público*, 28 September 2012. Available at http://www.publico.pt/politica/noticia/os-muitos-numeros-da-manifestacao-de-15-de-setembro-em-lisboa-1565022). On 2 March 2013, similar figures in Lisbon, around 1.5 millon in the whole country ('Mais de um milhão e meio de portugueses saíram à rua', *TSF*, 2 March 2013. Available at http://www.tsf.pt/PaginaInicial/Portugal/Interior.aspx?content_id=3084756&page=1).

284 Pierre Guibentif

secondary role. Nonetheless, these social movements, even if they stimulated public debate, had no impact on the course of the reforms. The European elections of 25 May 2014 revealed that, apart from a moderate increase in votes for the Communist Party (in alliance with the Portuguese ecological party), none of the established political parties benefitted from these movements, compared with previous elections for the Portuguese or European parliaments (see Table 12.1). No new political force comparable to Podemos in Spain or Syriza in Greece emerged.

As a reaction to the lack of political debate, a broad set of political groupings and personalities organized a *Congresso Democrático das Alternativas* (Democratic Congress of the Alternatives)[34] on 5 October 2012 to debate political options in the face of the country's economic situation. The initial success of this initiative showed the frustration of part of the population at the hollowing of institutional political procedures. Meanwhile, the *Congresso Democrático das Alternativas* has established itself as a relevant player in the Portuguese public sphere. Its political impact, however, remains to be demonstrated. People linked to this initiative did later set up, in partnership with a newly created left-wing political party, LIVRE, a 'citizen's candidature' (*candidatura cidadã*) for the general election in the autumn of 2015.[35] The results of this election revealed that this initiative failed to attract votes and to renew the scope of the Portuguese political parties: the new party obtained 0.72 per cent of the votes and did not elect any deputy to the Parliament. One could argue, however, that the dynamics created by the Congresso did partly benefit another, already established party, Bloco de Esquerda. This party defended a programme on many points identical to those of LIVRE, and became at that election the third political party in the country, growing from 5.17 per cent to 10.22 per cent (see Table 12.1), and from 8 to 19 deputies elected. It succeeded in maintaining this position in the later presidential elections of January 2016. (See in particular the newspaper *Público*, editions of 5 October 2015 and 25 January 2016).

So one could scarely argue that the measures required by the Memorandum were backed by a democratically formed political will. True, the right-wing parties, whose political programmes were the most compatible with the rationale of this document, won the parliamentary elections of 2011. But this victory happened after it had been signed. It could be interpreted as a ratification, but also as a discouraged acceptance of a fait accompli. In any event, the results of the 2014 elections, after the many previous popular demonstrations, confirmed the weak legitimacy of the government whose main task was the implementation of the Memorandum. In addition, as far as the process that led to the signing of this document is concerned, it was not a process of forming a political project; it was

---

34 'Congresso democrática das Alternativas – Resgatar Portugal para um futuro decente'. Available at http://www.congressoalternativas.org/p/o-congresso_9.html.

35 'Candidatura Cidadã – Tempo de Avançar'. Available at http://www.tempodeavancar.net/.

The experience of the European periphery 285

a sequence of reactions to economic pressures. These economic pressures took three specific forms:

1 First, there was the 'pressure of the financial markets', that is, the soaring of Portuguese government bond yields. The Portuguese case illustrates a mechanism resulting from the deregulation of global financial markets in the 1990: markets were put in the position of monitoring national governments.[36] In the Eurozone, this mechanism is likely to have a particularly strong impact given the fact that the central banks of the individual member states have lost most of their means of intervention, and that the European Central Bank was not supposed, until its most recent initiatives in this domain ('quantitative easing'[37]), to acquire government bonds on the markets, according to the principles defended by ordoliberal economists who played a crucial role in the setting up of the institution.[38]

2 Second, the less direct, but strong impacts of economic dynamics are the result of the creation of the euro. The implementation of a single currency in the Eurozone had, in particular, two direct effects. On the one hand, in countries which have recently experienced high levels of inflation (which was the case at the periphery of the continent), the cost of bank credit dropped to an impressively low level, strongly encouraging private and public indebtedness. In 2009–2010, the level of private and public Portuguese debt, mainly as a consequence of this mechanism, was one of the reasons the markets put Portuguese government bonds under pressure. On the other, firms already trained to operate transnationally – many of them based in the centre of Europe – could rapidly take advantage of the improved possibilities of creating subsidiaries in other countries in order to take advantage of low labour cost and of a strong demand for the goods or services they offered,[39] hindering the development of domestic productive capacity.[40] In the face of these two trends, states' means of action were restricted by European rules

---

36 Abreu *et al.*, *A Crise*, p. 181; Boyer, 'The unsustainable divergence', pp. 10, 40 f. Interestingly, the necessity for the Portuguese state to maintain its access to the financial markets is explicitly mentioned as corresponding to an 'aim of exceptional public interest' by the Portuguese Constitutional Court (Case 396/2011, quoted by António Casimiro Ferreira and José Manuel Pureza, 'Estado de Direito ou Estado de Exceção: a justiça constitucional face ao questionamento do Estado social', in Reis, *Economia Política*, p. 300).

37 For a Portuguese comment on these measures, see Alexandre Abreu, 'A bazuca não é o que parece', on the blog *Ladrões de Bicicleta*, 30 January 2015. Available at http://ladroesdebicicletas. blogspot.pt/2015/01/a-bazuca-nao-e-o-que-parece.html.

38 Brunkhorst, 'Beheading of the legislator'; Boyer, 'The unsustainable divergence', p. 30; Reis *et al.*, 'Compreender a crise', p. 28.

39 Abreu *et al.*, *A Crise*, p. 38.

40 Boyer, 'The unsustainable divergence', p. 34; Santos, 'Convergence and imbalances', p. 47; Miguel St. Aubyn, 'We'll still be here in the long run: Austerity and the peripheral growth hypothesis', in Mamede, Silva and Teixeira, *Structural Change*, p. 69 f.

286   *Pierre Guibentif*

previously enacted in the name of the liberty of consumers,[41] free competition and the principle of non-intervention by the state in the economic dynamics.[42] Thus, the possibilities for Portugal to adapt and strengthen an industrial policy likely to counterbalance these dynamics was very limited.[43]

3   Third, actors in the financial systems took decisions which directly impacted on the financial markets and, thereby, on the political system. One case is the decision of the Portuguese private banks to cease buying Portuguese government bonds at the moment when the Portuguese government was facing the effect of negative reactions by other investors on the markets.[44] Another example of a decision with direct impact was the downgrading of the Portuguese sovereign debt by rating agencies. One could also include in this category the wrong decisions taken by the management of banks with an important role in the country's economy, decisions that led to nationalization or other costly bail-out measures at the expense of the state's budget and affecting the country's credibility on the markets.[45]

This direct impact of economic forces on Portuguese politics was strongly felt in Portugal as a loss of sovereignty, the country being qualified as 'protectorate'.[46] The weak role of Parliament has been manifest,[47] as well as the increasing power of 'the non-elected'.[48] An experience of a partial recovering of the sovereignty of the Portuguese state during this period was provided by the decisions of the Portuguese Constitutional Court, which, in several cases, ruled against measures taken on the basis of the Memorandum, as violating the Portuguese Constitution.[49] However, these decisions gave rise to critical comments on

---

41 A mechanism critically assessed by Everson and Joerges, 'Reconfiguring the politics', p. 658.

42 St. Aubyn, 'We'll still be here', p. 79.

43 Manuel Mira Godinho, Ricardo Paes Mamede and Vítor Corado Simões, 'Assessment and challenges of industrial policies in Portugal: Is there a way out of the "stuck in the middle" trap?', in Mamede, Silva and Teixeira, *Structural Change*, p. 271.

44 Abreu *et al.*, *A Crise*, p. 60.

45 In the course of the bank crisis, the Portuguese government had to bail out two banks at the end of 2008: see Costa and Caldas, 'A União Europeia e Portugal', p. 92. More recently, during the summer 2014, it had to cope with the collapse of the Banco Espírito Santo: see Berrigan, Kuhnert and Weiss, *The Economic Adjustment Programme*, p. 50 f. On the role of the banks, see also, Kumm, 'The cosmopolitan turn', p. 627.

46 Among many other references, Daniel Oliveira, 'A democracia ou o euro', in *Que fazer com este euro? Portugal na tragédia europeia* (Lisbon, Portugal: Edições 70/*Le Monde diplomatique – Edição portuguesa*, 2013), p. 97 f.

47 Leite *et al.*, 'Austeridade, reformas laborais', p. 125.

48 António Casimiro Ferreira, 'A sociedade de austeridade: Poder, medo e direito do trabalho de exceção', *Revista Crítica de Ciências Sociais* 95 (2011); António Casimiro Ferreira, *Sociedade da Austeridade e Direito do Trabalho de Exceção* (Porto, Portugal: Vida Económica, 2012).

49 For detailed references and a discussion of the relevant cases, see Gonçalo de Almeida Ribeiro and Luís Pereira Coutinho, eds. *O Tribunal Constitucional e a Crise. Ensaios Críticos* (Coimbra, Portugal: Almedina, 2014); Jorge Reis Novais, *Em Defesa do Tribunal Constitucional. Resposta aos Críticos* (Coimbra, Portugal: Almedina, 2014); Ferreira and Pureza, 'Estado de Direito'.

The experience of the European periphery   287

the part of European Commission officials, challenging the legitimacy of the Court.[50] Some months after these decisions, a group of Portuguese lecturers in jurisprudence issued a book defending a 'constitutionalism limited to the principles',[51] and warning against 'constitutional dirigism'.[52] The main argument is that decisions taken by specialists in the financial markets should not be questioned by jurists with no appropriate training and support.[53] Interestingly, one paper included in this book[54] quotes extensively from *The Financial Crisis in a Constitutional Perspective*, in particular Teubner's contribution to that volume,[55] to support this argument. Another book, published some months later, defends the Court.[56] It quotes Habermas in several places, in particular, his book on the European Constitution.[57]

Factually, when confronted with the theoretical approaches introduced above, what happened in Portugal during these years fits rather well with the analysis proposed by the systemist approach, which is confirmed by the mentioned quotations of Teubner's work in this context: the dynamics of the financial markets did collide with the functioning of the Portuguese political and legal systems. It can also be considered as a situation corresponding to what the critical approach takes as its cognitive starting point. It calls for the kind of political action which could be defended on the basis of that approach: one way to re-equilibrate the financial and the political dynamics would be to develop European political institutions which could give democratic legitimacy to the decisions of European bodies and within which Portuguese citizens could maintain equal political rights with the citizens of other European countries, whatever the measures to be taken at a national level. Habermas, whose ideas, as we have seen, played an important

---

50 See, for example, José Manuel Durão Barroso's declaration emphasizing the possible consequences of these decisions on the trust of the financial markets, quoted by Novais, ibid. p. 5. Critical statements questioning the impartiality of the Portuguese Constitutional Court are to be found in a document issued on 15 October 2013 by the EC Representation in Portugal, 'Will the Constitutional Court put at risk the MOU Implementation?'. Available at http://www.publico.pt/ficheiros/detalhe/relatorio-da-comissao-europeia-na-integra-20131018-151213. On the heated debate in Portugal on this document, see 'Relatório da Comissão Europeia diz que decisões do TC influenciam sucesso do programa da troika', *Público*, 18 October 2013. http://www.publico.pt/politica/noticia/bruxelas-diz-que-nao-e-hora-para-activismos-politicos-do-tc-1609564. For an appreciation of the Court's role, in the view of the officials of the European Comission, see also, Berrigan *et al.*, *The Economic Adjustment Programme*, p. 22.

51 Gonçalo de Almeida Ribeiro, 'O Constitucionalismo dos Princípios', in Ribeiro and Coutinho, *O Tribunal Constitucional*.

52 Rui Medeiros, 'A Jurisprudência portuguesa sobre a crise. Entre a ilusão de um problema conjuntural e a tentação de um novo dirigismo constitucional', in Ribeiro and Coutinho, ibid.

53 Ribeiro, 'O Constitucionalismo dos Princípios', p. 93 f.

54 Medeiros, 'A Jurisprudência portuguesa'.

55 Gunther Teubner, 'A constitutional moment? The logics of "hitting the bottom"', in Kjaer, Teubner and Febbrajo, eds. *The Financial Crisis*, pp. 3–42.

56 Novais, *Em Defesa*.

57 Habermas, *The Crisis*.

288   *Pierre Guibentif*

role in the recent public debate in Portugal,[58] came to Lisbon in October 2013 to defend them.[59]

On the other hand, it is more difficult to relate what happened in Portugal during this period to the law and politics centred approach, at least in the version presented in the papers analysed here. What has been experienced here has little to do with a transnational effort to defend individual rights. The only individual rights directly taken into consideration by the measures implementing the Memorandum were those of the holders of Portuguese government bonds.[60] Conversely, in Portugal, the measures taken under the pressure of an international entity did impact upon the legally grounded expectations of many people: civil servants, pensioners and the beneficiaries of social assistance provisions. This forces us to give prominence, while reflecting on recent development in transnational law, not only to the measures taken in favour of individual rights but also to those taken in favour of markets, sometimes with severe impacts on the individual rights of members of entire populations. Such measures are far from exceptional. In Europe, they currently concern four countries; similar measures were taken in recent decades in Africa and Latin America, under the auspices of the IMF and the World Bank. In fact, the continuity between the successive interventions of these entities is emphasized in many analyses of the current Portuguese crisis.[61] So, it seems at least debatable to hold that the development of international constraints on national sovereignty is mainly the result of constitutional dynamics in defence of the individuals' rights. Individual rights are far from being the only motive of international pressures on national sovereignty.[62]

---

58   It is fair to note that literature on the crisis in Portugal contains many highly critical references to a federal Europe, which are implicitly directed against the position of Habermas. The tension between two approaches inspired by twentieth-century critical social theory is most clearly revealed by the fierce critiques by Perry Anderson of Habermas in *Le Monde diplomatique*, also published in the Portuguese edition: Perry Anderson, 'A Europa face à hegemonia alemã', *Le Monde diplomatique – Edição portuguesa*, December 2012.

59   In a public speech delivered at the Fundação Calouste Gulbenkian, Lisbon, 29 October 2013, on 'Democracy in Europe today'.

60   António Manuel Hespanha, 'A revolução neoliberal e a subversão do "modelo jurídico"', *Revista do Ministério Público*, No. 130 (2012).

61   Abreu *et al.*, *A Crise*, p. 72; Boyer, 'The unsustainable divergence', p. 13; Costa and Caldas, 'A União Europeia e Portugal', p. 110.

62   Kumm discusses the recent transition to a period in which the legitimacy of international law has become an issue (Kumm, *Legitimacy of International Law*, p. 910 f.). Without questioning his argument as a whole, one should remember that the rise of this legitimacy issue, with the transition from the GATT to the WTO, and in Europe with the White Paper on 'Completing the internal market' (June 1985), was also when international law became, to an important extent, a tool for the implementation and extension of markets. From that moment on, international legal instruments had, among their other functions, to frame answers to financial crises – the causes of which also need to be discussed, a discussion outside the scope of this chapter. In several countries, measures were taken by international agencies which severely constrained their political systems. No wonder that the legitimacy of international law – a tool increasingly used for such purposes – had become an issue.

The experience of the European periphery 289

One could argue, on this point, that the financial measures alluded to here are taken in the long-term interest of the populations. Even if such a long-term general benefit could be demonstrated,[63] it remains to be seen whether the initial sacrifices are fairly distributed, in time and across categories of people.

On top of the economic and financial dynamics, the force of organizations

So, the Portuguese case seems to confirm what the critical approach denounces and what the systemist approach has carefully analysed,[64] namely, the impact on the Portuguese political and legal systems of transnational financial and economic dynamics: unbalanced trends of industrial development and of credit transfers within the Eurozone, and later the bank crisis, followed by the sovereign debt crisis. Therefore, Portugal can be used as an empirical terrain for the detailed observation of the processes theoretically reconstructed by systems theory, in particular, in Teubner's version.

Let us remember the main thesis in Teubner's recent work on constitutionalization, applied to the analysis of the financial crisis: the 'hitting the bottom' thesis. Systems would 'exhibit an intrinsic compulsion to growth', which could lead to the: (1) collision of the growth imperative of one system with the integrity of other social sub-systems; (2) collision with a comprehensive rationality of world society; and (3) collision of the growth acceleration of a system with its own self-reproduction.[65]

The 2007–2008 bank crisis could be qualified as a process of pathological growth – uncontrolled growth of credit allocated and the uncontrolled dissemination of toxic assets by financial products precisely aimed at a better circulation of this credit – which led to the sudden worldwide shrinking of the banks' funds in the aftermath of the American subprime crisis. This process can be qualified as an example of Teubner's process (3): the growth of a system colliding at a certain moment with the self-reproduction of the system itself (banks cease to be in a

---

63 For an assessment of the long-term impact of austerity in Portugal, see Abreu *et al.*, *A Crise*, p. 143f.; Costa and Caldas, 'A União Europeia e Portugal', p. 118f.; Pedroso, *Portugal and the Global Crisis*. It makes sense to relate this Portuguese debate to other contributions to the international debate on the impact of structural adjustment programmes, in particular in the field of health: among others, see Alexander E. Kentikelenis, Thomas H. Stubbs and Lawrence P. King. 'Structural adjustment and public spending on health: Evidence from IMF programs in low-income countries', *Social Science and Medicine* 126 (2015).

64 Even if they draw radically different normative conclusions ('Let the systems function in their differentiated ways' – 'Let's promote a world-polity'), these two approaches share a significant part of their cognitive foundations. These affinities can be related to the Habermas-Luhmann debate of the 1970s, which probably had a strong impact on the 'systems' component of Habermas's theory of communicative action. In Habermas's recent papers, the analysis of the globalization processes uses many concepts borrowed from systems theory (one example among many others: Habermas, 'Eine politische Verfassung', p. 341f.).

65 Teubner, 'A constitutional moment?', pp. 4–7.

290   *Pierre Guibentif*

condition to allocate credit). The later sovereign debt crisis – 'A Constitutional Moment?',[66] presented at a meeting held in Frankfurt in March 2010, was presumably written at its very beginning – could offer an example of process (1): governments, obliged to support the banks threatened by the crisis, in order to limit the consequences on the remaining economic activity, had to indebt themselves. When the public debt reached unsustainable levels, as was the case in Portugal, international support had to be requested, which was granted provided national sovereignty was temporarily limited. Thereby, the pressure of the economic system did impact on the political system.

The two processes described did indeed take place in Portugal. There were bank bankruptcies, which obliged the state to inject a considerable amount of money in the national banking system.[67] Because of these unexpected expenses, in addition to the indebtedness boosted by the introduction of the euro, public debt became unsustainable and international help had to be negotiated, with the consequences described above. However, the processes to be observed during this recent period of crisis and austerity cannot easily be reduced to – in systems theory terminology – the effects of a compulsive growth of communications in the financial system. Such a qualification could aptly fit the reduction of wages and pensions, as well as the reallocations in the state's budget, aimed at making funds available to pay the yields on government bonds, as a direct answer to the pressures of the financial markets. On the other hand, what about measures such as the reform of the justice system,[68] tighter monitoring of civil servants or the reform of labour law, allowing the dismissal of employees on the grounds of unfavourable work evaluation results and so on?[69] Obviously, such measures may have an indirect financial impact insofar as they may improve productivity, and this was definitely one motive for their promotion in the present period. Their content, however, cannot be derived solely from the impositions of the economic and financial systems. Moreover, if we analyse Portuguese recent history more carefully, we will see that they were already planned and partly implemented before the crisis. The need to solve the financial crisis gave new momentum to social processes which may have had causes outside the financial domain.

How could these other social processes be qualified, in the light of the 'hitting the bottom' thesis, if they are not the direct and only consequence of financial communication? Indeed, they could well be characterized as the compulsory growth of certain communication chains, but not, or not just, the growth of financial communication. Rather, I would argue, they are the growth of organizational communication.

---

66 Ibid.

67 The estimated cost of the bail-out of the *Banco Português de Negócios* is said to be around 3.4 billion euros (Costa and Caldas, 'A União Europeia e Portugal', p. 92).

68 See Santos, 'Novas reformas'.

69 Among other sources: 'A nova proposta do governo não convence', *Público*, 30 January 2014. Available at http://www.publico.pt/economia/noticia/nova-proposta-do-governo-nao-convence-e-gera-duvidas-de-aplicacao-1621640.

The experience of the European periphery 291

Let us remember this crucial component of Luhmann's theory of social systems in modern society. There are mainly two types of social system, apart from the two extreme cases of society as such and of temporary interactions: functionally differentiated social systems on the one hand and organizations on the other. Luhmann emphasizes this difference dedicating different works to the two types of system,[70] and in the books devoted to functional systems, there are chapters addressing specifically the organizations involved in and sustaining the functional system.[71] His account of recent social evolution can be reinterpreted as a symmetrical explanation of the development of both realities: functional systems and organizations. Organizations with pre-modern characteristics did sustain the process of functional differentiation, that is, of the emergence of differentiated functional systems. The other way round, functionally differentiated systems – namely, the economic, legal, scientific and political systems – favoured the shaping of our late modern disembedded and abstract notion of organization. As a result of this evolution, most functional operations – economic, legal, scientific and so on – generate on the one hand, economy, law, science or any other functionally differentiated social activity and, on the other, one or more of the organizations which supply the material conditions for these operations (companies, law firms, courts, research centres and so on).

If we admit this distinction between organizations and functional social systems, it is worth, at least as a *Gedankenexperiment*, to attempt a generalization of Teubner's 'hitting the bottom' argument. Compulsion to grow can affect functional systems – which is the issue explicitly discussed by Teubner. It could also affect organizations and, beyond single organizations, the universe formed nowadays by large formalized organizations, connected to each other by complex,

---

70 For the functional systems, see mainly Niklas Luhmann, *Die Wirtschaft der Gesellschaft* (Frankfurt, Germany: Suhrkamp, 1988); Niklas Luhmann, *Die Wissenschaft der Gesellschaft* (Frankfurt, Germany: Suhrkamp, 1990); Niklas Luhmann, *Law as a Social System* (Oxford, UK: Oxford University Press, 2004); Niklas Luhmann, *Art as a Social System* (Stanford, CA: Stanford University Press, 2000); Niklas Luhmann, *Die Politik der Gesellschaft* (Frankfurt, Germany: Suhrkamp, 2000). Niklas Luhmann, *Die Religion der Gesellschaft* (Frankfurt, Germany: Suhrkamp, 2000); Niklas Luhmann, *Das Erziehungssystem der Gesellschaft* (Frankfurt, Germany: Suhrkamp, 2002). For the organizations, see mainly Niklas Luhmann, *Funktionen und Folgen formaler Organization* (Berlin: Duncker & Humblot (1994, 5th edition, with a new epilogue) and Niklas Luhmann, *Organization und Entscheidung* (Opladen, Germany: Westdeutscher Verlag, 2000).

71 The complementarity between functional systems and organizations is clearly stated in Luhmann, *Die Wirtschaft*, p. 308, in a chapter on 'Medium and organization'. The discussion of this relation is less clearly differentiated in Luhmann, *Die Wissenschaft*; Luhmann, *Law*; and Luhmann, *Art*. Interestingly, it becomes an almost standardized motive in the three volumes dedicated to functional systems which were more recently published, and presumably written in a later time: see the following chapters: Luhmann, 'Political organizations', in *Die Politik*; Luhmann, 'Religious organizations', in *Die Religion*, p. 226; Luhmann, 'Re-specifications: Organization and professionalization', in *Das Erziehungssystem*, p. 142. See also, Niklas Luhmann, *Die Gesellschaft der Gesellschaft* (Frankfurt, Germany: Suhrkamp, 1997), p. 840 f. For additional references, see Pierre Guibentif, *Foucault, Luhmann, Habermas, Bourdieu. Une génération repense le droit* (Paris: Lextenso-Librairie générale de droit et de jurisprudence, 2010), p. 112 f.

292   *Pierre Guibentif*

plural and multi-layer processes of listing, cooperating, networking, standardizing, certificating, ranking and so on. On this second aspect, Teubner's work is less useful, since it gives little room to the discussion of the articulation between organizations and functional systems. Poul F. Kjaer touches a sensitive point when stating that 'left-luhmannians systematically tend to disregard the organizational aspect'.[72]

The issue of the compulsory and pathological development of organization gave rise to intense discussions decades ago, under the heading 'bureaucratization'. The fight against bureaucratization, in the narrow sense of a pathological development of state agencies, has stimulated the comparatively young science of organizations.[73] This scientific development, in turn, has inspired, among other dynamics, the promotion of the so-called new public management. This trend contributed to the disembeddedness of the organization in different domains where existing agencies were, at their origins, strongly shaped by their specific mission (health, education, science, justice), bringing about a sharper differentiation of organizations, on the one hand, and functional systems, on the other. See, in the legal domain, the trend that has been called the 'managerialization of the law'.[74] This could have favoured the addiction of organizations to organizational communication. In this sense, Kjaer refers to 'structures, which increasingly acquire a life of their own', mentioning as examples 'evaluation schemes and auditing systems'.[75] A concrete example of such structures, at the European level, is the Open Method of Coordination, with the sophisticated interplay it requires between national and European governmental agencies, research entities, stake-holders and project management, favouring a 'technocratic' approach, which gives 'few signs that the strategy has been successful in stimulating popular participation in the project'.[76]

More concretely, cases of the growth of organizational communication are: the differentiation and strengthening of management functions, for instance, in health centres, courts or universities; the superposition of legal and organizational norms (such as, for example, ISO-norms); the expansion of evaluation and monitoring mechanisms; the feeding of management with data on all aspects of the organization's functioning; and the setting up of new forms of inter-organizational networks. These are evolutions that are seen in Portugal, and which are intensified

---

72 Kjaer, 'Law and order', p. 405.

73 For a short overview of these debates, see Erhard Friedberg, 'Organization', in *Le dictionnaire des sciences humaines*, eds. Sylvie Mesure and Patrick Savidan (Paris: Presses universitaires de France, 2006), p. 836.

74 Lauren B. Edelman, Sally Riggs Fuller and Iona Mara-Drita, 'Diversity rhetoric and the managerialization of the law', *American Journal of Sociology* 106 (2001); see also, as an example of empirical research on the managerialization of the penal justice system in France, Benoit Bastard and Christian Mouhanna, *Une justice dans l'urgence. Le traitement en temps réel des affaires pénales* (Paris: Presses universitaires de France, 2007).

75 Kjaer, 'Law and order', pp. 421, 423.

76 Bengt-Åke Lundvall and Edward Lorenz, 'The euro crisis and the failure of the Lisbon strategy', in Mamede, Silva and Teixeira, *Structural Change*, p. 98.

The experience of the European periphery   293

by the factual 'state of exception' that resulted from the financial crisis. They are particularly visible in the university and in the domain of academic research,[77] but do also concern domains such as social assistance.[78]

Certainly, there is a link between this organizational development, and economic and financial dynamics. Private firms or governmental agencies, which have to dismiss part of their staff to reduce costs, have necessarily to redefine the division of labour in the organization. If internationally operating firms are encouraged by the single currency to relocate part of their activities and create subsidiaries in a country like Portugal,[79] monitoring mechanisms have to be set up. The point is that the process of the development of such mechanisms has its own organizational logic, which deserves to be properly grasped by specific conceptual tools if we want to give an accurate account of what happens in contemporary society.

Revisiting the organized/spontaneous divide

If there is such a process as a compulsive operating of organizations, the question is to appreciate more precisely its nature and impact. Luhmann's way of relating organizations and functional systems obliges us here to make a distinction. If we admit that organizations are both involved in certain functional systems and form part of networks of organizations, there are at least two possible kinds of impact by organizations on their environment. The examples of impact mentioned up to now belong to a first category: the impact – call it external – of the universe of organizations (perhaps we could identify 'organization' as one among the functional systems of late modernity)[80] on the other functional social systems. The sophistication of organizational measures taken in domains, such as health,

---

77 On the recent reform of the universities in Portugal, see Maria Eduarda Gonçalves, 'Changing legal regimes and the fate of autonomy in Portuguese universities', in *Higher Education in Portugal 1974-2009 – A Nation, A Generation*, eds. Guy Neave and Alberto Amaral (Dordrecht, The Netherlands; Heidelberg, Germany; London, New York: Springer, 2012). For a critical appraisal of a recent evaluation exercise addressing Portuguese research centres, see 'The flawed evaluation of Portuguese research units conducted by the ESF and FCT', *De Rerum Natura*, 2014. Available at http://dererummundi.blogspot.pt/2014/08/facts-about-fctesf-science-evaluation_29.html.

78 Hespanha, Ferreira and Pacheco, 'O Estado Social', p. 210f.

79 Abreu *et al.*, *A Crise*, p. 38; Boyer, 'The unsustainable divergence', p. 36; Lundvall and Lorenz, 'Failure of the Lisbon strategy', pp. 85, 97.

80 Teubner suggests the existence of such a system when referring to the 'anonymous Matrix' (Teubner, *Constitutional Fragments*, p. 142f. [p. 215f.]). To admit the existence of such a system raises a tricky question, not clearly answered in Luhmann's work: the relationship between politics and organization. In many aspects, these two realities have the same characteristics. In both cases, what is at stake are binding decisions. And politics, to a significant extent, more than other functional systems, is made out of organizations. It is, in a certain sense, an organization of organizations. Three characteristics, at least, distinguish politics from the remaining part of the organizational universe: the relevance of the government/opposition code; the place, among the organizations forming the political system, of organizations specialized in the legitimate use of violence; and a special form of inclusion of individuals. We shall come back to these characteristics later in the chapter.

294 *Pierre Guibentif*

science or law, is detrimental to the appropriate treatment of the patients,[81] or to a responsive and creative scientific business, or to the production of fair decisions on cases submitted to the justice system.[82] In these cases, the problems are due to: (i) the differences between organizational communication and the particular functional communication at stake; (ii) the fact that organizations that are supposed to operate mainly as sustaining a certain functional activity are conditioned by their links to other organizations, are less involved or not involved at all in that activity.

Since organizations do participate in the operations of functional systems, a second type of impact has to be considered: the – one could say internal – impact of organizations, within a certain system, on its other components. Here, we encounter an issue directly addressed by Teubner at one precise moment in the development of his theory of constitutions. In one of the first papers where the topic of constitution is centrally addressed, 'Global private regimes',[83] he introduces the idea of a difference between organized and spontaneous domains of social systems.[84] The operations of social systems would require a combination of organization and spontaneity. An important step in the development of functional social systems, historically, is said to be the moment when these two domains are both clearly separated, but somehow protected one against the other. Indeed, there is a risk that the organization may condition excessive spontaneity. This is the risk highlighted by Teubner: 'The precarious balance between the spontaneous and the organized sphere needs to be continually recalibrated, particularly countering the tendency of the organized sphere to dominate the spontaneous sphere'.[85]

One example of the impact of organizations on the remaining components of a social system is the distance between formalized political organizations – organs of sovereignty, political parties – and the public, identified empirically in researches on trust in the institutions. This distance could be interpreted as an effect of a trend towards political groupings focusing excessively on organizational communication. In Portugal, as in other countries, the issue of trust in the institutions has raised serious concerns for years.[86] In recent times, one more specific example of such a trend could be the current discussions, among noncommunist political movements to the left of the Socialist Party, on the need for

---

81 For empirical research on exactly this topic: Tiago Correia, *Medicina. O Agir numa Saúde em Mudança* (Lisbon: Mundos Sociais, 2012); Thomas Ginsbourger and Philippe Terral, 'Dynamiques "d'humanisation" puis de "managérialisation" d'un projet d'activité physique sur un site de lutte contre le cancer', *Sociologies* (2014).

82 See the critique of the 'managerial mindset' in international law by Martti Koskenniemi, 'Constitutionalism as mindset. Reflections on Kantian themes about international law and globalization', *Theoretical Inquiries in Law* 8 (2006).

83 Teubner, 'Global private regimes'.

84 This difference is also discussed in Teubner, *Constitutional Fragments*, pp. 22 [p. 44], p. 88f. [p. 139f.]), but a convincing introduction to this motive is still the one to be found in 'Global private regimes'.

85 Ibid. p. 90 [p. 141].

86 Jorge Vala, Alice Ramos and Pedro Silva, 'Confiança na Justiça', paper presented at the Centro de Estudos Judiciários, Lisbon, November 2012.

The experience of the European periphery   295

new parties in this political field, on the relationship between these parties and between organized groups within these parties. These debates are considered by some observers as contributing to the difficulties parties in this segment of the political spectrum experience in attracting voters.[87]

Admitting that the organized component of social reality has already given rise to extensive debate, as alluded to above, what is at stake for the approach of the current European crisis – and here, more specifically in the case of Portugal – is how to identify more exactly what corresponds to the concept of the spontaneous domain of a functional social system. Teubner refers concretely to the market in the economic system and to public opinion in the media system.[88] But, the question remains: what constitutes more precisely this spontaneous domain? If we take the public, it is composed of people receiving the messages produced by the media. The social part of this public is made up of communications, asking for messages in interactions with agents of media providers, or commenting on the contents in smaller or larger groups of people receiving the same messages. It is the aggregated demand of such people and the diffuse combination of comments, which may have an impact on the writing of future messages, which will attempt to anticipate the demands and interests perceived. What feeds these communications, however, are individuals who perceive the messages and link these perceptions to memories or projections composed by other perceptions. These readers' perceptions are actually a matter of communication within the media, where the interests and emotions of people in the audience are a topic of leading articles, readers' letters and answers to them, or codes of conduct. The communicational dynamics of the public are linked to myriad psychic processes. What makes up the spontaneity of the spontaneous domain is – to a significant extent – the role played in it by these psychic processes.

Such an impact by psychic processes requires, however, at least two conditions. First, specific mechanisms are necessary for the coupling of these psychic processes with communication, since communication and perception are the operations of systems of a different kind.[89] Among such mechanisms, we have highly personalized roles in particular. But the consequence of such a coupling could be the long-term conditioning of the minds involved, which could lead to a standardization of the relevant psychic processes, just the opposite of spontaneity. This is why a second condition has to be fulfilled: the existence of mechanisms, on the level of the social systems and structures, creating some distance between the psychic and the communicational processes, thus favouring psychic processes

---

87 André Freire, *Austeridade, Democracia e Autoritarismo* (Lisbon, Portugal: Vega, 2014), p. 74.

88 Teubner, 'Global private regimes', s. IV; Teubner, *Constitutional Fragments*, p. 23 [p. 44].

89 Among many other references, Luhmann, *Art*, ch. 1. For additional references, see Pierre Guibentif, 'Rights in Niklas Luhmann's systems theory', in *Law and Intersystemic Communication – Understanding 'Structural Coupling'*, eds. Alberto Febbrajo and Gorm Harste (London: Ashgate, 2013), p. 267, as well as Pierre Guibentif, 'Theorien und Menschen im Werk von Gunther Teubner/Theories and human beings in Gunther Teubner's work', *Zeitschrift für Rechtssoziologie* 35 (2015): 5.

296   *Pierre Guibentif*

likely to cause new irritations to communication. Regarding the media's public, this decoupling is the result of a separation between organizations: on the one hand, the broadcasting or newspaper company, on the other, single individuals in their private sphere, or involved in other organizations, which require them to consult news produced by the media. The stimuli experienced by psychic systems in these multiple and diverse social settings are likely to generate communicative reactions in the readers, which will surprise or challenge the communication circulating within the media-producing organizations.

Taking this example as a starting point, it is worth trying to give more substance to the concept of the spontaneous domain of functional systems, applying it to other systems. The most obvious candidate for such an exercise is science, since we can take advantage of our own researchers' experience here. One component to be considered is, again, the public, which plays a role in science comparable to the one it plays with the media. There are journals and other publications, produced by organizations that sustain scientific activity. The reactions of their public have some impact on the scientific publication business.

But there are at least two other phenomena to be taken into account: one is the opening, by organizations, and within them, of spaces of less formalized interaction. It is commonly assumed, among scientists, that the informal gatherings that take place at formal conferences are a fruitful source of new chains of scientific communication. This effect is due to the potential of the interaction order discussed years ago by Goffman,[90] which imposes specific norms to the people involved, 'in modern societies at least', not directly linked to the surrounding social structures, and which exposes people involved to immediate stimuli emanating from other persons. Even if the interaction can never be direct communication between minds, it is communication immediately conditioned by the simultaneous and, at many points, necessarily corresponding perceptions of the participants, which stimulate, at that very moment, the formation of their states of minds.

Another component of the spontaneous domain of science is formalized situations in which strong requirements for originality are addressed by organizations to personal contributions (sticking to the example of the scientific conference, the expectations directed at the papers to be presented).

A combination of the two mechanisms identified is meetings of boards composed of people chosen on the basis of their personal scientific qualities. Such meetings open a space where people will feel challenged: (a) to interact; and (b) to interact in their quality of scientific personalities.[91]

---

90 Erving Goffman, 'The interaction order', *American Sociological Review* 48 (1983): 11.

91 For elements of a sociological analysis of public commissions, see Pierre Bourdieu, *Sur l'État. Cours au Collège de France 1989-1992* (Paris: Raison d'Agir/Seuil, 2012), pp. 47f., 61f. This work is based on a different conceptual framework, but it corresponds on several points to the analysis outlined here: displayed independence of such bodies; relevance of the personal status of their members; non-direct coupling between the particular interests of the people involved and the arguments in the commission's debate. And it follows the same sociological aim: to understand the generation of social force.

The experience of the European periphery   297

What is experienced in Portugal in the scientific domain in these times of crisis, is indeed a reduction in the spaces of interaction (through the reduction of self-government structures, through the individualization of evaluation schemes), a dismantling of publics (by the marginalization of national scientific journals) and a disqualification of the substance of personal contributions (by almost exclusively quantitative schemes of evaluation). These trends are coupled with an impressive development of organizational devices for the funding and the evaluation of programmes, projects, teams and individuals; the rationalization of the links with the broader community; the certification of research entities and training programmes; and so on.

Similar processes are taking place elsewhere in Europe. However, the semi-peripheral characteristics of the country[92] could play a certain role and favour the preponderance of the organized over the spontaneous components of science. Definitely, the public for science is, in proportion, less numerous than in countries at Europe's centre, and habits of collegial interaction have had less time to build an appropriate culture, notably in the social sciences, whose development started after the 1974 Revolution. Under these conditions, processes that still have a moderate impact elsewhere in Europe already have more severe and visible consequences here.

Data in line with the hypothesis of increasing pressure by organizations on individuals have emerged from a quantitative analysis of the evolution of working conditions in Europe, based on a typology derived from a cluster analysis of forms of work organization.[93] This research identifies four systems of work organization according to their potentials in terms of workplace learning: discretionary learning, lean production, Taylorist organization and traditional organization. Of main interest here, and calling for further characterization, is the category 'lean production': it includes a majority of workers who state 'that their work pace is determined by quantitative production targets'. While they are challenged to learn and to solve problems, the problems appear to be more narrowly defined and the space for possible solutions less wide. The pace of work is more constrained, notably by constraints linked to the use of numerical production targets or performance targets.[94]

The countries with the highest proportion of workers subjected to 'lean production' conditions are Ireland and the United Kingdom (40.9 per cent and 45.1 per cent, against a European average of 28.2 per cent). Even if Portugal's score is significantly lower (22.4 per cent), the country shares with these two countries

---

92 Describing Portugal as a semi-peripheral country, Boaventura de Sousa Santos, 'Social crisis and the state', in *Portugal in the 80's. Dilemmas of Democratic Consolidation*, ed. Kenneth Maxwell (New York/Westport CT/London: Greenwood Press, 1986). For a discussion of this concept and its application to Portugal, see Pierre Guibentif, 'Law in the semi-periphery: Revisiting an ambitious theory in the light of recent Portuguese socio-legal research', *International Journal of Law in Context* 10 (2014).

93 Lundvall and Lorenz, 'Failure of the Lisbon strategy'.

94 Ibid. p. 84.

298 *Pierre Guibentif*

one characteristic: lean production is more frequent than discretionary learning (18.9 per cent).[95] The crucial question here is: how have these proportions evolved recently? The figures presented by Lundvall and Lorenz fit the hypothesis of the increasing pressure of the organized on the spontaneous component (in this case, of the economic system): in Europe, from 2000 to 2010, discretionary learning dropped from 35.1 per cent to 31.8 per cent, and lean production increased from 28.2 per cent to 31.3 per cent.[96]

To conclude this section: the spontaneous domain of a functional system would be the heterogeneous universe of small organizations and individuals (singles) playing a role in the operation of the systems in parallel to large organizations, and of spaces, embedded in large organization, for more or less informal interaction, and for creative individual performances, with the vocation of coupling the system with a plurality of non-standardized and hopefully intense psychic processes. These are the social devices likely to generate, according to a radical formulation inspired by Foucault, the 'tension between human subjectivity (irrationality) and the power of rationality'.[97]

This model of the relationship between the organized and spontaneous components of social systems has been here applied to recent evolutions in Portugal, which illustrate the possible impact of organization on spontaneity. The reverse effect – spontaneity impacting on organization – should also be envisaged.[98] The setting up of events such as, in May 2013, a conference entitled *Vencer a Crise com o Estado Social e com a Democracia* (Let's defeat the crisis with the welfare state and democracy)[99] was the result of strategies of involving people marginalized by the current functioning of the formal political system, of giving voice to their experiences and of gathering these very heterogeneous experiences with a view to the formation of new political projects. The Portuguese example, however, also allows us to identify what could be 'compulsive growth', or acceleration of psychic processes: emotionally motivated acts of violence. Only on one occasion, on 14 November 2012, has a

---

95 Ibid. p. 85.
96 Ibid. p. 92.
97 Everson, 'The fault of (European) law', p. 112.
98 There are obvious parallels between Teubner's opposition of organized and spontaneous components of functional systems, and the opposition in Jürgen Habermas, *Theory of Communicative Action* (Boston, MA: Beacon Press, 1987), of systems and lifeworld. Even if differences between these two theoretical proposals deserve a more expanded discussion, Habermas's opening statement to the 1983 edition of his work is worth recalling here: all aspects of the relationship between the two spheres have to be considered. Having identified signs of 'colonization of the lifeworld', the theory of modern society should not neglect the opposite processes: dynamics generated within the lifeworld, which may condition the systems (for more references on this reappraisal by Habermas himself, of his own theory, see Guibentif, *Foucault, Luhmann, Habermas, Bourdieu*, p. 183).
99 For materials on this meeting, see 'Vencer a crise com o Estado Social e com a Democracia' (2013). Available at http://www.congressoalternativas.org/2013/05/vencer-crise-com-o-estado-social-e-com.html.

The experience of the European periphery 299

demonstration led to acts of real physical violence.[100] So, in Portugal, in this period of crisis, violence has remained a marginal phenomenon. But these few cases of violence remind us that the strong impact of forces emanating from the spontaneous part of social reality can take such forms. Actually, the historical process, which led to attributing to the state a monopoly on the exercise of legitimate violence, could be considered as one mechanism guarding against the risk of this kind of impact.

The place of individuals in the sociology of constitutional processes

The conceptual scheme for the analysis of the societal processes triggered or accelerated by the current economic crisis, tentatively and summarily outlined in the three previous sections, has implications for the agenda of social sciences. For sociology to be in a position to analyse these processes, some changes are advisable.[101] Such changes are actually already on the way, as we shall see. What is important is to better connect the development of socio-legal research and, in particular, the sociology of constitutional processes, to these changes.

What has been identified here are processes and mechanisms by which social forces or dynamics relate to – are generated by their intertwinement with – psychic dynamics. The essential lessons of systems theory are by no means undermined by the recognition of such phenomena. However relevant psychic processes might be for social processes, what we observe obliges us to admit that there are no direct relations between these two realms of reality, only sophisticated and non-trivial mechanisms of coupling and accidental irritations. The mechanisms concerned are, in part, communicational structures building notions of perception within communication (notions as personality or privacy,[102] scientific disciplines as psychology and so on). Their analysis belongs to the sociological domain. Sociology should also pay attention to the social facts likely to be interpreted as revealing the impact of psychological processes on social processes. This is the aim, in particular, of the sociology of emotions.[103]

---

100 On this demonstration, see 'Carga policial foi "proporcional" ou houve abusos e ilegalidades ?' *Público*, 16 November 2012. Available at http://www.publico.pt/portugal/jornal/carga-policial-foi-proporcional-ou-houve-abusos-e-ilegalidades-25596943.

101 A challenge explicitly taken up by the 2016 Congress of the Association internationale des sociologues de langue française: '*Sociétés en mouvement, sociologie en changement*' ('Moving societies, changing sociology'). Available at http://www.aislf.org/spip.php?article2663.

102 On this notion, in a systemist approach, see Pierre Guibentif, 'Studying the emergence of the right to privacy. A suggestion for the future agenda of sociology of law', paper presented at the 'Global-Regional-Local, Institutions, Relations, Networks. Past and Future of the Sociology of Law' conference, Oñati, Spain: International Institute for the Sociology of Law, May 2014.

103 For a recent assessment of the development of this branch of sociology see 'Emotional labor around the world: An interview with Arlie Hochschild', *Global Dialogue. Newsletter for the International Sociological Association* (2014). Available at http://isa-global-dialogue.net/emotional-labor-around-the-world-an-interview-with-arlie-hochschild/.

300 *Pierre Guibentif*

But beyond the treatment of these more conventional sociological research objects, sociology should also develop, together with disciplines specialized in the analysis of psychic processes (psychology, cognitive sciences, neurosciences), knowledge of the real operation of the existing mechanisms of coupling. The state of the art in the disciplines likely to be involved suggests that, in the future, we probably will be in a position to produce knowledge of the cognitive impact of social structures and of the impact of cognitive structures – acquired, at least partly, as an effect of certain social structures – on (other) social structures. Whatever the pace of such scientific development, sociology has to provide itself with the conceptual schemes to enable it to participate constructively in these advances. It must develop the conceptual apparatus to address individuals in society.[104]

Systems theory is, I would argue, a strong candidate for inspiring such sociological evolution. Teubner, in particular, has given high relevance to individuals in his writings, rightly emphasizing the potential of Luhmann's work on the divide between psychic and social systems.[105] This part of Teubner's work, however, still needs to be expanded. As far as the law and politics centred approach is concerned, it offers promising possibilities of connection with such an agenda, given the attention it gives to the issue of individual rights. However, individuals holding these rights only appear as marginal references in the literature considered here. Again, it would seem advisable to develop concepts addressing the individual. The critical approach is inspired by works which have for years given prominence to the individual in their theoretical framework, after the seminal inputs of Horkheimer[106] and Marcuse.[107] One recent development of special relevance is proposed by Axel Honneth, who grounds the analysis of recent evolutions in politics on the concept of social freedom. This concept, which can be viewed as a specification of the concept of recognition, should enable critical theory to take the experience of individuals into account better.[108]

---

104 For examples of efforts in this direction, see Margaret S. Archer, *Structure, Agency and the Internal Conversation* (Cambridge, UK: Cambridge University Press, 2003) or, taking the opposite perspective of a sophisticated sociological analysis of devices addressing individuals, Alfons Bora and Peter Münte, eds. *Mikrostrukturen der Governance. Beiträge zur materialen Rekonstruktion von Erscheinungsformen neuer Staatlichkeit* (Baden-Baden, Germany: Nomos, 2012).

105 For an early and strong statement, see Gunther Teubner, *Law as an Autopoietic System* (London: Blackwell, 1993), ch. 3, s. VI. For additional references, see Pierre Guibentif, 'Theorien und Menschen'.

106 Max Horkheimer, 'Traditional and critical theory', in his *Critical Theory. Selected Essays* (New York: The Continuum Publishing Company, 2002).

107 Herbert Marcuse, 'Some social implications of modern technology', *Zeitschrift für Sozialforschung/Studies in Philosophy and Social Sciences* 9 (1941); Herbert Marcuse, *One-Dimensional Man* (London: Routledge & Kegan Paul, 1991).

108 Axel Honneth. *Freedom's Right. The Social Foundations of Democratic Life* (New York: Columbia University Press, 2014).

Possibilities of self-constitution

In Portugal, as elsewhere in the contemporary world, we can observe the impact of the strong dynamics of the economic and financial systems on all other social systems, in particular, the political system, severely conditioning – even threatening – the operations of these systems. Definitely linked to this dynamic is a strong trend towards rationalizing organizations of all types, by the imposition of a design essentially inspired by the practices of corporate business. Let us focus as a first step on the economic and financial dynamics. If we follow Teubner's hypotheses derived from systems theory, the economic and financial dynamics call for an internal answer, a constitutionalization from the inside. Internal constitutional processes may be triggered by irritations to the system as a result of reactions from part of its environment. One obvious lesson from the Portuguese experience, however, is that reactions do not easily affect the economic and financial system.

So the question is: under what conditions will societal reactions be strong enough to counterbalance the current dynamics of the economic and financial systems? This is one more point on which Teubner's approach deserves some elaboration. Teubner gives central relevance to the differentiation between functional systems; he also insists on the intriguing differences in their modes of operation;[109] finally, and departing significantly on this point from Luhmann's theory design, he admits that the functioning of social systems generates forces. This is most clearly formulated in the following definition of the 'constitutional moment', which is: 'the experience of a liberated social *energy*, yielding destructive, even self-destructive, consequences that can only be *overpowered* by their reflection and by the decision to self-limitation'.[110]

These three assumptions should lead to the following question: are there differences in the force of the different systems? In view of current evolution, it seems obvious that the forces generated by the operations of the financial system are much stronger than those generated by the operations of most other social systems.

Here, we have to come back to a realistic intuition shared by the law and politics centred as well as the critical approach. Even if the political system can no longer be qualified as an instance of central coordination of the social reality, it could play a special role in the framing of societal reactions towards the excesses of economic and financial dynamics, for three reasons. First, national political systems and international (political) organizations, taken together, command financial resources that can, at least partly, counterbalance the economic dynamics of the shareholder-value motivated strategies of other players in the economic system. In addition, they are in a position to support, in part, the economic circuits

---

109 Gunther Teubner, 'Exogene Selbstbindung', IV. 4.
110 Teubner, 'A constitutional moment', p. 11 (emphasis added). On this point, as we know, there are similarities between systems theory and Bourdieu's theory of social fields: see Pierre Bourdieu, 'The force of law: Toward a sociology of the juridical field', *Hastings Law Journal* 38 (1987).

302   Pierre Guibentif

necessary for the maintenance of social activities beyond the economy. This is emphasized in this volume by Brunkhorst (see Chapter 11), who remembers how ordo-liberalism, and later neo-liberalism, imposed a notion of the state that bets on the radical reduction of these resources.[111]

Second, as rightly emphasized by Thornhill, the main characteristic of modern states is their ability to reproduce power 'from highly singular processes of coercion',[112] as a result of a long historical evolution in which a crucial step is the 'suppression of private violence'.[113] In most states in the world, political systems command the legitimate use of violence. This means that political systems have a particularly high potential for social force, likely to threaten the whole social reality, as we learned during the twentieth century. But this potential is also the condition for the proper functioning of all other social systems.[114]

Third, the political system gives a prominent role to human individuals. It is, as already mentioned, in its essence a complex of organizations, and organizations require members. But there is a more important feature, which distinguishes politics from the remaining organizational universe. The organizations at the centre of the political system aim to act for, or against, or even to 'produce',[115] human individuals. This is why it makes sense to classify political systems as 'inclusive'.[116] It means that the political system, together with the legal system, contributes to re-establishing a place for individuals in a society in which the functional differentiation of activities – and no longer of persons – has deprived individuals of a clear notion of their social location.[117] Following another of Luhmann's arguments, explicitly developed in the case of the law, the political systems, in

---

111 Brunkhorst, 'Beheading of the legislator', p. 9 f.
112 Thornhill, *Sociology of Constitutions*, p. 375.
113 Ibid. p. 63.
114 The programme of systems theory could be summarized in the following terms: to concentrate on the incredibly diverse and complex consequences of the fact that physical violence could effectively have been banned from many spheres of normal human togetherness, across large regions of the world, over the last four centuries. However, as Reemstma has convincingly argued, human violence has not been suppressed; it can acquire new and more destructive forms precisely in this violence-negating context, and – this appeal should be taken up by future developments of systems theory – Luhmann's theory can contribute to the understanding of the strange coexistence between functional systemic normality and the possibility of extreme forms of violence. See Jan Philipp Reemtsma, *Trust and Violence: An Essay on a Modern Relationship* (Princeton, NJ: Princeton University Press, 2012), ch. 1, s. 9 [p. 87f.]: discussion of Luhmann on the modern notion of trust and its implications; ch. 3, s. 5 [p. 209 f.]: discussion of Luhmann on the position of individuals in modern society, at the margins of the functional systems.
115 An aim addressed by the concept of 'biopolitics', proposed in Michel Foucault, *Birth of Biopolitics. Lectures at the College de France, 1978–79* (London: Palgrave MacMillan, 2008).
116 See Thornhill, *Sociology of Constitutions*, p. 17 and throughout. For a particularly explicit definition of his notion of 'inclusivity' (p. 54), see pp. 74 f. See also, Thornhill, 'The Future of the state', p. 371.
117 Niklas Luhmann, 'Subjektive Rechte: Zum Umbau des Rechtsbewusstseins für die moderne Gesellschaft', in *Idem, Gesellschaftsstruktur und Semantik 2* (Frankfurt, Germany: Suhrkamp, 1981), p. 84.

The experience of the European periphery   303

articulation with the legal system, could play a central role in the coupling, on a large scale, of psychic systems and social systems.[118]

The Portuguese case, however, reveals at least three factors which limit the potential of the political system to generate reactions likely to favour the self-containment of the economic and financial systems. First, in Portugal as well as in most other European countries, political debate and practice are focused on the country itself and take European or global issues only marginally into account.[119] So it is unlikely, cognitively and practically, to favour reactions of direct relevance for global economic and financial communication. Second, the Portuguese state has already been profoundly conditioned by the requirements of the economic and financial system. This is due, to a significant extent, to institutional arrangements made at EU level. This has also to do with the impact of managerial dynamics throughout the Portuguese administration. Third, as the decline in political participation shows (see Table 12.1), and as abundantly debated by politically interested groups in Portugal, many people do not trust the political system and are no longer motivated to channel their demands to political instances.

This analysis of the Portuguese situation deserves two comments. The first is that the identification of the last two points corresponds exactly to one of the situations described by Gunther Teubner as requiring constitutionalization: the weakness of the spontaneous component of the national political system, compared with the strength of its organized part. In this case, the prominence of the organizational component is due to a significant extent to the intertwining between Portuguese state organizations, as they have recently evolved, and global economic and financial dynamics. If we accept Teubner's qualification, this means that the self-constitution of the economic system calls for the self-constitution of politics at the national level in the first place. In addition, self-constitution, in this specific context, means mainly strengthening the spontaneous component.

The second comment is that the first factor brings us back to the issue of a transnational polity, which, for the time being, exists only as a rather precarious reality. Taking the organized/spontaneous divide as a frame, what we may find, at a global level, is a heterogeneous set of states, international organizations and other politically relevant organized players, on the one hand; and an almost non-existent transnational public sphere on the other. At the European level, we find a much denser organizational arrangement with effective supranational entities,[120] but a still extremely frail and fragmented public sphere. Here, again, prospects of

---

118 Luhmann, *Law*, [p. 487] p. 416.
119 One example of this lack of interest: commercial publishers in Portugal avoid publishing books on European issues, knowing that there is no demand for such books. Another example: in the first version of a list of topics to be discussed for preparing the programme of a political organization, the seventh and last topic was 'International relations and Europe'. This seventh topic disappeared in a second version of the list, with some sub-topics being included under other headings.
120 For a survey of the debates on the European polity, see Přibáň, 'Self-referential European polity', p. 444f.

304   *Pierre Guibentif*

effective political dynamics likely to favour economic self-constitution depend on the self-constitution of politics, this time at a transnational level. At this level, however, what is at stake is not only the balancing of the organizational and the spontaneous components but, first of all, to give consistence to both components. As far as the organizational component is concerned, this raises complex questions about the nature and evolution of existing institutional arrangements, an issue that we shall not tackle here. As far as the spontaneous component is concerned, there is certainly much more to be done at the transnational than the national level,[121] but, admittedly, the essential issue is the same and has already been duly identified:[122] to give consistence to a public sphere.

This brings us back to this inescapable statement: the emergence of social forces – political forces – effective enough to successfully pressure the global economic and financial system in the sense of its self-constitution requires transnational public spheres, not as a sufficient, but as a necessary, condition. Here it is worth returning to the analysis of the spontaneous components of the social systems, since public spheres are the spontaneous component of political systems. Developing Teubner's conceptual scheme, we were led to reconstruct this spontaneous domain as a mix of interactions and informal organizations on the one hand, and psychic processes on the other. The emergence of social forces in these spontaneous domains depends crucially on the interplay between these two elements. In the absence of appropriate communicational arrangements, psychic processes will have no effect.[123]

The analysis of the current situation of political systems, shortly summarized here, suggests that structures which, in other times and at a national level, could give expression to personal emotions – spaces for debate, discourses and actors likely to effectively represent certain concrete individual experiences – are no longer fit for this role, or only to a limited degree. The question, therefore, is: what other social structures, apart from those supplied by the political systems, are likely to contribute to the formation of social forces based on psychic processes? This is, as Habermas would put it, an empirical question, and empirical research will certainly disclose very diverse phenomena, such as social movements of a new kind, communicational dynamics sustained by electronic communication devices, as well as violent expressions of social force, such as terrorism.

The history of modern politics and our own researchers' experience, however, compel us to pay special attention to one specific set of mechanisms, what

---

121 William Outhwaite, 'European democracy', paper presented at the 'Self-constitution of Europe: Symbols, politics and law' conference, Cardiff, June 2013.

122 Paul Blokker, 'A political–sociological analysis of constitutional pluralism in Europe', chapter 3 in this volume.

123 This statement could be related to the old lessons of conflict sociology: see the distinction in Lewis A. Coser, *The Functions of Social Conflict* (Glencoe/London: Free Press/Macmillan, 1956), p. 79, between hostile feelings (psychic processes) and conflicts (on the level of communication).

The experience of the European periphery 305

we could call the cultural systems:[124] mainly science, art and law. It is worth remembering that their early differentiation gave rise to a new type of personality (*l'honnête homme*), able to communicate with a broad network of people, sharing with them their specialist interest, competing with them in the practice of the distinguishing virtues identifying a certain system and, as a side effect of that competition, acquiring a distant view of the surrounding social reality.[125] This type of personality played an important role in the development of modern economy, as well as modern politics, precisely by causing the spontaneous components of these two systems to vibrate. Or, perhaps better put, as generating a spontaneous domain – an 'internal environment'[126] – which was institutionalized in a later evolutionary step, as a crucial moment in the constitution of economy and politics.[127] Science, art and law are types of communication, corresponding to strong professional identities, which might be viewed as playing an important compensatory role in all other social systems, strengthening individual positions.

As we saw, however, these cultural systems nowadays are also under pressure from the economic and financial systems, pressures partly mediated by public policies reshaping the organization of parts of these domains. This leads us to the following statement: among the factors for the self-constitution of politics, which are required for the self-constitution of the economic and financial systems, there is the self-constitution of art, law and science. In addition, we should ask ourselves: what should be done to give the self-constitution of our own domain – science – a chance? The model of social reality outlined above suggests six lines of action:

1   In the strengthening of the spontaneous component of our academic business, we should give more space to effective debate, and this debate should include the issue of the self-constitution of our domain. In more concrete terms, this could commit socio-legal scholarship to place, as part of a broader contribution by the social sciences,[128] its expertise in matters of regulation, rights, effectiveness of social rules and so on, at the service of a debate that should include all scientific disciplines.

---

124 To justify this terminology, one could refer to Jiří Přibáň, 'Symbolism of the *Spirit of the Laws*: A genealogical excursus to legal and political semiotics', *International Journal of the Semiotics of Law* 22 (2009), p. 191, and to the concept of culture defended there: 'permanent communication of the same with the other'. Within this broader framework, art, law and science would be discourses supplying means for differentiating and relating the same and the other, and symbolizing, by their own differentiation within the realm of culture, the functional differentiation of society. For reflections that could correspond to such an understanding of contemporary culture, see Přibáň, *Legal Symbolism*, pp. 133f., 195f.; Jiří Přibáň, 'European legality and its critique: On Bauman's concept of an adventurous Europe', in *Liquid Society and its Law*, ed. Jiří Přibáň (Aldershot, UK: Ashgate, 2007), p. 139.

125 See Bourdieu's theory of the formation of the scholastic reason: Pierre Bourdieu, *Pascalian Meditations* (Cambridge, UK: Polity Press, 2000).

126 Kjaer, 'Structural transformation'.

127 Teubner, 'Global private regimes', s. IV.

128 Jacques Commaille and Françoise Thibault, *Sciences with the Science* (Paris: Alliance Athena, 2015).

306 *Pierre Guibentif*

2 Obviously, we have to take the best possible advantage of the transnational features of our domain. Given the differences between the organization of science in different countries, effective cooperation between individual scholars is likely to be less directly conditioned by organizational and political requirements and, more centrally, by scientific criteria. Moreover, we have to take into account that our transnational debates do build, even if in modest measure, elements of a global public sphere.[129]

3 The relationship between the different cultural systems has to be intensified, in order to pool, as far as possible, the forces emerging from these domains. Sociology of law, one bridge among others between law and science, has here an obvious role to play (the present volume contributes to these three first types of actions).

4 Taking advantage, apart from other relevant materials and experiences, of our own reflection on our working methods, of the comparison between scientific organizations in different regions of the world, as well as the comparison with the other cultural functional systems, we must better identify the specificity of scientific organization and oppose it, in a constructive interplay, to managerial modes of scientific organization. These could be steps on the way to a better articulation between spontaneous and organized scientific business, and could contribute to widening the scope of the general debate on organizations and to the pluralism of the organizational experience in the late modernity.

5 Science has to rethink its relationship to politics and to the economy, and work for more autonomy in a post-national context. For the moment, it is difficult to imagine a scientific business without any public support, and any modern human cooperation will probably have to count on scientific resources, the production of which it will have to support. Science, therefore, will probably always have strong links to political organizations. For two centuries, it was almost completely owned by nation-states, which brought abundant resources, but also massive cognitive and normative constraints. Nowadays, we have to relocate ourselves in a social universe where more or less formalized political entities are forming themselves at very different levels, from local to global initiatives. Private players are also setting up research units. Much of our self-constitutive potential depends on the means we develop to allow effective cooperation between researchers working in these many different contexts. In our relationship with states and with private companies, we should value our scientific way of organizing our activity and preserving its creativity. This could contribute, ideally, to the reshaping of democracy and the welfare state on the one hand, and to the invention of effective practices

---

129 The International Institute for the Sociology of Law offers valuable illustrations of this potential for the internationalization of our scientific practices and legal reflections. For some additional reflections on this example, see Pierre Guibentif, 'The force of science and the force of organizations: Some exploratory thoughts applied to the example of the Oñati institute for the sociology of law', *Sortuz – Oñati Journal of Emergent Socio-Legal Studies* 6 (2014).

The experience of the European periphery 307

of corporate social responsibility on the other. This could both enrich our organizational skills and maintain spaces for spontaneous scientific acts.

6 Science has to develop its relationship to people untutored in science. On the one hand, in particular with the media and education, it has to provide cognitive tools likely to be used in the most diverse social contexts, to help people orient themselves in complex contemporary social reality and to give expression to their experiences. Social sciences have to operate as one more mediator, beyond the media, political representation, social movements and other means of expression, between the experiences of individuals and the socially relevant communication. In additon, they have to operate, as far as possible, where these experiences do not already find means of expression, making it difficult for social systems to be aware of their own excesses. This is what social sciences have done, in their specific way, since their beginnings. There are now plenty of new reasons for continuing these efforts.

Bibliography

Abreu, Alexandre, Hugo Mendes, João Rodrigues, José Guilherme Gusmão, Nuno Serra, Nuno Teles, Pedro Delgado Alves and Ricardo Paes Mamede. *A Crise, A Troika e as Alternativas Urgentes*. Lisbon, Portugal: Tinta-da-China, 2013.

Anderson, Perry. 'A Europa face à hegemonia alemã'. *Le Monde diplomatique – Edição portuguesa*, December 2012.

Archer, Margaret S. *Structure, Agency and the Internal Conversation*. Cambridge, UK: Cambridge University Press, 2003.

Bastard, Benoit and Christian Mouhanna. *Une justice dans l'urgence. Le traitement en temps réel des affaires pénales*. Paris: Presses universitaires de France, 2007.

Berrigan, John, Stefan Kuhnert and Peter Weiss, dirs. *The Economic Adjustment Programme for Portugal 2011–2014. European Economy – Occasional Papers 202*. Brussels, Belgium: European Commission – Directorate-General for Economic and Financial Affairs, 2014. Available at http://ec.europa.eu/economy_finance/assistance_eu_ms/portugal/index_en.htm.

Blokker, Paul. 'A political–sociological analysis of constitutional pluralism in Europe', chapter 3 in this volume.

Bohman, James. 'Volkerrechtsverfassung und Politik'. In *Habermas-Handbuch*, edited by Hauke Brunkhorst, Regina Kreide and Cristina Lafont. Stuttgart, Germany: J.B. Metzler, 2009, pp. 291–300.

Bora, Alfons and Peter Münte, eds. *Mikrostrukturen der Governance. Beiträge zur materialen Rekonstruktion von Erscheinungsformen neuer Staatlichkeit*. Baden-Baden, Germany: Nomos, 2012.

Bourdieu, Pierre. 'The force of law – Toward a sociology of the juridical field'. *Hastings Law Journal* 38 (1987): 814–853.

Bourdieu, Pierre. *Pascalian Meditations*. Cambridge, UK: Polity Press, 2000.

Bourdieu, Pierre. *Sur l'État. Cours au Collège de France 1989–1992*. Paris: Raison d'Agir/ Seuil, 2012.

Boyer, Robert. 'The unsustainable divergence of national productive systems'. In *Structural Change, Competitiveness and Industrial Policy. Painful Lessons from the European Periphery*, edited by Ricardo Paes Mamede, Ester G. Silva and Aurora A.C. Teixeira. London and New York: Routledge, 2014, pp. 10–42.

308 *Pierre Guibentif*

Brunkhorst, Hauke. 'Zwischen transnationaler Klassenherrschaft und egalitärer Konstitutionalisierung. Europas zweite Chance'. In *Anarchie der kommunikativen Freiheit. Jürgen Habermas und die Theorie der internationalen Politik*, edited by Peter Niesen and Benjamin Herborth. Frankfurt, Germany: Suhrkamp, 2007, pp. 321–349.

Brunkhorst, Hauke. 'Cosmopolitanism and democratic freedom'. In *Legality and Legitimacy: Normative and Sociological Approaches*, edited by Chris Thornhill and Samantha Ashenden. Baden-Baden, Germany: Nomos, 2012, pp. 171–195.

Brunkhorst, Hauke. 'The European dual state: The double structural transformation of the public sphere and the need for repoliticization', chapter 11 in this volume.

Brunkhorst, Hauke, Regina Kreide and Cristina Lafont, eds. *Habermas-Handbuch*. Stuttgart, Germany: J.B. Metzler, 2009.

Cohen, Jean L. 'Völkerrechtsverfassung'. In *Habermas-Handbuch*, edited by Hauke Brunkhorst, Regina Kreide and Cristina Lafont. Stuttgart, Germany: J.B. Metzler, 2009, pp. 87–94.

Commaille, Jacques, and Françoise Thibault. *Sciences with the Science*. Paris: Alliance Athena, 2014.

Correia, Tiago. *Medicina. O Agir numa Saúde em Mudança*. Lisbon, Portugal: Mundos Sociais, 2012.

Coser, Lewis A. *The Functions of Social Conflict*. Glencoe/London: Free Press/Macmillan, 1956.

Costa, Ana, and José Castro Caldas. 'A União Europeia e Portugal entre os resgates bancários e a austeridade: Um mapa das políticas e das medidas'. In *A Economia Política do Retrocesso. Crise, Causas e objectivos*, edited by José Reis. Coimbra, Portugal: Almedina/Centro de Estudos Sociais, 2014, pp. 87–126.

Edelman, Lauren B., Sally Riggs Fuller and Iona Mara-Drita. 'Diversity rhetoric and the managerialization of the law'. *American Journal of Sociology* 106 (2001): 1589–1641.

Everson, Michelle. 'The fault of (European) law in (political and social) economic crisis'. *Law and Critique* 24 (2013): 107–129.

Everson, Michelle and Christian Joerges. 'Reconfiguring the politics-law relationship in the integration project through conflicts-law constitutionalism'. *European Law Journal* 18 (2012): 644–666.

Ferreira, António Casimiro. 'A sociedade de austeridade: Poder, medo e direito do trabalho de exceção'. *Revista Crítica de Ciências Sociais* 95 (2011): 119–136.

Ferreira, António Casimiro. *Sociedade da Austeridade e Direito do Trabalho de Exceção*. Porto, Portugal: Vida Económica, 2012.

Ferreira, António Casimiro and José Manuel Pureza. 'Estado de Direito ou Estado de Exceção: A justiça constitucional face ao questionamento do Estado social'. In *A Economia Política do Retrocesso. Crise, Causas e objectivos*, edited by José Reis. Coimbra, Portugal: Almedina/Centro de Estudos Sociais, 2014, pp. 283–308.

Foucault, Michel. *Birth of biopolitics. Lectures at the College de France, 1978–79*. London: Palgrave MacMillan, 2008.

Freire, André. *Austeridade, Democracia e Autoritarismo*. Lisbon, Portugal: Vega, 2014.

Friedberg, Erhard. 'Organization'. In *Le dictionnaire des sciences humaines*, edited by Sylvie Mesure and Patrick Savidan. Paris: Presses universitaires de France, 2006, pp. 835–838.

Ginsbourger, Thomas and Philippe Terral. 'Dynamiques "d'humanisation" puis de "managérialisation" d'un projet d'activité physique sur un site de lutte contre le cancer'. *Sociologies* 2014. Available at http://sociologies.revues.org/4790.

The experience of the European periphery 309

Godinho, Manuel Mira, Ricardo Paes Mamede and Vítor Corado Simões. 'Assessment and challenges of industrial policies in Portugal: Is there a way out of the "stuck in the middle trap"?'. In *Structural Change, Competitiveness and Industrial Policy. Painful Lessons from the European Periphery*, edited by Ricardo Paes Mamede, Ester G. Silva and Aurora A.C. Teixeira. London and New York: Routledge, 2014, pp. 258–277.

Goffman, Erving. 'The interaction order'. *American Sociological Review* 48 (1983): 1–17.

Gonçalves, Maria Eduarda. 'Changing legal regimes and the fate of autonomy in Portuguese universities'. In *Higher Education in Portugal 1974–2009 – A Nation, A Generation*, edited by Guy Neave and Alberto Amaral. Dordrecht, The Netherlands; Heidelberg, Germany; London, New York: Springer, 2012, pp. 161–178.

Guibentif, Pierre. *Foucault, Luhmann, Habermas, Bourdieu. Une génération repense le droit*. Paris: Lextenso-Librairie générale de droit et de jurisprudence, 2010.

Guibentif, Pierre. 'Rights in Niklas Luhmann's systems theory'. In *Law and Intersystemic Communication – Understanding 'Structural Coupling'*, edited by Alberto Febbrajo and Gorm Harste. London: Ashgate, 2013, pp. 255–288.

Guibentif, Pierre. 'Law in the semi-periphery: Revisiting an ambitious theory in the light of recent Portuguese socio-legal research'. *International Journal of Law in Context* 10 (2014): 559–561.

Guibentif, Pierre. 'Studying the emergence of the right to privacy. A suggestion for the future agenda of sociology of law'. Paper presented at the 'Global-Regional-Local, Institutions, Relations, Networks. Past and Future of the Sociology of Law' conference, Oñati, Spain: International Institute for the Sociology of Law, May 2014.

Guibentif, Pierre. 'The force of science and the force of organizations: Some exploratory thoughts applied to the example of the Oñati institute for the sociology of law'. *Sortuz – Oñati Journal of Emergent Socio-Legal Studies* 6 (2014): 67–81. Available at http://opo.iisj.net/index.php/sortuz/issue/view/51/showToc.

Guibentif, Pierre. 'Theorien und Menschen im Werk von Gunther Teubner/Theories and human beings in Gunther Teubner's work'. *Zeitschrift für Rechtssoziologie* 35 (2015): 5–27.

Habermas, Jürgen. *Theory of Communicative Action, Volume 2*. Boston, MA: Beacon Press, 1987.

Habermas, Jürgen. 'Hat die Konstitutionalisierung des Völkerrechts noch eine Chance?' In *Idem, Der gespaltene Westen*, by Jürgen Habermas. Berlin: Suhrkamp, 2004, pp. 113–193.

Habermas, Jürgen. 'Eine politische Verfassung für die pluralistische Weltgesellschaft?'. In *Idem, Zwischen Naturalismus und Religion*, by Jürgen Habermas. Frankfurt, Germany: Suhrkamp, 2005, pp. 324–365.

Habermas, Jürgen. *The Crisis of the European Union*. Cambridge, UK: Polity Press, 2012. Published in Portugal as *Um Ensaio sobre a Constituição da Europa*. Lisbon, Portugal: Edições 70, 2012.

Habermas, Jürgen. 'Demokratie oder Kapitalismus?' In *Idem, Im Sog der Technokratie*, by Jürgen Habermas. Berlin: Suhrkamp, 2013, pp. 138–157.

Habermas, Jürgen. 'Democracy in Europe today'. Speech delivered in Lisbon, Fundação Calouste Gulbenkian, 29 October 2013.

Hespanha, António Manuel. 'A revolução neoliberal e a subversão do "modelo jurídico"'. *Revista do Ministério Público*. No. 130 (2012).

Hespanha, Pedro, Sílvia Ferreira and Vanda Pacheco. 'O Estado Social, crise e reformas'. In *A Economia Política do Retrocesso. Crise, Causas e objectivos*, edited by José Reis. Coimbra, Portugal: Almedina/Centro de Estudos Sociais, 2014, pp. 189–281.

310 *Pierre Guibentif*

Honneth, Axel. *Freedom's Right. The Social Foundations of Democratic Life.* New York: Columbia University Press, 2014.

Horkheimer, Max. 'Traditional and critical theory'. In his *Critical Theory: Selected Essays.* New York: The Continuum Publishing Company, 2002, pp. 188–243.

Joerges, Christian. 'Europäische Staatsbürgerschaft'. In *Habermas-Handbuch*, edited by Hauke Brunkhorst, Regina Kreide and Cristina Lafont. Stuttgart, Germany: J.B. Metzler, 2009, pp. 312–315.

Kentikelenis, Alexander E., Thomas H. Stubbs and Lawrence P. King. 'Structural adjustment and public spending on health: Evidence from IMF programs in low-income countries'. *Social Science and Medicine* 126 (2015): 169–176.

Kjaer, Poul F. 'Law and order within and beyond national configurations'. In *The Financial Crisis in Constitutional Perspective: The Dark Side of Functional Differentiation*, edited by Poul F. Kjaer, Gunther Teubner and Alberto Febbrajo. Oxford, UK: Hart Publishing, 2011, pp. 395–430.

Kjaer, Poul F. 'The structural transformation of embeddedness'. In *Karl Polanyi. Globalization and the Potential of Law in Transnational Markets*, edited by Christian Joerges and Josef Falke. Oxford, UK: Hart Publishing, 2011.

Kjaer, Poul F., Gunther Teubner and Alberto Febbrajo. *The Financial Crisis in Constitutional Perspective: The Dark Side of Functional Differentiation.* Oxford, UK: Hart Publishing, 2011.

Koskenniemi, Martti. 'Constitutionalism as mindset. Reflections on Kantian themes about international law and globalization'. *Theoretical Inquiries in Law* 8 (2006): 9–36.

Kumm, Mattias. 'The legitimacy of international law: A constitutionalist framework of analysis'. *European Journal of International Law* 15 (2004): 907–931.

Kumm, Mattias. 'The cosmopolitan turn in constitutionalism: An integrated conception of public law'. *Indiana Journal of Global Legal Studies* 20 (2013): 605–628 (contribution to *Transnational Societal Constitutionalism*, symposium edited by Gunther Teubner and Anna Beckers).

Leite, Jorge, Hermes Augusto Costa, Manuel Carvalho da Silva and João Ramos de Almeida. 'Austeridade, reformas laborais e desvalorização do trabalho'. In *A Economia Política do Retrocesso. Crise, Causas e objectivos*, edited by José Reis. Coimbra, Portugal: Almedina/Centro de Estudos Sociais, 2014, pp. 127–188.

Luhmann, Niklas. *Grundrechte als Institution. Ein Beitrag zur politischen Soziologie.* Berlin: Duncker & Humblot, 1965.

Luhmann, Niklas. 'Subjektive Rechte : Zum Umbau des Rechtsbewusstseins für die moderne Gesellschaft'. In his *Idem, Gesellschaftsstruktur und Semantik 2.* Frankfurt, Germany: Suhrkamp, 1981, pp. 45–104.

Luhmann, Niklas. *Die Wirtschaft der Gesellschaft.* Frankfurt, Germany: Suhrkamp, 1988.

Luhmann, Niklas. *Die Wissenschaft der Gesellschaft.* Frankfurt, Germany: Suhrkamp, 1990.

Luhmann, Niklas. *Funktionen und Folgen formaler Organization.* Berlin: Duncker & Humblot (1994 5th edition, with a new epilogue; original publication 1964).

Luhmann, Niklas. *Die Gesellschaft der Gesellschaft* (2 vols). Frankfurt, Germany: Suhrkamp, 1997.

Luhmann, Niklas. *Art as a Social System.* Stanford, CA: Stanford University Press, 2000.

Luhmann, Niklas. *Die Religion der Gesellschaft.* Frankfurt, Germany: Suhrkamp, 2000.

Luhmann, Niklas. *Die Politik der Gesellschaft.* Frankfurt, Germany: Suhrkamp, 2000.

Luhmann, Niklas. *Organization und Entscheidung.* Opladen, Germany: Westdeutscher Verlag, 2000.

The experience of the European periphery 311

Luhmann, Niklas. *Das Erziehungssystem der Gesellschaft*. Frankfurt, Germany: Suhrkamp, 2002.

Luhmann, Niklas. *Law as a Social System*. Oxford, UK: Oxford University Press, 2004.

Lundvall, Bengt-Åke and Edward Lorenz. 'The Euro crisis and the failure of the Lisbon strategy'. In *Structural Change, Competitiveness and Industrial Policy. Painful Lessons from the European Periphery*, edited by Ricardo Paes Mamede, Ester G. Silva and Aurora A.C. Teixeira. London and New York: Routledge, 2014, pp. 80–101.

Mamede, Ricardo Paes, Ester G. Silva and Aurora A.C. Teixeira, eds. *Structural Change, Competitiveness and Industrial Policy. Painful Lessons from the European Periphery*. London and New York: Routledge, 2014.

Marcuse, Herbert. 'Some social implications of modern technology'. *Zeitschrift für Sozialforschung/Studies in Philosophy and Social Sciences* 9 (1941): 414–439.

Marcuse, Herbert. *One-Dimensional Man*. London: Routledge & Kegan Paul, 1991 (original publication 1964).

Medeiros, Rui. 'A Jurisprudência portuguesa sobre a crise. Entre a ilusão de um problema conjuntural e a tentação de um novo dirigismo constitucional'. In *O Tribunal Constitucional e a Crise. Ensaios Críticos*, edited by Gonçalo de Almeida Ribeiro and Luís Pereira Coutinho. Coimbra, Portugal: Almedina, 2014, pp. 263–288.

Neves, Marcelo. *Tranconstitucionalismo*. São Paulo, Brazil: Martins Fontes, 2009.

Novais, Jorge Reis. *Em Defesa do Tribunal Constitucional. Resposta aos Críticos*. Coimbra, Portugal: Almedina, 2014.

Oliveira, Daniel. 'A democracia ou o euro'. In *Que fazer com este euro? Portugal na tragédia europeia*. Lisbon, Portugal: Edições 70/Le Monde diplomatique – Edição Portuguesa, 2013, pp. 93–109.

Outhwaite, William. 'European democracy'. Paper presented at the 'Self-Constitution of Europe: Symbols, Politics and Law' conference, Cardiff, June 2013.

Pedroso, Paulo. *Portugal and the Global Crisis. The Impact of Austerity on the Economy, the Social Model and the Performance of the State*. Lisbon: Fundação Friedrich Ebert, 2014. Available at http://www.feslisbon.org/conteudo.php?AHsKYwpo=AGUKbQp7 BmsBZFZqUmdUVVViDGdVcFdgAT0EaVU7&AGIKZgtela9Xr1tela9Xr1=ADkK Ogtela9Xr1tela9Xr1&AGcKawphBmUBclZi.

Přibáň, Jiří. 'European legality and its critique: On Bauman's concept of an adventurous Europe'. In *Liquid Society and its Law*, edited by Jiří Přibáň. Aldershot, UK: Ashgate, 2007, pp. 131–151.

Přibáň, Jiří. *Legal Symbolism. On Law, Time and European Identity*. Aldershot, UK: Ashgate, 2007.

Přibáň, Jiří. 'Symbolism of the *Spirit of the Laws*: A genealogical excursus to legal and political semiotics'. *International Journal of the Semiotics of Law* 22 (2009): 179–195.

Přibáň, Jiří. 'The juridification of European identity, its limitations and the search of EU democratic politics'. *Constellation* 16 (2009): 44–58.

Přibáň, Jiří. 'The self-referential European polity, its legal context and systemic differentiation: Theoretical reflections on the emergence of the EU's political and legal autopoiesis'. *European Law Journal* 15 (2009): 442–461.

Přibáň, Jiří. 'Constitutionalism as fear of the political? A comparative analysis of Teubner's *Constitutional Fragments* and Thornhill's *A Sociology of Constitutions*'. *Journal of Law and Society* 39 (2012): 441–471.

Reemtsma, Jan Philipp. *Trust and Violence: An Essay on a Modern Relationship*. Princeton, NJ: Princeton University Press, 2012.

312 Pierre Guibentif

Reis, José, ed. *A Economia Política do Retrocesso. Crise, Causas e objectivos*. Coimbra, Portugal: Almedina/Centro de Estudos Sociais, 2014.

Reis, José, João Rodrigues, Ana Santos and Nuno Teles. 'Compreender a crise: a economia portuguesa num quadro europeu desfavorável'. In *A Economia Política do Retrocesso. Crise, Causas e objectivos*, edited by José Reis. Coimbra, Portugal: Almedina/Centro de Estudos Sociais, 2014, pp. 22–85.

Ribeiro, Gonçalo de Almeida. 'O Constitucionalismo dos Princípios'. In *O Tribunal Constitucional e a Crise. Ensaios Críticos*, edited by Gonçalo de Almeida Ribeiro and Luís Pereira Coutinho. Coimbra: Almedina, 2014, pp. 69–103.

Ribeiro, Gonçalo de Almeida and Luís Pereira Coutinho, eds. *O Tribunal Constitucional e a Crise. Ensaios Críticos*. Coimbra: Almedina, 2014.

Santos, Boaventura de Sousa. 'Social crisis and the state'. In *Portugal in the 80's. Dilemmas of Democratic Consolidation*, edited by Kenneth Maxwell. New York/Westport, CT/London: Greenwood Press, 1986, pp. 167–195.

Santos, Susana. 'Novas reformas, velhos debates. Análise das políticas de justiça e dos seus impactos no sistema judicial'. *Configurações* 13 (2014): 11–25.

St. Aubyn, Miguel. 'We'll still be here in the long run: Austerity and the peripheral growth hypothesis'. In *Structural Change, Competitiveness and Industrial Policy. Painful Lessons from the European Periphery*, edited by Ricardo Paes Mamede, Ester G. Silva and Aurora A.C. Teixeira. London and New York: Routledge, 2014, pp. 67–79.

Supiot, Alain. 'Towards a European policy on work'. In *Resocializing Europe in a Time of Crisis*, edited by Nicola Countouris and Mark Freedland. Cambridge, UK: Cambridge University Press, 2013, pp. 19–35.

Teixeira dos Santos, Fernando. 'Convergence and imbalances in the EMU: The case of Portugal'. In *Structural Change, Competitiveness and Industrial Policy. Painful Lessons from the European Periphery*, edited by Ricardo Paes Mamede, Ester G. Silva and Aurora A.C. Teixeira. London and New York: Routledge, 2014, pp. 43–66.

Teubner, Gunther. *Law as an Autopoietic System*. London: Blackwell, 1993.

Teubner, Gunther. 'Legal pluralism in the world society'. In *Global Law Without A State*, edited by Gunther Teubner. Brookfield, VT: Dartmouth, 1997, pp. 3–28.

Teubner, Gunther. 'Global private regimes: Neo-spontaneous law and dual constitution of autonomous sectors?' In *Public Governance in the Age of Globalization*, edited by Karl-Heinz Ladeur. Ashgate, UK: Aldershot, 2004, pp. 71–87.

Teubner, Gunther. 'A constitutional moment? The logics of "hitting the bottom"'. In *The Financial Crisis in Constitutional Perspective: The Dark Side of Functional Differentiation*, edited by Poul F. Kjaer, Gunther Teubner and Alberto Febbrajo. Oxford, UK: Hart Publishing, 2011, pp. 3–42.

Teubner, Gunther. *Constitutional Fragments: Societal Constitutionalism and Globalization*. Oxford, UK: Oxford University Press, 2012.

Teubner, Gunther. 'Exogene Selbstbindung: Die Konstitutionalisierung von Gründungsparadoxien gesellschaftlicher Teilsysteme (Exogenous self-binding: How social systems externalise their foundational paradox)' *Zeitschrift für Rechtssoziologie – German Journal of Law and Society* 35 (2015).

Teubner, Gunther and Anna Beckers. 'Expanding constitutionalism'. *Indiana Journal of Global Legal Studies* 20 (2013): 551–603 (introduction to *Transnational Societal Constitutionalism*, symposium edited by Gunther Teubner and Anna Beckers).

Thornhill, Chris. *Sociology of Constitutions. Constituitions and State Legitimacy in Historical-Sociological Perspective*. Cambridge, UK: Cambridge University Press, 2011.

The experience of the European periphery 313

Thornhill, Chris. 'The future of the state'. In *The Financial Crisis in Constitutional Perspective: The Dark Side of Functional Differentiation*, edited by Poul F. Kjaer, Gunther Teubner and Alberto Febbrajo. Oxford, UK: Hart Publishing, 2011, pp. 357–393.

Thornhill, Chris. 'Politische Macht und Verfassung jenseits des Nationalstaats (Political power and constitution beyond the national state)'. *Zeitschrift für Rechtssoziologie – German Journal of Law and Society* 32 (2011): 205–219.

Thornhill, Chris. 'National sovereignty and the constitution of transnational law: A sociological approach to a classical antinomy'. *Transnational Legal Theory* 3 (2012): 394–414.

Thornhill, Chris. 'A sociology of constituent power: The political code of transnational societal constitutions'. *Indiana Journal of Global Legal Studies* 20 (2013): 551–603. Contribution to *Transnational Societal Constitutionalism*, symposium edited by Gunther Teubner and Anna Beckers.

Thornhill, Chris, and Samantha Ashenden, eds. *Legality and Legitimacy: Normative and Sociological Approaches*. Baden-Baden, Germany: Nomos, 2010.

Vala, Jorge, Alice Ramos and Pedro Silva. 'Confiança na Justiça'. Paper presented at the Centro de Estudos Judiciários, Lisbon, Portugal, November 2012.

13 The empire of principle[*]

Petr Agha

Introduction

The aim of this contribution is to recentre our thoughts, which have recently shifted in favour of the 'end of politics' and the consolidation of the post-political condition in the wake of the Eurozone crisis. I shall consider the rapidly accelerating decline of the political topography since the 1990s into a post-democratic arrangement, in which expert administration, the naturalization of the political into the management of a presumably inescapable economic ordering by an administrative elite in tandem with an economic oligarchy, has occupied and filled out the very meaning of Europe. The chapter will demonstrate the need for the European project and the spaces for democratic engagement, to be taken back from the post-political oligarchic constituent order, represented by the austerity measures. It will revisit a handful of key components of the process of self-constitutionalization, in the light of the austerity measures imposed after the outbreak of Eurozone crisis, in order to see how and if Europeans, under these novel conditions, can still constitute their own Europe. If Europe is really going through substantive transmutation, as this chapter argues, this will not be revealed by the analysis of positive laws, constitutional texts and institutional arrangements alone. We need to dig deeper into the 'hidden abode' of European discursive practices, its ideas and ideologies. I will particularly focus on the role one of the primary tools of the European project, so-called 'integration through law', plays in the consolidation of austerity measures as a part of the post-2008 constitutional landscape of Europe and the effect it has on the generative matrix of the European project.

Before we start, let me make a couple of initial remarks. The very process of self-constitutionalization is quite paradoxical from the outset, since the

---

[*] An earlier draft of this chapter was presented in June 2013 at the Cardiff one-day 'Self-constitution of Europe: symbols, politics and law' conference. I am indebted to Jiří Přibáň and the other participants for providing valuable comments. I would also like to thank Marija Bartl, Christian Joerges, Jan Komarek and Johan van der Walt for their helpful comments on the earlier draft.

The empire of principle   315

self-constitution of a not-yet-constituted Europe can only take place retroactively.[1] That is why the project of Europe we have now not only disguises the original heterogeneity of ideas (and the many possible and different versions of Europe there could have been) but, more importantly for our purpose, reflects a series of choices which gradually became the Europe we have today and in the same vein, presupposes the many different versions of Europe that we may have.[2] If the European project does not exist before its declaration, before the founding moment, it still means we need to postulate its existence as a possibility, even before it comes to life. The imaginary Europe is therefore a strong and sometimes forgotten dimension in the European integration project and a dimension with important social, political and democratic implications for the construction of the European identity and constitution.

Europe really comes to life when a certain (European) frame of reference manages to capture our imagination and we begin to think within it; this framework consequently begins to govern how the objects of our discourse are formed, or what modes of observation and formulation become available in which to speak of Europe. This set of relations becomes a structure of meanings formed from (discursively) established relations between its numerous elements. This is why the European project emerges, when events are linked up and retrospectively analysed against the backdrop of how we imagined Europe to be, materialized in the paradigmatic structure of values, institutions and procedures; this is when 'the European' begins to embody a certain necessity and foster a sense of solidity. Such discourse enables us to speak (about) Europe, but also constrains what could be said (and how) by de-limiting the scope of positions. This Foucauldian interpretation of the European project helps us to cast a different light on the impact of the debt crisis on the process of self-constitutionalization. If Europe is foremost a series of discursive practices, a (definite) set of relations between myriad everyday events, then it is of the utmost importance how these events are connected, and what and who connects them.

The ideology of Europe

The present-day quest for Europe is framed by two substantial failures: the failure of the Constitutional Treaty in 2005 and the outbreak of the Eurozone crisis in 2008. Crouch, as early as 2004, showed how the logic of business activity, the logic of the

---

1 'All representations of political unity lead back to a representational act that is not mandated, yet without which no genesis of a polity is possible. Not only does this suggest that there is a core of irreducible groundlessness at the heart of every political community, but also that no polity is contemporaneous with its own genesis'. Hans Lindahl, 'Sovereignty and representation in the European Union', in *Sovereignty in Transition*, ed. Neil Walker (Oxford, UK: Hart Publishing, 2003), p. 133.

2 'The collective subject is always in a state of continuing self-constitution, and the judgments it makes will have a reflective effect upon its own identity as a community'. Ronald Beiner, *Political Judgment* (Chicago, IL: University of Chicago Press, 1983), p. 143.

316   Petr Agha

market, is the core reference point for the institutional architecture of the political systems of Europe. Since the mid-1980s, political discourse has imploded into 'a tightly controlled spectacle, managed by rival teams of professionals expert in the technique of persuasion',[3] with the global firm being the central player in the post-democratic society. Even before the current crisis fully started, three judgments of the European Court of Justice in 2007–2008 – the Viking, Laval and Rüffert judgments[4] – set new market-oriented standards and criteria, reframed labour rights in terms of market rights, becoming 'no less and no more than the judicial toppling of the post-war acquis of the common European labour law constitution'.[5] This arrangement was later elevated, thanks to the new Fiscal Compact,[6] to the new fundamental principle of the emerging EU constitutional order. It seems to me that the idea of Europe and the praxis of European integration is nowadays most visibly represented by one particular set of relations: the austerity paradigm of Angela Merkel, which represent a marked culmination of a tendency dating from before the outbreak of the crisis.

The shift of power from political representatives to independent experts and the judiciary, as seen in the strengthened position of the European Court of Justice (ECJ) for economic issues, is described as the 'judicialization of politics'[7] and represents a substantial change in the political landscape of Europe.[8] While institutions keep working with reference to the same rules and procedures, an increasing number of fundamental political decisions are made literary 'behind the closed doors' of expert bodies, mainly justified as inherent economic necessities.[9] Across the EU, austerity has been presented and imposed on the basis of its being necessary, mainly for reasons of overall economic necessity.

The struggle for discursive power in the explanation of the causes of the crisis and the right economic policies to overcome it, takes place on many different levels and in different arenas, ranging from (scientific) debates about the economic causes and consequences of the crisis to debates in the mass media.[10]

---

3 Colin Crouch, *Post-Democracy* (Cambridge, UK: Polity Press, 2004), p. 4.

4 ECJ, Case C-438/05 Viking [2007] ECR I-10779-10840; ECJ, Case C-341/05; Laval [2007] ECR I-11767-11894; ECJ, Case C-346/06; Rüffert [2008] ECR I-1989.

5 Christian Joerges, 'What is left of the Integration through Law project? A reconstruction in conflicts-law perspectives', in *The European Rescue of the European Union? The Existential Crisis of the European Political Project*, eds. Edoardo Chiti, Agustín José Menéndez and Pedro Gustavo Teixeira (Oslo, Norway: ARENA, 2012), p. 46.

6 Formally, the 'Treaty on Stability, Coordination and Governance in the Economic and Monetary Union'; also the 'Fiscal Stability Treaty'.

7 Ran Hirschl, *Towards Juristocracy* (Cambridge, MA: Harvard University Press, 2004).

8 'The reliance on courts and judicial means for addressing core moral predicaments, public policy questions and political controversies – (judicialization of politics, ed. note) is arguably one of the most significant phenomena of late twentieth and early twenty-first century government'. Ran Hirschl, 'The judicialization of mega-politics and the rise of political courts', *Annual Review of Political Science* 11 (2008): 94.

9 Rebecca Adler-Nissen and Kristoffer Kropp, eds. *Special Issue: Making Europe: The Sociology of Knowledge Meets European Integration, Journal of European Integration* 37(2) (2015).

10 Marc Pilkington and Christine Sinapi, 'Crisis perception in financial media discourse: A concrete application using the Minskian/mainstream opposition', *On the Horizon* 22 (2014).

The empire of principle 317

This power has been critical in legitimating the adopted solutions[11] embedded in social practices, norms and institutions. Public statements like, 'there is no alternative' tell us as much about our common lived relation to reality than about this reality itself; rather, they express our reflective sense of commonality with others who are capable of being similarly affected by such a proposition and then analyse the current state of affairs. At the same time, however, this does not mean that such a paradigm could survive without appealing to deeper convictions that we all share; such descriptions of our reality must yet appear to be objective representations of the way the world is. In *The Sublime Object of Ideology*, Žižek cites Marx's analysis of being King in *Das Capital* to illustrate his meaning: a King is only King, because his subjects loyally think and act as if he is King (think of the tragedy of Lear). Yet, at the same time, the people will only believe he is King if they believe that this is a deeper truth about which they can do nothing. In this way, ideology moves from wielding merely the power to construct this or that particular statement, to acquiring the 'power of constructing [the whole of social] reality'.[12] Žižek makes a very simple yet powerful observation here. Ideology does mystify the real state of affairs, but it does not operate primarily at the cognitive level: ideology becomes the very foundation of our reality; it is 'a fantasy-construction, which serves as a support for our "reality" itself'.[13] Ideology is primarily a discourse whose primary function is not to make correct theoretical statements about our reality, but to orient our lived relations to and within this reality.

A particular vision of the social world has the capacity to transform the world it enters, as such visions are performed by actors and thus call into being the very thing they seem merely to represent.[14] These ideas gradually become more fundamental, encompassing social structures and defining the terms of the debate; they legitimate certain frames over others and create 'the given' of, for example, Europe while defining away alternative solutions, forms and imaginaries as unthinkable. This monopoly is centred on the ability to construct the problem in a certain way, to define the issues at hand as well as their solutions. Such fields[15] are structured so that one dominant set of actors will acquire a definitional monopoly over the issue at hand.

Such principles, by naming things, give our world meaning(s). The present moment, I think, is absolutely crucial in the context of our debate on the self-constitutionalization of Europe, in which the law and its general principles are the

---

11 Pierre Bourdieu, *Distinction: A Social Critique of the Judgement of Taste* (London: Routledge, 1984); Pierre Bourdieu, *The Field of Cultural Production* (New York: Columbia University Press, 1993); Michel Foucault, *Discipline and Punish: The Birth of the Prison* (London: Penguin Books, 1977).

12 Pierre Bourdieu, *Language and Symbolic Power* (Cambridge, UK: Polity Press, 1991), p. 166.

13 'The fundamental level of ideology, however, is not of an illusion masking the real state of things but that of an (unconscious) fantasy structuring our social reality itself'. Slavoj Žižek, *The Sublime Object of Ideology* (London and New York: Verso, 1989), pp. 33–45.

14 Judith Butler, *Bodies that Matter: On the Discursive Limits of 'Sex'* (Abingdon, UK and New York: Routledge, 1993).

15 Bourdieu, *Field of Cultural Production*.

318 *Petr Agha*

facilitators of the integration of diverse European societies.[16] This order becomes the internal law of things, a hidden web existing through perception and language. This is why we need to carefully examine the foundations of the process and the principles that govern the process of self-constitutionalization, since they have a decisive effect on how we conceive of ourselves as Europeans and of Europe as a whole, and how the respective components of the EU are produced in public debates along with the relations that arise between such components and their recipients.

Integration through law

These discourses, as they are juridified, cease to be political (organic) and become subsumed under the governance of (legal) principles. The strategy of European integration called 'integration through law' was made possible mainly by the postulation of the supremacy doctrine, vindicated by the Treaty amendments, from Maastricht through Amsterdam to Lisbon. The emphasis on law's integrative force runs parallel to the tendency, in the broader field of EU studies, to treat the process of integration as quasi-teleological and as self-evidently a good thing.[17] The foundational principles of European integration by law are presented as almost real entities, not as products of our democratic imagination, which possess an inherent meaning and (authoritatively) prescribe conduct. Against this backdrop, when the austerity paradigm enters EU constitutional law as one of its principles, it is naturalized and becomes a generally accepted knowledge – and is materialized as the ruling ideology.

Jeremy Bentham noticed that (legal) concepts are 'fictitious entities',[18] a remark which may help us to move our debate away from mechanized, quasi-teleological, principles of EU law and to conceive of them, rather, as (intellectual) constructs and question their ontological status. If principles establish what conclusions should follow, facts are subsumed under the remit of the principle, not vice versa; the consequences prescribed by principles then simply follow; and what they do is to perform primarily a prescriptive and classificatory function. They describe a fragment of reality with universalizing ambitions in order to establish the application itself. Whenever an event occurs, the established patterns include the circumstances described by the principle, and the possibility of using the principle for the purpose of deciding the matter at hand becomes activated. This is a very tempting strategy for dealing with problems Europe encounters on its way to self-constitutionalization. The usage of the distinctively apolitical, universal and principled vocabulary which is found in pre-existing authoritative statements (treaties, conventions and ECJ decisions) allows us to conclude that it

16 Part Three of the Treaty on the Functioning of the European Union, OJ 2007 C 306.
17 Joseph Weiler, 'The constitution of the common marketplace: Text and context in the evolution of the free movement of goods', in *The Evolution of EU Law*, eds. Paul Craig and Gráinne de Búrca (Oxford, UK: Oxford University Press, 1999).
18 Jeremy Bentham, *Of Laws in General* (London: Athlone Press, 1970), p. 251.

The empire of principle 319

has been properly justified. It is the use of certain legal principles, the presence of particular words in the justification, which gives the decision its legitimacy.

The idea of 'cosmopolitan constitutionalism' developed by Kumm (or European constitutionalism beyond the state) seems to be the epitome of the recent developments in European integration and its constitutional order[19] – it (seemingly) steers clear of hierarchies, embraces pluralism and entrenches itself in a thick set of substantive and procedural norms, such as subsidiarity and due process. It presents itself as a mere 'cognitive frame' in which legal and political practice unfolds. This overarching frame is anchored in universal moral ideals embedded in respective European fields of shared values (human dignity, liberty, democracy, equality, the rule of law and respect for human rights), which are embedded in the EU's legal order and are, by their very nature, not dispositional; they are immanent in the concept of EU law itself. What Kumm presents as a mere 'structuring device'[20] nonetheless ensures the optimization of the uniform application of EU law by providing a framework for 'mutual deliberative engagement'.[21] Even though it presents itself as a mere frame of reference, it fiercely subsumes everything under its frame of reference and defines the field for decision making – it tries to colonize the entire discursive field of the European project. The role of such principles is amplified by the role of the Court as a body far removed from the daily affairs of Europe and its strict adherence to a style of formal reasoning that emphasizes logical deduction from legal principles within the Court-defined frame of legal reasoning that might justify one particular interpretation as opposed to other means of creating Europe.[22]

The formalization of the complex decision-making apparatus of creating and sustaining Europe by the means of EU law, buttressed by reference to the primacy of principles operating under the umbrella of a 'cognitive frame of reference', transforms the entire idea of a self-constituting Europe into a mechanism working on the basis of cogs and wheels. The entire apparatus therefore builds towards a decision that had been determined to a large extent even before the case was made subject to it. This mechanism of justification at the same time avoids the need to offer deeper substantive justification – paradoxically, justification by way of substantive values is, in the end, more superficial. Pierre Rosanvallon laments the obsession with (good) 'governance' as the idea of governance replaces 'politics by widely disseminated techniques of management, leaving room for one sole actor on the scene: international society, uniting under the same banner the champions of the market and the prophets of law'.[23] It elevates a certain kind of

---

19 Mattias Kumm, 'The jurisprudence of constitutional conflict: constitutional supremacy in Europe before and after the constitutional treaty', *European Law Journal* 11 (2005).

20 Ibid.

21 Ibid.

22 Miguel Poiares Maduro, *We the Court -The European Court of Justice and the European Economic Constitution* (Oxford, UK: Hart Publishing, 1998), pp. 16–25.

23 Pierre Rosanvallon, *Democracy Past and Future*, ed. Samuel Moyn (New York: Columbia University Press: 2006), p. 228.

320   Petr Agha

rationality (namely, means-ends rationality) as well as accompanying functional necessities into the position of the governing principle of Europe.

This is demonstrated by the *Pringle* judgment, which has profoundly transformed the existing constitutional constellation of the Union by merely stating the commitment to 'the financial stability of the euro area as a whole' as well as to new modes of economic governance. The Court perceives the economic integration of European communities as an autonomous and apolitical process, taking place *beyond* the influence of the communities it, in turn, governs. Moreover, it does so by virtue of the very tool which is supposed to govern the Europeanization of European states – constitutionalized commitment to price stability and rules against inappropriate budgetary deficits. This decision shows the possible effects of Kumm's 'cognitive frame of reference' within which economic criteria and economic expectations, social and political life are all reframed in terms of the supreme principle governing the governance of European affairs. Commentators on European affairs characterize this development with different terms, such as 'executive federalism',[24] 'distributive regulatory state'[25] or 'authoritarian managerialism'.[26]

Europe as post-political arrangement

Böckenförde[27] was among the first in discussions of the European crisis to refer to the concept of the 'state of exception' in which the European treaties transformed the European constitutional foundations into 'soft law' and allowed for a new paradigm to be introduced, one which is governed by a huge increase in arbitrariness and self-referential logics. Europe, as imagined by Weiler and many others, has been destabilized, and legal processes have steadily developed an autonomous dynamic, entering into new alliances with European bureaucratic machineries and interest groups. What has consequently emerged is a new assemblage of power capable of dictating standards and norms that increasingly restrict the field of action of any politics: a web of soft law and governmental standards, best practices and administrative procedures that channel and articulate the needs of financial capital, making its command immediately effective.

The ECJ, which plays the role of apolitical, supra-national body legitimated precisely by its modus operandi which disregards the local and particular, is the principal engine of further integration. Furthermore, since it can only present the outcomes of its decision making as products of interpretation, the claims it adjudicates have to be formulated in universal terms with reference to overarching frame(s) of

---

24   Jürgen Habermas, 'A pact for or against Europe?', in *What does Germany Think about Europe?*, eds. Ulrike Guérot and Jacqueline Hénard (Berlin: ECFR, 2012).

25   Damian Chalmers, 'The European redistributive state and a European law of struggle', *European Law Journal* 18 (2012).

26   Christian Joerges and Maria Weimer, 'A crisis of executive managerialism in the EU: No alternative?', Maastricht Faculty of Law Working Paper 2012/7 (2013).

27   Ernst-Wolfgang Böckenförde, 'Kennt die europäische Not kein Gebot?', *Neue Zürcher Zeitung*, 21 June 2010.

The empire of principle 321

reference, its decision justified by reference to the principled constraints.[28] This, in turn, legitimizes the position of the Court as the guardian[29] of the overarching framework, which justifies the position of the Court and the European project firmly embedded in the very 'cognitive frame'.

The ECJ is not merely the law applier but the *Treaty interpreter*, which creates the medium of communication, namely, the language and structures in which the decision making takes place and claims are articulated.[30] It creates the terminology (and symbolic language) without which no conversation about the issues with which it is entrusted to adjudicate upon can meaningfully occur, even outside the halls of the Court. Austerity seems to have become an invisible hand that guides, conducts, restrains and holds us together and, most importantly, captures our democratic imagination.

Here we encounter a fully codified symbolic system – our laws and our lives are interpreted, applied and typically produced by a body of trained experts, and these processes are restricted to an institutional arena of the Court in which issues of coherence and consistency are paramount. Such a code[31] implies the legitimate(d) right to impose classificatory principles which enjoy a compulsory validity or, at least, adjudicate on the validity of all such principles.[32] It is these principles which determine what goes on in our social reality, so it is not simply a matter of the form: it establishes the very terrain of any public deliberation, the scope and limits of what might be undertaken politically and symbolically 'in the precise sense of determining the structure of the material social processes themselves'.[33]

In this manner, the decision-making process is transposed onto a body of neutral, widely shared principles enforced by a neutral, beyond the state, body. Recall that Kumm characterizes the development of constitutional law in the EU as an experimentalist process in which, against the backdrop of polyarchic decision making, the ECJ establishes framework rules. National courts conditionally apply them in differing ways; however, differences are gradually contained and resolved in iterated exchanges between the ECJ and national legal systems. Europe, no longer tied to any (specific) constitutional order, founds its legitimacy in substantive overarching and widely accepted principles. However, law, especially in the form

---

28 'The . . . emphasis is that each individual judgment must on its face appear to be politics-free. Abidance of this requirement is not possible without strict judicial allegiance to prevailing canon for legal reasoning, judicial methodology and logics of presentation'. Hjalte Rasmussen, *The European Court of Justice* (Copenhagen, Denmark: Gadjura, 1998), p. 335.

29 Damian Chalmers, 'Judicial preferences in the Community Legal Order', *Modern Law Review* 60 (1997): 169–170.

30 Alec Stone Sweet, 'The European Court of Justice', in *The Evolution of EU Law*, eds. Paul Craig and Gráinne de Búrca (Oxford, UK: Oxford University Press, 1999).

31 Pierre Bourdieu, *The Logic of Practice* (Stanford, CA: Stanford University Press 1990), pp. 79–80.

32 Ibid. pp. 136–137.

33 Pierre Bourdieu, 'Cultural reproduction and social reproduction', in *Power and Ideology in Education*, eds. Jerome Karabel and Albert H. Halsey (Oxford, UK: Oxford University Press, 1977), p. 276.

322 Petr Agha

of (supra-)constitutional law, tends to obfuscate its highly ideological nature – it denies both its biases, hiding the contingent political and economic values embodied in the 'higher' principles it puts forward.

The analogy of a 'machine' employed by Hardt and Negri helps us to understand how the interplay between the myriad everyday events unfolds under the umbrella of austerity measures. The current European project is immaterial and intangible, and yet it regulates the internal constitutions of member states through a contractual process made up of 'networks of agreements and associations'.[34] Just as a machine is a self-contained entity that executes its tasks and procedures within its own authoritative rationale, so does the austerity paradigm produce an 'imperial constitutionalization of world order'[35] operating upon a pre-ordained foundation of principles, frames and networks. Paradoxically, integration through law sustains a very peculiar dynamic, a trend that Christian Joerges referred to as the 'de-legalization' of economic and monetary union.[36]

When the market begins to function as a focal point of our deliberations,[37] it immediately begins to produce specifically demarcated sets of authoritative values, concerns and interests. Other forms of judgement are displaced as possible modes of evaluative discernment; the epistemological mechanisms of the economy become the practice of judgement[38] as it brings out a utilitarian rationality to bear on all practices of government, thereby transforming the very meaning of 'nature' to refer to the specific logic at work in governmental practices. This is how 'the financial stability of the euro area as a whole' becomes the only acceptable mode of evaluation. This crucial transformation of our democratic landscape replaces the social contract as a site of (political) truth within the market. Once market principles manage to capture the tools with which we decided to build our European project, namely, law and the European constitution, we begin to imagine Europe according to the social rationality of neoliberalism. Codification of something akin to a 'cognitive frame of reference' thus amounts to an 'objectification' or 'crystallization' of divisions that could otherwise only be generated spontaneously, since it implies a principle which can be applied to particular cases without a remainder.[39] Such structuring of social space forms the ultimate substrate of our lives.[40]

---

34 Antonio Negri and Michael Hardt, *Empire* (Cambridge, MA: Harvard University Press, 2000), p. 182.
35 Ibid. p. 14.
36 Christian Joerges, 'Law and politics in Europe's crisis: On the history of the impact of an unfortunate configuration', EUI Working Papers LAW No. 2013/09.
37 'prices can only be regulated in markets, because it is only there that the gathered citizens, by comparing their interests in exchanging, can judge the value of things relative to their needs . . . it is only in markets that one can judge the relationship of abundance and scarcity between things that determines their respective prices'. Michel Foucault, *The Birth of Biopolitics: Lectures at the Collége de France*, 1978–1979, ed. Michel Senellart, trans. Graham Burchell (Basingstoke, UK: Palgrave Macmillan, 2008), p. 48, n. 6.
38 Ibid. p. 16.
39 Bourdieu, *A Social Critique*, p. 480.
40 Bourdieu, *Logic of Practice*, p. 138.

The empire of principle 323

Katechontic Europe

The economic crisis in the Eurozone and the frenetic activity of its bureaucratic machinery makes it easy to forget that the EU as a constitutional and political project has been in limbo. At the same time, pro-European legal and academic discourses and political rhetoric are shaped by an unwavering conviction regarding further integration.[41] It is true that euphoria and triumphalism are now replaced with silence from some quarters,[42] but the European Union had, we were told, attained a 'stable constitutional equilibrium'.[43] Is it possible to conclude from the reactions to the 2008 crisis that the success of the European project of today is predominantly determined by the perceived need to safeguard a strong or 'sound' economy?[44] At the beginning, we asked what holds Europe together and it seems that the answer is, next to austerity, nothing more than the concept of integration, assembly and the process of further unification of the economy.

The idea of constitutionalism beyond the state perfectly matches the essentially non-political, economic arrangement that has clothed itself in political discourses of human rights, rule of law and democracy. It becomes obvious that self-constituting through procedure has worked as poorly as self-constituting through prosperity, as much as the European policy makers have tried to spin a formalistic and procedural framework for the EU, much like Kumm's influential account. The forms and procedures put forward by Kumm conceal the initial lack of substance and proximity to the life of Europeans and their daily dealings and the relations which the framework were designed to merely formalize. The Union postulates the a priori conditions of unity which do not dynamically (organically) emerge from within the heat of political life – unity appears as extraneous layers superimposed on the disarray of European communities.[45] As often happens, the vacuum of political existence is filled with formal structures referring to higher overarching values, a necessary supplement to 'the fiction of absolute normativity'.[46] What remains within the framework the European Union is an expression without

41 'Europe matters. We know it matters because whenever reference is made to the presence of an EU provenance, lay perceptions of a legal provision change. Debate shifts to its general economic costs, the economic benefits or costs for particular individuals; how it threatens or reinforces perceptions of nationhood; and the degree of national political unity or disunity it generates. These extra associations constitute the cumbersomeness of EU law. They are the added significance or resonance attributed to a provision simply by virtues of its having an "EU"'. Damian Chalmers, 'Gauging the cumbersomeness of EU Law', *Current Legal Problems* 62 (2009): 405.
42 Armin von Bogdandy, 'The European lesson for international democracy: The significance of Articles 9 to 12 EU Treaty for international organizations', *European Journal of International Law* 23 (2012), pp. 322, 323.
43 Andrew Moravscik, 'Reassessing legitimacy in the European Union', *Journal of Common Market Studies* 40 (2002): 603, 618. Andrew Moravscik, 'The European constitutional compromise and the neofunctionalist legacy', *Journal of European Public Policy* 12 (2005): 349, 366.
44 Jan Werner-Müller, *Contesting Democracy: Political Ideas in Twentieth-Century Europe* (New Haven, CT and London: Yale University Press, 2011), p. 147.
45 Carl Schmitt, *Constitutional Theory* (Durham, NC: Duke University Press, 2008), p. 62.
46 Ibid. p. 155.

324   *Petr Agha*

anything to express, devoid if not of meaning then of a connection to the sources of meaningfulness. The relegation of constitutional substance to the background and its replacement by constitutional details played out in a very formalistic register serves to substantiate the highly formal institutional arrangement where unity does not actually exist, and which is not in any way bound to the texture of political existence.

On the other hand, if there is one purpose for the continuation of the current European project, it is precisely what Carl Schmitt meant by his *katechon*,[47] that is, an empire entrusted with averting apocalypse, in this case, by keeping economic catastrophe at bay. Schmitt shows that the legacy of Roman law and temporal political orders established over the centuries is katechontic: what is the best possible order that prevents decay, the victory of 'evil' and resists the Antichrist, the end of finite time? The katechon, the 'restrainer', is always prepared to act against catastrophe.[48] It holds the 'end of the world'[49] at bay and suppresses the power of the Antichrist. Its main task is to restore and maintain the existing social, economic and political order. As such, it is not a passive figure, it is a symbolic representation of an imperial sovereign who insists that 'time is limited', confronted with the coming defeat of the existing social, economic and political order. Katechontical forces are not simply reactionary forces; rather, they proactively prevent the victory of the Antichrist on Earth. It is this active awaiting of the believers which includes the necessity of taking decisions, including (or especially) political decisions. Schmitt's katechon invites us to imagine the end of the empire, to imagine ruins and ruination as that which will be – sometime in the future, not now, not yet.

The concept of the katechon touches upon a central issue in Schmitt's work: his attempts to re-theorize the concept of the *Empire*, and of the imperial imaginary. In the new post-euro crisis discourse, we find a new 'nomos',[50] the nomos of austerity. In the new global constitutional order, this economic theology[51] has replaced the political one. Therefore, the preservation of the euro justified the decisions taken and taken beyond the constitutions of the member states.[52] The austerity paradigm became the modern version of the fight against the katechon in the medieval Christian Roman Empire, as the ultimate political justification. This

---

47 Pauline verse, II Thessalonians 2.6–7: 'And you know what is restraining him now so that he may be revealed in his time. For the mystery of lawlessness is already at work; only he who now restrains it will do so until he is out of the way'. Carl Schmitt, *The Nomos of the Earth in the International Law of the Jus Publicum Europaeum* (New York: Telos Press, 2003), pp. 59–60.

48 Empire, according to Schmitt, 'meant the historical power to restrain the appearance of the Antichrist and the end of the present eon'. (ibid. p. 60).

49 Ibid.

50 Ibid.

51 Giorgio Agamben, *The Kingdom and the Glory. For a Theological Genealogy of Economy and Government* (Stanford, CA: Stanford University Press, 2011), p. 46.

52 See the special issue of the *German Law Journal*, dedicated to the OMT Decision of the German Federal Constitutional Court: *German Law Journal* 15(2) (2014). Available at http://www.german-lawjournal.com/.

The empire of principle 325

perhaps explains the radical change in the European constitutional and symbolic landscape, with the rise of the new 'holy alliances' against the crisis of the common currency which has to be fought because 'there is no alternative'.

Conclusion: 'Whom do you believe, your eyes or my words?'

Each of our own ideologies, the ideology we believe in, is usually perceived by us not as an ideology but rather as neutral knowledge, something that is common sense. In other words, dominant discursive structures naturalize power structures and stabilize them, so that they are taken as 'given'. As Žižek reminds us in his essay, 'With or without passion', in one of the Marx brothers' films, Groucho Marx, when caught in a lie, answers angrily: 'Whom do you believe, your eyes or my words?' This remark demonstrates perfectly the logic behind the functioning of the existing order of conduct, in which the formal reference to substantive principles of the 'cognitive frame' satisfies the requirements laid down by the substantive principles of the European project.[53]

The postulated absence of alternatives justifies the alliances between administrative elites and the economic oligarchy and justifies the primacy of austerity principles within 'integration through law'. Therefore, the nomos of the euro, the preservation of the common currency (and the institutional order that is founded on it) justifies all the adopted measures. Given that the European Union has become an agent of austerity and that Europe's constitutional landscape has radically changed in the name of fiscal consolidation, with very doubtable legitimacy, the answer to the critical question of this collection – how can Europe constitutionalize itself – becomes really problematic, since politics in the Eurozone has rapidly shifted towards a 'state of emergency'. The choices that led to the establishment of the nomos of the euro are presented to Europeans as a necessity with no alternatives.

The rule of law plays a central role in the process of the self-constitutionalization of Europe, and this means that the whole process is to a large extent subsumed under the normalizing discourse of the imperatives of economic order,[54] represented by the 'integration through law' framework. Consequently, this framework regulates our very ontological freedom. The common political identity of Europeans is assumed, with the help of the very same structures designed for the de-politicization of public affairs. If we accept this, we must confront an urgent ethical challenge: how does one create deep and affirming communities outside the (economic) logic of the dominant paradigm ruling European affairs? In this chapter, I asked what, if anything, the principles of 'austerity' might mean for our understanding of Europe and the process of the self-constitutionalization of Europe. I suggested that an adequate understanding of today's European project

---

53 Slavoj Žižek, 'With or without passion: What's wrong with fundamentalism? Part I', Lacanian Ink, (1997/2005). Available at http://www.lacan.com/zizpassion.htm.
54 Foucault, *Birth of Biopolitics*, p. 295.

326   Petr Agha

necessitates a reconceptualization of the location of the sovereign power – Marx's 'hidden abode' – which is nowadays found within expanded circuits of global 'immaterial' capital and governance.[55]

The relationship between agency and the process of self-constitutionalization informed by the austerity paradigm is perhaps best characterized by Marx's famous dictum that men make their own history, but not under the circumstance of their own choosing. Furthermore, since any agency presupposes structure against which it can be performed, so European agency is always embedded in pre-existing social relations that constitute that agent's milieu. At the beginning, a range of choices, formats or doctrines were available; however, at one or several critical junctures, one or several of these choices gained an advantage and this advantage is continuously reinforced through adaptation and naturalized. Therefore, although the metaphor of 'self-constitution' often remains a useful one, it is also one that is very limited in its ability to capture the dynamics of contemporary Europe. The ideas that form the European project do not float about in a universe of meaning, but are produced by human agency and social power relations. Theorizing the role of ideas in this way brings us to the concept of ideology, namely, as 'a set of beliefs which coheres and inspires a specific group or class in the pursuit of political interests judged to be desirable'.[56] Ideologies – and the knowledge structures they entail and cognitive shortcuts they encourage – are, to some degree, inevitable since they are a manifestation of associations, implicit motives and affective reactions as well as careful reasoning and explicit choices. Ideology defines these interests for the group in question, but at the same time it seeks to legitimate these interests vis-à-vis other groups. It is equally important to link ideological discourse to agency, that is, to acknowledge that it is dependent upon human practice for its reproduction or transformation. Action always takes place through the medium of some pre-existing forms; structure (that is, the law) is thus not only constraining but also enabling.[57]

But more importantly, the domination of immaterial production in today's global capitalism has had far-reaching effects on our society, perhaps explaining the present state of the European project. The new organization of immaterial capitalist production in fact defines a new way, in general, that we build our common projects.[58] European law will continuously develop, through interpretation and application, but it will do so along 'pathways' traced by the dominant, governing principles.

---

55 'Social reality changes ... then the old theories are no longer adequate. We need new theories for the new reality ... Capitalist production and capitalist society has changed': Antonio Negri and Michael Hardt, *Multitude: War and Democracy in the Age of Empire* (London: Penguin Books, 2009), p. 140.

56 Terry Eagleton, *Ideology: An Introduction* (London: Verso, 1990), p. 44.

57 Anthony Giddens, *Central Problems in Social Theory: Action, Structure, and Contradiction in Social Analysis* (Berkeley/Los Angeles: University of California Press, 1979), pp. 51, 69–70.

58 Negri and Hardt, *Empire*, p. 58.

The empire of principle 327

The EU has slowly transformed into a 'post-democratic regime of bureaucrats'; politics proper has been reduced, as Jacques Rancière[59] would say, to police-logic, the mere administration of the closed social body. The constitutions of the member states are no longer the supreme source for the organization of political power, as they have been transformed into 'partial orders'.[60] Moreover, the European level, the beyond-the-nation-state milieu, creates the space for a huge flexibility of 'governance' and for the development of multi-level regulations, which would have been impossible at the nation-state level. These 'beyond-the-state' arrangements are presumably constituted as interactive relations between independent and interdependent actors that share a high degree of consensus and trust, within inclusive institutional or organizational settings, as Kumm would argue. They imply a common framework of shared values, founded upon an institutional configuration dominated by a particular rationality of governing. But in reality, this post-political frame, the technocratic dream of a pure post-politics, reduces the process of self-constitutionalization into the sphere of governing and polic(y)ing within a given distribution of what is possible,[61] and set out by the principles which serve the austerity paradigm:

> In post-politics, the conflict of global ideological visions embodied in different parties which compete for power is replaced by the collaboration of enlightened technocrats (economists, public opinion specialists . . .) and liberal multiculturalists; via the process of negotiation of interests, a compromise is reached in the guise of a more or less universal consensus. Post-politics thus emphasizes the need to leave old ideological visions behind and confront new issues, armed with the necessary expert knowledge.[62]

There is no contestation over the givens of the situation; there is only debate over the technologies of management. The power of post-political democracy resides, in other words, in the declaration of its impotence to act politically,[63] which is ultimately reflected in the institutional configurations.[64] Although the formal configuration of democracy is still intact, there is a proliferating arsenal of new

---

59 Jacques Rancière, *Disagreement: Politics and Philosophy*, trans. Julie Rose (Minneapolis, MN: University of Minnesota Press, 1999).

60 Dieter Grimm, *Die Zukunft der Verfassung II. Auswirkungen von Europäisierung und Globalisierung* (Berlin: Suhrkamp, 2012). Compare Johan van der Walt, *The Horizontal Effect Revolution and the Question of Sovereignty* (Berlin: de Gruyter, 2014).

61 Slavoj Žižek, *Welcome to the Desert of the Real!* (London and New York: Verso, 2002), p. 303.

62 Slavoj Žižek, *The Ticklish Subject: The Absent Centre of Political Ontology* (London and New York: Verso, 1999), p. 198.

63 Jacques Rancière, *Disagreement: Politics and Philosophy*, p. 113.

64 'Postdemocracy is the government practice and conceptual legitimation of a democracy after the demos, a democracy that has eliminated the appearance, miscount, and dispute of the people and is thereby reducible to the sole interplay of state mechanisms and combinations of social energies and interests . . . It is, in a word, the disappearance of politics'. Ibid. p. 102.

328   *Petr Agha*

processes that bypass, evacuate or articulate with these formal institutions.[65] This crisis management then becomes the real unifying thread of the constitutional development of the EU. The European project, which is continuously created and which is non-existent unless created by the community which decided to become Europe, is slowly being transformed into a meaning given to it by investment banking, determined by the practice of conducting 'expertise' entirely disjoined from democratic decision making.

The emphasis on 'beyond-the-state' management impacts heavily on the relations of power. We saw how, in the wake of the global economic crisis, the financial command of austerity affirmed not merely its autonomy but also its direct constitutional relevance. The Fiscal Compact and European Stability Mechanism (ESM) narrowed the field against which the process of self-constitutionalization can be played out – a vast centralization of 'executive' institutions goes hand in hand with budget cuts at the expense of democratic criteria of legitimization. The so-called Fiscal Compact endowed the Commission with new – and it is important to highlight, eminently negative – powers through the ESM to scrutinize national budgets and impose fines on deficit violators.[66] It is beyond doubt that a fundamental transformation occurred within the very institutional framework of the EU in the wake of the global economic crisis;[67] even from a juridical point of view, it is easy to see that the whole project of 'integration through law', the trademark of European integration, has been confronted with its limits and contradictions in recent years.[68]

The idea of Europe is in crisis, so are European countries, and European Union scholarship is no exception. Our scholarly conceptualizations of the EU – as a community of law, as a democracy, as a post-national sui generis polity – are also in need of a radical rethink. The incumbent task for Europeans is thus clear: to confront the political question directly and not hide behind its principles. The big question – which we must now work to answer for ourselves, for we must not rely on others to answer it for us – persists: how can Europeans become citizens of Europe? If we are to answer this question responsibly – as Europeans – we must decisively refuse the false choice offered to us and instead redefine it altogether. In so doing, we will redefine ourselves.

The main challenge Europe is facing, one that is more fundamental than solving the financial and political crises it is embroiled in, is to attain its political existence, to constitute itself. The question at stake in the coming years will not be:

---

65 Crouch, *Post-Democracy*.

66 Giandomenico Majone, 'Rethinking European integration after the debt crisis', UCL, European Institute Working Paper no. 3/2012.

67 Some scholars speak of a transition from the 'democratic deficit' to a 'democratic default' (ibid. p. 21), while others denounce a 'pre-emption of democracy' (Fritz Scharpf, Monetary Union, Fiscal Crisis and the Preemption of Democracy', MPIfG Discussion Paper 11/11 (2011) or the 'elitist' and 'post-democratic' nature of the EU (Wolfgang Streeck, *Buying Time: The Delayed Crisis of Democratic Capitalism* (New York: Verso Books, 2014).

68 Joerges, 'What is left?'.

The empire of principle 329

'What is the best form for the EU constitution?' but, rather, 'Who is the (self-) constituting subject?' – the people or establishments?

Bibliography

Adler-Nissen, Rebecca and Kristoffer Kropp, eds. 'Making Europe: The sociology of knowledge meets European integration'. Special Issue, *Journal of European Integration* 37(2) (2015).

Agamben, Giorgio. *The Kingdom and the Glory. For a Theological Genealogy of Economy and Government*. Stanford, CA: Stanford University Press, 2011.

Beiner, Ronald. *Political Judgment*. Chicago, IL: University of Chicago Press, 1983.

Bentham, Jeremy. *Of Laws in General*. London: Athlone Press, 1970.

Böckenförde, Ernst-Wolfgang. 'Kennt die europäische Not kein Gebot?', *Neue Zürcher Zeitung*, 21 June 2010.

Bourdieu, Pierre. *Distinction: A Social Critique of the Judgement of Taste*. London: Routledge, 1984.

Bourdieu, Pierre. *The Logic of Practice*. Stanford, CA: Stanford University Press 1990.

Bourdieu, Pierre. *Language and Symbolic Power*. Cambridge, UK: Polity Press, 1991.

Bourdieu, Pierre. *The Field of Cultural Production*. New York: Columbia University Press, 1993.

Butler, Judith. *Bodies that Matter: On the Discursive Limits of 'Sex'*. Abingdon, UK and New York: Routledge, 1993.

Craig, Paul and Gráinne de Búrca, eds. *The Evolution of EU Law*. Oxford, UK: Oxford University Press 1999.

Chalmers, Damian. 'Judicial preferences in the community legal order'. *Modern Law Review* 60 (1997): 164–199.

Chalmers, Damian. 'Gauging the cumbersomeness of EU law'. *Current Legal Problems* 62 (2009): 405–439.

Chalmers, Damian. 'The European redistributive state and a European law of struggle'. *European Law Journal* 18 (2012): 667–693.

Chiti, Edoardo, Agustín José Menéndez and Pedro Gustavo Teixeira, eds. *The European Rescue of the European Union? The Existential Crisis of the European Political Project*. Oslo, Norway: ARENA, 2012.

Crouch, Colin. *Post-Democracy*. Cambridge, UK: Polity Press, 2004.

Eagleton, Terry. *Ideology: An Introduction*. London: Verso, 1990.

Foucault, Michel. *Discipline and Punish: The Birth of the Prison*. London: Penguin Books, 1977.

Foucault, Michel. *The Birth of Biopolitics: Lectures at the Collége de France, 1978–1979*, edited by Michel Senellart, translated by Graham Burchell. Basingstoke, UK: Palgrave Macmillan, 2008.

Giddens, Anthony. *Central Problems in Social Theory: Action, Structure, and Contradiction in Social Analysis*. Berkeley/Los Angeles, CA: University of California Press, 1979.

Guérot, Ulrike and Jaqueline Hénard, eds. *What does Germany Think about Europe?* Berlin: ECFR, 2012.

Hirschl, Ran. *Towards Juristocracy*. Cambridge, MA: Harvard University Press, 2004.

Hirschl, Ran. 'The judicialization of mega-politics and the rise of political courts'. *Annual Review of Political Science* 11 (2008): 93–118

Joerges, Christian. 'Law and politics in Europe's crisis: On the history of the impact of an unfortunate configuration'. EUI Working Papers LAW No. 2013/09.

330   Petr Agha

Joerges, Christian. 'What is left of the Integration through Law project? A reconstruction in conflicts-law perspectives', in *The European Rescue of the European Union? The Existential Crisis of the European Political Project*, eds. Edoardo Chiti, Agustín José Menéndez and Pedro Gustavo Teixeira (Oslo, Norway: ARENA, 2012).

Joerges, Christian and Maria Weimer. 'A crisis of executive managerialism in the EU: No alternative?', Maastricht Faculty of Law Working Paper 2012/7, 2013.

Karabel, Jerome and Albert H. Halsey, eds. *Power and Ideology in Education*. Oxford, UK: Oxford University Press, 1977.

Kumm, Mattias. 'The jurisprudence of constitutional conflict: Constitutional supremacy in Europe before and after the constitutional treaty'. *European Law Journal* 11 (2005) 262–307.

Lindahl, Hans. 'Sovereignty and representation in the European Union'. In *Sovereignty in Transition*, edited by Neil Walker. Oxford, UK: Hart Publishing, 2003, pp. 87–114.

Majone, Giandomenico. 'Rethinking European integration after the debt crisis'. UCL, Working Paper No. 3/2012.

Moravscik, Andrew. 'Reassessing legitimacy in the European Union'. *Journal of Common Market Studies* 40 (2002): 603–624.

Moravscik, Andrew. 'The European constitutional compromise and the neofunctionalist legacy'. *Journal of European Public Policy* 12 (2005): 349–386.

Negri, Antonio and Michael Hardt. *Empire*. Cambridge, MA: Harvard University Press, 2000.

Negri, Antonio and Michael Hardt. *Multitude: War and Democracy in the Age of Empire*. London: Penguin Books, 2006.

Pilkington, Marc and Christine Sinapi. 'Crisis perception in financial media discourse: A concrete application using the Minskian/mainstream opposition'. *On the Horizon* 22 (2014): 280–296.

Poiares Maduro, Miguel. *We the Court – The European Court of Justice and the European Economic Constitution*. Oxford, UK: Hart Publishing, 1998.

Rancière, Jacques. *Disagreement: Politics and Philosophy*, translated by Julie Rose. Minneapolis, MN: University of Minnesota Press, 1999.

Rasmussen, Hjalte. *The European Court of Justice*. Copenhagen, Denmark: Gadjura, 1998.

Rosanvallon, Pierre. *Democracy Past and Future*, edited by Samuel Moyn. New York: Columbia University Press, 2006.

Scharpf, Fritz. 'Monetary union, fiscal crisis and the preemption of democracy'. Max-Planck-Institut für Gesellschaftsforschung Discussion Paper 11/11, 2011.

Schmitt, Carl. *The Nomos of the Earth in the International Law of the Jus Publicum Europaeum*. New York: Telos Press, 2003.

Schmitt, Carl. *Constitutional Theory*. Durham, NC: Duke University Press, 2008.

Stone Sweet, Alec. 'The European Court of Justice'. In *The Evolution of EU Law*, edited by Paul Craig and Gráinne de Búrca. Oxford, UK: Oxford University Press, 1999, pp. 121–154.

Streeck, Wolfgang. *Buying Time: The Delayed Crisis of Democratic Capitalism*. New York: Verso Books, 2014.

Van der Walt, Johan. *The Horizontal Effect Revolution and the Question of Sovereignty*. Berlin: de Gruyter, 2014.

Von Bogdandy, Armin. 'The European lesson for international democracy: The significance of Articles 9 to 12 EU Treaty for international organizations'. *European Journal of International Law* 23 (2012): 315–334.

The empire of principle 331

Werner-Müller, Jan. *Contesting Democracy: Political Ideas in Twentieth-Century Europe.* New Haven, CT and London: Yale University Press, 2011.

Žižek, Slavoj. *The Sublime Object of Ideology.* London and New York: Verso Books, 1989.

Žižek, Slavoj. 'With or without passion: What's wrong with fundamentalism? Part I'. Lacanian Ink, 1997/2005. Available at http://www.lacan.com/zizpassion.htm.

Žižek, Slavoj. *The Ticklish Subject: The Absent Centre of Political Ontology.* London and New York: Verso, 1999.

Žižek, Slavoj. *Welcome to the Desert of the Real!* London and New York: Verso, 2002.

Index

Abizadeh, Arash 142
absolutism, and managerialism 219
absolutist fallacy 72
Ackerman, Bruce 82
acquis on values 161, 165, 168, 170, 171–2
administration, and government 41
administrative law 128, 198
administrative science, new 220
agencies, European 187–92
agency, European 326
Ahmed v. HM Treasury (2010) 30
Alter, Karen 125
Amtenbrink, Fabian 229
anti-politics 78
anti-terrorism directives, UN 30
Assembly of Estates 256
associative obligations 138–9, 140–1, 144–7
associative relations, and NCC 147
asylum policy 2
austerity, nomos of 324
austerity paradigm 316, 321, 322, 326, 327, 328
austerity politics 258, 266–7
austerity regimes 218–19, 220, 262
authoritarian liberalism 253
authoritarian managerialism 320
authority: constitutional 70; judicial 15, 32; multiplication of sites of 117, 119, 123; public 80
autonomy: democratic constitutionalism 74–5; of global social sectors 130; public 126, 127, 128; social 131; statist or foundationalist constitutionalism 69; universal constitutionalism 71–2, 73

autopoietic social systems theory 58, 59
Avbelj, Matej 70, 106

banking sector: and capital maximization 224; Portugal 286, 290; regulation 226; risks 223–4, 231–2
Bank of International Settlement 228
Barroso, José Manuel 81–2
Basel III Accords 226, 227
Basque Country, secessionist movement 96
Beck, Ulrich 113
behavioural economics 208
belonging, cultural sense of 263
benchmarks 192–3, 197
Bentham, Jeremy 318
Berlin, Isaiah 41
Berman, Paul Schiff 121–4
best fit universal constitutionalism 70
best practice 193
'beyond-the-state' management 328
Big Bang 223, 224, 230
Bloco de Esquerda, Portugal 284
Böckenförde, Ernst-Wolfgang 320
Bologna Process 261
Boltanski, Luc 78, 81
Bomhoff, Jacco 197–8
bottom-up constitutional order 85
bovine spongiform encephalopathy (BSE) crisis 187
Brok, Elmar 37
Brunkhorst, Hauke 67, 77, 80, 277, 302
Bundesverfassungsgericht 169
bureaucracy 44
bureaucratization 292

Index 333

calculemus-based governance 50
Canada: human rights 31; minorities in 99
Canada (Justice) v. Khadr (2008) 31
Canadian Charter of Rights and
Freedoms 31
capital, democratization of 230–1
capitalism, global 326
capitalist hegemony 230
Capps, Patrick 127
Catalonia, secessionist movement 96
charter for Europe 86
Charter of Fundamental Rights 22, 103,
173
China, use of sample rulings 29–30
citizenry, European 246
civic solidarity 263, 264
Civil Procedure Code, Russia 27
civil society, transnational 81–6
class: and inequalities 100, 257; struggle
and social integration 267
coercion: and enforcement 147; and joint
patterns of action 149–50; normative
conception of 8, 139, 146–7; and
political associations 144–5, 147;
proto-legal relations 153; and scope of
obligations 146; standard account of
144–5; state 144, 145, 302
comitology 119, 187
Commission Guidelines on Better
Regulation 188–9
commissions, EU 259–60
common goods 84
commons constitutional order 87
Commons Sense project 83
communication: electronic 260;
organizational 290, 292–3, 294, 295;
and perception 295–6
communicative power 80
communities: imagined 53; and individuals
209
competition 124, 203, 215
competition law 207, 254
complexity: European society 2–3; of
governance 196, 198; within markets
222
compliance, presumption of 171
Comte, Auguste 40
conditionality principle 170
conflict-of-laws perspective 127

conflicts: avoidance of 264; within the EU
56; political and social 123, 133; public
243, 259–60; transnational 277; *see also*
contestation
Congresso Democrático das Alternativas,
Portugal 284
consent, and legal obligations 138, 140
constituent power 14–24, 79, 133, 249,
251, 255–6
constitution: economic of Europe 247;
political 248
constitutional analysis 33
constitutional deficit 86
constitutional democracy 69
constitutional evolution, and economic
hegemony 244–8
constitutional facticity 243–4
constitutional formation 25, 31, 33
Constitutional Fragments 129
constitutionalism: beyond the state 323;
as commonality 53; cosmopolitan
319; democratic 73–6, 87, 196;
depoliticization of 51; European 4–9,
38, 48–9, 133–4; and expertise 184–7,
196; holistic 198; legal theories 87;
liberal 83, 133; multi-level 196–7;
political 56, 130, 133; post-constituent
38, 39, 60; post-national 74, 77; and
power 55; societal 5, 39, 48–51, 52,
55, 58–9, 131; sociological concept of
58–60; state-based 130, 131; statist or
foundationalist 68–70, 76, 80, 86, 87;
theories of 67–70; transnational 275–9,
288; universal 70–3, 76, 80, 86, 87;
Westphalian 68
constitutionalization: European 23;
integration as 55, 60; and juridification
131; rule-of-law 247
constitutionalizations 4–6
constitutional law 25, 212, 321
constitutional moment 301
constitutional orders, European 87
constitutional pluralism 4, 6, 7, 8, 95,
97–108, 116–21; *see also* legal pluralism
constitutional politics 4–5, 8, 9, 66, 76–81,
86–7, 88
constitutional polity, European 52–5
constitutional processes, sociology of
299–300

334   *Index*

constitutional rights 28, 31
constitutional sociology 76, 130
constitutional systems, national/European 17
constitutional technocracy 253–5, 257, 258
Constitutional Treaty 37–8, 58, 82, 315
constitution-interpreting subjects 69–70, 72–3
constitutions: breach of 256; democratic 254; developed after WWII 245–6; development of 24; European Constitution 15, 16, 24–33, 56, 66, 266, 267; European social welfare and security 248; extraterritorial 31; fragmented 129–32; making of 14; material 134; national 276; Portuguese 286; rights-based 18; rule-of-law constitution 247; societal 130; sociological turn in 4–5; supranational 38; United States 107–8, 254
constraints of permissibility 148, 149–50
consultation, and policy making 189–90
contestation: dealing with 128; and global legal pluralism 126; and the internal market 203–6; public 243, 259–60; *see also* conflicts
Copenhagen Commission 172–3
Corte Costituzionale 169
cosmopolitan constitutionalism 319
Cosmopolitan Europe 113
cosmopolitan Europe, and hermeneutic pluralism 112–14
cosmopolitan theories, constitutional polity 52–3
Costa case 248
Council of Europe (CoE) 95, 103, 173, 174
Court of Auditors 192
courts, and contestation 128
crises: economic 10, 244, 263, 328; in the EU 48, 81–2, 295; Eurozone 9, 220, 315, 316; financial 222, 225–6, 289, 323; global economic crisis 244, 263, 328; Greek crisis 2015 1, 262, 266–7, 280; Portugal 279–89, 303; refugee and migrant crisis 1–2; sovereign debt crisis 222, 280, 290
critical approach, transnational constitutionalism 277–9
critical discourse theory 104

Crouch, Colin 224, 315–16
cultural diversity 99–100
cultural pluralism 97–105
cultural systems 305, 306
culture: civil democratic 96; human rights 97, 111; legal 97–105; regional 130

debate: need for 305; silencing of 264, 266
debt: Portugal 280, 281, 285, 290; and risks 230; and the single currency 285
decentralisation 194
decision-making 316, 319, 321
de-juridification, of the EU 48–51
deliberative democracy 242–3, 266–7
democracy: compliance with 170; constitutional 69; Copenhagen criteria on 172; deliberative 242–3, 266–7; and the EU 283; participatory 194; and policy making 210; political 71; post-national 126
democratic circle 239–43, 249
democratic constitutionalism 73–6, 87, 196
democratic constitutions 254
democratic deficit, EU 47
democratic government 69
democratic legitimacy 37, 242, 265–6
democratic power 96, 240
democratic project, European 97
democratic socialism 246
democratic value, of the EU 96
democratization, of capital 230–1
demonstrations, Portugal 283–4
depoliticization: of constitutionalism 51; of the EU 48–51; politics of 45–6; through societal constitutionalization 52
deregulation: of financial markets 223, 285; and liberalization 230
Derrida, Jacques 266
deterritorialization, of law and politics 60
differences, recognizing and accommodating 101
directly-deliberative polyarchy (DDP) 193–5
Directorate for Impact Assessment and European Added Value 191
discourse, and power 241
discrimination, and minority groups 100
discursive power 240, 316–17
dispute resolution 110

distributive regulatory state 320
diversity: cultural 99–100; within the EU 98; of institutional normative orders 109–10; national 184, 185–6; of pluralism 112–13
Draghi, Mario 255, 256, 259, 267
Dublin Regulation 2
Durkheim, Emile 57
Dworkin, Ronald 138, 139–41, 143–4

economic activity, regulation of 205
economic conditionality 218, 219, 220
economic constitution, of Europe 247
economic crisis 10, 244, 263, 328; *see also* crises
economic dynamics 301
economic hegemony, and constitutional evolution 244–8
economic integration 163–4
economic morality 233
economic power 252
economic pressures, reactions to in Portugal 285–6
economics: behavioural 208; discipline of 220–1; neo-classical 222; and scientific method 233
economies, and the EU 203–4
economy: global 258; and science 306
Ehrlich, Eugen 50, 94, 109
elections: European Parliamentary elections May 2014 97; Greece 267; Portugal 281–2, 284; turnout at 257
electronic communication 260
elites 37, 78, 97, 261
emphatic republicanism 71
empiricism 208
energy policy 255
enforceability: of obligations 147–8, 151, 153–4, 155–6; proto-legal relations 153–5
enforcement: and coercion 147; excessive focus on 161; of legal obligations 152–3; and principles of political morality 145; proto-legal relations 153–7; public or omnilateral 156; state 144–5; of values 165–6, 168, 171, 174
Enlightenment philosophy 40
epistemic pluralism 118
equality 101

ethical fragmentation 111
ethical relativism 111
ethnic minorities 100; *see also* minority groups
ethnological and ethnographic studies, turn to 50
euro 244, 285, 324
Eurogroup of Eurozone finance ministers 250
Europe: ideology of 315–18; as post-political arrangement 320–3
European Alternatives 85
European Banking Union 229
European Budgetary Regime (EBR) 250–1, 252, 260
European Central Bank (ECB) 218–19, 229–30, 250, 252, 253, 259
European Charter of the Commons 83–4
European Citizens' Initiative for the Right to Water 84
European Commission 190–1, 193, 218–19, 250, 328
European Commons Movement 82–3
European Constitution 15, 16, 24–33, 56, 66, 266, 267
European Convention on Human Rights (ECHR) 18–19, 20, 30–1, 95, 105
European Convention on the Future of Europe 85
European Council 170, 193, 250
European Court of Human Rights (ECtHR) 18, 22–3, 103–4, 128, 166, 172, 266
European Court of Justice (ECJ): and the ECHR 18–19, 20; and economic conditionality 218; and European Budgetary Regime (EBR) 251; and human rights 20–1, 172; interpretation of the Treaty 202; and judicial institutions 16; and market integration 211–14; Opinion 2/13 167; and pluralism 103, 104; and politics 212, 213; power of 13–14, 15, 19, 213, 214, 316, 320–1; and regulation 216; single rights 17–18; supremacy of 118; *Viking, Laval* and *Rüffert* judgments 316
European demos 105
European Economic Governance 132; *see also* governance
European integration *see* integration

336 *Index*

Europeanization: economic 204; and
   sovereign state's powers 57
European labour law constitution 316
European law *see* law(s) 13–14
European Ombudsman 192
European Parliamentary elections, May
   2014 97
European Parliamentary Research Service
   191
European periphery 274
European project 315, 319, 325, 326, 328
European society: complexity of 2–3; and
   the EU 39
European Stability Mechanism (ESM) 218,
   252, 328
European System for Financial
   Supervision (ESFS) 231
European Union directives, national
   deviations from 22
European Water Movement 84
europhobia 97
Eurozone crisis 9, 220, 315, 316; *see also*
   crises
evaluative approaches, within the pluralist
   field 102–5
Everson, Michelle 277
executive federalism 244, 248, 249–50,
   320; *see also* federalism
executive power 252
existence conditions, for legal obligations
   142
existentiality, test of 81, 82–3
expertise: and constitutionalism 184–7,
   196; constitutionalization of 8; and
   governance 183, 186, 195; for impact
   assessments (IAs) 189; and open method
   of coordination (OMC) 193; and policy
   making 183, 186, 188, 196, 198; and
   politics 215; role of 183, 186
expert knowledge 48
exploitation, and joint patterns of action
   149–50
expulsion procedure, Council of Europe's
   (CoE) 174
extraterritorial constitutions 31

Fabius, Laurent 1
Factortame (1989) 20
facts, and norms 243–4

fascism, emancipation from 245–6
federalism 48, 58, 162, 163, 173; executive
   244, 248, 249–50, 320; post-democratic
   executive 88
federalists 47
financial crises 222, 225–6, 289, 323;
   see also crises
Financial Crisis in a Constitutional
   Perspective, The 287
financial dynamics 301
financial instability 231
financial markets: deregulation of 223,
   285; Portugal 285; systemic risk within
   227
financial sanctions, effectiveness of 174
Financial Services Act 1986 230
financial system, force of the 279–89
first-order rules 131
Fiscal Compact 250, 316, 328
Forst, Rainer 79
Fossum, John-Erik 15–16, 80–1
foundationalist constitutionalism 68–70,
   76, 86, 87
four pillars of the European market 17
Fraenkel, Ernst 250
France, Front National 97
freedoms: four basic 17; hindrance of 150
free movement of peoples 2, 204, 208
free-standing constitutionalism 70–1, 87
Friedman, Lawrence 97
Frontini (1973) 20
Front National, France 97
functional differentiation 184–5
functional systems 291, 296, 298, 301
Fundación de los Comunes 85
fundamental rights, proportionality relating
   to 23
futurization 223–6, 227, 232

Galán, Alexis 123
Geertz, Clifford 106
genealogical fallacy 72
Gerhards, Jürgen 263
German Constitutional Court 117
Germany: *Grundgesetz* 245; ordo-
   liberalism 247; supreme court 213;
   wages in 258
Gerstenberg, Oliver 195
global administrative law 128

Index 337

global economic crisis 244, 263, 328; *see also* crises
globalization: of banking governance 224; and joint patterns of action 148; and the nation state 130; and normative hybridity 122; and sovereign state's powers 57; and transnational governance 42; as transnational processes 277
global legal pluralism 121–9, 134; *see also* pluralism
global regulatory bodies 125, 127; *see also* regulation
Goffman, Erving 296
goods, common 84
governance: banking market 224; calculemus-based 50; complexity of 196, 198; and constitutionalism 196; democratic 194; depoliticization of constitutionalism by 51; EU 188; European Economic Governance 132; multi-actor 197, 327; multi-level governance system 94; new 110; open method of coordination (OMC) 192–5; and politics 45, 319–20; polyarchies of 53; private 197; reflexive 194, 198; role of expertise and knowledge in 183, 186, 195; scientification of 229; technical 44–8; technocratic 218, 229; theories of transnational 42–4; weakness of 265
government: and administration 41; democratic 69
Gower Report 230
Grande, Edgar de 113
grassroots constitutional order 87
Greece: crisis in 1, 262, 266–7, 280; elections 267; and the EU 218; sovereign debt crisis 219–20
Grimm, Dieter 14, 69
growth: compulsive 298; pathological 289
Gurvitch, Georges 49

Habermas, Jürgen 38, 88, 249, 265, 277, 287–8
happiness, collective 40
Hardt, Michael 322
Hart, H.L.A. 120, 142
Hauer (1979) 18
Hayek, Friedrich 247

hermeneutic pluralism, and cosmopolitan Europe 112–14
Hirsi case 266
'hitting the bottom' thesis 289, 291
Hoechst (1989) 19
Honneth, Axel 300
Horkheimer, Max 300
HR Agency 103
human rights: Canada 31; culture 97, 111; defence of 276; and the EU 163, 167; and EU governance 48; and EU laws 168–9, 170; and European Court of Justice (ECJ) 20–1, 172; and post-war constitutions 245–6; principles 111
Human Rights Act (HRA) (1998), United Kingdom 28–9
human rights law 17, 18, 20–1, 27, 28–9, 103
Hungary: ideologically informed non-compliance 165, 166, 167; and refugees 1

identities: and constitutionalism 69; within the EU 96; European 263, 264, 315, 325; thick 164
identity politics, and constitutional theory 51
ideologically informed non-compliance, with EU values 165–8
ideology: constitutional pluralism as 106; of Europe 315–18; and the European project 326
imagined community, European polity as 53
impact assessments (IAs) 184, 188–92, 196, 197
inclusion 24, 101–2, 112, 113
inclusionary structure building, formation of constitutional laws 25
incommensurability 111
independent experts, power of 316
indicators, measurable 192–3
individual rights 288, 300
individuals: and communities 209; and organizations 302; and sociology of constitutional processes 299–300
inequality(ies): class 100, 257; within the EU 204, 209, 248; in Europe 244; social/political 208, 257–9; in wages 258

338   *Index*

injustice, and the EU 172
inner-juridical constituent power 16, 17, 18, 20, 21, 25, 28, 33
institutional capacity, of the Copenhagen Commission 172–3
institutionalist theory of law 118
institutionalized politics 132
institutional normative order, law as 109
institutional orders, tests of 81–2
institutional pluralism 124–5
institutional theory of law 7, 120
integration: as constitutionalization 55, 60; economic 320; EU 163, 201; European 187, 210–11, 315; resistance to 97; through law 318–20, 322, 325, 328; values of 103
integration theory, neo-functionalism 185
interface norms 127
internal market 163–4, 203–9, 212–14
Internationale Handelsgesellschaft (1970) 18
international instruments, autonomous use of 18–20, 28–9
internationalism 219
International Monetary Fund (IMF) 218–19
internet 260
investment treaty law 123
Italian Constitution Court 20

Joerges, Christian 51, 322
joint patterns of action: and globalization 148; reasons for 154; success/pathology of 149–50
journalism 260, 261
Journal of Law and Society 197
judicial authority 15, 32
judicial constituent power 16
judicial elites 97
judicial institutions: and the ECJ 16; of the EU 7
judicialization of politics 316
judicial minimalism 128
judiciary, power of 214, 316
Juncker Commission 191
Juncker, Jean-Claude 266
juridification, and constitutionalization 131
jurisprudence: ECHR as source of 18–19; EU 212; transnational 8, 277

justice 79, 143
justification: basic structure of 79; mechanism of 319; and normative conception of coercion (NCC) 146–7; and obligations 146; of public authority 80

Kadi (2005) 22, 31
Kant, Immanuel 151, 152
katechon 324
Keck and Mithouard 212
Kenya, democratic transition in 28
Keynesian economics 222, 230
Kjaer, Poul F. 292
Knight, Frank 220, 221, 232
knowledge: expert 48; and governance 183, 186, 195; and open method of coordination (OMC) 193; and policy making 183, 186, 188, 196, 198; role of 8, 183, 186
Komarek, Jan 106
Koskenniemi, Martti 219
Krisch, Nico 124–8
Kumm, Mattias 68, 70, 71–2, 119–20, 276, 319, 320, 321, 323, 327
Kymlicka, Will 164

labour costs 255
labour law constitution 316
Laing, Ronald D. 264
laissez-faire conception, trade 206
Larik, Joris 174
Laval judgement 316
law and politics centred approach, transnational constitutionalism 276, 278–9, 288
law(s): administrative 128, 198; competition law 207, 254; and constituent power 14–15; constitutional 25, 212, 321; deterritorialization of 60; EU 319; European 326; European labour law constitution 316; and human rights 168–9, 170; human rights law 17, 18, 20–1, 27, 28–9, 103; informal/ formal 50; as institutional normative order 109; institutional theory of 7, 118, 120; integration through 318–20, 322, 325, 328; law making 193–4; legitimacy of 104; national 20; plasticity

of 168–71; and politics 248; private 260; proportionality in 22–4; public 14, 16, 23, 25–6, 30, 33, 256, 259–60; reflexive law 193–4; relation law 68–9, 71, 73–4; and rights 247; rise of European 13–14; scope of 168–71; single rights 17–18; and social reality 121; societal 40; sociology of 306; state 109–10; transnational 48–9, 54–5, 117, 256; of the Treaties 253–4; validity of 110–11; and values 8, 161–3, 169

lean production 297–8

left wing political parties 258

legal culture 97–105

legal hybridity 122

legal norms 151, 154, 167

legal obligations: associative 138–40; enforceability of 155; enforcement of 152–3; interactions generating 151; pedigree tests for 142, 143, 145–6; site/scope of 141–3

legal order: cosmopolitan 113; supremacy of EU 118

legal pluralism *see* pluralism

legal reasoning 128

legal theories, constitutionalism 87

legislation, democratic 243–4

legislative competence, of internal market provision 205–6

legislative power 252

legislative process, EU 9

legitimacy: challenges to 287; democratic 37, 242, 265–6; of EU 15; of the law 104; normative 73; of normative orders 110–11; political 80–1; of private governance 197; sociological 78, 80; through legality 239; of transnational law 117

legitimation crisis, EU 37

Lehman Brothers bankruptcy 280

Lengfeld, Holger 263

lex mercatoria 94

liberal constitutionalism 83, 133

liberal constraints, to pluralism 123–4

liberalism: authoritarian 253; neo-liberalism 247, 255, 302; ordo-liberalism 247, 255, 302

liberalization, and deregulation 230

Liebert, Ulrike 77

L'Internationale 85

Lisbon Strategy 2000 188

Lisbon Summit 2000 192

Lisbon Treaty 19, 37–8, 48, 57, 82, 106, 248, 249, 250, 254, 266

living conditions 244

LIVRE, Portugal 284

Lorenz, Edward 298

Luhmann, Niklas 129, 184–5, 274, 279, 291, 293, 300, 301

Lundvall Bengt-Åke 298

Maastricht Treaty 19, 117

MacCormick, Neil 93, 109, 117–18, 120

macro-prudential supervision 228

Maduro, Miguel 82

Majone, Giandomenico 190

management, technologies of 327–8

managerialism: and absolutism 219; authoritarian 320

managerialization 292, 306

Manifesto for the Commons in the European Union 84–5

Manifesto of Ventone 246

Marcuse, Herbert 261, 300

margin of appreciation 123, 128

market integration, and European Court of Justice (ECJ) 211–14

markets 206, 208, 222–3, 224, 232, 257; *see also* internal market

Marx, Karl 40

material constitution 134

Maus, Inge 249

media 260–1, 264

member states 105–6

Memorandum of Understanding 2011, Portugal and the Troika 279, 281, 283, 284, 286, 288

Menéndez, Augustín José 15–16

Merkel, Angela 259, 266, 316

Method Monet 246

Meuwese, Anne 197–8

microeconomic politics 255

migrant crisis 1

minority groups 99–101, 103–4

monetary policy 255

money, role of 222; *see also* euro

monitoring mechanisms 293

monitoring, pre-accession 170

340 *Index*

moral hazard 231
morality: economic 233; political 141, 145; public 140
moral principles 111
moral project, Europe as 3
movement, restrictions on 204–5; *see also* free movement of peoples
M.S.S. v. Belgium and Greece 166
Mueller, Jan-Werner 83, 173
multiculturalism 99, 102, 111
multi-level governance system 94
mutual recognition, principle of 167

national courts 20–2, 29, 30–1
nationalism, and the internet 260
nationalist europhobia 97
nationalist populism 105
nation states: constitutional formation of 25; demise of 46, 47, 57; and globalization 130; persistence of 60; political constitution of 130; power of 251
natural law theories, and sociological theories 40
Negri, Antonio 322
neo-classical economics 222
neo-functionalism, integration theory 185
neo-liberalism 247, 255, 302
networks: within the EU 95–6; European Alternatives 85; inter-organizational 292–3
Neumann, Franz 247
Neves, Marcelo 276
new administrative science 220
Nold (1974) 18
non-compliance: with EU values 165–8, 169, 170
normative associative relation 145
normative conception of coercion (NCC) 8, 139, 146–7
normative hybridity 121–2
normative individualism 98
normative legitimacy 73
normative orders 110–11, 114
normative pluralism 109
normative principles 125
normative structure, of joint patterns of action 148
normative theory, multiculturalism as 102

normativity 240
norms: acceptance of 211; European 247; and facts 243–4; interface norms 127; legal 151, 154, 167; publicly (omnilaterally) authorized 151; types of 101–2, 109
North American Free Trade Agreement panels, and US state courts 123
North-South divide 258

obligations: associative 138–9, 140–1, 144–7; enforceability of 147–8, 151, 153–4, 155–6; and justification 146; proto-legal relations of 147; of the rightful condition 153–4, 155; of states 138–41
Offe, Claus 254
Ombudsman, European 192
omnilateral authorization, proto-legal relations 152
On Critique 81
open method of coordination (OMC) 184, 192–5, 197, 198, 292
Opinion 2/13 167
Orbán, Viktor 1
ordo-liberalism 247, 255, 302
organization: impact on spontaneity 298; scientific 306
organizational communication 290, 292–3, 294, 295
organizational development 293
organizations: and individuals 302; internal/external impact of 293–5; networks of 293; power of 289–93
outsourcing, of key constitutional issues 173

Palombella, Gianluigi 160
parliamentarianism 254
parliamentary power 254
Parsons, Talcott 184
participatory democracy 194–5
participatory processes 194
Patterson, Dennis 123
(Peace and) Security and Cooperation at the European level (OSCE) 103
pedigree tests, for legal obligations 142, 143, 145–6
permissibility, constraints of 148, 149–50

Pernice, Ingolf 15, 16
personality, new type of 305
Peters, Anne 15
Plato 241
plural demos 105–7
pluralism: challenges to 105–8;
constitutional 4, 6, 7, 8, 95,
97–108, 116–21; cultural, legal and
constitutional 97–105; diversity of
112–13; epistemic 118; and European
Court of Justice (ECJ) 103, 104; as
fragmented constitutions 129–32; global
legal 121–9, 134; institutional 124–5;
legal 7, 97–105, 112, 116–17; liberal
constraints to 123–4; normative 109;
politics of 133; and proportionality 120;
radical 121–9; systemic 124–5, 126;
traditional 94
pluralist field 99–105
police-logic, politics as 327
policy(ies): asylum policy 2;
constitutionalization of 214; energy
255; monetary 255; and politics 214–15;
resistance to 97
policy making: and consultation 189–90;
and democracy 210; European Union
(EU) 203; and knowledge/expertise 183,
186, 188, 196, 198; process of 193–4;
rational technical model of 191–2
political action: and legal and
constitutional pluralism 116, 133; and
supranational and global law 129
political associations, coercive nature of
144–5, 147
political conflict, avoiding 123, 133
political constitution: European 248; of the
nation state 130
political constitutionalism 56, 130, 133
political constitutionalization, of social
systems 131
political debate, lack of 284
political decision-making 316; *see also*
decision-making
political deliberation, and pluralism 125
political democracy 71
political disenchantment 44
political elites 37, 97, 261; *see also* elites
political inequality 257–9
political legitimacy 80–1

political morality 141, 145
political parties, left wing 258
political power 60, 134, 255
political right 257–9
political–sociological approach, to
constitutional politics 66, 76–81,
86–7, 88
political sociology 76–7
political sovereignty 256
political systems: European 316; and
psychic/social systems 302–3; use of
violence 302
political will 239
politics: anti-politics 78; austerity 258,
266–7; constitutional 4–5, 8, 9, 66,
76–81, 86–7, 88; constitutional
rights in domestic 31; defining
40; democratic constitutionalism
73–4; of depoliticization 45–6;
deterritorialization of 60; and European
Court of Justice (ECJ) 212, 213; and
expertise 215; and governance 45,
319–20; governed by laws 41; of
identity 51; institutionalized 132;
judicialization of 316; and the law
248; within market systems 131;
microeconomic 255; of modern
economies 224; national 210–11; of
pluralism 133; as police-logic 327; and
policy 214–15; post-politics 320–3, 327;
of power 41; right wing politics 257–9;
and science 306; self-constitution of
304; self-limitation of 59; shotgun
218–19; statist or foundationalist
constitutionalism 68–9; transnational
54–5, 277–8; universal constitutionalism
71
polities: constitution of 40, 52–5; in
European constitutionalism 7; and
political power 134; and societal self-
constitutionalization 49
polytheism, new 45
popular sovereignty 69
Portugal: banking sector 286, 290; Bloco
de Esquerda 284; crisis in 279–89, 303;
debt 280, 281, 285, 290; demonstrations
283–4; elections 281–2, 284; financial
markets 285; LIVRE 284; Memorandum
of Understanding 2011 279, 281, 283,

342 *Index*

284, 286, 288; Social Democrat Party 280; Socialist Party 280–1, 294–5; social movements 283–4
Portuguese Constitution 286
post-constituent constitutionalism 38, 39, 60
post-democratic executive federalism 88
post-national constitutionalism 74, 77
post-national democracy 126
post-politics 320–3, 327
pouvoir constituant, permanent 15
poverty, and social inequality 257
power: communicative 80; constituent 14–24, 79, 133, 249, 251, 255–6; and constitutionalism 55; contradicting systems of 248–53; democratic 96, 240; and discourse 241; discursive 240, 316–17; economic 252; of the EU 37, 174; of European Commission 328; of European Court of Justice (ECJ) 13–14, 15, 19, 213, 214, 316, 320–1; of external entities 282–3; of independent experts 316; inner-juridical constituent 16, 17, 18, 20, 21, 25, 28, 33; of judiciary 214, 316; legislative and executive 252; limitation of 59; mixed constituent 249; of nation states 251; new assemblage of 320; of the non-elected 286; of organizations 289–93; parliamentary 254; political 60, 134, 255; politics of 41; private-regulatory 197; of self-constitutionalization 55; societal constitution of 51–2; sovereign 57, 251, 326; state 60; techniques of 241; technocratic 251, 266
pragmatic sociology 78
preliminary rulings, to national courts 20, 29
principles: conditionality 170; human rights 111; of mutual recognition 167; normative 125; political morality 141, 145; public autonomy 126, 127, 128; public morality 140; rule of law *see* rule of law; toleration principle 125
Pringle judgment 320
private governance 197
private law 260
private-public partnerships 260
privatization 260

privatized Keynesianism 224
procedural sovereignty 249, 251, 256
profit motive 232
proportionality: in European law 22–4; inner-juridical constituent force of 32–3; and pluralism 120
protectionism, elimination of 206
proto-legal relations 140, 147–57
Prudential Regulatory Authority (PRA) 231, 232
psychic processes, impact of 295–6, 299–300
psychic systems, and political systems 302–3
psychological processes, impact on social processes 299
psychology, and markets 208
public autonomy 126, 127, 128
public conflict and contestation 243, 259–60
public debate, silencing of 264, 266
publicity, of enforcement 156
public law 14, 16, 23, 25–6, 30, 33, 256, 259–60
public-legal order, of EU 15
public morality 140
public opinion 239, 260–2
public or omnilateral enforcement 156
public reasoning 124
public sphere 7, 9, 80, 239, 240, 259–67
Putin, Vladimir 27

radical pluralism 121–9
Rajoy, M. 96
Rancière, Jacques 327
rationality, means-ends 320
rationalization, as social differentiation 45
rational technical model, policy making 191–2
Raz, Joseph 120
reality, test of 81, 82
Reding, Vice-President 173
reflexive governance 194, 198
reflexive law 193–4
reform, of the EU 174
refugee and migrant crisis 1–2
regulation: banking market 224; banking sector 226; of economic activity 205; EU 187–92, 210; and European Court

Index 343

of Justice (ECJ) 216; global regulatory bodies 125, 127; macro-prudential 228; state 206; transnational private 197
regulators, types of 110
regulatory risk management 224
relation law 68–9, 71, 73–4
relationships, in the internal market 96
religious groups 100
repressive tolerance 261
republicanism, emphatic 71
requirement of publicity, of enforcement 156
reserved powers 254
rightful condition 151–2, 153–4, 155
rights: Charter of Fundamental Rights 22, 103, 173; as constituent power of the EU 23; constitutional 28, 31; individual 288, 300; and the law 247; practice 72–3; protection of 19; to self-governance 197; single 17–18, 23, 26–8; of single persons 17–18; through groups 98
rights-based proportionality 22–3
rights-based public reason 73
right wing politics 257–9
risks: banking sector 223–4, 231–2; of constitutional pluralism 121; and debt 230; management of 187, 188, 224, 226; in markets 222–3; risk analysis 232; systemic 227; and uncertainty 232
Risse, Mattias 143
Romantic sociology of community 50
Rosanvallon, Pierre 319
Rüffert judgement 316
Ruiz Zambrano 17
rule of law: compliance with 170, 172; in the EU 159–60, 164, 168, 169; and self-constitutionalization 325; systemic deficiency in 161
rule-of-law constitutionalization 247
rules, first/second order 131
running constitutional code 23
Russia: proportionality 32; rights derived from international law 27
Rutili (1975) 18

Sabel, Charles F. 195
Saint-Simon, Henri de 40, 41
Salgoil (1968) 17
sanctions 174

Schäuble, Wolfgang 255, 267
Schengen regime 252
Schengen Treaty 2
Schilling, Theodor 14
Schmitt, Carl 324
science: and economics 221; new administrative science 220; of organizations 292; politicisation of 192; and politics/the economy 306; spontaneous domain of 296–7
scientification, of modern governance 229
scientific discourse 240
scientific domain, in times of crisis 297
scientific method, and economics 233
scientific objectivity, new 222–5
scientific organization 306
Sciulli, David 49
scope, of legal obligations 141–3
secessionist movements 2, 96
second-order rules 131
Second World War, and formation of the EU 244–5
Security and Cooperation at the European level (OSCE) 103
self-constitution, possibilities of 301–7
self-governance, rights to 197
self-management, of society 41
self-rule: democratic constitutionalism 74–5; statist or foundationalist constitutionalism 69; universal constitutionalism 71–2
Shaw, Jo 74, 75, 77
Sieyès, Emmanuel Joseph 256
silencing, of debate 264, 266
Simms (1999) 29
SINAPSE 189
single currency *see* euro
single rights 17–18, 23, 26–8
Sinzheimer, Hugo 247
site, of legal obligations 141–3
social autonomy 131
Social Charter 103
social classes, underprivileged 100; *see also* class
Social Democrat Party, Portugal 280
social differentiation: in public opinion 262; rationalization as 45
social forces, emergence of 304
social freedom, concept of 300

344 *Index*

social inclusion 24, 101–2
social inequality 208, 257–9
social integration, and class struggle 267
socialism, democratic 246
Socialist Party, Portugal 280–1, 294–5
social-market economy 209
social modernization 44–5
social movements, Portugal 283–4
social practices, and public autonomy 126
social processes: during crisis/austerity
    290; impact of psychological processes
    on 299
social reality: and law 121; model of
    305–6
social rule of recognition 142
social sciences 307
social stasis 2
social sub-systems, global 130
social systems: organized and spontaneous
    domains of 294, 295, 298, 304; political
    constitutionalization of 131; and
    political systems 302–3; theory 291
social systems theory, autopoietic 58, 59;
    see also systems theory
social welfare and security constitution
    248
societal constitutionalism 5, 39, 48–51, 52,
    55, 58–9, 131
societal constitutions 130
societal laws 40
societal reactions, to economic and
    financial dynamics 301
society: fragmentation of world 130;
    modern 58; self-management of 41
sociological concept, of constitutionalism
    58–60
sociological legitimacy 78, 80
sociological studies, of the EU 185
sociological theories, and natural law
    theories 40
sociological turn, in constitutions 4–5
sociology: constitutional/political 76–7,
    130; of constitutional processes
    299–300; of emotions 299; of law 306;
    new science of 41; pragmatic 78
Solange method 20–2, 30–1
Somek, Alexander 45, 164
sovereign debt crisis 219–20, 222, 280,
    290

sovereign power 57, 251, 326
sovereignty: within the EU 106, 251; loss
    of 279–89, 286; national 210; originally
    shared 47; political 256; popular 69;
    procedural 249, 251, 256; state 105,
    214; transnationalization of 46
Spain, and the Basque Country/Catalonia
    96
speech acts, performance of 240–1
Spencer, Herbert 57
spontaneity, impact of organization on 298
Stability Growth Pact, Lisbon Treaty 250
stakeholders, involvement of 189–90
standard setters 110
standard setting, by the ECtHR 103–4
state agencies, pathological development
    of 292
state coercion 144, 145, 302
statehood, in Europe 105–6
state law 109–10
states: coercion by 144, 145, 302;
    obligations of 138–41; power of 60;
    regulation 206; welfare function of 224
statist constitutional order 87
statist fallacy 72
statist paradigm, constitutionalism 68–70,
    76, 80, 86, 87
Stauder v City of Ulm (1969) 18
Stone Sweet, Alec 105, 113
Stork v. High Authority [1959] ECR 17
    169
structural constitutional vulnerability
    160–1
subjects, constitution-interpreting 69–70,
    72–3, 75
Sublime Object of Ideology, The 317
subprime crisis 280
substantive reasons, as grounds of
    obligations 146
Sunstein, Cass 128
supervision, macro-prudential 228
supranational constitutions 38
supranational legal systems 29, 30, 129
supranational primacy 106
supremacy, challenges to 105–8
supremacy doctrine 318
Swiss Confederation 254
symbolism, and uncertainty 221
systemic deficiency, rule of law 161

systemic pluralism 124–5, 126
systemic risk, certainty of 227
systemist approach, transnational
    constitutionalism 275–6, 278–9
systems theory 129–30, 186, 274, 278,
    279, 289, 299, 300

technical governance 44–8
technocracy, constitutional 253–5, 257,
    258
technocratic governance 218, 229
technocratic power 251, 266
territorial autonomy challenges 105
test of existentiality 81, 82–3
test of reality 81, 82
test of truth 81–2
Teubner, Gunther 5, 49, 51, 59–60,
    129–32, 133, 193, 275, 287, 289, 291–2,
    294, 295, 300, 301, 303
Thatcher, Margaret 247
theory, constitutional 183
Thornhill, Chris 276, 302
timidity trap 257, 258
Tobacco Advertising judgment 206
toleration principle 125
totalitarianism 131
trade, laissez-faire conception 206
Transatlantic Trade and Investment
    Partnership (TTIP) 259
transconstitutionalism 276
transnational civil law 256
transnational civil society 81–6
transnational constitutionalism 275–9, 288
transnational debates 306
transnational governance 42–4
transnational jurisprudence 8, 277
transnational law 48–9, 54–5, 117, 256
transnational markets 206
transnational politics 54–5, 277–8
transnational private regulation 197
treaties: debate regarding 202; European
    320; and the European Court of Justice
    321; law of 253–4; *see also* names of
    individual treaties
Treaty of Amsterdam 253
Treaty of European Union (TEU): Article
    1 96; Article 2 161, 163, 164, 165,
    166, 167, 168, 169, 170, 172–3, 174;
    Article 6(1) 170; Article 7 165, 166,

174; Article 49 170; and constitutionally
    pluralism 108
Treaty of Lisbon *see* Lisbon Treaty
Treaty on the Functioning of the European
    Union (TFEU): Article 26(2) 204–5;
    Article 114 206, 207, 209, 212; Article
    125 255; Article 127(1) 230; Articles
    258, 259, 260 165; interpretation of 202,
    216
Trenz, Hans-Joerg 77, 80–1
Troika, the 252, 279, 280, 281, 283, 284,
    286, 288
trust: in institutions 263, 294; and market
    building 208; in political systems 303
truth: speaking the 240; test of 81–2
Tully, James 68–9
Tuori, Kaarlo 111

UKIP 97
uncertainty: in markets 222–3, 232; and
    risks 232; and symbolism 221
UN Charter 46
UN directives, anti-terrorism directives 30
unemployment, European 259
unification, European 245, 246
United Executive Bodies of Europe (UEB)
    244, 251–2, 253, 255, 259–60, 264, 266,
    267
United Kingdom: and accession to the
    European Convention of Human Rights
    105; Commission on a Bill of Rights
    105; constitution 31; Human Rights Act
    (HRA) (1998) 28–9; proportionality 32;
    and Scotland 96; UKIP 97
United States: constitution of 107–8,
    254; impact assessments (IAs) 190–1;
    proportionality 32; state courts 123;
    supreme court 213
universal constitutionalism 70–3, 76, 80,
    86, 87
universalism 230–1
universal validity 111

validity, of the law 110–11
value-at-risk methodology (VaR) 226
values: *acquis* on 161, 165, 168, 170,
    171–2; compliance with 170; content
    of 166; democratic 96; enforcement of
    165–6, 168, 171, 174; European Union

346 *Index*

(EU) 3; fundamental 105; ideologically informed non-compliance with 165–8, 169, 170; of integration 103; and the law 8, 161–3, 169; market-based approach to 164; and market making 211; and self-constitutionalization 56–7; substance of 171, 173; systemic deficiency in 161
Van Duin, Kees P.S. 229
Van Gend en Loos (1963) 13, 247, 248
Vencer a Crise com o Estado Social e com a Democracia 298
Venice Commission 173
Viking judgement 316
violations, of Article 2 TEU 165
violence: emotionally motivated acts of 298–9; political systems use of 302; suppression of private 302
Voßkuhle, Andreas 15–16
vulnerability, structural constitutional 160–1

wages, inequalities in 258
Walker, Neil 15, 53–4, 118–19, 120, 196
war, prevention of 201

water, as a public good 84
Weber, Max 44–5
Weiler, Joseph 162, 170
Weisskopf, Walter A. 221, 222, 233
welfare, and competition law 207
welfare function, of states 224
welfare maximization, within scientific economic process 233
welfare states 246
West German Constitution Court 21
Westphalian constitutionalism 68
We the People 107–8
White, Jonathan 251
Wilkinson, Michael 70, 77, 79–80
Wilkinson, Mike 134
Williams, Andrew 164
withdrawal, from the EU 97; *see also* secessionist movements
Wolin, Sheldon 39–40
work organization, in Europe 297–8
World War II, and formation of the EU 244–5
wrongdoing 150, 151, 156

Žižek, Slavoj 317, 325